The Diary of Mr. James Melvill, 1556-1601

THE DIARY

OF

MR JAMES MELVILL.

1556—1601.

PRINTED AT EDINBURGH,

M.D.CCC.XXIX.

TO

SIR WALTER SCOTT, BART.

President,

AND THE MEMBERS OF THE

BANNATYNE CLUB,

THIS WORK IS PRESENTED

BY

VISCOUNT MELVILLE,

SIR WILLIAM ARBUTHNOT,

SIR HENRY JARDINE,

ROBERT DUNDAS,

COLIN MACKENZIE,

JOHN BORTHWICK

EDINBURGH, JULY, 1829.

THE BANNATYNE CLUB.

M DCCC.XXIX

SIR WALTER SCOTT, Baronet.

PRESIDENT

THE EARL OF ABERDEEN, K T.

RIGHT HON WILLIAM ADAM, LORD CHIEF COMMIS-
SIONER OF THE JURY COURT

SIR WILLIAM ARBUTHNOT, BARᵀ

5 JAMES BALLANTYNE, ESQ

SIR WILLIAM MACLEOD BANNATYNE

LORD BELHAVEN AND STENTON

GEORGE JOSEPH BELL, ESQ

ROBERT BELL, ESQ.

10 WILLIAM BELL, ESQ.

JOHN BORTHWICK, ESQ

WILLIAM BLAIR ESQ

REV PHILIP BLISS, D.C L.

GEORGE BRODIE, ESQ

15 THE DUKE OF BUCCLEUCH AND QUEENSBERRY.

JOHN CALEY, ESQ.

JAMES CAMPBELL, ESQ.

HON JOHN CLERK, LORD ELDIN

WILLIAM CLERK, ESQ.

20 HENRY COCKBURN, ESQ.

DAVID CONSTABLE, ESQ

ANDREW COVENTRY, ESQ

JAMES T GIBSON CRAIG, ESQ

WILLIAM GIBSON CRAIG, ESQ

25 HON GEORGE CRANSTOUN, LORD COREHOUSE

THE EARL OF DALHOUSIE.

JAMES DENNISTOUN, ESQ

ROBERT DUNDAS, ESQ

RIGHT HON. WILLIAM DUNDAS, LORD CLERK
    REGISTER.

30 HENRY ELLIS, ESQ.

CHARLES FERGUSSON, ESQ

ROBERT FERGUSON, ESQ

LIEUT.-GENERAL SIR RONALD C FERGUSON

THE COUNT DE FLAHAULT

35 HON JOHN FULLERTON, LORD FULLERTON.

LORD GLENORCHY.

THE DUKE OF GORDON

WILLIAM GOTT, ESQ.

SIR JAMES R. G. GRAHAM, BART

40 ROBERT GRAHAM, ESQ.

LORD GRAY.

RIGHT HON. THOMAS GRENVILLE.

THE EARL OF HADDINGTON

THE DUKE OF HAMILTON AND BRANDON.

45 E. W. A. DRUMMOND HAY, ESQ.

JAMES M HOG, ESQ

JOHN HOPE, ESQ. SOLICITOR-GENERAL
COSMO INNES, ESQ.
DAVID IRVING, LL.D.
50 JAMES IVORY, ESQ.
REV JOHN JAMIESON, D D
ROBERT JAMESON, ESQ
SIR HENRY JARDINE
FRANCIS JEFFREY, ESQ
55 JAMES KEAY, ESQ
JOHN G. KINNEAR, ESQ
THOMAS KINNEAR, ESQ , TREASURER
THE EARL OF KINNOULL
DAVID LAING, ESQ. SECRETARY
60 THE EARL OF LAUDERDALE, K T
REV JOHN LEE, D D
THE MARQUIS OF LOTHIAN
COLIN MACKENZIE, ESQ
HON. J. H. MACKENZIE, LORD MACKENZIE.
65 JAMES MACKENZIE, ESQ.
JAMES MAIDMENT, ESQ
THOMAS MAITLAND, ESQ.
GILBERT LAING MEASON, ESQ
THE VISCOUNT MELVILLE, K T.
70 WILLIAM HENRY MILLER, ESQ
THE EARL OF MINTO.
HON. SIR J. W MONCREIFF, LORD MONCREIFF
JOHN ARCHIBALD MURRAY, ESQ
WILLIAM MURRAY, ESQ

75 JAMES NAIRNE, ESQ.

MACVEY NAPIER ESQ

FRANCIS PALGRAVE, ESQ

HENRY PETRIE, ESQ

ROBERT PITCAIRN, ESQ

80 JOHN RICHARDSON, ESQ

THE EARL OF ROSSLYN

ANDREW RUTHERFURD ESQ

THE EARL OF SELKIRK

RIGHT HON SIR SAMUEL SHEPHERD, LORD CHIEF
BARON OF SCOTLAND

85 ANDREW SKENE ESQ

JAMES SKENE, ESQ

GEORGE SMYTHE, ESQ

THE EARL SPENCER K G

JOHN SPOTTISWOODE, ESQ

90 THE MARQUIS OF STAFFORD, K G

MAJOR-GENERAL STRATON

SIR JOHN ARCHIBALD STEWART BART

HON CHARLES FRANCIS STUART

ALEXANDER THOMSON ESQ

95 THOMAS THOMSON, ESQ   VICE PRESIDENT

W. C TREVELYAN ESQ

PATRICK FRASER TYTLER, ESQ

ADAM URQUHART, ESQ

RIGHT HON SIR GEORGE WARRENDER, BART

100 THE VENERABLE ARCHDEACON WRANGHAM

PREFATORY NOTICE.

MR JAMES MELVILL'S DIARY, comprehending the period from 1556 to 1601, has long been known as a work of authority and importance in the ecclesiastical and political affairs of Scotland: From it Mr David Calderwood enriched his History of the Church, and, latterly, Dr M'Crie his interesting Life of Mr Andrew Melvill. While it comprises the autobiography of a man, whose mild and conciliating disposition, yet honest and stedfast principles, rendered him peculiarly fit, amidst the violence of conflicting factions, to advocate and describe the interests of the Reformed Church of Scotland, it forms a faithful record of a momentous period in the ecclesiastical and civil polity of the nation,—interspersed with many valuable notices regarding the state of learning in our universities and schools, and the characters of the more eminent men in church and state, during the latter part of the sixteenth century.

Although this work may be more strictly denominated *Memoirs* than a *Diary*, the latter term has been assumed on account of its being the title under which it is most generally known, and also to avoid confounding it with SIR JAMES MELVILLE'S MEMOIRS

The original Manuscript is preserved in the Library of the Faculty of Advocates, and consists of 371 folio pages, closely written in the author's hand, in a small but distinct character, of which a fac-simile is prefixed   It would appear from the following notice, in an unknown hand, inserted in a copy in the possession of Adam Gibb Ellis, Esq , that the original MS at one time belonged to Mr David Calderwood, who, it is well known, drew largely on its contents in compiling his History of the Church of Scotland. ' The following, " At Anstruther,' &c. and " The ' Historie of the Life of J M." were tran- ' scribed from an old MS lent to me by Sir Wm Calderwood of Poltoun, one of ' the Judges in the Courts of Session and Justiciary, who had it among other ' papers that belonged to his grand-uncle, Mr David Calderwood, author of ' Altare Damascenum, History, &c '

Sir William Calderwood was elevated to the bench in 1711, and having died in 1733, Mr Ellis's copy must have been prepared between these periods ; and as it bears internal evidence of having been transcribed from the Faculty MS , it would, therefore, appear that the " old MS " alluded to in the above notice, is the one now in the Advocates' Library—more particularly as there is no other copy of the Diary of an earlier date than the beginning of the eighteenth century. It is probable that Sir William Calderwood afterwards presented this MS. to the Faculty of Advocates, of whose body he was a dis- tinguished member

There is another transcript of the Diary in the Signet Library, apparently of the same age with Mr Ellis's copy   Excepting these no other is known to exist ; and in preparing this work for the press, both of them have been con- sulted ; but, being inaccurately transcribed, they have not afforded much as- sistance in elucidating any ambiguous expression in the original   Mr Ellis's MS is contained, along with a copy of Mr John Maule's HEAVEN NO HELL, OR DEATH NO DANGER, in a folio volume, which formerly belonged to the late Rev. Adam Gibb, and which bears the inscription, ' James Erskine's Book,' on the inside of the board   The copy in the Signet Library, contained in a small quarto volume, belonged to Mr Patrick Cuming, minister in Edinburgh, at the sale of whose books it was purchased by the late Mr George Paton, at whose death it was transferred to the Signet Library. From various corrections and interlineations in this copy in the well-known handwriting of Mr Robert Wodrow, it appears to have been at one time in his possession.

It may be observed that, throughout the following pages, the abbreviations of the MS have been for the most part avoided : while the orthography of the original has been scrupulously retained, even occasionally at the expense of perspicuity In some instances, however, it was found necessary to depart from such strict accordance, where errors of a clerical nature occurred Where these have been corrected, they will be found in a list of ALTERATIONS AND COR-RECTIONS at the end of the book, from which the reader may judge of the propriety of the change from their original to their altered form

MR JAMES MELVILL'S DIARY.

1556—1601.

JAMES SMITHL, JHON DYKS, AND MR SWIIT
STRANG EXERCEISLS TO MY SPRLIT ;
BAI DOWY MII UIN-ANDRO'S I LIGHT
OI MYND AND BODIE MAR'D THL MIGHT

MR JAMES MELVILL'S DIARY.

At Anftruther, the 10 of Auguft, in the yeir of the laft age 1600.

FORSAMIKLE as the corruption of man is readie not onlie vngratlie to forget the benefittes of God, bot alfo moft facrilegiuflie to afcrybe to thamfelues the praife of anie thing commendable and weill done, I haiff thought it maift neceffar to inregiftrat in this book the warks of God for the minifterie of his worfhipe, and faluation of his peiple within this congregation of Kilrynnie. for amendment of vnthankfulnes, and remembring and fteiring vpe the hartes of all the members thairof to acknawlage fra tyme to tyme the graitnes of his cair, loue, guidnes and grace ; and that all thanks and praife may be giffen to his Maᵗⁱᵉ, all haill and alleauerlie

In the yeir 1583, Mr Wilyeam Clark of maift happie memorie for godlines wefdome, and loue of his flok, departed this lyff, leaving four congregationes wharof he haid the charge, deftitut of minifterie, vᶻ. Abercrombie, Pittenweim, Anftruther, and Kilrynnie, whafe defolat mifenie was the mair, that it fell in the yeirs of feirfull plages and confufion bathe vpon the kirk and comounweill ; to wit, the yeirs fourfcore four, and fourfcore tyve yeirs, in the quhilk vnhappie tyme Biſhop Adamſone of St Andros. tyrannizing in the kirk, obtrudit to thame ane of whome they lyked nathing. whafe name I fpair, for the maift part, be occafion wharof thair enterit in verie grait diffentioun in thair bowelles, quhilk vexed tham with anguifh of mynd, grait peanes and expences during the faid twa yeirs, and mikle of the fourfcore fax alfo.

To the remead and compofing wharof fupplicationes war gevin in to the prefbyterie of St Andros, of the mercie of God newlie erected and reftored againe, whilk directed commiffionars at dyvers tymes to vifit the efteat of thefe kirks, and travell to draw the peiples hairts togidder in ane, and aggrie vpon a paftor Amangs the quhilk commiffionars was James Meluill, ane of the maifters of the Collage of Theologie whafe doctrine and dealling when they haid haid and war acquented withe, they condifeudit all in ane to craue at the preſbyterie that his peanes might be imployed and continowed with thame, nocht onlie for compoſing of thair controuerſies, and reconceiling tham in Chryſt, bot alſo for vndertaking of a paſtorall charge amangs tham So the ſaid Mr James being erneſthe delt withall, bathe be the preſbyterie and the congregatiounes, yeildit to the calling of God and his kirk, and enterit in the ſimmar feaſone, in the mouethe of July 1586, to teatche at the kirk of Anſtruther, ſituat in the middes of the ſaids congregatiounes

It pleaſit the Lord of the herveſt to bliſ his travelles, ſa that all debattes and controuerſies amangs the congregatiounes, and within the bowelles of euerie ane of thame (quhilk war bothe grait and in number,) being takin vpe and removit, with grait ioy and comfort the communioun was miniſtrat in the kirks of Anſtruther and Kilrynnie in the Spring tyme of the yeir 1587

Therefter finding the foir congregationes a burding intolerable and importable with a guid conſcience, whowbeit the ſaid Mr James haid brought with him at the beginning a fellow laborar, v Mr Robert Durу, yit nather could the ſaid Mr Robert be provydit of a ſtipend, nather could they find thamſelues able to diſcharge ſo grait a cair of ſaulls; therfor, the ſaid Mr James ſett himſelf cairfullie for the ſeparating and ſeuerall planting of the ſaid congregatiounes, reſoluing to tak himſelf to Kilrynnie alean; and delt with Pittenweim, and cauſit thame prepeare ane auditorie and kirk within thair awin town, in the quhilk he teached to theme bathe on the Sabathe and ouk dayes, nocht intermitting his ordinarie doctrines in the vther kirks, vntill Pittenweim was prouydit and planted with a miniſter of thair awin, and that without hurt or impeairing of the ſtipend of the kirk of Anſtruther Waſter; the quhilk be grait fatherie and trauell at the Plat, and dyvers actiones of pley befor the Lords of Seſſioun and Exchacker, be the ſpeciall bleſſing of God he haid augmented from tourſcoir pounds to a hunder lib and thrie chalders victuall, with gleib and manſe recouered and repeared And ſa Pittenweim being planted with Mr Nicol Dalglſh, the ſaid Mr James quyttes and reſignes the ſaid new purchayſt ſtipend, with the kirk of Anſtruther, gleib, and manſe, to his fellow-laborar Mr Robert Dury, and freithing himſelff of the charge bathe of Anſtruther and Pittenweim, with all the ſtipend and commodities thanof, whowbeit diſpoint to him ſtedfaſthe vnder the Kings priuie teall, and tuik him to the kirk of Kilrynnie alleanerlie

1589.—For ſoone therefter the parochinars of Abercrombie aggreit with Mr Alexander Forſythe, and crauit of me their vicarage, with ſaxtein pounds money pevit out of thair teind ſcheaves, quhilk I haid alſo diſpoint to me for my lyſſ-tyme, bot I quyt all in lyk maner, and incontinent efter admiſſion of the ſaid Mr Alexander to that miniſterie, delyvert him my pices and rights of vicar-age and ſtipend, togidder with the burding of the ſaid peiple and congrega-tion.

Now in this mean tyme, the ſtipend of Kilrynnie was but fourſcore lib but ather gleib or manſe, but God moved the peiples hartes to haue a cear of me, and mak me ſufficient ſecuritie of four hounder markes in ſtipend, the town of Anſtruther Eiſter bund for the twa part, and the gentlemen to Landwart for the thride, and fordar obleſit thamſelues to big me a hous vpon a piece of ground, quhilk the Laird of Anſtruther gaiff frælie tor that effect   This was vndertakin and begoun at Witſonday in an 1590, bot wald neuer haiff bein perfyted, gift the bountifull hand of my God haid nocht maid me to tak the wark in hand myſelff, and tuinſhed ſtraughe to my conſideratioun all things neidfull, ſa that neuer ouk paſt bot all ſort of workmen was weill peyit, never a dayes intermiſſion fra the beginning to the compleitting of it, and never a ſoar fingar during the haill labour   In June begoun, and in the monethe of Merch efter, I was reſident therin.   It exceides in expences the ſoum of thrie thowſand and fyve hounder marks, and of all I haid nought of the paroche, bot about a thrie thowſand ſleads of ſteanes, and fourtein or fyttein chalder of lyme; the ſtanes from the town, and lyme from the landwart, ſkarſlie the half of the materialles, lyme and ſtean, and thairfor iuſtlie I may call it a ſpectakle of Gods liberalitie

The hous being endit, and I reſident than in, I becam mikle in deat, and my familie than withall to increas; for bearing the burding wharof I fand my four hounder marks to com far ſchort, ioyning than withall a grait part tharoff vn-pleaſendlie peyit, and out of tyme, quhilk did caſt me in grait heavines and perplexitie, ſa that I was mightelie tempted to haiff abandonet this miniſterie of Kilrynnie, and yeildit to maiſt erneſt callings in vther places; for Edinbrugh, Sterling, Dondie, and St Andros alſo, haid dyvers tymes erneſtlie dealt with me   Yit finding my dear peiples hartes, than obedience to my miniſterie, and the wounderfull bleſſing of God growing alwayes with me, I durſt na wayes waver or mint away, bot ſtand ſtedfaſt in that roum and ſtation wher he haid placed me; and ſa tand in notable experience the treuthe of Chryſtes words, ſaying " Seik firſt the kingdome of God and the righteouſnes tharof, and the reſt ſalbe caſtin in to yow '   As to the grait glorie of his name I continow this narration

For the fam yeir 1590, meining my felt to the Plat, I gat foufcore pounds in augmentatioun, and the yeir following, maift cafelie, by expectatioun, four chalders of victuall. Sa I fand be fure experience that it was gnid to len and giff to God, and nocht ftand for his honor to quyt whatfumeun, for he wald repey twyfe als gnid, and nocht ly lang in na mans comoun. Whowbeit, alas! what can we giff him bot his awin. Bot behauld yit the gonne.

It pleafed his grace indeid to twitche my confcience with a folift cear of my charge and flok. fa that whowbeit my diftractions and occupations war in grait and maift weightie and neceffar efteares of the knk, yit his fear fuffert me nocht to leaue my peiple without dayhe attendance and confort, and fa of unfpeacable mercie and fawour the Lord ftenit vpe a young man, indewing him with fingular graces, and fetting the canfull affectioun of his hart to fupplie my abfence and weaknes, yea as a fathfull yok fellow to vndertak the halff of my burding, vᶻ. Mr Johne Doig, in whafe roum in the fchole, the Lord fend another youthe alfo of fpeciall godlines, and cair of Chryfts honor and of the weill bathe of young and auld. Thir twa, my happie halff marrow (of whome I man wryt to the glorie of God, as he is witnes I do in all this reherfall, that fche euir haid als grait a cear of my calling as I haid myfelf, delyting aboue all things to fie the wark of God to grow and go fordwart, and efteiming that onlie rightlie and weill beftowit that was want that way, neglecting and cafting afyde the cair of prounfion for hirfelff and childring, whowbeit now growing feikhe and impotent) hald a fpeciall cair of, and delyt into for the helpe of my charge bathe amangs the young and auld, and thairfor interteaned them in houfhauld; fa that the burding of houfhaulding and deattes contracted in liging, with verie grait expences in the comoun efteares of the knk, wherin almaift the halff of fum vens I was employed, maid me aboue fit æque at the yens end.

Bot my gnid God and maifter, whom I feruit, and whofe turn and wark I haid in hand, prouydit ane vther helpe be a purpofe, and in a maner, quhilk I could nocht haiff deuyfit nor luked for; firft, he moued the Lard of Anftruther to be willing to difpone and quyt the right of the teind fifche to the paroche and toun, ane or bathe, for the foum of thre thowfand marks, quhilk annes being beftowit, might purchas a ftedfaft ftipend to than minifter for euer. Nixt, when bathe toun and paroche haid refufit the blok, it pleafit God to moue the Lard to offer it to myfelff a thowfand marks better cheape, to be acquyrit to me and myne. And God alfo put in my hart to accept of the blok: bot nocht facrilegiuflie to purchas a leiving to me and myne, of that quhilk fuld fuftein the minifterie of God's worfchipe and faluation of the peiple, but to acquyer it for the fuftentatioun of the minifterie of the town of Anftruther Efter When we haid aggreit vpon the blok for twa thowfand mark, the ane halff to be peyit befor and at Mertimes in an. 1592, and the vther at Witfonday in an 1593, I knew nocht whar nor whow to gett the foumes. I conveint tharfor the haill Eldars of the paroche to brouche and land within the feffioun-hous in the kirk, and thair I maid them this offer; to be content with my prefent leiving, and let the revenew of the temd fifches be taken vpe yeirlie till twa thowfand marks and the profit war peyit compltie, and thereftir to quyt them thair augmentation, and tak me to my affignation and thefe fifches, to line vpon and fuftein a fellow-labourar with me, quhilk might be thereftier a conftant prouifioun for thair minifterie in all tyme to come Manie fhew guid will to the mater, when they faw that I was na way feiking my awin commoditie, bot the weill and prouifion of thair minifterie; bot in end and effect. as it feares with comoun turnes, when it cam to the preparing and deburfing of founes it fealled. And then giff it haid nocht pleafit God to moue the hart of a fpeciall freind of myne (to whom I was regirating the mater, and to whome, in that ceas, the minifterie of Kilrynnie is mair behauldin nor to all the paroche and parochinars) to get me the foum I fould delyver at the firft term, I wald haiff bein forcit to quait the blok againe, and left the purchas of the fpeciall moyen and prouifioun of this minifterie, quhilk now, of the fpeciall gift and prouidence of God, is acquired vnto it.

Now the firft termes foum being delyverit, and the Lardes right put in my hand, it could haiff avealit the minifterie nathing, vnles I haid the tytle of the vicarage, quhilk was in Jhone Anftruthers poffeffioun, with whome it beho-ued me to blok of new againe for his difmiffioun, the quhilk I did, and contented him with thrie hounder marks and referuatioun of the dewtie of the Siluerdyk. Sa yit I haid threttein hounder marks to delyver and purchas, for the quhilk I meined myfelf againe to my feffioun, and was compellit in end to fell tham my augmentatioun, quhilk they war bund to pey me yeirlie, to thair grait eafe and my grait hurt, (war nocht thair eafe culd nocht be my hurt, whafe eafe and weillfear in God was all my can and refpect in the mater,) for haiffand the town of Anftruther bund be fufficient contract in wiant to me, for twa hounder marks yeirlie, during my minifterie, and the gentlemen to land-wart for a hounder, I quat tham bathe for thrie yeirs dewtie, v'. nyne hounder marks, wharas fen fyne I might haiff gottin of tham twyfe famikle, and my right ftanding to the fore. The quhilk I wald nocht fa particularlie

fett down, war not fum, forgetting themfelues and the giait benefit of God, hes
alleagit that they deburfit founes for acquyring of the teind filches to the minifterie, quhilk is far from the treuthe; for indeid, giff God haid nocht done
that turn without thair founes or cair, thair haid fkaiflie bein a minifterie in
Kilrymne this day   And this I wryt nocht to impear the praife of guid men in
the paroche, wharof I thank God than is a guid number, and als weill affected
as in the land agean, bot to reprefs the vnwarrie ingratitud of fum that confidders nocht the bountifull guidnes of God in the planting and preferuation of
thair minifterie

Bot to return to the narration —With this nyne houndrethe marks, and four
hounder of my brethin founes gear, I fatiffeit the next termes founn, and enterit be prefentation, collation, and inftitution of the vicarage, as actuall minifter in poffeffion of the faid teind filches, and na way be the tytle recevit fra
the Laird as Taxman, to mak it clen and fure that I fought the promifion of the
minifterie, and nocht a leiving to me and myne   Quhilk I fett down parthe to
ftope the mouthes of calumniators, giving out my doing as a conquaift of the
kirk gear to me and myne, parthe to refolue my warldlie frindes, who thinks
I wald never be fa daft as to tak on founes fa giait to acquyre and bring
hame to the kirk hir teinds agane: bot it is not the warlde, bot my God
whome I teik to pleafe, and I thank his bontè continualie, hes in fa doing fund
mair of the warlde, nor fic as hes done vtherwayes, or euer I fought or luked
for   The haill expences of the proces and pices of the tytle lyand in a feuerall buft be themfelues in my lettron, I eftimat to a houndrethe marks, fà in
deburfit money the haill is to me four-and-twentie houndrethe marks

The quhilk founn, by the fpeciall blefling of God, in the filchings I might
haifl eafehe vtreade fen my firft poffeffioun, gift the burding of my torfaids fellow-laborar and fcholmaifter haid nocht lyen vpon me, the grait expences of the
comoun effeares of the kirk, and the lang and heavie diftres of my wyff. Now
this my frind wald afk, What I haiff for my releiff of fic founes ? I anfwer
the fawour and prouidence of my guid God   For giff God fpear my dayes
with reft in his kirk, I hope he fall vtreade all my deattes, that it may be left
frie to the intrant. Giff nocht, and the intrant be worthie of the roum of this
minifterie, God and his confcince will moue him to pey the deat refting   Giff
he will nocht, the greiff and lofs wil be graitter to haiff fic a man in that roum,
nor of myne to pey my deattes, whowbeit they fell the books and plenefhing
for that effect   As for the bernes, giff they lern to be Gods fervants and
bernes, he will provyde for them as he hes done for me : giff nocht (as God for-

bid) they ar mair worthe to beg nor to bruik (Nehem v ver 4) For my reward at the hands of God, the Lord of his infinit mercie and grace frethe me from the ruft defert of my vyle finnes, for the merit of the deathe and pretius bloode of his Sone my Sauour, the Lord Jefus Chryft, wha is God over all, blefïit for euer For when all is done, as he and my confcience beares witnes againft me, a maift wretched, vyle, vnworthie feruand in his fight, vnles he behauld me in his Chryft, whas I am, and nocht my awin And far be it fra me to glore in ame thing bot his cros, wharby, wald to God, this warld war fulhe crucified to me, and I to it

As for the town and paroche, the benefit indeed is thairs, let them tharfor as I hope they will, confidder than dewtie in confcience befor thair God, to whome for than minifterie. I am fun they ar man addettit nor ame paroche I know, the Lord mak them to acknawlage it and be thankfull This onlie I befeik them for the mercies of Chryft, let neuer that he takin away or abufit from the right ufe quhilk God hes ames applyed it vnto, fa far as may ly in thame, as they loue the honour of God, and his worfchipe to ftand in the middes of tham, iovint with the faluation of thair faulles. And namlie I man ernefthe admonifche the hous of Auftruther neuer to mein to acclame agame the tytle or poffeffion of thay teinds, whowbeit they might find a corrupt and facrilegius perjured perfone to put in the roum, be whome they might gett a new fett and poffeffion of thay teind fitches; for I promince heir a curs and maledictioun from God vpon whofeuer fall interinet and draw away the commodities tharof from the right vfe of fuftening of the minifterie of Gods worfchipe, and of the faluatioun of Gods peiples faulles within the town of Auftruther, and congregation of Kilrynnie And God forbid that euer that hous fhould bring on it the terrtull effect of this curs, quhilk of dewtie I man loue beft of ame hous in the Land

In the yeir 1598, I cawfit print my Catechifine for the profit of my peiple, and beftow it thar vpon fyve hounder marks, quhilk God moued the hairt of a maift godlie and lowing friind to frihe offer to me in len for that effect Of this I remean addettit, bot could neuer, to my knawlage, attein to a hounder marks agam for the buiks.

THE HISTORIE OF THE LYFF OF J. M.

Thow does manie things, O Jehoua, my God Thy merveals and thoughts toward ws cannot ordour be be recompted befoie thie , giff I wald fet me to fchaw and fpeak tham out, they ar mo in number than I can relicarte — Psalme XI VERSE 6

I will fing the mercies of the Lord for euer with my mouthe will I declare thy treuthe from generation to generation.—Psalme LXXXIX.

Thow art my hope, Lord Jehoua my confidence fra my beirnhead.

I lean vpon thie from the wombe , from my mothers bowels thow eacht me , in thie fall my praife be continualie.

Let my mouthe be filled with thy laude, even all the day with thy glorie.

Caft mie nocht away in my auld age , when my ftrainthe fealls me, leaue mie nocht —Psalme XCI. VERSES 5, 6, 8, 9.

O whow den ar thy thoughts towards mie, O ftrong God whow grait is the foum therof

I wald recount tham, bot they are ma then the fand : I wake that I may bie yit withe thie —Psalme CXXXIX. VERSES 17, 18.

I KNAWE a man in Chryft, brought from the wombe of his mother be God, the 25 day of the monethe July (dedicat of auld to S. James the Apoftle and Martyr) in the yeir of our Lord 1556 ;* wha, for thanktulnes of hart to the praife and honour of his gratius God and den father in Chryft, and for edification and comfort of his childring, and fic as fall reid the faming hereefter, is movit to fett down in monument of wryt the benefits of God beftowit on him fen his firft conception and day of his birthe foremarked, fa far, at leift, as his weak vnderftanding and ticall memorie in maters that ar efteemed of importance can conceaue and recompt Whow beit, as I haiff profeffed, in the words of the Pfalme with Dauid. that the fmalleft of his vnknawin benefits paffes the gratteft reatche of my apprehenfion and vtterance.

And firft, God wald haift me begottin of godlie, tathfull, and honeft parents, bathe lightned with the light of the gofpell at the firft dawming of the day tharof within Scotland, knawing and beleving that Couenant of Grace, and fa the feid of the fathfull, exprefhe mentioned in that covenant, quhilk affures

* My vncle, Mr Andro, haulds that I was born in an. 1557

me of the benefit tharof, yea of that root and wealfpring of all his benefites, my eternall election in his Chryft befor the foundation of the warld.   Thefe parents be name war Richard Melvill of Baldowy, and Hobell Scrymgeour, fiftar to the Laird of Glafwell for the tyme   My laid father, brought vpe in letters from his youthe, and gentlemanne effeares till he was paft twentie yeirs of age, therefter chofine Pædagog to James Erſkine appenand of Donne, he paft with him to Germanie, whar he remeaned at the ftudie of letters, namlie, Theologie, firft with Doctor Macabeus, in Denmark, and theretter a heirar of Philip Melancton in Wittenberg, be the fpace of twa yeirs   Of the grait mercie of God hauffing the happe of fic maifters as war the gratteft lights of that age within the countrey in the toune of Montrofe, and companie of that Lard of Donne,* and the maift godlie, lerned, and noble Scots martyre Mr George Wyſhart, and thefe nominat in Germanie   And the Lord bleffing the feid fawin be tham in his hart, at laft, foone etter the firft reformation of religion, thruft him out into his herveft, and placed him minifter of his evangell at the kirk of Mariton, a myle from Montrofe, harde adiacent to his awin houfe and roum of Beldowy, in the quhilk he continowed faithfullie vnto his lyffes end   He died the 53 yeir of his age, in the moneth of Junie, an. 1575, in a Icterik fewar, maift godlie; for etter manie moft comfortable exhortationes maid to the noble and gentlemen of the cowntrey, wha all reforted to vifit him during his diſtres, and to his breither and frinds wha remeaned about him, about the verie houre of his deathe, he caufed reid to him the 8 chap of the Epiftle to the Romans, and immediathe etter his brother, Mr James, minifter of Arbrothe, afking him what he was doing; lifting vpe eies and hands toward hevin, with reafonable might of voice he anfwerit, " I am glorifeing God for the light of his gofpell, and refting in affurance of his fweit promifes of lyff maid vnto me in my Samour, the Lord Jefus Chryft," and na ma intelligible words therefter   He was a man of rare wefdome, iudgment and difcretion, and therfor mikle imployed in the tryfts and effeares of the noble and gentlemen of the countrey, quhilk diftracted him fra his calling, hinderit his vertew and fhortened his lyff   The recompence quhilk he had, was eftimation and affection of all. Ther was nane of his rank, and verie few aboue it, that was fa honored and loued as he, quhilk kythed fpecialie at his buriall, and hes bein often tauld me be men of all degries fen fyne.

My mother died about a thrie quarters, or at leaft within a yeir, etter I was

* Jhone Areſkin of Dun, fuperintendent of Angus and Mernes

born. a woman exceidinghe belouit of hir hufbands frinds and mbouis I haiff
dineis tymes haird when my fathei breithei Rogei, Jhone, Mr James and Robeit, could nocht fatifhe thamfelues in comending his godlines, honeftie, vertew and affection toward thame And I haiff often haird Mr Andio fay, that
he being a bern veiie feiklie, was maift lowinglie and tendeihe treated and
cared toi be hir, embrafing him and kiffing him oftentymes with thefe woids,
" God gift me an vther lad lyk thie, and fyne tak me to his ieft ' Now fihe
haid haid twa laddies befor me, whaiof the eldeft was dead, and betwix him
and the fecond, fihe bure thrie laffes, fa in end God granted his defyre, and
gaiff his an wha wald to God he war als lyk to Mr Andio in gitts of mynd as
he is thought to be in proportion of bodie and lineaments of face, foi ther is
nane, that is nocht vtherwayes particularlie infoimed, bot taks me for Mr Andios brother

 The nixt benefit is of my education till I cam to the age of a man, and entered in my calling, whaim als manie moments, als manie benefits ; bot the
maift remarkable to my iudgment and memoire I will record. And firft in
generall to the praife of my heavinlie parent, I man confefs with Dauid, " My
mother has now left me, bot Jehoua hes receauit me," and with Efai, " The
mother hes forgot the frint of his wombe, bot the Lord hes iemembent me
alwayes " I haid an evill inclyned woman to my nuris ; therefter fpeaned
and put in a cottar hous, and about foui or fyve yeir auld brought hame to a
ftep-mothei ; yit a verie honeft burges of Montios,* hes oft tauld me, that
my father wald ley me down on my bak, pleying with me and lauche at
me becaus I could nocht rys, I was fa fatt ; and wald afk mie what ealed
mie ; I wald anfwer, " I am fa fatt I may nocht geang " And trewhe fen my
remembeiance, I cam never to the place, bot God moued fium an with a mo-
therlie affection towards me About the fyft yeir of my age, the Grate Buik
was put in my hand, and when I was feavine, lytle therof haid I leimit at hame :
therfor my father put my eldeft and onlie brother Dauid, about a yeir and a
halff in age aboue me, and me togiddei to a kinfman and brother in the minifterie of his to fcholl, a gund, leined, kynd man, whome for thankfulnes I
name Mr Wilyam Gray, miniftei at Logie, Montrofe. He haid a fiftar, a
godlie and honeft matron, rewlai of his hous, wha often rememberit me of my
mothei, and was a verie lowing mother to ws indeid Thei was a gund nomber of gentle and honeft mens berns of the cowntiey about, weill tieaned vpe

* Robert Claik

bathe in letters, godlines, and exerceife of honeft geams. Ther we lerned to reid the Catechifine, prayers, and fcripture. to rehers the catechifine and prayers par cem, alfo nottes of Scripture efter the reiding therof; and ther furft I fand, (blyfed be my gud God for it) that fpirt of fanctification beginning to work fum motiones in my hart, even about the aught and nynt yeir of my age, to pray going to bed and ryfing, and being in the feilds alan to fay ower the prayers I haid leirnt with a fweit moving in my hart, and to abhore fwearing, and rebuk and complean vpon fic as I haird fweai. Whervnto the exemple of that godlie matron, feirklie and giften to reid and pray in hir bed, did mikle profit me, for I ley in hir chamber and haird hir exerceifes. We leirned ther the Rudiments of the Latin grammair, withe the vocables in Latin and Frenche, alfo divers fpeitches in Frenche, with the reiding and right pronunciation of that toung. We proceidit fordar to the Etymologie of Lilius, and his Syntax, as alfo a lytle of the Syntax of Linacei : ther with was ioyned Hunteis Nomenclatura, the Minora Colloquia of Erafmus, and fum of the Eclogs of Virgill and Epift. of Horace ; alfo Cicero his epiftles ad Terentiam. He haid a verie gud and profitable form of refoluing the authoirs, he teatched grammaticalie bathe according to the Etymologie and Syntax, bot as for me, the trewthe was, my ingyne and memorie war gud aneuche, bot my iudgment and underftanding war as yit finored and dark, fa that the thing quhilk I gat was mair be rat ryme nor knawlage. Ther alfo we haid the ane gud. and feilds reafonable feai ; and he our maifter wai teached to handle the bow for archerie, the glub for goff, the batons for fencing ; alfo to rin, to loope, to fwoum, to warfell, to proue pratteiks, euerie ane haiffing his matche and andagonift, bathe in our leffons and play. A happie and golden tyme indeid, giff our neghgence and vnthankfulnes haid nocht moued God to fchorten it partlie be deceying of the number, quhilk caufed the maifter to wenie, and partlie be a peft quhilk the Lord, for finne and contempt of his gofpell, fend vpon Montrofe, diftant from Ouer Logie bot twa myles ; fa that fcholl fkalled, and we wai all fend for and brought hame. I was at that fcholl the fpace of almoft fyve yeirs, in the quhilk tyme, of publict news I remember I hard of the mariage of Hendrie and Marie King and Quen of Scots, Seingnour Danies flauchter, of the Kings mourder at the Kirk of Field, of the Quens taking at Carbaiii, and the Langfyd feild. Wherof reid Mr Bowchannan Cornicle, lib 17, 18, 19.

Even at that tyme me thought the heiring of thefe things moued me, and ftak in my hart with fum ioy or forow, as I haird they might helpe or hender the religion, namelie, I remember the order of the faft keipit in an 1566;

the evill handling of the mmifterie, be taking away of ther ftipends. toi Mr James Meluill, my vncle, and Mr James Balfour, his cufing-german, bathe mmifters and ftipendies, with gud, godlie, and kynd Patrik Forbes of Cors The Laird of Kinnaber, and the godlie and zealus gentlemen of the countrey, parthe for thair bernes caufe, and parthe for that notable inftrument in the Kirk of Scotland, Jhone Erfkine of Done, fuperintendent of Merns and Angus, his refidence in Logy at certean tymes, did oftentymes frequent our hous, and talk of fic maters   Alfo, I remember weill whow we paft to the head of the mnir to fie the fyre of ioy burning vpon the ftiple head of Montrofe, at the day of the King's bnrthe.   Thefe things I mark for the grait benefit of that place and companie, wherin the Lord wald haiff me treaned vpe in my firft and tender age.

Now, when my brother and I war come hame, our father examined ws, and was glad to fie that we haid profited reafonablie : Neuertheles, the efteat of the countrey was fo vncertean and trublefome, the moyen he haid (wanting his awin ftipend, and helping diuerfe that wanted of his breithing) bot mean and finall, and the occafione of fcholles nocht ferving, we remeaned a wintar at hame, rememberit of our bniks bot now and then, as our father haid leafer, quhilk was bot verie feindle   Yit the Lord fuflerit nocht that tyme to be fruitles nather, bot I remember them twa benefites ; ane the reiding of the Storie of the Scripture that wintar, quhilk ftak in my mynd, and of Dauid Lindfayes book, quhilk my eldeft fiftar, Ifbell, wald reid and fing, namelie, concerning the letter iudgment, the peanes of Hell, and the ioyes of Heavin, wherbe fche wald caus me bathe to greit and be glad   I louit hir, theirfor, exceeding deirlie, and fche me by the reft   Sche fchew me a day amangs vtheris, a ballet fett out in print againft mmifters. that for want of ftipend left thair charge, beginning—

> Who fo do put hand to the pleuche,
> And therfra bakward goes ,
> The Scripture maks it plean aneuche—
> My kingdom is nocht for thofe, &c

With this fche burft furthe in teares, and fayes, " Alas ! what will com of thir at that letter day ? God keipe my father, and Mr James Meluill, and Mr James Balfour fra this "   And efter, cryes out the verfe of Dame Lindfay :—

> Alas ! I trimble toi to tell
> The terrible torments of the Hell ,
> That peanfull pit who can deplore ,
> Quhilk fall indure for euermore.

With hir fpeitches and teares fche maid me to quak and chout bitterlie, quhilk left the deipeft ftampe of God's feai in my hart of anie thing that euer I haid haid befor   I was giffen to a bernhe euill and dangerus vfe of pyking, the quhilk fche perceaving, of purpos gaift me the credit of the key of hir kift, and haiffing fum fmall filuer in a lytle fhottle, I tuk fum of it, thinking fche fould not haif mifteit   Bot be that occafion fche enteint fa vpon me with fa foar threatnings, and thei withall fa fweit and lowing admonition and exhorta- tions, that I thank thie my God, I abfteunt from it all my dayes thereftei : and whereuer I was, gif I could haiff gotten anie thing to bv, worthie of hir, I was accuftomed to fend it hir in taken of oui affectioun, fa lang as fche leivit This benefit I haid of God by hir meanes that wintar, for incres of his fear and honeftie of lyff   The vther was for cuill converfation and prudence   My father, that wintar, put in oui hands Palingenius, wherin he delyted mikle himfelf inioyning to ws, at his rydings fra hame, to lern fa manie verfes par ceur.   Therby I leirnt weill, and euer keipit in memorie, for dayhe practife fenfyne, thefe precepts for winning of hartes, conciliating of affectiones, and peaceable converfation, quhilk he hes in Cancro from thefe verfes following to the end of the buik :—

> Quicumque ergo cupit multum dum vivit amari
> Ant ftudeat delectare, aut prodeffe vel in fe
> Vututes habeat quas compellimtin et ipfi
> Commendare mah, et quamuis odere, verentur, &c.

Onlie a thing in the end (quhilk, he wald nocht haif ws to lern) for fubtill re- venge is nocht Chriftian, bot vit manft neidfull to be market, it is fa in vfe in the warld in this our age, and eftemied a mean point of prudence

> Nimimm magna eft prudentia vincere blande
> Atque animi ad tempas preftum cœlare dolorem

Machiauel himfelff could nocht haif preferyvit it fa weill as I haiff knawin it practifed in this countrey, and as vit it is working on : God mak ws fimple as dowes, and wyfe as ferpents   I thank God fra my hart, that maid me to ken it fra my youthe to bewar of it, bot nocht to vfe it, as I bles my Chryft I deteaft all revenge as deuillrie, and namelic ferpentine

About the fpring tyme, my father refolued to keipe my eldar brother at hame withe him, to leir him houffandrie and experience of the warldlie lyff, now almoft paft from the age of bernheid ; and to fend me to the fcholl againe for a veir or twa, that thereftir he might acquent me alſo with houſbandrie, and prepear for me a roum, and that becaus he nather ſaw the meanes to mak ws attein to ſic lerning as we might liue vpon, nor when we haid gottin it, anie ſure intertemment in the countrey for it. Sa I was put to the ſcholl of Montroſe, finding, of God's gud providence, my auld mother Marjorie Gray, wha parting from hir brother at his mariage, haid takin vpe hous and ſcholl for laſſes in Montroſe ; to hir I was welcome againe as hir awin ſone. The maiſter of the ſcholl, a lerned, honeſt kynd man, whom alſo for thankfulnes I name, Mr Andro Miln ;* he was verie ſkilfull and dilligent ; the firſt yein he cauſit ws go throw the Rudiments againe, thereftir enter and pas throw the firſt part of Grammer of Sebaſtian, therwith we haid Phormionem Terentii, and wai exerceiſd in compoſition ; efter that entered to the ſecond pairt, and haid therwith the Georgics of Wirgill, and dyvers vther things I never gat a ſtrak of his hand, whowbeit I committed twa loud faultes, as it war with fyre and ſword : Haiffing the candle in my hand on a wintar night, before ſax hours, in the ſcholl ſitting in the claſs, beinhe and neghgentlie pleying with the beut, it kendlit ſa on tyre, that we haid all ado to put it out with our feit The vther was being moleſted by a condiſcipile, wha cutted the ſtringes of my pen and ink-horn with his pen-knyff, I minting with my pen-knyff to his legges to fley him, he feared, and lifting now a lag, now the vther, raſht on his lag vpon my knyff, and ſtrak himſelff a deipe wound in the ſchin of the lag, quhilk was a quarter of a yeir in curing In the tyme of the trying of this mater, he ſaw me ſa humble, ſa feard, ſa greived, yeild ſa manie teaires, and by faſting and murning in the ſcholl all day, that he ſaid he could not find in his hart to puniſhe me for dar Bot my righteus God let me nocht ſlipe that fault, bot gaiff me a warning and remembrance what it was to be defyld with blude, whowbeit neghgenthe ; for within a ſchort ſpace efter I haid cauſit a cutlar, new com to the town, to poliſhe and ſcharpe the ſan pen-knyff, and haid bought a penniе-wourthe of aples, and cutting and eatting the ſam in the Linkes, as I put the cheiue in [my] mouthe, I began to lope vpe vpon a litle ſandie bray, haiffing the pen-knyff in my right hand, I fell and therwithe ſtrak myſelff, miſſing my wombe, an inche deipe in the inwart ſyde of the left knie, even to the bean, wherby the æquitie of God's iudgment and my conſcience ſtrak me ſa, that I was the mair war of knyffes all my dayes.

In Montroſe was Mr Thomas Anderſone, miniſter, a man of mean gifts, bot

of fingular gud lyff, God moved him to mark me, and call me often to his
chalmer to treat me, when he faw ame gud in me, and to inftruct and admonife me vtherwayes: he defyrit me ever to rehearfe a part ot Calvin's Catechifine on the Sabothes at efternoone, becaufe he haid the perple lyked weill of
the clerrnes of my voice and pronuncing with fum feilling; and therby God
moued a godlie honeft mation in the town to mak mikle of me therfor, and
called me hir lytle fweit angle   The minifter was able to teatche na ofter
but annes in the ouk: but haid a godlie honeft man rerdar,* wha read the
Scripture diftincthe, and with a religius and deuot feilling, wherby I fand
myfellf mount to giff gud eare and lern the Stories of Scripture, alfo to tak
plefure in the Pfalmes, quhilk he haid almoft all by hart in profe   The Lard
of Done, mentioned befor, dwelt oft in the town, and of his charitie interteined
a blind man, who haid a fingular gud voice, him he caufit the doctor of our
fcholl teatche the wholl Pfalmes in inter, with the tones therof, and fing tham
in the knk: be hen ing of whome I was fa delyted, that I lernit maine of the
Pfalmes and toones therof in inter, quhilk I haiff thought euer fen fyne a
grait blefling and comtort.   The exerceife of the minifterie was kepit ouklie
then in Montrofe, and than affemblies ordinarlie, quhilk when I faw I was
movit to lyk fellou weill of that calling, bot thought it a thing vnpoffible that
euer I could haiff the abilitie to ftand vpe and fpeik when all helde thair toung
and luiked, and to continow fpeiking alean the fpace of an houre   Ther was alfo
ther a poit† that frequented Edinbruche, and brought ham Pfalme buikes and
ballates, namlie, of Robert Semples making, wherin I tuik pleafour, and lernit
fum thing bathe of the efteat of the countrey, and of the miffours and cullors
of Scottes ryme. He fchew me firft Weddeiburn's Songs, wharof I lerned diuerfs
par cem with grait diuerfitie of toones   He frequented our fcholl, and of him
alfo I lerned to vnderftand the Callender etter the comoun vfe thairof   And,
finalie, I receavit the communion of the bodie and blud of the Lord Jefus
Chryft firft at Montrofe, with a graitter reuerence and fence in my faull then
oft therefter I could find, in the 13 yeir of my age, whar, coming from the
table, a gud honeft man, ane eldar of the kirk,‡ gaiff me an admonition concerning lightnes, wantonnes, and nocht takin tent to the preatching and word
read, and prayers, quhilk remeaned with me ever fen fyne; fa God maid
euerie perfone, place, and action, to be my teatchers: bot, alas! I vfed tham

* Jhone Beatie   † Jhon Finheavin   ‡ Richart Anderfone, brother to the former
Mr Thomas Anderfone.

neuer fa fruitfullie as the gud occafiones feruit, bot was caried away in vanitie
of mynd with young and fullifhe conceattes, quhilk is the heauie challange of
my confcience   The tyme of my being in Montrofe was about twa yeirs, during the quhilk the comoun newes that I hard was of the grait praifes of the
gouernment, and in end the heauie mean, and pitifull regrat amangs men in
all efteatts for the traiterus murdour of James Erle of Murro, called the Guid
Regent, anent the quhilk, fie the 19 book of the fornamed Cornicle

1571.—The efteat of Montrofe fchol changit be occafion of the mafters taking
of him to the miniftene. I cam hame to Baldowy about the Lambes in an 1571
the fourtein yeir of my age, now expyred, whar my father fetts me about the
herueft-labour, wherin I haid litle pleafoun, for whowbeit I fpendit nocht the
tyme fa truetfullie as I might at fcholl yit I lyked the fchollars lyff beft; bot
my father held ws in fic aw, that we durft nocht reafone with him, bot his
will was neidfull obedience to ws   Sa to the glore of my God, I remember a
certean day my father fend me to the fmiddy for dreffing of hewkes and fum
yron inftruments, the way lying hard by Mariekirk, wherin my father pretched, I begoude to weirie foar of my lyff and as my couftome had bein fra my
beirnheid to pray in my hart, and mein my efteat to my God, coming torrent
the kirk, and luking to it, the Lord fterrit vpe an extraordinar motion in my
hart, quhilk maid me atteans, being alean, to tall on gruiff to the ground, and
pour out a fchort and erneft petition to God, that it wald pleas his guidnes to
offer occafion to continow me at the fcholles, and inclyne my father's hart till
vfe the fanning, with promife and wow, that whateuer miffour of knawlage
and letters he wold beftow on me, I fould, by his grace, imploy the fanning for
his glorie in the calling of the minifterie ; and ryfing from the ground with ioy
and grait contentment in hart, again fell downe and worfchipped, and fa paft
on and did the earand, retourning and praifing my God, finging fum Pfalmes
Within a few dayes therefter, Mr James Meluill, my vncle, comes to Baldowy,
and brings with him a godlie lernit man, named Mr Wilyeam Collace, wha
was that fam yen to tak vpe the clafs as fuft regent of S Leonard's Collage,
within the Vniuerfitie of St Andros ; efter conference with whome that night,
God moues my father's hart to refolue to fend me that fam yeir to the Collage   Trew it was I was bot weaklie groundit in grammar, and young of
yeirs, yit the lowingnes of the gentleman, and promife of the benefeit of a
burfare's place, and of taking peanes on me, maid the mater to go fordwart,
wherof, when I was informed be my faid vncle, and haid fein and fpoken a

lytle with the man. Rebecca was never blyther to go with the servant of Abraham, nor I was to go with him. And trewlie this finding of God at a nead, was the beginning of a ritche treaffour of the pruiff of his prouidence, mercie and grace continowallie increaffing fen fyne, that I wald nocht giff for ten thowfand warlds.

Sa I cam to St Androis about the fift of November in the forfaid yeir 1571, and entent in the courfe of Philofophie, vnder the regenterie of the faid Mr Wilyeam, wha haid the eftimation of the maift folide and lernit in Ariftotle's Philofophie. And first haid vnder him Caffander his Rhetorik: but at the beginning, nather being weill groundet in grammer, nor com to the yeirs of naturall iudgment and vnderftanding, I was caft in fic a greiff and difpear becaufe I vnderftood nocht the regent's langage in teatching, that I did nathing bot burfted and grat at his leffones, and was of mynd to haifl gone ham agean, war nocht the luiffing cear of that man comforted me, and tuik me in his awin chalmer, caufit me ly with himfelff, and euerie night teatched me in privat, till I was acquented with the mater * Then he gaiff ws a compend of his awin of Philofophi and the partes thairof, of Dialectik, of Definition, of Diuifion, of Enunciation, and of a Syllogifine Enthymen, and Induction, &c., quhilk I thought I vnderftood better About the quhilk tyme, my father coming to the town, begoude to examine me, and finding fum beginning was exceidinglie reioyfit, and vttered fweittar affection to me then ever before; he intertemed my regent verie harthe in his ludging, and gaiff him grait thanks; he fend me to him, efter he haid taken leue, with twa pieces of gold in a neapkine; bot the gentleman was fa honeft and lowing, that he wald haifl non of his gold, but with aufteire countenance fend me bak with it: Na, never wald receaue gold nor filuer all the tyme of my courfe. We enterit in the Organ of Ariftotle's Logics that yeir, and lernit till the Demonftrations. He haid a lytle boy that feruit him in his chamber, called Dauid Eliftone, wha, amangs threttie and fax fchollars in number, (fa manie war we in the clafs,) was the beft This boy he caufit weat on me, and confer with me, whase ingyne and iudgment paft me als far in the wholl courfe of philofophie, as the aigle the howlet In the multiplication of Propofitiones, Medalles, Couerfion of Syllogifines, Pons Afinorum, etc, he was als read as I was in telling an-and-threttie This I mark for a fpeciall caufe of thankfulnes following.

Bot of all the benefites I haid that yeir was the coming of that maift nota-

* We hard the Oration pro rege Deiftaro.

ble profet and apoftle of our nation, Mr Jhone Knox to St Andros, wha, be
the faction of the Quein occupeing the caftell and town of Edinbruche was
compellit to remoue therfra with a number of the beft, and chufit to com
to St Andros. I hard him teatche ther the prophecie of Daniel that fimmer
and the wintar following. I had my pen and my litle book, and tuk away
fic things as I could comprehend In the opening vpe of his text he was moderat the fpace of an halff houre ; bot when he entert to application, he maid
me fa to grew and tremble, that I could nocht hald a pen to wryt I haird him
oftymes vtter thefe thretenings in the hicht of ther pryde, quhilk the eis of
mome faw clerlie brought to pafs within few yeirs vpon the Captean of that
Caftle, the Hamiltones, and the Quein himfelff He ludgit down in the Abbay
befyde our Collage, and our Primarius, Mr James Wilkie our Regents, Mr
Nicol Dalglefe, Mr Wilyeam Colace, and Mr Jhone Dauidfone went in ordinarlie to his grace efter denner and fupper. Our Regent taried all the vacans
to heir him, whowbeit he haid vrgent effeares of his brother fonnes to handle,
to whom he was tutor Mr Knox wald fum tyme com in and repofe him in our
collage yeard, and call ws fchollars vnto him and blefs ws, and exhort ws to
knaw God and his walk in our contrey, and ftand be the guid caufe, to vfe our
tyme weill, and lern the guid inftructiones, and follow the guid exemple of our
maifters Our haill collage, maifters and fchollars, war found and zelus for the
guid caufe ; the vther twa collages nocht fa ; for in the New Collage, whowbeit
Mr Jhone Dowglafs, then Rector, was guid aneuche, the thrie vther maifters
and fum of the Regentes war euill myndit, vz Mrs Robert, Archbald and Jhone
Hamiltons, (wharof the laft twa becam efter apoftates) hated Mr Knox and
the guid caufe ; and the Commiffar Mr Wilyeam Skeir could nocht lyk weill
of his doctrine. The auld collage was rewlit be Mr Jhon Rutherfurd, then
Dean of Facultie, a man lernit in philofophie, bot invyus corrupt. This I mark
for the fetting furthe of the benefit I receavit in the collage and compame I
was into The public newes I hard that yen was of the Englifs armie that
cam in vnder the conduct of Mr Drur, and brunt and flew throuchout Clid-
difdall and all the dominiones of the Hamiltones, for the flauchter of the Guid
Regent ; they brunt the caftell and palice and town of Hamiltone, and caried
away grait pray ; they wracked all the Bordars waft and eft, and tuik the
caftell of Hume. Alfo Mathew Stewart, Eile of Lennox was fchofine Regent
wha that herveft cam to Breachine, befeigit the caftell tharof, haldin be the
fuddarts of the Erl of Hountlie, compellet tham to rander, and hangit threttie
tharof, qlk was callit the Bourde of Breachine.

This yeir in the monethe of July, Mr Jhone Dauidsone, an of our Regents, maid a play at the mariage of Mr Jhone Colum, quhilk I saw playit in Mr Knox presence, wherin, according to Mr Knox doctrine, the castell of Edinbruche was besiged, takin, and the Captan, with an or twa with him, hangit in effigie

1572.—The second yeir of my course we haird the Demonstrations, the Topiks and the Sophist Captiones. And the Primarius,* a guid, peacable, sweit auld man, wha luffed me weill, teached the four speaces of the Arithmetik, and sumthing of the Sphere; bot the graittest benefit I haid of him, was his daylie doctrine at the prayers in the kirk everie morning, for he past throw the twa buiks of Samuel and twa of the Kings verie pleanlie and substantiuslie, quhilk I remembent the better ever since. He causit sing comounlie the 44 and 79 Psalmes, quhilk I lernt par ceur, for that was the yeir of the bludie massacres in France, and grait troubles in this countrey, the warres betwix Leithe and Edinbruche being verie hat. The castel of Dumbarten was notablie tean, and Jhone Hamilton, Bischope of St Androis hangit

In the monethe of August, the Blak Parliament of Stirling haldin,† whan the second Regent was slean in Wolmistones armes, &c. vide Buchan Chro

1573.—The thrid yeir of our course we haird the fyve buiks of the Ethiks, with the aught buiks of the Physiks, and De Ortu et Interitu. That yeir we haid our Bachlar art according to the solemnities then vsed of Declamations, banqueting and playes. And in the mean tyme thatof my father maried my said eldest sistar Isbell and second, Marione, bothe on a day; bot efter that festing, we gat hard newes of the defeat of the Forbesses at the Crab-stean besyd Aberdein

1574.—The fourt and last yeir of our course, quhilk was the 17 yeir of my age outpast, and 18 rinning, we lerned the buiks De Cœlo and Mateors, also the Spher, more exacthe teachit be our awin Regent, and maid ws for our Vices and Blakstens, and haid at Pace our promotion and finissing of our course. The beginning of this yeir was also maist dulfull to me by the departour of my deirest sistar Isbell, wha died of hir first bern, in whom I lossit my naturall mother the second tyme

* Mr James Wilkie.   † The parliament was haldin in August 1571, befor I cam to the Vniuersitie

The ordour of four kirks to a minifter then maid be the Eil of Morton, now maid Regent, againft the quhilk Mr Jhone Damdfone, an of the Regents of our collage, maid a buik called the " Conference betwix the Clerk and the Courtieur,' for the quhilk he was fummoned befor the Juftice-ear at Hadintoun this wintar, the laft of our courfe, and bamfihed the cowntrey

In the thrid and tourt yeirs of my courfe, at the direction of my tather, I hard the Comiffar, Mr Wilyeam Skein, teatche Cicero de Legibus, and diuers partes of the Inftitutiones of Juftinian I was burdet in the houfs of a man of law, a verie guid honeft man, Andro Greine be nam, wha louit me exceiding weill, whafe wyfl alfo was an of my mothers ; I am fure fche haid nocht fone nor bein fche loued better This lawier tuk me to the Confiftorie with him whar the Comiffar wald tak pleafour to fchaw ws the practife in judgment of that quhilk he teatched in the fcholles. He was a man of fkill and guid confcience in his calling, leirnit and diligent in his profeffion, and tuk delyt in na thing mair nor to repeat ower and ower agane to anie fchollar that wald afk him the things he haid bein teatching Lykwayes my oft Andro acquentit me with the formes of fummonds and lybelling of contracts, obligatiounes, actes, &c , but my hart was nocht fett that way

Man ower in thefe yeirs I leirned my mufic, wherin I tuk graitter delyt, of an Alexander Smithe, fervant to the Primarius of our collage, wha haid bein traned vpe amangs the mounks in the Abbay I lerned ot him the Gam, Plean fong, and mome of the treables of the Pfalmes, wherof fum I could weill fing in the kirk ; bot my naturalitie and eafie lerning by the ear maid me the mair vnfolide and vnreadie to vfe the torne of the art I louit finging and playing on inftruments paffing weill, and wald gladhe fpend tyme whar the exerceife therof was within the collage, for twa or thrie of our condifciples played fellon weill on the Vuginals, and another on the Lut and Githorn Our Regent haid alfo the Pinalds in his chalmer, and leirnit fome thing and I eftn him : bot perceaving me ower mikle caried efter that, he difharted and left of It was the grait mercie of my God that keipit me from anie grait progrefs in finging and playing on inftruments, for giff I haid attemed to anie reafonable miflure therin I haid never don guid vtherwayes, in refpect of my amorus difpofition, wherby Sathan fought even then to deboiche me, bot my God gaifl me a piece of his fear, and grait naturall fhamfaftnes, quhilk by his grace wai my preferuatines Als I haid my neceffars honeftlie aneuche of my father, bot nocht els ; for archerie and goff, I haid bow, arrofe, glub and bals, but nocht a puifs for Catchpull and Tauern, fic was his tatherlie wefdom for my

weill   Yit now and then I lernit and vsit sa mikle bathe of the hand and
Racket catche as might serue for moderat and halfome exerceife of the body

I wald hauff gladlie bein at the Greik and Hebrew toungs, becaus I red in
our Byble that it was translated out of Hebrew and Greik , bot tha langages
war nocht to be gottine in the land   Our Regent begoud and teatched ws the
A,B,C, of the Greik and the simple declinationes, bot went no farder   Be that
occasion he tauld me of my vncle Mr Andro Melnill, whom he knew in the tyme
of his course in the New Collage to vse the Greik logicks of Ariftotle, to the
quhilk was a wounder to tham that he was sa fyne a fchollar and of sic expectation   This maid me inquyre for Mr Andro when I cam ham the fecond and
thrid yen of our courfe , bot my father and Mr James fchew me they fearit he
was dead, becaufe of the grait cruill waries in France, and that they hard he was
in Poicteors befeiged ; that it was aught or nyne yens fen he pafl to France,
and four or tyve yens fen they gat anie letters or word from him.   This
twitched my hart wounder foar in refpect of the grait comendation I haird of
him be my Regent and diuerfe vthers   Bot foon efter, about the middes of
our thrid yen, Alexander Young cam ham from Geneu, from his vncle and
my neir kinfman Mr Hendrie Scrymgour of honourable memorie, with fum
propynes to the King, and letters to Mr Georg Bowchanan and Mr Piter
Young, that an the Kings maister, that vther his pædagog, and amangs the
reft brought letters from the faid Mr Andro to my father and his brother Mr
James, and therwithall word of his weilfear and fingular eftimation in Geneu,
whar he haid four yens profeffit.   Of thefe newes my hart was exceiding glade,
and the faid Alexander being with all diligence to return agane to Geneu, I
haid a letter in readines pennit at lamthe in Latin, the beft I could, quhilk I
delyverit to my cowfing Alexander, wha within a twa monethes put it in the
hands of my faid vncle Mr Andro.   And he tauld me at meitting, and oft
fen fyne, it was a fpeciall motion of his ham coming, then the quhilk I, nor
Scotland nather, receavit never a graitter benefit of the hands of God, as will
better appeir henefter.

Bot becaufe in all my courfe, the graitteft benefit was the fight and heiring
of that extraordinar man of God Mr Jhone Knox, fa far as I then knew and
haird of him, I man hen record.   In the tyme of his being in St Andros, ther
was a Generall Affemblie hauldin in the fcholles of St Leonards, our Collage.
Thair, amangs vther things, was motioned the making of Bifchopes, to the
quhilk Mr Knox opponit himfelff directhe and zealufhe.   Yit a number of

commiffionars of the kirk meatt at Leithe* with the lords that haid the guid caus in hand, (wharof euerie ane was hounting for a fatt kirk leiving, quhilk gart tham feght the faſtar,) and ther aggreit to mak Biſchopes the warſt turn that euer was done for the kirk leiving, as experience atteanes declared, when they war named *Tulchains*, that is, calffis ſkinnes ſtuffed with ſtra, to cauſe the cow giff milk ; for euerie lord gat a biſchoprie, and fought and preſented to the kirk ſic a man as wald be content with leaſt, and fett tham maiſt of fewes, takes, and penſions   Amangs the reſt the Erle of Mortoun gat the biſchoprik of St Andros, efter the hanging of Jhone Hamiltone, and preſented thervnto that honorable father of the Vniuerſitie, as Rector therof for the preſent, Mr Jhone Dowglaſs, a guid, vpright-harted man, bot ambitius and ſimple, nocht knawing wha delt with him   I hard Mr Knox ſpeak againſt it, bot ſparinghe, becauſe he lout the man, and with regrat, ſaying, " Alas ! for pitie, to lay vpone an auld weak man's bak, that quhilk twentie of the beſt gifts could nocht bear   It will wrak him and diſgrace him."   And indeid it cam to paſs ſa, for within twa or thrie yeirs he died, during the quhilk he haid nather that ho-nour, welthe, nor helthe as he was wount to haiff, euer repenting that he tuk it on   That was the firſt tyme I hard Mr Patrik Conſtantine, wha then new retourned out of France with young Mr James Macgill, the Clark Regiſter eldeſt ſone, thought, be the ſaid Clarks court, wha was grait with the Erle of Mortoun, to haiff bein preſent to the biſchoprik, bot coming ſchort, becam a zealus preatchour againſt biſchopes. I hard a ſermont of his the ouk efter the biſchope was maid, vpon ane extraordinar day that he might haiff the graitter audience, wherin he maid thrie ſorts of biſchoppes : my Lord Biſchop, my Lord's Biſchope, and the Lord's Biſchope.   " My Lord Biſchope," ſaid he, " was in the papiſtrie ; my Lord's Biſchope is now, when my Lord getts the benefice, and the Biſchope ſerues for na thing bot to mak his tytle ſure ; and the Lord's Biſchope is the trew miniſter of the goſpell."   Mr Patrik was then weill lyked, and of guid expectation with ſic as knew him nocht intus.   The yeir efter was maid biſchope Geordie of Murro, whom I ſaw a haill wintar mumling on his pretching af his peapers euerie day at our morning prayers, and haid it nocht weill par ceur when all was done ; and efter him Biſchope Patone of Dunkell.† This greivit the hairt of the men of God to the dead : bot the warres war ſa hatt, and the Lords cryed they behind to leaue tham giff they gatt nocht the kirk

* The Conſcience at Leithe was in Januar, and the General Aſſemblie in Merche therefter, 1571
† I ſaw tham bathe gett impoſition of hands be B. Dowglas and Mr Jhon Woundrom, ſuperin-tendent, whom I ſaw alſo inaugarat (as they cald it) B. Dowglas.

leiving, and monie knew nocht yit the corruptioun and vnlawfulnes of that in-
ventioun of men, and sa the mater paft fordwart

At Mr Knox comming to St Andros, Robert Lekpriuik printer, tranfported
his lettres and prefs from Edinbruch to St Andros, whar firft I faw that excellent art ot printing, and haid then in hand Mr Patrik Conftant's Catechifine
of Calvin, converted in Latin heroic vers, quhilk with the author was mikle
eftimed of

About the fame tyme cam to St Andros to vifit Mr Knox, Johne Durie, fellow minifter at Leith with Mr Dauid Lindfay, wha was then for ftoutnes and
zeall in the gud caufe mikle renouned and talked of; for the gown was na
fooner af, and the Byble out of hand fra the kirk, when on ged the corflet, and
fangit was the hagbot, and to the fields   Him I faw firft at St Andros with
Mr Knox

The town of Edinbruche recouered agane, and the gud and honeft men
therof retourned to thair houffes, Mr Knox with his famihe paft hame to
Edinbruche, being in St Andros he was verie weak   I faw him euerie day
of his doctrine go huhe and fear, with a furring of martriks about his neck
a ftaff in the an hand, and gud godlie Richart Ballanden his feruand, haldin
vpe the vther oxtar, from the Abbay to the paroche kirk, and be the faid Richart and another feruant, lifted vpe to the pulpit, whar he behouit to lean at
his firft entrie, bot or he haid done with his fermont, he was fa active and vi-
gorus, that he was lyk to ding that pulpit in blads and flie out of it   Sa foone
efter his comming to Edinbruche, he becam vnable to preatche; and fa inftitu-
ting in his roum, be the ordinar calling of the kirk and congregation, Mr
James Lawsone,* he tuk him to his chamber, and moft happelie and comfortablie departed this lyff   Vide concerning his lyfi and dathe, Mr Thomas
Smeton's buik againft Hamiltone the Apoftat

Ther was twa in St Andros wha war his aydant heirars, and wrot his fermonts, an my condifciple Mr Andro Yowng, now minifter of Dumblean, wha
tranfleated funi ot tham in Latin, and read tham in the hall of the Collage in-
ftead of his orations: that vther was feruant to Mr Robert Hamilton, minifter
of the town, whom Mr Robert caufit to wrait, for what end God knawes   The
threatenings of his fermonts war verie fowr, and fa particular, that fic as lyket
nocht the caufe, tuk occafioun to reprotche him as a rafhe raler without war-

---

* A man of fingular lerning, zeal and eloquence, whom I neuer hard preatche bot he melut my
hart with teares.

rand   And Mr Robert Hamilton himselff being offendit, conferrit with Mr
Knox, asking his warrand of that particular thretning aganist the Castell of
Edinbruche, that it sould run lyk a sand glass ; it sould spew out the Captan
with sham, he sould nocht com out at the yet, bot down ower the walles—and
sic lyk. Mr Knox answert " God is my warrant, and yie sall sie it " Whill
as the vther was skarsse satisfeit, and tuk hardlie with it, the nixt sermont
from pulpit, he repeates the thretnings, and addes therto, " Thow that will
nocht beleive my warrand sall sie it with thy eis that day, and sall say, What
haif I to do heir ?" This sermont the said Mr Robert's servand wrot, and
being with his maister in Edinbruche a twa yeir therefter at the taking of
the Castell, they ged vpe to the Castell hill, saw the forwark of the Castell all
demolished, and imning lyk a sandie bray ; they saw the men of wear all sett
in ordour. The Captan, with a lytle cut of a staff in his hand, takin down
ower the wals vpon the leathers, and Mr Robert, troublet with the thrang of
the peiple, sayes to his man, " Go, what haif I ado heir !" and in going away,
the servant remembers his maister of that sermont, and the words , wha was
compellit to glorifie God, and say, he was a trew prophet

Ane vther strange particular was recompted to me be Mr Dauid Lindsay,
minister of Leithe · That efter Mr Knox haid taken bed, he cam in to visit
him, as he was accustomed, and asked him whow he did   He answent,
" Weill, brother, I thank God ; I haiff defyrd all this day to hait yow, that I
may send yow yit to yon man in the Castell, whom yie ken I haif loued sa deirlie : Go, I pray, and tell him that I haif send yow to him yit annes to warn and
bid him, in the nam of God, leave that euill caufe, and gif ower that Castle ;
giff nocht, he salbe brought down ower the wals of it with shame, and hing
aganist the sune : Sa God has assurit me "   Mr Dauid, whowbeit he thought
the message hard, and the thretning ower particular, yit obeyit, and past to
the Castell ; and meiting with Sir Robert Meluill walkin on the wall, tauld
him, wha was, as he thought, mikle movit with the mater   Therefter com-
muned with the Captan, whom he thought also sumwhat moved : but he past
from him in to the Secretar Lithintone, with whom, when he haid conferrit a
whyll, he cam out to Mr Dauid agam, and said to him, " Go, tell Mr Knox
he is bot a drytting prophet "   Mr Dauid returning, tauld Mr Knox he haid
dischargit the commissioun faithfullie, but that it was nocht weill accepted of
efter the Captan had conferrit with the Secretar.   " Weill (sayes Mr Knox) I
haif bein ernest with my God anent tha twa men ; for the an I am sorie that
sa sould befall him, yit God assures me ther is meicie for his saul ; for that

vther I haif na wairand that euer he falbe weill " Mr Dauid fayes, he thought
it hard, yit keipit it in mynd till Mr Knox was at reft with God.   The Englifs armie cam in with munition meit for the feage of the Caftell, and within
few dayes the Captean is fean to rander, and com down the leathers ower the
wals : he is committed to a ludging in the town with a cuftodie of fouldarts
Mr Dauid, becaufe of grait acquentance, comes to vifit him, whom he employes to go to the Erle of Morton and offer him his haill heritage, the band
of manrent of all his frinds, and to pafs at the countrie in exyll during his
will.   Mr Dauid goes that night and fpeakes the Erle, then being Regent.
proponing to him the offers   The Regent goes afyde and confultes with the
Abbot of Dumfermling and Clark Regifter, therefter Mr Dauid comes craving
his anfwer   It was giffen, It could nocht be ; the peiple could nocht be fatiffeit.
nor ther caufe cleir and crowned, with[out] exemplar punifment of that man
and his counfellour the Secretar.   Mr Dauid the morn be nyne houris comes
agean to the Captean, the Lard of Grange, and taking him to an fore ftare of
the ludgin apart, refolues him it behoued him to fuffer.   "O then, Mr Dauid,'
fayes he, " for our auld frindfchipe and for Chryft's feak. leaue me nocht "   So
he remeanes with him, wha paeffing vp and down a whyll, cam to a fchot, and
feeing the day fear, the fune cleir, and a fkaffald preparing at the Corfs in the
Hiegcatt, he falles in a grait ftudie, and alters countenance and cullour :
quhilk, when Mr Dauid perceaved, he cam to him and afkes him what he was
doing   " Fathe, Mr Dauid," fayes [he], " I perceaue weill now that Mr Knox
was the trew fervant of God, and his thretning is to be accomplifled ;" and
defyred to heir the treuthe of that againe   The quhilk Mr Dauid reherfed.
and addit thervnto, that the fam Mr Knox at his retourning had tauld him
that he was erneft with God for him, was forie, for the loue he buir him.
that that fould com on his bodie, bot was affurit ther was mercie for his faull
The quhilk he wald haiff repeated ower againe to him, and thervpon was
grnitlie comforted, and becam to be of guid and cheirfull cowrage ; fa that he
dyned moderathe, and therefter tuk Mr Dauid aparte for his ftrenthning to fuffer that dethe, and in end befeikes him nocht to leaue him bot convoy him to
the place of execution ; " And tak heid," fayes he, " I hope in God, efter I falbe
thought paft, to giff yow a taken of the affurance of that mercie to my faull
according to the fpeakine of that man of God.'   Sa about thrie houres efter
none, he was brought out and Mr Dauid with him, and about foure the fune
being wall about af the northwert nuk of the fteiple. he was put af the leddar.
and his face firft fell to the eft, bot within a bonie whyll turned about to the

weft, and ther remeaned againft the fune ; at quhilk tyme Mr Dauid, euer prefent, fayes, he marked him when all thought he was away, to lift vpe his hands
that war bund befor him, and ley tham doun agam fafthe, quhilk moued him
with exclamation to glorihe God befor all the peiple This laft part of his execution I hard alfo of Jhone Durie, wha was prefent with him on the fkaffald
    Sa in lyk maner whateuer he fpak concerning the Hamiltones and the Quem,
whowbeit in appeirance in the mean tyme bot contrar, and mome guid folks
thought hard and ftrange, yit cam to pafs, and was marked in particular to the
grait glorie of God, terrour of the enemies, and ioy of the godlie

    Thus ending my courfe of Philofophie in St Andros, whar vpon the part of
God I haid offerit to me all guid occafion of godlines, lerning, and wefdome
fa mikle as was in the countrey for the tyme, and might fall in my age ; bot
on my part, wha throw wantones and vanitie neglected and mifpent the occafiones, haid gottin na thing bot a nam and opinion of lerning, a babling of
words without wit, at leaft wefdome ; for my light young nature was giffen
mair to be fuperficiall nor folid, circumferentiall nor centrik, defyring to heir
and haiff the names of maine things, bot never weill degefting nor ryping out
the nature of anie, bot fleiting and flowing, foon lyking and foone lothing euerie
thing   Onlie now and then I fand fum fweit and conftant motiones of the
feir and loue of God within me
    I cam to Doudie, whar my vncle Roger, a man godlie, kynd, and wyfe, en-
terit with me to vnderftand to what calling my hart inclynd, and gaiff out
that my father's intention was to haiff me a lawer. I faid nocht mikle againft
it, bot wiffed at God I might haiff the gifts and grace to be a minifter. Coming ham my father tented me in the fam maner, bot nocht fa familiarlie ; nather durft I vtter anie thing againft his opinion and iudgment, bot faid I was
readie to obey his will and direction in all things. He commandit me then
to occupie my tyme weill amangs his books till the vacans, at what tyme he
wald haiff occafion to meit with fum guid man of law in Edinbruche, to whom
he wald put me in feruice ; giff fa he meinde indeid, becaufe he faw na promifion for the minifterie, or to effay my refolution, I can nocht tell. Going a day
to Bomtone, I paft by the kirk of Maritone and place wher I haid prayed, and
wowed to God, the fam cam in my memorie with a grait motion of mynd
and determination to pay my wow giff God wald giff the grace and moyen
Sa praying and worfchiping befor God, it cam in my mynd to pen a fermont
vpon a part of Scripture, and leaue it in a buik of my fathers, whar he might

find it. and fa I tuk the beginning of the nynt of Jhone's Euangell of the blind man, and ftudeing his comentares theron, Mufculus and Marlorot, wrot it and left it in Mufculus Comentars, quhilk when he fand it, lyked him weill ; yit fpak na thing, bot left me in fufpence till it pleafit God to gift me full refolution   For a lytle befor Lambes word cam that Mr Andro was com to Edinbruche, and within twentie dayes efter he cam to Baldowy, with whom when my father had content, and knawin what opinion he hand of me, he delyvert me ower vnto him   thinking he was difburdenit of me ; and fa indeid he was, as the continuation of this narratione will declar   This was in the yen of God 1574

Becaufe I faid befor that Scotland receavit never a grautter benefit at the hands of God nor this man, I will fchorthe fett down, fuft, a litle difcours of his lyff befor his coming ham   and fyne what he brought with him.   He was born in Baldowy, a place pleafand, tertill, and weill aired, lyand within a myll to the town of Montrofe, vpon the fouthweft, hand be the Æftuarium flummis Æfkæ meridionalis, in the yen of Chryft's bnthe 1545, the 1 day of the monethe Auguft, begottin of gentill and honeft parents, Richard Melull of Baldowy, brother-german of Jhone Melull of Dyfart, and Gills Abercrombie, douchter to Thomas Abercrombie, burgefs of Montrofe, of the houfs of Muthle.   He was the youngeft of nyne brether, all left alyve when than father was flean with the graitteft part of the gentilmen of Angufs, in the vangard of the field of Pinkie   His mother leivit an honorable widow till he was twall yeir of age, traned vpe in letters in the fcoll of Montrofe, vnder Mr Thomas Anderfone, efteemed the beft maifter in his tyme, whowbeit nocht the maift lernit   Sche left fax of his fonnes in honeft rounes, all even then or fchorthe therefter, bearing office in kirk or comoun weill, and with the beft eftimed in thair rank and aboue ; they war Richart Melull of Baldowy, and minifter of Chryft's Euangell fone efter, the eldeft : Mr Thomas, a tyne fchollar, weill trauelit in France and Italie, Secretar-deput of Scotland . Walter, burgefs, and efter bailyie of Montrofe, a wyfe and ftout man : Roger, burgefs of Dondie, a man of fingular giftes of nature and God's grace, bot was nocht traned vpe in lettres   I haird that faithfull paftor of Dondie, Wilyeam Chryftifone, a lytle efter his deathe, with teares fay, " Alas ! when God tuk this Roger Melull, he tuk from me my father, and the carefuleft father that euer Dondie haid   His nam wilbe remembent fa lang as Dondie is a town "*   Mr

* I haiff hard Mr Robert Bruce fay oft of Roger, that giff he haid haid Mr Andro's lerning, he wald be the oddeft man in Europe.

James, minifter of Chryft's Euangell: Jhone, then gudman and rewlar of his
mother's effeares, and efter a minifter in the kirk · the reft war Robert, Dauid, and Andro, wharof the firft twa was kept at the fcholl till they tyrde,
and war put to Crafts; the laft was a feikhe tender boy, and tuk pleafur in
na thing fa mikle as his buik   Sa with the portion that was left him, he
fpendit a ven or twa in Montrofe, namlie, heirring a France man, called Petrus
de Marfihers, teache the Greik grammer, and fum thing of that langage, honefthe conduct to the fam as a rare thing in the countrey, nocht haird of befor, be that notable inftrument in the kirk, Jhone Erfkine of Done, of maift
honorable and happie memorie; wherin he profited fa, that entering therefter
in the courfe of Philofophie within the Vniuerfitie of St Andros, all that wes
teatched of Ariftotle he lerned and ftudeit it out of the Greik text, quhilk
his maifters vnderftood nocht   He paft his courfe in the New Collage, tenderlie belouit of Mr Jhone Dowglafs, provoft of that Collage and rectour of the
Vniuerfitie, wha wald tak him betuix his legges at the fyre in Wintar, and
warm his hands and cheiks, and bleffing him, fay, " My fillie fatherles and
motherles chyld, its ill to wit what God may mak of thie yit "   Sa ending his
courfe of Philofophie, he left the Vniuerfitie of St Andros with the commendation of the beft philofopher, poet, and Grecian, of anie young maifter in the
land; and with all poffible dihgence maid his preparation, and paft to France
Be the way he was extreamlie tormented with fie feiknes and ftorme of wather, fa that oft tymes, whylls he danger of fchipwrak, whylls he infirmitie and
feiknes, he luked for deathe, he arryvit firft in England, and again imbarking
cam to Burdeaux, wher he taried nocht lang, bot embarking from that cam to
Deipe; from that to Paris, whar he remeanit in the Vniuerfitie twa yeirs at his
awin ftudies, heirring the Lightes* of the maift fcyning age in all gud lettres,
the king publict profeffors, Andreas Tornebus in Greik and Latine Humanitie; Petrus Ramus in Philofophie and Eloquence; Jo: Mercerus in the Hebrew langage, whervpon he was fpecialie fett. In the laft yeir of they twa, he
grew fa expert in the Greik, that he declamit and teatchit leffones, vttering
never a word bot Greik, with fie readines and plentie, as was mervolus to the
heirars. From Paris he paft to Poicteors, whar he regented in the Collage
of St Marceun thrie yeirs † Ther he haid the beft laweis, and ftudeit fa mikle

---

* Salmacus, Pafcafius, Forcatellus, Mathematiciens; Baldumus the lawer   Duretus, Medicine,
Carpentarius, Quinquarborius, Hebrew.

† Ther was grait emulation and contention in verfes, and harangs betuix the twa Collages, S.

therof as might ferue for his purpofe. quhilk was Theologie, wherto he was dedicat from his mother's wombe And when the Collages war giffen vpe, becaufe of the feage leyed to the town, quhilk was lang and fenfull, he was employed be an honourable councellar to inftruct his onlie fone. The bern profited exceiding weill, and was of a fweit inclination, takin away from him and his parents be a fchot out of the campe, quhilk parted the wall of his chalmei and woundit him deadlie in the thie He called incontinent for his maifter. whom, whow foone he faw, he caucht him in his armes, and vttered the words of the Apoftle in Greik ; δ διδασκαλε, τὸι δρομοι μοῦ τετελικα,—" Maifter, I haiff perfytted my courfe ;" and fa with mome vther godlie and fweit words he died That bern gaed neuer out his hart, bot in teatching of me, he often remembert him with tender compaffion of mynd. He taried in that houfs, quhilk was weill furnifit, during the tyme of the feadge. Ther was a corporall with a few fuddarts put to keipe the houfe, who efpyed him in his prayers and fpeitches to be halie and deuot ; and on day (being a Papift and man of wair,) with a grait aithe he challengit Mr Andro that he was a Hugonot, and wald helpe to betray the town, thertor becaufe the alarme was ftrikken, he could nocht truft him in that houfs Mr Androw anfwers incontinent, " I am als honeft a man to my God and magiftrat and eftet of the town, and maifter of this familie, as thow art, and fa fall proue this day—do thy beft " And with that ftarts to the nixt armour and on with it, and all in armes to the ftable, and takes the beft horfs be the heid. This when the corporall faw, he comes with fellon fear termes and intreats him to leaue of and forgiff him " O no, no !" fayes he, " I fall proue als honeft and ftout as thyfelff " " O Monfieur," fayes the vther, " my Captean and the maifter of this houfs will rebuk me and put me from it, giff yie be thus troublet ; thertor I pray yow tak me obleffit to my vttermaift, and tarie and forgiff me." Sa he tuk eafe in gud part, and was neuer troublet thereftei. Giff it haid com to the warft, he was refolued, being weill horft, to haiff gottin him to the campe of the Admirall, wha was in perfone befeageand the town.

The feage of the town being raifit, he left Poicteors, and accompanied with a Frenche man, he tuk iorney to Geneu, leaving buiks and all ther, and caried na thing with him bot a litle Hebrew Byble in his belt Sa he cam to Geneu all vpon his fut, as he haid done befor from Deipe to Paris, and from that to Poicteors ; for he was fmall and light of body, but full of fprites, vigourus

Marcenn and Pharcan, bot during his prefence thei, S Marcenn haid without queftion the vpper hand.

and cowragins. His companiones of the way, when they cam to the Ine wald
ly down lyk tyred tyks, bot he wald out and fight the townes and vilages
witherfoeuer they cam. The ports of Geneu wer tentelie keipit becaufe of
the troubles of France, and multitud of ftrangers that cam. Being therfor
inquyrit what they war, the Frenche man his companion anfwernt, " We ar
pure fcollars" Bot Mr Andro perceaving that they haid na will of pure folks,
being alreadie owerlaid therwith, faid. " No, no. we are nocht pure ; we haiff
alfunkle als will pay for all we tak fa lang as we tane. We haiff letters from
his acquentance to Monfieur di Beza : Let ws delyver thefe—we craue na
fordar ;" and fa being convoyit to Beza, and then to than ludging, Beza, perceaving him a fchollar, and they haiffing neid of a Profeffour of Humanitie
in the Collage, put him within a twa or thrie dayes to tryell in Virgill and
Homer, quhilk he could acquait fo weill, that but farder he is placed in that
roum of profeffion, and at his firft entrie, a quarters he peyit him in hand. Sa
that whowbeit thair was but a crown to the fore betwix tham bathe, and the
Frencheman weak fprited, and wift nocht what to do, yit he fund Gods prouidence to releue bathe himfelff and helpe his marrow till he was prouydit
In Geneu he abead fyve yeirs. during the quhilk tyme his cheiff ftudie was
Diuinitie, wheranent he hard Beza his daylie leffons and preatchings ;—Cornelius Bonauentura, Profeffour of the Hebrew, Caldaik, and Syriac langages ;—
Portus, a Greik born, Profeffour of the Greik toung, with whom he wald reafone about the right pronuntiation therof ; for the Greik pronuncit it efter the
comoun form, keiping the accents ; the quhilk Mr Andro controllit be precepts
and reafone, till the Greik wald grow angrie and cry out, " Vos Scoti, vos
barbari, docebitis nos Græcos pronunciationem linguæ noftræ, fcilicet !" He
hard ther alfo Francis Ottoman, the renownedeft lawer in his tyme Ther he
was weill acquented with my Eam, Mr Hendrie Scrymgeour, wha, be his lerning in the lawes and polecie and fervice of manie noble princes, haid atteined
to grait ritches, conquefit a prettie roum within a lig to Geneu, and biggit
theron a trim houfs called the *Vilet*, and a fear ludging within the town,
quhilks all with a douchtar, his onlie bern, he left to the Syndiques of the
town. About the end of fyve yeirs the Bifchope of Brechine and Mr Andro
Pulwait with him cam ther, and tareing a whyll, purpofit hamwait, with
whom Mr Andro Meluill, efter the receaving of letters from his brethering
and me, with grait difficultie purchaffit leaue of the kirk and magiftrates of
Geneu,* and takin iorney cam hamwart. From Lions they traverfit the

* Wha wald on na wayes haiff contented to part with him, giff his confcience haid fuffered him

Franche Compté to the head of the riuer of Loir and cam down the sam be
water to Orleans, hauffing in companie. lewm or aught dayes, a captean, a me-
diciner, and a preist, superstitius papists at than meitting kythed in ther
speitche and meattes, bot be minie and solid reasoning withall, becam flech-
eatters on Fridday, and the captean nocht far from the kingdome of heavin or
they parted   The portes of Orleans wer streat kerpet, (being bot a yeir and
halft efter the horrible maslacres) Brechine and Mr Andro Polwart was on
fut, and Mr Andro weill mounted on horss, becaufe he haid wraisted his leg,
they past the twa futmen and deteining the horsman, the souldarts inquyres
what he was   He answerit a Schottes man   " O ! yie Scottes men are all Hugonotes." fayes the gard. " Hugonotes !' fays he, " What s that ? we ken nocht
fic "   • O," fayes the souldart, " vie haiff nocht mefs "   " Forsuthe,' fayes he
minriche, ' our beirns in Scotland gaes dayhe to mefs '   " Gud companion,"
fayes the vther, lauching, " go thy way."   Coming to thair ludging he tells
his inbours and garres them lauche : • Bot siuhe,' fay they, " we war verie
fleyed our pasport sould haiff bein loked, and finding ws com from Geneu,
sould haiff bein troublet." • Yea," fayes thair host, " tak it for a speciall prouidence of God, for within this twall monethe moine thowsands for les hes
lost than lyves ' Going out of the town again at the turn of a vew, they meit
the procession, Brechine and his Pædagog was befor, Mr Andro a lytle efter
Brechine turnes bak and fayes, " What sall I do !"   " Fordwart,' quod he,
and so he does   Mr Andro haulds out his fyde clok with his armes als thought
he haid bein bearing fum thing vnder his oxstars, and so passes by   But his
hart bet him therefter oft and fear that he sould haifl sa stouthe counfelht
the vther, and vsit a piece of diffimulation himfelff   Coming to Paris, ther
they remeaned dyvers dayes, where Mr Andro, meitting with the Lord Ogilbie
his countreyman, is requeisted be him to go to the Jesuits Collage whar he
reafonit with father Tyrie sindrie dayes ; bot the tyme being sa dangerus, and
of sum innassing speitches of the Bischope of Glafgw, he was counfelht to haft
af the town *   Sa they cam from Deipe ower to Ry in England, from thence
to Londone, whar they remaint a space, and bying horsses, cam hame Loudon
way be Berwik to Edinbruche.   And this for a schort recitall of his lyff till
his coming ham.

to referv his gifts anie langer onoffered to his cowntrey, and imployed for the benefit of his
frinds.   Beza, in his letter to the generall kirk of Scotland alleages that as the grauteft taken of
affection the kirk of Geneu could fchaw to Scotland, that thev haid suffered thamfelues to be
fpuiled of Mr Andro Melull, wherby the kirk of Scotland might be mritched

* At Whitfonday he cam out of Paris, the quhilk day King Charles, that maid that horrible maf-

As to that he brought ham with him.—It was that plentifull and inexhauft theaffour of all gud letters and lerning bathe of humen and devyne things ; and that quhilk fuperexcelles, ane profund knawlage, vpright fincentie, and fervent zeall in trew relligion, and to put the fam in vfe for the profit of his kirk and countrey ; ane vnwearied peanfulnes and infatiable pleafour to giff out and beftow the fam without anie recompence or gean   Yea, rather fa far as his fmall moyen might reak, conducing and inviting all gud ingynes to receave and inbrace the famng.   Wherby within thefe fax and twentie yers he hes inritched his nation with incorruptible fubftance, mor without all compear nor in anie age fen it was a kingdome, or manie nations in the waild this day, giff ther wan honour and mentinance for lerning, quhilk the diduction of this Stone will verifie and cleir at large   The nixt fimmer cam ham his librarie, ritche and rare, of the beft authors, in all langages, artes and fciences, cleirlie declaring be his inftruments what a craftes man he was.

He was nocht well come to Edinbruche, when word was of him at Court, and the Regent Eile of Morton called vnto him Mr George Buchanan. Mr James Halliborton, coronall, and Alexander Hay, foone efter Clark Regifter, and directes tham to dell with Mr Andro to content to be my Lord Regents grace domeftic inftructour, and to giff a few notes vpon his chaptour read daylie, and he fould be honorablie advanced at the firft occafion   The Regents menning was to haiff him and his giftes framed for his purpofe, to reftrean the friedome of application in preatching, and authoritie of the Generall Affemblies, and bring in a conformitie with England in governing of the kirk be Bifchopes and innunctiones without the quhilk he thought nather the kingdome could be gydet to his fantafie, nor ftand in gud aggriement and lyking with the inbour land   For this form of polecie he vfit to mak fchofe of the men of beft giftes, and fuft try tham at Court giff they would be conformable and ferue his purpofe, and fyne prefer thame to bifchopries and government of the

Naribus, ore oculis atque auribus vndique et ano,
Et pene erumpit qui tibi Carle, cruor.
Non tuus ifte cruor   Sanctorum at cede cruorem,
Quem ferus haufifti, concoquere haud poteras.

At neafe, at mouthe, at ein, at ears, at wand,
That blud that buiifts from all thy conduits weaft
Is nocht thyne, Charls bot of that holie band,
Quhilk thow did drinke, bot could nocht weill digeaft.

kirk, as he did with twa therefter, and haid proceidit ferdar giff God had nocht disapointed him. Mr Andro, whowbeit nocht weill acquented with thir purposes then, yit lyked nocht to be in Court, bot rather to be in sum Vniuersitie, and protests thair as the Kings Lectors in Parise, and sa as God directed him, refusit, and cravit his graces fawour to repose a whyll with his frinds till God callit him to fix a roum quhilk he thought meittest.

Sa he cam to Baldowy to his brother, my father, whar he remeaned that herveft quarter, and whar, within a few dayes efter his coming, I was resigned ower be my father haillelie vnto him to weak vpon him as his sone and servant; and, as my father faid to him, to be a pladge of his loue. And furhe his service was easie, nocht to me onlie, bot euen to the fremdeft man that ever serued him, for he schosed for his servantes onlie schollars; and giff they haid done ame gud at thair book, he cared nocht what they did to him That quarter of yeir I thought I gat graitter light in letters nor all my tyme befor, whowbeit, at our meitting, in my conceat, I thought I could hauff taked to him in things I haid haird, as he did to me as a maifter of Arts, bot I perceavit at annes that I was bot an ignorant bable, and wift nocht what I faid, nather could schaw ame vse therof, bot in clattering and crying He fand me bauche in the Latin toung, a pratler vpon precepts in Logik, without ame profit for the right vse, and haifling fum termes of Art in Philofophie without light of folid knawlage; yit of ingyne and capacitie gud aneuche, wherby I haid cunned my dictata and haid them readie aneuche. He enterit therfor and conferrit with me fum of Bowchanans Pfalmes, of Virgill and Horace, quhilk twa, namlie Virgill, was his cheiff refrefchment efter his graue ftudies; wherin he lat me fie, nocht onlie the proper Latin langage and ornaments of poefie, bot alfo mair guid Logik and Philofophie then euer I haid hard befor. I had tean delyt at the Grammer Schole to hen reid and fung the verfes of Virgill, taken with the numbers therof (whowbeit I knew nocht what numbers was till he tauld me) and haid mikle of him par ceur; bot I vnderftud never a lyne of him till then He read a Comedie of Tyrence with me, fchawing me that ther was bathe fyne Latin langage and wit to be lernit: That of langage I thought weill, bot for wit I merveled, and haid nocht knawin befor. He put in my hand the Comentaries of Cæfar, comending him for the fimple puritie of the Latin toungc, alfo Saluft, and read with me the Conuration of Catelin. He haid gottin in Paris, at his by coming, Bodin his Method of Hiftori, quhilk he read ower himfelff thryfe or four tymes that quarter, annes with me, and the reft whill I was occupied in the

Greik grammer, quhilk he put in hand of Clenard, causing me vnderstand the
precepts onlie, and lear the παραδειγματα exacthe ; the practise wharof he schew
me in my buik, going throw with me that Epistle of Basilius, and cawsing me
lern it be hart, bathe for the langage and the mater : therefter to the New
Testament, and ged throw sum chapteis of Mathew and certean comfortable
places of the Epistles, namlie, the Romans And last. entering to the Hebrew, I gat the reiding declynations and pronons, and sum also of the conu-
gations out of Martinius grammer, quhilk he haid with him, and schew me
the vse of the Dictionan also, quhilk he haid of Reuchlins with him. And all
this as it war bot pleyng and craking, sa that I lernit mikle mair by heiring
of him in daylie converiation, bathe that quarter and therefter, nor euer I
lernit of anie buik, whowbeit he set me euer to the best authors

The Generall Assemblie was haldin in the monethe of August, soone efter
his hame comming, whar ther was grait word of him, aryfing be the commendation of the Bischope of Brechine, and Mr Andro Pulwart. Sa commissionars from dyverse partes of the cowntrey maid sutt to the Assemblie for
him ; namlie, they of Fyff wald haiff haid him to St Andros in the roum of
Mr Jhone Dowglass, newlie departed this lyff, and ther indeid was he marked
be the Regent to haiff bein maid Bischope of St Andros, giff he haid bein capable of Court Bischopriks ; bot the maist erneft instance of Mr James Boid
Leslie, maid Bischope of Glasgw, and Mr Andro Hay, superintendent of thaise
partes, obteined of the Assemblie and sum of his frinds ther present, that he
sould come and visit Glasgw, and sie the beginning of a Collage ther, and heir
what conditiones sould be offered to him, that giff he lyked he sould condi-
send till abyde with tham. This Mr James Boid was a gentle man of the
Lord Boids kin, a guid man and lower of lerning and lernd men, inducit be
his cheiff to tak the Bischoprie, the gift wharof the said Lord Boid, being a
grait counsallour to the Regent, haid purchassit for his commoditie ; bot within
a yeir or twa, when he fand nocht his bischope plyable to his purpose, he
caufit his sone, the Maister of Boid, tak the Castell, and intromeat with all
therin, keipe it and gather vpe the rents of the Bischoprik to intertein the
faining, and this was done impune, nochtwithstanding the Regents streat justice.
becaufe the Tulchain caufit nocht the kow giff milk aneuche to my Lord. Sa
that I haiff hard the honest gentle man new whill fear that euer he tuk on that
Bischoprie efter he haid vnderstud be Mr Andro of the vnlawfulnes therof,
and fand sic a curss vpon it. The vther, Mr Andro Hay, was an honest, zealus,

frank harted gentleman, perfone of Renthrow, and Rector of the Vniuerfitie of Glafgw, wha lyked never thofe Bifchopries, and wha fpecialie was the erneft futtur for Mr Andro Meluill   Sa vpon their lettres he tuk iorney, accompanied with twa of his breither, Mr James and Roger, and Mr James Balfour, then minifter at Edinbruche his cowfing german, and cam vnto Glafgw, whar he contented, at the end of vacance, to enter and teatche in the Collage as principall maifter, and thus aggrieng he returned ham again to Baldowy   At the tyme apointed, about the end of October, we tuk iorney, accompanied with his brother Jhone, and cam to Doudie, from that to St Johns Town, the firft tyme I faw it; from that to Stirling, whar we remaned twa dayes, and faw the King, the fweiteft fight in Europe that day, for ftrange and extraordinar gifts of ingyne, iudgment, memorie and langage.   I haid him difcours, walking vpe and down in the auld Lady Maris hand, of knawlage and ignorance, to my grait mervell and eftonifhment.   Ther Mr Andro conferrit at lynthe with Mr George Bowchanan, then entering to wriat the Storie of his Countrey; alfo with Mr Piter Young, and Sanders his brother; Mr Gilbert Moncreif the Kings Medicinar, whome with he haid bein weill acquented in Geneu.   Alfo with Mr Thomas Bowchanan, then fcholmafter the wha accompanied ws of his kyndnes to Glafgw

We cam to Glafgw about the firft of November 1574, whare we fand Mr Piter Blakburn, a guid man, new com from St Andros, enterit in the Collage, and begoun to teatche conform to the ordour of the courfe of St Andros   But Mr Andro entering principall maifter, all was committed and fubmitted to him, wha permitted willinghe to the faid Mr Piter, the can of the Collage Leiving, quhilk was but verie fmall, confifting in litle Annualles then, and fett him baillche to teatche things nocht haid in this Countrey of befor, wherin he traucht exceiding dihgentlie, as his delyt was therin alleanerhe   Sa talling to wark with a few number of capable hemars, fic as might be inftructars of vthers therefter, he teatched tham the Greik grammer, the Dialectic of Ramus, the Rhetorie of Taleus, with the practife therof in Greik and Latin authors, namlie, Homer, Hefiod, Phocilides, Theognides, Pythagoras, Ifocrates, Pindarus, Virgill, Horace, Theocritus, &c.   From that he enterit to the Mathematiks, and teatched the Elements of Euclid, the Arithmetic and Geometrie of Ramus, the Geographie of Dyonifius, the Tables of Hunter, the Aftrologie of Aratus; from that to the Morall Philofophie, he teatched the Ethiks of Ariftotle, the Offices of Cicero, Ariftotle de Virtutibus, Cicero's Paradoxes, and Tufculanes, Arift Polyt. and certean of Platoes Dialoges; from that to the Naturall Philofophie he teatched the buiks of the Phyfics, De Ortu, De Cœlo, &c alfo of Plato and Fernelius With this he ioyned the Hiftorie, with the twa lights thereof, Chronologie and Chrographie, out of Sleidan, Menarthes and Melancthon. And all this, by and attoure his awin ordinar profeffion, the holie tonges and Theologie, he teacht the Hebrew grammar, firft fhortlie, and fyne mor accurathe, therefter the Caldaic and Syriac dialects with the practife therof in the Pfalmes and Warks of Solomon, Dauid, Ezra, and Epiftle to the Galates. He paft throw the haill comoun places of theologie verie exactlie and accurathe; alfo throw all the Auld and New Teftament, and all this in the fpace of fax yeirs, during the quhilk he teatcht euerie day cuftomablie twyfe, Sabothe and vther day, with an ordinar conference with fic as war prefent efter denner and fupper. His lerning and peantulnes was mikle admired, fa that the nam of that Collage within twa yeirs was noble throwout all the land, and in vther countreys alfo Sic as haid paffed ther courfe in St Androus cam in nomber ther, and entered fchollars again vnder ordour and difcipline, fa that the Collage was fa frequent as the roumes war nocht able to receaue tham. The fcolmaifter of the town, Mr Patrik Scharpe, was his ordinar heirar and contubernall, whome he inftructed, and directed in the maift commodius bringing vpe of the youthe in grammer and guid authors; whom I haid oftentymes profes that he lerned mair of Mr Andro Melvill craking and pleying, for vnderftanding of the authors quhilk he teatched in the fcholl, nor be all his comentares. Sic lyk Mr Piter Blakburn, wha tuk vpe the firft clas Finalie, I dar fay ther was na place in Europe comparable to Glafgw for guid letters during thefe yeirs for a plentifull and guid chepe mercat of all kynd of langages, artes and fciences.

In the Simmer of the firft of thefe fax yeirs, about the 18 yeir of my age compleit, God opened my mouthe firft in publict vpon the exerceis, with fic comendation out of the mouthe of Mr Andro Hay, rector and fuperintendent, namlie even ther in publict in his addition, as I was wounderfullie incouragit to go fordwart In the middes of that ouk, I dreamed that I haid maid the exerceis in Montros, and being demifled from the breithring with confortable commendation, I cam ower to Baldowy to my father, and entering in the place ther was nan that knew me. I paft vpe to the hall, and enter it in the chalmer at the end therof, whar I met with my father, and tauld him whow I haid bein occupied, wha tuk me in his armes and kiffing me, faid in my ear, " Jamie, ferue God, for thow art behauldin to him :' and with that he goes and fitting down on a bedfyde, he keaues bak ower, fa that his feit flak out ftiff and dead. With that I walkned with grait feir and commotion, quhilk abaid with me the fpace of an houre. Bot the burding of the exerceife lyand vpon me, maid me to forget it, till going to the rector, Mr Andro Hay, his ludging to delyver certean buiks I haid borrowit, and at the firft fight he takes me in his armes, and thrufting and kiffing me, he fayes, " My hart, ferue God, for thow art behaldin to him." This is my dreain, thought I, and tauld it to my companion going to the Collage agane. Bot within twa days, my vncle, Mr Andro, returning from Edinbruche, whar he haid bein taking ordour with his buiks new com hame, by his countenance fuft, and efter a fweit and confort-able delling with me, therefter tauld me that his brother, my father, was de-perted this lyff, and efter inquifition, fund it was the fam verie night I haid dreamed Sa it pleafed God to mak me warning, and furneife me confort againft the heavieft newes that euer I haid hard befor in all my lyff ; for as I haiff fchawen befor, he was a rare man, and a maift lowing father to me, at the clofing of whafe mouthe God thus opened myne.

Be eccafion of the recounting of this dream to my vncle Mr Andro, he re-memberit me of an vther I haid dreamed, and tauld him the ouk befor his go-ing to Edinbruche, that my brother Dauid was hangit, with certean circum-ftances, quhilk troublit me. The quhilk at the verie inftant I tauld him, he interpreted of my brothers mariage, whilk wald nocht be to his weill and con-fort, knawing na thing of that mater, till with the newes of my fathers dethe he was infomit that he haid maried his fone Dauid in a fummar and haftie maner a few dayes befor his depairtour, quhilk was almaift a wrak to him and his hous, as hereften we fall declare

Nocht lang efter Mr Andro receavit letters from Monfieur du Bez, and therin amangs the reft, " Colaceus vefter, exemplar omnium intutum, nuper apud nos rita functus eft" This was my guid Regent, wha, efter the ending of our courfe, had gean to France, and coming to Genen, ther died ; a grait los to the Kirk of God in his countrey, for he was foidlie lernit, hailelie addicted to diuinitie, with a fincear and zealus hart. Ther was never twa thinges befor that, quhilk ofter and mair heavilie I regreated in my mynd, nor the deing of thefe my fathers, befor I haid teftified my thankfull hart to thame, efter the atteining to fum light of letters and knawlage of God ; quhilk when I was even then about to do be fum litle effay in the thrie langages, I was be the newes of thair deathe cutt aff.

That yein alfo, in the monethe of Merche, I haid the benefit to be prefent with my vncle, Mr Andro, at the General Affemblie haldin in Edinbruche. At the quhilk the queftion being movit about the Jurifdiction and polecie of the Kirk, Mr Andro Melvill, withe certean vther brethring, war ordeamt to tak peanes theranent, and giff in ther iudgment to the nixt Affemblie. And in deid that mater coft him exceiding grait peans bathe in mynd, body, and gear,* during the fpace of fyve or fax yeir, with the gean of the Regent, Erl of Morton, and his bifchopes vtter indignation Yit, with the wounderfull affiftance of God, he bure it out till the abolifhing of bifchopes, and eftablifing of the prefbyteries according to the word of God Wharby he gatt the nam of επισκο- πομαστ.ξ,— epifcopor um exactor,—the flinger out of bifchopes Ther I hard firft in Edinbruche Mr James Lawfon, a godlie lernit man, of a wounderfull moving vtterance in doctrine, whom I delyted mikle to heir, and whom I never haird bot withe teares bathe of remors and ioy. As alfo Jhone Durie, newlie tranfported from Leith to Edinbruche, a man zealus and mightie in fpreit, with Mr Walter Balcanquall, ane honeft, vpright hairted young man, lathe entent to that miniftene of Edinbruche. Thir, informed man throwhe be Mr Andro of the vnlawfulnes of bifchopes, and the right maner of governing of the Kirk be prefbyteries, dealt dilligentlie and forciblie in ther doctrine againft that ane, and for that vther wakned vpe the fpreits of all gud brethring, and crabet the court ftranghe Bot furhe ther minifterie and exemple of lyff movit me, and tuk fie hauld vpon my hart, that I went never to na place with better will nor to Edinbruche, and tyred never les in ame place nor in than companie.†

1575 —Being at the Affemblie therefter in Auguft at Edinbruche, 1575, the queftion was proponed, " Giff Bifchopes, as they war at that tyme in the Kirk of Scotland, haid a lawfull calling or office by the word of God?" Efter advyfe of certean breithring thervpon, and reafoning in publict, it was refolut negatiue ; and that the nam bifchope was comoun to euerie paftor, and ordeimt that breither fould inquyre ferdar bathe in that and vther poinctes of the difcipline and polecie of the Kirk.

Etter the Affemblie we paft to Angufs in companie with Mr Alexander Arbuthnot, a man of fingular gifts of lerning, wefdome, godlines, and fweitnes of nature, then Principall of the Collage of Aberdein ; whom withe Mr Andro

* Keiping Affemblies and dyettes of conference, reafoning and advyfing with brethring anent that wark

† The tym was verie fauorable for God haid glorefied his nam woundertullie of leat, in performing ftrange things forfpoken be Mr Knox againft the Caftell of Edinbruche.

I

communicat anent the haill ordour of his Collage in doctrine and difcipline,
and aggreit as therefter was fett down in the new reformation of the faid Collages of Glafgw and Abeidein. In Angus we maried my youngeft fiftar Bar-
bara vpon Mi James Balfour, then minifter at Guthrie ; and buried guid auld
Thomas Meluill of Dyfart, the murrie man ; and fa, efter vacans, returned to
Glafgw.

About Michaelmas, in the yeir 1575, in the 19 yeir of my age, I enterit
Regent, and tuk vpe the clafs, and teatched the Greik grammer, Isocrates Pa-
ranefis ad Demonicum, the firft buk of Homeis Iliads, Phocylides, Hefiods
εργα και ημεραι, the Dialectic of Ramus, the Rhetorik of Taleus, with the practife in Ciceros Catilinars and Paradoxes, &c

Thei was then refident in Glafgw Mr Patrik Adamfone, alias Conftant, minifter of Pafley, a man of notable ingyne, letters, and eloquence, wha was Mi
Andioes grait fiind and companion ; and, efter he haid craftelie infinuat himfelff in Mr Androes fawour, and the miniftrie of Edinbiuche, he began to ftep
on fordwart to the firft degrie of a bifchope, and leaving Pafley paft to Court,
and becam minifter to the Regent, Erle of Mortoun. About the quhilk tyme
the perfonage of Giffen vaked, a guid benefice. lyand hard befyde the town of
Glafgw, peying four and twentie chalder of victuall   This benefice is offered
to Mr Andro, piovyding he wald be the Regents man, and leaue aff the perfut of the bifchopes ; quhilk he refufit. bot delt erneftlie with the Regent himfelff, and be all moyen, namlie, of the faid Mr Patiik, to haifl it annexit to the
Collage, the rent wharof was veiie finall, nocht able to fuftein twa maifters.
without ame buifares. The Regent keipit the benefice in his hand vndifpomt
mikle of twa yeir. alleaging, that Mi Andro haid the wait, wha wald defraud
that Collage, and himfelff bathe, of fic a benefit. becaufe of his new opiniones.
and owerfie dreames, anent the Kirk difcipline and polecie. Yit, at laft, the
Regent, feing he could nocht be broken be boft, be advyfe of the faid Mr Patrik, he effayes to moue him be benefit, and makes a new erection and reformation of the Collage of Glafgw, annexing and mortefeing thairvnto the faid benefice of Giffen ; quhilk was the beft tuin that ever I knew ather the Regent
or Mr Patrik to do. Bot the fpeciall drift was to demeanit Mr Andro, and
caufe him relent from deallmg againft bifchopes ; bot God keipit his awin
fervant in vprightnes and treuthe, in the middes of manie heavie tentationes,
(whilas his coleg, Mr Piter, and vthers, nocht onlie furmeifit, bot fpak out,
that he was a grait hinder of a guid wark,) and by his bleffing effectuat the
turn be crowked inftruments.

1576.—The fecond yeir of my regenting, I teatchit the elements of Arithmetic and Geometrie out [of] Pfellus for fchortnes; the Offices of Cicero; Ariftotles Logic, in Greik, and Ethic, (and was the firft regent that ever did that in Scotland,) alfo Platoes Phædon and Axiochus; and that profeffion of the Mathematiks, Logic, and Morall Philofophie, I keipit (as everie ane of the regents keipit thair awin, the fchollars ay afcending and paffing throw) fa lang as I regented thei, even till I was, with Mr Andro, tranfported to St Andros.

That yen, in Apryll, the Generall Affemblie, conveint in Edinbruche, refolued, concerning bifchopes, the nam and office to be comoun to all the paftois of the Kirk, out of the quhilk might be fchofin commiffionars for vifitation, planting, &c. Item, All bifchopes war ordeanit to tak thamfelues to a particular flok. Item, Contribution ordeanit to be maid for releiff of the exylit Frenche kirks. Item, Nominat for making overture of the polecie and iurifdiction of the Kirk: for the Weft countrey, James, bifchope of Glafgw, Mr Andro Melvin, Mr Andro Hay, Mr James Grig, Mr Dauid Cuningham; for Lawdien, Mr Robert Pont, Mr James Lawfone, Mr Dauid Lindfay, and, adioynit to tham, Mr Clement Lytle, and Mr Alexander Sim, lawers, for Fyff, Mr Jhone Windrame, fuperintendent, with the principall maifters of the Vniuerfitie; for Meins and Anguff, the Laird of Din, Wilyeam Chryftifone, Mr Jhone Row, Mr Wilyeam Rind, Jhone Duncanfone; for Aberdein, Mr Jhone Crag, and Mr Alexander Arbuthnot; the places ordeanit whar they fould meit, and thair diligence to be giffen in to the nixt Affemblie, to be haldin at Edinbruche in October.

In this mean tyme the Chancellar, Lord Glammis, being a gud, lerned noble man, wryttes to Geneua to Theodor Bez, craving his iudgment in the queftiones moued at our Generall Affemblies; and, be that occafion, we gott hain Bezaes Treatifs *De triplici Epifcopatum*, quhilk did mikle gud.

All the tyme I could get, by my ordinar calling, I employed to the ftudie of the Hebrew toung and theologie. I read Bezaes Confeffion, giffen me be my vncle, diligenthe, and hard his Leffons according to Caluins Inftitutiones: and, being myndfull of my wow, and finding God to haiff bleffed the firft and fecond opening of my mouthe in publict on the exerceife, I thought guid to continow. The ordour of the Collage was, that euerie regent, his ouk about, convoyit the fchollars to a kirk hard adiacent whar the peiple convenit, and that regent red the comoun prayers, with a chaptour or twa. I, for my part, contented nocht fimplie to reid, bot taking fum pean, when I might haiff fliped, the night befor, indeuorit to tak vpe the foum of the chaptour, and giff fum notes of doctrine, with exhortation. This pleasit and comfortit guid peiple verie mikle, sa that they resorted verie frequentlie my ouk, quhilk alsa movit the rest of the regents to essay and follow the sam form ; and sa bathe profited thamselues and vthers. All the quhilk I record to the praise of the grace of my guid God alleanerlie ; for vther wayes, a veaner, fulishar, corrupter youthe was ther nocht in that Collage ; sa that giff my God haid nocht put in me sum bit of conscience, and fear of his nam, in discharging my office, and a peice of honestie and scham befor the warld, I sould never haiff done guid, bot, by sluggishnes and wandering fantasies, easelie caried away to all debourherie

The breithring apointed be the Assemblie convenit at Glasgw, in Mr Dauid Cunnghames hous, then Subdean of Glasgw, and dean of our facultie of artes ; a man learnit and of verie guid accompt at that tyme, haid fear hous and yeards wherin an erle micht haiff dwelt, and a thowsand mark of rent with the better. Nan was sa frak in the caufe as he. He moderat the reasoning, gathcrit vpe the conclusiones, and put all in wrait and ordour to be reported to the Assemblie. Bot, to mark the strange sagacitie of my vncle Mr Andro, he ever suspected bathe Mr Patrik Adamsone and this Mr Dauid, and said, he feart they sould nocht proue frinds in the caufe, they war sa courtlie. And sa fell out, indeid, as we sall heir

The Generall Assemblie, convened at Edinbruche in October, ordeanit the travelles of the breithring to be sighted and advysit vpon, that, being brought in open Assemblie, they might procede to determine. In the mean tyme, compenres Alexander Hay, Clark of Registar, and giffes in, from my Lord Regents grace, a number of questiones to be resolut be the Assemblie, anent the polecie and jurisdiction of the Kirk, quhilk sett tham to farder consultation. Ther was Mr Patrik Adamsone, presented to the bischoprik of St Andros ; and being inquyrit, in the publict Assemblie, giff he wald receaue that bischoprik, he answerit he wald receaue na office judgit vnlawfull be the Kirk : and as to that bischoprik, he wald na wayes accept of it without the advyfs of the Generall Assemblie. And, neuertheles, or the nixt Assemblie, he was seasit hard and fast on the bischoprik, wherby all gossoprie ged vpe betwin him and my vncle Mr Andro. Ther was at Court then, Captin Mongumerie, a guid honest man, the Regents domestic, wha market an accustomed phrase of Mr Patriks in his doctrine ; " The prophet wald mein this." And whow soone he faw Mr Patrik gripe to the bischoprie, he cryes out amang his companions :

" For als oft as it was repeated be Mr Patrik, ' The prophet wald mein this,
I vnderftud never what the *profit* mems whill now," quod he.

To mak the Affembhe lyk the better bathe of the prefenter and prefented,
the Regent directs his minifter to the Affemblie, fchawin he had receav it a letter from the Quein of Eingland, informing his grace that the Princes of Germanie war to keipe a Generall Convention at Magdeburg. for ratefieng of the
Auguftan Confeffion, whar wald be prefent lermt Commiffionars from all Proteft-
ant princes; and that hir Matie was to fend, requyring him to do the fam
The Regents grace, thertor, defyrit the Affemblie to nominat the perfones,
and he fould mak prouifion. The Affemblie nominat Mr Andro Melull, Mr
Alexander Arbuthnot, and Mr George Hay; bot when ther was an appenance of the bifchoprie, the ambaffadrie fealit.

Mr Patrik taking him to the bifchoprie, the fuffragantes roum is filled atteanes be Mr Dauid Cunninghame, wha leived Glafgw and the guid caufe, and
becomes the Regents minifter, bot with a curs accompaning him; for he haid
never that wealthe nor eftimation efter quhilk he haid befor, whow beit within
a yeir advancit to the bifchoprik of Aberdein; and nocht onlie fa, bot be-
came, foone efter the Eile of Mortons execution, an of the [maift] miferable
wretches in all the weft countrey, lyand debochit and out of credit, in a cot
hous, himfelfl at the an fyde of the tyre, and his cow at the vther. Thus
God curfed that bifchoprie of his; but as for Mr Patriks, we will haiff men
ado with it hereftei

This yeir, in the wintar, appened a terrible Comet, the ftern wharof was
verie grait, and proceiding from it toward the eft a lang teall, in appenance,
of an eall and a halff, lyk vnto a biffom or fcurge maid of wands all fyrie
It reafe nighthe in the fouth weaft, nocht aboue a degrie and an halff afcending aboue the horizon, and contmowed about a fax oukes, or twa monethe, and
piece and piece wen away. The graitteft effects wharof that out of our countrey we hard was a grait and mightie battell in Barbaria in Afric, wharin thrie
kings war flean, with a hudge mulutud of peiple And within the countrey,
the chafing away of the Hamiltones. For whowbeit the Regent, foone efter
the taking of the government vpon him, maid a law of obhuion; yit the Hous
of Mar confentit nocht therto, thinking the young king, whom they haid in
keiping, could neuer be fure fa lang as the Hamiltones keipit than rounes,
and therfor maid a Read againft them the fam fimmer, wherby the Lords of
Arbrothe and Pafley, with the fpecialles of thair frinds, namlie, fic as war
giltie of the guid Regents murthour, fled away in Eingland. The Caftell of

Hamilton, keipit a whyll be Arthour of Mirritoun, was takin and demoliffed to the ground, and the faid Arthour execut at Stirling in my fight, wha died verie penitentlie and weill, to my grait edification ; being the firft execution that euer I faw, except of a witche in St Andros, againft the quhilk Mr Knox delt from pulpit, fche being fet vpe at a pillar befor him · Lyk as I haiff hard the fam maift notable feruant of God almoft ordinarlie threttin thefe Hamiltones maift terfullie for the murder of the gud Eile of Murray, Regent The Lord Arbrothe maried the Countes of Caffels, fiftar to the Lord Glammes then chancellar, wharby he gat tolerance for a fchort tyme.   But the wintar befor the faid chancellar being cut of at Stirling, in the fimmer following he was fean to flie away.   The minifter of Hamilton, Mr Jhone Dauidfone, a gud man, haud admoniffed and thretned that Caftell for ryot, hurdome, &c. and faw in a vifion, as I hard him record, a grait arm, with a fword in the neff, ftanding aboue the Caftell, quhilk, with fwift force ftricking down vpon it, did overthraw the fam to the grund, and therefter coming down throw the wood and town, did fpoile and hurt the fam

1577.—The year following, 1577, the Generall Affemblie conuened at Edin-bruche in October. whar the heades of the polecie war ordeamit to be drawin in conclufiones, and certean breither apointed to gather togidder the trauelles of the brething from all partes, and digeft and put the fam in ordour, drawing tham in certeane propofitiones for breintie

At that Affemblie, Mr Patrik Adamfone is fund to haiff intrufit himfelff in the bifchoprik of St Andros againft the actes and ordinances of the Kirk, and therfor ordeanit to be proceidit againft be his Synodall Bot, as he was wounderfull craftie, he offerit to ley down all, at the feit of the brething, and be ordourit at the pleafure of the Affemblie whow foone the fam war throuche and at a point with the mater of the polecie ; and fa with fear promifes, drifted and pat aff till he gat his tyme

About the end of that fam October, ther was an vther Affemblie haldin at Edinbruche. at the quhilk the heids of the polecie war reported, digeft in order. They war ordeanit. efter reufing, to be put in mundo, and prefented to the Regents grace ; and certean breithring nominat to confer with his grace theranent, and a dyet fett at Stirling for the fam.

During all thefe Affemblies and erneft endeuors of the breithring, the Regent is often requyrit to giff his prefence to the Affemblie, and fordar the caufe of God ; bot nocht onlie in effect refufes, bot vfes grait thretning againft

the maift zelus breithring, fchoring to hang of thame, vtherwayes ther could
be na peace nor ordour in the countrey. Sa, euer refifting the wark of difcipline in hand, bure fordwart his bifchopes, and preffed to his iniunctiones and
conformitie with Eingland; and, but queftion, haid fteyed the wark, giff God
haid nocht fteined vpe a faction of the nobilitie againft him, wha maid a grait
convocation at the Fall kirk, and haid almoft com to ftraks, giff the Einglis
Ambaffatour, a guid, godlie man, and louer of our nation, Mr Robert Bowes,
with the Chancellars guidnes and wefdome, haid nocht fteyit for taking ordour; wherwith a Convention was fett in Stirling of the Efteates, and the
breithring nommat and apointed be the Affemblie weating on, fell out that vnhappie murdour of that lerned and guid noble man, Lord Glammes, Chancellar, flean in a tumult be a fchot of a piftolet in the head * Whom when God
had fa taken away from the Regent Mortoun, his contrar faction drawes a
diaught at annes to caufe the King, now about fourtein yeirs of age, to tak
the goveinment in his awin perfone; wharby Mortoun is compelht to go to the
Market Crofs of Edinbruche, in folemne maner, and giff ower his Regentfchipe,
and all publict adminiftration of the realme.

This Regent Erle of Mortoun was a man ever caft vpon the beft fyde,
and did honefthe and ftouthe in the caufe. He lowit Mr Knox whill he was
alyue At his deathe and buriall he gaiff him ane honorable teftimonie,
" That he nather fearit nor flatteit ane fleche ," and, efter his deathe, was
frindlie to his wyff and childring. He was verie wyfe, and a guid Juftitiar in
adminiftration. His fyve yeirs war eftimed to be als happie and peaceable as
euer Scotland faw. The name of a Papift durft nocht be hard of; ther was
na theiff nor oppreffour that durft kythe. Bot he could nocht fuffer Chryft to
reing frielie be rebuking of finne, bot maid oppofition to the miniftrie of
Edinbruche in publict place; nor, be the right government of his Kirk be the
Prefbyterie of his lawtullie callit paftors and eldars, miflyked the Affemblies
Generall, and wald hairf haid the name therof changit, that he might abolifhe
the previlage and force therof Wharvnto my uncle, Mr Andro, fpecialie opponit himfelff, and therby, and for the bifchopes, incurrit his fpeciall indigna-

---

* Mr Andro maid vpon him this Epigram.—

Tu, Leo magne, iacis inglorius; ergo manebunt
Qualia fata canes? Qualia fata fues?

Sen lawlie lyes thow noble Lyon fyne,
What fall betyde behind to dogges and fwyne?

tion, and therabout firſt diſcordit with Mr Dauid Lindſay, to whom he was
comounlie contradictor, ſaying that Maiſter Knox haid commendit him to the
Court all his dayes, that he was a guid mid man, and maker of brues amangs
men, bot ſould nocht haiff place betwix God and man. Yit in effect the ſaid
Mr Dauid keipit honeſt in the cauſe of the diſcipline till it was concludit, and
efter. He ſought to inſinuat himſelff, efter the leying down of his Regentrie
in the Kings fawour and ſum Counſallours, be twa things in ſpeciall that con-
cernit the Kings weill and the realmes. Ane, that the King might be a frie
king and monarche, haiffing the iewell and power of all Eſteates, quhilk the
Kirks Generall Aſſemblie empeared. Ane vther, to be conforme with England
in the Kirks polecie; to haiff biſchopes to rewll the Kirk, and they to be an-
ſwerable to the King, and ſa the trie preatching repreſſed. With this, he was
wounderfullie giſſen to gather gear, therby, as he ſaid, to mritche the King
withall. Thir things, whoweit humblit, yit he amendit nocht, bot keipit out
his courſe till he might do na man, and then gloriſiet God, as in the awin
place ſalbe declarit.

This yeir, in the ſimmer, God brought hain Mr Thomas Smetou, a man of
ſingular giftes of lerning and godlines, a grait benefit to his kirk, and ſpeciall
bleſſing of my guid God, for me in particular.

1578.—The Generall Aſſemblie convenit at Edinbruche in Apryll 1578 in
the Magdalen Chapell * Mr Andro Melull was ſchoſin Moderator, whar was
concludit, That Biſchopes ſould be callit be thair awin names, or be the names
of Breither, in all tyme coming, and that lordlie name and authoritie baniſſed
from the Kirk of God, quhilk hes bot a lord, Chriſt Jeſus. Alſo the haill heids
of the polecie, put in propoſitiones, and ſett in ordour, war rateſied and allowit,
except a litle of the Diaconat to be farther adviſit. Item, That na biſchope
ſould be elected or maid therefter, nor na miniſter conſent therto, vnder the
pean of depriuation. Item, The leat murdour of the Lord Glames, Chancellar,
regreted; and for that blud and vthers, for the Kings proſperus government,
vndertaken newlings in his awin perſone, and for the guid acceptation of the
wark of the polecie and diſcipline of the Kirk, now concludit, and to be preſented to his Maᵗⁱᵉ and Counſall, their was a generall faſt concludit to be zeal
uſlie keipit throwout the land †

* At this Aſſemblie war a number of queſtiones giſſen in from Court be Alexander Hay, Clark
Regiſter, and the anſweis therof craut at diuerſs Aſſemblies thereſter, for the Courtes effect
† When the Aſſemblie haid concludit the diſcipline, diueiſe of the breithring, as namlie, Mr

The Affemblie therefter conveined at Stirling in July that fam yeir, wherin the form of conclufion, as in all the former Affemblies, fa in that, was, That the Kirk all in a voice, hes concludit the haill articles and propofitiounes of the buik of the policie of the Kirk, to be conform to the Word of God, and meit for the Efteat of the Kirk in this land, and ordeanes the fam with a fupplication, to be prefented to the Kings Ma⁶⁶. The quhilk was done, and his Hienes gaiff a verie confortable and gud anfwer theranent, nominating certean of his Counfall to confer with the breithring apointed be the Kirk thervpon

That yeir my vncle dedicat to the King his CARMEN MOSIS with certean Epigrames, and a chap. of Job in vers, quhilk put all men in hope of grautter warks ; but parthe his giant occupationes and diftractiones, parthe, as he wes wount to fay, Scribillantium et fcripturientium turba ; and cheiflie that he thought the tyme maift profitablie beftowit in doing, teatching, and framing of gud inftruments for the meantinence of the treuthe and wark of the minifterie and fcholles, moved him to neglect wraitting, except of verfes and epigrammes, as his humor and occafiones moved him : wharof he hes in his peapers a grait number, and nocht a few, as Carmina Sybillina, loft. Bot for commendation of thrie notable verteus in him, thrie things amangs manie ma I man re-compt :—Interpretation of Dreames, Patience, and Heroic Stoutnes

The Collage haid mome pleyes in law depending that veir, and Mr Piter Blakburn was œconomus and fpeciall actor : yit becaufe the æftimation of Mr Andro was graitter, he defyrit him at certean perempter dyettes to be prefent in Edinbruche. For fic a dyet being to go to Edinbruche, Mr Piter comes in to his chalmer in the morning heavie and grim lyk. Being inquyrit be the Principall what ealed him, he anfweirit, " I haiff dreamed an vnfall dream, and I am fiun thing folift efter it.' —" What is it ?" fayes he. " Methought we

<hr>

Andro Meluill and Andro Hay, defyrit the fam to be fubfcryvit be the haill breithring. To the quhilk Mr Patrik Adamfone anfweired, " Nay—we haif an honeft man, our Clark, to fubfcryue for all, and it war to derogat to his fathfulnes and eftimatioun gif we fould all feneralie fubfcryue." ' Weill," fayes Mr Andro Hay, " gif anie man com againft this, or deny it hereftei, he is nocht honeft." And to Mr Patrik he faid, befor thrie or fower, " Ther is my hand, Mr Patrik, gif yie com againft this hereftei, confenting now fa throwhe to it, I will call yow a knaue, and it war never fa publiethe." Mr Patrik receaues the conditioun. Bot at the prefenting of the conclu-tiounes befor the Regent and Counfall, the Regent afkes Mr Patrik gif he haid affented therto. He denyit it, and that he haid refufit to fubfcryve it. Wherypon the faid Conclufiones of Difcipline war refufed be the Counfall. The caufe wharof, when Mr Andro Hay haid inquyred at diuerfs honor-able Counfellars, they leyed the wait on the faid Mr Patrik, wha coming by in the mean tyme, Mr Andro Hay takes him be the hand befor the faid Counfallour, and difpytfulhe to his face fayes ' O knaue, knaue ! I will croun thee the knaue of all knaues !'

G

war fitting at our Collage burde, and a cap full of barme drink befor ws I luked to the cap, and I thought I faw a read headit tead lope out of it, and craled vpe vpon the wall, the quhilk I percewed and dang down, and tramped vnder my feit, and as I turned I faw an vther lope out alfo, quhilk, whowbeit I followed, it gat away in a holl out of my fight"—' Be nocht fobft,' fayes he, " Mr Piter ; I will interpret your dream, and warrand the interpretation trew, for a pynt of wyne ? —" For futhe,' fayes the vther, " and it be gud, a quart"—" The Collage burd and cap is our Collage leiving, into the quhilk twa read nebbit teades lies intrufit thamfelff They ar the twa read neafed compeditours of our Collage, againft the quhilk yie hauff prefenthe the actiones, viz Jhone Grame, the fift whom yie perfewing at this dyet, chin als weill as he will on the wall of the law, yie fall ding down and owercome. The vther is the read faced Commiffar, Mr Archbald Beaton, wha be fome wyll fall efchew prefenthe, and win away Affure thyfelff, man thow fall find it fa " Mr Piter lauches, and fayes he was worthe the wyne, whow euer it was, for the twa men war verie read and tead lyk faced for ploukes and lumpes. And in deid it cam fa to pafs, for they brought hame a notable decreit of reduction of a few of the freires yeard againft Jhone Grame ; and the vther, by moyen and erueft folifitation, gat the action delayit, and brought to arbitrament *

Now for his patience, whowbeit he was verie h. t in all queftiones, yit when it twitched his particular, no man could crab him, contrair to the comoun cuftome, as amangs maine vther, I marked this —My Lord Hearife haid a fone in the Collage named Jhone, wha was drawin away from his ftudies and ordour be fum young men of the town, namlie, a burgefs an named Andro Heriot The principall calles for Jhone, and reproving him, fayes, " What ? hes my Lord your father fend yow hen to fpend your tyme with debauchit perfones of the town, &c This was tauld Andro Heriot, wha, parthe of intemperat difpofition, and partlie, as was fuppofed, be the Collage mflykers

* I hauff alfo marked maine experiences in him of wounderfull figacitie and fmelling out of mens naturalls and difpofitiones, fa that tho fum haid bein never fa fair fairand and curtens, he could nocht gif tham a gud countenance nor word , quhilk, indeid, wald proue ill men Vthers, altho nocht of fa gud appearance, he wald lyk of, and be hamhe with, wha wald proue weil Of bathe the fortes I could racken diuers be nam and fournam, but it is nocht expedient , onlie an I can nocht omit, wha about this tyme was ordeanit be the Generall Affemblie to be tean ordoun withall be the Synod of Glafgw for deferting of his minifterie , wha be his tear ciuill factons fund fawour with all except Mr Andro, wha, delling tcharphe with him for his defertion of the minifterie gat this anfwer —" I will nocht profes pouertie "—" O then," fayes Mr Andro to him, " yow will deny nocht onlie the minifterie, bot alfo trew Chriftianitie " This man was Mr Jhone Colum, firft apoftat fra the minifterie, and fyne fra trew Chriftian rehgion to foull Papiftrie.

ftired vpe, cam to Mr Andro, the Principall, a day efter fermont, coming out
of the Kirk, haiffing all his fchollars and Regents at his bak, and quarrels him
fchamtullie with manie thows and lyes, continowing from the Kirk almaift
down to the Collage, quhilk is a grait fpace, yea, with fword about him, with
menaffings and brawlles, but Mr Andro verie patienthe and meiklie anfwers
never a word bot " God facher, what hes mun it yow, yie neid to boft? We ar
ma nor yie' The fchollars war out of than wittes, and tean wald haift put
hands on him, bot he rebuked tham in fic fort that they durft nocht ften
As for myfelff for als patient as I am called, I doucht nocht fuffer it, bot
withdrew myfelff from him

Within a fchort fpace etter, the faid Andro contractes a fiver, or the quhilk
he died ; and a day or twa befor, he fend for the Principall, wha gladlie cam
and vifit him ; wha, with grait remorfe, conteffit his offence, and commendit
the vthers grait patience, faying, " That he haid win a graitter victorie of
him, nor gift he haid fuffent his fchollars to ding out his harnes ;" and oft
tymes embrafing and kiffing him for the fweit contort he beftowed on him,
being fa vnworthie, crved ay for him fa lang as the breathe was in him, and
fa gaift vpe the ghaft, being a luftie youthe in his mide age

The young man, Jhone Maxuell, parthe efchewing difcipline, and parthe,
as was fuppofed, caried away be the cownfall of Papifts, (for he haid gottin
euill groundes therof, and all his fathers houfs, be Mr Gilbert Broun, Abbot
of New Abey,) left the Collage, and abaid in the town   Bot whow foone the
Lord Heres, his father, haird of it, he cam to the town, fcharplie rebuked his
fone, and brought him to the Collage, etter he haid lowinghe and maift cur-
tefhe delt with the Principall, caufit the haill maifters and difciples convein in
the verie clofs of the Collage, and ther, in prefence of all, aufterlie commandit
his fone to fitt down vpon his knees, and humblie offer himfelff to what fort
of difcipline the Principall of the Collage and his Regent (againft whome cheiff-
lie he haid bein refractar,) wald put him to   The young man obeyit humblie,
and the Principall lifted him vpe be the hand etter promife of amendment ;
and efter reconciliation he enter it him to his Regent agane, humblie prefenting to him a piece of golde   What that Lord Heres was vther wayes I leaue
it to the Cornicle ; bot in this he left a notable exemple to all noble men and
fathers to follow.

For forear verification of his grait patience, becaufe he wald fem verie
hat and impatient   At our table, comonlie at mealles and efter, was movit
be him fum queftion of philofophie or artes, namlie, for this end to fchaw that

Ariftotle could er, and haid erred, contrar to the S Andros axiom, Abfurdum
eft dicere eriaffe Ariftotelem.   Mr Piter Blakburn, our coleg, was a bitter
propugnar of Ariftotle, a verie guid and lerned man, bot rud and carbffe of
nature : and when he could nocht bear out his defence be reafone, he wald do
it be coler and invection vpon the perfone of Mr Andro. that he was arro-
gant, proud, and full of his awin fence ; but when it cam to that the argument feaffed, for the Principall never fpak a word mair   And be this form of
doing he wan Mr Piter from mome, bathe wrang opiniones and evill fatones :
for the guid, honeft harted man, trie from his coler. efchamed of himfelff.
amendit himfelff   And this I marked euer to be Mr Andros maner : Being
fure of a treuthe in reafoning he wald be extream hat, and fuffer na man to
bear away the contrar. bot with reafone, words, and geftnre, he wald carie it
away, caring for na perfone, whow grat foener they war, namlie, in maters
of relligion   And in all companies, at table or vtherwayes, as he vnderftood
and tuk vpe the neceffitie of the perfones and mater in hand to requyre, he
wald frielie and bauldlie hauld than cares low of the treuthe : and tak it as
they wald, he wald nocht ceas nor keipe filence ; yea, and nocht onlie anes or
twyfe, bot at all occafiones, till he fand than better inftructed, and fett to go
tordwart in the guid purpofe   And verche be lang experience I haiff knawin
him to haiff done as mikle guid in fic conferences and meittings as be his publict doctrine ; for fic as war willing to vnderftand in fa doing, he pleafin it than
man and mair : and fic as wer nocht, he fuffered never to reft till he ather
brought than from ther contrarie mynd, or els difconered a perverfs difpofition againft the treuthe   Giff he haid nocht bein throuche and refolut himfelff
in a mater, he wald haiff heard verie patienthe and quethe, and reafonit thervpon caldlie and camlie aneuche till he war fullie refolut, and fand his grounds
fure.   But for his awine particular, in perfone, gear, or fame, I knew him
never haid in publict with ame man to this houre

  Now for his heroic cowrage and ftoutnes :—The Regent, feeing he could
nocht diuert him [be] benefites and offers. he calles for him a day indirecthe
and, efter lang difcourfing vpon the quyetnes of the cowntrey, peace of the
Kirk, and advancment of the Kings Maties Efteat, he braks in vpon fic as war
difturbers therof be thair conceats and owerfie dreames, imitation of Geneu difciphne and lawes ; and, efter fum reafoning and grundes of Gods Word alleagit,* quhilk irritat the Regent, he braks out in coler and bofting :—" Ther

---

* This Regent obiected againft the General Aflemblie, That it was [a] conuocation of the Kings

will never be quyetnes in this countrey, till halff a dissone of yow be hangit or banished the countrey '—" Tushe, sir ' sayes Mr Andro : ' Purpuratis tuis ista minitare mihi, idem est humi au sublime putrescam : Domini est terra Patria est vbicunque, est bene. I haiff bein ready to giff my lyff whan it was nocht halff sa weill wared, at the pleasour of my God I leived out of your countrey ten yeirs as weill as in it Let God be glorified, it will nocht ly in your power to hang nor exyll his treuthe ' Monie sidyk hes he haird, and for me reported in mair ferfull form ; bot for all nevir rangeda sot athei from the substance of the caute, or forme of proceiding therin. Bot a piece of stoire I man report, steirit vpe in particular againit him in my persone.

The Lord Boid was grait with the Regent, and haid a cusing in our Collage named Alexander Boid, a youthe of a grait spreit and ingyne, bot verie commersom and refractar He haid pleyit the companion wickedlie with the maister in the grammar school, and sic lyk with the first regent the first yeir of his course in the Collage The nixt yeir he comes to me : At his entrie I delt with him fearlie, and besought him to be weill conditioned, and he sould find na thing in me bot speciall courtessie and affectione ; bot giff he sould preass to missuse me, and mak trouble as he haid done to his maisters befor, for alsmeik as I sensed he wald find me scharper nor anie he haid delt with Vpon this premonition he continows halff a yeir as guid a bern as was in the seage Till taking occasion of Mr Thomas Smetones companie, in the quhilk I mikle delyted I past with him to Edinbruche to fetche ham his wyff ; and befor my going, I tuk exact ordour with my schollars, inioyning large tasks to tham, and apointing of censurers and deleattors of all their behauiour Conning ham agan I fand the said Alexander often deleated in grait faultes, namlie, absenting himselff from the kirk, and pleying the loun on the Sabbathe I begin to deall with him in words : he disdeanes and vilipends with misbehauiour in words and countenance ; I command him to correction—he rebelles : to be

leiges Mr Andro answeirt, ' That Chryst and his Apostles war giltie of that cryme, wha conveinit with houndrethes and thowsands, taught tham, and gouerned without anie leiue of the magistrat and vit did all dewtie to Cæsar, and bade gif him that quhilk was his Item, Mr Andro alleaging a place of the Actes to the said Regent the Regent tayes tantinghe, " Read me euer of sic an Act as we did at St Jhonstoun ?' Answeres Mr Andro ' Gif vie be escheamed of that act, Chryst wilbe escheamed of yow ' The Reformatioun of Religioun in Scotland was don as the men in the Gospell wha, bringing a man seik of the palsey, careid he toursome in bed, brak the housf aboue what Chryst was, vnasking leiue of the gudman and maister therof, for the grait desyre quhilk they haid to com to Chryst for the mans helthe Yit Chryst fand na fault therwith, bot being than fathe, approued the fam, and healed the man. Sa throw zeall the kingdom of Heavin suffered violence at the beginning, and men fought to com to Chryst without asking leiue of King or Cæsar

fchort, I wald nocht be detorcit ; and he gat his deat peyit, bot indeid far
within his demeant   He fittes down in a nuk fra my fight, and whill I was
teatching my leffone, he takes his pen and ink horn, and ftiks himfelff on the
face and neas till effufion of blud ; he ryves his buik, and dightes his neas
with the leaves therot, and drawes the blud athort his face, and fpots his
clothes with the famng ; and incontinent efter the leffone, rinnes out of the
Collage, and away and compleanes to his frinds he was fa infulit crewalie be
me   The principall and maifters at the bruit, and my defyre, takes tryell, and
finds it as is spoken   He byds away fra the Collage a monethe, about the
end wharof, on a fimmer evening efter fupper, I was comng out of the Caftell
with twa of my compamons, whar we had bein vifiting a guid gentleman,
wha, vnbefet be twafum, had defendit himfelff notablie, being weill fenfed till
his dagger cas cut in pices, and brought to extream danger of his lyft, was compellit ather to flay an of tham or be flean , for the quhilk apprehendit, he was
detened in preflone in the Caftell whar we cuftomablie vifited him, and lernt
of him to fence   Sa, comng from him in the kirk yeard, my fchollar lying in
weat with an Alexander Cunngham, fiftar fone to the Lord Boid, wha hounds
out the youthe with a baton in his hand to flink me behind my bak.   Hening
the found of his feit, I turned and fpak a few words, at the quhilk the boy
rinnes by me and luiks for his helper, Alexander Cunnghame, wha cam with
fpeid efter him with a drawin fword and mome bludie words.   The twa that
war with me faw nocht this Alexander, bot ran and tuk the boy , fa Alexander leyes out a ftrak at me with the fword, quhilk, declynng my bodie a
litle, I efchewed, and clofing with him, I gripped his fword arm vnder my left
oxter, and with my right hand caucht his quhingar, haffing na kynd of wa-
pean vpon myfelff, and bids him ftand   Withe this, incontinent my twa com-
panoines commes and finders ws , fa my God keipit me that night, bothe from
doing or receaving anie tordar harme   Coming to the Collage, I fchew the
mater to the Principall, wha firft commandit all the fchollars to ther bedds,
perceaving tham incenfit, and fearing a wark of the deuill to deborche
tham from ther ftudies, enter tham in blud, and wrak the wholl Collage
Yit wald nocht fuffer the preparatiue to pafs vntean ordour with : Vpon the
morn convenes the Rector and Magiftrats of the Town, according to the ordour, and cites the parties befor tham   I compein ; the vther is contumax,
and perfeueis in his boft   The mater is tryed exactlie   They decern Alexander Cunnghame for his wrang to come to the place whar it was done, and
ther, humblie, bear futted and bear headit, to craue the Rectour, the Principall,

and me, the perfone offendit, torgiffnes This being notefied to Alexander, he
malings, and wowes ther fould be grantter caufe maid or anie forgiffnes cravit
Ther na thing was noy fit fa mikle in the countrey, as the Bouds and Cunning-
hams wald flay the mafters and burn the Collage Bot the Princepall rarget
never a whit, nor movit himfelff, whowbeit fum of ws war right fleyd, but
fend and reafit Letters, and fummoned Alexander befor the king and fecret
counfall, wha compened with a grait number of his frinds, thinking to bost
ws fra it ; bot we cam befor the king and counfall at S Andros, producit the
proces and decreit of the rector and bailyies of Glafgw, and obteined the fam
to be ratefiet , and the faid Alexander chargit to fulfill and obey it fic a day,
or then to enter in ward within the Caftell of Blaknes. Coming ham to
Glafgw and the day approtching, our fpeciall frinds dealt with ws, namlie
the Rector, Mr Andro Hay, a man of grait moyen in the countrey, to quyt
that decreit and forgifl it, feing ther was na evill done, vtherwayes he was
certified it wald com to war , for the man was neir in blod on the father fyde
to the Eil of Glencarn, and on the mothers to the Lord Boid, the naturall and
fafones wharof he knew, that they wald nocht fufler ther blud fched (as they
alleagit) vnreuengit. The Principall anfweis, ' Giff they wald haiff forgiffnes let tham crave it humblie, and they fall haiff it ; but or that preparatiue
pafs, that we dar nocht correct our fchollars for fear of bangftars and clanned
gentlemen, they fall haiff all the blud of my body firft " Sa the day comes,
at the quhilk the Lord Boid comes to Glafgw, accompanied with all his frinds ,
fo comes my Lord of Glencarn with his, to the number of four or tyve houn-
diethe gentilmen   The Principall is delt with be diuers interceffors nocht
to prefent the place ; bot terrifie as they wald, he fayes, " They that will
go with me go : they that are fleyd, let them tarie " And fa the Rector, the
Principall, and I, with our fchollars at our bak, in our gowns, com to the kirk
yeard and ftude at the place whar I was vnbefett ; the kirkyeard being full of
gentlemen, giffes place   Then comes Alexander, arrayit in his beft abulyi-
ment, in the muddes of twa gentlemen, wharof an was the eldeft brother of
my fchollar the vther his neneft frind , and the faid Alexander, bear headit
and bear futed, and offers to fulfill the decreit giff ame wald accept of it.
" Dout nocht of the acceptation," anfwers the Principall, we are hen readie '
And fa the faid Alexander, in prefence of all his frinds, to bear him witnefs,
recited the words of the decreit, and obeyed contorm to euerie circumftance.
The quhilk, when the gentilman faw, wha, for the maift part, knew nocht for
what caufe they cam, luche him to fkorn, fpendit thrie or four hounder mark

in the town. and returned, as they confeffit. grautter fulles nor they cam a
field

Now to Mr Thomas Smeton, of whom I maid mention befor.—I marked the
wounderfull gudnes and prouidence of God towards his Kirk in this realme.
wha, as firft efter the blud of thefe martyrs, Mr George Wifchart and Walter
Miln. ftened vpe Mr Knox to effectuat the wark of Reformation ; and taking
him to his reft, fend ham Mr Andro Meluill for continuance of zeall and fin-
ceiritie, with exquifit literature and knawlage, and for putting on of the coap-
ftean of the trew and right difcipline and polecie   Sa, when the courfe of
Papiftrie begoud againe to crepe in be the alteration of the government, and
Gurfan Counfall entering about the King, then God plucked out from amangs
the Jefuifts, a wadge of thair awin timber, wherwith to rent and crofs than
deccaits   This was Mr Thomas Smeton wha, in that iorney to Edinbruche.
recompted to me the ftrange wirking of God with him ; this in fonm :—That
at the Reformation of religion, he being put from the Auld Collage of S Andros. paft to France. whare in Pars he thought mikle vpon the trew way of
faluation, and be dealling of diuerfs of his acquentance. namlie, Mr Thomas
Matteland, a young gentilman of guid literature and knawlage in the treuthe
of religion, was brought to ken and be inclynde to the beft way   Whar alfo
he was acquentit with my vncle Mr Andro, and Mr Gilbert Moncreiff   Yit
lothe to alter his mynd wherin he was brought vpe, and faind himfelfi fum
tyme fullie perfwadit in the mater of his fathe and faluation, he thought he
wald leaue na thing vntryed and effeyit perteining therto   And vnderftanding
that the ordour of the Jefuifts was maift lerned, halie, and exquifit in the Papiftrie, he refolut to enter in thair ordour during the years of probation ; at
the end wharof, giff he faind himfelfi fatteled in his auld fathe, he wald continow a Jefuift ; and giff he faind nocht amangs tham that might remoue all the
douttes he was caft into. it was bot tohe to feik fordar, he wald yeild vnto
that light, that God, be the erneft delling of his lowing friuds and companions.
haid enterit him into   And fa he enterit in the Jefuifts Collage at Paris
whar he faind Mr Edmont Hay, a verie lowing frind, to whom he communicat all his mynd   Mr Edmond, feing him worthie to be win to tham, and
giffen to lerning and fight, directes him to Rome, and be the way he cam to
Geneu, whar Mr Andro Meluill and Mr Gilbert Moncreiff being for the tyme.
he communicat with tham his purpofe, and cravit thair prayers. Of his purpofe they could fie na guid warrand, but thair prayers they promifit harthe

Sa, making na stey ther, he past tordwart to Rome, whar he was receavit in
the Jesuits Collage gladlie   In the quhilk Collage was a father hauldin of
best lerning and prudence wha was ordeanit to travell with hie as wer de-
temed in preflone for religion, to convert tham , of him he cravit that he
might accompanie him at sic tymes when he went to deall with these presòn-
ers, quhilk was granted to him   Be the way as they cam from the presoners
to the Collage, quhilk was neir a mvll, Mr Thomas wald tak the argument
of the prefoners, and mentem it againft the Jesuit for reafonings caufe, and
indeid to be refoluit, and the more he infisted he taind the treuthe the
ftrangar, and the Jesuits anfwers never to fatiffie him.   This way he continowit about a yeir and a halff in Rome, till at laft he becam fufpitius, and
therfor was remitted bak to Paris, throw all the Collages of the Jesuits be
the way ; in all the quhilks he endewoirt mair and man to haiff his douttes
refoluit, bot fand himfelff ay fordar and fordar confirmed in the veritie   Coming to Paris agam, he abaid ther a fpace verie lowinghe interteined be Mr
Edmond, till at laft he could nocht bot difcover himfelff to Mr Edmont, to
whom he faves he was alfimikle behauldin as to anie man in the warld ; for
nochtwithftanding that he perccavit his mynd turned away from thair ordour
and relligion, yit he ceafed nocht to counfall him frindlie and fatherlie, and
fuffered him to want na thing.   And being a verie wyfe man, he thinks to
keipe Mr Thomas quyet, and nocht to fuffer him to kythe an adverfar againft
them   Perceaving, therfor, the young man giffen to his buik he gifles him
this counfall, to go to a quyet collage, fituat in a welthie and pleafant part
in Lorain, whair he fould haiff na thing to do but attend vpon his buiks, whan
he fould haiff all the Antient Doctors, and fic buiks as yie pleafit to reid , he
fould leak na neceffars ; than he fould keipe him quyet till God wrought fordar with him, vtherwayes he wald caft himfelff in grait danger   Thair was
na thing that could allure Mr Thomas man nor this, and therfor he refolued
to follow his counfall , and taking iorney, went towards Lorain, whan be the
way the Lord leyes his hand vpon him, and vifites him with an extreain fever,
cafting him in vttermaift pean and perplexitie of body and mynd   Than he
fought a maift ftrang and ferfull battell in his confcience, bot God at laft
prevealing, he determines to fchaw himfelff, abandone that damnable focietie,
and vtter in plean profeffion the treuthe of God, and his enemies falfhods,
hypocrafie and craft.   Sa coming bak to Paris agam, he takes his leue of Mr
Edmont wha yit, nochtwithftanding kythes na thing bot loving frundfchipe
to him, and at his parting gifles thrie counfalles.   1. To reid and ftudie the

Ancient Doctors of the Kirk, and nocht to trow the ministers   2 To go ham
to his awin countrey ; and thridlie, To marie a wyff From that he manifested
himselff amangs the profeffours of rehgion, till the tyme of the maffacre quhilk
fchorthe enfewit, at the quhilk being narrowlie fought, he cam to the Englif-
Ambaffator, Mr Secretarie Walfingham, in whafe houfs lyand at Paris for the
tyme as in a comoun guthe, he, with manie ma, war feaff With whome alfo
he cam to Emgland foone efter, whar he remeaned fcholinaifter at Colchefter
till his coming to Scotland

At his coming in Scotland, he was gladlie content to be in companie with
my vncle Mr Andro, and fa aggreit to be minifter at Paifley, in place of Mr
Andro Pulwart, wha enterit to the fubdeannie of Glafgw when Mr Dauid
Cuninghame was bifchopit in Aberdein A litle efter his placing, Mr Andro
Prmcipall of the Collage, put in his hand Mr Archbald Hamiltones apoftats
buik De Confufione Caluianæ Scitæ apud Scotos : and efter conference theranent, movit him to mak anfwer to the fam, quhilk was publifhed in print
the yeir following, to the grait contentment of all the godlie and lernit   Mr
Thomas was verie waciyff and peanfull, and fkarfhe tuk tyme to refreche nature   I haiff fein him oft find fault with lang denners and fuppers at General
Affemblies ; and when vthers wer therat, he wald abftein, and be about the
penning of things, (wherin he excellit, bathe in langage and form of letter,)
and yit was nocht ruftic nor aufter, bot fweit and affable in companie, with a
modeft and naine grauitie ; verie frugall in fude and reyment, and walked
maift on fut, whom I was verie glad to accompanie, whylls to Sterling, and
now and then to his kirk, for my inftruction and comfort   He lout me exceiding weill, and wald at parting thruft my head in his bofome and kis me

He being weill acquented with the practizes of Papifts, namlie, Jefuifts,
and thair deuyces for fubuerting of the Kirk of Scotland, bathe publiche and
priuathe ceaffit nocht to cry and warn minifters and fchollars to be diligent
vpon ther charges and buiks, to ftudie the controuerfies, and to tak head they
neglected nocht the tyme, for ther wald be a ftrang vnfeatt of Papifts Alfo
he was cearfull to know the rellgion and affection of noble men, infinuating
him in thair companie in a wyfe and graue maner, and warning tham to be
war of euill companie, and nocht to fend thair berns to dangerus partes. And
finalie, Mr Andro and he, maruelouflie confpyring in purpofes and iudgments,
war the firft motioners of an antifeminarie to be erected in St Andros, to the
Jufuift femmaries, for the courfe of theologie, and ceffit never at Affemblies
and Court till that wark was begoun and fett fordwart.

The Generall Affemblie convenit at Edinbruche, October 1578   Therin
the noble men frequenthe conveinit war defyrit to allow of the policie of the
Kirk by grait peanes and deliberation concludit, and, as they haid accepted the
right and trew confeffion of the Chriftian fathe, fa of the difcipline alfo drawin
out of the word of God.   They accepted therof, and promifet to meantein the
fam to ther powar, except in fa far as the Kings Matie and Counfall was nocht
refolut, namlie, of the Diaconerie   Thir noble men war the Erles of Atholl,
Argyll, Montrofe, &c. wha haid drawin the faction againft the Regent Mortoun; fa it pleafit God to work.

    That yeir arryvit Monfieur d'Obignie from France, with inftructions and
devyffes from the Houfs of Guife, and with manie Franche fafones and toyes,
and in effect, with a plean courfe of papiftrie, to fubuert the efteat of the Kirk
new planted, bathe with trew doctrin and difciplne   He brought with him
an Mons. Mombnineau,* a fubtill fpreit, a murrie fellow, verie able in bodie,
and maift meit in all refpects for bewitching of the youthe of a prince   They
within few dayes infinuat thamfelffs fa in fawom of the young king, that they
gydit all, brought in be Mortones mifflykers, bot to the wrak bathe of him and
thame   Vnder than winges crape in craftie fellowes, wha maid the reformation of relligion, and all the gud feruice done for the king befor, to be bot turbulent and treafonable delling, &c , againft the quhilk the minifters of Edinbruche, lyk fathfull watchmen, maid loud and tynius warning.

1579 —The Affemblie convenit at Edinbruche in the new kirk, July 1579,
to convoy the man craftelie and quyetlie the courfe intendit, thair is prefentit
from his Matie a letter to the Affemblie, fchawing his hienes guid mynd towards
the Kirk, and craving the heads of the policie to be prefented to the parhament
inftant, to be paft therat   This was to conciliat the fawour of the Kirk. and
mak Mortoun mair odius till they war ftranger. Item, Bifchopes and Super-
intendents haiblie remouit, and commiffioners from affemblie to affemblie in
number fufficient for the haill realm, according to the feuerall prouinces, placed
in ther roum. The bifchopes ther began to withdraw thamfelues fra the
Affemblies, and ordour takin theranent. The reformation of the Vniuerfitie
of St Andros intendit, and futt maid to the Kings Matie theranent   Prefbyteries ordeanit to be erected. and that the exerceifes fould be as prefbyteries
in the mean tyme

* Mr Nicol Dalgles tauld me that this Monbirneas mother was a verie godlie lady, and fchew
grait curteffie to tham in France at Burge in Berie, and warnit tham of M Obignies fending in
Scotland, wherupon he maid aduertifment to the minifters of Edinbruche

It was a maift pleafand and confortable thing to be prefent at thefe Affemblies, thair was fic frequencie and reuerence, with holines in zeall at the doctrine quhilk foundht mightehe, and the Seffiones at euerie meiting, whar, efter erneft prayer, maters war granhe and clerlie propomt ; overtures maid be the wyfeft : douttes reafomt and dificuflit be the lernedeft and maift quik ; and finalie all withe a voice concluding vpon maters refolued and clerrit, and referring things intricat and vnclenred to farder advyfment. Namlie, it is to be noted, that in all thefe Affemblies anent the polecie, ther was nocht fic a thing as a careing away of ame pomct with a number of vottes, an or ma, or by a preoccupied purpofe or led courfe : bot maters indifferentlie propomt, and efter beging light of God, and teafing the Scripture by conterence and reafoning dificuflit, with large and fufficient tyme takin and diligenthe employed for that effect, all with a voice, in an content and vmtie of mynd, determines and concludes.

God glorified himfelt notablie with that minifterie of Edinbruche in thefe dayes The men haid knawlage, vprightnes, and zeall ; they dwelt verie commodiuflie togidder, as in a Collage, with a wounderfull confeat in varietie of giftes, all ftrak on a firing and foundet a harmonie. Jhone Duiy was of fmall literatuie, bot haid fem and marked the grait warks of God in the firft Reformation, and bein a doer bathe with toung and hand He haid bein a diligent heirar of Mr Knox and obferver of all his wayes. He conceavit the beft grounds of maters weill, and could vtter tham teanhe, fullie and ferfullie, with a mightie fpreit, voice, and action. The fpeciall gift I marked in him was halmes, and a dayhe and mighthe ceaifull, continuall walking with God in meditation and prayer. He was a verie guid fallow and tuk delyt, as his fpeciall confort, to haiff his table and houfs filled with the beft men Thefe he wald gladhe heir, with tham conter and talk, profeffing he was bot a buik bearer, and wald tean lern of thame : and getting the ground and light of knawlage in ame guid pomct, then wald he reioyfe in God, praife and pray theirvpon, and vrge it with fa clear and forcible exhortation in affemblies and pulpit, that he was eftimed a verie forderfum inftrument. Ther ludgit in his houfe at all thefe Affemblies in Edinbruche, for comoun, Mr Andro Melvill, Mr Thomas Smeton, Mr Alexander Arbuthnot, thrie of the lernedeft in Europe , Mr James Melvill, my vncle, Mr James Balfour, Dauid Fergufone, Dauid Home minifters , with fum zelus, godhe barrones and gentilmen In tyme of mealles, was reafoning vpon guid purpofes, namhe, maters in hand ; thereftir erneft and lang prayer ; thereftir a chaptour read, and euerie man about gaift his not and obſeruation therof : Sa that gift all haid bein fett down in wryt, I haiff hard the lernedeſt and of beſt iudgment ſay they wald nocht haiff wiſſed a fuller and better commentar nor ſum tymes wald fall out in that exerceiſe Therefter was ſung a Pſalme : efter the quhilk was conference and deliberation vpon the purpoſes in hand ; and at night, befor going to bed, erneſt and zealus prayer, according to the eſteat and ſucceſs of maters. And often tymes yea, almoſt daylie, all the Collage was togidder in an or vther of than houſſes : for, befor Mr James Lawſone and Mr Walter war maried, they war burdit with Jhone Dune, and efter entring to than awin houſſes, keipit exceiding guid fallowſchipe togidder.

Heir I man remember a ſingular benefit of Gods prouidence and government towards me I was then in the floure of my age, about a twa and twentie and thrie and twentie yeirs , a young man nocht vnlowhe, and of nature verie lowing and amorus, quhilk was the proped ſchot of Sathan wharby to ſnare me, and ſpoill the haill wark of God in me Manie lovers haid I, and ſum loves alſo ; ſome occaſiones, in dyvers places and ſortes of perſones and nocht of inferior rank : Yit my guid God, of his trie grace and loue towards me, a vean, vyll, corrupt youthe, parthe by his fear wrought in my hart, parthe by neceſſar occupation in my calling, and parthe be a certean ſchamfaſtnes of a baſhfull nature, quhilk he pat in me, ſa keipit me that I was nocht owercome nor miſcaried be na woman, offenſiulie to his Kirk, nor greivſlie to my conſcience, in blotting of my bodie. I markit befor the occaſion I haid of lerning to ſing and play on inſtruments of muſic in S Andros, wharof my hart was verie deſirus, bot from grait ſkill wher in God keipit me ; far graitter and ſwerttar haid I in Glaſgw of a gentilmans houſ in the town, wha interteined maiſt expert ſingars and players, and brought vpe all his berns therin, namlie, his eldeſt dauchter, a verie pleaſand gentilwoman, endewit with manie guid verteus. I haid euerie yein ſum of this gentilmans ſonnes my ſchollars, and be that occaſion was hamlie in his houſ, and maiſt lowinghe and harthe interteined Affection enterit verie extreamlie betwix that gentlewoman and me, bot as God and man bathe knew, honeſt and cheaſt ; yit ſie as giff my God, and the cairfull and fatherlie admonitiones and conforts of my vncle, haid nocht ſupplied, it haid vndone me Manie fear battels and greiws tentationnes did my God vphauld me in, and carie me throw, and at laſt put in my hart a purpoſe to ſeik and vſe that holie and lawfull remeid of mariage, and therin, namlie, to reſpect a helpe and confort for that calling, whervnto I haid adwowit myſelfl. Sa be my haunting to the General Aſſem-

blies in Edinbruche, and takin with the godlie ordour and exerceife in the familie of Jhone Durie, and with that canfull walkine with God I faw in him;
as alfo with fum appeirance of Gods face and honeftie I faw in the face and
fafones of the bein, being bot about alleavin or twall yeirs of age, I refolut
with my God to fettle my hart ther, tak hir for my loue, and put all vther
out of my hart: And this almoft a four yeir befor our mariage

1580.—The Generall Affemblie convenit at Dondie, July 1580, wharat Mr
James Lawfone was moderator: The Kings Commiffionars war ther   Ther
Epifcopatus was vtterlie abolifched, and all brukand that office ordeaunt to
demit the fam   and with dew tryall to be receavit as paftors of particular
congregationes de nouo, and that vnder pean of excommunication; and the
provinciall Synods immediatlie following to put the act in execution   Item,
Anent the office of Reidars, that ther is nocht fie an office in the Kirk of God
as of fimple reiding; and therfor, all Reidars to be tryed within twa yeir,
and gift they haiff nocht profited fa that they ar able to exhort with doctrine,
to be depofit, and that nan fould be admitted, in tyme coming, to anie benefice
that could do na mair bot reid.   Alfo manie delationes was maid of Papifts
that had flocked hame with and efter Monfieur d'Obignie wha haid prefence
and credit at Court: wheranent the Kings minifters. Mr Jhone Crage and
Jhone Dunkanfon war admonifed.

At that Affemblie, Captan Robert Anftruther, father brother to the prefent
Lard of Anftruther, wha haid fpendit his haill lyff in the warres in France,
and haid atteined ther to honour and ritches, moved of confcience, cam hame
to end his lyff in his awin countrey, in the Reformed Kirk therin, and offerit
himfelff as a penitent to the faid Affemblie, for being fa manie yeirs prefent at
Mefs with his maifter, the King of France, knawin the ydolatrie therof, and
profeffing the trew religion in his hart.   The Affemblie remitted him to the
Synod of Fyff and Prefbyterie of St Andros, to be receaued in the tawour of
the Kirk, as he was the wintar thereifter, and within a yeir died happelie full
of dayes.   He was a verie wyfe and valiant man in armes, fpendit all his
tyme in the warres with grait honour, and yit haid the hape never to fched
blud with his awin hand, nor to haiff his blud fchede   He left to the pure of
the congregation of Kilrinny, whare he was born, and whare he died, the foum
of a thowfand maiks

That yeir was the Kings firft progrefs and promene athort his countrey,
with folemnities of entrefs in manie of his Hienes brouches; and amangs the

reft of St Andros, whar we war for that prefent com from Dondie with the fupplication and articles of the Affemblie, and keiping a dyet befor the Counfall about Alexander Cunnghame, in the mater mentioned befor. Whar, on a day, the gentilmen of the countrey about, haid a gyfe and farce to play befor the King: His Matie was in the new limes of the Abay, befor the windowes wharof, the fchow was to be maid Grait confluence of peiple convened, and the place read with a fear circuit : It continowed void for the fpace of a lang houre, wither that his Matie was nocht readie to behauld, or the playars to prefent thamfelues, I can nocht tell, bot, whill all ar gafing and langing for the play, in ftappes Schipper Lindfay, a knawin frenetic man, and paeffes vpe and down in the circuit with a grait grauetie, his hands in his fyde, looking verie big and hiche The man was of a grait telyie, weill bigged, of a large face, and guid manlie countenance, all rouche with heire his browes grait tuftes of heire, and als grait a tuft vpon the verie neb of his neafe ; his look was verie reafit and hiche : Wherat firft the peiple maid a noyfe with lauching . bot when he began to fpeak, he movit fic attention as it haid bein to a preatcher, and indeid, for my part, I was man movit with it then with monie preatchings Ther he difcourfit with grait force of fpirit and mightie voice, crying vpon all of all ranks and degries to heir him, and tak exemple be him, whow wicket and ryottous a man he haid bein : what he had done and conqueift be the fie, and whow he had fpendit it. and abofit himfelff be land ; and what maift mifthe for that the grait God and iudge of the warld haid brought vpon him. He haid wit, he haid ritches, he haid ftreuthe and abilitie of body ; he haid fam and eftimation paffing all of his tread and rank , bot all was vanitie, that maid him mifken his God, wha wald nocht be mifkenned, namlie, be the hicheft. And turning himfelff to the bofs windo, whar. in the nedinaift, the Erle of Morton was ftanding gnapping on his ftaff end, and the King and Monfieur d'Obigme aboue, he makes fic application to him in fpeciall as movit him throw the hart, and was marvellus in the eares of the heirars · For myfelff, I was eftonifched and movit to tears, heiring and feing the man. Amangs the reft, he warned him. nocht obfeurlie, that his iudgment was neir, and his dome was dichten. And indeid, the verie fain tyme was the platt a dreffin againft the Erle of Morton. na wayes knawin nor fufpected of anie in comoun. Sa that the plat leyers wald haiff fufpected a difcouerie, giff they haid nocht knawin the man to be lunatik and bereft of his wit. I market the Erle, ftanding iuft fornent him. mikle movit with this firft interlude, as erneft and nocht play, fa that during

all the fportes that followed, he altered never the grauitie of his countenance

In the monethe of October immediathe thereftei, the Generall Affemblie
conveinet at Edinburche   Ther bifchopes callit vpon ; all war fund abfent
The actes maid againft them ordeanit to be put in operation   Mr Andro
Melvill, fear againft his will, decernit and ordeanit to tranfport himfelff from
Glafgw to St Andros, to begine the wark of Theologie ther, with fie as he
thought meit to tak with him for that effect, conform to the leat reformation
of that Vniuerfitie, and the New Collage therof, giffen in be the Kirk and
paft in Parliament   Wharvpon compulfatoris of homing paft out againft him,
and Mr Thomas Smeton ordeanit to be placed in the Collage of Glafgw in
his roum

About this tyme refted happelie in the Lord, Mr Jhone Row, minifter of
St Jhonftoun, a wyfe, grave father, and of guid literature, according to his
tyme, wha, be information of my vncle, Mr Andro, haid firft, in a Generall
Affemblie, be doctrine, clenit all the heads of the difcipline, to the grait contentation of the haill Kirk ; and thereftei continowit a conftant promoter
therof to his end

The vacans befor, and all that yein, I was refolued haillelie to haiff gean to
France ; bot could na wayes obtein my vncles guid will, nor yit the guid
breithrings, whafe iudgments I reuerenced ; yit I haid almoft prevealed till
this tranfportation was concludit   And then, parthe moued with the low and
reuerence of my vncle, whom I could nocht leaue, fo erneftlie defyring me to
tak a part of that charge with him , and parthe glad to be frie from the daylie labor of regenting in Philofophie, to afcend to the profeffion and dayhe
trauell in Theologie, wharin I was blythe to fpend my haill lyff, I caft away
that purpofe of France, and tuk me haillelie to tak part with my vncle,
namhe, finding the approbation of all the guid breithring and calling of the
Kirk to that purpofe   Yit a benefit quhilk I haid of that purpofe, to pafs in
France, was the ftudie of the Frenche toung, wharto I was mikle giffen that
yeir, and wherin, to fatiffie me, my vncle helped me graithe, be confering
with me textes of Scripture ; alfo fum thing of the beft authors in the Frenche
toung, as of Plutarches Lyves and Heliodors Ethiopic Hiftorie, confering the
Greik with the Frenche   wherby I profited in bathe, namhe, in the right
pronunciation of the Frenche langage, quhilk is hardeft to attein vnto   Be
quhilk occafion I tuk mikle delyt, and reade manie things in the Frenche
langage.

We tuk leiue from Glafgw with infinit teares on bathe fydes, fa that fie as war our miflykers befor, (wharof, except fum Boyds and that Alexander Cuninghame, thei was nan,) wald haiff tean kythed frindfchipe then ; and leaving Mr Thomas Smeton in the Principalls, and my cwfing, Mr Patrik Melvill (fone to gud Roger, wha leathe haid paft his courfe in Philofophie ther,) in my roum, we cam to Edinbruche about the end of November, whaire I fand my bein growand in grace and fawour with God and man, quhilk eafed me fum what of the langour of our frinds at Glafgw

But the grait fein and cear quhilk was in my hart of my inhabilitie to vndertak and bear out fa grait a charge as to profefs Theologie and holie tounges amangs minifters and maifters, namlie, in that maift frequent Vniuerfitie of St Andros, amangs diuers alterit and difplacit, and therfor, malcontents and miflykers, occupied me fa, that I behouit to forgett all, and rin to my God and my buik

Mr James Lawfone, Jhone Dury, with the Lairds of Bread and Faldownfyde, convoyit ws to Londy, and fa with the Lard therof, to St Andros, and enterit ws in the Collage in the monethe of December, 1580. Mr Andro, principall maifter, Mr Jhone Robertfone, wha haid bein lang in that Collage befor, and haid ftudiet fum thing in Theologie, a gud weil conditionet man, but of finall literature and giftes, and me. Mr Andro maid his preface, and entent to the comoun places : Sa did I, and entent to the Hebrew Grammar Mr Jhone did as he could in the New Teftament, bot was fupplied therin be the Principall, wha remitted na thing of his wounted peanes

At our firft entrie, ther was a ftudent chalmerit abon a lafted leache feller, in the quhilk fellar wrights war working, and it was full of dry timber and fpealles, grait and finall. The ftudent colling his candle in a morning, the coll falles throw the laft, and kendles the finall fpeals lyand alangs a pleaning burde, and fa athort the houfs ; he comes out greitting and crying, quhilk, my chamber being nixt, I heir, and coming down with fpeid, lookes in at a window, and fies all the houfs athort in tyre, and the key of the dure could nocht be gottin Giff I haid a dammift fear hart, God knowes, luiking for na thing bot the burning of the haill place at our firft entrie, to the grait difcourage and greiff of all gud men, and the ioy of the wicked, and fie as heated the wark Wharfor, crying mightilie to God in my hart, I, with the auld portar, prefles the breaking of the dur in vean ; bot it pleafed God mercifullie to luik on and pitie the mater, fending the wright boy with the key onlukit for, and twa or thrie with watei, wherby we quenched the fyre befor it tuk

I

hald of the gefts and latting aboue : and indeid, the houfs being fa full of dry
timber and fpealles, it was a wounder to fie the fyre fa foone flokned , and
that, quhilk I thought a fpeciall benefit, befor ame thing was haird therof in
the town or noyfe maid therabout ; bot it fank fa in my hart, that I could
nocht forget nor conceill it, for danger of vnthankfulnes to God, wha fa mercifullie keipit that wark from fklander and difcuragment at the firft entrefs
therto.

Ther was nan that welcomde ws mair nor Mr Patrik Adamfone, called
Bifchope, wha reforted to our leffones, and keiped verie familiar frindfchipe
with Mr Andro, promifing what could ly in him for the weill of that wark
He haid takin him to the minifterie of St Andros, and teatched twyfe in the
ouk exceiding fweitlie and eloquentlie ; but the Sabothes at efter noone,
vaked becaufe of Mr Robert Hamiltons feiklines, wha was ordinar minifter
And therfor, at the defyre of fum of the eldars of the kirk fend from the Seffion, I occupied the pulpit on the Sabaths at efter noone, lyk as the Principall
did oftentymes in the forenoone, in abfence of the Bifchope   Thus it pleafed
God, of vnfpeakable grace, to hald the mouthe quhilk he haid opened, founding his treuthe and praife, quhilk was done with grait tentationes and mikle
trembling and fear in the prefent tyme, bot now rememberit to the grattest
ioy of my hart   And thus we wer occupied all the ouk in the fchoolls, and in
the Kirk on the Sabothe, quhilk was my onlie releiff againft mome toolifhe
thoughts and languiffing ceais, and held me faft vpon my God, with erneft
wakryffnes, to beg his grace

Ther was twa things that day he ftereit me vpe to thankfulnes toward God,
and erneft indewour in my calling   That an when I lewked vpon fie as haid
bein maifters and regents when I was a fchollar, now to be receavers of inftruction out of my mouthe, faying oft with Dauid, "Thow has maid me
wyfar nor my teatchers"   Another, I faw a condifciple of myne, mentioned
befor, Mr Dauid Elifon be name, wha was the beft fchollar of his clafs all the
tyme of our courfe, and going to France with the Claik Regiftar fonnes, ther
he falles in a phrenefie and daffing, quhilk keipit him to his deathe ; whom,
when I beheld out of the pulpit in the fcholles, and rememberit the mercifull
working of my God with mme, my breift could nocht contein my breathe nor
my eis teares   Then I had the honour of him, to whome all honour aperteines,
to be the teatcher of Mr Robert Rolloc, of moft worthie memorie, the Hebrew toung, wha reforted ordinarlie to my leffone and chalmer for that effect.

1581 —The Generall Assemblie convenied at Glasgw in Apryll, 1581, wherat, throw distance of place, and the new beginning of our wark in St Andros.
Mr Andro thought lang nocht to be; bot at last, borrowing a guid horß from
the Bischope, afthand takes iorney and keipes that Assemblie.   Therin the office of Bischopes, as they war mentioned, iudged damnable.   The Act of Dondie
cleirliar expomt and ordeanit to be put in execution   The ordour of Presbyteries, in all prounces, sett down, and Commissionars apointed for establissing
of the sam.   The Kings Confession, publissed for removing suspition of Papistrie from the Court, sighted and allowit.   This Confession is maist notable
bot becaufe it is publict and comoun in the houses and hands of all, I haue
omitted it   Bot, namlie, the buik of the Polecie, efter almaist a ten yeirs labours, was throwlie, and in everie poinct, ratified and ordeanit to be unregistrat
in the buiks of the Assemblie, and copies therof giuen turthe to all prounces.
The quhilk, becaufe this declyning age is beginning to forget and slype fra, I
thought guid to insert in this place, wharof the tenor followes :—

THE HEADS AND CONCLUSIONS OF THE POLECIE OF THE KIRK, 1581.

CAP I

Of the Kirk and Polecie therof in generall, and wherin it is different from the Ciuill Polecie.

I CONCLUSION

PROPOSITION 1   The Kirk of God is sum tymes larghe tean for all them that professes the
Euangell of Jesus Chryst ; and sa it is a companie and fellowschipe, nocht onlie of the Godlie, bot
also of hypocrites professing, alwayes outwardlie, a trew religion.

2. Vther tymes it is taken for the godlie and elect onlie, and sum tymes for them wha exerceises
the spirituall functiones amangs the congregation of them that professes the treuthe.

3. The Kirk, in the last sence, hes a certean powar granted be God, according to the quhilk, it
vses a propir iurisdiction and government exeirceit to the comfort of the haill Kirk.

4. This powar ecclesiastical, is a powar and authoritie granted be God the Father, throw the
Mediator Jesus Chryst, vnto sic wha hes the speciall government of the Kirk committed to them
be lawfull calling, according to the Word of God

5. The polecie of the Kirk, flowing from this powar, is an ordour or form of spirituall government, exeirceit be the members apointed therto be the Word of God giften be Chryst vnto his office
bearers, to be vsit for the weill of the haill bodie of his Kirk.

6   This powar is diuersfie vsit, for sum tymes it is seueralhe exerceit, (cheifhe be the teatchers,)
sum tyme coniunctlie be mutuall consent of them that bears the office and charge efter the form of
iudgment   That an is comounlie callit, Potestas ordinis, that vther, Potestas iurisdictionis

7 Thefe twa kynds of powar hes bathe a author and ground, and a finall caufe, bot ar different in the form and maner of execution, as is euident in the fpeaking of our Maifter in the 16 and 18 of Mathew

8. This powar and polecie ecclefiafticall is different and diftant in thei awin nature fra that powar and polecie quhilk is callet Ciuill, aperteinand to the ciuill government of the Comoun weill, albeit they be bathe of God, and tend to a end, giff they be rightlie vfit; to wit, to advance the glore of God, and to hauft guid fubiects

9 For this powar ecclefiafticall flowes immediathe from God, throw the Mediator Jefus Chryft, and is fpirituall, nocht haifing a temporall head on either, bot onlie Chryft the fpiritnal king and governour of his Kirk, now in glorie within the heavines, at the right hand of his father.

10. Therfor, this powar and polecie of the Kirk fould lein vpon the Word immediathe, as the onlie ground therof, and fould be takin from the pure fonteans of the Scripture, heuing the voice of Chryft the onlie king of his Kirk, and therfor fche fhould be rewlit be his lawes alleancthe.

11. It is a tytle falfhe vfurpit be Antichryft, to call himfelff head of the Kirk, and aught nocht to be attribntit to angell or man, of what efteat foeuer he be, faving to Chryft Jefus, the onlie head and monarche of his Kirk

12. It is proper to kings, princes, and magiftrates, to be callit Lords and Dominators ower than fubiects, whom they govern onlie, bot it is proper to Chryft alean to be callit Lord and Maifter in the fpirituall government of the Kirk   Not aught anie that bears office therin to vfurpe dominion or be callit Lords within the Kirk, bot onlie minifters, difciples, and fervants, for it is Chryfts proper office to command and reull his Kirk vniuerfall, and euerie particular Kirk, throw his fpreit and word be the minifterie of men.

13 Nochtwithftanding as the minifters and vthers of the ecclefiaftical efteat ar fubiect to the magiftrat onlie, fa aught the perfone of the magiftrat to the Kirk fpiritualie, and in ecclefiafticall government and difcipline.

14 The exercefe of bathe thir iuridictiones can nocht ftand in a perfone ordinarlie.

15. The ciuill powar is callit the powar of the fword, the vther is callit the powar of the keyes

16 The ciuill powar fould command the fpirituall to exercefe and do thair office according to the Word of God   The fpirituall reulars fould require the Chriftian magiftrat to minifter iuftice and punithe vyce, and to meantein the libertie and quietnes of the Kirk within than boundes

17. The magiftrat commandit externall things for externall peace and quietnes amangs the fubiects   The minifterie handlit onlie externall things for confcience caufe.

18. The magiftrats handlit onlie externall things and actiones don befor men, bot the fpirituall rewlars iudge bathe inwart affectiones and externall actiones, in refpect of confcience, be the Word of God

19. The ciuill magiftrat crawes and gettes obedience be the fworde and vther externall meanes, bot the minifterie be the fpirituall fword and meanes.

20 The magiftrat nather aught to pretche the Word, minifter the Sacraments, nor execut the Cenfouris of the Kirk, nor vit prefcryve anie form or reull whow it fould be done, bot command the minifter to obferue the reull commandit in the Word of God and punithe the tranfgreffours be ciuill meanes.   The minifter, on the vther part, exerces nocht the ciuill iurifdiction, but teatches the magiftrat whow it fould be done according to the Word of God.

21 The magiftrat aught to affift meantein, and fortifie the Jurifdiction of the Kirk   The minifter fould affift thair prince in all things aggreiable vnto the Word of God, provyding they neglect nocht than awin charge be involuing themfelues in ciuill effeares.

22. Finalie, As ministers ar subiect to the iudgment and punisment of the magistrats in externall things if they offend, sa aught the magistrates to submit themselues to the discipline of the Kirk, if they transgress in maters of religion and conscience

CAP. II

Of the parts of the Policie of the Kirk, and persons and office beareris, to whome the administration thereof is committed.

1. As in the ciuill policie, the wholl comoun weill consistes in the governours or magistrats, and sic as ar governit or subiects, sa, in the policie of the Kirk, sum ar apointed to be reulars, and the rest of the members therof to be reuled and obey acording to the Word of God and inspiration of his spreit, alwayes vnder that an head and governour, Chryst Jesus

2. Again, the haill policie of the Kirk consistes in thri things —In doctrine, in discipline, and in distribution   With doctrine annexit the administration of the Sacraments

3. And according to the partes of this diuision ar thre a thrietauld sort of offeiars in the Kirk, to wit, of ministers or preachours, of eldars or governours, and of deacones or distributars   And all these may be called be a generall word, Ministers of the Kirk

4. For albeit the Kirks of God be reuled and governed be Jesus Chryst, wha is the onlie King, hie priest, and head therof, yit he vses the ministerie of men as a maist necessarie midds for his purpose

5. For sa he hes, from tyme to tyme, befor the Law, vnder the Law, and in the tyme of the Evangell, for our grait comfort reased vpe men indewed with the gifts of the Spreit, for the spirituall government of his Kirk, for the exerceising and bearing of his awin powar, throw the Spirit and Word to the building of the sam

6. And to tak away all occasion of tyrannie, he will that they sould rewell, with mutuall consent of brethring and æqualitie, euerie an according to thair functiones

7. In the New Testament and tyme of the Euangell, he hes vsit the ministerie of the Apostles, prophets, euangelists pastors, and doctors, in administration of the Word, the Eldarschip for guid ordour and administration of discipline, and the Deaconschipe to haue cure of the Kirk guiddes.

8. Sum of thir ecclesiasticall functiones ar ordinar, and sum extraordinar or temporall

9. The office of Apostles, Euangelists, and Prophets, ar nocht perpetuall, bot serving for the first planting of the Kirk, now haiff ceassit, except when it pleasethe God extraordinarlie to steire vpe sum of tham for a tyme againe

10. Ther ar four ordinar functiones, or offices, in the Kirk of God   The office of the Pastor, Minister, or Bischope, the office of Doctor or of the Presbyter or Eldar, and of the Deacon

11. Thir offices are ordinar, and aught to continow perpetualie in the Kirk, as necessarie for the government and policie of the sam, and na ma offices aught to be receavit or suffent in the trew Kirk of God establissed acording to his Word.

12. Therfor, all the ambitius tytilles inventit in the Kingdome of Antichryst, and in his vsurped Hierarchie, quhilk ar nocht of thir sortes, togidder with the offices depending thairpon, in a word, aught to be reiected.

CAP. III

Whow the perfons that be in ecclefiafticall offices ar admitted to thair functions.

1. Vocation or calling, is comoun to all that fould bear office within the Kirk, quhilk is a lawfull way be the quhilk qualefiet perfones ar permitted to anie fpirituall office within the Kirk of God

2 Without this lawfull calling it was neuer leifome to anie peifone to middle with anie function ecclefiafticall

3. Ther is twa fortes of calling, ane extraordinar, immediatelie be God, as wer the Prophets and Apoftles quhilk, in Kirks eftablifled and alreadie weill reformed, hes na place

4 That vther calling is ordinar, quhilk, befyde the calling of God, and inwart teftimonie of guid confcience hes the lawfull approbation and outward iudgment of men according to Gods word and ordour eftablited in his Kirk.

5 Nan aught to prefume to enter in anie ecclefiafticall office without he haift this guid teftimonie of confcience befor God, wha onlie knawes the harts of men.

6 This ordinar and outward calling hes twa partes. Llection and Ordination.

7. Election is the chufing out of a perfone or perfones maift habill to that office that veakes, be the iudgment of the eldaitchipe and content of the congregation, whervnto the perfone or perfones ar to be apointed.

8. The qualities in generall requifit in all them wha fould bear chaige in the Kirk, confiftes in foundnes of religion and godlines of lyft, according as they ar fufficientlie fett furthe in the Word

9. In this ordour of Election is to be efchewit, that na perfone be intrufit in anie of the offices of the Kirk againft the will of the congregation, over quhilk they ar to be apointed, or without the vot of the eldarfchipe.

10 Nan aught to be intrudit or put in the places aheadie planted, nor in anie roum that veakes tor anie warldlie refpect. And that quhilk is called the benefice, fould be nathing els bot the ftipend of the minifter wha is lawfullie called and elected

11. Ordination is the feparation and fanctefeing of the perfone elected to God and his Kirk etter he be weill tryed and fund qualifiet

12 The ceremonies of Ordination ar, fafting prayer, and impofition of the hands of the eldaitchipe

13. All this, as they ar ordinat of God, and maid able be him for the wark whervnto they ar limited within Gods word, fa aught they nocht to pas the bounds therof.

14 All thefe office bearers fould haift ther awin particular flocks, whom amangs they exercerie thair charge, and fould mak refidence with tham, and tak the infpection and owerfight of tham euerie ane in his vocation. And generalie this twa things aught they all to refpect: the glorie of God, and edifeing of his Kirk in difchaiging the dewties in ther calling.

CAP IV

Of the Office bearers in particular, and firft, of the Paftor or Minifter

1. Paftors, or bifchops, or minifters, ar they wha ar apointed to particular congregationes and kirks, quhilk they reull be the Word of God, and ower the quhilk they watche In refpect wharof,

tum tymes they are called paftors for feiding of than flocks, fum tym *επισκοπαι*, or bifchopes, be - caufe they watche over the congregation, fum tum minifters, be reafone of thair fervice and office, tum tyme alfo prefbyters, or feniores, or eldars, for than age, graunte, and maners, quhilk they aught to haift in taking care of the fpirituall government, that aught to be maift den vnto tham

2 They that ar called to the minifterie, or that offer thamfelues thervnto, aught nocht to be elected without a certean flocke be affigned vnto tham

3. Na man aught to ingyre himfelft, or vfurpe this ofhce, without a lawfull calling

4 They wha ar annes callit be God, and dewlie elected be man, efter that they haiff annes accepted the charge of the minifterie, may nocht leaue than function

5 The detertours fould be admonifched, and, in cafe of obftinacie, finalie excommuniceat

6 Na paftor may leaue his flock without licence of the Provinciall or Nationall Affemblie, giff he do vtherwayes, efter admonition nocht obeyit, let the cenfouris of the Kirk ftrik vpon hun.

7. Vnto paftors of the Kirk apertemes the teatching of the Word of God, in feafone and out of feafone, publhelie and privatlie, alwayes teatching to edifie and difcharge of his confcience be Gods Word prefcryvit to him

8 Vnto the paftors onlie apertemes the adminiftration of the Sacraments in lyk maner as of the Word, for bathe ar apointed be God as meanes to teatche ws, that an be the ein, that vther be the ein and vther fenfes, that by bathe knawlage may be tranfferrit to the mynd

9. It apertemes be the fam reafone to the Paftor to pray for the peiple, and, namlie, for the flock committed to his charge, and to blifs tham in the nam of the Lord, wha will nocht fuffer the blefing of his fathfull fervands to be without effect

10. He aught to watche aboue the maners of his flock, that he may the better apply to tham in rebuking diffolut perfones, and exhorting the godlie to continow in holines and the feir of the Lord

11 It appertemes to the minifter, efter lawfull proceiding be the eldarfchipe, to pronunce the fentence of binding and lowfing vpon anie perfone according to the powar of the keyes granted to the Kirk.

12. It belanges to him in lyk wayes, efter lawfull proceiding of the eldarfchipe, to folemmize the band of mariage, and blifs the perfones iovnet therin

13 And generalie all denunciationes that ar to be maid in the kirk, befor the congregation, con- cerning ecclefiafticall offences, belanges to the office of the minifterie, for he is the mouthe, mef- finger, and herauld of God, betwix him and his peiple in all there effeares.

CAP. V

Of Doctors and than office, and of the Scholles

1 Ane of the twa ordinar and perpetuall functiones that trauelles in the Word, is the office of a Doctor, wha may alfo be called a Prophet, Bifchope, Eldar, or Catechifar, that is, a teatcher of the Catechifme and Rudiments of Religion

2 His office is to opin vpe the mynd of the fpreit of God within the Scriptures, fimphe with- out fie application as the minifter vfes, to that end that the fathfull may be inftructed in the right warrands of halfome doctrine, and that the puritie therof may abyde in the Kirk, vncorrupted be ignorance and euill opiniones.

3 He is different from the Paftor, nocht onlie in name bot in diuerfitie of giftes, for to the Doctor is giffen the word of knawlage, to open vpe, be fimple doctrine, the myfteries of fathe To the paftor the gift of wefdome, to apply the fam be exhortation to the maneis of the flocks, as occafion feruit

4. Vnder the name and office of a Doctor, we comprehend the ordour of Scholes in Collages and Vniuerfities, quhilk hes bein meantemed carfullie, alfweill amang the Jewes and Chriftianes as profane nationes.

5. The Doctor being an Eldar, as faid is, fould affift the Paftor in the government of the Kirk and conceiue with the eldars, his breithing, in all Affembhes, be reafone the interpretation of the Word, quhilk is onlie iudge in ecclefiaftical mateis, is committed to his charge.

6. Bot to preatche vnto the perple, to miniíter the Sacraments, and to celebrat mariage, perteines nocht to the Doctor, vnles he be vtherwayes callit ordinarlie, whowbeit, the Paftor may teatche in the Scholles as he wha hes the gift of knawlage, oftentymes meit therfor, as the exemple of Policarpus and vthers does teftifie

CAP VI

Of the Eldars and thair office

1. The nam of Eldar in the Scripture is fumtyme the nam of age, and fumtyme of office

2. When it is the nam of office, fumtyme it is taken larghe, comprehending alfweill the paftors and doctors, as thair wha ar comounlie callit Seniors or Eldais.

3 In this our diuifion, we call thofe Eldars, whom the Apoftle tytilles Prefidents or Gouernours

4 Thair office, as it is ordinan fa it is perpetuall, and alwayes neceffar in the Kirk of God

5 The Eldarfchipe is a fpirituall function as the miniíterie

6 Eldars annes called to the office lawfullie, and haifing the gifts of God meit to exerceife the fam, may nocht leaue it againe

7 Albeit fue a nomber of eldars may be fchafin in certean congregations, that an part of them may releiue an vther for a reafonable fpace, as was amangs the Leuites vnder the law in ferving of the temple

8 The number of Eldars in eueiie congregation can nocht be limitat, bot fould be according to the bounds and neceffitie of the peiple.

9. It is nocht neceffar that all the eldars be alfo teatchars of the Word, albeit cheiflie they aught to be fic, and fa worthie of double honnour

10. What maner of perfones they aught to be, we referre it to the expreís Word, namlie, the Canons wrytten be the Apoftlles.

11. Thair office is alfo, feueralie as comunelie, to watche dihgenthe vpon the flock committed to thair charge, bathe publicthe and priuathe, that na corruption of relligion or maners enter therin

12 As the paftors and doctors fould be diligent in fawing the fied of the Word, fa fould the eldars be cairtull in feiking the fruitt of the fam amangs the peiple.

13 It aperteines to thaim to affift the paftors in examination of them that comes to the Lords Table, and in vifiting of the feik.

14. They fould be cairfull to caufe the Actes of the Affemblie, alfweill particular as prouinciall or generall, to be put in execution.

15 They fould be diligent in admonifing all men of thair dewtie, according to the reull of the Evangell

16. Things that can nocht be corrected be priuie admonition, they fould bring and deleat to the Elderfchipe

17. Than principall office is to hauld affemblies with the paftors and doctors, wha ar alfo of thair nomber, tor eftablifhng of guid ordour and execution of difciplme   Vnto the quhilk affemblie all men ar fubiect that remeanes within thair bounds.

CAP. VII

Of Eldarfchips, Affemblies, and of Difciplme.

1. Elderfchipes or Affemblies ar conftitut of Paftors, Doctors, and Eldais, that labour nocht in the Word, of whom and of whafe feuerall powar has bein fpoken.

2 Affemblies ar of four fortes, for ather ai they of particular kirks and congregationnes, an or ma, ather of a prouince, ather of a naill nation, or of all and findrie nationes profeffing Jefus Chryft

3 All Ecclefiafticall Affemblies hes powar to conuern lawfullie togidder, for treating of things concerning the Kirk and thair charge.

4 They haifl powar till apoint tymes and places to that effect, and a Affemblie to appoint dyet, tyme, and place for an other.

5 In all Affemblies a Moderator fould be chofin be comoun confent of the haill breithring conuent, wha fould pray, propone maters, put in reafoning, gather the vottes, and keipe the Affemblie in guid ordour

6. Tent fould be tean be the Moderator, that onlie ecclefiafticall maters be handlit in Affemblies, and na melling with anie thing perteining to the Ciuill Jurifdiction

7 Euerie Affemblie hes powar to fend furthe from them a romber, an or ma vifitors to fie whow maters ar handlit in the bounds of thair iurifdiction.

8. Vifitation of ma Kirks is na ordinar office ecclefiafticall in the perfone of a man   nather may the name of a Bitchope be attributit to the vifitour onlie, nather is it neceffar to abyde alwayes in the perfone of a man, bot it is the part of the Elderfchipe to fend out qualefiet perfones to vifeit

9 The finall end of all Affemblies is, firft to keipe the relligion and doctrin in puretie, without errour and corruption, next, to keipe comlie and guid ordour in the Kirk.

10 For this ordours caufe they may mak certean reulles and conftitutions aperteining to the guid behauiour of all the members of the Kirk, in thair vifitation

11 They haift powar allo till abolifhe and abrogat all ftatutes and ordinances concerning ecclefiafticall maters that ar fund noyfum or vnprobtable, and aggrie nocht with the tyme, or abbufed be the peiple.

12 They haift powar till execut ecclefiafticall difciplme and punifment vpon all tranfgreffours and proude contemners of all guid ordour and polecie of the Kirk   And fa the haill difciplme is in thair hands

13. The firft kynd and fort of Affemblies, albeit they be within particular congregationes, yit they exerceife the powar and iurifdiction of the Kirk with mutuall confent, and therfor bears the nam of the Kirk.

14. When we fpeak of particular congregationes, we mein nocht that euerie particular paroche

K

kirk can, or may, haiff thair awin particular elderschipe specialie to Landwart, bot we think thre, foui, ma or fewar, particulai kirks may haiff a comoun elderschipe vnto tham all to iudge in ecclesiasticall caufles

15 Albeit it is meit that fum of the Eldars be chofin out of euerie particulai congregation, to concur with the reft of thair brethring in the comoun affemblie and to tak vpe the delationes of offences within their awin kirks, and bring tham therto

16 This we gather of the practise of the primitiue Kirk, whair eldars, or Collages of Seniors, war conftitut in cities and famous places

17. The powar of the particulai elderschipe, is to giff diligent labours in the boundes committed to than charge, that the kirks be keipit in guid ordour, to inquyre diligenthe of naughtie and vngodlie perfones, to trauell to bring tham in the way agane, be admonition, threatning of Gods iudgments or be correction of cenfoms.

18 It apperteines to the Elderschipe to tak heid that the Word of God be puilie teatched within thair bounds, and Sacraments dewlie minniftrat the difciphne mentemed, and the ecclefiafticall guids vncorrupthe diftribut

19. It belanges to this kynd of Affemblies to canfe the ordonnances maid be the provincialles Nationall and Generall, to be keipit and put in execution.

20 To mak conftitutiones concerning το πρέπον in the Kirk, for decent ordour of the particulai kirks whar they govern, prouyding they alter na rewles maid be the Provinciall or Generall Affemblies And that they mak the Provinciall Affemblies reulles to fie as they fall mak and abolithe conftitutiones tending to the hurt of the fam

21 It hes powar to excommunicat the obftinat

22 The powar of election of tham wha beares ecclefiafticall charges, perteines to this kynd of Affemblie within thair awin bounds, being weill erected and conftitut of paftors and doctors of fufficient abilitie

23 Be Elderschipe or Prefbyterie, is memed fie as ar conftitut of Paftors, doctors, and fie as ar now called Eldars.

24 Be the lyk reafone than depofition aperteines alfo to this kynd of Affemblie, as of tham that teatche erronius doctrin and corrupt, that be of fklanderus lyff, and efter admonition, amend nocht; that ar giffen to fchifme, or rebellion, againft the Kirk, to blafphemie manifeft, to fymonie, and all corruption of brybes, falthode, peiurie, hurdom, thift, drunkennes, flyting, feghting, worthie of punifment be the law, vfurie danfing, and fie diffolutiones and crymes that importes eiuill infamie, and all vthers that deferues feparation tra the Kirk

25 Thefe alfo, wha ar fund altogidder infufficient to exeent thair charges, fould be depofit, wharof vther Kirks wald be aduertifed that they receane nocht the perfones depofit

26 Albeit, they aught nocht to be depofed, wha, throw age, feiknes, or vther accidents, becomes vnmeit to do than office, in the quhilk cais, than honom fould remean vnto tham, than kirks fould meantein tham, and vthers aught to be prouydit to do than office.

27. Provinciall Affemblies we call lawfull conventiones of the Paftors Doctors, and Eldars of an province, gathered for the comoun effeares of the Kirk therof, quhilk alfo may be callit the Conference of Kirk and breithring

28 Thir Affemblies ar conftitut for weghtie maters, neceffar to be intreated be mutuall confent and affent of breithring within that province, as neid requyres.

29 This Affemblie hes powar to handle, ordei, and redrefs all things committed or done amifs in the particular affemblies or prefbyteries

30. It hes powar to depose the office bearers of that province for guid and iust caufles, deferuing deprivation.

31. And, generalie, this Affemblies hes the haill powar of the particular elderfchippes wherof they ar collected.

32. An Nationall Affemblie, (quhilk is our Generall of this realm) is a lawfull Convention of the Kirks of that haill realme or nation, whar it is vfit to be gaddent for the comoun effeares of the Kirk, and may be callit the Generall Elderfchipe of the haill Kirk within the realme

33. Nan ar fubiect to repeare to this Affemblie to wot thefin, but ecclefiafticall perfones in fic number as falbe thought guid be the fam Affemblie, nocht excluding vther perfones that will repeare to the faid Affemblie, and ther propone, heir, and reafone ordourlie

34. This Affemblie is conftitut, that things omitted or done amifs in the Provinciall Affemblies may be redreffit, and things generalie ferving for the weill of the haill body of the Kirk in that realme may be torefein, intreated, and fett furthe to Gods glorie.

35. It fall cair that Kirkes be planted in places whar they ar nocht.

36. It fould prefcryve the reull whow the vther twa kynd of Affemblies fould proceid in all things

37. This Affemblie fould tak heid that the fpirituall iurifdiction and ciuill be nocht confoundit, to the hint of the Kirk.

38. That the Patrimonie of the Kirk be nocht diminifched nor abbufit.

39. And, generalie, concerning all weghtie effeares quhilks concernes the weill and guid ordour of the Kirk vniuerfall of this realm, it aught to interpon his authoritie thervnto

CAP. VIII.

Of the Deacones and thair office, the laft ordinar function in the Kirk

1. The word Deacon is fum tyme larghe takin, comprehending all them that bear office in the minifrie and fpirituall function of the Kirk.

2. Bot now as we fpeik, it is tean onlie for tham to whom the collection, and diftribution, of the almes of the fathfull and of the Kirk guids does belang.

3. The office of the Deacon, fo takin, is an ordour and perpetuall ecclefiafticall function in the Kirk of Chryft.

4. Of what properties and beauties he aught to be that is called to this function, we remit to the manifeft Scripture

5. The Deacon aught to be elected and called as the reft of the fpirituall officiars, as was fpoken of befor

6. Thair office and powar is to collect and diftribut the haill ecclefiafticall guids vnto tham to whom they ar apointed.

7. This they aught to do according to the iudgment and apointment of the prefbyteries and eldarfchips, of the quhilks the deacones ar nocht, that the patrimonie of the Kirk and puire be nocht interuerted to privat mens vfes, nor wrangfullie diftributed.

CAP. IX.

Of the Patrimonie of the Kirk, and distribution therof

1. Be the patrimonie of the Kirk we mein whatsumeuer thing has bein at anie tyme befor, or salbe in tyme coming, doted and giwen, or be consent and vniuersall custom of countreyes pro-fessing Christian religion, apointed to the publict vse and vtilitie of the Kirk.

2. Sa that vnder this patrimonie we comprehend, first, all things gewin, or to be gewin, to the Kirk and seruice of God, as lands, bignngs, possessiones annualrents, and all sic lyk wherwith the Kirk is dotted, athei be donation fundation, or mortification, or anie vther lawfull tytles, be kings, princes, or anie inferiour persones, giwen to God and his Kirk, with the continuall oblationes of the faithfull

3. We comprehend also all sic things as be Lawes, Custome, or vse of Countreyes, hes bein applyed to the vse and vtilitie of the Kirk, of the quhilk sort ar the Teinds small and grait, Manses, Gleibs, and sic lyk, quhilk, by comoun and municipall lawes and vniuersall custome, ar possessed be the Kirk

4 To tak away onie thing of this patrimonie be vnlawfull meanes, and conveit it to the parti-cular and profean vse of anie man, we hald it a detestable sacrilege befor God

5 The guids ecclesiasticall, aught to be collected and distribut be the deacones, as the Word of God apomts, that they wha beais office in the Kirk may be prony dht for without cear and sollicitude

6 In the Apostolicall Kirk the Deacones war apointed to distribut whatsoeuer was collected of the faithfull to the necessitie of the sanets, sa that nan lakit amangs them

7 These Deacones was nocht onlie collectors of that quhilk was gathered in maner of Almes, (as sum suppose,) bot of vthers guids monable and vmmouable, of lands and possessiones, the pryce wherof was brought and leyit at the feit of the Apostles.

8 This office continowed in the Deacones hands, wha intromeated with the haill guids of the Kirk, ay whill the esteat therof was corrupted be that Antichryst, as the ancient Canones does witnes

9 The sam Canones makes mention of a foui fauld distribution of the patrimonie of the Kuk, wharof a part was apointed for the pastors or bischopes. for than suitentation and hospitalitie. the second to the eldais and deacones, and all the clargie, the thride to the puir seik persones and strangers; the fourt for the fabric and vphauld of the Kuks and vthei esteates, namlie extraordinar

10 We ad heir vnto the Scholles and Scholmaisters, quhilk may be weill suitemed of the sam guids, and ar comprehendit vnder the clargie, to whom we ioyne the Clerks of the Assemblies, ali-weill particular as generall, Syndics or Procurators of the Kuks esteates, Takers vpe of the psalme, with sic lyk vther ordinar offices of the Kuk, sa fai as they ar necessar

CAP. X.

Of the Office of a Christian Magistrat

1. Albeit all the members of the Kirk be haldin euerie an in thair vocation, to advance the Kingdome of Jesus Chryst, sa fai as lyes in than powar, yit, cheislie and namlie, Christian princes, kings, and magistrates, ar hauldin to do the sam.

2 For they ar callit in the Scriptures, Nurishars of the Kirk, forsamikle as be tham, (at leaſt aught to be,) meantened, ſoſtert, vphauldin, and defendit againſt all that wald procure the hurt of the ſam

3 Sa it aperteines to the office of a Chriſtian magiſtrat till aſſiſt and fortefie the godlie proceidings of the Kirk in all behalffs , and namlie, to ſie that the publict eſteat and miniſterie therof be meantemed and furtemed as aperteines, conform to the Word of God.

4 To ſie that the Kirk of God be nocht invadit nor hurt be falſs teatchers, or hyrlings, nor the roumes therof occupied be dum dogges and ydle bellies

5. To aſſiſt and meantem the diſcipline of the Kirk, and puniſhe tham (inihe that will nocht obey the cenſures of the ſam, without confounding alwayes the au iuriſdiction with the vther.

6. To ſie that ſufficient prouiſion be maid for the miniſterie, ſcholles, and pure , and giff they haiſt nocht ſufficient for avating on than charges to ſupport than indigences, euen with than awin rentes, giſt neid ſa requyre

7. To hauld hand to them alſweill concerning thair awin perſones, ſaueing tham from opin iniurie and violence, as concerning than rentes and poſſeſſiones, that they be nocht defraudit, rubbet, nor ſpoiled therof.

8 Nocht to ſuffer the patrimonie of the Kirk to be applyed to profean and vnlawfull vſes, or to be deuoirt be ydle bellies, and ſic as haiſt na lawfull function in the Kirk, to the hurt of the miniſterie, ſcholles, and pure, and vther godlie vſes, whervpon the ſaming aught to be beſtowit.

9 To mak Lawes and Conſtitutiounes aggreiable to Gods Word, for the advanſment of the Kirk and polecie of the ſam, without vſurping vpon anie thing nocht perteining to the ciuill ſword, but belanging to the offices that ar mere eccleſiaſticall, as is the miniſterie of the Word and Sacraments , vſing of eccleſiaſticall diſcipline and ſpiritnall execution thereof, or anie part of the powar of the ſpirituall keyes, quhilk our Maiſter gaiff to his Apoſtles and than trew ſucceſſours.

10 And altho kings and princes, that be godlie, ſum tymes be than awin authoritie, (when the Kirk is corrupted, and all things out of ordour,) place miniſters and reſtore the trew ſervice of the Lord, efter exemple of ſum godlie Kings in Juda, (the quhilk they did be direction of prophets,) and diuers godlie Kings and Emperours, in the light of the Goſpell , yit when the miniſterie of the Kirk is annes lawfullie inſtitut, and they that ar placed in offices lawfullie callit, then all godlie princes and magiſtrates aught to heir and obey thair voice, and reuerence the Maieſtie of the Sone of God be them ſpeakand

CAP. XI

Of the preſent Abbuſes remeaning in the Kirk, quhilk we deſyre to be reformed

1 It is the dewtie of the godlie Magiſtrat to meantem the preſent libertie, quhilk God, of his mercie, hes granted to the pretching of the Word, and the right adminiſtration of the Sacraments within this realm, ſa it is to prouyde that all abbuſes quhilk as yit remeanes within the Kirk be remouit and vtterly takin away.

2 Therfor, firſt, the admiſſion of men to Papiſticall benefices, ſic as ſerues nocht, nor hes na function in the Reformed Kirk of Chryſt, as Abates, Comendators, Pryores, Pryoreſſes, and vther tytles of Abbayes, whaſe places ar now, for the maiſt part, be the iudgment of God, demoliſhed and

puigit of Idolatrie, is plean abbution, and is nocht to receane the Kingdome of God in Chryft amangs ws, bot rather to refufe it

3 Sic lyk they that wai called of auld the Chaptours and Convents of Abbayes, Cathedrall Kuks, and lyk places, ferue for na thing now, but to fett Fewes and Takes, (if anie thing be left,) of the Knk lands and teindes, in hurt and preiudice therof, as daylie experience teatches, and therfor aught to be alluterlie altent and abolifhed

4 Ot the lyk nature ar the Deacones, Archdeacones, Chantors, Thefauraris, Chancellouris, and vthers haifland the lyk tytle flowand from the Pape and Canon Law onlie, quhilk hes na place in a reformed Kirk

5. Mikle les is it lawfull, that perfones amangs thir men haiff fyftein, faxtein, twentie, or ma Kirks, all haifhng charge of faulles, and brouk the patrimonie therof, ather be admifhon ot the Prince, or of the Kirk, in this light of the Luangell, for it is bot mocage to crane reformation whar fic lyk hes place.

6. And albeit it was thought gud for avoidhng of grattei inconvenients, that auld pofletfours of fic benefices wha embraffit the religion, fould emoy, be permifhon, the twa part ot the rentes quhilk they poffeffit ot befor, during than lyft tyme, vit it is nocht tolerable to continow in the lyk abufs, and giff than places and vther benefices of new to als vnmeit men, or rather vnmeittar, wha ar nocht myndit to ferne in the Kirk, bot leme an ydle lyft, as the vthers did wha bruiked them in tym of blindnes

7 And in fa far as in the ordour tean at I eithe, anno 1571, it appeiris that fic may be admitted, being found qualefiet, &c, ather that pretendit ordour is againft all gud ordour, or els it man be vnderftud nocht of tham that be qualefied to wouldhe effeares to ferue in the Court, bot fic as ar qualefiet to teatche Gods Word, haifhng the lawfull admifhon of the Kirk.

8 As to the Bifchope, if the nam ἐπίσκοπος be properlie takin, they ar all an with minifters, as we befor declarit, for it is nocht a name of fuperioritie and lordfchipe, bot of office and watching.

9. Yit becaufe in the corruption ot the Kirk this nam, as vthers, hes bein abbufit, and yit is lyk to be, we can nocht allow this fachion ot chufing of Bifchopes, nather of the Chaptours that ar electores of tham, to fic a fort of office as they ar chofine

10 The trew bifchopes fould addict thamfelues to a particular flok, quhilk findrie of tham refufes nather fould they vfurpe lordfchipe ower than breithring and inheritance of Chryfte, as thefe men do.

11 Paftors, in fa far as they ar paftors, hes nocht the office of vifitation of ma kirks ioyned to the paftorfchipe, without it be giffen to tham.

12. It is a corruption that bifchopes fould haiff fordai boundes to vifit nor they may poffiblie or lawtulhe

13. Na man aught to haiff the office of Vifitation, bot he that is lawfulhe chofine by the Prefbyterie thervnto

14 The Elderfchipe, being weill eftablifled, hes powar to fend out Vifitors, an or ma, with commifhon to vifit the boundes within than elderfchipe, and fic lyk, efter compt tean of tham, ather to continow or remoue them, as the Prefbyterie thinks meit, to the quhilk they falbe alwayes fubiect.

15. The temporall iurifdiction, ioynit in the perfon of a paftor, is Corruption

16 It agreis nocht with the Word of God, that a bifchope fould be a paftor of paftores of manie flockes, and yit without a flock certean, and without ordinar teatching

17 It agreis nocht with the Scriptures, that they fould be exemed fra correction ot thair breithei, and difciphne of the particular elderfchipe of the Kirk whai they fould ferue, nather that they

fould vfurpe office of vifitation of vther kirks, nor anie vther function befyde vther ministers, bot
ta far as beis committed to tham be the Kirk.

18 Heiroi, we defyre the Bischopes that now ar, athei to aggrie to that ordoui that Gods
Word requyres of tham, and as the generall Kirk will preferyve vnto tham, nocht paffing the
bounds, nather in ecclefiaftical noi ciuill cfleares, or els to be depoht from anie function of the Kirk.

19 We deny nocht, in the meantyme bot mnafters fould athfi than Prince, when they ar requyrit, in all things aggreiable to the Word and thair calling, whither it be at Counfall, Parliament,
or vtherwayes, provyding that they nather neglect than awin charges, nor, be flaterie of Princes,
hurt the publict eftcat of the Kirk.

20 Bot, generalie we fay, na perfone, vnder whatfoeuer tytle of the Kirk, and fpecialie the ab-
bufit tytilles of Papiftrie, as Prelattes, Convents, and Chapters, aught till attempt anie act in the
Kirks name, athei in Counfall, Parliament, or without, haiftand na Commiftion of the reformed
Kirk within this realme.

21 And be Act of Parliament, it is prouydit, that the Papifticall Kirk and Jurifdictiou fould
haift na place within the fam, and na bifchope, nor vthei prelat, in tyme coming, fould vfe anie
Jurifdiction flowing fra that authoritie.

22. And again, that na vther ecclefiafticall iurifdiction fould be acknawlagit within this realm,
bot that quhilk is and falbe within the reformed Kirk, and flowing therfra.

23 Sa we efteim holding of Chaptars in Papifticall maner, athei in Cathedrall Kirks, Collages,
or vthei conventuall places, vfurping the name and authoritie of the Kirk, to hurt the patrimonie
therof, or vfe anie vthei act to the preiudice of the fam, fen the yeir of our Lord 1560, to be ab-
bufion and corruption, contrar the libertie of the Kirk reformed of Jefus Chryft, and lawes of this
realme, and therfor aught to be annullit and reducit, and in tymes coming, alluterlie difchargit.

24 The dependances alfo of this Papifticall iurifdiction ar to be abolifhed, of the quhilk fort ar
the mingled iurifdiction of the Commiffars, in fa far as they mell with ecclefiafticall maters, and
haiff na commiffion of the Kirk therto, but war erected in the tyme of our Soveraine Lords mother, when things war ont of ordour. It is an abfurd thing, that findrie of tham haifing na function of the Kirk, fould be iudges to minifters, and depofe tham from thair roumes. Therfor, they
wald athei be difchargit from ecclefiafticall maters, and anie melling therwith, or it wald be limitat
to tham in what maters they might be iudges, and nocht hurt the libertie of the Kirk.

25. They, alfo, that war before the ecclefiafticall efteat in the Papes Kirk, or that ar admitted of
new to Papifticall tytilles, and now ar toleratit be the Lawes of the Realme, to place the twa part
of thair ecclefiafticall rents, aught nocht to haift anie fordar libertie bot to intromet with the portion
affignet and granted to tham for than lyft tyme, and nocht vnder the abbufit tytles quhilk they hade,
difpone the Kirk rents, fett takes and feues therof at than pleafure, to the wrak of the Kirk and
of the pure laborars that dwell vpon the Kirk lands, contrar to all guid confcience and ordour.

CAP. XII

Certean fpeciall Heids of Reformation crauied.

1 Whatfoeuer hes bein fpoken of the offices of the Kirk, the feuerall powars of the office bearers,
than coniunct powar alfo, and laft, of the patrimonie of the Kirk, we vnderftand it to be the right

retormation that God craues at our hands, that the Kirk be ordourit therto, as with that ordour
quhilk is maist aggreiable vnto the Word of God.

2. Bot becaute fum things wilbe twitched in particular anent the esteat of the countrey, and
that quhilk we feik principalie to be refoimed in the fam, we haist collected tham in thir heids
following.—

3 Firft, feing the haill countrey is deuydit in provinces, and thir provinces agam ar deuydit in
paroches, alfweill to Bruche as Land, and in euerie parochine a reionable congregation, ther wald be
placed an or ma paftors to feid the floks, and na paftor or miniftei to be burdeanit with particular
charge of ma flocks or kirks then an alleancrhe

4 And becaufe it wilbe thought haid to find out paftors to all the paroche kirks of the realme
alfweill to landwart as in townes, we think, be the advyis of fic as commiffion may be giffen to be
the Kirk and the Prince paroches in landwart or finall villages m. , be ioyned twa or thrie, or ma
in fum places togidder, and the principall and maift commodius kirks to ftand and be repeairt fufficienthe, and qualefiet miniflers placed therat, and the other kirks nocht fund neceffarie, fuffent
to decay, than kirk yeards alwayes being keipit for buriall places, and in fum places, whar neid
requyres, ane parochine, whar the congregation is ower grait, may be deuydit in twa or ma

5 Doctors wald be apointed in Vniucrfities, Collages, and vther places neidfull, and fufficienthe
prouydit for, to open vpe the meining of the Scriptures, and to haift the charge of faulles, and to
teatche the rudiments of religioun.

6 As to the Eldars, ther wald be fum to be Cenfors of the maners, ane or ma, in euerie congregation, but nocht an Affemblie of eldais in euerie particular kirk, but in townes onlie and famous
places, whar refort of men of iudgment and abilitie, to that effect may be haid, whar the Eldais
of particular kirks about may convein togidder, and haift comoun Eldaifchipe and Affemblie place
amangs them, to treat of all things that concernes the congregationes ower whom they haift the
owerfight

7. And as ther aught to be men apointed to viut and denyde the paroches as neceffitie and commoditie requyres, fa wald ther be apointed be the generall Kirk, with the affent of the prince, fic
men as feires God, and knew the efteat of countries, that war able to denominat and affinge the
places whar the Affemblies of particular elderfchipes fould convein, taking confideration of the Dio-
ceifes as they war denydit of auld, and of the efteat of the counties and prouinces of the realme.

8. Lykwayes as concerning Prouinciall or Synodall Affemblies, confideration war allwa to be
haid, whow manie and in what places they war to be hauldin, and whow often they fould convein
aught to be referrit to the libertie of the generall Kirk, and ordour to be apointed therin

9. The Nationall Affemblies of this Countrey, callit comounlie the Generall Affemblies aught
alwayes to be reteined in than awin libertie, and haift ther awin place, with powar to the Kirk to
apoint tyme and places convenient therfor. And all men, alfweill magiftrats as inferionis, to be
fubiect to the iudgment of the fam in ecclefiafticall caufes, without anie reclamation or appellation
to anie Judge, ciuill or ecclefiafticall, within this realme.

10. The libertie of election of ecclefiafticall perfones callit to beai function in the Kirk obferuit
without interrupted continowance vnto the corruption of Antichryft, we defyre to be reftored and
reteined within this Realm, fa that nan be intrufit vpon anie congregation, ather be prince or anie
inferiour perfone, without lawfull election and confent of the peiple ower whome the perfone is to
be placed, as the practife of the Apoftolicall primitiue Kirk, and all guid reafone and ordour craues

11. And becaufe this Ordour, quhilk Gods Word and all guid reafone craues, can nocht ftand
with patronages and prefentationes to benefices, vfit in the Papes Kirk, we defyre all fic as trewlie

tenes God, erneftlie to confidder, That forfamikle as the names of pationages and benefices togidder with the effect therof, flowed from the Pape and clofit of the Cenon Law, wharby vnmeit
and corrupt perfones ar intrufit and placed in kirks haiffand curam animarum, and forfamikle as
the maner of proceiding hes na ground in the Word of God, bot repugnes flatlie to the faming,
owerthrawing the ordour and libertie of election, they aught nocht to haiff place in the light of
Reformation, and therfor, whafoeuer will trewlie embrace Gods Word, and defyre the Kingdome
of his Sone Jefus Chryft to be advanced, they will alfo embrace and receaue the polecie and ordour
quhilk the will of God and vpright efteat of his Kirk craues . Vtherwayes it is in vean that they
haiff profeffed the Gofpell

12 Nochtwithftanding, as concerning vther benefices and patronages therof, that hes nocht curam animarum, fic as ar thefe altarages, prebends foundit on temporall lands, annuels, and fic lyk,
may be referuit to the ancient pationes to difpone thervpon when they veak to fchollars and bur-
faies as they are requyred be Act of Parliament.

13 As to the Kirk rents in generall, we defyre that ordour to be admitted and meanteined
amangs ws that may ftand with the incentie of Gods Word and practife of the Kirk of Chryft.

14 To wit, that was befor fpokin, the haill rent and patrimonie of the Kirk, (excepting fmall
pationages befor mentioned,) may be deuvdit in tour portiones, ane therof to be affigned to the
Paftor, for his interteinment and hofpitalitie, ane vther to the Eldais, Deacones, and vther officiars
of the Kirk, fic as Clarks of Affembhes, Takeis vpe of the Pfalmes, Beddels, and kirk maifters and
keipars, fa far as they ar neceffar, ioyning in fpeciall maner the Doctors and Scholles, that thair
ancient foundationes may be helped whar neid requyres. The third portion to be beftowit vpon
the pure members of the fathfull and hofpitalls The fourt and laft, for reparation of the kirks, and
vther extraordinar charges as ar profitable for the Kirk, as alfo for the comoun weill, as grait neid
fall requyre

15. We defyre, therfor, the ecclefiafticall guids to be vplifted and diftributed fathfullie to whom
they apertein, and that be the minifterie of the Deacones, to the quhilk office properlie the collection and diftribution therof belanges , that the pure may be anfwerit of than portion therof, and
they of the minifterie left without care and follicitude , as alfo the reft of the treaffours of the Kirk
may be referuit and beftowit on the right vfes.

16 Gift thefe Deacones be elected with fic qualeties as Gods Word craues to be in tham, ther
is na feir that they fall abbufe thamfelues in thair office, as the profean collectors did of befor , yit
becaufe that this vocation appeares to manie to be dangerus, let tham be oblnit, as they war of auld,
to a yeirlie compt to the Paftors and Eldarfchipe , and iff the Kirk and Prince think expedient, let
cautioners be oblift for thair fidelitie, that the Kirk rents na way be delapidat

17. And to the effect this ordour may tak place, it is to be prouydit that all vther intromettours
with the Kirk rents, collector generall or fpeciall, whither it be apointment of the prince or
vtherwayes, may be difchargit of fordar intromiffion therwith , and fuffer the Kirk rents, in tyme
coming to be hailelie intrometit with be the minifterie of the Deacons, and diftributit to the vffes
betor mentioned. And alfo to the effect, that the ecclefiafticall rents may fuffice to thofe vffes for
the quhilk they ar apointed, we think it neceffar to be defyrit that alienationnes, letting of fewes or
taks of the rents of the Kirk, alfweill landes as teindes, to the hurt and diminution of the auld
rentalles, be reducit and annullit, and the patrimonie of the Kirk reftorit to the auld integritie
In lyk maner, that the teinds, in tyme coming, be fett to nane bot to the laborars of the ground, or
els nocht fett at all, as it was aggreit vpon and fubfcryvit be the Nobilitie in the firft Buik of Difciphne, anno 1560.

L

CAP XIII.

The Vtilitie that fall follow of this Reformation to all Esteattes.

1. Seing the end of this fpirituall government and polecie whatof we fpeik, is that God may be glorified, the Kingdome of Chryft Jefus advancit and all they that ar of his myfticall body may hue peaceblie in confcience. Therfor we dar bauldlie affirm, that all fie wha hes trew refpect to thefe ends, will, evin for confcience caufe, gladlie agrie and conform themfelues to this ordour, and advance the fam fa mikle as lyes in them, that thair confcience being fett at reft, they may be rephnifhed with fpirituall gladnes, in dewtifull obedience to that quhilk Gods Word and the teftimonie of thair awin confcience does craue, and refufing all corruption contrare vnto the fam.

2. Nixt, we fall becom an exemple and patron of guid and godlie ordei to vther nationnes, countries, and kirks profefiing the fam religion with ws, that as they haiff glorihed God in continowing in the finceritie of the Word hitherto without all ermours, praife be to that grait keippar, fo they may haiff the lyk occafion in our converfation, when, as we conform ourfelues to that difcipline, polecie, and guid order, quhilk the fam Word and puritie of Reformation craues at our hands. Vtherwayes that fearfull fentence falbe ruithe faid and fein —" The feruand that knaws the wil of his Maifter and does it nocht, falbe beatin with mame whipps.'

3. Mairower, gift we haiff anie pitie or refpect to the pure members of Chryft, wha fa granthe incieas and multiplie amangs ws, we will nocht fuffer tham to be lang defiandit of that part of the patrimonie of the Kirk quhilk rufthe belangs vnto tham. And be this order, gift it be dewhe put in execution, the burding of tham falbe takin af ws, to our grait comfort, the ftreites falbe elengit fiom the crying and murmuring of tham, as we falbe na man a fklander to vther nationes as we hithertiles haiff bein, for nocht takin ordour with our pure, and caufing of the Word quhilk we profes to be euill fpokin off, gifting occafion of fklander to the enemies, and offending the confcience of the fimple and godlie.

4. Befyd this, it falbe a grait eafe and commoditie to the comoun peiple in releiving of than burdings, and vphaulding than kirks for than inftruction and faulles helthe. and refidence of God amangs tham, as alfo for the farftie of ther bodies in biging and haulding vpe of briggs and vther publict warks, for the comlines and polecie of the countrey, alfo ane eafe to the laborars of the ground in pevment of than teinds and all vther things whereinto they haiff bein hithertils rigurufhe handht be thefe fals callit kirk men, thair takfmen, futters, and extortioners.

5. Finalie, to the King Matie and haill commoun weill, this profit fall redounde, that the curfe of facrilage, (quhilk wounderfulhe eates vpon and confumes all that auld luk and welthe in the patrimonie of his croun and rents, guid and geai of all his leiges,) being remount, the Lord fall blifs all in fu fort as ther falbe na want, bot plentie and ftore of all guid things. The Lord wil open the heavines, the erthe and fie fall gift than incres, and all falbe fatiffeit with aboundance. And when the ordinar neceffarie efteares of the Kuk, fcholles, and pure, ar fatiffeit, the fuperplus being collectit and put in the threafors of the Kuk, may be profitable imployed and liberalie beftowit vpon the extraordinar fupport of the efteares of the Prince and Comoun weill, and fpecialie of that part of the Kuk rents quhilk is apointed for the reparation of the kirks and fabric therof.

6. Sa we conclud, all being willing to apply thamfelues to this order, the peiple fuffering thamfelues to be rewht therby, the Prince and Magiftrats thamfelues nocht being exemmit, and they wha ar placed in ecclefiafticall efteat, rightlie rewling and governing, God falbe glorifiet, the Kirk ædifiet, the bounds therof inlargit, Chryft Jefus and his Kingdom fett vpe, Sathan and his fub-

ueitit, and God fall dwell in the middes of ws, to furnife all guid and keipe fiom all euill, in his Sone the Lord Jefus, wha, with than eternall fpiit, abyds hohe and bleffed for euer.   Amen

INDS THE CONCLUSIONS OF THE POLECIE

In the yeir 1580, in the wintai, brak out a notable effect of Monfieur d'Obignie's courfe and coming in Scotland.   For the King, fitting at Coun-fall a day with his nobles, amangs the quhilk the Erle of Moitoun laft Re-gent was, in comes Captean James Stewart, a brother of the houfe of Ochil-trie, advancfit in creadit of Court be d'Obignie, and maid Captean of the Kings Gaid, quhilk of new was then tean vpe. and tallin down on his knies, accufed the Erle of Moitone of hic treafone: Whairvpon the faid Erle was incontinent committed to warde in the Caftle of Edinbruche; the Erle of Angus, his cufing, chaigit to waid benoithe Tay, with ceitean cheiff men of that nam And thereifter Moitoun was tranfpoited from Edinbruche to Dinbartane, whar he remeaned till the monethe of May.   In the mean tyme his landes and gear war difpoint to Mon Obignie, maid and called then Duc of Len-nox; fa of a noble and ritche prince as ever governde in Scotland, he becam a puie prefonei, wha fkaifhe haid to furnife his neceffitie.   In the monethe of May he was brought till Edinbruche, and keipe in Robin Guilayes houfe, with a band of men of wear, and the verie dayes of his puting to affys and execution, I hapned to be thei in Edinbruche, and haid and faw the notableft exemple, bathe of Gods iudgment and mercie, that to my knawlage evei fell out in my tyme   For in that Tolbuthe whar oftentymes, duiing his govern-ment, he haid wryfted and throwin iudgment, parthe foi geain, wharto he was gein, and partlie for particular fawour, was his iudgment owerthrown, and he, wha aboue anie Scotfman haid maift gear, frindfchipe, and cheutell, haid nan to fpeak a woid foi him that day, bot the giaitteft pait of his affy-fars being his knawin vnfiendis, he was condamned to be headit on a fklaf-fauld; and that head, quhilk was fa wittie in warldlie effeares and polecie, and haid commandit with fic anthoiitie and dignitie within that town and iudgment feat, to be fett vpe on a prik vpon the hicheft ftane of the geavell of the Tolbuthe, that is towards the publict ftreit.   The quhilk fentence, in my fight, was put in execution vpon the moine.   But in grait mercie, when the Lord haid ftiyped him naked and bear of all thefe things warldlie, and of a cable maid a twynde thride to go in at the narow ei of that neidle, he gaiff him, efter vnfenyit repentance, fic fathe and affurance of his fawour in Chryft, that he maift magnanimufhe contemned infulting of enemies, bevaling of frinds, all warldlie dignitie, ritches and pleafures, and tuk him with his Chryft be deathe to owercom and gett the Croun of Lyff.   The minifters war at him that night of his condemnation, and the morn befor he was brought out, whom he fatiffeit verie weill, be iuftefeing God, his Word and minifterie therof, and acknawleging his finnes ; bot na airt nor part of the kings fathers murdour wherfor he was condemnt.   Jhone Durie and Mr Jhone Dauidfone, whom he haid hardlie vfit, the an for his pretching, the vther for his buik againft the four kirks, cam to him, of whom he crauit pardone ; and wha taried with him, and was maift movit for his ceas.   He keipit the fam countenance, geftour, and fchoit fententius form of langage vpon the fkaffalde, quhilk he vfit in his princlie government   He fpak, led about and vrgit be the commanders at the four newkes of the fkaffald ; bot efter that, ance he had verie fecttulhe and grauelie vttered, at guid lanthe, that quhilk he haid to fpeak, thereftter almaift he altered nocht thir words.   " It is for my finnes that God has iuftlie brought me to this place, for gif I haid feruit my God als trewlie as I did my King, I haid nocht com hen ; bot as for that I am condemd for be men, I am innocent, as God knaws   Pray for me "   All men and peiple of all rankes bevalit his deathe exceidinglie, except onlie they wha haid particular hatred againft him ; for papiftrie durft nocht be hard of in his dayes of government, and the land inioyed neuer graitter peace and plentie   I could wreit mukle mair of my heiring, feing, and knawlage, anent this mater and the things that followed, giff my purpose war to wrait the Storie of ciuill efteares in our tyme ; but that nocht being, I content to haiff recordit the wark of God, quhilk I faw with my eis, and hard with my eares ; for the quhilk I could nocht bot at my returning to St Androis glorifie God, be rcherfall thereof in opin audience from pulpit.

That yer, 1581, the Generall Affemblie conveint in October at Edinbruche ; in the quhilk, certean breither war apointed to confult whow the Parliament fould nocht inleak the fpirituall efteat. bifchopes being removit   To the quhilk deliberation the Affemblie was dryven vnto be court, the grait gydar wharof, the Duc of Lennox, by Guifean counfall and direction, nocht daring put at religion pleanlie, preffit the reftoring of the efteat of bifchopes, and haid lathe intrufit Mr Robert Montgumerie in the bifchoprik of Glafgw, without all ordour of the Kirk, *pleno iure principis*, (quhilk vexit the breithring of Glafgw wounderfullie, fa that I wat nocht whow manie fcore of dyettes they war compellit to keipe in that eareud) The breithring apointed be the Affemblie returnes thair advys in that mater; the quhilk being confiddent be the Affemblie, all in a voice determines, That concerning vot in parliament, and vfing of Ciuill and Criminall Iurifdiction, commiffioneis fould be directed fiom tyme to tyme from the Generall Affemblies to the Parliaments, to difcharge the Kirkes dewtie, and do for the fam in all hir effeares. And the heritable bailyies of Regalties fould vfe all things perteining to the iurifdiction of ciuill and criminall caulfes

The minifters of Edinburche all this whyll was maift fathfullie and wacryfhe giffing the warning to all, anent the cours and practife of papifts; and therfor, at this Affemblie, Mr Walter Balcanquall was accufit be the Court. *fed fi uftia.*

At that tyme it was a pitie to fie fa weill a brought vpe prince till his bernhead was paft, to be fa miferablie corrupted in the entrefs of his fpringall age, bathe with finiftrus and fals information of all proceidings in his minoritie, and with euill and maift dangerus grundes and principalles in gouernment of Kirk and Comoun weill. Then was he maid to think warft of the beft men that euer feruit in this Kirk and Countrey: to think the haill maner of Reformation of religion to haiff bein done be a prime faction, turbulenthe and treafonablie; to fufpect the noble men and haill minifterie that ftude for the caufe of religion and his croun againft his mothers faction; yea, to tak courfe againft them, and put at tham as his vnfrinds. Amangs the reft, Captan James put the opinon of abfolut powar in his Maiefties head; whom, in fa doing, I can compear to nane fa weill as to Philomelus, the Captean of the Phocenfis, wha being about a maift facrilegius purpofe to owerthraw and fpulyie the Kirk of Delphus, and cut out of the pillars therof the deceits of the Amphictrons, whafe facrat iudgment governed the comoun weill of all Greice, and fa to subuert bathe religion and polecie, he compellit the Pythian preift to go vpe on the Tripos, to giff him a refpoufe The woman, vrgit violentlie, fayes, "Yow may do what yow will." The quhilk wourds Philomelus gripped at, and taried na langer for the oracle, but gaiff out amangs his armie, and to all, that he haid gottin a plean licence of Apollo to do what he wald * Sic lyk Mr Patrik Adamfone, bifchope of St Andros, a grait counfellour in thefe dayes,

---

* Diodor. Sicul Bibhoet. Hift. lib 16. Lyk as Stratocles, in Athens, maid a decree of Demetrius, παν ὁτι ὁ Βασιλευς Δημητριος κελευση τυτο και προς θεους ὁσιον και προς ανθρωπους ειναι δικαιον—Whatfumeuei King Demetrius commandath, that to be holie toward God and iuft toward men. Plut. in vita Demetu

amangs manie vther euill grounds what of we will heir heirefter, inculcat this :
" That a Chriftian King fould be the cheif governour of the Kirk, and behouit to haue bifchops vnder him, to hald all in order, contorm to antiquité and
maift flurifling efteat of the Chriftian Kirk vnder the beft emperour, Conftan-
tine And that the difcipline of the Kirk of Scotland could nocht ftand with
a frie kingdome and monarchie, fic as was his Maieftie in Scotland," &c
Mutche lyk bifchope Caiphas, wha thought that Chryfts kingdome and the
Roman impyre could nocht ftand togidder : Or Herod, wha heiring that
Chryft the King was borne, was troublit, and all Jerufalem with him, and
therfor fend, &c.

Bot nochtwithftanding of this conftitution of Court, by a remarkable prouidence of God cam furthe the Cornicle of Mr Georg Buchanan printed with
priuilege and the Buik of the Polecie of the Kirk concludit in Affembltie.

That September, in tyme of vacans, my vncle, Mr Andro, Mr Thomas Buchanan, and I, heiring that Mr George Buchanan was weak, and his Hiftorie
vnder the pres, paft ower to Edinbruche ames earend, to vifit him and fie
the wark When we cam to his chalmer, we fand him fitting in his chaire,
teatching his young man that feruit him in his chalmer to fpell a, b, ab; e, b,
eb, &c Efter falutation, Mr Andro fayes, " I fie, fir, yie are nocht ydle."
" Better this," quoth he, " nor ftelling fl.eipe, or fitting ydle, quhilk is als ill "
Thereftei he fchew ws the Epiftle Dedicatorie to the king ; the quhilk, when
Mr Andro had read, he tauld him that it was obfcure in fum places, and wanted certean words to perfyt the fentence. Sayes he, " I may do na mair for
thinking on another mater " " What is that ?" fayes Mr Andro " To die !"
quoth he ; " bot I leaue that and manie ma things for yow to helpe "*

We went from him to the printars wark hous, whom we fand at the end
of the 17 buik of his Cornicle, at a place quhilk we thought verie haird for the
tyme, quhilk might be an occafion of fteying the haill wark, anent the buriall of Dame Therfor, fteying the printer from proceiding, we cam to Mr
George agam, and fund him bedfaft by his cuftome, and afking him, whow
he did, " Even going the way of weilfare." fayes he. Mr Thomas, his cufing,
fchawes him of the hardnes of that part of his Storie, that the king wald be
offendit with it, and it might ftey all the wark " Tell me, man," fayes he,
" giff I haue tauld the trenthe ?" " Yis," fayes Mr Thomas, " Sir, I think fa.'
" I will byd his fead, and all his kins, then," quoth he : " Pray, pray to God

* He was telling him alfo of Blakwods anfwer to his buik, De iure regni.

for me, and let him direct all." Sa, be the printing of his Cornicle was endit. that maift lerned, wyfe, and godlie man, endit this mortall lyff.

Efter that Generall Affemblie in October, Mr Patrik Adamfone aggreit to all the poincts of the Buik of Policie, and concerning the office of a Bifchope; and calling to dinner Mr Andro Melvill, my vncle, Mr Alexander Arbuthnot, and vthers diuers, he fubfcryvit therto, quhilk his fubfcription is yit in my vncles cuftodie. Item, that wintar he paft ower to a Convention of the Eftteates; and efter he fand nocht cuit as he luiked for, he dreft him to the minifters of Edinburche, fchawing tham whow that he cam ower to Court with Balams hait, of purpofe to curfe the Kirk and do euill, bot God haid wrought fa with him, that he haid turned his hart to the contrare, and maid him, bathe in reafoning and votting, to ftand for the Kirk, promifing to fchaw fordar and fordar fruicts of his converfion and guid meaning. Wharat Jhone Duiy was fa reioyfit, that he treated him in hous, and wrot ower at lainthe to me in his fawour. Whervpon I paft down to his Caftell at his hame coming, and fchew him what information concerning him I haid gottin from the breithring of Edinburche, thanking God therfor, and offering him, in cais of continuance, the right hand of focietie. Wherat reioifing, he tauld me the mater at lainthe, and, namlie, concerning the grait motiones and working of the Spreit. " Weill," faid I, " that Spreit is an vpright, habe, and conftant Spirit, and will mair and mair kythe in effects; bot it is a fearfull thing to lie againft him'

But to retoun to Mr Andro Melvin. The light of his lerning, and hatt of his zeall to hairf reformation in the kirk and fcholles in St Androis, brak nocht foonner out, when the darknes of ignorance and cauldnes of Chriftian profeffion vttered themfelues in his contrare. Manie and grait adverfaries he haid; but the Lord, wha haid fanctefeit him for his wark, gaiff him notable victories ower all. Firft, the Maifters wha war difplaot out of the New Collage, as Mr Robert Hamilton, minifter of the town, commandit be the Generall Kirk to leaue the office of principalitie in the Collage, and tak him to his minifterie, vexit him with perfut of compts of the Collage; but he reiected that vpon the Commiffionars wha haid the powar of the Reformation, whom be moyen and importunitie the faid Mr Robert maid to relent, and direct him again vpon Mr Andro, to his great vexation, till it pleafit God to cutt fchort the lyff of the faid Mr Robert, even when he was about to intend action againft Mr Andro. Yet that caufe ceaffit nocht, bot was followit out in the perfonnes of his weidow and beirnes, be a man of grait wit, peanes, and moyen, an of Mr Androes awin compamones, whafe confort he had fund in Glafgw, and now luked for, comng to St Andros, to fie a gud wark. This was Mr Thomas Buchanan, firft Scholmaifter in Stirling, and fyne Proveft of Kirkheuche in St Andros, and mnnifter of Syres. A man of notable gifts of lerning, natuiall wit, and ypiightnes in the caufe of the Kiik againft the bifchopes, but haid his awm impeifectiones, namlie, of extream partiabtie in the caufe of his frinds and dependais, quhilk maid him to alter with Mr Andro, and in that caufe of Mr Robeit Hamiltones, whafe relict he maried, and his collegges, to often greue Mi Audio; bot, in end, a glib of the Collage gear fettlet that, allowit be the fauds Commiffionais, Mr Andro bearing with it, becaufe he could nocht mend it. Ane vthei that haid bein Regent in that Collage vnder Mr Robeit Hamilton, was Mr Jhone Caldcleuche, a daft woufteu man He bofted that he wald *houche* Mr Andio, with mikle mair daft talk; and a day he comes in to Mr Androes chalmer, being alan in it, and afkes him weill rudlie, giff he knew him. " Na," fayes Mr Andro, " I knaw you nocht." " I fould be knawm," fayes he. " as a Maifter in this Collage; my nam is Mr Jhone Caldcleuche." " Ho!" quoth Mr Andio, " is this yie that will houche men ?" And with that put to the chalmer dure, and fayes, " It is even beft tym now " Bot the vther cahnit atteanes, and beginnes to fpeak with mair reuerence; whom Mr Andro, by manhe courage and force of ieafone, fa dantoned and tamed, that the Maifter was fean to tak a buifaies place in the Collage, and hue therin as a humble ftudent. I was in the chalmer abou and hard all, and cam doun at laft to the ending of it.

Thir fafcheries war fkarflie weill fattelit, when out braks a graitter contiadiction This was of the Regents of Philofophie, namlie in St Leonards Collage, wha heirring, in Mi Androes oidinar publict leffones of Theologie, thair Ariftotle, amangs the reft of the philofophers, the patriaiches of heiefie as ane of the ancients termes tham, mightehe confuted, handling the heids auent God, Prouidence, Creation, &c, maid a ftrange fteir in the Vniuerfitie, and cryed, Grait Diana of the Ephefians, thair biead winner, thair honour, thair eftimation, all was gean, giff Ariftotle fould be fa own harled in the hening of than fchollars; and fa dreffit publict Orationes againft Mr Androes doctrine. But Mr Andro infifted mightehe againft tham in his ordinai leffones; and when thair counned haranges cam at thair Vickes and promotiones of Maifters, he lut tham nocht fhpe, bot af hand anfwerit to tham prefenthe with fic force of treuthe, euidence of ieafone, and fpirituall eloquence, that he dafhit tham, and in end convicted tham fa in confcience, that the cheift coi yptyeis amangs tham becam grait students of Theologie, and speciall professed frinds of Mr Andro, and ar now verie honest vpright pastors in the Kirk; whom, for honour, I nam in speciall Mr Jhone Malcolm, minister at St Johnfe Town, and Mr Andro Duncan at Carell   And certeanlie the treuthe was, that ignorance, with a proude opinion of knawlage, becaufe they knew na better, wrought all this. For efter the first zeall of Reformation, in Mr Knox and Mr Gudmans dayes, the cauldnes of Mr Robert Hamiltones ministerie, and ignorance and neghgence of tham that sould haiff teatched Theologie, maid, that Regents and schollars cairt na thing for Diuinitie ; yea, it was evin a pitie to sie that ignorance and profannes that was amangs tham.   And as for Langages, Arts and Philosophie, they had na thing for all, bot a few bukes of Aristotle, quhilk they leirnit pertinatiuslie to bable and flyt vpon, without right vnderstanding or vse therof   Bot within a yeir or twa, Mr Andro, be his delling in publict and priuat with euerie an of tham, preualit sa, that they fell to the Langages, studeit than Artes for the right vse, and perusit Aristotle in his awin langage, sa that, certatim et serio, they becam bathe philosophers and theologes, and acknawlagit a wounderfull transportation out of darknes vnto light.   Bot, indeid, this was nocht done without mikle teghting and taiherie, and the authoritie of the Generall Affemblie interponit in end

     The thrid thortar and debat quhilk he haid, was with the prouist, bailyies, and counfall of the town, about thair ministerie   The Seffion of the Kirk haid a custome to fend twa of thair eldars euerie ouk to defyre Mr Andro and me to helpe tham on the Sabbathe, during the want of a minister and abfence of the bifchope   Sa Mr Andro coming in the pulpit, fpak the treuthe of all things with grait ardentnes and zeall ; and being acquent with fum corrupt proceidings of the newlars againft equitie and iuftice, and perceauing they lyked nocht of gud men to be than minifter fic as Mr Andro wald haiff haid, bathe for the weill of the Town and Vniuerfitie, namlie of that wark of Theologie, fic as Mr Thomas Smeton or Mr Alexander Arbuthnot, he cantit tham heir thair doings in the deafleft eare.   This was takine fa huche, that a grait fpace ther was na thing bot affixing of plackarts vpon the Collage yett, bofting with batoning, burning and chaffing out of the town : wherwith, to fpeak the treuthe, I was mikle feairt, feing Town, Vniuerfitie, and all malcontents againft ws att annes, and luikit for na thing, day for day, but ftening vpe of fum tumult for ane euill turn   But Mr Andro, with an heroicall fpreit, the mair they ftirit and boftit, the mair he ftrak with that twa eagit fword, fa that a day he mouit the Proveft, with fear rubbing of the ga of his confcience, to ryfe

out of his featt in the middes of the fermont, and with fum muttering of words
to go to the dure, out throw the middes of the peiple ; for the quhilk being
delt with be the Prefbyterie, and convicted in his confcience, the faid Proveft
maid publict fatiffaction be acknawlaging of his offence, and craving God and
the congregation forgiffnes. Another day he tuk a placcard, affixed vpon the
Collage yet, knawin be the Italian and Frenche toung to be wrytin be James
Lermont, appeirand of Balcomie, and in the application of his doctrine, quhilk
was wounderfull perfing and vehement, he produces the wryt, and haiffing
the faid James fittand betor him in the kirk, he thretnes him in particular
with a iudgment, that manie years efter was marked to ftrik vpon the faid
James, to this effect ; " Thow Frencherft, Italiamft, jolie gentleman, wha has
defyled the bed of fa manie marred, and now bofts with thy baftonados to defyll his Kirk, and put hands on his feruants, thow fall neuer inioy the fruicts
of mariage, be haifing lawfull fucceffion of thy bodie ; and God fall baftone
thie in his righteous iudgments " This was remembirit when the faid James,
being Lard of Balcomie, leiued manie yens in mariage without chyld, and taken be the Heiland men coming out of the Leaws, was ficcerlie baftoned, and
fa hardlie vfed, that foone therefter he died in Orkney, in the yeir 1598

The fourt feght that he haid was againft the Pryor and his gentlemen pen-
fioners, wha colluded with the rewallars of the town to hald the minifterie
vacand ; and in the mean tyme tuk vpe the ftipend, and fpendit the fam, with
the reft of the kirk rents of that Pryorie, at the goff, archerie, guid chein, &c
Thir things be Mr Andro and I war rounden out of pulpit to tham , quhilk
for to ftay, they prepant a purs with a nomber of fourtie fhilling pieces in it,
and fending for me to the Chalmerlings hous, efter guid intertenment they
offerit it to me for my peanes takin in pretching and fuppleing the default of
a minifter I anfwerit, it was trew my peanes haid deferuit that and mair at
thair hands, whowbeit I haid recompence in all aboundance at the hand of
God, in honoring me with the meffage of his Word and fervice, bot my peanes
was nocht takin for the hinderance of that minifterie, bot for forderance of the
faming ; and I fearit, giff thay gat a fafon of a minifterie fa eafche prouydit,
they wald be lang of bringing in an of the notable men nominat to that minifterie, vnder whafe feit I wald be glad to fit with my pen, and with whom
I wald be blaithe to helpe as I could for nought : And fa refufit thair money
This, when the Prefbyterie vnderftud be Mr Andro and me, and efpying that
our helping on the Sabathes hinderit the placing of a man of giftes in that
minifterie, for they haiffing George Blak to minifter the facraments and ma-

rie, and we to teatche, wald content therwith and leik na mair, therfor the Prefbyterie difchargit ws from pretching anie man, and ordeanit me to pen a letter to be red the nixt Sabbathe, fchawing the reafoues of our leaving at pretching: Quhilk being done and publicthe read, certean of the rewlars of the town, namlie Mr. Dauid Ruffell and Wilyeam Lermont, ragit therat, and pennit againft the nixt day an anfwer, in effect and termes vincuerent, denying the authoritie of the Prefbyterie, calling it pretendit, and inveyng againft the fam ; for the quhilk caufe the perfone that red it, Ringand Rewll, taker vpe of the pfalmes, being callit befor the Prefbyterie, fchew that Mr Dauid Ruffell and Wilyeam Lermont commandit him to reid it : bot, pure man, he gat his reward, for he never threane nor did guid efter that, bot died with madnes and miferie.   The lairds Mr Dauid and Wilyeam being callit, the Pryor and Proveft compeires with tham, thinking to bang out the mater, bot God affiftes Mr Andro fa, that he dafht them all, and maid them fean to go packing.   The Generall Affemblie nocht being far to, the Prefbyterie remittes the mater therto, and fummoned the faid Mr Dauid and Wilyeam to compeir befor the Affemblie, quhilk they did with thair affiftars ; bot they war condemnit be the Affemblie, and ordeanit to mak publict repentance in the Kirk of St Andros, and Mr Andro to receaue the faming ; the quhilk they did folemlie, and fa becam better conditioned therefter *   By this occafion I man mark be the way, it was a confortable thing in thefe dayes to haiff a guid caufe in hand, and ftand be it ; for whowfoeuer it was refifted and croffed in particular feffiones, prefbyteries, or affemblies, yit fure it was to be redreffed and brought to a guid poinct at the Generall Affemblies, becaufe of the friedome, grait authoritie and vprightnes in zeall that was therin, to the grait terrour of the wicked, and confort of the godlie : Sa mikle the mair is the lofs therof to be deplored in this declyning age and tyme.

The fyft and graitteft enemie of all was the bifchope, Mr Patrik Adamfone craftelie and quietlie concurring with the Court, bot alwayes as yit vnder profeffion of grait friudfchipe, and fa maift dangerufhe feikand his diftruction, with the vtter owerthraw of the libertie of Chryfts Kirk and Kingdome   But the Lord notablie vpheld and preferuit his awin fervant, and brought his enemies to confufion, as in the haill narratiue and Storie following will be manifeft.

---

* Mr Dauid Ruffell, for falfhod, was efter, in the yeir   , depofit from his office of Commiffar Clarkfchipe with a not of infamie, and Jhone Arnot placit in his roum

1582 —The Generall Affemblie convenit at St Andros the 24th of Apryll, anno 1582; Mr Andro Melum fchofin Moderator To it was Mr Robert Mongomerie, intrufit bifchope of Glafgw, fummoned, wha compered, with Letters of Horning to difcharge the Affemblie · yit he durft nocht vfe tham. fie was the frequencie of barrones and breithring, with fa grait authoritie and zeall And fa, for acceptation of the bifchoprik *pleno iure*, and troubling of the breithring of Glafgw, he was depofit in perpetuum, and thretnit with excommunication, till he humblie prefentit himfelff with teares befor the Affemblie; and then Jhone Dury, wha was maift feneire againft him reafe out of his feat, and caught him in his armes.* But at that fam tyme Mr Wilyeam Clark, my predeceffour a wyfe godlie, fweit man faid vnto me, "It will neuer be this man that will trouble and hurt the Kirk, bot yie will find that Mr Patrik Adamfone will do it wha is this mans counfallar, and cauffes him now to yeild for the tyme " At that Affemblie was apointed a generall Faft, to be keiped in the monethe [of] Junie following, the cauffes wharof was confpiracie of Papifts, oppreffion and thraldom of the Kirk, &c.

In the monethe of Junie that fam yeir, an vther Generall Affemblie was convenit in Edinbruche, wherat Jhone Dury, for his plean fpeitches againft the Duc, and proceidings of the Court was accufit, bot hoping for na fpeid than, he was callit befor the King and Counfall at Dalkethe, whar narrowlie efchaping the Duc, his cookes, (wha cam out of his kitching with fpeittes and grait knyves,) with his lyff, as he often tauld me, he was, be act of Counfall, banifched out of Edinbruche, bot the Generall Affemblie commandit the Prefbyterie of Edinbruche to keipe his roum frie and place nan thern In this Affemblie, manie greiffes and articles war pennit, and commiffionars apointed to prefent tham at the Convention of the Efteats, to be haldin at Perthe in the monethe of July nixt following.

The Convention keiping at Perthe, Mr Andro Melum, Moderator, with the reft of the Commiffionars, went thither with the Greiffes and Articles of the Kirk,† wha gat verie cull countenance, and manie fecret terrors To that

* Yit the fam Mongumerie infifted and troublet the breithring of Glafgw therefter, and therfor was excommunicat, and the excommunication annullit be ane act of Counfall, and letters publifched thervpon, receavit therefter in Court and intertemed in the Kings prefence be the Duc, and the fam fentence therefter, in the Parliament 1584, be an act therof annullit

† *Greiffes of the Kirk, giffen in at Perth.*

Vnto your Maieftie maift humblie memes and fchawes your Graces maift fathfull and obe-

Convention cam the Erle of Hountlie, weill accompaned with his frinds, in whase fauours, to the grait hurt of the Forbasses, the King gaifl out a decreit arbitrall.   Newes war sparpeht athort the countrey, that the ministers war

dient subiects, the haill Ministers of Gods Word within this your Graces realme, convent in the Generall Aflemblie, haldin at Edinbruche the 27th of Junij   That wharvpon the occasion of dinerss grait and evident dangers appering to the haill Kirk of God, and profeflours of his treuthe in this countrey, finding the authoritie of the Kirk abrogat, ecclefiasticall censures contemnit, and violence vfit aganist sum of our breithring vnpunished, wharof the lyk hes neuer bein sein within this realme, nor in anie vther what trew relligioun hes bein pretclut and reflenvit   And fearing lest vour Maieftie, for leak of informatioun, might neglect in tyme to prouyd remedie for the inconveuments lykhe to enfew theirspon, we convent ourfelues in the fear of God and your Hienes obedience, and efter diligent confideration of the prefent efleat, be comoun confent thought necefar be our Commiflionars, to open vpe and prefent to your Grace certean of our cheiff and weghtie greiffes, without haftie redrefs wharof the Kirk of God and his trew relligion can na wayes ftand and continow in this vour Maiefties countrey

Firft, That your Maieftie, be denys of sum counfallours, is cauffit to tak vpon vour Grace that fpirituall powar and authoritie quhilk properlie apertienes to Chryft as onlie king and head of his Kirk, the miniftene and execntioun wharof is giffen to fic only as beares office in the ecclefiasticall gouernment of the faming, fa that, in your Graces perfone, sum men preffes to erect an new Papedom, as thought your Maieftie could nocht be full head and king of this comoun welthe, vnles alfe weill the fpirituall as temporall fword be put into your Graces hands, vnles Chryft be bereft of his authoritie, and the jurifdictionis confoundit quhilk God hes denydit, quhilk directlie tendes to the wrak of all trew relligioun, as be the fpeciall heades following is manifest   For benefices ar giffen be abfolut powar to vnworthie perfones, intrufit in the office of the minifterie without the Kirks admiffioun, directlie aganist the lawes of God and acts of Parliament, wharthrow the Kirks levinges comes in profean mens hands, and fichvk as fell their faulles, and mak schipwrak of confcience, for pleafur of men   and obteaning fum wardlie commoditie

1   Eldarfchips, Synodall and Generall Affemblies ar difchargit, be Letters of Horning, to proceid aganist manifeft offendars, and to vfe difcipline of the Kirk, and cenfures therof, according to Gods Word.

2   Jhone Dune, be act of Counfall, is fufpendit from pretching, and banifched from his flock

3   Excommunicat perfones in contempt of God and his Kirk, ar intertemed in cheiff lords houffes, and namlie, Mr Robert Mongumerie authorifed and cauflt to pretche, and brought in your Maiefties hous and prefence, quhilk is a fear wound to the confcience of tham that loues vour Maieftie, and knawes vour Graces vpbringing, and a heavie fklander to all nationnes profeffing the trew relligioun

4.   An Act of Delyverance of Counfall is maid aganist the proceidings of the minifterie, withe a fklanderus narratiue fufpending fimphe, and difannulling, the excommunicatioun rufthe and ordourhe pronuncit aganist Mr Robert Montgumerie, an rebell and obftinat offendar and troublar of the Kirk of God, and open proclamatioun maid according therto.

5   Contempt of ministers, and dinging of manie doing ther offices, and efpecialie the violent drawing of Mr Jhone Howyfone out of the iudgment featt, whan he was placed Moderator of the Prefbyterie of Glafgw, his crewall and vttragins handling and carcing to preafone, lyk a theift, be

all to be thar maffacred, quhilk moued me go repear to Perthe with diligence, to tak part with my vncle and father in Chryft. Coming ther, Sir
James Melvill of Halhill fchawes me whow euill my vncle and I was thought
of at Court, becaufe of our fermonts in St Andros the tyme of the faft, and
our doings and fayings at Affemblies, and counfallit ws to depart af the town,
quhilk I fchew Mr Andro, and wilht fa to do, bot in vean ; " For I thank
God," fayes he, " I am nocht fley'd nor terble fpirited in the caufe and meffage
of Chryft ; com what God pleafes to fend, our Commiffion falbe difchargit."

the Proveft and Balies of Glafgw, and ther complices   And, efter complent maid, na ordour takin
with the doers therof, but contrarwayes intertenning tham as gif the faming haid bein guid fervice.

6 and 7. The Minifter of Glafgw was, be force of armes, difplaced out of his roum, quhilk,
without reprotche, he hes occupied thir manie yeirs, the gentlemen of the countrey being convocat
for that effect   Alfo violence was vfit, be an of your awin gward, to pull him out of the pulpit
the day of Communioun, in prefence of the haill congregatioun, in tym of fermont, and na fault
fund therwith

8 The Officiar of the Kirk was cuftin in preafone. your Grace being prefent, and ther keipit a
lang tym, for executing of Letters directed againft a fklanderus man

9 The Minifters, Maifters of Schoolles and Collage of Glafgw, the verie fchollars therof, in
tym of publict faft, war, be Letters of Horning, compellit to leaue ther flockes and fcholles deftitut ;
and fenfyne, from tyme to tym, and place to place, haue bein continowit and deleyit, therby to
confum tham be exorbitant expences, and to wrak the kirks and fcholles wherof they haue the
charge

10. The Students of the Collage war invadit, and ther bluid crewallie fched, be the Bailyie
and commonitie, gatherit therto be found of comoun bell, and ftruck of drum , and be certean feditius perfones inflambet to haue flean tham all, and brunt the Collage . And yit na thing don to the
authores of the tumult and fedioun

11. Hands fchakin with the bludie murderars and perfecutors of the perple of God, be letters
and propynes reftraint and fent.

12 The Duc oftymes promifit to reform his hous, and na thing don therin.

13. The Lawes maid for mentenance of the trew relligioun, and punifment of the enemies
therof, ar nocht put to executioun, fa that all things gaes loufe, and wars lyk till enfew

Monie vther things ther be that craue prefent reformatioun, wherwith we think nocht expedient to trouble your Maieftie, vntill we fie what ordour beis takin with thefe greivs compleants
beferkhand your Maieftie maift humblie, for the loue of God, wha hes placed and eftablifed your
Maieftie in this royall throne, hitherto wounderfullie mentened and defendit, cearfullie to luk vpon thir maters as becomes the heutenant of God, and thankfull Chriftian King ; and withe the advys
of tham that feir God, and tenders your Graces efteat and weill and quietnes of this comoun
welthe, fa to redres the premifles, that firft Chryft aboue all may be acknawlagit, his meffingers,
without feir or ftope, to execut their office, the cours of the Gofpel advancit, and fic exemple maid
of punifment of tham wha fa licentiuflie and contemptuuflie haue wrangit and minurt the minifters
and profeffours of Gods Word, that vthers heirefur be effrayit to interprvfe the lyk

At laft the Commiffionars ot the Kirk war callit, wha, comming in befor the King and his Counfall, delyverit than Greiffes and Articles, quhilk being read, Captan James beginnes to threttin, with thrawin brow, and bofting langage " What!" fayes he, " wha dar fubfcryve thir treafonable articles?" &c.   Mr Andro anfweres, " We dar, and wil fubfcryue tham ; and git our lynes in the caufe"   And withe all ftarts to, and taks the pen fra the Clark, and fubferyves, and calles to the reft of the breithring with couragius fpeitches, wha all cam and fubfcryvit   This bauldnes, when the Duc and Captan perceavit, they gathent theron that the Kirk haid a bak, and becam effrayit · and, efter fum calmer langage, difmiffit tham in peace, whom euerie an fuppofed they fould haiff bein hardliar delt withall.

In the monethe of Auguft thereftei, certean of the nobilitie and barrones of the realme repearit to the King at Ruthven, in the Eile of Gowries hous, and fchew his Maieftie whow all things went wrang be the mifgoverning of that new Counfall com lathe from France, to the grait offence and greiff of all his guid fubiects, the heavie vexation of the Kirk, and extream perrell of the co-mounweill, cravit, therfor, maift humblie of his Maieftie, that he wald content till abandone the faid Counfall, and tak him to be counfallit be his auld nobili-tie, as his princelie progenitours haid done, and the fundamentall lawes of Scot-land craust, and fa furthe, as at man lainthe is contened in a Declaration of them, publifed foone therefter in print.   And fa the King and the Duc war diffiuered, and neuer faw vther againe

This brought a grait relenue to the Kirk, and the honeft breithing of Glaf-gw and Edinbruche, that war foar troublit be the faid Duc: whowbeit, the treuthe is, for aught I know, (and I know whateuer the fpecialles of the Kirk knew, that I am fure,) the Kirk was nather art, part, read nor counfall in that mater, nather lurket for anie fic thing at thair being in St Johnftone And what euer the inftruments war and refpected, they could nocht bot re-iois in God, and thank him for delyvering King, Kirk, and Comounweill of fic Cownfall, as fett thamfelues plainlie to perveit all.

Within few dayes therefter, Jhone Durie gat lenue to ga ham to his awin flok of Edinbruche, at whafe retourning ther was a grait concurs of the haill town, wha met him at the Nather Bow, and, going vpe the ftreit, with bear heads and loud voices, fang to the prais of God, and teftifeing of grait ioy and confolation, the 124th Pfalm, " Now Ifrael may fay, and that trewlie," &c till heavin and eithe refoundit. This noyes, when the Duc, being in the town haid, and ludgit in the Hiegat, luked out and faw, he raue his beirde for anger. and hafted him af the town, and remeaned in Dumbartan, at the Waft Sie, whare, or he gatt paffage, he was put to als hard a dyet as he caufit the Eile of Morton till vfe ther, yea, evin to the tother extremitie that he haid vfit at Court: For, wheras his kitching was fa fumptuus that lumpes of butter was caft in the fyre when it foked, and twa or thrie crownes wart vpon a ftok of keall dreffing, he was fean till eat of a magre gus, fkowdrit with bar ftra

In that monethe of October, the Generall Affemblie convent at Edinbruche, whar, with freche courage, the Infchopes war fett vpon, and fenere ordour takin with tham: alfo fic as haid been ewill inftruments to the Due againft the Kirk war takin ordour with Amangs the reft, Mr Dauid Macgill, Aduocat, tor penning of fklanderus and wicked proclamation, publhffed againft the Kirk This was a man of als grait, fohde, and naturall a wit as in our tyme, excelling therin all his colleages of the Seffion and Lawers, bot without all fenfe of God, and with a prydfull difdean and contempt of the miniftene I hard him als difpytfulhe and lightfulhe, being in his awin houfe, tak vpe my vncle Andro being fend with vthers from the Affemblie to him, as mount me, being prefent, vtherwayes eftimed nocht verie impatient, to almaift debord, nocht onlie with toung, bot hand Bot, or he died, with a terrible ftrak of confcience, God tamde him lyk a lamb; fa that Mr Andro coming to him againe, and I with him, was as the Angell of God in his eis, cuft his hat to the ground, and could fkairfhe luik him in the face, till he haird out of his mouthe the words of confolation, the quhilk he gaped for as a gorbet, and receavit as Cornelius the inftruction of Piter: yea, the meeneft of the miniftene that cam to vifit him, was mair to him than giff the King and the Lords haid com to him I thought often that was a cleir accomphfinent of Efaias prophecie, " The lyon fall eat ftra lyk a bullok, &c He died maift happelie and fweitlie, efter diuers yeirs humiliation, with thefe words in his mouthe, " Lord, in thy light, let me fie light '

At that Affemblie, I was ernefthe futed, be the Town of Stirling, to be than Paftor, bot the wark of Theologie being yit in the tender budding leaff, my vncle, Mr Andro, could nocht confent therto, nor the Kirk with his mifcontintment command; whowbeit, my mynd was to the miniftene, remembering euer my wow, and nocht the man vnwillinghe, that I haid the purpofe of my mariage in hand

1583 —The yeir following, 1583, in the end of Apryll, and beginning of

May, the Generall Affemblie convenit at Edinbruche. That Affemblie was frequentlie keipit be the nobiltie, (for ther was prefentlie a Convention of the Efteats at Edinbruche,) wha requefted the Affemblie to approue than proceidings, in repeaning to his Maieftie at Ruthven, &c. The brethrings iudgment was, That God haid glorified his nam, and wrought therby to the grait eafe and comfort of his Kirk, as they haid fund hithertils: as for the inftruments, they could nather approue nor difproue, bot wiffit with than hartes they might be fund fanctified veffalles of mercie to the Lord. To the quhilk effect at leaft, they defyrit an act to be infert in the Buiks of the Affemblie, to the quhilk the Kirk wald nocht condifcend till they haid the Kings gud will and confent thervnto. The quhilk his Maieftie, fending Coronell Wilyeam Stewart, new cam ham, and of grait credit, and Mr Dauid Lindfay, to the Affemblie, in large termes and maner affented vnto; and fa it paft, as is extant in the Buiks of the Affemblie. Amangs the reft, Jhone Dury had a day in his doctrine a verie clear and pertinent companifone for the purpofe, of the blind man in the 9th of Jhones Euangill. When the Pharifies faid that Chryft was but a finner, Whow could he do anie guid? "I can nocht tell," fayes the blind man, "bot a thing I am fu of, that I was blind, and now I fie." This he applyed with grait euidence and approbation of the henars.

At that Affemblie I maried my wyff, the firft day of May, and gat the bleffing of the beft brething of the Kirk; the quhilk, my bleffed God of Heavin be bleffit for, I haif fund wonnderfull effectuall to this houre, for als grait helpe and comfort in my calling, euen in the middes of hir heavie difeafe and impotencie, as anie brother in the land hes. And whowbeit, the haill courfe of my lyff fen fyne has bein, in outward appeirance, bot a fcholl of afflictiones, yit (alas! for thankfulnes) a maift halfome and happie fcholl, with a mixture of als manie prouifiones, preferuationes, priuat profits, pleafurs, ioyes, and confolationnes, as euer anie of the fecret annes of the Lord receauit.

In the monethe of Junne therefter, at the beginning therof, a heavie Tertian fever, called comounlie the *Exees*, owertuk me, quhilk pynned me extreamlie, namlie in the hat of it, that ten or twall houres I wald ly burning therin and reaving, and ryfe again without anie fwet. This continowed till the middes of the monethe of Auguft.

All this whyll, fen the Generall Affemblie in Apryll, an. 1582, and befor, vntill this Auguft, a lytle befor Bifchope Adamfone keipit his caftle, lyk a tod in his holl, feik of a difeafe of grait fetiditie, and ottymes vnder the cure of women fufpected of witchcraft, namlie an, wha confeffit hir to haiff lernit medecin of an callit Mr Wilyeam Simfone, that appeired diuers tymes to hir efter his dead, and gaiff hir a buik, &c. This woman being examined be the Pref-byterie, and fund a witche in thair iudgment, was giffen to the Bifchope to be keipe in his caftle for execution, bot he fufferit hir to flipe away, bot within thrie or four yeirs therefter fche was takin and execut in Edinbruche for a witche * Nochtwithftanding, the King coming to St Andros about the end of July, and feparating himfelff ther from the Lords that haid feafit about him at Ruthven, the Bifchope becomes a baill man atteanes, and occupies the pul-pit befor the King, luftelie declaming, as it was markit, in a poffeffit and inra-git maner, againft Minifterie, Lords, and all thair proceidings; and he that often profeffit from pulpit betor, that he haid nocht the fpirit of application, gat the gift of application be infpiration of fic a fpirit as never fpak in the Scriptures of God And becaufe it was reported for treuthe, that the Duc in Paris haid deid a Papift, he maid opin contradiction therto, affirming, tor cer-tean, that he deid a guid Proteftand, quhilk he provit be fchawin of a fkroll in his hand, quhilk he callit the Duc his Teftament, bot an honeft merchant woman fitting befor the pulpit, and fpying it narowlie, affirmed it was a compt of a four or fyve yeir auld dett that, a few dayes befor fche haid fend to him. Wharof fche gat na man peyment nor the Duc his executors maid hir.

At that tyme, Sir Robert Meluill cam to the Collage to Mr Andro, and, as a friend, fchew him whow euill the King was infoirmit of him, befaught him thertor to go to the King, and purge himfelff of thefe calumnies. Quhilk Mr Andro refufit to do, faying, purgation prefupponit foulnes, wherof his con-fcience, nor na man, was able iufthe to accufe him in anie kynd of vndewti-fulnes to the Kings Maieftie; giff his Maieftie defyrit his coming to him for his advys in maters of the Kirk or Comounweill, or anie vther dewtifull obe-dience, he wald maift humblie do it with all obfervance, but he wald nocht be an indirect accufar of himfelff to his Soverain.

The Counfallors and Courteours now gifles out, that the King captiued be-for, thought himfelff at libertie, and fa fettes thame to be evin, bathe with the Lords of the Read of Ruthven and with the Kirk, quhilk they fklanderlt as allowars of treaffone Yit craftelie, for the fpace of halff a yeir or mair, dif-

---

* It was reported for veritie to ws, that the Bifchope confulted with thefe witches anent the Kings efteat, of the countrey, and his awin, and gat a refponfe, that he fould ftand fa lang as the King ftud Bot the Deuill, as he vfes to do, deceauit him ther. Bot, verelie, about thefe witches we war plane and fcharpe with him, bathe from pulpit, in doctrine, and be cenfur of our Prefby-terie.

sembling with the Lords, they begin to put at some of the Kirk.   And, in the
monethe of Nouember, Jhone Durie of new is dischargit Edinbruche; and
coming ower to St Andros, whar I haid takin vpe hous, efter the vacans, he
finds his douchtar, my wyff, bot beginnand to convales of a deadlie hat fiver.
(wharout of sche haid cullit with a bleding excessiue, sa that, for ought the
medicineis could do, it steyed nocht four and twentie hours till lyff was almost
flitting: bot the Lord haid mercie on me, and spairt hir for a speciall wark
of comfort to me againft the day of a grait euill;) and tareing bot a few dayes,
behoued to go to his ward in Montros, to the quhilk I convoy it him   Be the
way, a lytle befor we cam to the furde of the Water of Lownan, a sow comes
in the lue rod befor ws, and trottes on toward the furd, swomes ower befor
ws   Now, the water was weill grait in speat, whar, we being in the middes
therof, my father, Jhone Duries hors lyes down in the water, and committes
his rydar to swoming with the stream: bot it pleasit God, I being nixt vnder
him, caught him be the cott neak, and taking a gripe of my hors mean, he
wad and wan to land: Whatof I miuragit him, speattes of afflictiones war to
seafe on ws, bot the Lord sould delyver out of them all   Sa, coming in
that countrey, I acquented him, and recommendit to all our frinds, whom he
finding thereftir euer lowing and frindlie, fand my mariage a speciall prouidence of God towards him

     That was a dark and heavie Wintar to the Kirk of Scotland, ecclipsed and
bereft of thrie grait lights, of Mr Alexander Arbuthnot in the beginning
therof, Mr Thomas Smeton in the middes, (of quhilk fort I wat nocht giff
ther was manie scores in all Christiandome for all sort of lerning and godlines:) and, in the end of the wintar, Mr Wilyeam Clark, my predecessour, a
man, whowbeit nocht in rank of lerning with the vther twa, yit the light and
lyff in the part he dwelt in, mikle belout and regratted of all sorts of persones that knew him, namlie that he had the charge ower: Ower sure a pre-
sage of a grait calamitie and oweithraw schorthe till ensew vpon the Kirk of
Scotland Amangs diueis Epitaphes wherwith Mr Andro beualit this so grait
a loss, I maun heir insert an, becaus it stiks recenthe in my memorie

              Vix heu! vix raptum, defleuimus Arbuthnotum;
                 Vix heu! iusta datis soluimus exequias.*
              Et premit altera mors, et funere funus acerbat,
                 Et magno extincto lumine, maius obit.

                         * Inferius.

Ille quidem Arctoa tenebras de nocte fugabat,
Fulgebas medio Glafgua ftella die
Quod fi luce fua fpoliata eſt noxque diefque
Noſtra, Eheu ! quantis obruimur tenebris
Aut ergo e tenebris renoca lucem, aut hominum lux
Chriſte, redi, et nobis ſtat fine nocte dies.

Turned in Scots

Yit ſkaiſe alas ! haid we bemean'de out den Arbuthnots dead,
Yea, ſkaiſe alas ! his exequies haid we and funerales mad,
When corps with corps does vin ws fear, and deathe with deathe does pres
And an giant light *extinguiſed*,* an other fealles alas !
That an the dark and drowſie might be northe did dryve away,
That ither as the† Sun did ſhyne be fouthe at mids of day
Gift fa then bathe our night and day be fpuhyet of thair light,
Sa fenfullie lies ws owerwhelm'de of darknes what an hight !
Then ather Chryſt from darknes now the light retourn againe,
Or com our light, that but all might, our day may ay remaine.

MR WEILIAM CLARKS EPITAPHE

That thow a Maiſter was, as yet thy Schollars ſkill can proue,
That thow art weill, full weill, confirmes thy godlines and loue
A cunning Clark, right cleirlie knawin, be nature and be art,
And all the thrie, in that thow play'd fa weill the paſtors part,
Then happie Maſter Weil I am Clark *by nam thow fall abyd*,‡
As Carell, with Anſter, Pittenweim lyes leauche by Fyffs coſt fyd

Biſchope Adamſon, for all his lang feiknes, becam then nocht onlie able to pretche, and keipe Conventiones of Counſall and Eſteates, and weat vpon Court, bot alſo, in the wintar, to tak iorney and go in ambaſſage to England and all to practife the alteration of the haill eſtent and diſcipline of the Kirk ‖ Coming to Londone about Yull, he informit the Quein the warſt of the miniſterie and gud nobilitie, and the beſt of the Court of Scotland, he practiſed with the biſchopes for confoimitie, and gaiſt tham dextra ſocietatis, he delt for lernit preatchouris to be placed in the beſt rowmes of Scotland, knawing

* Alas ! put out   † Thow Glaſgw ſtar as.   ‡ Thy nam als lang fall byd
‖ The Preſbyterie had enterit in proces with him, and remitted him to the Synodall, and that to the Generall, in the quhilk he was fuſpendit from the office of the miniſterie, as corrupt, bathe in doctrn and lyſt, and oidemed to be forder proceidit againſt   In the meantyme, to eſchew the cenfors of the Kirk, and practife the wrak therof, he vndertaks this iorney

weill the beſt men of the miniſterie of Scotland war to be diſplaced, he wrot
verie craftelie to Geneua and Tigurie, and ſend tham propoſitiones and queſtiones defyring to haiff thair iudgment; and, finalie, left na ſtan onturned
ower that might mak for the wark of Sathan, to beſeige and demoliſhe the
walles of Jeruſalem

Whill he is a biſſie biſchope about thir things in outting, as the cours was
layed, they war nocht ydle at hame; for, in the beginning of Februar, Mr
Andro Meluin is ſummoned to compeir befor the King and Counſall within
les nor thrie dayes,* to anſwer to ſic things as war to be levit to his charge
anent certean ſpeitches vttered be him from pulpit, ſeditius and treaſonable.
Mr Andro compeired, accompanied with ſum of his ſchollars and frinds,
amangs whom was Mr Robert Bruce; and I being in Angus, convoying my
mother in law to hir houſband, gou away a day befor his ſummounding, maid
diligence, and cam to Edinbruche the day of his ſecond compeirance The
quhilk day he declyned the iudicatory of the King and Counſall, being accuſit
vpon na ciuill cryme or tranſgreſſion, but vpon his doctrin vttered from pulpit The quhilk, when the King and Captan James, then maid Grait Chancellar, with roarings of lyones, and maſſages of deathe, haid taken ſa hat, that
all the Counſell and Courtes of the Palice war filled with fear noyes, and
bruttes, Mr Andro neuer iarging nor daſcht a whit, withe magnanimus courage,
mightie force of ſprit, and fonthe of euidence of reaſone and langage, planlie
tauld the King and Counſall, that they preſumed ower bauldlie in a conſtitut
eſteat of a Chriſtian Kirk, the kingdome of Jeſus Chryſt, paſſing by and diſ-
deaning the prophets paſtors, and doctors of the Kirk, to tak vpon tham to
iudge the doctrin, and controll the ambaſſators and meſſingers of a King and
Counſall grratter nor they, and far aboue tham   " And that," ſayes he " vie
may ſie your weaknes, ouerſight, and raſhnes in takin vpon yow that quhilk
yie nather aught nor can do," (louſing a litle Hebrew Byble fra his belt, and
clanking it down on the burd befor the King and Chancelar.) ` Thain is.'
ſays he, " my inſtructiones and warrand: let ſie quhilk of yow can iudge theron, or controll me therin, that I haiff paſt by my inſtructiones " The Chancelar, opening the buik, findes it Hebrew, and putes it in the Kings hand, ſaying, " Sir, he ſkornes your Maieſtie and Counſall." " Na, my lord,' ſayes Mr
Andro, " I ſkorn nocht; bot with all erneſtnes, zeall, and grauitie, I ſtand for
the cauſe of Jeſus Chryſt and his Kirk." Manie tymes put they him out, and

* Summoned on Setterday, to compeir on Monenday nixt

callit him in againe; whylles delling with minacings, and whylles with fear
words, to brak him, bot he grew man and mair in weïdome, ſtrengthe, and
courage, whowbeit, nan was ſufferit to com in with him: and when he cam
out, haid ſkarſlie leſour to draw his end, mikle les to tak ame advys with his
frinds and breithring In end they proceids: admittes an accuſar, wha bruikit
that nam for ignominie manie yeirs efter, " Wilyeam Stewart the Accuſar," a
penſionar of the Pryor of St Andros; receaves the articles of accuſation; admittes and takes the depoſition of a number of witneſſes, ſummoned out of St
Andros, namlie his graitteſt miſlykers, Mr Andro euer adheiring to his declinator, and at all tymes, as occaſion ſeruit, telling tham his mynd mightelie
anent the treuthe and weght of the cauſe of Chryſt and his Kirk, and wrangs
done thervnto, quhilk he wald be avengit of ſum day And when they haid
don all, lytle or na thing for than purpoſe gat they provin, bot deceirnes that
Mr Andro, for his vnreuerent behauiour befor his Maieſtie and Counſall, ſould
be put in waird in the Caſtle of Edinbruche during the Kings will In the
mean tym, Mr Androes breithring and frinds is informit, be ſie as knew the
plattes leyed, that ther was na guid meined to Mr Andro, and, if he war
annes faſt, he wald nocht be lowſit again, vnles it war for the ſkaffald This
maid him to keipe him quyet a night and a day, during the quhilk tyme I
trauelit amangs the counſallars. Manie gaiff me fear words, and ſaid thei was
na danger, bot our beſt frinds read a dictum, wrytten on the wall, ſounding,
Loufs and Leiving We vnderſtud, fordar, that the deceit of the Counſall
was alterit, and the waird apointed to be Blaknes, a toull holl, keipit be Captan James men. Sa, whill we was all in grait and heavie anxietie, and maiſt
dulfull doutſomnes, what to counſall,—vpon the an part, thinking it a hard
and fear mater to bereaue the Scholles and Kirk of Scotland of ſie a light and
leadder, and thinking that moyen and tyme might mitigat the King, and procure his libertie; vpon the vther part, knawing the courſe and plattes leyed
be the enemies, and ſeing the violent form of Captan James government, we
thought it haidar to jeopeird the lyff of ſie a man, as might be reſerued for a
better tyme,—being, I ſay, in this dutfull debeat amangs ourſelues, and euerie an with his awin hart nocht knawin weill whairto to inclyne, Mr Andro
himſelff comes out in publict, reſolut and cheirfull, and bad ws all be of guid
cowrage, for God haid reſoluit him of the beſt, and he was aſſurit wald be with
him Sa we go to dinner in Mr James Lawſones hous, wha with all his
gheaſts war exceiding heavie hairted, and oftentymes could nocht contein, bot
mix thair teares with thair drink Onlie Mr Andro eat, drank, and crakked

als merrehe and frie myndit as at anie tyme, and mair ; and (accoiding to his continuall form at meat, and in all companie,) tuk occasion of guid conference and discours, pertinent for the tyme and flat of mateis, to his awin woun- derfull incouragment, and our grait comfort, interlasing alwayes sum minie interludes, and drinking to his Captean and waidfellowes, bidding ws mak ws ready to follow, &c   Sa, eftei denner, he gaiff it out, and non knew ither. bot a venie few, that he wald obey the charge, and enter in waid, giff the King commandit, and God sa diiected him.   Wheirpon the Measlar gettes acces, giffes him the charge, with his warrand, till enter in the Castell of Blaknes within four and twentie houres, the quhilk he receaues reueienthe ; bot, within an houie or twa, his brothei Roger and he slippes out at the Port. hand foi hand, and ludges that night whaie God haid prepaiit, and within foui and twentie houres enteiit in Bervik, in place of the Blaknes *

Ther was na thing behind bot bitter teares and heavie lamentation, parthe for the present lofs, bot mikle mair for the esteat that was till ensew vpon the Kirk, quhilk euerie an apprehendit in graitter and graitter missour of hor- rour and fenfulnes. Bot aboue all, that notable and maist fathfull minister of God, Mr James Lawsone, wha, feing sa teiiible a tempest bieiding and co- ming on the schippe of the Kiik, and the wycsest, stouttest, and ableast schip- pars and marineis reinowit, appichendit the dangei sa liuely, and diank in the greiff and melancholie sa deiplie, quhilk being augmentit, and na wayes mitigat. be that quhilk followit, namlie, the vndewtifulnes of his flock, wasted his vi- tall sprites be piecemeill, and, within few monethes therefter, cutted the thrid of his maist stedable and comfortable lyff to the Kiik of Scotland.

As for my felff, to confes the treuthe I was almaist exanimat with heavines of hait, the quhilk, gif it haid nocht resolut in aboundance of teaies, my lyff haid bein suffocat ; for the quhilk cause I tuk me to a chalmei. and closing the dure, let my affectiones brak out, and go louss at iandom, quhilk a speciall lowing frind of myne, wating on me, suffeiit foi the space of an houie, bot efter knok- kit sa, and spak to me, that bathe for loue and reueience it behouit me till opin ; wha nocht onlie vsit all the comforts he could, bot wated vpon me, and convoyed me ham to St Andios : This was Andio Wod of Strevithie.

Mr James Lawsone, and Mr Walter Balcanquall, his onlie colleg that ie- meaned, maid, accoiding to thair disposition, the pulpit of Edinbiuche to found

* A certean of Captan James horsmen haid immediathe befor riddin out at the sam port till attend vpon him, and convoy him to Blaknes, ther annes to mak him sure

mightelie in the praife of Mr Andro, and to the deteftation of the fact of the
Counfall, that had fa proceidit agamft him; alfo, they prayit for him in particular, at all thair ordinar fermontes, quhilk moued the peiple verie mikle,
and gallit the Court

At my comming to St Andros, my wound, fkarfhe flemit, begoud to blude
apace, finding na thing, whar euer I cuft my ei's, bot mater of melancholie His
bookes war in danger, being put to the horn, and therfor I addreffit me with
diligence to pak tham vpe, and put tham afyde, and fkarfe was ther ane
quhilk I haid knawin in his comoun vfe that ranckled nocht my wound againe,
fa that that labour was fellon peanfull and heavie to me. Bot, aboue all, it
was a dayhe hart brak to me to fie that notable wark, fa weill begoun, yeilding, in the fuft fpring tyme of it, fie appenrance of plentifull fruicts, with fic a
calamitie cuttit of from all hope of herveft I thought I felt continualie a
cauld heavie lumpe lyand on my hart, lyking for to chok me; and fure I am it
haid coft me my lyff gift the mightie hand of my God haid nocht cuirt bathe
bodie and faull; and efter the cuiring therof, fun nelit, by all confcience of abilitie
and expectatioun, fum miffour of ftrynthe and gitts to tak a piece of courage,
and hald in the fpunk of lyff in the wark, till God fould haif mercie, and retoun for the reftauration therof

For finding as in the fpring tyme, nature beginning to purge, I helped the
fam with a melancolique purgation, quhilk wrought lang, and in grait quantitie, euidentlie be the cullor, kything the peccant humour And foone therefter, finding fum curage, bathe naturall and fpirituall, I fell to wark, and by
my awin houres for the langages quhilk I keipet befor, I fupplied, as I could,
the thrie dayes of Mr Andros publict Leffones in the comoun places of Religion, and teatched the twa cheiff controuertit heads *De verbo et Ecclefia*, in
the monethes of Merche and Apryll.

By and befyde the inward hand of my God, to whom alan perteines all
praife, I haid twa vtward fpeciall comforts An was the Maifters and Members of the Vniuerfitie, wha kythed an vther mynd to the wark then I luiked
for, and ganf than prefence and gud countenance and affiftance to my Leffons, to my grait comfort and incuragment The vther was of twa fpeciall
dayhe friends and companiones: the ane Mr Robert Bruce, the vther Mr Robert Durie, wha keipit companie with me continualie, to my grait vphald and
forderance in Gods Word.* Of that an wharof, namlie, for the grait praife

---

* Mr Thomas Buchannan alfo was my gud nibour and frind at that tyme, and all his dayes

of the caire and proudence of God towards his Kirk, I man remember sum thing man at lainthe

Mr Robert Bruce, second sone to the Laird of Airthe, brought vpe in letters. past his cours of Philosophie in the Vniuersitie of St Andros, and therefter be his father furnesit, was sent to France, whar, and in the Vniuersitie of Lovan, in the Low Countreyes, he studiet, namlie till Humanitie and the Jurisprudence, quhilk his father and frinds haid sett to be the end of his studies Therefter coming hame, he is directed till attend on Court and Session, for his fatheris effeares and his frinds, till the Lord began to call vpon him, and wouk strangle in his conscience, sa that he haid na rest nor confort, bot in the Word of God and companie of guid men Yit the manifold effeares of his father and frinds continualie importuning him, maid him to striue againft the working of his hart; bot in vean, for he was fean at last plainlie to schaw his father, that ther was na reft nor lyff for him, vnles he haid leine to go to the studie of Theologie, and be in companie of Mr Andro Melvill in St Andros Sa his father permitted at laft, and he cam to ws at the beginning of that sam wintar, at the end wharof Mr Andro was put att, whom maist lowinglie and fathfullie he assisted till his departour out of the countrey, and syne retourned again to ws and sett himselff mair erneftlie then euer befor to his studies : and that nocht onlie to be a hearar, but to essay what gift God wald giff him of vtterance of that quhilk he studeit. And all this mouit, yea, drawin as it war perforce, with a mightie inwart working, quhilk suffent him never to gett rest bot when he was about that purpose He said to me a day, in releiving of his mikle and fear occupied mynd, in privat conference purmencing in the fields, that or he cust himselff again in that torment of conscience quhilk was leyed on him for resisting the calling of God to the studie of Theologie and Ministerie. he haid rather go throw a tyre of brimston halff a myll lang.

Sa, befor he wald open his mouthe at our table, whar ordinarlie ther meall about, the students opened vpe a chapter, and gathered sum nottes thervpon. he desyrit to haiff sum exerceis in privat with me and Mr Robert Dury, and sa annes in the ouk first, therefter thryse. our tyme about in a large wyde hous of the Collage, we handlit a chapter, till that way we past throw the Epistles to the Romanes and Hebiews, but or we cam anie way fordwart in the Hebiews, Mr Robert tuk the haill exerceis to himselff, and haid vs auditors, to our grait ioy and comfort. Therefter we drew him to the Scholl, whar the students haid ther privat exerceifes befor the Maisters ; from that to the Table

o

and fyne to the morning doctrine on the Sabbathe. to quhilk a multitude of
the beft peiple of the town reforted.   Sa it pleafed God at that tyme, to my
fingular vphauld and menuagment in his fervice, to begin to trean vpe and
fram that maift notable preatchour for the tyme of reftitution of his deceyit
and captiued Jerufalem

During this tyme, the firft intelligence be wryt I gott of Mr Andro, was of
the Bifchopes biffinefs, a iuft cope of whafe Articles he fend me hame , the
quhilk I haiff thought meit heir to infert, for cleiring of the controuerfie betuix the Kirk and him, and to fchaw whow craftelie and malitiuflie that fy-
cophant calumniattes the ordour and conclufionnes of Difcipline befor fett down,
therby to haiff catchit a vantage, giff he could haiff gottin, be fic information.
a cenfour of the breithing of the French Kirk. Geneu. Tygurie, &c., and to
mak ws and our Difcipline odius to the Quein and Kirk of Eingland.

ARTICLES QUHILK THE BISCHOPF OF ST ANDROS GAIF OUT IN EINGLAND TO THE FRENCH
KIRK AT LONDONE, SEND TO GENEU, TYGURIE, &c   1583.

The Ordour apointed be the Minifters of Scotland obtrudit to the King be tham

1 As thei [is] a difference betwix the Ciuill polecie and gouernment of the Kirk, fa is thei
diuers gouernours apointed for the an and for the vther

2 The ciuill magiftrat rewlit in his politik efteaues only, and the fpirituall gouernours in the
efteaues of the Kirk.

3 As fpirituall rewlaies does exceid thair boundes, if they interpoys vpon ciuill and politik
matters , fo does the Prince or ciuill magiftrat, it he pretend in maters ecclefiafticall

4 The exemple of Vzziah, King of Juda, declares that kings fould be affiayed to middle with
maters perteining to the Kirk

5 It is an herefie to a Prince to vfurpe the tytle to be called the Head of the Kirk.

*Thefe aboue wryttin concern the Princes dewtie — Thefe that follow concern the
government and polecie of the Minifitie*

1 The Ordour wharby the Kirk fould be gouernit, alfweill in preatching of the Word, miniftration of Saciaments, as difcipline ecclefiafticall, is fufficientlie and tullie fett further in the Scriptures, and hes neid of na larder , and the Minifters of the Word of God fould haift na iniunctiones
giffen to tham in pretching of the Gofpell, bot fould fpeak as the Word of God puttes in than
mouthe.

2 The government of the Kirk confiftes in thrie fortes , in Paftor, Doctor, Senior, wha aught to
haiff the haill difcipline of the Kirk in than powar, and Paftors to be fic as hes a particulai flok
wha lykwayes fould be called Bifchopes.

3 The office and extent of Bischopes, as they ar of provinces and dyocris, can nocht stand with the Word of God

4 Euerie Pastor within his awin congregation sould haiff a nomber of Seniores or Eldars, of laic men, to assist tham in counsall for the government of the Kirk, and in euerie compas, or reasonable precinct of boundes, thair sould be erected a Presbyterie, consisting in the Pastors and Doctors, and sic vther laic persones, as be election may be associat within the sam. And these Presbyters sould haiff cair of the doctrine and maners within than boundis, and of the election of Pastors, when anie of tham fall happin to vnleak , and powar of excommunication, and dispositioun of benefices

5. The Synodall Assemblie does consist in manie Presbyteries, lyk as the Presbyteries in manie particular kirks , and in the Presbyteries and Generall Assemblies, an Moderator is to be chosin be the consent of the rest at euerie meitting, and his powar to continow to the next Assemblie therefter.

6. Thair is appellation from the particular to the Presbyterie, from the Presbyterie to the Synodall, and from the Synodall to the Generall, if anie man be hurt and greivit   And the Generall Assemblie does consist of the Commissionars, quhilk ar directed from the Synodall Assemblies to the Generall And in lyk maner the Assemblie Generall sould haiff a Moderator chosin at euerie meitting.

7. The Assemblie Generall hes powar to mak lawes, canones, and constitutionnes, for the effeares of the haill Kirk, and to determine in all maters ecclesiasticall, in election of Pastores, deposition, suspension, excommunication, heresie, and whatsumeuer effeares perteining to the Kirk

8. The Assemblie Generall may appoint tymes of than convention from Assemblie till Assemblie, and convein thamselues without anie licence impetrat of the Prince for that effect.

9. The Assemblie Generall hes also powar to direct Commissionars to the Kings Parliament, quhilks Commissionars sould haiff the powar and authoritie of the Kirk, and nocht sic as ar Bischopes, except they be from tyme to tyme authorised with than commission

10 The Assemblie Generall hes also powar to direct, of than awin nomber, certean to visit the Kirks as occasion fall fall. And ther is na ordinar powar to visit, except they haiff commission of the Kirk, and be directed from the General Assemblie to that effect

11 Beneficis ar the invention of the deuill, and na man aucht to posses rent or leiving , bot Deacones sould lift vpe the Kirk rents, and distribut the sam, according to the ancient canones

12 Patrones and patronages ar nocht to be tolerated in the reformit Kirk, as occassiones of intolerable corruptionnes Bot the patrones sould resing in fawours of the Deacones . And giff patrones sould be permitted, they sould nocht haiff the choise of the election of the persone , bot efter the persone is elected be the parochine or Presbyterie, then the patrones aucht to confer the leiving onlie to the persone intiant, and the distribution of the said leiving immediathe to be giffen to the Deacones.

13. Ther belanges to the patrimonie of the Kirk all sic temporall and spirituall lands, teinds rents, as hes bein at anie tyme foundit or dotted thervnto   And it is a sacrilage to the Prince, or anie inferior persone, to middle therwith, except the Deacones onlie to the vse forsaid.

14. Giff the Prince wald contravein the Actes of the Generall Assemblie, he may be alsweill excommunicat as anie inferiour in the realme

Followes the Judgment of the Bischop of St Andros, quhilk he pressed to haif had confirmed be the lerned Doctors and Ministers of Gods Word in England, Geneu, or alsquher, for supplanting of the Kirk of Scotland

1. For the Prince

1 It is ane of the graittest parts of the Prinche office, to appoinct a godlie Ordour to the Kirk, and to tak head that the sam be meanteined and keipit *

2 It proceidit from the tyrannie of the Paipe, till arrogat to the Clergie the haill government of the Kirk, and to exclud thertra Christian princes and godlie magistrates, wha sould be nurishes of the Kirk, and keipars of bathe the Tables.

3 Princes in than awin cowntries ar cheiff heades vnder Chryst, as weill in ecclesiasticall policie as temporall, and thair iudgment in bathe is soveran

4. Giff the rewlars of the Kirk hes done wrang, appellation is lawfull to the Prinche powar, be whase authoritie the saming sould be redressit.

2 For the Ministrie

1 It is maist necessar that a guid ordour and form be preseryvit in the Kirk, als weill in the service of God as in publict doctrin, that all things may be don ordourlie, and na man transgres the limites and bounds apointed in the Scripture, vnder pretext of the libertie of the Spreit of God

2 The government of the Kirk does consist in the authoritie and powar of the Bischope, to whom ar committed the dyoceis and provinces in government

3. The office of Bischope is of the Apostolic institution, and maist aggreable to the primitiue puritie of the Kirk of God

4. The ordination and ordinarie Judgment of Pastors belangit to the Bischope, without whase authoritie whasoeuer does presume to the Pastorall cure, enters nocht at the dur, bot ower the dyk

5. Doctors hes na powar to preatche, bot be the apointment of Bischops, nather haiff they anie fordar powar in gouerning the Kirk.

6. Seniors or Eldars, of the laic sort, is nocht agreable with the Scripture, nor ancient puritie of the primitiue Kirk.

7. Presbyteries to be apointed of gentilmen, or lords of the ground, and vthers associatt with the Ministers, is na vther thing bot till induce a grait confusion in the Kirk, and an occasion of continuall sedition

8. The ordour of apointing Moderators in Presbyteries or Assemblies to be alterit at thair meitting, is nather canonicall efter the Scriptures, nor aggreiable to the ordour of the primitiue Kirk, in the quhilk it hes bein locall in the Bischopes seat, and nocht electiue and variable, as was the Wardeanes of the Tures.

9. The Synodall Assemblie sould be moderat and governed be the Bischope, in euerie province and dyoeie, and be him sould ordour be takin that the Kirks be weill servit.

10 The Generall Assemblie of a realme hes nocht powar to conveen thamselff bot vpon a grait and weghtie occasion intimat to the Prince, and licence granted therto.

11 Ther is na Assemblie that hes powar to establis lawes and constitutiones within the realm, bot sic as ar allowit of the Prince and his Esteat.

12. The resort of the Prelates of the Kirk to the Kings Parliament and grait Counsall, for the

---

* Giff this grunds be fast stuken to or nocht, this tyms experience may tell.   1600 weghtie efteares of the realme, is maift neceffar, and that Minifters fall piefum to direct of thair number to the Counfall and Parlament, it is an intolerable arrogancie

13 Vifitation is an office neceffar in the Kirk, and proper to the function of a Bifchope, and fic as ar apointed be him for that effect

14 Benefices and patronages hes bein zealuffie and godlie apointed be our anteceffours, and Chriftian Paftors may with faiff confcience mioy the faming And the Deacones to be apointed ower the Kirk rents is an prepofterus imitation of the primitive Kirk, without anie kynd of reafone

15. The patrimonie of the Kirk is that, quhilk, be the lawes and efteates of countreyes, belangs to the Kirk and intertemnent thairof, and nocht that aboundance wherwith the Roman Kirk did ow erflow

Thir laft Articles, plean contradictorie to the eftabliffed difcipline of the Kirk of Scotland, the faid Bifchope of St Androis prefented to the Bifchopes of Canterbery and London ; alfo to the Minifters of the Frenche Kirk at Londone, and to fundrie vther lernit men, alleaging tham, to be foundit vpon the Scriptures, and maift finceare antiquitie, willing tham, be vertew of a commiffion giffen to him be the Kings Maieftie of Scotland, to intreat of thir mateis, to confirm the fam be than fubfcription and approbation.

And mairower, he wrot to Geneu and Tigurie finiftrus infoi mation of all our proceidings, and as beft might ferue to purchas, and haid bein neuer fo lytle a hinkling of ther pen till haiff born out his courfe, and maid vant of for his creadit at Court Bot, as my vncle directed me, I maid his biffines knawin at hame, and informit all the guid breithring of his proceidings, and fend copies of his Articles abrode throwout the countrey And, on the vther part, Mr Andro, wha waired him far in credit without the countrey, amangs the beft and maift lerned, namlie at Geneu and Tigurie, wrot vnto the Kirks at lamthe in the breathrings nam, and informit tham of the man, and all his proceidings and purpofe, in his delling with thame The quhilk epiftle, becaufe it cleires bathe the caufe and ftorie better nor I can fet it down, I haiff tranflated, and thought maift meit to be infert in this place

To the maift Reuerend Fathers, and our maift lowing Breithring in the Lord Jefus, the Paftors of the Kirk of Geneua and Tigurie.

It is now almaift fyftein yeris, Reuerend Fathers in God, and Breithring in the Lord, maift worfchipfull, fen that graue and lerned men, and that quhilk is cheiff burning with wyfe and fincere zeall of the glorie of God, and helthe of his Kirk, informed with your precepts, and inftructed with your exemples, hathe in the fift planting of our Kirks comioyned with the puritie of doctrine the holines of difcipline And that than vniforme confent and aggreiment in all poinctes witneffed vnto the haill warld, might left vnto the pofteritie, they fubfcryvit your Confeffion In the futtfteppes of the qubilk guid and godlie renouned men, we thereffer mifting haift, nixt efter the heavinlie oracles of the Word of God, following the doctrine and conftitution of your Kirk, keip the fam courfe vnto this prefent day, and farther, alfo leanning on the mercie and guidnes of our God, and in the ftrynthe of his Holie Spreit we dout nocht conftantlie, without weneing, to hald the fam vnto the end   Of the qubilk our purpofe and conftant aggriement with yow in doctrine and difcipline we haiff fund of Gods guidnes this finiet, that induring fa manie yeirs na herefie hes fprung out in our Kirks, nan com from vther places hes taken rut, entered anie thing deiplie, or remeaned anie fpace of tyme in the hart of anie man mikle les to haiff growin vpe or cropen abrode   Na obftinat Papift or trefpaffom, publictlie knawin, hes it fufferit lang to converfe amangs ws, vntean or doun withe.   Sa it hes pleafit the Lord to bles the labours of his feruantes, vndertakin according to the direction of his Word, and vnto this day to heape fa grait and incredible happines, of his awin fingular guidnes, vpon the congregationnes of Scotland

But in the mean tyme, alas! whill as we anfwerit nocht vnto fa grait and rare a grace and guidnes of God toward ws, be that thankfulnes of mynd, obedience to his Word, and diligence in our deu-ties, that becam ws.   Behauld of the feartall iudgment of God, but indeid infthe deferuit, Sathan fa blinds with auarice and ambition, ane nocht of ws, albeit amangs ws, bearing the office of a mi-nifter, that forgetting, as fayes the poet, bathe his awin fchiam and the helthe of his breithring, and that qubilk is man miferable, cafting at all guid confcience, and making fhipwrak of his fathe, goes fordwart without ceafing to mix heavin with erthe, and with vtter confufion to trouble all things For when he haid left his flok, and vnwitting of the Kirk haid croppin in Court, when he haid nocht onlie with fubtill craft and polecie intrudit himfelft in the efteat of tals bifchopes, of new fprung vpe agane from the holles, the qubilk he haid oppugned of befor, bot alfo haid taken planlie vnto him, that fals vfurped authoritie qubilk in his fermonts publiclie he haid damned, qubilk opin-lie in a maift frequent Affemblie Generall of the Kirk he haid oftentymes abiurit, and the qubilk, be findrie fubfcriptiones and hand wryttes, he haid renuncit and giffen ower, when, as he haid addict-ed himfelft to the maift vyle feruitude and flauerie, and with the fworn enemies to the guid efteat of the Countrey, Kirk, and Relligion, in a maift filthie caufe ioyned and bandit himfelft, when, that in doutfull maters and difpant helthe of his body he haid nocht onlie confulted with witches concern-ing the efteat of King and Comntrey, bot alfo for releiff of his feiknes he haid erneftlie fought the helpe and fupport of deuilrie and witchcraft, when, that efter a ftubburn fylence from pretching the fpace of a haill yeir vnder clok of feiknes and infirmitie, he haid, to fofter and flen vpe the per-nitius affectionnes of the Court, maid twa maift turbulent and feditius fermonts, when he haid, with the Machiavellians of the Court, and the Papes trafecturs at ham, deuyfit maift crewall coun-falles againtt the lyff, lands, and efteat of the beft and maift zealus noble men, and vthers guid gen-tilmen and fubiects of the countrey, when he haid don monie vther things qubilk nather tyme fuf-feres, and fchiam forbiddes, to wryt, and now, when formall proces vpon the fornamed maift odius, hynous crymes was lead and deducit againft him befor the Prefbyteries and Affemblies, and for that caufe, efter that he was inhibit, as maift fklanderus and vnworthie till vfe the function of minifterie, vnto the tyme that the laft cenfor of the Kirk might ftrik vpon him, to cut him of from the body of the fam as a maift contagius and corrupt member, he obteines a trie legacie from his Matie to pas to vther nationnes, whar, vnder pretence and clok of curing his difeafes and feiking of his helthe, he might moyen all the meanes and wayes he could (as his verie deids hes declarit) to vex and trouble the Kirk, the qubilk now he haid leyit in his hart to flay and diftroy as his deadlie enemie.   Yie will giff ws, as we hope, this leiue, (reuerend fathers and breithring in the Lord,) in the caufe of God and his Kirk, fimplie and planlie to deall with yow, for that onlie a cearffar of the hait is witnes that we veild na thing in this present narration to our privat affections, bot rather owerpas manie things of iett purpose, quhilk the caufe itfelff requyres

In London, then, letting himfelff out as Ambaffator for his Ma{tie}, he thrfteoufhe intreated oftentymes of feeret purpofes with the Ambaffators of France and Spean. Withe our nibour bifchopes (for ther amangs our nbours he remeaned, nather purpofed he at the beginning to go ame farder,) he haid fic conference, be the quhilk he traducit the beft of our nobilitie and fubiects as feditius and treafonable. He giftes himfelff to fic deviffes and coumfalls, be the ftrainthe and effect wharof, at this tyme, the maift lernit and fathfull paftores, in bathe the kingdomes, ar forced ather haillehe to keipe fylence and leane the miniftene, or then by flight and exyll to faft thair lyves, or els to effav the filthie wemmes of ftinking pietlones, or then of necefhtie to do that quhilk onlie remeanes agains than dewtie and confcience, to fubferyve to the ambitius tyrannie of the tals bifchopes, and to the impietie of manie corrupt rytes and ceremonies. Of this comes thofe Archiepifcopall Letters, written to yow and the breithring of Tygurie, be the quhilks that me nelus, cunning, and fyne artifice, in femveing and diffembling what he will, bathe does burding ws with fals and forgit crymes, and bring the government of our Kirk, traducit be manie calumnies, into dout and queftion. Albeit, he is les ignorant then anie man. and our awin confcience beares ws record, ws to haift preffed erneftlie to that, that the difciplne of the Kirk might be taken out of the Word of God, fa far as could be, and that it fould nocht pas a iot from the iudgment of your Kirks. Wharfor, lyk as it fould be fuperfluus to ws to open vpe and declare our iudgment vnto yow, namlie concerning maters of difcipline, feing whatfoeuer we haift in that mater, we willinglie and planlie confes to haift receaned it of yow, and that we altogidder agrie with vow in all poincts, fa metueloufhe does our mynds and willes, be the vertew of Gods Spient, concent in an harmonie. Sa will we nocht, for fear bathe of temeritie and impudence, preferyve vnto yow anie form of anfwering, or manor of wrytting againe to the Bifchopes Letters and Queftionnes. Of this onlie at this tyme, wald we haift vow perfuadit, that the gind ordour of the Kirk the quhilk Adamfone durft firft vndermynd fecretlie, and thereftter opinlie oppung, and now at laft wickedlie to calummiat, fathlefhe to mean fwear, and malitiulhe to deteaft as Papall tyrannie, mother of confufion and faggot of fedition, hes bein receavit within our Kirks contoum to the Word of God, and maner of the conftitutionnes of your Kirks, euer fen the firft tyme that Papiftrie was chaffit away, and incontinent approwit be the vottes of the haill efteates of the countrey in Parliament, and, piece and piece, at laft, of the mercie of God, hes bein brought to fum mediocritie of perfection fa far, at the leaft, as the fmalnes of that miffour quhilk God hes beftowit vpon ws might attein vnto, and quhilk thrie yeirs ago hes bein approvin, fealled vpe, and ratefeid be the profeffion of the mouthe, holie and feinfull aithe of the Lord interpoinit, and fubfcription of the hand of the King himfelff, and euerie ane of his fubiects, giant and fmall, or what ordour, rank, and efteat foeuer they war. and that be the expres letters patents of his Ma{tie}, commanding all and findrie, vnder the hieft pean, to do the fam.

Now, altho thefe things be fa in verie deid as is declarit, and this our difcipline be corroborat be diuers and manifold vfe and experience, maifter of toolles, in all partes and in euerie occafion fallin out continuallie thir xxv yeirs bypaft. Neuertheles the aduerfar, efter that he haid maid the maift godlie and ftout, allweill of the nobilitie as of interiour efteates, wha haid bein the fpeciall inftruments of God in the defence and eftablifment of Relligion and the caufe of the King, be conducit and fuborned accufars, wailht out of the number of fic men wha haid fauld thamfelues in faull and body, to work all kynd of iniquitie and villanie for waildlie preferment, and be fals forgit crymes maift craftelie and deceatfulhe leyit vpon tham, ather to be accufit of thair lyves and want

the head, or to be comprehendit and casten in prisson, banished, and forfault, to the intent, that
nan sould be lett to ganstand than godles comse This aduersar, I say, taucht the Kings Matie incontinent, and these Papisticall epicureans and bludie clients of the Hous of Guise and Quein Mother, be the quhilks his Grace is hauldin in fearfull bandes and abus, to convocat a Parliament of
the thrie Estets of the countrey, to bring the saming into vyle and bund slauerie For nather durst
they reasone of the maters proponit, nor thereftir gift than vottes and iudgment trulie, according
to the wounted libertie of the Estaetes of Scotland, and the laudable government of our nation. Bot
in a new and maist strange maner, the Kings will being maid a law and reasone for all things, the
Presbyteries at vtterlie perueersted, the pseudo episcopall tyrannie restout, the King, be a plean
law, receaves a full and absolut powar to command and rewll in maters, alsweill ecclesiasticall as
ciuill. The sentences of excommunication, lawfullie pronuncet be the Presbyteries, be than authoritie is dissanulled and declarit to be of na fors or effect And finalie, all ecclesiasticall iurisdiction, and nixt vnder the King, all powar of rewling in the Kirk, is giffen to the fals bischopes,
quhilks war of befor, when the Kirk flude, athir maist ruslie excommunicat, or lying vnder the proces of the Kirks centours, as knawin maist iklanderus and vnhonest persones throwout all the
countrey.

Amang the quhilk the cheiff captan and rewlar, even the author, and torger, and cheiff executor
of all this wickednes, is Patrik Adamsone, the fals Bischope of St Andros, wha steying vpon this
perpetuall and pontificiall dictatura, meruelus it is whow euattehe he rages againt the pastors of
the Kirk, and all guid men, for bathe he propynes certean Articles, (skartit togidder be him,) or
rather blottes of that comlines and ordour, quhilk sould be in Chrystis Kirk drawin newhe out of
the dregges of the cupe of the Antichryst vnto the lawfull pastors to drink, and als be the authoritie of the King, obtrudis thame to be subteryvit vnder the pean of banisment, incarceration, or de-
prywing of thame from thair ministerie Be the quhilk Articles, bathe that libertie of preatching the
Word being opprest, is attemperat vnto the lusts and pleasures of men ; and stent of publict
prayer, with the simplicitie of ryttes, in ministration of the sacraments and celebrating of mariage,
is filthelie adulterat, and manie vther things againt the expres Word of God is committed. He
hes pitifulie destroyed the Collage a fyve yeirs since, at the command of the King , and be a speciall Act of Parliament, consecrat to holie erudition and vertew, that onlie a antismarie, of the
knawlage of the toungges and sincere theologie, in all the realme of Scotland, sett doun and planted
againt the manifold seminaries of the bislie Jesuites, casting out therof all the professors and students, and spulyeing the Bibliothek and wryttings therof, it nocht being obscure what Sathan purposes by this doing , to wit, that the light of heavinhe knawlage being extinguisht, we be involued
again in the mist and darknes of Jesuiticall sophistrie , that we, wha began in the sprit, may end in
the flesche , that the wynyeard of the Lord, spoilled of the sauegards and defence of his hedge,
might be eatten vpe of wyld beasts , and, finalie, the walles of Jerusalem cast down, the sanctuarie
may be brunt and defylit Vnto the holie peace, concord, and vnitie with our nibours, to whase
trindschipe we ar ioyned sa streathe, first be bands of religion, libertie, and conquest therof by than
speciall helpe and meanes, and thereftir confirmed with manifold benefites, they prefer the sauour
and sundschipe of the Gusians, and the rest of these monstruus Readeattins in France, quha celebrat
that bludie drunken teast of Bartholomew in Paris, with that horrible butcherie of the holie mar-
tyres of God, the quhilk our Court now affirmes mislie to haiff bein massacred Yea, they haue
persuadet our Joas to receane in Athalia in the association and fellowschip of the Sceptor and
Croun, without whase guid will, benediction, and full delyverance, they contend that nather can
he happelie ring and lawfullie at hame, nor obtein the empyre of the whole Ill of Britannie Be

the bludie counfall and direction of the quhilk Athalia, all things hes proceidit, fen Monfieur Obignies firft coming in Scotland, in fic fort, that according therto, a thrie yeirs ago, the Life of Morton, Regent of Scotland, and now lathe the Eile of Gowrie, bothe moft ftout and valiant aduengars and defendars of Relligion and the Kings caufe, be the tals fentence of corrupted iudges, war circumvenit and oppreffed. At whafe pleafure and will albeit captine, the beft nobilitie and peires of the land, the frakeft and maift zealus in relligion, in dicta caufa vnhaid, ar forfaulted, apointed for the flauchtar and drawin to the gibets and comoun place of execution, and all than guids and geare, as the clothes of the innocent to the hangman, ar giffen to the faulles clyent of Guife and Athalia. To quhilk mercies men, with the guids and gear of the nobleft, beft, and maift innocent, as with the fpuilzie of than enemies, ar gorgiuflie array it, and accompanied warlyke with a fort of Immeirs and godles fuddartes, moft feirfull and dolorus to the guid and godlie and profitable and plefand to the vngodlie and wicked. They abrogat and braks Gods lawes, and maks wrang and vmuft, and puts tham fcharplie in execution, fa that in na place euer could that be man treulie fpokin,

> Jam late impietas graffatui libera, paffim
> Omnia plena malis.
> Cum penes inniftos ius eft, et iuffa molorum
> Sunt metuenda bonis.

> Now rages loufs vngodlines in land,
> In euerie place all is *full of** moleft,
> Whill as the right is in the wrangfull hand,
> And wait mens lawes ar feirfull to the beft

Sie now, altho we fould keipe filence, reuerend fathers and maift lowing breithring in the Lord, what memes the queftiones of Adamfone anent the powar of the Prince in making of ecclefiafticall lawes, and conftituting of the polecie of the Kirk, in convocating of Synods and Generall Affemblies and in proclaming of Faftes, to wit, that na thing be fa fin and faciat amangs vs quhilk be the wickednes of thefe mifchant men fall nocht be violat and vndone. He knawes weill aneuche, nather can he be ignorant of that quhilk he hes fo often read and lerned of your maift godlie and lerned wrytings, That it perteines nocht to the Prince to prefcryve ather relligion to the Kirk, or difciplme to the Paftors therof, bot be his authoritie to confirme bathe the an and the vther apointed be God, and finceirlie declarit out of his Word be the miniftrie of his fervantes, to reuenge and punifhe all corrupting of clean doctrin, contempt of holie difcipline, and perturbation of lawfull ordour, for the quhilk vfe and purpofe he hathe receavit the fword, to decore the Affemblies, gift neid beis, with his prefence; to arme the innocence of this miniftrie be his faftigard and defence, ift thei aryfe controuerfies amangs the Paftors fumtymes, to compofe and agrie the fam be his authoritie interponed, to promoue, be guid lawes maid for that effect, thefe things quhilk ar lawfullie conftitut be the Affemblies, and to do maine vther things for the weill of the Kirk, quhilks wer lang to reheirs, and vnneidfull. Bot far vtherwayes does he fitt in the Synods amangs the Paftors, then he does in the throne of the kingdome amangs the Efteattes—hen to mak lawes for fubiects and command, bot ther to receaue lawes from God to obey. And finalie, the coming

---

* Or, *ill and*

of the enemie to be declairt be the found of the trumpet of the watchmen, as Ezechiell and Joel commands.

And albeit, that fum things be callit ecclefiaftically, and vther things ciuill, and the ciuill apertean to the Comoun weill, the vther to the Kirk, yit it is nocht fa mikle to be confident what things is handlit as whow, feing the knawlage of an and the felff fame thing, a way, and in fum refpect, apertenies vnto the magiftrat, and an vther way to the Senat Leeclefiafticall, and vit fie a mater nather does the Kirk curhe, nor the Counfall or Parlament ecclefiafticallie, intreat ἀλια γλαυκας ἡς Ἀθηνας—falt to Dyfert, or colles to Newcaftell And as twitching the Convention of the nobilitie at Ruthven, and the iudgment of the Affemblie concerning that mater, What neid is ther to wryt? The halheft and beft part of the nobilitie and efteates of the realme, without anie tumult or flauchter, comprehending and putting in prifloue ane or twa wicked men, remoued a peft from the Comoun weill, a fure mifcheift fra the Kirk, and delyvent the King from prefent danger, bathe of body and faull. The King callit a Convention of the Efteates He declairt the danger wherin himfelff, the Kirk of God, and Comoun welthe, was brought in by the counfall of wicked men—he commends the faithfulnes and ftoutnes of the nobilitie, wha haid delyverit his Matie, the Kirk, and Comoun weill, from fa prefent a danger—fire and graue fentences and vottes ar fpoken—all with a voice commends the deid Ane Act is maid be the Efteates, be the quhilk the convening of the nobilitie at Ruthven is approuen as guid fervice done for King and Comoun weill And at the fam tyme the Generall Affemblie of the Kirk was conveuit, vnto the quhilk was fend tra the noble men that tuk fa guid a wark in hand to purge tham from the calumnies of euill willars, and from all fufpition of privat factionnes and fedition, and to notifie and approue the deid to the Affemblie and all guid men Ther is alfo fend to the Affemblie ane or twa Commiffionars from the King From the Affemblie alfo vnto the King ther is directed lykwayes fum of the breithring with his Maties Commiffionars, to vnderftand the Kings awin mynd in that mater, and report it again to the breithring In the Kings awin nam and words, it is reported to the Affemblie againe, that his Matie acknawlegit in verie deid himfelff, the Comoun weill, and the Kirk of God, to haiff bein releiued of a maift grait and extream danger, and for that caufe thanked God haithe, and willit the Affemblie, and cnerie an of the breithring, according to than office, diligentlie to trauell that the comoun danger, now being remouit be the ftoutnes of the nobilitie, the wark of delyverance begoun fould be bauldlie profecut and perfyted, fa that bathe in than prayers to God, and fermontes in publict to the peiple, they fould haiff in fpeciall recommendation fa guid, fa holie and wholfome a caufe of the King, Kirk, and Comoun weill The Affemblie obeyes, and giffes thanks to God in a fingular maner, for hearing of the prayers of the Kirk, quhilks haid bein powred out with a folem faft and humiliation a lytle befor the aryfing of the delyverance from the fworn fuddarts of the Hous of Guife, and of our Athalia, Obigme being captan to tham, wha haid fa fearlie oppreffed the Kings Matie, Kirk, and Comoun weill, with a miftie night of captiuitie and blak darknes of fchamfull fervitude And this is that quhilk our guid Bufchope exagitates, to bring the breithring in hatred and invy, wha efchames nocht befor yow to plead the caufe of the Papifts, whom he can nocht fuffer to be counted for goattes be the trew Paftors, whafe office is to feid the Lambes of Jefus Chryft But the bearer preffes ws, and peraduenture this is over mikle, namlie vnto yow wha is acquented with the fmelling out of the craft and fubtelue of fic wolffes. And therfor in end we pray yow, bathe in your privat and publict prayers, to commend to our comoun Father the Kirks in bathe the countries, for the graiteft part is deftitut of thair Paftors, and fa exponit to the intrufion of bludie wolffes, and that yie wald, in this grait darknes, fchvne befor ws be your faithfull counfall, wha, fear againft our willes, ar pullit away from our awin dear flockes. From, &c.

1584.—Bot to turn bak agane, and deduce the Storie of our esteat till we followed Mr Andro, and war all fean to the efter him About the beginning of Apryll that yeir, 1584, the deuill essayit the stay of my werk, trauelles for halding vpe the wark of the Collage of Theologie, or rather hadding in ane spark of lyff in it. For the Œconomus of the Collage, wha held the hous, and intro-meted with the haill leiving therof, being a flight and war man, and percea-ving the esteat of the Knk deceying, and graithe to be hated be the Court, he thought it wald nather be profitable nor sure for him to be in that place of service in the Knk : for he haid his intelligence and collusion with the Bischope alwayes.   And therfor, whowbeit in the middes of the yeir, when all thinges war at the deirest, and he haid vplifted the best and surest part and peyment of the Collage leiving, yit he comes to me, and wald neides giff ower his of-fice, and leane the halding of our hous in the Collage. This was wounderfull heavie to me, being owerburdent with teatching and governing of the stu-dents in thair disputes, exerceises, and conversation : for the hous of the Col-lage, annes giffen vpe, the students behoued to skatter, and all exerceis ceas Yit it pleased God to gift me a hart resolued to be doing what I could, think-ing it the best, when euer the visitation of the Lord sould com, to be fund oc-cupeit in his wark Therfor, with the advys of Mr Robert Bruce, wha maist lowinglie and cearfullie assisted me in all, I called the said Œconomus to his comptes, gaiff him a discharge of his intromission, sa far as he clared him be iust compt, and vndertuk my selff the furnesing of the hous, wherunto my wyff was a right and stedable helpe, and sa put af that monethe.

This monethe of Apryll was a most anxius and perplext monethe to the Kirk and haill countrey of Scotland : Wherin about the Pasch, the Erles of Angus and Mar, the Maister of Glammes, accompaned with than frinds, oc-cupied the town and castle of Strueling, luiking for the concurrance of the countrey to stand be the giud caufe, and repres Captan James insolence. Bot finding cauld concurrance, and hering of the King with grait forces to be merching from Edinbruche to Striling, war fean to flie and etchape into Eing-land.   At the sam tyme, the breithring from all partes assembling to St An-dros, whar the Generall Assemblie was aponcted to be keipit, they fand a bosting tyrie Commissionar* directed from the King, to craue a retractation of the approving of the Read of Ruthven, and a condamnator and excommu-nication of the noble men conveined at Striling ; bot the graitest part of the

* My Lord Litle Justice, Mr Johne Grahani

breithring departed, and fie as remeaned refufed to hald an Affemblie, and fa fuffered the fam to defeit. I haid then bathe the comfort and difconfort to haifl Mr James Lawfone to be my gheft : To haiff the man to whom, for his grait affection, I was mikle addetted, and wha was cheiff for lerning, holines, powar in doctrine, and all guid vertues amangs the haill miniftere, in my hous interteaned the beft I could, it was a grait comfort and ioy to me : bot to fie him in fic perplexitie, forow, and melancholie, it wald hauff grievit the hart of ame wha loued the caufe of Chryft.

The King, with his forces, coming to Stirling, the town receaves him obedienthe. The Caftle nocht being funefit, was fean to rander, luking for ther lyves, bot gat na grace   The Erle of Gowrie, apprehendit in Dondie a whyll befor, is brought to Stirling, and ther beheadht

About the beginning of May, I was compellit throw neceffitie, bathe of the furnefing of the foundat perfones in the Collage, and my awin famelie, to tak iorney athort Angus and Merns, whar the Collage leiving lyes, and gather in the rent dew to the Collage.   In this mean tyme, the Bifchope is retourned from his embaffage. A Parliament is keipit at Edinbruche, in the quhilk lawes is fett down for reftraining of the fre pretching of the Word, and owerthraw of the haill eftabliffed difcipline of the Kirk ; and that of fpeciall purpofe to be fnares to tak the fathfull minifters in, for do what they could, they fould nocht efchape ather treaffone againft Chryft or the King   For preatching frihe the treuthe, they fould fall vnder the danger of thefe lawes ; and keiping fylence, or pretching to the pleafour of men, they fould betrey the caufe of Chryft   Thefe lawes ar promulgat at the Mercat Cros of Edinbruche, and wowes maid be Captean James, the Chancellar, and cheiff hand of that cours, that giff Mr James Lawfones head war als grait as a hay ftak, he fould caufe it lope from his haufe. The quhilk, when Mr James perceavit, he advys of his breithring of the Prefbyterie, and of the beft of his flok, and godlie barones and gentlemen about, with his brother and coleag, Mr Walter Balcanquall, withdrew himfelff fecrethe from Edinbruche, and paft in Eingland   Bot befor they paft, Mr Robert Roul, accompanied with Mr Walter Balcanquall, and certean of the breithring, cam to the Mercat Cros at the verie publication of the Actes of Parliament, and tuk publict documents, that they protefted againft the faid Actes, (fa far as twitched the Kirk,) in the nam of the Kirk of Scotland, &c.

Returning from Angus, all thir newes is tauld me, and that the bruit was, that I was away with the reft ; whowbeit, indeid, as yit it cam na wayes in my mynd to leaue the Collage, bot was refoluit to be fund ther when euer it pleafit God to vifit me   Sa the Sabbathe efter my ham coming. I went to the Kirk, and efter noone my vncle Roger, knawing fordar nor I did, comes ower from Donche, and finding a frind of his in St Andros, tauld him that the Bifchope was coming hame with a commiffion to tak me ; and therfor befought him nocht to leaue me till I aggreit to go ower to Donche with him. Sa he delt with Mr Robert Bruce and vthers my frinds, and importuned me fa, that it behoued me to go with him, as I did that night to Donche   The newes that comes to me the morn was, that the Bifchopes men, with the Magiftrats, haid bem cerfing the Collage and my hous for me. and haid fought out all my lettrones and wryttes ; and that my dittay was allready macted. interteining of intelligence with my vncle. the Kings rebell, &c.

Sa feiking refolution can fulhe of my God what to do, a cufing of my awin name, of his awin frie motion and accord, offerit to me, be the affiftance of God, to put me faiff in Bervik within twentie four houres be fie.   To this alfo my vncle Roger, and vther frinds, aggreit   Sa efter confultation with my God, and finding of his warrand in my hart, I concludit to go, albeit nocht without grait tentationes and mikle heavines ; yit on the part reioyfing, that God gaiff the hart to leaue natiue countrey, houfe, and fwent lowing new maried wyff, and all for the loue of him and his Chryft.   Thus my cufing being a mariner, conducit a bott to carie a town of his portage wyn about to Carell, and decking me vpe in his fie attyre betymes in the morning, about the fimmer folftice, tuk me in down vnder Donche as a fhipbroken fie man ; and rowing about, behouit to go to the heavin of St Andros, to los a certean of fkleatt fteanes, and becaufe it was law water, we behoued to ly a whyll in the road till the water grew, whare the bott wanting ane owerlaft, the feall was caffen ower hir ta end, and ther I leyed vpe, left I fould be fpyed of fum fhipes rydding befyde. Bot within fhort fpace, parthe be rokking in the fie, and parthe for want of eare, I grew fa extream feik, that mane a tyme I befaught my cowfing to fett me a land, fchofin rather ane fort of dethe for a guid caufe, nor fa to be tormented in a ftinking holl.   And yit, whowbeit it was extream peanfull, I gatt ther notable mediem of vomitine, quhilk was a preferuatiue to my helthe all that yeir   Sa coming haird to the fteppes of the Archbifchopes peare at St Andros, we loffit our fkleattes. and tuk in vmers, and rowit out agean immediathe, and cam that night to Pitmilhe burn mouthe, wher I gead a land, and repofit me in my fie abbat.   And efter offers of grait kyndnes be

the Lard, and fuinitour of a iubbei of ftaik Merche eall, betymes in the morning we rowit out about the Nes. The day was hat Ther was bot twa men
in the bott, by twa cufings of myne with myfelff : Of thefe twa we haid an at
our deuotion, the vthei was the awner of the bott, and veiie euill affected : bot
the hat rowing, and the ftope with the ftaik eall hard befyd him, maid him
atteans to keaue ower afhpe. And it pleafit God to fend a piettie puihe of
wound, wherby getting on a feall vpon hin, oi euei our fchippei waknied we
was a guid fpace befouthe the May : wha feing he could nocht mend himfelfl,
was fean to yeild and agrie with his meichant foi a hyie to Beivik. Bot being af and on with Dumbar, about ane eftei noon comes af the hilles of La-
mermuie age a giait mift, with a tempeftous fchoure and diow, quhilk, or we
could gett our fealles takhlt, did caft ws about, and, or my cufing was awar,
caiied ws bak almaift to the May, with fic a how wa and fpene diift, that the
bott being opin, he lukit foi grait danger gitt the ftoiniie fchoure haid continowed Bot the young man being veiie fkilfull and able ftarts to his kift,
and tuk out a compas, and finding ws contiare our couife, with mikle ado,
wanting helpe, and fchipping of mikle watei, he cuft about and pykit on the
wind, halding bathe the helme and fcheit, fufteining in the mean tyme euill
langage of the fchippai in ftead of helpe, till it pleafit God meicitullie to luik
vpon ws, and within an houie and an halff to diyve away the fchoure and
calme the diow, fa that it fell downe dead calme about the fun diawing leache.
To keipe the fie all might in an opin litle bott, it was dangerus, and to go to
Dumbar we durft nocht, fa of neceffitie we tuk ws towaid St Tabs Heid. Bot
we haifing but twa eaics, and the boat flaw and heavie, it was about alleavin
houres of the night or we could win ther, whowbeit, na man was ydle, yea,
I iowit myfelff till the hyd cam af my fingais, mair acquented with the pen
nor working on an aie Coming vndei the crag, we rowit in within a prettie
lytle holl betwix the mean and the head, whaie eafehe going a land, we re-
fiefchit ws with cauld watei and wyne ; and ietuining to our boot, fleipit the
dead of the night, bot neidit nan to wakin ws, for foone be the day light pi-
ped, ther was fic a noyfe of foulles on the ciag, and about ws, becaufe of thair
young annes that we war almaift pieffed to lainche out. Now we haid Caw-
dingham bay and Hay mouth to pas by, and that but flawhe rowing be the
land, whai was the iefidence of Alexander Houie of Manderfton, an of our
cheiff confederat enemies, and wha baid inteicepted a boot of the Eile of Angus coming about from Tamtallou to Beivik nocht long befor. This put ws
in grait feir ; but our guid God gardit ws, making a fweit thik mift till aiyfe,

wherby we might bot fkaifhe gis at the fight of the land, and therfia nane could fie ws.   Sa we cam on hulie and fear till we wan within the bounds of Beivik, whar we was in graiteft danger of all vnbefett in the mift be twa or thrie of the cobles of Beivik, quhilk war fa fwift in rowing, that they ged round about ws; bot we being tyve within burd, and haiffing twa piftolets, with thrie fwords, and they na armour, they were fean to let ws be, namlie when they vnderftud that we was making for Bervik.

Thus gratiuflie protected be my guid God, I cam to Bervik, whar I fand Mr James Lawfone and Mr Walter Balcauquall, my vncle Mr Andro, Mr Patrik Forbes, appeirand of Cois, and fum vther gentlemen, but twa dayes befor entred in their iorney fouthe ower. And Mr James, with his colleg, war evin vpon thair voyage to follow, as they did within thrie or four dayes, acquenting me with thair frinds, and leaving me in than rowm to pretche in the Kirk, as I was defyiit.

Being in Beivik, I remembeit the fweit tender haited young las that I haid maried, and thinking our burding was nocht yit giait, nathei knew I that fche was with chyld, I refolued with my God to fend for hir, and tak fic part togidder as it fould pleis his guidnes to beftow.   And fa fatiffeing the botmen to thair contentment, I fend bak with tham my cufing, Mr Alexander Scrymgeour (being then bot a fchollar, and now a man of guid giftes and eftimation in the miniftene,) with a letter to my wyff, wha, cafting all things afyde, cam to me with diligence, be the conduct of a fervant of the Einghs Ambaffatour, lying in Edinbruche for the tyme, and tuk part with me during all my foiouning in Emgland, to my giait confort. My cowfing, James Melvill, returned nocht bak to Scotland, bot tareid in Emgland, and occupied his calling ther all the tyme of our exyll.   I tareid at Beivik about a monethe, and teatched twyfe eune ouk, wherby I gat verie giait freindfchipe, namlie of a maift cuiteus and godlie lady, my Lady Widdringtoun, fpoufe to Sir Harie Widdringtoun, Knight, and Maifter Governour of the town, vnder my Lord of Houndesdean, wha defieyed me of all my charges during the tyme I was ther, and offerit me ten crownes of gold at my paiting, bot I haid na neid of tham, and therfor refufit tham thankfulhe.   I haid alfo offered me, be diuers guid men and weimen of the town, bot haiffing of the bountifull liberaltie of my God aneuche brought with my wyff, I wald nocht meur ame likhhead of a mercenar; bot trewlie I fand fic fectfull profeffioun of trew Chriftianitie in Bervik, as I haid nevei fein the lyk in Scotland.

Efter rype and lang advyfinent with my God, I refolued to tak iorney futhe owei, and as God fould call me to anie condition to teatche a fcholl, and theiwithe keipe the mouthe quhilk he haid opened, in catecheifing and pretching of Chryft occupied, till thefe afflictiones war paft in Scotland, quhilk I luiked nocht indeid fould haiff bein quartei fa fchort as they war

In the mean tyme, the Erles of Angus and Mar. lyand at Newcaftell, wryttes for me ans, and the fecond tyme veiie inftanthe, to com and pretche the Word vnto tham foi thair comfoit. To whom I anfwerit I could nocht, becaufe I was nocht entered in the miniftene ; nathei was I of anie experience of knawlage in ther maters, being but a young man biought vpe in the fcholles, and therfor haid refolued to keipe my awin calling. The tieuthe was alfo, that my hait abhoirit and feant to haiff to do with thame, being the Kings rebelles, and nocht knawing ther caufe weill, and difpotition of thei hart.

Yit 1 could nocht bot vifit tham in my ioiney at Newcaftell, wher I purpofed to tak fchipping fouthwait to London. Sa paiting from Bervik, harthe iecommendit to the bleffing and grace of God, be manie godhe men and women, and be him fett and convoyet a gind way on our iorney, we cam that night to Anweik, and ludgit in the houfe of a weidow, whofe fone in law, gind man of the hous, was lyand feik of manie deadhe wounds, giffen him be the Scottes theives on the Boidar : And yit we ieceavit never an euill countenance of them, bot be the contiar war veiie weill treated, and ieafouabhe, and at our departing, gat bathe fiom the auld woman and hir douchtar manie bleffings

Comming the nixt night to Newcaftell, we refoluit on the moin incontinent to feik foi fhipping, and na wayes maid anie lang taieing, a piece of dewtie annes difchargit to the noble men   Bot Mr Jhone Dauidfone, being ther with the Lords, infoimes me fa in all maters, yea, and being my Maifter in St Andros, and a man of authoritie in the Word and Spreit of God, and namhe fchawing me it was nocht his indgment onhe, but of the haill breithring that haid paft by, that I fould abyd with the noble men, exerceifing tham in the Word of God, till that ather they all, oi fum of tham at leaft, fould ieturne bak agame, biakes me from my purpofe and refolution, that at the eineft delhng of the Loids, and clening of thair caufe, purpofe, and confeience vnto me for that effect, I yeildit till abyde with tham.

Thus finding the warrand of God fattelit in my hart, efter diueis dayes deliberation and eineft prayer, I followed the fam   And foone efter Mr Jhone Dauidfones paffing away, wha haid bein deteined be tham onhe to abyde my coming and enter me, thinking it beft to fett down the ordou meit to be

keipit amangs tham at the beginning, I put the fam in wryt with ane exhortation, direction, and fathfull warning prefixed, as followes :

To the right godlie, zealus, and noble, my Lords of Anguis and Marie, the Master of
Glammes, and other noble and gentle men in companie with tham at this
prefent in Newcaftle, in England, your honors moft humble Minifters
and fervants in the Lord, wifheth grace and peace from God
the Father, and from the Lord Jefus Chryft

Forsamikle as at the erneft defyre of your godlie and noble honors, and the apointment of
the reft of our breithring, confirming that inwart calling whilk we haift of God in our harts, we ar
placed hen to ferne your lordfchips and your companie in the minifterie of the Word of God in a
tym fa neceffar Lyk as in maift tender lone and affection we ceafe nocht in our exhortationes to
put yow in mynd of all things, according as the occafion of the portion of Scripture intreated offers. Sa we haift thought it expedient, for the mair faithfull ditcharging of our dewtie and confcience
befor God and his Kirk, fchort he in wryt to call to your continuall remembrance fome fpeciall
things, the diligent confideration and often meditating wharof may ferue grathe to the furtherance
of the wark of God put in your weak hands

It behoued ws firft, in verie deid, till acknawlage in our confciences, and confes, as the treuthe
is, that the Lord hes maift ruifhe, and yit in grait mercie, corrected ws, nocht onlie for vther our
manifald finnes and offences, be the quhilk we haift ftrayed away from him, to bring ws hame again
be his rod of humiliation, to the fauld and obedience of that guid Paftor of our fuilles, the Lord
Jefus, therby making ws to feill and perceaue in experience the fatherlie cear quhilk he hathe of
ws, in chafterfing ws as his awin deire childring, but alfo, and maift fpecialhe at this tyme, for
over lightlie regarding, and negligenthe vfing, the occafiones offered, of performing the guid wark of
the Lord, quhilk we haid in our hands. For nather at that tyme, as becam ws vprightlie, was the
glorie of God fought, nather yit afauldlie and ardenthe was procured the preferuation advancement, and further eftablifment of his Kirk, the kingdome of his Sone Chryft Jefus, fa notablie of
his grait mercie planted within our countrey, but then as now brought in extream danger, be craftie
and wicked Papifts. Nather was the Kings perfone and efteat diligenthe gardit from pernitius
flatterars, carnall Atheiftes, feditius and bludie idolaters, licentius libertines, filthie harlotes, hel-
lifhe witches, and fie vther duehthe counfallours, as ceaffed nocht to nurifhe and flen vpe the poifone quhilk they had inftilled in his voung and tender breift Nather was ther maid anie redres of
the innumerable abbufes and mifordours croppen in within the body of our miferable comoun
welthe. But contrare wayes, fum haifting na thing bot the Word of Gods glorie in than mouthe,
lacked all loue and defyre therof in the hart, the quhilk appered plainlie in than warks and proceidings, to the difhonour of God, and fklander of his guid caufe. Sum thought it a fmall mater
to flatter the King in all his conceattes and affectiones, and mak his eares patent to fie wha could
alienat his mynd from the guid caufe and inftruments therof, and hald his hart and fauour bund
and bent to the former faction of the enemies, and than vngodlie courtes Some regarding nought
at all bot than awin ftanding and guid efteat wardlie, as though ther haid beine na thing in hand
but a comoun alteration and change of Court, played prettelie the part of Jak on bathe the fydes
The compleants, greiffes, and petitiones of the Kirk was hard, but with deaft eares, and lurked on

Q

with winking ers, in sic sort, that the King now triumphes in that pointt, affirming with manie at-
testationes and aithes, that never annes was mount to him be the nobiltie a word of the Kirks effeares Na remeid nor redres for sacrilage, wherwithe the grattest part was defylt, no provi-
sion for the ministerie, scholles, and pure, no ministration of Justice, nor punithement for maist
odius and horrible crymes, quhilk aboundit in euerie quarter of the countrey, and synahe, all was
find to haist focht thin awin particulars, becaufe na better appeired in deid.

And yit nochtwithstanding thir our great sinnes, quhilk, gift God wald enter in judgment to pu-
nishe, mght deferue a thowsand tauld man nor he hes yit leyde on ws, yea, the verie helles fyre,
we may be weill atimed, if we be rightlie humblit and vntemedhe turned to him with all our harts,
with deliberat, ardent mynds and willes, to trauell till amend all thir misses, in cais God again ans
in his mercie fall offer the occation, that of his superaboundant grace wathing away all our iniqui-
ties in the blood of his Sone Chryst Jesus, he will, for the glorie of his awin name, and that com-
passion quhilk he hes ever haid of his awin deir childring, luik vpon the oppression of his awin Kirk,
and the miserie of that pure afflicted nation and realme.

For trenthe it is, when we luik at our awin deseruing, we can find na thing but mater of mere
desperation But I pray yow, what hes the glorie of the Lord deseruit, that is trode vnder tutt be
these wicked instruments of Sathan, wha, without all schame and teir of Gods iudgments, hes bein
sa bauld as to place a vanishing scheddow, a breathe going and nocht retourning again, with absolut powar and authoritie in the roum and seatt of the most hie God? What hes the kingdome of
the Lord Jesus and libertie therof, merited? The quhilk by vyle dogs turning to thair vomit, and
filthie swyne waltring in the toull pudle of thair abominnable vyces and corruptiones, is polluted,
defylt, and led schamfulhe captiue to the slauerie of the corrupt and cancered affectiones of profean Jeroboams, that hes gean about with knawladge againtt consceuce to force the trew worschip-
ping of God, sett down and stablished with all triedome, liberties and primledges of the Word, in
his awin Sanctuarie at Jerusalem, as a captiue slaue to serue to be a pernitius kynd of government
as thair vndantoned breanes and vnbrydelt affectionnes hes against all prietie, iustice, and honestie,
blasphemulie forgit and impudentlie obtrudit to God, and the Kings faithfull and obedient subiects.
Wha hes pulled away the ordinarie sacrifices of contreit and brokin harts for repentance, the
peace offerings for remission of sinnes and reconciliation, and oblation of the calues, of the lippes for
ioy of conscience and thanksgiffing of the peiple of God, from Chryst Jesus, the hohe altar of the
Lord placed in the middes of his Kirk, as in Mount Sion, and hes tyed the sam to thair newhe
erected goldin calffes and abominationnes of Bischopes seattes, and residence of court, as in Dan
and Bethell Wha haithe ruggit away, but wisdome or reasoning, the administration and government
of the Lords Tempell from his lawfulhe called Ministers, Doctores, Eldars, and Deacones, to the
quhilks onhe be the Word of God, it is giften as to his schosme Leuittes, and anointed Priests of the
childring of Aaron and be plain law hes applyed the sam to thair bellgodes, fals priests of Baal,
maist infamus amangs the peiple, theists, drunkards, gluttones, whure and witch mungars, periurit,
sacrilegius, deboushit persones, to mean holyglasses, comoun trickers and deceaners, and finalie, men
shamles, and maist sklanderus in all thair lyfl and doings And all becaufe, say they with Jeroboam,
the sone of Nobat, wha maid Israell to sin, vtherwayes our kingdome can nocht stand, our courfe
can nocht go fordwart, for the peiple will go to Jerusalem, they will adheire to the hous of Dauid, they wilbe instructed be the priests of the leiving God, wha can nocht comport with our
doing

They haist pulled the Croun of Royall Authoritie within the spirituall kingdome, and thrawin the fword of the Word of God, and fchepter of ecclefiaticall government, af the head, and from the hands of Chryft Jefus the onlie head and King of his Kirk. And fa, with open found of trumpet calling down, fa far as in tham lay, the eternall Sone of God King immortall of heavinlie glorie, from his throne, wherout of he rewlethe his Kirk hes placed in his fteade a chyld of corrupt Adam, even an erthlie mortall creatoure. They haiff followed the fullthe exemple of Achaz the King of Juda, and Uria the preift, in removing of the brafen altar of the Lord and placing in the roum therof an vther, according to the form of the altar of Damafcus. They haiff followed the pervers dealling of the curfed apoftat Julian againft the Kirk of Chryft, in taking away the levings from the Minifters to deftroy tham be houngar,—man crewelly nor Diocletian, wha cuft the Chriftianes to wyld beaftes,—and making wafte and defolat the fcholles of Divinitie and all holie eruditiontioun. They haiff faid with the foy and defperat Jewes to the Sters, "Sie noit" and to the Prophets "Prophefie na langer to ws in the nam of the Lord, but fpeak vnto ws pleafand things according to our lyking." And, whilles the faithfull fervantes of the Lord, in love of thair amendement and fervent zeall of the glorie of God difchaiged trule thair commiffiones, receaued of the Lord vnto tham, they haiff forced tham, for fear of thair lyves, to flie and abandone thair natiue countrey with crewall Jezabell, cuft tham in preffoure with wicked Achab, and thretned tham with death, as did foolithe Amazia, when the Lord haid taken counfall to deftroy him. They haiff plucked the keyes of the kingdom of Heavin from the trew Apoftles of Chryft, and giffen tham to the wicked Pharifies, his enemies, wha nather will enter in thamfelues, nor fuffer vthers till enter. And finalie, they haiff caft down the dyk, cutted the hedge, demolithed the toure, brokin the wynepres, banithed the watchmen and laboraris, the fredders and delvers of the wyneyeard of the Lord, to mak it to be trumped vnder fute of wyld Atheifts, yea, an opin prey to the bloodie and crewall locufts of the botomles pit.

Can the Lord fuffer thefe things lang, and be nift in executing of his iudgments, and paring out of his plages vpon his curfed enemies? Can the Lord fuffer his Sanctuarie to be defyld, and his awin to fmart, and be the Father of Mercies, God of Confolation, and maift faithfull keipar of his promifes? Can the Lord fuffer his glorie to be giffen to an vther? Can He, wha hathe promifed to mak the enemies of Chryft Jefus his futtfool, fuffer tham to tread on his head?

Na, na! right honourable and den breathing, he hes anointed him King on his holie montean, he hes giffen him all nationes for an inheritance, he hes put in his hand a fchepter of yron to brufe in poudre thefe erthen vefhalles. When his wrothe fall annes begin to kendle bot a lytle he fall mak it notortiuflie knawin till all the warld, that they onlie ar happie wha in humilitie kiffes the Lord Jefus and truifts in him. Now, therfor, feing the Lord hes maid your lordfchipes to haift thefe places and rowmes be in the within your natiue countrey, wher throw it lyes on your fhoulders of fpeciall dewtie, wherof yie fall giff a compt to God, to procure and feik to the vttermaift of your powar the releifl, delyverance, and weil of your naturall nation and Prince lying this day in fa pitius efteat of captiuitie,—and feing, in lyk maner, it hes pleafed the Lord of his guidnes to call vow to be his gude inftruments in this maift acceptable wark of vindicating of his glorie defaced, and delyverie of his Kirk, brought in fa miferable boundage, as alfo of the reclaming of your natiue King from fa dangerus a companie and courfe,—and feing yow haift alfo, ance or twyfe, employed yourfelff in the caufe, but for the iuft reafones befor reherfed, and multitud of our fecret finnes, wherwith the Lord hathe bein hihie offendit, it hes nocht as yit haid an expected fuccefs and vit, as becomes valiant warriours and capteanes of the Lords armie, ar nocht difcuragit, but purpofes, efter trew humiliation and affurance of Gods mercie and fauour, to go fordwart,—we, your Ministers in the fen and nam of the Lord our God, and in loue and reuerence of your honours, defyre thir prefentes to be a witnes and teftimonie befor God and his Kirk, of the faithfull difcharge of our confcience and dewtie towards yow, exhorting yow maift erneftlie

By the Lord our God, and his Sone Chryft Jefus, that withe trew repentance, internyit humiliation, reformation of lyff and maners, inftruction and welcdome of the Buk of God, ardent prayer and meditation, feruent loue and zeall toward God, his Kirk, and your King, yie fall frache and curaguiflie to the wark of God, and, following furthe the fam directlie, vprightlie, faithfullie, conftantlie, and with all can and diligence fearing alwayes that wa, quhilk the Prophet pronunces againft hie as does the wark of the Lord negligentlie and deceitfullie, yow may yit hope for a happie fucces of the mercie and bleffing of God, for his awin glorie and names fak   Yie fie the enemies never ceaffes to denyte, dehberat, reafone, tak countall and put in execution thair malice and crewcltie againft the Kirk of God, his treuthe and profeffours therof, whow grathe then fould we be efchamed to be found flipperie and flaw in the guid cauie of our Chryft

Bot this a thing in fpeciall we man denunce vnto yow, taking God, his Kirk and yom felues to record, that we forwarn you, faithfullie, and in tyme, That in cais (as God forbid) yie ga to this wark againe, mooued cheiflie with your awin particulars, as vengeance on your enemies and to be reftored to fic honours rowmes poffeffionnes, and commodities quhilk yie moyed of befor making Gods glorie the caufe of his Kirk, of your King and Comoun weill, to be bot pretences and fkugges, and as bot flaues and guidates feruing therunto ather the Lord fall curfe the wark in your wicked hands and mak it turn to your grattar fchame and difaduantage then of befor, or, in ceas for his awin names feak, he work the wark of his glorie in mercie for deliverance of his Kirk, (as he is accuftomed to do with maift rouftie and crooked inftruments and dellings,) vit will he nocht feall in his inftice to reward yow with the corrupt and hypocriticall workers of iniquitie, at fic tyme thereafter as he thinks conuenient   Bot in ceas (as we hope weill and calles to God maift ardenthe that fa may be) efter trew repentance and effectuall reformation of yourfelfis and companies, yie go to wark, fetting directlie befor your eis the honour and glorie of God, according to his will, framing your willes and affectiones vnto the fam, and fa vprightlie, trewlie and zealouflie, be all guid meanes and waves feik God to be glorified, his Kirk to be deliverit, reformed, and trulie eftablifhed, your tender King, and fweit natiue countrey, to be reddie from the abbufes and mifeulares of the fam, and mak your awin particulars to follow efter, as the feruant and theddow, and nocht go befor as the maifter and body, and be maift willing and erneft to fchaw the fam, in effect when God fall offer the occafion.   And finalie, if yie go to with vpright delibrat mynds and bent willes till amend all things neglected of befor, then we dar be bauld, be the warrand of the Word of God, till affure yow of the prefence and blefing of God to be withe yow, and vndoutedlie to perform the wark in your hands, whow weak that euer they be and whow manie, craftie and puiffant to euer they be, that geanitands the fam, to his awin glorie, the grait confort of his Kirk, and your honour and weilfear, nocht onlie temporall, but perpetuall and euerlafting.

And to that intent, that maters may this wayes happlie proceid, we ar in conclufion maift erneftlie and lowinglie, in the bowelles of Chryft Jefus, to exhort you and all your companie, that in the mean tym, whill as occafion of bodelie exercife in the mater is nocht vit offered, that yie gift yourfelues diligentlie and feruenthe to fpirituall exerceis, in hering, reiding, and meditating continowalie of the Word of God, wherby yie may be mooued to vnfeinved repentance, trew humiliation, amendment of lyff, and deuot and ardent prayer to the Lord, for his grace mercie, and fauour, and for the working of his powerfull Spreit in yow, yie may out of the Word of God, as out of the fontean and thereaffor of all wesdome draw out sic store and aboundance of all guid knawlage, wesdome, and wholsome counsall, as may direct yow alwayes aright, and wharby yie may find strenthe, courage, comfort, patience, hope, and perseverance in all your battels, bathe within and without, to the end, and assure victorie and glorie in the end

For the quhilk caufe, we haist sett down to your lordsehips and companie the order, bathe of doctrin and discipline, quhilk aucht to be obserut in effect in all the companies and fellowschippes of the faithfull but specialie with all reverence and can be ws now in this present esteat, wharby we ourselues may be marmed prepared, and maid fitt in all things for the wark of God, the enemies hering of it, difuragit, and sie as loued God and his guid caufe, prouocked be our exemple, be moued to praise God, and baldlie ioyne themselues with ws, being persuadit that we seik vnfenedlie the Lord

The leiving God of heavin and eirthe, in the tender loue and mercies of his Sone Chryst Jesus, mak his guid Spreit to dwell sa plentiouslie in your noble harts, that yie may be fund worthie and notable instruments of his glorie, bathe in this and all vther guid warks of the Lord God, and that nocht onlie at this tyme, but enduring the haill course and tyme of your lyves, that efter all the battels of this present miserie, yie may inioy with him that everlasting croun of glorie, quhilk he hes leyde vpe in store for all his faithfull servands and valiant warriours   AMEN.

At Newcastell, the 2 of August, 1584

The Order and Maner of Exerceife of the Word for Instruction, and Discipline for Correction of Maners, vsed in the Companie of thofe Godlie and Noble Men of Scotland, in tyme of thair aboad in Englands, for the quid caufe of Gods Kirk, thair King and Countrey.

FIRST, ther shalbe four sermones in the ouk   twa on the Sonday, and twa on the ouk dayes, ane befor noone, and an vther efter, on the Sabothe   and, on the ouk dayes, an on Wedinsday, and an vther on Fredday.

The sermont on the Sabbathe sall begin at halff houre befor ten, and continow whill efter alleavin, sa that the haill exerceise sall nocht pas the space of ane houre and a halff, and efter noone it sall begin at halff houre to four, and end befor fyve

The sermones on the ouk dayes sall begin at ten houres, and be endit be alleavin, sa that the haill exerceise pas nocht the space of an houre.

Ther salbe daylie comoun prayers twyse euerie day, before noone at ten homes, and efter at foure, at quhilk tyme a Psalme salbe read and handlit, sa that the roum therof be schorthe gathered, the partes sett doun in ordour, and some schort notes of doctrine, with exhortation, bot in sie schortnes, that the haill tyme occupied exceid nocht the space of an halff houre

Ther salbe at euerie meall, immediathe efter thanksgiffing at denner and supper, a chapter read of the historie of the Bible, and handlit schorthe as tyme and occasion sall requyre, and thereffer a Psalme, or reasonable lection therof, being lang salbe soung.

Ther salbe a ouk in the monethe dedicat till abstinence and publict humiliation, spent in prayer doctrine, meditation with sic modest, temperat, and humble behauiour as effeires, the order wharof salbe obserut according to the prescript of the buik of fast and publict humiliation vsed in the Kirk of Scotland, wherof the present caufses salbe the miserable esteat of our Kirk and countrey of Scotland, and, amangs the rest of the Kirks in Europe, of France and Flanders.

At the quhilk tyme, vpon the laſt Sabbathe of the ouk immediathe following the exerceiſe of faſting, the Super of the Lord ſalbe miniſtrat, efter that niſt tryell and examination haid paſſed befor

On the Satterday, at the houre of euening prayer, or the Sabathe, at efter noon, or bathe, ſalbe a lecture, or plean leaſone in the Catechiſme, and principall grounds of Chriſtian religion

The Miniſters, according as they fall agrie amang thamſelues, ſall haiſt there ordinarie Texts out of the cheiſt partes of the Scripture, ſom of the Law, ſum of the Prophetes, ſome of the Euange-liſts and Actes of the Apoſtles, and ſome of the Epiſtles and Reuelation And the ordinar exer-ceiſe at prayers and mealles ſalbe in the Pſalmes Salomones Warks, and Hiſtorie of the Auld Teſtament

Euerie an in ſpeciall is erneſthe exhorted to his priuat exerceiſe of feruent prayer reiding and meditation of things haird and read. that therby he may be fleued vpe to grow, day by day, man and man zealus and deuot in ſpreit, familiar with his God armed with ſpirituall armour againſt all aduerſitie, and diligenthe moued to practiſe of doctrine in a godhe lyſt and hahe conuerſation And this mikle for the exerceis of doctrin and prayer, for the quhilk it is neceſſar that euerie an that can reid haiſt a Byble and Pſalme Buik.

Of Diſcipline

Ther ſalbe a day in the ouk, Tuſiday or Turiſday a Convention of ſic as ſalbe choſin Eldars and Deacones, for ordering of all things perteining to the comlie maner of all exerceiſes of the Kirk, and all vther things neceſſar to a hohe Chriſtian congregation. And namlie to watche ouer the maners of thamſelues and the reſt and ſpy out the tructes of the Word in all behauiour, and giff anie opin vyces and ſklanders talk out in the perſones of anie man, to bring that perſone to re-pentance and redres, and remoue the ſklander from the companie, as alſo to haiſt a can of the ſeik and diſeaſed, pure and indigent

Ther ſalbe then ſax Eldars choſin and ordourlie callit to that office, quhilk conſiſtes ſpeciahe in cenſuring and oweriſing of maners, and rebuking in priuat of all ſic as behaues thamſelues in ſpeaking, doing geſtoure, or vther wayes, then it becomes hohe and faithfull Chriſtianes And in ceas of na amendment, efter twa or thrie admonitiones, or publict offence or ſklander inſewing, to deleat them to the Aſſemblie or Seſſion, wherby they may be brought to repentance and mak publict ſatiſfaction

Ther ſalbe twa Deacones an till attend vpon the box, that ſall ſtand on the table at euerie meal, to collect and diſtribut to the outward puir that ar nocht of our nomber, ane vther to haiſt the can of our awin inward indigent or diſeaſed, to recommend tham to the Seſſion for prayer, or collection to be maid for reheſt of ther neceſſitie

Gift in the audience of an Eldar, ather at meat, play. or elſwhare, a gentilman ſall nam the De-uill banning pronunce an athe, filthie talk, or anie euill fauored ſpeiche, the Eldar ſall cauſe him pey to the box and in cais of diſobedience deleat him to the Seſſion And gift a fallow or lad be fund with ſic ſpeiches as faid is, or anie wayes making noyſe or moleſtation, the Eldar ſall ather correct him preſenthe or deleat him to his maiſter, wha, gift he correct him nocht conuenienthe to his fault he ſalbe cenſured be the Seſſion

All, bathe maiſter, ſeruant, and boy, ſalbe preſent at all the exerceiſes of the Word and Prayer, except ſic as ſalbe occupied efter meals. abſent from Chapter and Pſalme, and the Eldars oukhe, thair tyme about, with ane of the Miniſters, ſalbe ſpeciall inſpectors and notars of the abſents, wha falbe for the firſt fault cauſed pey to the box ſax pence, for the ſecond, a ſchilling, and, for the thrid, ſummoned befor the Seſſion, and cauſit mak publict repentance.

Iff an haiſt a neceſſar earand to do, wherby it behouethe him to be abſent, let him aduertiſe ane of the Miniſters or Eldars, and he ſalbe excuſit.

The Miniſters, Eldars, and Deacones, ſhall haiff in wryt the names of all the companie, an and vther, for the effect forſaid.

The reſt, referring to farther deliberation and to be concludit and ſet down be comoun advys, as tyme and occaſion ſall miniſter mater.

FINIS.

This exhortation, warning, and direction, with the ordour of exerceiſe of Doctrine, Prayer, and Diſcipline, being preſented to the noble men, they accepted verie weill therof, and gaiff me grait thankes, and cauſing it to be notified to all thair companie, they ſubmitted themſelues harthe to the ordour, humblie embracing the admonition and direction. And ſa making choſe of our Eldars and Deacones we conſtitut a Seſſion, the noble men thamſelues being magiſtrats and ciuill rewlars, euerie an of ther awin companie, and togidder of the haill. And about the beginning of Auguſt, 1584, we entered to the practiſe and keiping of the order, wherin we continowed, by the grait grace of our merciful God, during the haill tyme of our ſoiourning in England, with ſic fruict of ſpiritual inſtruction, contort, and ioy, as bathe grait and ſmall thought it the happieſt tyme that euer they ſpent in all than lyff. Gud, godlie, wyſe, and ſtout Archbald, Erle of Angus, hes oft tymes ſaid to me, " Befoir my God, Mr James, giff the conſcience of the guid cauſe we haiff in hand moued me nocht, and giff I haid bot ſa unkle of my awin leiving as might bot in this maner ſuſtein ws, I wald be harthe content to ſpend all my lyff in this eſteat and forme.'

This noble man was tellon weill myndit, godlie, denot. wyſe, and graue ; and by and beſyde thir comoun exerceiſes, was giffen to reiding. and priuat prayer and meditation, and ordinarlie efter dinner and ſuper, haid an houres, and ſum tyme man nor twa houres, conference with me about all maters, namlie concerning our Kirk and Comoun weill ; what war the abbuſes therof, and whow they might be amendit. Wherof he was ſa carfull, that he cauſit me ſett tham down in wryt and preſent tham to him, being in companie with the reſt, quhilk, when he haid red himſelff and conferrit theron with tham, he cauſit wryt a copie in guid wrait, quhilk he put in a litle coffer, wharin his ſpeciall writtes and lettres war carried about with himſelff continualie, that he might haiff tham in memorie, and as occaſion ſervit, confer and reafone theron with his confortes : The quhilk, alfo, I thought nocht amifs heir to infert.

PSALME LXXXI

HEAR, O my peiple, and I will witnes vnto thie Ifrael, if thow will harken vnto my voice, if ther fall nocht be anie ftrange God amang yow, or fall nocht worfchipe anie vther God

I am the Lord thy God, wha brought thie out of the land of Egypt Open thy mouthe wyd, and I fall fill it

But my peiple wald nocht heir my voice, and Ifraell wa'd nocht obey me,

Wharfor I gaue them ower vnto thair awin harts luft, and lut them follow thair imagirationis

O thet my peiple wald haift harkned vnto me, if Ifraell wald haue walked in my wayes !

I fould foone put doun thair enemies, and turn my hand again thair aduerfaries

The haters of the Lord fould willinglie haif veildit vnto h m , and the gude extent of my peiple fould haiff indurit for euer

I fould hau fead tham alfo with the fynneft whait floure, and with the ftonie roks honie fould I haif filled thie

Certean grut Abbuffis and Corruptions in the Kirk and Comoun weill of Scotland, quhilk partlie the leat mifreulars hes brought in partlie as the hie places in Juda hes remeaned vnreformed vnto this day, giffen vpe to the noble men cryled in England to wey and confidder, that they might be repented for thair part, and indevor it to redrefs, when it fould pleafe God to grant abilitie and occafion At Newcaftell, 10 Auguft, 1584

JESVS CRYST the onlie King ot his Kirk, withe the libertie and fredome of his fpirituall kingdome in preatching of the Word, and exerceifing of Difcipline, is brought lathe in maift abominable flauerie to the corrupt affectiones of fleſche and blude

For, what as Chryft aucht onlie to command and bear rewll in the Kirk be his Word and Spreit, and be the minnifrie of his lawfulhe called othcrais and feruants, to whom he hes concredit the difpenfation of his heavinlie myf enes, the gydding and tending of his lambes, with the keyes of the kingdom of heavine, of binding and lowfing, the King takes vpon him to rewll and command alſweill in Chryfts fpirituall kingdome as in his awin crull, quhilk is maift facrilegius, and war nor Papifticall , and hes apointed, not feruands, but vnder lairds and commanders, whaſe authoritie and powar flowes nocht from Chryft or his Kirk, but from the King, (as the bull giffen to the Biſchope of St Androis planlie teftifies), and wha nocht onlie ai maift fklanderus perfones them-felues, bot alfo whaſe office hes na thing at all to do with the Scriptures of God, bot mere Anti-Chriftian, to tyrannife ower the Lords inheritance, and vex the bodies and confciences of Chryfts flok. And that quhilk is maift dangerus, and almaist defperat, this feitfull and horrible fpoliation of Chryft Jefus, and tyrannie ower his Kirk, is maid and confirmed be plan lawes in Parliament

Henby is the libertie of Gods Spirit bund in the mouthes of the preachouris, the gift and fredom of cutting and deuyding of the Word aright, and applying till euerie an than part as they haiff neid, without fpearing of the graitteft becauſe of graitteft neid, fa mikle commendit in the Storie and Wryttingis of the Apoftles reftrant and oppreft , the reanes of Difcipline, Excommunication with all the fpirituall cenfouris and correctiones of the Kirk, Election, Ordination, depriuation of

Minifters, apointing of Affemblies, and giffing of warning to the peiple to efchew plages be fafting and prayer, togidder with the haill government of the Hous of God, ar put in the hands of the Comt and than corrupt Bifchopes The quhilk of all vther hes maift neid of difcipline, wha, for than odius crymes, ar maift fubuert till excommunication and cenfors of the Kirk, wha hes nather fkill nor will to elect guid and qualefiet Paftors, wha ar readier and mair willing to depriue and put away the faithfull and edificatiue, nor the mercenar and fklanderus ; wha, fleiping in thair finnes, hes nocht waeryff eis to fie the plag coming, and therfor cares nocht for fafting and prayer, and finalie, wha being the cheiff corruptars and deformers of the Kirk, can nocht fuffer fие Affemblies to be haid for reformation and ordouring therof. The rentes and reuennes of the Kirk, the bread of the minifterie, fcholles, and pure, is giffen to dogs and fwyne, to the graitteft contemners, vex- ars, and oppreffars therof And, in a word, the hous of God is maid a den of theines, and the flockes of Chryft committed to hyrlings, whom the forfaid wolffs lies at thair deuotion

The haill body of the nation, and namlie the graitteft members therof, wha fould be gydders and guid exemples to vthers, ar defylt with facrilage, fwearing, blafphemie, blud, adulteries, reaf and oppreffion, &c., fa that na mervell it is tho the fleing buik of Gods iudgments enter in than houfles, and confume timber with flean

Lawes nather throwlie weill maid for punifhment of fic hynous crymes, and manie weill maid wantes execution, lyk athercape wobbes that taks the fillie flies, bot the bumbarts braks throw tham

Be the infatiable facrilegius auarice of Erles, Lords, and Gentlemen, the Kirk, Scholles, and Pure ar fpulveit of that quhilk fould fuftein tham The materiall Kirks lyes lyk fheipe and nout faulds rather then places of Chriftian congregationes to affemble into. The parochmars will haiff a couple of fkores of hirdes for than cattell, bot fkarfe a paftor to teid thrie thowfand of thair faulles. Whar- of cumes tenfull darknes of ignorance, fuperftition, and idolatrie, with innumerable filthie and exe- crable finnes, quhilk procures Gods mft advengance vpon the haill land

The fmall number that is of the minifterie, can haiff na certeantie of the pure ftipend affignet vnto tham, but yeuheit man be caft in the Lord Modifiers hands, and of new fchapin and affigned ower again, to fie whow mikle may be win in to the collector Of this comes that fic wha hes court and credit, and avaites theron, gets weill mikle, namlie giff they can comport and flatter vthers, and the beft gets nocht for than neceffitie

Ther is na promfiion maid for the pure reliefs and fatherles of the Minifterie. But nochtwith- ftanding than erneft, faithfull, and maift wakryff ceai over thair flockes, quhilk maid them to caft away all vther induftrie and vertew for warldlie prouifion to than wyffes and childring, they ar fuffered to beg and ly in miferie efter ther departour

The Scholles, and in fpeciall the Collage of Theologie, quhilk fould be the Seminarie of the Kirk and Minifterie, lenkes prouifion bathe for maifters and ftudents, for the haill rents therof ftanding in Teinds, ar fparpeled in findrie parts and provinces of the countrey, far from the Collage, and the gentilmen tenants, accuftomed to pay a fmall filuer dewtie, will na wayes grant till augment vncompellit be law, the quhilk the exception of omnium intereft fteyes from taking effect, fa that honeft, graue, and lernit men, fic as fould be the profeffours of Theologie, can nocht haiff thair neidfull and honeft inftentation. And as for ftudents, the childring of the grait and riche ar nocht defyrus of diuinitie The mid rank thinks it an vnthrift to beftow thair childrings berns part of geare in fuftening tham at the ftudie of Theologie, and when they haiff paft the courfe therof, to haiff na guid roum or moyen of lyff preparit for them in Kirk or Comoun weill. And as for the pure, quhilk ar comounlie beft griffen to that ftudie, and wharof comes maift fruict to the

R

Kuk of Chryſt, they haiff na thing to ſuſtein tham withe of thair awin, nather is ther prouiſion of burſars places for them; ſo that na mervell it is whowbeit ther be bathe grait raritie and ignorance amangs the Miniſterie. And in verie deid it is of the extraordinar beneſit of God that ther is ather lerning or religioun in Scotland, being therin nather fundationes or moyen to trean vpe ſchollars, nor honour and profit for ſie as hes attemed to lerning.

Of this comes it, that the guid ingyns, wharof na nation hes graitter ſtore nor ours, ather is applyed for neceſſitie to handie crafts and counting ſervice, or then gaes furthe of the Countrey, whar the graitteſt part is corrupted and abbuſit, and maid maiſt dangerus enemies to the Kuk and Eſteat of than countrey.

The Nobilitie and Gentlemen ar vnlerned them ſelffs, and takes na delyt to haiff than childring and frinds brought vpe in lettres, to the grait reprotche and ſchame of the Countrey, and thair awin grait hurt and diſhonour.

Ther is manie noble and gentilmen that hes prebendaries, alterages and vther rents and caſualities, be the quhilk they pleaſure ther ſervands and frinds in gifting them lytt rents therof. The quhilk, giff they war a lytle mendit, rightlie vſed, and maid burſſes in the Scholles of Philoſophie and Theologie, euerie noble man might haiff a ſeminarie of the youthe of thair awin frinds or ſervands within few yeirs weill inſtructed in guid letters, nocht onlie to ſerue themſelues in thair houſies, but alſo than vther frinds and haill peiple of thair lands and dominiones.

Dilapidators of than beneſices, and anuallers therof, from the right vſe, vnto thair wyffes childring and frinds, etter they are depoſit iuſtlie be the Kuk from the office, yit neuertheles, in diſpyt of God, the Kuk and guid ordour, the Prince and the Law makes him to poſſes the beneſice. And in ceas a houndrethe yeirs ſen ſyne, the laborars or factors haid peyit victuall or fourtie pennies money for the boll, giff they ſet it now in few or lang taks for fourtie pennies the boll, or change the victuall in ſiluer, it is nocht eſteimed diminution of the rentall. Albeit the treuthe be that fourtie pennies money now is diminiſhed in valour ſax fauld from that it was a hounder veir ſyne yea, that fourtie pennies growes now toward fourtie ſhillings, and the boll of victuall that was then bought for fourtie pennies will nocht be bought now, communibus annis, for ten tymes our fourtie pennies at this day. Yea, ſa hes the grait abbus growin, that in ceas the predeceſſour, being a waiſter of his beneſice, hes ſett lang takks and fewes with plean diminution, and alſo conteining nuſt cauſes of reduction, ther is na remeadie to be gottin altho the law be plan, becauſe Judges, Lawers, Lords and all is infected with the ſam ſeiknes, ſa that the remead falles amang impoſſibilities lyk the Hieland or Bordour theift.

The rents, lands and hevings of the Hoſpitalls, Almes houſies and Maſone Dieus, ar lyk wayes tean in few be gentilmen and burgeſſes for right nocht, in ſie ſort that thair buildings is alwhare deceyit, and than fundations loſt and aboliſhed.

The Pure, parthe for want of than awin patrimonie, and parthe for yeuhe increaſhng of thair number, be wrang and oppreſſion, goes throw the countrey in ſwarmes, war nor Turks or Infidelles, godles and lawles, without mariage, bapteſme, or knawlage of dewtie to God or man.

The Nobilitie neglects and caſtes af than publict callings, leiving nocht as ſie as ſould haiff a ſpeciall cair and charge of thair Countrey and Comoun weill, and whom God hes callit to be counfallours to than King, fathers of the peiple, and defendars and meantemers of his Kuk in this cleir light of the Goſpell, for the quhilk calling Chryſt ſall a day call them till acompt, bot rather as privat men, thinking it aneuche to keipe that quhilk than fathers hes left tham, and tak thair paſtyme and pleaſur, or to conquerſe mair to thair childring, or to be redouted of than nibours, and pley the oppreſſours and bangſters, &c

As for the rewlling of the Comoun weill, hald in hand till execution of Justice, reforming and establishing of the Kirk, counsalling and assisting of than Prince to that purpose, they cair na mair therfore nor sa mikle as may be a pretence for than particulars. Sa that whar they sould be rewlars and halders of vthers in guid ordour and dewtie bathe in Knk, Court and Comoun weill, they ar becom degenerat slaues to Courteours, and corruptors of Judges, men of Law, and Kirk men, for bringing to pas manie vnniust and wrangfull turn, or to be suffert to sit at hame for thair eaise and pastyme, as thouche they war born for ther awin bellie lyk beasts. Wharof hes proceidit this misicheiffs following :

Ambassatours of Babel, Clyentes of the Pape, our Athalia and the Hous of Guis, and the Court of Spean protest Papists, hes bein and is suffert to carie away the Kings hart from the cheiff professiours and meanteiners of the Gospell, to rinne a cours direct against religion, weill of his Countrey, and standing of himselff in guid esteat of kinghe honour, bodie and saull. Sa that it is thought and spokin, that the vndewtifulnes and negligence of the Nobilitie hes indangerit and almaist lost that rare perle of sa notable expectation.

Debauscht men, godles flatterers, wha haid sauld themselues in body and consicience to do anie thing for warldhe preferment, was suffert till insinuat thamselues in the Kings fauour, wha withe violence, outtragius pryd, craft, talsed and flatterie, war meit to execut the plat leyed down be the Papists, and now, ingratfulhe indeid, und musthe vpon the part of men imployed to wrak than advancesars, bot in respect of God maist insthe to punisthe the owersight of the nobilitie. Yea, thair degenerat harts, wha ceasit nocht for purchasing of thair particulars to becom seruants and courters of flattering courteours, and permit the haill government of the Comoun weill to be cast lous and turn in tyrannie to thair iust deservit wrak in the end.

Of this hes sprung the absolut powar, whaibe as a monster never hard of in anie mist government, the haill priuileges of the thrie Esteates of the Realme is weakned and almost takin away. Be the quhilk Esteates, according to the louable custom of the Kingdome of Scotland, fra the beginning therof, all things with mature deliberation, fiie reasoning and votting, all things was done. And be the quhilk Kings passing than bounds to the wrak and oppression of the Comoun weill, war corrected and brought in ordour. In lyk maner the priuilages of Towns and Vniuersities, yea of the holie Kirke itselff, established be sa manie guid Rewlars and Parhaments, according to the Word of God, ar owerthrawin.

All the Judgments of the Realme, Secret Countall, Session, Justice Courts, Consistories, Scheriffs Courtes, Provost, Baillies and vthers, ar rewlit, nocht be law ciuill or municipall, right or reasone, *sed principis placitum legis habet rigorem.* It is the Kings will, for now Captean James, as Stratocles in Athens, hes maid a law "That whatsoever the King commands, that is halie towards God, and iust anents men."

From thence ar sa manie score of slauchters and murdours, hearschips and oppressiones, lying on the head of the King and bak of the Countrey, crying to the heauennes for iust vengeance from the righteus God, for as euerie an hes moyen at Court sa comes his mater to pas. And becaufe the Court is godles and wicked, the maist vngodlie and wicked finds the grattest moyen therin. Wharof it comes that the wicked thus triomphe, and the guid and godlie is oppressit and wracked ; sa that na meruell it is to sie the countrey thus plagged, yea whowbeit it sould vtterhe pearisthe in Gods righteus iudgments.

The Kings patrimonie and casualities ar gratthe hurt and abbusit, whilk causes nocht onhe his povertie, to the grait scham of the Countrey and hinderance of comoun warks, bot alfo sa monie intolerable taxationnes, exactiones and imposts to be maid vpon his subiects, to the tyring of thair harts, and wrak of the pure laborars, for Lords, Lairds, and Prelates exacts twyfe fa mikle from thair pure tenents vpon that occafion

Of the tormentioned papifticall courfe and this, comes fa manie forfaultries and banifment of the beft and maift noble men of the realme, felling of flauchters and blud, grait foumes of compofitiones exacted for na faults bot weill doing, the quhilk all of Gods iudgments turnes to mifcheifs, whill as be thn diuelithe feductors it is abufit to execut all kynd of violence againft the guid men of the land

The reft referring to your Lordfchips experience and wefdome, and to fie as hes graitter infight be yeirs and iudgment, I ceas nocht to pray God to gift your Lordfchips an vpright and conftant refolution to fie thir things fum day redreffit and amendit.

ZACHARIE I.

Thus fayes the Lord of hoftes,

Turn vnto me with all your harts,

And amend your euill wayes,

and I will turn vnto

yow, fayes the

Lord of

Hofts

Now becaufe amangs thefe hoirrible corruptiones, we haiff affirmed that quhilk wald feim incredible in a reformed and fattled efteat of a Kirk, That thefe monftruus infiewllars wald caufe the King tak vnto him to be the onlie Head and Monarche in the Kirk as in the Comoun weill: and that the cheiff rewlars of the Kirk, the Bifchopes, fould tak the authoritie and warrand of thair calling from him, (quhilk is pleane Popifh hierarchie, and is mikle wars, as the Pape is a bifchope, an ecclefiaftik perfone and officebearer, prouyding he and his Kirk war trew,) as indeid I could fkairflie a lang whyll beleiue my-felff that the Deuill durft fa foone and planlie vtter himfelff in Scotland, whill I gat the Actes of Parliament formentioned ; and efter diligent intreatie, a iuft copie of the Archbifchope of St Andros Bull cam in my hand, quhilk for the warrand of fa hiche alleageance it behoued me to heir till infert.

A Copie of the Bull quhilk the Archbifchope of St Andros gat of the King as
Supream Gouernour of the Kirk, wherby he has powar and authoritie
to vfe his Archepifcopall office within the Kirk and his Dioeefe.

OUR SOUERAN LORD, with advys and confent of the Lords of his Hienes Priuie Counfall, ordeanes a Letter to be maid vnder the Grait Seall in dew form, geuand, grantand to his weilbelouit Clerk and Orator Patrik, Archbifchope of St Andros, powar, authoritie and jurifdiction to exerceis the faming Archbifchopric, be himfelff, his Deputes, and Commiffionars, in all maters ecclefiafticall with-in the dioceafe of St Andros, and Shreffdomes quhilk hes bein heirtofore annexed thervnto. With powar to the said Archbischope vnder his Hienes to call and convein Synodall Assemblies of the ministerie within the diocease for keiping of gud ordour, meanteining of trew doctrine and reformation of maners alleancerhe. To plant ministers of Kirks, quhilks sall happin to be desolat and vacand To gift admission and collation of benefices to persones qualefiet ather presentit be the lawfull patrones or ws To depose persones vnqualified and vnable in lyff or doctrine for discharging their cure, the quhilk persones being sa deposit, than rents, stipends and benefices to veak in the hands of the lawfull patrones, to be conferred of new to qualetiet and godhe persones: To reform Collages, Kirks and sic vther places apointed for lerning. To place and displace Maisters of Collages vnqualefiet according to the tenour of thair fundationes or euill affected to our seruice and obedience, contrauening be word or wryt our Royall powar and priuilage establisied in our leat Actes of Parliament, or sklandering ws be erroneus doctrine To visit the Hospitales within the diocease, and Kirks, and sie tham weill furnesit, menteined and apperelled. Commanding our faithfull and trew subiects to yeild vnto the said Patrik, Archbischope of St Andros, dew obedience: And that the sam may be better renerenced and obeyit, We haiff giuen and granted power to the said Archbisc hope to haift an of the maist verteus, godhe, and honest officers of armes within the said Diocease, wha salbe callit the Officer of the Kirk, wha sall in Our nam and authoritie assist the forsaid Archbischope, and sall command all and sindrie contrauenairs and brakars of the gud and godhe ordour of the Kirk, of what degrie or qualitie soeuer they be vnder Ws, with sic penalties, mulcts, imprisonments, repentances and maner thereof, as We, our Counsallours and Esteates sall agrie vnto, vpon the humble sutt of the said Archbischope, and vther Bischopes and Commissionars in ecclesiasticall maters, in the quhilk gift the said Bischope and officer be disobeyit, We will accompt the iniurie don to Our awin persone, and punische the saming with all rigour in exemple of vthers. PROUYDING alwayes, that gift anie persone or persones receaue anie intolerable wrang, or, without cause or iust deseruing, be vther wayes vsit be the said Bischope, that as the Law of God and louable Constitution of this Realme does permit, it salbe leisome to the persones sa inormhe hurt, to appell to Ws, and our Soueran authoritie to be interponit for remead therof, for gift the seat and image of Emperours in ancient tyme was a sufficient girthe, azill and protection to them that haid refuge thervnto, it becomes Ws mikle mair in our awin persone to be a confort, aid and releiff to tham that fall seik vnto our cleamencie against whatsumeuer oppression be spirituall or temporall persones, to whom we promise our princelie fawour, the quhilk we mynd alwayes till administrat be the grace of God in sic sort as We may be answerable to him, whase image and leiutennantrie We bear in this Realm And fordar becaufe it is necessar for the Kirk of God, and preseruation of gud ordour to be menteined therin, that, when necessitie requyres, the bischopes of euerie dyocease, and sic vther lerned men of thair diocease as salbe thought meit for that purpose, assemble togidder for taking of an vniform ordour to be obseruit in the Realm, in form of Comoun Prayer and vther things requisit, for the comoun esteat of the Kirk, We of our prinche powar grantes the priuiladge vnto the said Archbisc hope to convein the rest, prouyding alwayes that befor anie Convention Generall of the clargie that the said Bischope sall mak Ws aduertised of the necessarie causses of the forsaid convention, that we may vnderstand the saming, to tend to the weilfear of the Kirk and polecie of the Countrey And that the said Bischope may haiff our speciall licence thervnto granted vnto him vnder Our priuie seall, and that na Act or Constitution maid be the Assemblie of Bischopes or Clerks haift anie force, strenthe or effect within our realm to bind anie of our subiects, without they be allowit, approvit and confirmed be Ws, our Counsall and Esteat: And efter the probation of Our Royall Authoritie, they to stand in full force and effect, &c.

Thus it pleaſed God of his grait mercie and grace to haiff me occupied the firſt monethe of my entrie with our Lords, about the end wharof Mr Patrik Galloway, returning bak agane from London, cam to ws, and vndertaking the Miniſterie of the compame with me, (wha traucht onlie in the Word and Diſcipline,) lyked weill of our ordour, and according to the faming, efter the exerceis of faſting a haill ouk going before, miniſtrat the Holie Communion the laſt Sabothe of Auguſt and ſa continowing conform to our ordour in euerie poinct the monethes of September and October, in the quhilk, becauſe my Wyff was becom grait with chyld of hir firſt birthe, and langit to be in Berwik, ther to ly for diuers reaſones, I, obteining leive of the flok, convoyed hir thither, and retourned to my charge till the monethe of November ; in the quhilk the Lords haiffing Mr Patrik with thame, thought it meit that I ſould remean a ſpace at Berwik, becauſe the halff of the compame and my Wyff was ther ; for ther was the Lords Abbots of Cambuſkinnott, Drybrouche and Patley, George Dowglas of Parkheid, and dyvers vther gentilmen. To this I aggreit, and entering with tham helde tham occupied als neir the ordour leyed down as could win.   And ſurlie I was never man diligentlie and fruitfulhe occupied nor that wintar : for by the exerceiſe quhilk I haid amangs our awin folks, to the quhilk reforted a number of godlie peiple of the town, becauſe the publict doctrin in the Kirk was diſchargit be a practeiſing betwix the Lord of Hounſdan, Gouernour, and Capteau James, gyddar of our Court, called then Eile of Arran and Chancellar of Scotland   The guid Lady Wedrington, of whom I maid mention befor, being cowſines, and in creadit with the ſaid Lord Gouernour, obteined licence to me, for hir confort and of a number of maiſt godlie and zealus peiple, to teatche in a certean hous of the Town thryſe in the ouk, to than and myne grait ioy and conſolation

During that tyme the Communion was to be celebrat in Berwik, and therfor a certean dayes I teatched to tham the doctrine of Prepaiation before the fam, wherin that guid Lady fand fic inſtruction and confoit, that ſche erneſtlie intreated me to ſett down the ſubſtance therof to hir in wryt : the quhilk I did, the quhilk alſo ſche ſchew me a ſpace therefter copied ower in her awin hand wryt, excending a thrie or four [leaves] throuche, for ſche wrot verie feair. Sic was hir diligence and cair to grow in knawlage and practiſe of trew relligion

The newes quhilk we haid in the meantyme out of Scotland war verie euill, for Arran with his authoriſed Archbiſchope began then to rage

Diuerſe gentillmen vpon naked and bear ſuſpitionnes was apprehendit and put to ſchamtull execution Amangs whom was the Lard of Drumwhaſill, wha drank a bitter cupe of his awin brewing, for he was a grait counſallour and doer in bringing hame Monſieur d'Obignie, and his ſone in law the Lard of Meanie, a gentleman of notable gifts of body and mynd, and therfor mikle hated and feant of theſe wicked men, whaſe deathe was als mikle lamented in Eingland as ever I hard Scotſman

The Archbiſchope, that he ſould nocht be behind fell to wark, and in tyme of modification of ſtipends, ſett down the form of a band, the quhilk all behoued to ſubſcryve that gat aſſignation of ſtipends ; yea, it was ſa proſecut that wha ſoeuer refuſed to ſubſcryve was thretned with the los of thair benefices and leivings, yea fordar, with impriſſonment and baniſment, in cais of ane ſpetches vttered in the contrar Heirvpon, and ſum vther forget cauſſes, Mr Dauid Lindſay was put in the preaſone of Blaknes, Mr Jhone Howiſone in the Spey Towre of St Jhonſtoun, Mr Andro Hay put in warde, and hardlie vſit ; yea, ther was nocht a gud man in Kirk or Countrey, but was put in ſic fear, and oppreſſed with ſic greiff, that they wenred of than lyvis, and thought ws happie wha was away, and had that libertie of body and mynd to ſerue our God and caſe our conſcience

A grait number of the Miniſterie kythed what they war, even ſum at the beginning went throuchlie with the Archbiſchope, but efter Mr Jhone Crag and Jhone Dunkeſone the Kings miniſter yeildit : wharof that ane Mr Crage* haid ſtand conſtant verie lang and ſuſteined grait thretnings and boſt of Arran , yit at laſt be weaknes and a ſort of ſophiſtication (caſting in a clauſe " according to the Word of God," making, manifeſt am repugnantiam in adicito, as gift ane ſould ſay, he wald obey the Pape and his Prelates according to the Word of God), he yeildit and ſubſcryvit, and drew with him the graitteſt part of the Miniſterie of Scotland, quhilk was the heavieſt newes that could com to ws : for alas ! then the enemies triumphed, and all the harts of guid men war broken and diſcuragit. Yit ther war a few guid brether in Mers and Lawthen, wha, as they might, bathe keipit thamſelues clein, and withſtude the aduerſar, making ſum ſtay to that grait defection, wha knawing that I was in

* Mr Crag at this tyme pronuncit a iudgment vpon the Eile of Arran in his face befor the King, ſaying, " As the Lord is iuſt he will humble yow." The Erle, mokking him, ſaid, ' I ſall mak the of a fals frier a trew profet ,' and ſa ſitting down on his kne, he ſayes, " Now I am humbht " Na," ſayes Mr Crag, " mok the ſervant of God as thow will, God will nocht be mocked , bot mak thē find it in erneſt when thow ſalbe humbht af the hiche hors of thy pryde ' Quhilk within a certean of yers thereſter (1598) cam to pas, when James Dowglas ran him af his hors with a ſpear, and flew him , and his carcas caſt in an open Kuke befyde, or it was buried was fund eattin with the dogs and ſwyne Mr Crag vtherwayes an excellent pretcher, had diſchargit a faithfull dewtie at court in all his miniſterie, bot heunn grevit ws all to the verie hart

Bervik, acquented me with the mater, and fend me the forme of the Band, with informatioun of all proceidings. Wharupon, with grait motioun and greiff of mynd, I pennit this Letter following and fend in, togidder with a Letter in Latine, and the Controuerfies gathered to a few conclufiones confirmed with manifauld reafones and places of Scripture, directed to the Archbifchopes meache and graittest affociat, Mr Alexander Home, Minifter of Dumbar, prouoking him to anfwer giff he could, or giff nocht to bid his ordinar the Archbifchope do it himfelff. Bot I haid nather anfwer of the an nor vther, and the guid breithring war therby mikle confoirted and incuragit

A iuft Copie of that quhilk the fubfcryving Minifters firft and laft did fubfcryve

WE the beneficed men, Minifters, Reiddars, Maifters of Scholles and Collages, vnderfubfcryving, teftifies and fathfullie promifes be this our hand wreittes, our humble and dewtifull fubmiffioun and fidelitie to our Soueran Lord the Kings Matie, and to obey with all humilitie his Hienes Actes of Parliament haldin at Edinbruche the xxij day of May 1584 yeirs, And that according to the fam we fall fchaw our obedience to our ordinar Bifchope or Commiffionar apointed, or to be apointed, be his Matie, to haue the exerceife of the fpirituall iurifdictioun in our diocefe according to the Word of God And in ceas of non obedience in the premiffis, our benefices, ftipends, and leivings to vac, ipfo facto, and qualefiet and obedient perfones to be prouydit in our rowmes, as giff we war naturalie dead, according to his Hienes Act of Parliament maid theranent in all poincts.

To the Breithring of the Minifterie of Scotland, wha hes lathe fubfervuit
to the Popifh Supremacie of the King, and ambitius tyrannie of
the Bifchops ower thair Brithring,

J. M wilfethe vnfenzit repentance

THER is ftrange newes lathe reported vnto vs (my breithring) that ye fould haift altogidder without ftreakes yeildit to the aduerfarie, and nocht onlie be word confentit, bot alfo be the fubfcription of your hands confirmed, that horrible boundage and fklauerie, wharinto our Kirk of Scotland is brought be the leat Actes of Parliament, and this prefent intolerable tyrannie of the tals Bifchopes, the quhilk, vndoutedlie brought vpon yow be Sathan the Aduerfar of Chryfts kingdome, hes bein wrought be the meanes athei of malice and hatred againft the treuthe knawin, or of ignorance, or then of grait weaknes

Trewlie, my breithring, albeit I knaw that of tham that wer Sathans inftruments be few and flatterie to bring yow to fo tenfull a tall and greiws fklander, fum be new Juhans, who altho they confes they knaw the treuthe of the finceare religion of Chryft, yit for malice and hatred conceavit againft it and the minifters therof, they haid rather bein of the Turks fathe then of the fathe of Minifters. And therfor following the fut fteps of Juhan, they perfecut the fam malitiuflie, taking the leivings from the minifters, cafting tham in preftone, banifhing tham the Countrey, owerthrawing the Scholles and Seminaries apointed for the continuance therof, and wald vndoutedlie, with fyre and fword, perfew the faming, gift force and powar anfwerit to than incenfit aire and bludie appetit. Sum ar mair leing, flattering and ambitius then was Amaziah, the Preift of the

Kings Chappell at Bethell, wha perceaving the prophets of the Lord to prophecie againft King Je-roboams new forgit relligion, be ferving to the quhilk his ambition and gluttonie was meantemed, he ceaffit nocht till invent treaffone, fedition and all fort of lies againft tham, and mak the King to bamfhe, impriffone and perfecut tham with all kynd of rigour,—man avaritius and war myndit againft Gods childring then Balaam the fals prophet, curfing and devyfing all meanes to mak the peiple of the Lord to fall in the hands of than enemies, and furnefhing to Balak wicked and dewl-luhe counfall to intyfe tham to detection from the trew worfchipping, and fa to fin againft God, to mak the tyre of his wrathe to kindle againft tham,—and, finalie, man rafhe and void of guid con-fcience in maters of Relligion then was Vrias the preift, wha thought idolatrus King Ahaz com-mand a warrand guid aneuche for him to difplace the altar of the Lord, and fett in the roum therof an new drefht according to the form of the Altar of Damafcus. Sum, wars nor the godles Atheift Machiavel, wha careing in than flewes maift cunning court craft, makes na thing of God, Chryft and Relligion with the Minifters therof, bot pages and flaues to ferue to than turnes For if they may mak for than cornie, and fic an efteat of government as they wald haift, O then they will fpeak weill and graithe efteim of tham, bot if they can do na thing for than purpofe, or can nocht fuffer thair wicked attempts or will nocht change and alter opiniones when they will,—then can they nocht be fuffeut in a Comoun weill, they ar enemies to princes and lawtull authorities, they ar feditius, proude and treafonable, and therfor man till exyll, bamfment, preafone and fkaffauld. To thefe Hell is but a boggill to fley barnes, and Heavin but a conceat to mak toolles fean And laft, man cthink nor Numa Pampilius, efteiming Relligion and worfchiping of God bot a fuper-ftitius terrour to the confcience of peiple to hauld tham in awe and vnder obedience This I fay, althought they be, that works in this mater be malice and hatred, iudgit and damnet of themfelues, and whafe portion falbe with the forenamed workers of iniquitie, to whom they ar lyk in lyff and doing, yit can yie nocht be pingit from communicating with than teirfull innes, in fa far as yie hauf confented thervnto be word and wryt, wharas yie fould rather hauf obeyit the Word of God, commanding be his prophet—" Say nocht, a confederarie with this peiple, nather fear yie than fear, nor be effrayit of tham, bot fanctefie the Lord of Hoftes, and let him be your dreid Surlie he fould hauf bein vnto yow as a fanctuarie, and vnto tham a ftumbling blok, and a rok to fall vpon "[*] Gladlie wald I purge you, my brethring, of this firft mean of malice and hatred againft the treuthe and the meantemars tharof. And alas ! that anie occanoun fould euer hauf bein of-ferit annes to think this of anie of that number. But what fall I fay when I hen that fum of yow hes nocht onlie fubftrayvit yourfelues, bot alfo, lyk defperat peft folks, deftitut of Chriftian charitie, travelles to feduce and infect fic as ar haill and wald keipe the right way, and betrayes the con-ftancie of the beft be delatting of tham to the Perfecutor, and that nocht onlie be telling the treuthe, bot be trattelles, lies and forgit tealles, lyk warldlie pykthanks, to mak your godlie brethring ather to mak defection with yow, or then to fuffer extenuatie in than bodies. Alas for forow ! what is the finicts of that doctrine of Loue and Charitie quhilk hes foundit fa often out of your mouthes ? Bot to let be charitie, what is the hatred of malice and homecid ! Alas ! thefe ar rather the marks of bludie burreaus and crewall buchars of Sathan, the her and murderar, then of the difciples of Chrift, the takens of Turks, Paganes and Papifts, then of Chriftian peiple, to let be pretchours and inftructors of vthers Wo is me for yow, vnles thir things be repented in tyme. Behauld what it is to flyde bot a litle from the treuthe, and mak a fchifme in opinion from the brethering When Sa-than getts ans enttes, to mak vntreuthe and falfhode feim to be born withall and yeildit vnto bot a lytle, he gaes fordwart incontinent and begets in the hart a hatred and malice againſt the treuthe and profeſſioun thereof. Bewar, bewar, my breithring, mark Sathans craftie dealings, caſt out with him and reſiſt him in tyme, leaſt he gett the vantage and preuaill, and mak the laſt wars noi the firſt, " For if we ſin willinglie efter we haiſt receavit the knawlege of the treuthe, ther remeanes na mair facrifice for ſin, but a fenful looking for of iudgment, and violent fyre to deuore the aduerſaries." *

Alwayes, my breithring, I wald willinghe heir yow all purgit of malice, bot I knaw ſum will ſay, I knaw na better, and vnderſtud neuer throwlie the maters of the diſciplne, and, if we haiff fellit, it is of ignorance and nocht malice. Certeanlie, albeit, I ſen that to be over tiew in over manie of yow, yit it is a ſ¨hamtull thing to be haid tellit in your awin countrey, and abrod in other nationes, that ye, wha hes bein brought vpe in ſa notablie conſtitut¨a Kirk this twentie ſax yeirs, in quhilk tum of yow alſo hes bein paſtors and teatchers nocht mikle les, and all hes born function and chaige, nocht onlie in pretchiug of the Word, but in diſchargiug of that vther als neceſſar poinct of your miniſterie, in rewling and governing of the Kirk with your fellow breithring thir manie yeirs bypaſt, to ſay that ye ai yit ignorant of the ecclefiaſtical iuriſdiction and ſpirituall authoritie of the kingdom of Chryſt, and whow it differs from the temporall, bodelie, and ciuill polecie, what is the part and dewtie of the Chriſtian magiſtrat in the Kirk, and, namlie, whither he aught to be maid a new Pape, to ſie tyrannie ower the Kirk, and conſcience of men of the eccleſiaſticall functiones, and gift that Satanical preſumption and pryde of fals biſchopes may be tolerat in the Kirk of Jeſus Chryſt, quhilk from the dayes of Conſtantin, be whaſe man zealus affection, than conſiderat wiſdome, they gat waildlie ritches and honour, hes infected the Kirk, nocht onlie with all kynd of vyces againſt the ſecond Table, but alſo hes rent and deuyd ht the ſaming, with ſects, ſchiſmes, hereſies, and diſſertiones, be than ambitious debeats, euer ſtryving for ſeat, wha might be hieſt and grateſt. Efter that annes that command and law of æqualitie giften be Chryſt was tranſgreſſed and violat, they neuer ceaſſit vnto the tyme they haid hoiſed vpe that Man of Sin into the throin and roum of that onlie ſupreain rewlar and head, the Lord Jeſus, for Biſchopes wald be Airchbiſchopes, and they Metropohtanes, and they Patriarches, and ſa Papes. Yie conveinit yourſelues in Generall and Provinciall Aſſemblies, and in Preſbyteries, to the quhilk yeuhe, half yeuhe, and oukhe, ye reſorted as ordinar members and charge beareis within the ſam, and yit can nocht tell what ground, warrant, or authoritie yie did the ſam vpon as tho yie ſould planlie ſay, yie did it nocht in fathe, and ſa ſo often ye ſinned and abbutit thoſe holy conventionnes of the Kirk of Chryſt.

To your giait repruff, I man call to mynd the notable occaſiones of atteining to ſolid knawlage in thir maters that God offerit vnto yow, bot in loue, as of God his glorie, ſa of your ſaules, as God mot loue myne Forby and attour your privat ſtudies in reiding of the Scriptures, and ſa mome leined mens wrytings on thir poincts, aggreing all in effect in maiſt ſweit harmonie, (wharinto, gift ye haid bein als diligentlie occupied as God gaiff tyme and occaſion, ye neidit nocht to alleage ignorance for an excuſe), whow war thir heads handlit publicthe in the Aſſemblies? Was nocht the Generall Aſſemblie, be the ſpace of ſax or ſeavin yeirs, almaiſt hailelie occupied in thir queſtiones? War nocht the miniſters, in all the quarters of the countrey, erneſthe exhorted, and be publict authoritie, commandit to ſears and ſeik the Scriptures diligenthe, and all kynd of wryttes, auld and new, for finding fuithe of the ſolide and vndoutted treuthe? Was ther nocht apointed conterences to be haid in all partes amangs the breithing, in thair oukhe exerceiſes and Provinciall

* Hebrews, x

Affemblies, from the quhilks men, weill inftructed with reafones and iudgment of the reft, war fend, from tyme to tyme, to the General Affemblies, whar, bathe be privat and opin reafoning, the opiniones and fentence of all men war examined and tryed, throw euerie head of the difcipline of the Kirk, and efter lang and often reafoning, all put in votting, and be baill and viniform content and agriement of the baill Kirk, in a General Affemblie, concluddit, and digefted in conclufion, and inregiftrat in the Books of the faid Affemblie, and extract thereof ordeanit to be giffen to euerie Prefbyterie throuchout the Realm, whidder gift this, ioyned with the continuall practife of the felff fam difcipline, thefe diuers years by paft, may mak ws inexcufable befor God, his Kirk, and Angelles, the verie blind warld may iudge

Alas ! deir breithring, ye may weill, for a fchort tyme, think yow in guid efteat that leirned nocht, becaufe, as yie think, with les prik of confcience, and danger of bodies and geire, yie may pas ower this euil days : But O, fulilhnes ! put the cais, yie might put af in this maner manie thowfand yeirs, ane fall com the day when yie fall be forcit to compeir befor that grait iudge, and giff an accompt of the difcharging of that manit lne calling, when a compt falbe cravit of all the ydle houres, words, and doings, that yie haift fpent. Sall yie nocht be then etchamit of that wheirinto now yie tak pleafour ? Sall nocht this filbe eate be turned in forowfull wanreft ? Sall ignorance then be an excufe befor him wha fall fchaw himfelft fiom heavin, with the angels of his might, in flambing fyre, to tak vengeance on tham that has nocht knawn him, namelie on fic as hes neglected and difpyfit fa manie guid occafiones of knawlage minnitrat vnto tham ? What fall the flatterie and authoritie of your King and Bifchop then availl ? Na thing, bot to be partakers of iudgment as of fine, except repentance intervein

Oh ! my breithring, yie ar farder in the mift with this ignorance then yie fuppofe. For what hope fall Sathan haiff now (of whafe force, craft, and bifines, yie fa oftentymes warn your heirars,) to mak yow to yeild in the verie poincts of the doctrine of Saluation, feing he hes fund yow fa eafie to be overcom in the cais of the difcipline, wharof yie haiff na les fure warrand and ground refeiing to the mater in the Word of God, if yow haid luft to haift lerned ? What incuragment fall it be to the Papifts, that hes nocht bein neghgent in lerning the vntreuthe, and ftudeing contiouerfies in than temmaries, and wha now daylie prouokes ws to the combat, when they fie but a lytle threatning of the Pince, nocht of lyfi, bot leving, and a fmall piece of flattarie of a fals bifchope, is able to fhak yow from your grounds, and mak yow to fall for leak of knawlage, yea, to fuffer the wull and blokhoufles of your difcipline to be demolifed and doung down, thinking (as indeid they may) it wilbe eafie to mak the branche, and win the hauld and citie of your doctrine and Kirk ? Sall they nocht, I fay, haift guid caufe to hope weill of the victorie and conquerit ? Sall they nocht haift reafone till affirme that quhilk they haiff fa often fpoken and wivttin, That the minifters of Scotland is bot a fort of ignorant and feible beafts, nather dow abyde reafoning nor thretning. My breithring, the Deuill hes maid a grait brak amangs yow, and with finall forces, and few ftiakes, gottin a grait victorie ouer yow, and yit vie will find that he will nocht content nor ftay ther, but as a victor putt vpe, will preas fordwait And, therefor, in the tender mercies of God, for the cair I haiff of your faluation, extreamlie indangerit now, when fame is loft and gone, I man apply vnto yow an extream and hirde remend, to pluk yow if poffible out of the claues of Sathan ; to wit, that fenfull commiuation of the Apoftle to the Hebrews, " It is impoffible that they quhilk war annes lightned, and haift tafted of the heavinlie gift, and war maid partakers of the Holie Ghoft, and hathe teafted of the guid Word of God, and of the power of the warld to come, if they fall away, falbe renewit againe be repentance feing they crucifie again to thamfelues the Sone of God, and makes a mok of him. The erthe, quhilk drinks vpe the rean that comes vpon it, and brings furthe herbes meit for tham be whome it is dreffit, receanes a bleffing of God. Bot that quhilk bears thornes and breires is reprobat, and neir curfing, the end wharof is to be brunt. * Yit breithing weilbelout, we are perfuadit of better things, and meit for faluation of yow, whowbeit, we thus, with the Apoftle, wryt to terrifie yow, and reclame and reafe from this fall, and keipe yow bak from farder and wars Alas! what a face fall yie haue to com befor the godlie and faithful breithring of the countrey, when it fall pleife God to delyver his awin Kirk and reftore it again to the former or better efteat or rather, What a confcience and mynd fall yie haift, when yie remember, and or ben that wa pronunced be Chryft vpon tham be whome fklander and offence comes ! And, O ! whow manie godlie hartes, bathe in Scotland and England, yea in France and all reformed Kirks, ar crewalhe wounted with this fact of yours, and that nocht without grait caufe. For, als lang as the haill nuintteue ilud conftant, ther was guid hope of a happie redres of maters, bot now, be this fact, yie haift gillen the Deuill entres within the walles of Jernfalem to fpoill and deftroy all the guid and conftant citemers therof wha will nocht detvll thamfelues, bow than knies to Baall, and eat twynes fleche with yow What will yie think when yie com to that vers of the 50th Pfalme 'Vnto the wicked this fayes God What hes thow to do to declair my ordonnances, that thow fouldeft tak my conenant in thy mouthe - feing thow hates difciphne, and hes caften my Words behind thie? Wald to God yie fould be fa moued thereby as was the leirned Origin, wha efter he haid ben induceit, throw weaknes to facrifice to Idols, therefter coming vnto the Kirk to preatche, cafting vpe the buik, he fell be Gods prouidence, on the fam place of the Pfalme, and burfting out in teares befor the peiple, he maid a maift dolorus and bitter lamentation and invection againft himfelff, as yie may read in his Lyfl, recordit be Sundas And finalie, what a dairt to your pure confcience fall that fentence of Chryft be, "He that denyes me befor men I will deny him befor my heavinlie Father? For yie knaw, that whofoeuer heues the Word of God and does it nocht, namlie in the tyme of tryall, fchawes nocht that he is fohdlie groundit in the fam, denyes Chryft, as he himfelff teatches in the 7th of Matthew, otherwayes Manie fall com vnto him on that day, and fay Lord, did we nocht prophecie in thy name? Did we nocht work miracles and caft out demiles?" Bot he will anfwer, "I knaw yow nocht, depart from me, yie workers of iniquitie?

Bot it may be that fum of yow, your vnhappie complices and counfallouns in this courfe, thinks and will fay, What neids all this ado? Why ar yie fa hat in threatning? the mater is nocht of fa grait weght, &c Alas! my breithring, miferable and lamentable experience, except God of his mercie prevent it, I feir fall teatche yow and the pure Kirk of Scotland what ye haift done, and whow grait and fearar the confequents that mfewes on your fact. For firft, be the approuing of that Act of Parliament anent the Kings fupremacie in all caufes ecclefiaticall as enull, and na appellation to be maid from him, yie haift nocht onlie fett vpe a new Pape, and fa become traitors to Chryft, and condifcendit to the cheaft error of Papiftrie, wherupon all the reft dependes, quhilk, giff it be nocht to deny and refute Chryft, I knaw nocht what it is fa to do. Bot farder, ye haift in fa doing granted man to the King then euer the Papes of Rome peaceblie obteined, whom tyrannuflie and ambitiuflie foeuer they fought the fam, for the Counfalles of Conftance and Bafil decreit in the Papes face, and be infinit argumentes of reafone and fcripture evicted, that it was nocht onlie a veritie bot a poinct of fathe The Councill to be aboue the Pape, and appellationes to be maitt lawfull from the Pape to the Councill And fa from the Pape ther was euer appellationes to the Councells, rewht be the Word of God and his Sprent, wherin the trew Bifchopes and Paftors, and Doctors of the Kirk fatt as Chryfts officiars, to iudge and difcern on maters ecclefiaticall, according

* Hebrews vi.

to the Word of God In the quhilk the best Christian Emperours that euer was, Constantin and Theodosius, sat in na hier degrie than the pastors as obedient members of the Kirk, humblie to be gouerned and rewled with the rest be the scepter of the Word of God, and nocht as Heads and Lords to commpand and rewll ower it, knawing the Lord Jesus Chryst was onlie King and Emperour than Bot vie haiff subtenent, that whosoeuer, in anie maters ecclesiasticall declynes the King and Counsalls iudgment, salbe reput and punished as a tratour. What I pray vow giff thesse profest Papistes and Jesuites that flockes ham out of France, Spean and Italie, and finds grantter fauour and credit in Court, then all the Ministers, what if they sall challange yow for the Doctrine of Justification, frie will, reall presence and the rest of the heids of religion, for these, as chieff maters ecclesiasticall, sall the King and his Counsall be iudge to vow, and na appellation be maid vnder the pean of treassone? What sall then, I pray vow, becom of religion and the professiours thereof? sall they nocht be ather forced to deny Chryst, or maid to disput with the torments apointed for trators? and syne this for a clok to be casten ower it, It is nocht for religion, but for hie treassoune that sic ar sa handlit Do vie nocht hen espy the craft of the crewall feind, wha dar nocht, in this age of knawlage and light of the gospell, oppon himselff against the treuthe, as the Scrybes and Pharisies durst not garnstand the doctrine of Chryst, bot teiks, vnder pretence of Lawes, and clok of iustice, to mak the godlie and trew professiours and preachours to be schamfull spectacles, that therbi men may be etchamit of the veritie of the Luangell, euen as Chryst was put to deathe vnder the nam of sedition and treassoune

 Secondlie, vie haiff taken away, be your subscriptiones, the lawfull powar of the Pastors and Doctors and Eldars of the Kirk, to convein thamselues in the nam of na erthlie prince nor temporall authoritie of King, nor for na erthlie nor temporall effears bot in the nam and authoritie of Jesus Chryst, King of Kings, Lord of Lords, the onlie Soveran rewlar and commander within the Kirk, quhilk is his kingdome spirituall, and nocht of this warld, till intreat of things heavinlie and eternall, quhilk directlie concernes the saules and consciences of men The quhilk powar they haiff of Chryst planlie in his Letter Will, ioyning a maist comfortable promise against sic grait difficulties that behouit till aryse in the discharge of sa hiche an office "Whansoeuer twa or thrie of vow salbe conuenit in my nam, I salbe in the mids of vow." Leaning vpon the quhilk powar and promise, the Apostles and Disciples conuened thamselues findrie tymes efter the resurrection of Chryst, and efter his ascension, to choise ane in the roume of Judas,* they assemblet the haill congregation to the election of the Diacons.† and now efter a grait manie kirks war planted, nocht onlie amangs the Jewes, bot also amang the Gentilles, the Apostles and Eldars assemblit thamselues in a Generall Countall at Jerusalem, to determin in the question moued about the circumcision, and sa furthe For when the command be Chryst is giffen ather to the heirars to heir, or the pastors to feid, or the doctors to teatche, or the eldars to govern or rewll, furhe be necessitie of relation, it man be that he gifes tham also authoritie and powar in his name to convein togidder and with than flockes for that effect Sa that be that act of Parliament quhilk discharges the Assemblies and Conventiones of ecclesiasticall office beareis, is restrant that fredome quhilk Chryst Jesus hes giffen to the officers of his kingdome, to convein for discharging of the dewties and callings quhilk he hes leyed on tham, to be vsit for his service, and saluation of his peiple. And trewlie als weill might they haiff dischargit the conventiones for heuring of the Word and ministration of the Sacraments, as for the exerceising of disciplne and government of the Kirk, seing this is na les leyed on the bak of the officiars of Chrysts Kingdom, as a speciall part of than dewtie and

<hr />

  * Acts, i.   † Acts vi.

charge nor the former, and hes the command and powar giffen to vfe it na les then the vther, without careing for anie authoritie or command of men.   For that quhilk Chryft fa erneftlie repeates to
Piter, quhilk alſo is commoun to all Paſtors, Feid ' feid ' feid ' is nocht onlie be Word and Sacraments, bot alſo be diſcipline, rewling, and government, as the mater itfelf declares, the word fig-
nifies, and the fimilitud planlie proues   And what, I pray yow, meines that comand of Chryfts
till the Kirk, that is, the ecclefiaftik ſenat or affemblie of the office bearers, as the lerned expones it,
' And if he refuſe to heir the Kuk, let him be unto thie as an Ethnic and Publican '" gift the
Kirk hes nocht powar and authoritie of iudgment giffen to it be Chryft ?   And that, ' I giue yow
the keyes of the kingdome of heauine, whatfouer yie loufe on erthe ſalbe lowſit in heavin, and
whatſoeuer ye bind on erthe ſalbe bund in heavin."   War thir keyes giffen to anie king or magiftrat ' or flowes the powar therof from humean ordination?   And finalie, what inemethe the
Apoſtle to the Romanes xiii. when he ſo erneftlie exhortes euerie officiar in the Kirk to diſcharge
than calling diligentlie?   Willes he than till abyde the commandiment of anie erthlie king or prince ?
Na, als frilie as the King hes his powar and authoritie of God the Creator to diſcharge his office
in things ciuill and temporall, als frilie hes the paſtors, eldars, doctores, and deacones of the Kuk
powar and authoritie of Jeſus Chryft the Redeemer to do thair office in things heavinlie and ſpirituall   But I purpoſe nocht, my breithring, to infift with yow in prouing of maters at this tyme,
bot taking things to be ſufficientlie tryed and concludit vnto the tyme I heir anie reaſones alleagit
be yow or anie vther in the contrar, I wald diſcouer vnto yow the feirfull conſequences of this your
yeilding, tending to the wrak of Chryfts Kuk and the libertie therof.

It was onlie the Aſſemblies and Preſbyteries, as all that fenes God, yea, and the enemies thamſelues knawes, that was the ordinarie mean to keipe the Kuk of Scotland from the pollution of
vyces, hereſies, and ſchiſmes, the quhilk now being takin away, vyce and wickednes fall owerflow,
for wha fall tak ordour therewith ?—the Court and bifchopes ' Als weill as Martin Elwod and Will
of Kinmont with ſtealling on the Bordours   Hereſie, Atheiſme, and Papiſtrie fall brak in, for wha
fall refift it ?—the bifchopes ' Put the cais, that fic wha hes fauld God, relligion, and heavin for
this preſent warld and the things therof, could haift the grace to gainſtand, the Atheiſts and Papiſts,
and cheiff meantemers of Atheiſme and Papiſtrie, wilbe grantter in Court (fin the quhilk the bifchopes hes than powar and authoritie, and can, nor dar do na thing without ſpeciall leiue and
command therof) nor the beggerlie bifchopes and all thair clergie can be   And laſt, the ſchiſmes
and controuerſies that aryſes and ar ſawin be Sathan falbe na wayes compomit nor extinguiſt be
the brotherlie and humble conventiones in æqualitie, (as the happie experience of ſax and twentie
yeir bypaſt hes proven our Aſſemblies till haue done,) bot contrarie wayes, be the proude ambition and vanitie of the bifchopes, they ſalbe daylie foſterit, increaſflit, and augmeitit, the pruif
and experience wherof yie may reid efter the firſt thrie hounder yeirs of Chryfts Kuk, when the
perſecutiones war endit, and the bifchopes began, vnder Chriſtian Emperours, to gett eaſe, honour,
and ritches, and braking the commandiment of Chryft, began till vſurpe lordlie authoritie and pre-
heminence over thair breithring.   Fra that tyme, as never of befor, miferablie hes the Kirk been
cut and deuydit be controuerſies, ſchiſmes, and hereſies, fa permitius hes it bein to ley aſyde the
Word of God, and right rewlles of governing of his Kirk be æqualitie amangs the paſtors.

Thridlie, yie haiff confentit and fubſcryvit that thir bifchopes fall haiff the owerfight and rewling
of all the Kirks, according to the powar quhilk they receaue of thair Pape and head.   Quhilk office hes na warrand in the Scripture of God, bot is an inuention of Sathan brought in be ambition
and auarice, yea that preſumptous and lordlie authoritie over the reſt of thei breithring is plat contrar to the word and commandiment of Chryft, Matth. 10. 19. and 26 24 28. and of Luc, 12.

11, 15, 16, 17 and Pet. 5 1 &c. And that mangrell melling with ciuill and warldlie maters, exerceiſing iudicatoiu in ciuill and criminall cauſſes, loudlie cryes that they war neuer of Chryſt, whaſe kingdome is nocht of this waild, wha refuſed to be maid King be the peiple, yea wald nocht ſa mikle as deuyd the inheritance amangs breithring, albeit a charitable turn, and all for eſchewing of incumbrance in eithlie maters, quhilk might hinder him from the ſpirituall and heavinlie wark of his Father for the quhilk he was ſend And by and attoure the vnlawfulnes of the office quhilk the Scriptiue and nature of the kingdome of Chryſt can nocht beir withall, the perſones that preſenthe yie haiſt ſubjery vit obedience vnto are infamus vyle men, nocht onlie of the bas and curſeſt ſort amangs the peiple, as war the preiſts of profan Jeroboam, bot maiſt diſſolut and ſklanderus in all than lyſt, be whaſe cairfulnes in gathering vpe the woll and milk, and cairleſnes in feiding of the floks, and evill exemple in all kynd of vyce, na mervell it is giff innumerable faulles drown in ignorance, periſhe in than ſinnes and hue without God or religion.

Therfor, now I beſeik yow, my breithring, rightlie to conſidder, and deiplie to pondre this mater Whidder haid it bein better to refuſe and vndertak the diſpleaſure of ane eithlie Prince, wha onlie hes powar ower the body, (and that na man rather nor it pleaſes God) and haiſt eſteemed all this waild but dirt and draft vnder your feit, in reſpect of his luiſt and obedience, wha could haiſt given yow again a houndrethe fauld in this lyſt, and the lyff eternall to the guid? Or to haiff conſentit, and incurrit the hiebe diſpleatuie of Chryſt Jeſus, the giant Heavinhe King, wha, efter the bodie is ſlean, may caſt bathe it and the ſaull in the fyre of Hell, and the offence and deteſtation of all the godlie and faithfull for the ſhamfull denying of ſa guid a maiſter, betraying of the friedome of his kingdome, ſklandering of his Kirk, and offering occaſion to the adueiſaris to triumphe and be incuiagit Again, I ſay, for Gods cauſe, and your awin ſaluation, enter in deiphe to wey and conſidder what yie haiff done, that the hynouſnes of the fact may mak yow to abhorre yourſelues and be vnſemyithe caſt down therfor. For haiff yie nocht be your hand wryt, the ſeall of your treuthe, bund yourſelues, as ſlaues, to the wicked appetit and affection of a blind godles Court, oueiflowing with all kynd of ſine and impietie? and to a Biſchope, O fy! to whom I can nocht giff a vicius epithet man nor another, and I am ſure a thowſand wald nocht expres his vyces, as yourſelffs, and all the waild, is witnes? And that quhilk is warſt of all, haiff yie nocht brought the libeitie of the ſpreit, and preatching of the Word of God, the diſpenſation wharof is concredit vnto yow, in maiſt abominable thraldome? Sa that yie dar nocht reproue vyce without exception of perſones, nor pretche the treuthe frihe, as your God, vour buik, and your conſcience, teatches yow, and commands. For, dar yie now rebuk the contemners of God and religion, and faithfull miniſters therof, the blaſphemers of Gods nam and his treuthe, dueilhthe diffimulation, yea, open dueilrie, periurie, perfecution, tyrannie, creweltie, oppreſſion, drunkennes, huredome, teirring of God and man, ambition, auarice, flatterie leing, braking of promiſe, tricking, taunting deceauing, profanation of the Word of God, ſacrilage, ſimonie, witchcraft, ſchamles obſcenitie, vilanie, apoſtaſie, and menſuaring of that quhilk the monthe hes profeſſit, and publicthe ſpoken and teatched, the hand hes often ſubſervit with the grait aithe of the Lord maid and interpoint therin? feing your new erected paprie, and, namlie your famus Ordinar, the Archbiſchope, to whom yie haiſt bund your obedience, is altogidder feſtered and owergean with tham

Now, as to that nam of obedience, quhilk is craiut in a fair and honeſt maner, to clok a maiſt filthie and vnhoneſt mater, miſter I to wryt ame thing to yow theranent? for can yie vnderſtand or teatche ame vther thing theranent nor this, Obedience, except it be in God, and according to his command, is na obedience, bot ſin, rebellion, and diſobedience, the quhilk is as the ſin of witchcraft, wickednes, and ydolatrie befor God, as Samuel teatched King Saul in his awin face. That quhilk man, following his awin iudgment and ill affection, calles rebellion, treafone, and difobedience, is allowit befor God as dewtifull dewtie, guid obedience, and feruice. And contra, was nocht Sydrach, Mifach, and Abednego caft in the fernace be Nebugednezar King of Babylon, for than difobedience, in nocht falling down to worfehipe his erected image? Was nocht Daniel caft in the den of Lyons for difobedience, becauf he brak King Darins godles law in making his prayer thryfe a day toward Jerufalem, and wald nocht gift fa mikle as a fecret content to fett vpe the King in Gods ftead? The gard of King Saul difobeyit him commanding be his awin mouthe to flay the prefts of the Lord. Sa did his awin fone guid Jonathan, and wald nocht bring in Dauid, bot conforted him, and fet him on his iornes. The Medwyfes, King Pharo, Ifada and the haill eftcates of Juda, bludie Athalia, Lobna, a citie of the Leuites prefts, the apoftat King Amazia, and innumerable ma in hohe Scripture, whate doings, neuerthelefs, the Spreit of God commends, and as dew obedience to God and than fuperiors, hes left tham inregiftrat in his Hohe Buik to be followit

In grateft humilitie and dewtifull reuerence of that manft lawfull authoritie giften be God to Kings and Magiftrats, and yit in curage and bauldnes of fpreit, for the glorie of my God and libertie of the Kingdome of Chryft, defaced alas! and brought vnder vill flauerie be the pernitius flatterers of princes wha doting tham in than conceattes, makes tham to tak vnto tham abfolut powar to do what they lift, and trampe the Kirk of Chryft vnder futt,—I will tak this propofition to defend againft the beft and manft lernit of than courteous, comt bifchopes and minifters, pronyding they difput be Scripture and guid reafone, and nocht be the Blaknes, Spey Touri, Gibet and Maden, That to obey the King of Scotland, as he craues prefenthe obedience according to his laft acts of parliament, is treafone againft Chryft, and difobedience yea rebellion to his Word and Command, and therfor whatoeuer may ftay and withftand him be refufall of obedience or vther wayes be ordinar and lawfull meanes of than calling and does nocht, is a treator to his Maieftie, Countrey and Kirk of Chryft within the fameng And leit yie, my brething, or anie vther fould tak this my plean fchawing of the treuthe in an euill part, the Lord God of heauin is witnes to my confcience that I mein na contempe or difdean to his Graces ather perfone or lawfull authoritie, nather does this proceide of anie euill will or defyre of reuenge for anie wrang done to vs, bot the Lord knawes, befor whom we walk, that the fiches and fobbes of our dolorus and manft affectioned harts toward his weill and amendment, is with teares powred out dayhe for that effect, and whom I knaw affuredlie that all the godhe in Scotland and England wald obey, loue and reuerence aboue all fleche as than awin naturall and born Prince, gift leaving thir godles Counfallors and courfes he wald rewll in the fen of God, and eftablis the kingdome of Jefus Chryft according to his Word. Therfor alas! my brething yie haift vnder the name of obedience defyht yourfelft with thefe crymes that Samuel conuicted King Saull of, for nocht obeying the Word of the Lord. And the exemples of Gods feruantes in than fen of his grait Maieftie and conftancie in ftanding in his treuthe and obedience flouthe, nochtwithftanding danger of lyfl, yea terrible torments, may be tearfull iudges fett befor your confcience to condemne yow, except yie repent Peter and Jhone ar bathe be word and exemple crying vnto yow, That it had bein better to obey God nor man.

But me thinks I heir fum of yow lamenting and faying, It was weaknes and feiblenes of this fi eall nature that maid yow do this thing Trewhe, my brething weaknes and infirmitie is naturall to fleche, and hes oftentymes maid the childring of God to flyde and fall, for fa did Dauid in adulterie and murdour, Peter in the threfauld denyall of his Maifter, and the zealus Origin of whate fall I fpak befor. Wharfor in that ceas onhe the remeadie incontinent without delay is to be fought, for it is manlie, and of weaknes to fall, bot to ly ftill and flcipe in fine without remorfe or amendiment, it is the rod of reprobation It is a thing maift fenfull to deny Chryft but far man nocht to confes him conftantlie agean vnto the deathe.   It is a horrible mater fa to fklander the Kirk of God, bot far man to continow therin, and nocht to repear and remoue the fam And therfor I exhort yow, dear brethring, maift erneftlie and tenderlie in the bowels of the Lord Jefus, and admonife yow, befor God, his Angelles and haill Kirk that yie pres with fpeidie repentance till amend this miferable mis, and repear fa mikle as can ly in yow this bealfull brak.   That vie meditat and cry with Dauid, that is, with the contrit fprit and broken hart of Dauid in that 51 Pfalme, yie go afyde with Piter! Yie lamentable! cry out and invey againft vourfelues with Origine, and mak the ftreames of your bitter teares delet and wafhe away that fubfcription, and the wound of your fiches and found of your fobbes, blaw abrod your repentance for that denyall of Chryft, and therefter conftanthe contes him with Piter vnto the deathe, and that fpedehe befor he cum in iudgment, and deny yow befor his heavinlie father.   And finalie, in conclufion, to remoue bathe the publict fklander and wa pronuncit againft he whar by it comes.   I fie nocht whow it can be don vther wayes, then giff yie com bauldhe to the King and Lords of Chacker again, and fchaw tham whow yie haift fallin throw weaknes, bot be God his powar ar rifin againe, and than, be publict not and witnes takin, frie yourfelnes from that fubfcription, and will the fam to be deleit, renuncing and detefting it planlie, and therefter publiethe in your fermonds and be your declaration and retractation in wryt prefented to the haill Kirk, and fathfull mamfeft the fam.   Let tham do with ftipend, benefice, and lyff itfelff what they lift, yie will ftik be Chryft, wha knawes what ye haift neid of, and will prouyde for yow fufficienthe, yie ferving him in this lyff, and bring vow henefter to his glorie in the lyft euerlafting.   The quhilk that yie may do, and therefter conftanthe ftand vnto the end, I fall erneftlie call to God for yow, to affift yow with his ftrong and almghtie fprit for the glorie of his awin name, the reparation of the grait offence and fklander of his Kirk, and your ioyfull receaving again in the number of Chryfts warioures and citiciners of his Kingdome, and Capteanes of his airme, with whome fechting lawfulhe in fuffring hen, with him we falbe crowint with immortall glorie in the heavines whar he leives and ringes with his father for euer

This Letter, with the conclufions and arguments befor mentioned fend hame, and going abrod, did mikle confort the conftant, and crab the enemie Twa of our ftudents in Theologie for copeing therof, and fending to breithring, war fean to flie, and com to me to Bervik, Mr James Robertfone, a verie gud brother, now minifter of Dondie, and Mr Jhone Caldcleuche, whom I receavit gladlie, and wha efter certean monethis abyding with me at Bervik, we paft fouthe togiddei to Londone.   Alfo an Wilyeam Erde, an extraordinar witnes fteired vpe be God ; wha being a mafone of his craft till he was paft twentie yeirs and maried, lernit firft of his wyff to reid Englis, and taken with delyt of letters he himfelff ftudeit the Latin, Greik, but fpecialie the Hebrew langage, fa that he haid his Byble als hamlie to him in Hebrew as anie vther langage : The quhilk being knawin to the Kirk, and the giftes he haid befyde, bathe of knawlage and vtterence of diuinitie, he was maid to leaue his handie craft and tak him heallie till attend vpon the Collage and exerceis, whar he profited fa that within few yeirs that he was callit and placed

r

in the Ministerie at the Kirk of St Cuthberts, vnder the Castell wall of Edinbruche, and is now a notable man for vprightnes and grait lerning and read-
ding. This brother for iust feir cam away also, and abaid with me a space in
Berwik. The caufe of his feir was the apprehending of his fellow laborar, a
graue and godlie brother, Mr Nicol Dalglaifhe, keiping of him in clos preffone
and putting him till ane effaife, of erneft and deliberat purpofe to haift execut
him as a trator, onlie for the fight of a certean letter com from Mr Walter
Balcanquall to his wyff, bot the faife wald nocht fyll him, wherat the Court
was verie crabbit That worthie brother, and now ancient father in the Kirk,
was verie euill handlit, and ftude wonderfull conftant

That fam wintar to thir hard newes from our awin countrey be northe,
cam vnto ws far harder newes from fouthe out of Londone, of the departour
of Mr James Lawfone ther : wha for giftes and eftimation was cheiff amangs
the ministerie : For, efter my vncle Mr Andro, with the faid Mr James and
certean vther of the breithring, haid in the monethe of July vifited the Vniuerfities of Oxfurd and Cambridge, and conferrit with the moft godlie and
lernit ther, retournit agane till Londone, parthe throw his trauell and alteration of the care, bot chieflie for the cauffes twitched befor of the behauiour of
fome of his awin flock, wha haid fubferyvit a Letter * calling tham wolffes and
hyrlings, Mr James, being a melancholian of conftitution, falls in a heavie
difeafe quhilk refolued in a melancolius dyfenterie, quhilk be na meanes of medecin (whowbeit he haid ther a number of maift lerned and godlie) could be
cured, bot efter dyvers monethes feiknes he died, fpeiking till his vtter houre
maift holilie to Gods glorie, and comfortablie till all the heirars ; bot his deathe,
and fpeitches, quhilk were maine and notable, I leaue to tham wha war prefent Bot verelie this was a grait los, and difharting amangs ws, and haid
vndone diuers of ws, giff God by his word and fpreit of confolation haid nocht
vphaldin ws. His wyff (whom for hir rare and maift fweit giftes of knawlage,
deuotion, tender and maift zealus loue towards God, his feruants and all that
loued the Lord Jefus Chryft, I can nocht of dewtie and confcience bot mak
mention of, for a happie memorie to the pofteritie,) was in readines to go to
him, and cam to Berwik euen about the tyme of tha dolorus newes, wharof
fhe knew na thing till fhe was by a convoy brought bak again to that maift
godlie and confortable hous to all the feruands of God, Huttonhall Bot, as
euer perfone in that eftcat. fche kythed the fruicts of trew Chriftiantie, nocht

* The copie of this Letter is amaigs my foralles

onlie at that tyme, bot all the dayes of hir lyff to hir death, leiving as a trew weidow and relict of sic a houſband, in faſting, prayer, meditation and exerceiſe of the warks of mercie and love, inſtructing the ignorant, ſweitlie admoniſing the offendars, conforting the afflicted, viſiting the ſeik and diſeaſed in body or mynd, and perſeuering in prayer with tham vnto the end : ſa that hir refreſhings and paſtyme was to tak peanes in theſe exerceiſes. Thus ſche leived in Edinbruche ſevin or aucht yeir efter our retourn, a remarkable mirroure of godlie weidowheid, and died with als grait mean and miſſing of the godlie in all degries, namlie the pure, as anie woman that euer I knew. Sche was my ſpeciall acquentance and confort in Chryſt from the deathe of hir houſband to hir lyves end.

My wyff was at the ſam tyme grait with chyld neir hir birthe, and hering of Mr James deathe, wha by the comoun and publict reſpect was to hir in affection a father, brought vpe dayhe in his hous and companie with his wyff, ſche dooht and burſted ſa, I being in Newcaſtell with the Lords, that they war all in grait fear ſche ſould hauff parted with her birthe. Amangs whom a godlie ſuddart, named Francis Goodwin, conforting hir, ſayes, " Tak heid what yow do, Miſtres Melun, that yow becom nocht an vnnaturall murderar of that quhilk is in your bellie, quhilk by appeirance is a man chyld, and yow knaw nocht if God may mak him to ſupplie a place in his churche agane.' Within a monethe therefter ſche was hchtar of a man chyld indeid, whom, be imitation of Joſephe, I callit Ephraim, becauſe God haid maid me fructfull in a ſtrange land , praying God of his grace, nocht regarding my ſinnes and vnthankfulnes, to mak anie mean inſtrument in his Kirk. I can nocht expres the cair, kyndnes, and tender affection quhilk God kindlit in the harts of that peiple towards me in behalff of my wyff and chyld : For certean I am, if all hir friinds and myn in Scotland haid bein about hir, it was nocht in thair powar to haiff vſed hir ſa cairfullie, lowinghe, tenderhe, and diligathe ; and namhe, I war maiſt ingrat if I ſould forget my guid, godlie, and maiſt courteus Lady, my Lady Wedringhton, wha wated on mair cairfullie then the maidwyff, and receavit him from the wombe in hir awin ſkirt, and finding him nocht luhe, maid haſt to the fyre, and thruſting in her curſhar, brunt it, and helde to his naiſthrilles, wherby he quicned and kythed ſignes of lyff. This I ſa particularlie ſett down, partlie till extoll the cair and prouidence of God towards me, and parthe to moue the chyld to ſett himſelff to the knawlage and ſervice of that God wha thus brought him from the wombe. He was boin the 15 day of Januar, in the yeir 1584.

About the middes of Februar, efter a grait humiliation and faft for all thir cauffes, and confort of the holie communion keipit at Newcaftell, the noble men, partlie becaufe they perceaut that than lyimg neir the Border indangerit than frinds, and parthe at the defyre of his Maieftie, paft fouthe, and efter they haid remanit about a monethe in Northwitche, they cam to Londone : and I returning to Bervik, as my calling requyrit, preparit my wyff and companie, and followed to Londone be water

My guid Lady Wedringtoun wald neids detein my young fone, and haiff him in plege till my retourning, wha lykwayes, with our vther maift cairfull and loving frinds in Chryft, maid gud provifioun for our voyage. Mr Walter Balcanquall cam down from Londone, and fending for his Wyff, went in company with ws. We war in nomber about twoll perfones paffingers imbarkit about the beginning of Merche, bot be contrarie windes, with grait fafcherie and feiknes, war put in in Tinmouthe, whar we ley fax dayes, and again launching furthe vpon the fourt day we arryvit at Londone, whar meitting with my Vncle and his companie, we war nocht a lytle comforted.

1585 — A lytle efter the noble men cam to Londone, and I entered againe to my awin charge, mikle helped and meuragit be my Vncle, whom the noble men drew to tham, and maid him than domeftic. Our tentationes then war verie grait, for be Ambaffatour efter Ambaffatour fend to hir Maieftie, firft we war callit a grait ftope bak from our frinds, quhilk maid tham and ws bathe to tyne hairt and almaift difpear : bot fyne it was erneftlie futed that we fould be put out of Eingland, and manie promifes maid for that effect. Sa that indeid we luiked for na thing bot to be put from Eingland as Scotland ; bot the Lord our God haid heirin a gud wark in drawing ws neirar and neirar vnto him, and making ws knaw that he was to wourk that wark himfelff for his awin glorie. And therfor, firft in the fimmer he fend a Peft. quhilk paft throw the principall Townes, and raget till almaift vtter vaftation in the Townes of Edinburche, St. Andros, St. Jhonftoun, and Dondie, in fic fort that the comoun clamer of the peiple was againft the Court. With this fic vtragius tyrannie was vfit be Arran and his licentius, proude, impudent Lady, that all efteates miflykit and wenied at the fam Thus God prepared the peiple at hame that fimmer ; and at the herveft, togidder with the raging peftilence increffing mair and mair, namlie in Edinburche, the Lord fend fic tempeft of wather and rean, that all began to cry, the Lords hand wald nocht ftey vnto the tyme the minifteris of God and noble men war brought hame againe. The quhilk

when our frinds perceavit, they maid ws aduertifment, bot the difficultatie
was in purchaffing of licence, quhilk our vnfrinds, confederates with Arran,
wald nocht fuffer to be granted, till God prouydit in lyk maner a motiue for
that, to wit, the flauchtar of the Lord Ruffell. Warden, at a day of Trewes,
vpon the Bordour. The quhilk, for all excufes could be maid, crabit fa the
Quem that fche licenced our noble men ioyned with the Hamiltones to return
to thair frinds in Scotland. And fa efter a verie erneft exerceife of humiliation, keipit be our haill companie at Weftminfter, wharin manie teares war
powred out befor the Lord, and the hartes of all weill prepared about the beginning of October, the Eiles of Angus and Mar, with the Maiftir of Glames,
and than companies, paft from Londone, and with thame my Vncle Mr Andro, Mr Patrik Galloway, and Mr Walter Balcanquall, wha coming to the
Bordour, the Lord Hamilton and thofe that war at Bervik cam to tham;
and as they enterit in the countrey, ther reforted vnto tham without deley the
haill Bordours eft and waft, conducted by thair Lords of Hume, Boduell, and
Maxuell, and merching foirdwart with diligence cam to St. Ninians Kirk, a
myll from Sterling vpon the firft day of Nouember, and ther camped to the
number of ten thowfand horfinen. In this mean tyme, proclamationes with
all diligence was fend athoirt the countrey, and double this number war conveinit within the town of Stirling, but nocht halff fa refolut and weill haitet
to feght in the quarrell as our men war. Sa, to be fchort, on the morn foone
be brak of day they vnbefett the town, and with grait quietnes and vnrefift-
able courage miniftred be God, fcaled and clam ower the walles. A lytle refiftance was maid be Captean James and Coronell Stewart be the fpace of twa
houres, bot feing the courage of the vther they fchrank bak, and reteiring,
gaiff libertie to all to enter and win the town. Captean James haiffing in his
poutche the key of the brig, fled away that gett incontinent; the reft, viz
Montrofe, Crafurd, Glencarn, Aroll, and Colonell Steward reteired to the Caftell, whar the King was, but our folks perfuing hathe, cam all to the Caftell
hill, and clos vnder forefnout of the blokhous planted thair ftanddars and
campe.

The King perceaving that he was nocht able to keipe the caftell, and knawing that the peiples affection was towards thefe noble men and miniftels, refolued to Parliament, and fend furthe vnto our Lords the Secretar and Juftice
Clark, requyring of tham, firft, That his lyff, honour, and efteat micht be pre-
fernit: Secondlie, That the liues of Montrofe, Crafurd, and Coronell Steward
fould be fparit: Thridlie, That all maters fould be tranfacted peacablie And

vpon thefe conditiones offerit himfelff to be governed be thair advys and counfall in tyme coming

The noble men anfwered to the Kings meffangers, That for the firft, the
God of Heavin knew that they haid neuer anie vther intention then to preferue his Maiefties perfone, efteat, and dignitie; and to delyver his Maieftie
from the handes of fic, wha vnder pretext of his name and authoritie, had fa
crenalhe oppreft the Kirk and Comoun weill, and haid exponed to danger
bathe his Maiefties lyff and croun: That haifing the feir of God befor thair
eis, they war com to do his Maieftie all dewtie and fervice, and to fchaw thamfelues faithfull and obedient fubiects, as they haid done of befor; expofing
thamfelues to the violence of fic as befor tyme taught with his mother againft
him with difpleyed baner, to depryue him of his efteat and honour, wha nochtwithftanding haid bein of leat, at leaft than fucceffours in that caufe, admitted
o the handling of all his effeares.

As to the fecond, feing the perfones befor named, whafe hues war defyrit
to be fpairt, haid troublet the haill countrey, and bein inftruments of fic confufion as the lyk haid nocht bein hard nor fein in Scotland, they could do na
les for his Maiefties honour, and affection they bure to thair countrey, then
feik the meanes wharby they might be put in the hands of Juftice, to be vfed
as they haid demerit.

As to the thride, they thamfelues declarit to the King, that they maid humble
fupplication to his Hienes, that he himfelff fould tak ordour and fic all things
to pas, and be wrought pacible in an opportune and convenient tyme to the
grait contentment of all his guid fubiects; and for that effect promifed all ayde
and affiftance: protefting that they approched nocht to his Maieftie in armes,
and with fic companies, bot be conftrant for faneing of thair lyues and leivings
from the tyrannie of fic as fought than ruine and vtter wrak

The Kings Meffingers being departed, the noble men fend in lyk maner
vnto the King, requyring of his Maieftie thrie things:

Firft, that the King fould gift his confent to reform the corruptiones and
abbuffes that war crouppen within the Kirk and Comoun weill, be the euill
government of tham wha haid abbufit his authoritie; and therfor he wald allow as lawfull and gud fervice thair proceidings in feiking the faid reformation, and for that caufe that his Maieftie wald fubfcryve the fchort declaration
quhilk they haid formed of thair caufe; and that for than grnitter affurance,
that the ftramthes and Caftells quhilk the troublers of the efteat haid in thair
handes fould be delyuered vnto tham, to be keipit be fic as the Efteattes of the

Realme thought meit —Secondlie, that the faid troublers of the Eſteat ſould be giffen in thair keiping, to be prefented to Juſtice; and—Laſt, that the Kings Gard might be changit, and an vther choſin of fathfull, modeſt and fobre men, vnder ſic a Captean and Commander as the noble men ſould nam.

All theſe things war granted.   The Lord Hamilton maid Captean of Dumbartan; the Laird of Cowdounknowes of Edinbruche, and Stirling reſtored to the Erle of Mar; and the Maiſter of Glames maid Captean of the Garde   In end a parliament was proclamed to be haldin at Linlithgow the tent of December following for reſtoring again of noble men, miniſters and all.

The King receavit all the noble men in fawour, and granted tham what they wald aſk for ther particular   Bot concerning the maters of the Kirk, that twitched his honour fa, that he wald nocht be controlled therin, nor grant to na thing bot efter his pleafour, and fa tuk vpe a heiche humor againſt all the guid breithring, partlie becaufe he perceavit that the noble men war nocht verie erneſt in tha maters, getting then awin turnes done, as indeid, (except the guid Erle of Angus, to whafe hairt it was a continowall grieff that he could nocht get concurrance), ther was lytle or fmall ccar amangs tham therof, for all the wowes and fair promifes maid to God and his fervants, the quhilk the Lord in mercie mak them to tak till hairt in tyme and repent, befor the laſt come, quhilk can nocht, in his uſt iudgment, bot be mair feirfull nor the firſt; partlie becaufe he eſtimed the Kirk to be the cheiff caufe of his controlment in his proceidings firſt and laſt, the difcipline whairof he could na wayes lyk, ex metu Herodiano et Jeroboanino.

About the end of Nouember, warning was maid according to the ordour of the Kirk be the laſt Moderator, athort the Countrey to the breithring. to convein in Generall Affemblie, conform to cuſtome befor the Parliament at Dumfermling, na vther meit town being frie of the Peſt   The breithring frequentlie furthe of all partes referting thither, the portes of the town war cloſit vpon tham be the Proveſt for the tyme, the Laird of Pitfirren, alleaging he haid the Kings expres command ſa to do.   Therfor the breithring, comending that wrang to God the righteus iudge, convenit ſa mome as might in the fields, and conforting themfelues mutualie in God, apointed to meit in Linlithgow a certean dayes befor the Parliament.   Bot God within few yeirs peyit that Lard and Proveſt his hyre for that piece of fervice, when for the halding out of his fervantes from keiping his affemblie in that town, he maid his awin hous to fpew him out   For a day in the morning he was fund fallen out of a window of his awin hous of Pitfirren, thrie or four hous hight, wither be a me-

lancolus difpear cafting himfelff, or be the violence of vnkynd ghefts ludgit
within, God knawes, for being taken vpe his fpeit-he was nocht fa fenfible as
to declar it, bot within few hours efter deit.

The newes of the taking of Stirling was at the Court of England and in
Londone within aught and fourtie houres ; for it being done on Tyfday in the
morning, on the Funfday thereefter Mr Robert Bowes tauld ws, and on the
Fredday it was comona in the mouthes of all Londone   At the quhilk we
graithmlie reioyfing in the foueran guidnes and mercie of our God, and reforting togidder to ftear ws vpe mutualie to thankfulnes ; fa with all convenient dihgence we maid for the iorney bame ower, in the quhilk as in going,
fa in returning we fund the bountifull and gratius hand of our God with ws,
fa that we had occafion diuers tymes to fing vnto the praife of our God that
126 Pfalme, with manie ma, but namlie at our coming to Anwik on the fecond Sabathe of ovr iorney   Ther we refted, and wat called to dinner be Sr
Jhone Foftar, Lord Warden, wha, at mides of dinner, began bathe to glorifie
God in recompting what he haid wrought already, and to prophefie concerning the ftay of foull wather and of the peftilence, whowfone all the minifters
of God war brought hame againe, as indeid it was marked and found within a
monethe, that we war eftonifhed to heir the mouthe of a wardhe euill man
fa opened to fpeak out the wounderfull warkes and prafes of God, wrought
for ws.   We war in companie a nine or ten horfes, and fand him the gratius
God of the land in retourning, as we fund him of the fies in our paffage
fouthwart

Coming in Scotland. I left my wyff, wearie of fa lang a iorney, to reft at
Hutonhall, in companie with the relict of Mr James Lawfone, guid, fweit and
godhe Janet Guthrie, and with Mr Robert Dune tuk iorney to Linlithgow
to the parliament, fwalleing vpe be hope, inquenchable ioy of reformation of
all things amis, and grant welcoming with manie guid morrowes   But as at
our going out of the countrey, we knew nor faw na thing that might reafe ws
in anie grant hope of promifion or confort, and yit by the guid prouidence of
our God, we fand far beyond expectation, fa be the contrar, at our retourning,
loking for all guid and confortable, we fund na thing les

For firft, ryding from Hadington to Smeton, repofing on our gyde, we went
fordwart, whowbeit vnder night far, bot when we war in graittelt danger of
coll pittes and finks, the darknes was fa grant, that our gyd knew nocht what

* My gud nidnus ceaes fen fyre and maift fine and faithfull brother and frind, Mr Robert Dury
was with me, wha haid a monethe er twa of befor com from the Rotchell to London to ws.

he was, nor whow to gyde, fa that iff God haid nocht gydet ws, we haid bein lyk Thales, wha compafed the eithe, and died in a draw well at his awin dur When we haid fpent a guid part of the night, at laft ane of our hors rafhed on his nes vpon a geuill of a hous, bot wither it was hous, or ftak, or heuche, we knew nocht, nather faw hors or man, na nocht our awin fingar end, till ane lightand down grapes ellanges, and finds a dui, and chapping we gat fum folks that tauld ws we war in Tienent, fra the quhilk conducing a gyde, with a lantern knit to his hors teall to fchaw ws the way, with grait fafcherie throw the Coll Hors Gett we cam to Smeton On the morn we maid haft, and coming to Leftarik, dhfiuned, and about alleavin hours cam ryding in at the Water Gett of the Abbay, vpe throw the Canow Gett, and red in at the Nether bow, throw the grait ftreit of Edinbruche to the Waft Port, in all the quhilk way we faw nocht thrie perfones, fa that I mifkend Edinbruche, and almoft forgot that euer I haid fein fic a town About euein we cam to Lithgow, to a nomber of heauie and grieved breither, and a miferable vyll pretone, the lyk wharof I was neuer in all my dayes.

The occafion of the breithings greiff was, that they war out of hope to gett anie thing vndone at that Parliament, quhilk was done at the Parliament of the 1584; and that becaufe the King haid fett himfelff difpytfulhe againft the Kirk, and thefe in fpeciall wha haid bein with the Lords, namlie my vncle Mr Andro, wha haid bein verie quik and plean with the King diuers dayes And as for the noble men, they requyred that, firft, they might be fattent in thair roumes, and fyne wald do aneuche; bot it was tauld them, that that wald bathe weaken and fcham tham and thair caufe with God and man Yit in effect the guid breithring wai left and deferted be tham, and behoued to bear thair reprotches that wald do na thing for Chryft But by this, a heavier caufe of greiff was giften be a bitter invention that Mr Crag maid againft ws befor the King and haill Lords of Parliament, ften ed vpe, as he alleadgit, be a fermont that James Gipfone haid maid, in the pulpit of Edinbruche, againft the fubfcryving miniflers, of whom Mr Crag was the cheiff, fa that ther was the fend of a feirfull fchirme, giff God, be the meanes of patient and wyfe breithring, haid nocht born down the fanning at the nixt Affemblie Togidder with this, the thrang of the town was fa grait that we haid na confort of meat, drink, or ludging, bot fa euill and miferable, and therwith fa extream deir, that we war rather brought from wealthe, eafe and libertie, and caft in a wretched foull preffone, nor from exyll till our natiue countrey, Yit the confcience of our caufe and feruice of Chryft vpheld ws, and maid ws

u

to keipe togidder, in a deceyit hous, that nather helde out wind nor weit, with confort furnefit be the mightie confortar, the fpace of ten dayes or fyftein, till the Parliament endit; efter the quhilk alfo I was conftreanit to tarie ither ten, parthe to gett our Letters of Reftitution exped, and parthe for my hors, whom, for want of ftabling, the firft night I foundert in bathe the twa former feit, to my grait los

Efter diuers hatt, rouche, and maift fcharpe reafonings, haid betwix the King and my vncle Mr Andro, in end the King defyrit ws to giff in in wrait what we haid to fay againft his Actes of Parliament maid in anno 1584 Vpon the quhilk we formed and gaif in to his Maieftie thir Animaduerfiones following :

Animaduerfions of offences conceaued vpon the Actes of Parliament maid in the yeir 1584, in the monethe of May, prefented be the Commiffioners of the Kirk to the Kings Maieftie at the Parliament of Linlithgow in December, 1585

In the Firft Act it is thought a grait impeaning of the libertie of the trew Kirk, in fa far as na thing therby is granted to the fam, bot the libertie of preatching and miniftration of faciaments, feing the powar of binding and lowfing, quhilk is called the powar of the Keyes of the kingdom of heauin, confiftes nocht onlie in thefe poincts, bot alfo in iudgment, iurifdiction and remouing of offences out of the Kirk of God, and excommunication to be pronunced againft the difobedient be tham that ar office bearers within the fam And fa the haill difcipline is left out And this act reftrictes the libertie granted be vther Actes of Parliament of befor concerning difcipline and correction of maners, quhilk war eftablifhed be a law in the firft yen of your Maiefties reing Our warrands of the Word of God for this part of the libertie of the Kirk, we ar to bring furthe when your Maiefbe pleafes

As concerning the Second Act, the narration therof apeires to be iklanders againft fum of the minifterie, quhilk we wald wis to be reformed, or vther wayes conceaued, except the treuthe therof war verefied And, as to the fubftance of the act itfelft, it attributes vnto your Maieftie a foueraine powar of iudgment, nocht onlie vpon the perfones of all vour fubiects, but alfo in all maters, wherin they, or anie of them falbe apprehendit, fummoned, or chargit, &c. Quhilk appeirs to be verie ftrange, the lyk wharof we heir nocht to haiff bein practifed in anie chriftian comounwelthe, and can nocht ftand with the Word of God For, although the perfones of men ar fubiect to your Maieftie and ciuill iudges, when they offend againft vour lawes, yit in maters mere ecclefiafticall, and concerning confcience, na chriftian prince can iuftlie clame, nor euer claimt, to himfelff fic powar to iudge, feing the prince in that behalft is bot a member of the Kirk, and Jefus Chryft onlie the Head, wha onlie hes powar to giff lawes in maters of confcience. And fa faid the godlie Ambrofe, " Imperator bonus intra ecclefiam non fupra ecclefiam eft " And to confound the Jurifdictiones ciuill and ecclefiafticall is that thing wherin all men of guid iudgment haiff iuftlie fund fault with the Pape of Rome, wha clamed to himfelft the powar of bothe the fwords, quhilk is als grait a fault to a ciuill magiftrat till acclam or vfurpe, and fpecialie to iudge vpon the doctrine, erionis, and heresies, he nocht being placed in ecclesiasticall function to interpret the Scriptures. The warrands heirof out of the Word of God we ar lykwayes readie to bring furthe

Anent the Thrid Act, it appeires to be obscure, bot vit the effect therof to tend to this, That nane defyre alteration of the form or custome of the conveining of the Estaets in Parliament as fam hes tought the fam to be innovat. Su, we vi derstand that the ancient libertie of the faid Thrie Estaets is louable and ancient, bot lykwayes it is of trenth that amangs vther corruptiounes that wai in tym of papistrie, the ecclefiasticall estaet was corrupted, and apointed to be of fic persones wha haid na lawfull function in the Kirk of God, and fpecialie aught nocht to haiff place, religion being reformed within this realme, we mein of Bifchopes, Abbots, and fic lyk Popifhe Prelacies, in confideration that be Actes of Parliament maid of befor, all authoritie and iurifdiction of the Pape of Rome, and of vthers flowing from him, nocht aggreeable to the Word of God, is abolifhed within this realme   Therfor, we think in our confcience, and haiff oft inted it of your Maieftie, that nane fhould vot in Parliament in nam of the estaet of the Kirk bot they that haiff thair calling of God, and ar conftitut in ecclefiasticall office and function according to his Word, and therfor dufcrent Committiouars, of the maift lernit bathe in the law of God and of the countrey, being of the function of the minifterie or eldais of the Kirk to reprefent that estaet, at whaie mouthe the law aught to be requyfit, namlie in ecclhiafticall maters, and it is nocht the grait rents er promotion to grait benefices, nor yit the dignitie of kmred or blood, that caries with it all knawlage or iudgment, bot vthei men, wha ar coumpted of interionr rank to the iudgment of the warld, may preveall therm. And thei is na inconvenient, that Committiouars may be fend fra the Kirk reprefenting the thrid estaet, alfweill as from the burrowes, to haiff vott in parliament   Therfor we humblie defyre your Maieftie to declar the faid act, and deny nocht vnto ws that libertie that Gods Word and the lawes of the countrey maid of befor, and æquitie and reaffone in this behalff craues

As concerning the Fourt Act, the tytle therof is difcharging all iurifdictiones and iudgments nocht approued be Parliament, and all affemblies and conventiounes without your Maiefties fpeciall licens and commandiment   And, in the narratiue, it appeires there is a fklanderus report reafed vpon the Kirk and office bearers within the fam, for vfing certean iurifdictiones nocht approned be the lawes of the realm, and alleaging ane Act maid in the dayes of your Hienes grandfyr, that all the heges aucht to be rewled be the comoun lawes of the realm, and be na vther lawes.   And, therfor, the faid act difcharges all iudgments and iurifdictiones, fpirituall or temporall, accuftomed to be vfed thir xxv yeirs bypaft, nocht approued be your Hienes and Eftaets in Parliament, with thretning of execution vpon all perfones that vfes or obeyes the fam, as vfurpers and contemners of your Hienes authoritie, and for convocation of your Hienes heges.   Su, we maift humblie craue your Hienes mynd to be farder declaied herin, for it appeires to ws to be verie ftrange, and a thing that can nocht ftand with the libertie granted be Jefus Chryft to his Kirk, and tham that bear function and office within the fam.   And, firft, as to the Act of King James the Fourt, your Hienes grandfyr, we fay, that the fam act appeires pleanlie to mein of the cmill iurifdiction, quhilk he and his predeceffours and fucceffours may clam within this realme be than Royall powar, and nocht of the ecclefiafticall iurifdiction, for that law was maid againft tham of the Ylles, that vfed the King of Dennraiks lawes in ciuill maters, and, in your grandfyrs dayes, thei was an vther ecclehiafticall iurifdiction within this realme, efter the maner of Papiftrie, vfed be tham that war called Kirkmen, vnto the days of reformation of relligion, as hes bein vfed continualie fen that tyme, with quhilk na fault was fund.   And it is of trenthe that ther is a fpritnall iurifdiction granted to the Kirk of God be his Word, (quhilk makes na derogation to the iurifdiction of erthlie princes,) wherof the office bearers within the Kirk in this realm hes bein in peaceable poffeffion and vfe

thir xxiiij yens bypaſt with the man, wherof followed na trouble, bot grait quietnes to the Kirk
and Comonnwelthe. And ther hes bein man trouble in the ecclefiaſticall eſteat within thir twa
yeirs laſt bypaſt, nor ener was fen the relligion was reformed within this countrey. Allwayes we
offer ws to proue, be guid warrands of the Word of God, that it is lawfull to the ecclefinſticall eſteat to convocat Aſſemblies, and to hauld the ſam, and till apoint an ordour, place, and tyme, for
conveining of the ſam, to treat vpon ſic maters as conceines the Kirks eſſeares, quhilk na wayes im-
peais your Maiefties cruill and royal inriſdiction, bot rather fortifies and decores the ſam   Nocht
denying, in the mean tyme, bot it is lawfull to your Maieſtie and Eſteates when ane extraordinar neceſſitie fall requyre, to call the members and office bearers within the Kirk in few or grantter number,
and cauſe tham be convened to reſolue vpon ſic things as conceines than eſteat, and neceſſitie of
the tyme   And tordai, conceining the Generall Aſſemblies of the Kirk, ther is an Act in the firſt
yen of your Hienes reing, rateſeing the authoritie therof, and deceining appellationes to be denoluit
therto, as to the laſt iudgment of maters conceining the Kirk   The ſam argument we vſe conceining
vther aſſemblies, alſwill particular, and of the Preſbyteries, as provinciall, be the paritie of
reaſone and guid grounds of the Word of God, quhilk we offer ws to ſchaw. Beſeikand your
Maieſtie to reform, or repeal and qualahe this act according therto, for, it it fall ſtand in the form
that it is, nocht onlie conventiones for diſcipline, bot alſo for heiring of the Word, wilbe therby
diſchargit.

As to the Fyft Act, we allow weill with our hartes, that all they that ar planted in the function
of the miniſtrie, if they commit ane offence worthie of deprivation, they be depriuit bathe of thair
functiones and reveneus, quhilk they poſſes for vſing the ſam   Bot to mak exception of perſones,
that they quhilk hanſt vort in Parliament fall nocht be controllit in that behalff, nor the lyk iudgment
execut vpon tham, we can nocht vnderſtand whow that can agrie with reaſone and guid lawes, ſeing we ar able to verefie the maiſt part of tham in that eſteat to be man ſklanderus, and wordy to
be depriued bathe of than function and beneſice than ane vther   And, as to the votting in Parliament, who they aucht to be that ſould hanſt place ther, we hauſt declarit our iudgment of befor
Therfor, this act appeires to mak exception of perſones, quhilk can nocht weill ſtand be the law of
God or man   As to the cauſſes of deprivation, it requyres alſo a conference, quhilk war ower lang
now to put in wait to your Maieſtie.   Therfor pleiſe your Hienes alſo till advys better hereupon
and qualeſie the ſam.

Now, for the Saxt Act, the dytter therof apeires to be verie canfull that miniſters ſall avait
vpon than function and office, and ſall vſe na vther function, iudgment, or office, that may abſtract
tham therfra   Giff it be ſimplie meined the act is verie guid   Bot, with your Maieſties licens,
they ar verie far in the wrang to your Hienes that wald burding yow with all function and iuriſdiction bathe in cruill and ecclefiaſticall maters, being bot a perſone, and mikle les able to diſcharge,
nor a ſimple miniſter of a kirk to diſcharge his cure. And, fordai, feing the ſam acte, and vther
actes of this Parliament, attributes iuriſdiction to Biſchopes ouer manie kirks and to be iudges in
ecclefiaſticall cauſſes alſo, they ar far man vnmeit to diſcharge themſelues therof nor a ſimple miniſter that hes onlie a flok or kirk, and, peradventure, an colleg with him in the ſam   And, fordar, in ſa far as the ecclefiaſticall eſteat is an of the Thrie Eſteates in Parliament, and as we ar able
to proue the office bearers and miniſters in the Kirk aught to repreſent the ſaid eſteat, it can nocht
weill ſtand that all iudicators ſould be taken from tham, ſeing it is the ſupream iudicator in this
realme, wherin bathe cruill and criminall cauſſes ar decydit, and, therfor, to tak away this iudgment from tham that ar of the ecclefiaſticall function it is verie hard, and can nocht weill ſtand

with the libertie granted to the Kirk of ancient tyme   As to the vther ciuill iudgments that may abstract ministers from thair cure, we think they aucht nocht to mell therwithe bot sa far as they ar called lawfullie by the Prince, and ar able to discharge the sam.*

Passing ower the rest of the Actes as nocht perteining to the Kirk, till we com to the thretteint, in the quhilk the first yeir fruicts of all benefices is decernit to be takin to your Hienes vse and your Gaird, na prouision being maid for the ministers that serues what the benefice lyes, and the hrst yeirs fruicts war neuer crauit within prelacies befor this Act   And also a grait yenhe taxation is leyed vpon the benefices, as appeires, bathe grait and smal, besydes the thrids   Remedie wald thertor be pronydit be your Maiestie whow the Kirks may be serued sufficientlie, and the ministers nocht disapointed of thair stipends, for the reveneus of the Kirk ar alreadv sa diminithed, that altho new impositiones be nocht leyed thervpon, it is difficill to keipe anie ordour within the Kirk quhilk mikle mair salbe impossible if they be farder diminithit   And as to the Munks portiones, it wald be a godlie ordinance to your Maiestie till apoint the sam, or els a guid part therof, for bursares in Collages, as sum tyme it was proponit and halffhe grantit

Sa, passing to the Twentie Act   The sam giftes commission to Patrik, called Archbischope of St Andros, and vther bischopes, or sic as your Maiestie sall constitut iudges in ecclesiatheall caufses, nocht specifeing of what efteat they sould be, ecclesiatheall or ciuill, and lyclyk mention is maid of sum Commissionars in the faxt act, to quhilk Commissionars powar is granted to put ordour to all maters and caufses ecclesiasticall, visit the kirks and stat of the ministrie, reform collages, receaue presentationes, and they onlie gift collationnes vpon benefices, and that Commissiones sould be extend-it hervpon, under your Hienes Grait Seall, conform to that quhilk diuerst Commissiones ar directet with powar to Bischopes alleanerlie in thair awin persones, without anie assessours or assistars, and, namlie to the Archbischope of St Andros, within his haill diocete, or to anie his deputes and com-missionars vnder him, with powar also to depose ministers, quhilk is nocht contened in the act, and lykwayes to place and displace maisters of Collages, attoure the tennour of the act   Sir, to speak our conſciences planlie concerning this act, we suppose your Maiestie be of guid mynde that the sam sall continow na langer nor this present Parliament, bot sall allutterlie be dischargit, for sa it is contened in the act itselff, in the end therot, in expres termes   wharbe we think your Maiestie and Estcates war of mynd it sould nocht continow when it was first maid.

And, indeid, gift it sould continow manie and grait inconvenients sould of necessitie follow to the Kirk of Jesus Chryst and esteat therof.   For, first, to deuolue that powar in a manes hand, al-tho he wer neuer sa wyse, lerned, and godlie, to do all things in the Kirk at his awin pleasure and authoritie, be himselff allanerlie, or his deputs, takes away that libertie and guid ordour quhilk the Spirit of God, be the mouthe of Pmll, willes to be in the Kirk, and wharof we haiff manie vther warrands into Gods Word, for it aperteines to the ecclesiasticall Senat, and nocht to anie a man to do those things.   Nather is it a ciuill thing, and to be committed to a ciuill magistrat, or to whome they pleise, to govern the Hous of God, quhilk is his Kirk, and can haist na exemple of anie vn-corrupt age or persone.   Therfor, we suppon your Maiestie will clam no fordar to the sam, nor yit suffer sic men to abbuse the Kirk in that sort.   And, as to vther iudges to be constitut in eccle-siastienll caufses be your Maiestie, nocht specifeing of what esteat they sould be, ciuill or ecclesiastik, that is indeid till vse the powar of bathe the swords, quhilk all men of guid iudgment lies damnit in the Pape   Sir, we ceas to mak fordar discourse vpon this act, or to declar the qualities of tham

---

* Notandum, That Mr Robert Pont penned this Animaduersion, and wald haiff it thus in, by the iudgment of my vncle Mr Andro, myne, and vthers, wha haid bein vpon the Session, and is of opinion yit that sa is lawfull.

to whom he commiſſiones ar giflen, becauſe we ſuppoſe your Maieſtie will willinghe reforme and abrogat alluterlie that act

Anent the Acts nocht imprented

SIR, We find amangs theſe Acts not imprented, the Act annulling the excommunication of Mr Robert Mongumerv, wherein your Maieſtie takes authoritie with your Eſtcates in Parliament, to mell with that thing quhilk can haiſt na exemple that anie prince ener melled with ſen the firſt planting of the relligion of Jeſus Chriſt   To pronunce excommunication vpon impenitent ſinners, or to abſolue tham therfra, or to decern the ſaming effectuall, or nocht effectuall, can na man pertein to prince, or anie ciuill magiſtrat, nor to preatche the Word of God, and miniſtrat Sacraments, for they are Lathe in lyk maner committed be Chryſt, our Maiſter to the trew offhce bearers within his Kirk, when, as he ſaid, Dic eccleſiæ, &c   Therfor, amangs all vther things, we can nocht merueil a lytle wha ſould be ſa bauld to put in your Maieſtics head till ſturpe that powar, or mell therwith, ſeing, for the kyk fact, Vzza, the King of Juda, was ſa terrible plagget, and his haill land ſhaken   God forgift tham that wald ſa reopen your Hienes without reſpect of conſcience, or the ten of God   We beſeik your Maieſtie to renok this, and mell na fordar therwith, as a thing nocht perteining to your offhce, or anie ciuill magiſtrat

Ther is an vther act amangs the nocht imprented concerning the payment of the miniſters ſtipends, of the quhilk we can ſpeak na thing becruſe we want the copie of it, beſeikand your Maieſtie to gift commandment to the Clark of Regiſtar that we may haiſt, and gift our reaſones in againſt it gift neid beis

The Supplicatione

SIR, We haiſt, in the ſen of God, at your Maieſties command, as ſchortnes of tyme wald ſuffer, giffen our animadueiſiones vpon the laſt actes of Parliament May 1584, beſeikand your Maieſtie to bear with our langunge, if in anie part it be nocht ſa perfytted and courtlie as ſome men wald wis, for we tend onlie vnto the end of theſe things wherof we war in conference with your Grace, to open tham vpe ſimphe and planlie, and to ſpeak the treuthe in our conſcience, (for it is nocht our dewtie to diſſemble with your Grace,) when we haiſt peruſed and read theſe actes ower and ower againe, ſa dilgenthe as we can, we can nocht think in our iudgment whow the ſam can ſtand as they ar formed, or whow anie interpretation that can be maid theivpone, viiles it was to contein contradiction, quhilk is an vncomlie thing in making or ſetting out of lawes, for the law itſelf ſayes, ' They that may ſpeak planlie in making of lawes, contracts, or anie ſic thing, and ſpeaks obſcurlie and ambigmithe, ſic contracts and lawes ar to be exponed againſt the maker or former thereof, ' quia potuerunt apertius dicere.'" Therfor ſawing the honors of your Maieſtie and your Eſteates, we think it man comlie to place new, reformed, and plean lawes in their roum, nor till interpret theſe quhilk can nocht be weill interpret in anie guid ſence. We truſt your Maieſtie will tak this our ſimple meaning in a good part, and do that quhilk is maiſt meit according therto. The Lord grant your Maieſtie the ſprit of trew and vpright iudgment. AMEN

There is a thing fordar, quhilk in maiſt humble maner we craue of your Maieſtie, that it be prouvdit be Act of Parliament, That lykas your Hienes is to reſtore tham of the Nobilitie to thair honours and leivings, ſa your Maieſtie will reſtore the Kirk of God, and Miniſterie therof, to thair former poſſeſhones, alſweill in diſcipline as than leivings, rounes, and offices, fra the quhilk they war difplaced be occafion of the taids actes, or anie thing following thervpon , and to than ftipends all-weill bygean as to cum, feing a giat part therof remeanes as yit on takin vpe

Thir Ammaduerfiones and Supplication, penned af hand becaufe of want of all commoditie, and prefented to his Maieftie be ws, the King tuk pean himfelff, be the fpace of foul and twentie houres, to tak him to his Cabinet, and, withe his awin hand, wrot and penned his Declaration following word be word :

The Kings Declaration and interpretation of his Actes of Parliament fet furthe

Nam eius est explicare, cuius est condere

THE Firft makes onlie mention of the pretching of the Word and Sacraments, nocht therby to abrogat anie guid fardar polecie or iurifdiction in the Kirk, bot, allanerlie to remit a pait therof to the actes infewing , and the maift quhilk as yit is vnaggreit vpon or concludit, I entend, God willing, to caufe to be perfyted be a godlie General Affemblie of Bifchopes, Minifters, and vther godlie and leined Imperatore prefidente And then fall the act be maid man ample, according to the conclufion aggreit vpon tham bathe in polecie and iurifdiction

The Second Act hes twa parts, an narratiue and a chaige The narratiue hes twa partes an afhrming that fum of your vocation haid appellt fra me, as nocht being than iudge ordinar. I dout nocht yourfelues will na wayes deny this, fen fum of yourfelues did it, and I dout be yit tkarie far from it. The vther part makes mention of the treafonable, feditius, and contumelius fpeitches vttercd be fum of your calling, in pulpit, againft me and my progenitors. This part lykwayes can nocht weill be denyit, fen it is man nor euident that it hes bein the maift part of fum minifters exercers thir foui or tyve yens paft. Allwayes, whowfoone the haill minifters of Scotland fall mend than maners in this poinct, the forfaid act falbe referndet. As to the fecond part of the Act, it contemes a charge that nan, being fummoned or accufed be me, fall declyne my iudgment in refpect I am declarit and confirmed Judge be the Parliament over all perfones within this realme, in all caufles that they falbe apprehendit or fummoned for , and in the lyne end it fayes, that nan fall declyne my iudgment in the premifles. Now, fay I, and declares, (quhilk declaration falbe als authentik as the Act itfelff,) that I, for my part, fall never, nather my pofteritie, aucht euer cite, fumond, or apprehend, anie paftou or preatchour for maters of doctrine in relligion, faluation, herefies, or tiew interpretation of the Scriptuie , bot according to my firft Act, quhilk confirmes the libertie of pretching the Word, miniftiation of the Sacraments, I awow the fam to be a matei mere ecclefiafticall, and altogidder impertinent to my calling , therfor neuer fall I, nor neuer aucht they, I mein my pofteritie, acclame anie powar or iurifdiction in the forfaids

The Thrid Act is fa reafonable and neceffar, that it neids na declaring nor explication, except onlie this, that my bifchopes, quhilk ar ane of the Thrie Efteates, fall haift powar, als tar as Gods Word and exemple of the primitiue Kirk will permit, and nocht according to that man of fine, his abominable abufes and corruptiones But I can nocht aneuche wounder whar yie fund that rewll or exemple, ather in Gods Word or anie reformed Kirk, that fum minifters, be commiffion of the reft, aught to be an of the Efteates in Parliament Weill, God purge your fpirits from ambition and

\thei indecent affectiones for your calling and giff vow grace to teatche, in all humilitie and fimphcitie, his Word and veritie.

In the Fourt Act I difchaige all iurifdictiones nocht approved in Parliament, and conventiones without my fpeciall licence. As to the difchaige of iurifdictiones, my meining and declaration is That they fall ceas whill a fetled polecie and iurifdiction be eftablilfied according to the miflour and lyne of Gods Word. As to difchaige of Affemblies, they ar nocht fimplie difchaigit bot onlie ordanit that they fould be halden with my fpeciall licence. And fuilie, I truft, that in all reformed Kuks, whan the princes and magiftiates war found in religioun vie fall find that the affemblies of the Kuk was nocht onlie be than fpeciall licence, bot evin be than calling, and they thamfelues Prefidents and Moderatois of tham. Yie do euill in making yourfelues to be ignorant of vou awin act, as to think the narratiue of this act fklanderus and vntrew.

As to the Fyft Act it exemes the bifchopes onlie for this caufe, for that it fpeakes onlie of deprivation of bifchopes be Synodall Affemblies wheras they fould be deprived be Generall. As to the caufies of deprivation, they falbe aggreit vpon be the Kuk, and therefter my act accordinghe qualefiet.

The hindmaid part of my declaration vpon the Third Act expones and with fufficient reafones proues the Saxt Act to be weill, and befyd the forfaid Saxt Act I am affinit na thing repugnant but intllie aggreiing with the Word of God.

As to the Thretteint, my intention was euer that all benefices of cure vnder prelacies fould be excepted, and fa fall they be referved in the Act. As to the xx Act, it is indeid bot temporall, and ten it is maid till induce onlie whill the Parliament, and farder during my will, it may be allweill callit bak without a parliament as with it. As indeid I mein, efter further conference with tuin of the miniftrie to tak a folide ordour theranents, but in a thing yie misconftrue it,—Wharas, vie alleage that it gifles authoritie to a perfone to reforme the Kuk quhilk is nocht, but it apomets euerie bifchope to reform his awin diocefe, and the Buchope of St Andros awin declaration apomtes ilk bifchope a counfell of his awin diocefe fa as in effect this act ordeanes ilk bifchope with his diocefe to reforme his awin diocefe. And as to the commiffionars nocht ecclefiafticall ioyned to tham, they ar ioyned to gift thair advyfles and nocht to interpone than authoritie, as vie vourfelues hes haid findrie men mare euill aflifling your Affemblies, and as it wilbe maift neceffar that fum men lerned and godlie be yit fchofin out for fattehng of the polecie.

As to the Act concerning the excommunication of the Bifchope of Glafgow, I man firft deleat the occafion fchorhe, and thervpon induce the anfwer and meining. Efter that he haid bein oft cited fummoned, and admonifhed vnder pean of excommunication to demit his benefice, and he, nochtwithftanding, ftill poffeffing the fanung, depending vpon me wha gaift it to him. At laft, fum of the miniftiers, fpecialhe fum of the Prefbyterie about Edinbruche was called (as oft befor they haid bein for the fam caufe,) before the Counfall and defyrit to leave at that form of proceeding whill it war tried be further conference wuther bifchopes was tolerable in the Kuk of God or nocht. This defyre was granted and promitt be the haill miniftiers prefent, bot immediathe therefter he was excommunicat at the kirk of Libbertoun, a landwart kirk againft promife * They being callit for againe, and accufed of ther promife, they all denyit the knawlage therof, and nocht onlie they but the haill miniftene of Scotland, except that onlie man Damdfone that pronunced the fentence the haill Kuk then difawowing, and that onlie man adwowing the deid. Chryft faying, Die ec-

---

* Lides hic penes principem.

clefire, and a onlie man ftellmg that dint in a quyet holl   The Act of Parliament reduces the
fentence for informalitie and nulletie of proces, nocht as iudges whidder the excommunication was
grundit on guid and iuft cauffes or nocht, but as witnes that it was informalie proceidit againft the
warrand of Gods Word, exemple of all reformed Kirks, and your awin particular cuftome in this
countrey.   And for approbation of the premifles, the forfaid bifchope falbe producit befor the firft
Generall Affembhe that I fall apoint, and thervpon the crymes that war leyed to his charge, fall
ather be peremptorilie abfolued or condemned.

Then fchorthe till end this my declaration, I mynd nocht to cut away anie libertie granted be
God to his Kirk . I acclame nocht to myfelff to be iudge of doctrine in relligion faluation, herefies, or trew interpretation of Scripture   I allow na Bifchopes according to the traditiones of men,
or inuentiones of the Pape, bot onlie according to Gods Word, nocht to tyrannife ower his brething,
or to do anie thing of himfelf, but with the advys of his haill diocesfe, or at leaft with the
wyfeft number of tham to ferue him for a counfall, and to do na thing him allean, except the
teatching of the Word, miniftration of the Sacraments, and votting in Parliament and Counfall.
Finalie, I fay his office is, folum ενισκοπειν ad vitam, haithng therfor fum prelation and dignitie
aboue his brething, as was in the primitiue Kirk. My intention is nocht to difcharge anie iurifdiction in the Kirk that is conform to Gods Word, nor to difcharge anie affembhes bot onlie thofe that
falbe haldin by my licence and counfall   My intention is nocht to mell with excommunication ,
nather acclame I to myfelff or my aires, powar in anie thing that is mere ecclefiafticall and nocht
αδιαφορον, nor with anie thing that Gods Word hes fimphe deuolut in the hands of his ecclefiafticall Kirk.   And to conclud, I confes and acknawlage Chryft Jefus to be head and lawgiffar to the
fam , and whatfumeuer perfones do attribut to thamfelnes as head of the Kirk, and nocht as member to fufpend or alter anie thing that the Word of God hes onhe remitted to tham, that man, I
fay committes manifeft ydolatrie, and finnes againft the Father in nocht trufting the words of his
Sone , againft the Sone in nocht obeving him, and taking his place , againft the Holy Ghoft, the
faid hahe fpreit bearing contrarie record to his confcience.

This mikle for my declaration, promifed at our laft conference, fa far as fchortnes of tyme could
permit   Wharin whatfoeuer I haiff affirmed, I will offer me to proue be the Word of God, pureft
ancients and moderns neoterics, and be the exemples of the beft reformed Kirks. And whatfoeuer
is omitted for leak of tyme, I remit firft to a convention of godlie and lerned men, and nixt till a
Generall Affembhe, that be tha meanes a godlie polecie being fatteht, we may vinformalie arme
our felues againft the comoun enemie, whom Sathan els feiling the brathe of God, makes to rage
in thir letter dayes. December 7 An. 1585

                                                            JAMES REX

Efter the receaving and reiding of this Declaration, the Parliament pofting
till an end, and all men mikle weiried in a cauld wintar fa ill eafed, and finding na affiftance nor confort, bot contrar bathe in nobilitie and brething, we
behoued till content, and tak that might be gottin for the prefent   And fa,
efter exhibition of this Supplication following, the meiting diffolued

The Commiffioner of the Kirks Supplication, giffen in efter the receatt of the former Declaration.

SIR, Let it pleafe your Hienes, we haiff fein and confidderit your Maiefties Declaration and in-

                                    X

terpretation vpon the mentioned Actes of Parliament. We praise God, as it becometh ws, for your Maieties iudgment and knawlage. Nochtwithstanding, we wald maist humblie craue that in this weghtie caufe concerning the eftablifment of a perfyt polecie and ftat of gouernment in the Kirk, to ftand to all ages and pofterities to cum, that the mater might be mair deiplie and digeft-lie confiddent, be conference of the maist lerned and godlie of your Hienes realme, and gif neid be, with confultation of the beft reformed Kirks in vther countries. That thereftter your Maief-tie, with advys of your Eftreats, may eftablifhe a perfyt and fetteht law in Parliament. And, in the mean tyme or at left to the nixt Parliament, your Hienes will grant ws libertie and freidome to hauld our ordinarie affemblies, and vfe he difciphne as we war in vfe of befor this leat Actes, for gouernment of the ecclefiafticall eficares, concerning the quhilk we falbe at all tymes reache to gif an accompt to God, your Maieftie, and guid Countall, if we do anie thing befyds our dewtie, or to pertuibe the Comoun Wealthe, fa far as lyes in ws. And in this mean tyme, that your Maieftie will grant to reftore all Minifters Maifters of Scholles and Collages to thair roumes and poffeffiones. And fpecialhe that our breithing, Mr Jhone Howdone and Wilyeam Watfone be delyverit out of warde, and that we be nocht troublet in the mean tyme, to impend and ftay all execution of the lait maid Actes of Parhament, mentioned la oft againft ws. And that the bifchopes vfe na thing bot that quhilk they war in vfe of befor the making of the forfaids Actes, and pertuibe nocht the Kirk nor Affemblies.

1586.—Thatt wintar my vncle fpent in Glafgw, being erneftlie intreated to vifit that Collage, quhilk was his eldeft berin; and I was occupied, firft, in tranfporting of my wyff from the Southe to the Northe whar hir father was in Montrofe. Thereftter, leaving hir ther, I was occupied in Edinbruche and vther places about the Collage efteares; in getting the leiving and ordour therof reftorit and reftablifhed, quhilk the Bifchope had altered and turned from Theologie to Philofophie, ab equis ad afinos; and be contentius pley be-twix Mr Jhone Robertfone, an of the Maifters wha remeaned behind ws, and Mr Dauid Achmoutie, claiming agane, efter my departing, the tytle and intro-miffion of Œconomer therof, was pitifulhe rent and confoundit.

Fra the Parhament the Peft abated, and began to be ftranghe and remark-abhe withdrawin be the mercifull hand of God, fa that Edinbruche was fre-quented agane that wintar; and at the entrie of the fpring, all the Townes al-moft defolat befor, repeipled, and St Andros amangs the reft; to the quhilk Mr Andro and I retourned and enterit in the Collage about the middes of the monethe of Merche. At our entrie we war put in mynd of the Prouinciall Affemblie, accuftomed to be keipit in the beginning of Apryll, intermitted du-ring the haill twa yeirs of our abfence; and vnderftanding that I had bein Moderator at the laft Synod quhilk was keipit, it ley on me to mak the doc-trine at the beginning of the Affemblie following. The text and purpofe wharof, be my vncles advys. I chufit out of the xii. to the Rom. 3, 4, 5, 6. 7,

8.   The Affemblie being convened in the place accuftomed verie frequenthe, and the bifchope placing himfelff hard befyde me that teatched, with a grait pontificahtie and big countenance, as he braggit he was in his awin citie, and haid the King his maifters fawour, he neidit to fear no man.   Efter incalling of the nam of God, entring on the doctrine, etter the deduction and opening vpe of the text, I intreated firft the groundes and poincts of the trew difcipline confirming the fam be clen warrands of Scripture ; thereftei refuted the contrarie corruptiones, namhe of the humane and deivilhfhe bifchoprik Thridlie, was difcoui fit the maner of planting and fettling with maift profitable, comhe, and confortable poffeffion of the right and trew difcipline within the Kirk of Scotland, vntill thefe twa or thrie yeirs laft bypaft :   Fourthe, it was deducit and declarit throwout the haill ages of the Kirk, fen the planting therof be the Apoftles, whow that the prefuming and fwalling of the cheiff corrupt members, be auarice and ambition, haid vitiat and wrakit the efteat of the Kirk from tym to tyme, bringing in fectes, fchifmes, herefies, and all kynd of corruption bathe in doctrine and maneis :   And laft, comming in particular to oui awin Kirk of Scotland, I turned to the Bifchope fitting at my elbow, and directing my fpeitche to him perfonalie, I recompted to him fchorthe his lyff, actiones and proceidings againft the Kirk, taking the Affemblie ther to witnes, and his awin confcience befor God, giff he was nocht an euident pruiff and exemple of that doctrine, whom being a minifter of the Kirk the dragon haid fa ftangit withe the poifone and venom of auarice and ambition, that fwalling exorbitantlie out of miffour, thretned the wrak and deftruction of the haill bodie, in ceas he war nocht tymouthe and with courage cut of   This particularlie confirmed and cleired, exhortation was direct to the Affemblie convenit ther to play the chirurgian for preferving of the body, namhe feing all meanes of amendment haid bein lang fyne vfed vpon that maift corrupt member and monftruus :   And this was done with fic powai of the fpieit and force of vtterance as it pleafed God to furneis for the wark he haid in hand

When I haid endit, the bifchope begoud with certean friuolus and forgit queftiones and chalenges againft me, adding thervnto thretnings that I fould be maid till anfwer befoi his Maieftie for my doctrine offenfiue againft the King and Actes of his Hienes Parliament, bot fa dafhit and ftrucken with terroi and trembling that he could fkarfe fitt, to let be ftand on his feit.   Bot the Affemblie, keiping thair ordour, chufit a Moderator, and therefter cenfurit my doctrine, and all in a voice glorified God, and approved the fam, praying God to

giff tham grace to byde be that treuthe quhilk haid bein cleirlie and mightelie delyverit to tham out of Gods Words, and to endewour to difcharge that
dewtie whairto they war fa movinghe exhorted   Therefter enterit in proces
with the bifchope, wha annes getting out of the Affemblie, wald na wayes giff
his prefence thairto againe, alleaging proudlie that it aperteined to him to
iudge it, and nocht to it to iudge him   Bot the treuthe was, he was dafhit
in confcience, and terrified with the number of gentilmen conveined, that,
nochtwithftanding his awin citie and his maifters fawour, he fenned to teir
eueire man he faw   To be fchort, the Affemblie proceiding with all grauitie,
leafor, and ordour, in end, for manie notorius crymes, troubling of the Kirk,
and prefent malignant contumacie, promuncit that fentence of excommunication againft him, the weght wharof he felt the farer therefter, that vphaldin
a whyll be the authoritie of man, he proudlie repyned againft the fam

A day or twa efter he penned an excommunication, and in a bifchoplie maner fend out a boy with ane or twa of his Jakmen, and red the fam in the
Knk, wherby be his archiepifcopall authoritie he excommunicat Mr Andro
Mehull, me, and a certean ma of the brethring   quhilk was as mikle thought
of, euen amangs the peiple, as gift he haid fylled the Kirk

Then with diligence he directs away to the King a heavie complent, with
a large and fchrewdlie penned Appellation, the quhilk I anfwered at lainthe,
as was thought maift neidfull for the tyme ; and to the quhilk, becaufe it con-
teines a full declaration of the haill caufe and proceiding therin, with the reafones and warrandes therof, I remit the reidar

The Sabathe following the Bifchope wald neids tak courage, and nochtwithftanding his fufpending from pretching of auld be the Generall Affemblie, and
now excommunication be the Synodall, yit he wald to the pulpit and preatche
But being com to the kirk, and the bell roung, and he readie to go to pulpit,
an comes and telles him, (vpon what mynd I knaw nocht,) that a number of
gentilmen, with certean citiciners, war conveined within the New Collage of
pupofe to tak him out of the pulpit and hang him   Wharat, calling for his
Jakmen and frinds to byde about him, he reafed a grait tumult in the kirk,
and for feir could nocht byd in the knk, but tuk him to the ftiple, out of the
quhilk, be the bailyies, accompanied with all his fauorars and fremds, fkairlie
could he be drawin to be convoyed faiffhe to his awin caftell : but being halff
againft his will ruggit out, and halff borne and careit away, fic as was neireft
him all the way war lyk to burft for ftink.   And it was reported for veritie
to me be manie honeft men that faw it with ther eis, that a heare brak out

amangs the multitude in the middes of the connoun Hie Gett and ftreit, and
ran before tham toward the caftell, and down throw the Noithe Gett. This
the vulgar callit the bifchopes witche. Vpon this he reafed and gaift out, yea
wrot to the King maift fals and malitius fklandeis on my vncle and me, alleaging that I haid pofted a day or twa befor athort the countrey to caufe the
gentilmen convein againft him : and that Maifter Andro haid tham convenit
in the Collage of purpofe to tak his lyff   When the treuthe was, that immediathe efter the ending of the Affemblie, a heavie feat of the Tertian ovei tuk
me, that caufit me keipe my hous twa dayes befor that Sabathe, and that fam
morning it feafed fa on me that I fwined and lay dead till by the grait and
pitifull cryes of my wyff, the inbours cam in for hir helpe and confoit; quhilk
convicted him of a malitius lie   And as to Maifter Andro, the treuthe was,
that the Lard of Lundy hanfand a fpeciall earand with his brother in law,
Pitmilbe, cam to St Andros with certean friuds, and about the laft bell, ged
in to the Collage to confer with Mr Andro, and haift exerceife of the Word
ther, becaufe he wald nocht heir an excommunicat man pretche ; the quhilk
the gud peiple of the town perceaving, left the kirk and drew tham to the
Collage, quhilk was all that was in that mater, vpon the part of Mr Andro,
wha, albeit he hated his wickednes, yit loued the faull and bodie of him better nor himfelff, the quhilk he wald never haid deftioyed, bot if it war poffible be all gud meanes win to God

The King at this mater was graithe incenfed, and knawing that a Generall
Affemblie was to be in Edinbrnche in the monethe of May following, trauelit
maift dihgenthe and cinefthe with couiteous, officiais, nobihtie, and minifterie, to haiff that fentence anulled, and his bifchope reftored and relaxed
And with fellon grait biffines, and mikle ado maid at the Affemblie. at laft
fkai fhe be a few number of ma vottes, threw out this conclufion, That the
Bifchope fould be haldin and reput in the fam cais and condition that he was
in befor the haulding of the Synod of St Andros, without preiudice. dicern-
ing or iudging anie thing of the proceidings. proces, oi fentence of the faid
Synod   Wherin, to the giait greiff of the godlie and zelus vpright haites, was
firft efpyed what the feir and flatterie of Court could woik in a Kirk amangs
a multitud of weak and inconfideiat breithring.

Na intimationes fiom pulpit was maid of this fentence, but with all fpeid
a proclamation with found of trumpet was maid theivpon. And therefter Mr
Andro and I called befor the King, and efter admitting to his gratius prefence
in his Cabbinet, and kiffing of his Hienes hand, yit Mr Andro was commandit

to ward in the place whar he was born, during the Kings will ; and I, becaufe I was feik of the Tertian fever, fend hame to the Collage   And the
Bifchope ordeant, by his preatching in the pulpit, to teatche publict leffones in
Latin within the Auld Collage fcholl, and the haill Vnuerfitie commandit to
frequent the faming Sathan mightehe ftryving therby to hauld vpe the ban-
ner againft the kingdome of Jefus Chryft.

    Thus with patience parting from Edinbruche, Mr Andro to his ward, and
I withe his directiones enteiing againe to that lang interrupted and almoft
ruyned walk of the Collage,—the bifchope to his teatching and preatching in
pulpit and fchooles, he triumphing and we almaift deiected,—thus remeaned
all that fummer   Yit in the mean tyme vnder graut weaknes, befor the warld.
God was working ftrongehe : wha turnefing fum helthe and courage to me on
the ane part, and graitter defyre of knawlage and hallines in the hartes of the
haill heirars of the Vnuerfitie, maid our auditorie and fchoolles to be frequented
againe I began till allure the auditor [with] a maift pleafand and fruitfull purpofe, to wit, the Hiftorie of the Byble, with the twa lightes for clering therof,
Geographie and Chronologie, and intermelling therwithe in thair ages as they
fell out, the cheiff poincts of the Greik and Latine Storie   Bot namlie myndfull of the walk of Chryft, everie vther day I teatched the Epiftle to Timothe,
intreatting, as I could, of the difcipline, and namlie infifting on the contra-
uerted queftiones, bringing in all the Bifchopes reafones, and retuting tham,
and eftablilling the treuthe to my vttermaift   Thefe difputes, at the defyre
of our ftudents, for thair memorie in the efter noone houres. I dytted to
tham.

    Bot fkantlie haid I bein a monethe thus wayes exerceifed to my graut con-
fort, and haldin in of fum fpunk of lyff in the Collage and caufe of Chryft,
when the Deuill deuyfes a diftraction   The Collage haid a Takifman of a
kirk of thais, named Jhone Yrewing. wha finding his Takes draw to an end,
and knowing that he could nocht gett tham renewed bot be moyen of Court,
dreffes him to attend theron ; namlie perceaving the King to be giffen to
halkin and hounting, wherin he was expert, he employes his fervice officiouf-
lie, fa that he becomes a man of credit, and feing Mr Androes ceas to ftand
fa, makes his futt that he fould nocht be receivit till his Tak was renewit : and
yit that he might haiff the turn done fearlie, cauffes the King to wrait for me
to come to him with diligence, and when I haid come twyfe or thryfe na thing
was meined to me of that mater be the King, bot onlie be his Maifter Haker.
This wayes being diftracted, the Vnuerfitie wanting the profit of Mr Andro.

and the finall thing I could do, alſo ſendes an erneſt ſupplication directed with the Dean of Facultie and a Maiſter of euerie Collage to his Maieſtie, ſchawing the grait loſ of Mr Androes trauelles and lerning amangs tham ; as alſo whow I was diſtracted fra my charge, humblie beſeikand his Hienes to releiue Mr Andro from ward, and to reſtore him to his teatching and office in the Collage, quhilk was ſa profitable for the Kirk and Comonnweill, and honourable for his Maieſties eſteat and realme.   The King, moued with this commiſſion and ſupplication ot the Vniuerſitie, promiſes to tak ordou with that mater and ſatiſſie the Vniuerſitie, prouyding the biſchope might be in quyetnes and reuerendlie haird and vſit, wherof Mr Andro making him ſure, he ſould be ſure   Whervpon I was directed to Mr Andro, and retourned anſwer, that as he haid euer behauit himſelſt befor, ſa he ſould do, troubling na man, bot attending on the diſcharge of his calling.   Nochtwithſtanding the moyen of the Maiſter Haker preuealed, and maid all our exerceiſes to veak except now and then for a monethe, and coſt me neir a couple of hounder mylles ryding ; till at laſt, about the beginning of Auguſt, I was directed ower to convoy my vncle to his Maieſtie, wha, coming to Falkland to his Hienes, was, be the convoy of the Maiſter of Gray, brought to his Maieſtie, and efter lang and fear conference, was receavit in fawour, and ſend hame to the Collage, bot ſa that vpon the Kings fathfull promiſe to better the Collage twyſe ſa mikle, the Maiſter Hakers Tak was ſubſeryvit.

   Thereftei, in the monethe of September, accompanied with my fathfull frind and companion, Mr Robert Dury, I tuk iorney to Bervik to bring hame my ſone Ephraim, on whome befor I haid ſkarſlie laſor to think ; and thanking that godlie guid courteus lady, and all our friinds ther, we retourned the neireſt way be the Ferrie of Noithe Bervik, paſſing the quhilk I was in the graitteſt perplexitie of ane that euer I was in my tyme befor, and haid the maiſt ſuddan and comfortable releiff of my guid and gratius God and father, to whaſe honour, as in all, I man record it   We ſchippit in weill vnaduyſedlie, becauſe the day was verie feare, in a mikle coll bott, wherin ther was bot a auld man and twa young boyes, we haiſſing twa hors, a boy, the nurſe, an Einghſs woman, a ſouldiers wyſſ of Bervik, wha haid a deſyre to com with the bern in Scotland, and whom I could nocht reſuſe, bathe becauſe of hir kyndlie offer, and the bern was ſa browdin vpon hir, that without danger he could nocht be ſpeaned from hir   We hoiſed ſeall with a lytle pirlie of eſt wind, and lanſhed furthe till almaiſt the third of the paſſage was paſt, and then it fell down dead calme.   For rowing nather was ther eares meit nor

handes, the boott was fa heavie, the man auld, and the boyes young. In this
mean tyme, the honeft woman becomes fa feik with fic extremitie and pieas
of vomiting firft, therefter with fwinings, that it was pitifull to behauld
Withe hir working, the barn wackens, and becomes extream feik, being nan
bot myfelff to cuire tham, for Mr Robert was rowing   This dieing for the
fpace of thrie houres, in end I becam dead feik myfelft, fa that then it becam
a maift pitifull and lamentable fpectakle, to fie a woman, a ftranger, an honeft
mans wyff com fra ham to pleafour me, to be with extream pres apeirand
eueiie minut to giff vpe the ghoft; an infant of thrie halff yeirs auld fpreaul-
ing in the awin excrements, and the father, parthe for feir and can of mynd,
and parthe for fear feiknes, lifting vpe pitifull handes and eis to the heavines,
voide of all eidlie confort or helpe of man.   Now, that quhilk maid our ei-
teat almaift difperat was if the calme remeamt, the woman could nocht haiff
indurit, bot, but dout, haid died, the extreamitie of hir pean and fwinng was
fik, and being fa far fra land in a halff of the night with that quhilk refted of
the day, nocht paft thrie houres, we could nocht haiff rowed to land, if anie
drow haid riffen, nather was ther handes to takle the fealles, nor was the
grathe haill and fiefhe to byd the wound And therwith, be hir tumbling and
yeawing, the maft fchonk fa loufe, that Mr Robert, the auld man being dam-
nift and machles, haid mikle ado to faften the fam ; fa that na releiff being
bot in the fweit meicie and helpe of our God, my hart maift vigentlie importuned him, and hoping patienthe, (for euerie houre was main nor the haill
tyme of our banifment,) at laft the Lord luiked mercifullie on, and fend, about
the fune going to, a thik ear from the Southeaft, fa that, getting on the feall
ther was vpon hir, within an houre and a halff, quhilk was ftrange to our
confideration, na wound blawing, we arryved within the Alie, and efter a
maift weirifome and fear day, gat a comfortable nights ludging with a godlie
lady in Carmuiy.

    I twitched befor the fermon that James Gipfone, minifter of Pencatland,
maid in the pulpit of Edinbruche, at the incoming of the Lords and taking of
Steiling   Therin, as he was thought to be fcharpe againft the fubfcryving
biethring, fo was he iudgit vehement and ouer peremptorie againft the King,
whom he threatned with the iudgments of Jeroboam, in thefe words, or verey
neir : " That if he perfifted in perverting the eftablifhed Difcipline of the Kirk,
and perfecuting of Gods faithfull fervants, his pofteritie fhould be cutt aff,
and he fhould be the laft of his race."   The King cauffed feik him lang ; and
at laft, by fum of his Gward apprehendit him and put him in prifone. And

at the Generall Affemblie, hauldin at Edinbruche in the moneth of October, travelit fa that by manieft vottes he was condemnit as rafche in application, and over particular and fair againft the King ; and fa removit from his minifterie whar he fervit. Yit could he by na meanes be moved to call bak or deny his doctrine, vnles he fhould he againft that warrand both of the Word and Spirit whar by he haid fpoken, &c

That wintar it pleafed God to repear againe the temple of his awin Jerufalem, opening the mouthe of his fervant Mr Andro again with fic grace and powar, that all began in erneft to be Theologes ; the treuthe bathe concerning doctrine and difcipline to be narowlier luiked vnto, and the Bifchopes fear fchawes, and fcheddowes, to vanifhe and wear away Then alfo God opened the mouthe of Mr Robert Bruce at a fpeciall remarkable tyme within the Collage For all was rufthe caften in dout wither they fould heir the Bifchopes pretching, being bathe fufpendit and excommunicat; yit manie yeildit for feir and fawour of the mans fmothe and pleafand vtterance, bot the beft, bathe of the Town and Vniuerfitie could nocht of confcience heir him, and therfor reforted verie frequentlie to the Collage euerie Sabothe, and fand of Mr Andro and Mr Robert Bruce exceiding grait edification and confort. As for me, I was then apointed be the Prefbyterie to teatche at Anftruther euerie Sabothe. and was in calling to that minifterie, wherin I enterit the fimmer following, about the fam age that the preiftes and Chryft himfelff enterit and began than minifterie Anent the occafion, maner and effects wharof, reid in beginning of this book, inregiftrat ther at lynthe, and of purpofe The quhilk narration, in this difcourfe of my lyff, and maift mercifull and gratius working of God with me, an vnworthie wratche, comes in in this place ordourlie.

Bot the memorie of my grait fafcherie and vexation wherin I was occupied in the fimmer of the 1586 yeir, haid almoft maid me forget a confortable benefit of God beftowit on me in the middes therof; to wit, of a pleafand fecond fone, in this refpect contrare to the vther, that the firft was gottin in Scotland, and born in England ; the fecond, gottin at London, was born in St Andros the nynt day of July Be occafion I haid the Erle of Mar to my goffope, whom I rememberit of his dewtie ; bot in loue and rememberance of him whom it was nocht thair part to let ly in ward from his calling, I called the bern Andro.

1587.—At the Generall Affemblie in the fpring tyme of the yeir 1587, Mr Andro moued the Kirk of Edinbruche to defyre the Affemblie to caufe Mr

Robert Bruce pretche, and efter to futt him att the faid Affemblie to be than paftor in the place of Mr James Law fone, and the faid Affemblie to grant and appoinet him therto Bot whowbeit that he and I bathe delt ernefthe with Mr Robert, he wald nocht affent therto, but contented to teatche ther, and tak a fey what God wald work with him ; the quhilk he did with the notable fruict that followed

That yeir, in the monethe of May, Guilaum Saluft S. du Bartas cam in Scotland to fie the King, of whome he was receavit according to his worthines. interteined honourablie. and liberalie propyned and dimiffed in the hervelt. to his Maiefties giait praife fa lauge as the French toung is vfed and vnderftind in the warld

About the end of June, his Maieftie cam to St Andros, and brought with him the faid Du Bartas, and coming firft without anie warning to the New Collage, he calles for Mr Andro, faying he was com with that gentleman to haifl a Leffone Mr Andro anfweres, " That he haid teatched his ordinar that day in the fornoone." " That is all ane,' fayes the King, " I mon haiff a Leffone, and be hen within an houre for that effect.' And indeid within les nor an houre, his Maieftie was in the fcholl, and the haill Vniuerfitie convenit with him, befor whom Mr Andro ex tempore intreated maift clenlie and mightelie of the right government of Chryft, and in effect refuted the haill Actes of Parliament mand againft the difcipline therof. to the giait inftruction and comfort of his auditor, except the King allean, wha was verie angrie all that night.

Vpon the morn the Bifchope haid bathe a prepared Leffone and feaft mand for the King His Leffone was a tichted vpe abregment of all he haid tetched the yeir bypaft, namlie anent the corrupt groundes quhilk he haid put in the Kings head contrarie to the trew difcipline. To the quhilk leffone Mr Andro went contrai to his cuftome, and withe his awin pen market all his fals groundes and reafones : and without farder cauflit ring his bell at twa efternoone the fam day, wharof the King heiring, he fend to Mr Andro, defyring him to be moderat, and haiff regaid to his prefence, vtherwayes he wald difcharge him He anfwered couragioufhe, that his Maiefties eai and tender breift was pittifulhe and dangerufhe filled with erionis and vntreuthes be that wicked man, tne quhilk he could nocht fuffer to pas, and bruik a lyff, vtherwayes, except the ftopping of the breathe of Gods mouthe, and preiudging of his treuthe, he fould behaifl himfelff maift moderathe and reuerenthe to his Maieftie in all refpects.   The King fend againe to him and me, defyring it fould be fa, and

fchawin that he wald haiff his four howrs in the Collage, and drink with Mr
Andro   Sa coming to that Leffone with the Bifchope, wha requyfted the
King for leiue to mak anfwer inftanthe in cais anie thing war fpoken againft
his doctrine   Bot ther Mr Andro, making him as thouche he haid na thing
to do but with the Papift, brings out thair works, and reids out of tham all
the Bifchopes grounds and reafones   The quhilk, when he haid at lainthe and
mairft cleirlie fchawin to be plean papiftrie, then he fettes againft the fam with
all his mean, and with innutible force of reafone, from cleir grounds of Scripture with a mightie parrhefie and fluide of eloquence, he dinges tham fa down,
that the bifchope was dafht and ftrukken als dum as the ftok he fatt vpon
Efter the Leffone, the King, in his mother toung, maid fum diftingoes, and
difcurfit a whyll theron, and gaift certean innunctiones to the Vniuerfitie for
reuerencing and obeying of his Bifchope , wha fra that day furthe, began to
tyre of his teatching, and fall man and mair in difgrace and confufion   The
King, with Monfieur du Bartas, cam to the Collage Hall, wher I caufit prepear,
and haiff in readines a banquet of wat and dry confectiones, with all fortes of
wyne, wharat his Maieftie camped verie merrelie a guid whyll, and therefter
went to his hors.   Bot Mon du Bartas taried behind and conferrit with my
Vncle and me a wholl houre, and fyne followed etter the King , wha inquyring of him that night, as ane tauld me, " What was his iudgment of the twa
he haid heird in St Andros ?" He anfweret the King, " That they war bathe
lerned men, bot the bifchopes war cunned, and prepared maters, and Mr
Andro haid a grait reddie ftore of all kynd of lerning within him , and by
that, Mr Andro his fpreit and courage was far aboue the other "   The quhilk
iudgment the King approued

That Witfonday I remouit my wyff and famelie from St Andros to Anftruther, quhilk was the twolt tyme I haid fhitted fen my mariage in the fpace
of four yeir ; wherby I was remembent this lyft to be but a forourning in a
wildernes, and was fett to confidder mair neirhe the hiftorie of the peiple of
God in thair iorney from Egypt to the Promift land, &c.

At my firft coming to Anftruther ther fell out a heavie accident, quhilk
vexit my mynd mikle at the firft, bot drew me mikle neirar my God, and
teatched me what it was to haiff a ccar of a flok   Ane of our Creares retourning from England was vnbefett be an Englis pirat, pilled, and a verie guid
honeft man of Anftruther flean therin   The quhilk lown coming perthe to
the verie roade of Pittenwenn, fpuilzied a fchipe lying therin, and ririfufit the
men therof.   This wrang could nocht be fuffered be our men, left they fould

be maid a comoun prey to sic limmers.   Therfor, purchassing a Commissioun, they riget to a propre she boot, and euerie man incuraging vther, maid almaist the haill honest and best men in all the Town to go in hir to the sie.   This was a grait vexation and greiss to my hart, to sie at my first entres the best part of my flok ventured vpon a pak of pirates, wharof the smallest member of the meinest was mair in valour then a schipfull of tham.   And yit I durst nocht stay sum les nor I steyed all, and all I durst nocht, bathe for the dangerus preparatiue, and the frinds of the honest man wha was slean, and of tham that war abbusit, wha war maine, in sic sort as the mater concerned the haill.   Bot my God knawes what a fear hart they left behind when they parted out of my sight, or rather what a hart they caried with them, leiving a bouk behind.   I nather eat, drank, nor sleiped, bot be constraint of natuie, my thought and cair always being vpon tham, and commending tham to God, till aught or ten dayes war endit, and they in sight retourning, with all guid takens of ioy,—flagges, streamers, and ensenigyie displayit,—whom with grait ioy we receavit, and went togidder to the Kirk, and praised God.   The Captean for the tyme, a godlie, wyse, and stout man, recompted to me trewlie ther haill proceiding   That they meiting with thair Admirall, a grait schipe of St Andros, weill riget out be the burrowes, being fyne of seale, went befor hir all the way, and maid euerie schipe they fargatherit with, of whatsumeuer nation, to strik and do homage to the King of Scotland, schawing tham for what caufe they war riget furthe, and inquyring of knaues and pirats   At last they meit with a proude stiff Einglisman, wha refufes to do reuerence : therfor the Captean, thinking it was a lown, commands to giff tham his nose piece, the quhilk delasht lightes on the tye of the Einglismans mean seale and down it comes ; then he yeilds, being but a merchant.   Bot ther was the mercifull prouidence of God, in steying a grait piece of the Einglisman lying out lin starn in readines to be schot, quhilk if it haid lichted amang our folks, being maine in litle roum without fence, wald haiff crewalie demeaned tham all ; but God directing the first schot preferued tham.   From them they approtched to the schore at Suffolk, and findes be Prouidence the lown, wha haid newlings takin a Crear of our awin town, and was spuleing hir   Whowsone they fpy ane coming war lyk, the lownes leaues thair pryce and rines thair schipe on land   Our she boot etter, and almaist was on land with tham ; yit steying hard be, they delaishe thair ordinance at the lownes, and a nomber going a land perfewes and takes a halffe a dissone of tham, and putes tham abord in ther boot.   The gentle men of the countrey and Townes besyde, heiring the noyes of fchoting gathers with haft, fuppofing the Spainyard haid landit, and apprehending a number of the lownes in our mens handes, defyrit to knaw the mater. The quhilk, when the Juftices of Peace vnderftude, and faw the King of Scotlands armes, with twa galland fchippes in war lyk maner, yeildit and gaiff reuerence therto, fuffering our folks to tak with tham thair prifoners and the puats fchipe, quhilk they brought hame with tham, with halff a diffone of the lownes ; wharof twa war hangit on our Pier end, the reft in St Andros ; with na hurt at all to anie of our folks, wha euer fen fyne hes bein frie of Einglis pirates.   All praife to God for euer.   Amen.

This yeir, rydmg vpe to Carnbie, in companie with the Lard of Balfour and his brother, to defing the Manfe and gleib of the Kuk to Mr Andro Hounter, minifter, vpon an kitle hat ridden hors,—approtching to a ftrype weill how of fevin or aught foot brod, I put at the hors to caufe him lope it. and becaufe he was euill mouthed and hat ridden, I held his head ftreat wharat he repyning in the middes of his lope, cuft down his head, fa that all the feddle gear braking, he cuft me ower on the vther bank with the fe-dle betwix my leagges, and his head going down, he lopes the fuperfault, and his buttokes lightes hard befyd me, with all his four feit to the Lift   The lyk wharof was neuer haird in the iudgment of the behauldars, and all that hathe confidderit it fen fyne, without anie hurt to the man or beift, except the fadle grathe braking

That yeir, about the end of July and beginning of Auguft, was haldin the firft Parliament be the King efter his perfyt age of twentie and a yeirs   Wher-in, except the ratefication of the Actes maid of befor for eftablifhing of the trew relligion and abolefhing of Papiftrie. na guid was done for the Kuk, bot be the contrar fche was fpuilyiet be a plane law of the ane halff of her patri-monie ; to wit, of the temporall landes of all her benefices be that Act of An-nexation: Hir ei in the mean tyme bleanit with twa fear promifes, ane of abo-lifhing of all bifchopries and prelacies ; and yit the bifchope of St Andros was a fpecial doar therin (and was the laft publict act that euer he was at) ·   Ane vther, that the haill teinds fould be peaceablie put in the Kuks poffeffion Bot of Gods iuft iudgment that annexation of the Temporalitie hes done the King alfmikle guid as fic promifes of the Kuks Spiritualitie.

The fam yeir, in the herveft, brak vpe a grait Peft in Leithe, and conti-nowit all that wintar, quhilk ftrak a grait terrour in Edinbruche and all the coft fyds   Be the occafion wharof we began the exerceis of daylie doctrine and prayers in our Kirk. quhilk continowes to this day with grait profit and confort, bathe of the teitchars and heirares.

This wintar I paft ower to Dakethe, and obteined the gift of the ftipend of Anftruther Wafter, whar God, be fum helpe of me, an vnworthie inftrument, called Mr James Nicolfone from the Court to the Minifterie And in retourning, of mere Prouidence, was the occafion of the mariage of Patrik Forbes of Cors with Lucres Spence, fiftar to the Laird of Wilmotfton, maried in Anftruther in the fummer following

1588 —That wintar the King was occupied in commenting of the Apocalypfe, and in fetting out of fermontes thervpon againft the Papifts and Spainyairds And yit by a piece of grait owerfight, the Papifts practeifed neuer mair biffiehe in this land, and maid graitter preparation for receaving of the Spainyarts nor that yen. For a lang tyme the newes of a Spanifhe name and armie haid bein blafit abrode : and about the Lambes tyde of the 1588, this Yland haid fund a fenfull effect therof, to the vtter fubuerfion bathe of Kirk and policie giff God haid nocht wounderfullie watched ower the fam, and mightehe fauchten and defeat that armie be his fouldiours, the Elements, quhilk he maid all four maift ferche to afflict tham till almoft vtter confumption Terrible was the feir, perling war the pretchings, erneft, zealus, and feruent war the prayers, founding war the fiches and fobbes and abounding was the teares at that Faft and Generall Affemblie keipit at Edinbruche, when the newes war credible tauld, fum tymes of thair landing at Dunbar, fum tymes at St Androis, and in Tay, and now and then at Aberdein and Cromertie firft And in verie deid, as we knew certeanlie foone efter, the Lord of Armies, wha ryddes vpon the winges of the wounds, the Keipar of his awin Ifraell, was in the mean tyme conuoying that monftruus name about our coftes, and directing thair hulkes and galiates to the ylands, rokkes, and fandes, wharvpon he haid deftinat thair wrak and deftruction. For within twa or thrie monethe therefter, earlie in the morning, be brak of day, ane of our Bailyies cam to my bedfyde, fayng, (but nocht with fray,) " I haiff to tell yow newes, fir. Ther is arryvit within our herbrie this morning a fchipe full of Spainyarts, bot nocht to giff mercie bot to afk " And fa fchawes me that the Commanders haid landit, and he haid commandit tham to thair fchipe againe till the Magiftrates of the Town haid advyfit, and the Spainvards haid humblie obeyit : Therfor defyrit me to ryfe and heir thair petition with tham. Vpe I got with diligence, and affembling the honeft men of the town, cam to the Tolbuthe ; and efter confultation taken to heir tham, and what anfwer to mak, ther prefentes ws a verie reuerend man of big ftatnre, and graue and ftout countenance, gray heared, and verie humble lyk wha, efter mikle and verie law courteffie, bowing down with his face nen the ground, and twitching my fho with his hand, began his harang in the Spanfe toung, wharof I vnderftud the fubftance, and being about to anfwer in Latine, he haiffing onhe a young man with him to be his interpreter, began and tauld ower agane to ws in guid Englis   The fum was, that King Philipe, his maifter, haid riget out a name and armie to land in England for inft caufes to be advengit of manie intolerable wrangs quhilk he haid receavit of that nation ; but God for ther finnes haid bein againft thame, and be ftorme of wather haid driyven the nauie by the coft of England, and him with a certean of Capteanes, being the Generall of twentie hulks, vpon an yll of Scotland, called the Fear Yll, wher they maid fchipewrak, and whare fa mome as haid efchapit the merceles fies and rokes, haid mair nor fax or fevin ouks fuffred grait hungar and cauld, till conducing that bark out of Orkney, they war com hither as to ther fpeciall frinds and confederats to kis the Kings Maiefties hands of Scotland, (and therwith bekkat euen to the yeard,) and to find releiff and confort therby to himfelff, thefe gentilmen Capteanes and the poore fouldarts whafe condition was for the prefent maift miferable and pitifull

I anfwent this mikle in foum . That whowbeit nather our frindfchipe, quhilk could nocht be grait, feing ther King and they war frinds to the graiteft enemie of Chryft, the Pape of Rome, and our King and we defyed him ; nor yit thair caufe againft our nibours and fpeciall frinds of England could procure ane benefit at our hands for thair releiff and confort . neuertheles, they fould knaw be experience, that we war men, and fa moned be human compaffione, and Chriftiannes of better relligion nor they, quhilk fould kythe in the fruicts and effect plan contrar to thais   For wheras our peiple reforting amangs tham in peacable and lawfull effeares of merchandife, war violentlie takin and caft in prifone, thair guids and gear confifcat, and than bodies committed to the crewall flaming fyre for the caufe of relligion, they fould find na thing amangs ws bot Chriftian pitie and warks of mercie and almes, leaving to God to work in than harts concerning relligion as it pleafed him.   This being trewhe reported again to him be his trunfhman, with grait reuerence he gaiff thankes, and faid he could nocht mak anfwer for thair Kirk and the lawes and ordour therof, onlie for himfelff, that ther war diuers Scotfmen wha knew him, and to whome he haid fchawin courtefie and fawour at Calles, and as he fuppofit, fum of this fam town of Anftruther   Sa fchew him that the bailyies granted him licence with the Capteanes, to go to

thair ludging for thair refrefchment, bot to nane of thair men to land, till the
ower lord of the town war aduertifed, and vnderftand the Kings Maiefties
mynd anent thame.   Thus with grait courteffie he departed.

That night, the Lord being aduertiffed, cam, and on the morn, accompanied
with a guid nomber of the gentilmen of the countrey round about, gaifl the
faid Generall and the Capteanes prefence, and efter the fam fpeitches in effect
as befor, receavit tham in his hous, and intertemed tham humeanlie, and fufferit the fouldiours to com a land, and ly all togidder, to the number of threttin fcore, for the maift part young berdles men, filhe, trauchled, and houngred,
to the quhilk a day or twa, keall, pattage, and fifhe was giffen ; for my advys was contorme to the Prophet Elizeus his to the King of Ifrael in Sama-
ria, " Giff tham bred and water," &c   The names of the Commanders war
Jan Gomes de Medina, Generall of twentie houlkes, Capitan Patricio, Capitan
de Legoretto, Capitan de Luffera, Capitan Maurtio and Seingour Serrano

Bot verelie all the whyll my hart melted within me for defyre of thankfulnes to Cod, when I rememberit the prydfull and crewall naturall of they peiple,
and whow they wald haiff vfit ws in ceas they haid landit with than forces
amangs ws.   And fall the wounderfull wark of Gods mercie and Juftice in
making ws fie tham, the cheiff commanders of tham to mak fie dewgard and
curteffie to pure fiemen, and thair fouddarts fo abiecthe to beg almes at our
dures and in our flreites.

In the mean tyme they knew nocht of the wrak of the reft, but fuppofed
that the reft of the armie was faifflie returned, till a day I gat in St Andros
in print the wrak of the Gahatcs in particular, with the names of the principall men, and whow they war vfit in Yiland and our Hilands, in Walles, and
vther partes of England ; the quhilk, when I recordit to Jan Gomes, be particular and fpeciall names, O then he cryed out for greiff, burfted and grat.
This Jan Gomes fchew grait kyndnes to a fchipe of our town, quhilk he fund
arrefted at Calles at his ham coming, red to court for hir, and maid grait rus
of Scotland to his King, tuk the honeft men to his hous, and inquyrit for the
Laird of Anftruther, for the Minifter, and his hoft, and fend hame manie commendationes.   Bot we thanked God with our hartes, that we haid fein tham
amangs ws in that forme.

That 88 yeir was alfo maift notable for the deathe of Quein Mother of
France, Catherin de Medicis, bludie Jezabell to the Sanctes of God, wha then
was callit to hir recompence.   As alfo the maift remarkable wark of Gods inftice in repeying the twa cheiff executors of that horrible carnage and maffa-

cre of Paris, making fiift King Hendrie to caufe his Gaid ftik the Duc of
Guife vnder treft with the Cardinall of Lorean.   And fyne a Jacobin frier of
that oidour, quhilk the King did maift for, maift treafonablie to ftik the King
The Loid woiking be maift wicked inftiuments maift wyfhe and iufthe *

Thus God glorifiet his name maift remarkablie in iuftice againft the graitteft enemies of his Kirk, and fweit mercie and fawour towards his; tor by the
continuance of pace in this Yll, the Kirks of Fiance, from almaift a defperat
efteat becam mah and mair to be confoited, betterit, and at laft releiiut   In
the 85 and 86 yeirs, all the Proteftants war chargit at France within fic a
day, vnder pean of lyff, lands, guids and gear; fa that the number of banifhed
in Eingland war fa grait, and the pure of tham fa manie, that they war compelled to feik releiff of ws for the faming   And to the gloire of God I remember it, in the pure bounds I haid vnder charge at the firft beginning of my in-
nifterie, we gatherit about fyve hounder marks for that effect; bot few or nan
did fannkle, as be the fmalnes of the foum may appeir.   The foum of the haill
collection quhilk the Fienche Kirks gat extendit bot till about ten thowfand
marks, as thair acquittances and Letteis of thankfgiffing beares, quhilk I haif
in cuftodie, delyverit to me be the Generall Affemblie to tranflat in Scottes,
and fett furthe to clofe the mouthes of invytull fklandeiars, wha gaiff out that
that collection was maid tor an vther purpofe   As alfo, the collection maid
for the Town of Geneua; whairfore we gat mair thankes by a Letter of Theodor du Bez in the name of the Senat and Kirk theirof, nor it was all worthe,
readie to be producit.

Nochtwithftanding of the Lords iudgments that yeir vpon Papifts, yit efter
the fpreit of the ferpent wharwith they ar led, altho cut and deadlie woundit in
diuers partes, neueitheles war euer fteiring and menaffing.   Sa that diuers
Practeifars and Trafectars, Jefuiftes, Seminarie Preifts, and vther emiffais of
the Antichryft crape in the Countrey, and kythed dangerus effects in diueis
paites, namlie in the Northe and Southe   And, theirfor, the maift wacryff
and cearfull of the breithring, euerie an warning and moving vthers as the
cuftome of the Kirk of Scotland was from the beginning, conveined at Edinbruche, in the monethe of Januar the fam yeir, and gaiff in to the King and
Counfall the Petitiones following:

* The Duc and Cardinall wer flean in Decem. 88, the Quein, for hartfearnes, followit in Januar, and the King was fticked the Auguft following

Z

The Kirks humble Petition to his Maieftie and Counfall for preuention of the dangers threatned
to the profeffion of the trew relligion within this Realme   1588, Jan.

THAT it may pleife his Maeftie guif command, bathe to particular Prefbyteries, and fic vther minifters and barrones and gentilmen as falbe thought meit to convein and confult vpon the readieft remedies of thir dangers appenand, fa oft as they fall think expedient, and to report thair opiniones and advytes to his Maeftie betwix this and the xx day of Januar.

That it may pleife his Hienes to forbeare in tyme to cum to interpon his Prime Letteris or difcharges to the Kirk for flcying of than proceiding with than cenfures againft Papifts, when as they can nocht be reclamed be lawfull admonitiones.

That Commiffiones may be directed to fum fpecialles of his Hienes Counfall, beft affected and of grauteft powar to ferche, feik, and apprehend and prefent to Juftice all Jefuitts and vtheris privat or publict feducers of his Hienes leiges, and that the faids Commiffionars may be inftantlie named, and a day apointed to the report of thair diligences in that behalff.

That fum fpecialles of the minifterie, afifted with fum weill affected barrones or vther gentilmen, may be authorized with his Hienes Commiffion and licence, to pas to euerie quarter of this Realme, and ther, be meanes that they find meitteft, try and explore what noble men, burrowes, Larrones, and vthers of anie rank or calling, profes the relligion, and will royne afauldlie in the defence therof, and wha will nocht, and that a day be appointed in lyk maner for reporting of thair diligence.

That feing the fpeciall occafion of the finifter fufpitiones conceavit of his Hienes fyncerutie in the treuthe, and that mantinates the Papifts maift is his authoritie and fervice put in the hands of papifts vnder whaife winges all Jefuitts, and vthers denoted to that fuperftitioun findes countenance and confort, That, for remead therof, it may pleis his Maieftie to purge his Hous, Counfall and Seffioun, and to reteire his powar of Lieutenantdrie, Wardanrie, and vther his auctoritie whatfumeuer, from all and whatfumeuer perfones, awowit or fufpected to be Papifts. And to let proclamationes be immediatlie directed for publication of his Hienes guid intention and meining in that behalff to the confufion of the Papifts and than patrones, and confort of the godlie offendit this tyme bygean, with than lang tolerance and ouerfight   FINIS

This Petitiones prefented be ws to his Maieftie and Counfall war granted, and therefter meitting. Commiffionars war nominat throuchout all the partes of this Land, to put in execution the things crauit, wharvpon an Act of Counfall and Proclamation paft out extant in print   The fam day it was thought guid that a certean fould be nominat to confult in privat concerning the beft and maift reddie way of the faid execution, wharof was ten of Noble men, Lawers and Burges, viz. The Erle of Angus, guid Archbald, the Erle Marefchall, Mr [of] Glames, Thefaurar, the Lard of Louchleaven, the Clark Regifter, Mr Jhone Scharpe, Mr Thomas Crag, Mr Jhone Nicolfone, Jhone Jhoneftone of Elphiftone, and Jhone Adamfone.   And ten of the Miniftrie, viz. Mr Andro Maluin, Mr Robert Pont, Mr Robert Bruce, Mr Dauid Lindfay, Mr Andro

Hay, Mr Thomas Bowchanan, Mr Patrik Galloway, Mr Nicol Dalglas, Mr Andro Mill and myfelff. Wha meitting the fam day at efter noone, efter lang reafoning and advyfiment, thought it maift expedient and neidfull, firft, that the faid execution fould be without deley, in refpect of the imminent danger.

Nixt, that forfamikle as ther war thrie rankes of enemies—the firft of cheiff meantemers of papifts and papiftrie ; the fecond of Jefuits, Seminarie Preifts and Trafectars ; the thrid of awowars, receauers and intertemers of thefe in thair houffes, and partakers of thair purpofes and ydolatrie,—it was thought beft that the firft fort fould be chaigit to warde ; the fecond apprehendit at vnwars and punifhed ; the thride proceidit againft conforme to the lawes of the Countrey, and being found culpable, to be punifhed accordinglie. And laft, to the intent that fa weghtie a mater might be folidlie advyfit and fett doun in all poincts, the Clark Regifter Alexander Hay, Mr Jhone Scharpe, Mr Thomas Crag and vthers war requeifted to tak tyme and paufe vpon the mater, and euerie ane feueralie fett down thair iudgment in wrait The quhilk being conferrit togidder, conclufion was taken and reported to his Maieftie, wharof proceidit the acts and proclamationes, and commiffiones foone efter publifhed in print.

At the fam tyme in that Convention war apointed certean Commiffionars and breithing to meit euerie ouk in Edinbruche for confulting vpon maters perteining to the weill of the Kirk in fa dangerus a tyme, viz Alexander Hay, Clark Regifter, Mr Jhone Lindfay, Lord of Seffion, Mr Jhone Scharpe, Mr Thomas Crag, Mr Jhone Skem, Mr Jhone Nicolfone, Aduocats, Wilyeam Lytle, Provoft of Edinbruche, Jhone Jhonftone, Jhone Adamfone, Hendrie Charters, burgeffes of Edinbruche, Mr Robert Bruce, Mr Dauid Lindfay and Mr Robert Pont, Minifters.

Alfo the Kings minifters, with fum vther breither, war apointed to trauell with his Maieftie for a proclamation to be fett furthe, to let all his fubiects vnderftand his Hienes zeall and cair for repurging of the land of Papiftrie and meantenance of the trew religion : And to defyre his Maieftie of new again now in his perfyt age to fubfcryve the Confeffion of Fathe maid, and renew the charge giffen in his minoritie to all his fubiects to fubfcryue the faming ower again. The quhilk alfo was obteined and publifhed in print.

It was fordar ordeamit that all Commiffionars and Moderators of Prefbyteries in all partes fould be cairfull to haift intelligence of all maters concerning religion and weill of the Kirk within thair boundes, and to mak aduertifment of the faming from tyme to tyme to the forfaid Commiffioneis apointed oukhe to convein in Edinbruche.

Item ther was a Generall Affemblie apointed to be hauldin at Edinbruche the faxt of Februai following : and the Prouinciall Affemblies in euerie fchyre to be endit befor the xxiij of that inftant Januar For the quhilk caufe it was thought neceffar that the Commiffionars of Provinces, and euerie minifter within thair awin bounds, fould inform all weill affectioned gentilmen to relligioun of the attempts of papifts and imninent danger therby, and of the libertie granted to convein be his Maieftie and Counfall, wherby thay may be moued to tak Commiffiones from Synods without feall to keipe the Generall Affemblie and mak it frequent.

And laft as concerning Jefuiftes, Semmarie Preifts and vtheis deceauers of the peiple, it was ordeanit that thair nixt Synods chaige fould be giffen to euerie minifter to declar tham excommunicat out of pulpit, at thair retuin immediathe to thair awin kirks, that the peiple may bewar of thame, and fic-lyk the companie of fic as fawours, intertemes tham in thair houffes, or hes ane thing to do with thame : And for that effect euerie minifter to haiff thair names in ollit. At this convention my vncle moderat and I wrot.

That Generall Affemblie in Februar was verie frequent of noble and gentlemen Therat the Greues of euerie province and prefbyterie wai giffen in, wherby it might be eafehe perceavit whow horriblie the land was defyled all throuchout, bot namhe in the Northe and Southe, with Papiftrie, Superftitione, blodfched, and all fort of villanie. Vpon the quhilk, regiates, griues, complents and petitiones wai formed and prefented to the King and Counfall for punifhment and redres, quhilk wai ower lang and tedius to be regiftrat And the breithing fteired vpe to wakryffnes and diligence in watching over thair floks and cairing for the haill Kuk

For conclufion of this meruelus yeir I can nocht forget my particular, feing that is my fpeciall purpofe to recompt the gratius working of my God with me He corrected me fweithe in taking from me at the beginning therof my litle fone Andro. Bot recompenced the fam again maift bountifullie in giffing me another Andro, born that fam yeir in the monethe of Auguft : Sa the Lord taks, the Lord giffes, bleffed be the nam of the Lord for euer.

The bern was fallon beautifull, lowing and mirrhie, and feimed to be of a fyne fanguine conftitution till a quarter efter he was fpeaned ; bot fyne, wither be wormes or a hectik confumption, I knaw nocht, bot his fleche and cullor

fealed, and be the fpace of a quarter of yeir confumed and dwyned away, keiping alwayes the fweiteft and pleafandeft ei that could be in annes heid   I was
accuftomed to fett him at the end of the table in tyme of denner and fupper,
as the Egyptiens did the picture of dead, till acquent me therwith ; and yit
when he died, I mervelit at my awin hart that was fa viened and moued
with it, fa that yit when I wrot this, I was nocht frie of the bowdings of the
bowelles of that naturall affection   And if we that ar erdlie wormes can be
fa affected to our childring, what a loue beares that heavinlie father to his '
He was my firft propyne and hanfell to heavin   I can nocht forget a ftrange
thing at his deathe.   I haid a peair of tyne milk whait dowes, quhilk I fed in
the hous : The ane whairof that day of his deathe could nocht be haldin af his
cradle, bot ftoped from fitting aboue it, crape in and fatt in vnder it, and died
with him : The vther, at my hamcoming on the morn, as I was wafhing my
hands, cam, lighted at my futt, and pitnifhe crying, " Pipe, pipe, pipe," ran a
litle away from me.   Then I called for peyes and beanes to giff it ; bot they
fchew me it wald na eatt   I tuk it vpe, and put pikles in the mouthe of it,
bot it fchuk tham out of the throt ; and parting from me with a pitifull pi-
ping, within twa or thrie houres died alfo.   I maid on him this Epitaphe.

> A foiournar in London, I thie gat,
>   At hame in tyme of trouble thow was born,
> The babbes for beautie thought maift dihgat,
>   Thy beautie feim'd yit farder till adorn.
>
> As Democrit thow firft the waild did fkorn,
>   For to refiaifhe the mynd a meakles marrow ,
> Syn to beveall my wickednes forlorn,
>   The tears of Heraclit thow feim'd to borrow.
>
> I fet thie in my fight at evin and morrow,
>   My hart till humble, acquenting me with deathe
> But O the loue of parents ! what a forrow
>   Did feafe on me, fra th' anes thow loft thy breathe '
>
> Oh ' firft lyk pleafand floure on erthe thow grew !
> Syne dwyn'd to dead, with dowes to heavin thow flew '

This page, if thow be a pater that reids it, thow wilt apardone me   If
nocht, fufpend thy cenfure till thow be a father, as faid the graue Lacedemo-
nian Agefilaus.

The minnftejie of Mr Robeit Bruce was veiie fteadable and mightie that yeii, and diuers yeirs following, maift confortable to the guid and godlie, and maift feifull to the enemies Sa that it was fenfabilie perceavit that as God haid fubftitut to Mr Knox, Mr Lawfone, fa haid he piouydit Mr Robert to fupplie that inleak. The godlie, for his puiffant and maift moving doctrine, lout him ; the waildlings for his parentage and place ieuerenced him , and the enemies for bathe, ftude in aw of him. The Chancellai, Mi Jhone Me-tellan, entent in fpeciall frindfchipe with him, Mr Andio and me, and keipit trew and honeft till the day of his deathe. He helde the King vpon twa gioundes fure, nathei to caft out with the Kirk nor with Eiingland. Whow-beit he haid maid infoimationes to him of guid men by the tieuthe, to win him couit at the beginning in the Duc his dayes, quhilk he wald fean haiff mendit, bot could nocht.

1589.—The yeir following ther fell out a mater in St Andros that wrought heavie and giait tiouble to the beft and honefteft men in all that town, and quhilk occupied me mikle and fear, bathe in mynd and body, manie yeis efter. The occafion wherof was this :

The Bifchope haid lurked a yeir oi twa lyk a tod in his holl, as his cuf-tom was when things fiamed nocht with him ; and indeid, be the Chancel-lars moyen, efter he was ioyned with ws, the Kings opinion and lyking was far diuerted fiom him   He deuyfes in this mean tyme a mifcheiff to be re-uengit vpon his miflykers, and fteires vpe a Jakman of his called Hendrie Ha-milton to quaiiell a Maifter of the Vniuerfitie, Mr Wilyeam Walwode, Pro-feffour of the Lawes, a man bathe in blude and affinitie ioyned neir to the maift honeft in all the town, knawing weill that bathe fic of the Vniueifitie and town that lyked him nocht, wald tak pait with the faid Mr Wilyeam. This Hen-drie comes vpon the Hie Gett, Mr Wilyeam going to the Principals Leffone of the New Collage, and efter quarreling words, touks him and ftriks him with the gaides of his fwoid. Mr Wilyeam plantes to the Rectoi, wha call-ing the faid Hendrie befor him, efter cognition, depryves him of his name of Maifter (for he was maid Maiftei,) and ordeanes him to mak a humble fatif-faction to Mi Wilyeam in the fain place whar he miourit him. This he re-tufing to do, the complainer memed his caufe to the Lords of Seffion, wha gaiff out compulfators vpon the Rectois decreit, whaiwith the faid Hendiie being chaigit, firft be the moyen of a cettein wicked men, mifgyders of the town, fauorars of the Bifchope, and haters of thair honeft and guid nibours onlie for their vertew, he is receaued in the number of the citiciners, and maid burges. Then he comes deffimulatlie to the Rector, defyring the execution of the chaiges to be superceidit, and promifit to mak amends to Mr Wilyeam on the Hie Streit fic a day. Be this Mr Wilyeam is fecoure, and within a day or twa addrefes him to his ordinar Leffone of the Lawes within the Auld Collage, and going from his hous in the town to the Collage, his gown on, his book in the a hand, and fand glas in the vther, meditating on his Leffone, Hendrie Hamiltone vfhes out of a hous, whare he lay in wait for bloode, and vnbefeatting Mr Wilyeam, with the firft ftrak wounds him in the hand and mutilats him, and had proceidit fordar, giff be fum gentle men paffing that way, he haid nocht been fteyed. Mr Wilyeam is lead to his mothers hous crewallie woundit, the newes wharof gaes amang his frinds, they ryfe and rine togidder in armes to affift the Bailyies for iuftice. Bot an of the Bailyies being vpon the confpuracie, refufing thair affiftance, brings the murdarer, accompanied with the Bifchopes guid brother, James Arthour, called comounlie Jaques, and a officer or twa and na ma, and in plane provocation, by the teithe of the partie, convenit befor Mr Wilyeams mothers ftare, yet whan he was lying with his wound bleading, fa that it could nocht be fteamide. The quhilk, his brother and brother in law feing, could nocht abyde, bot making a mint, maid the town to fle, and ftenit vpe a grait tumult of all fort rinning togidder in armes. Vniuerfitie, citie, and gentle men being in the town for the tyme. In this tumult nane is fa biffie to fchow his manreid in feghting as the faid Jaques Arthour, and meitting with his marrow, with rapper and dagger, miffing his ward, he gettes a porh at the left pape, wharof he dies. His corps is brought to a chirurgians boothe and fighted ther, and fought be his frinds and a number in publict, and fund to haiff that onlie a poinct ftreak of a rapper fword, be whom giffen na man could certeanlie knaw, fum fufpecting an, and fum another. Mr Wilyeams brother Jhone perfewes efter Hamiltone, wha crying for mercie, and randring himfelff, obtemes mercie at the faid Jhones hand, and be him is brought out and delyverit to the Bailyies againe.

The tumult fteying, the honeft men goes to thair houfes, ignorant altogidder of anie euill done, namlie of the flauchter of the faid Jaques. Amangs the reft, an James Smithe, a man of fingular qualities, grmtlie beloued of all godlie and guid men for his vertew and guid conditiones, and almikle mvyed and hated be the wicked, is warned be diuers that loued him, that ther was a man flaine, and the mater was dangerus, prayed him therfor to hauld himfelff

quyet and out of the way for a tyme. The quhilk he refufed, repofing on his
innocencie, and faying they haid fuffeit wrang in the perfone of thair frind,
bot haid done nane   Incontinent, the bailyies comes to the hous of the faid
honeft man, better accompanied nor when they convoyit Hamiltone to the
Tolbuthe, and charges him in the Kings name to go to warde with thame   He
willinglie obeyes and gaes with thame, and fa does the reft, to the number of
nyne or ten.

Thefe fimple foulles this wayes fangit in the net of thefe craftie hountars,
(wharin the partes of all I could pent out particularlie giff my purpofe permitted) war from the Tolbuthe brought to the Provefts hous, wha, withe
the Bifchope and reft of the mifcaullars of the town, war all vnder a complot,
refolving then to be weill renengit vpon thefe honeft men, wha, at the ham
coming of the Lords out of England, haid fought redres of manie grait abufes
and mormities committed be the faids mifrewlars of St Andros, luking that
all things then fould haiff bein corrected and fett in gud ordour,—that Zuill
comoun they thought to repey weill now at Pafch.

Sa they are fummoned to a day of law in Edinbruche, whar, vnderftanding
the law to be ftreat, and wanting the Prince fawour, quhilk was caried by
tham be the Bifchopes faction, and therwithall craftelie abbufit be tham fen-
yied frinds, they ar brought in effect to com in the will of the partie, wha
decernes vpon thame all banifment futhe of the town during thair will ; and
vpon twa in fpeciall, to wit, James Smithe, to whafe worthie praife I fpak
befor, and Jhone Walwode, brother to the faid Mr Wilyeam, banifment out
of the countrey, vpon grait fommes of contiouention and fure caution. By this
malitius craftie denys and convoy war thefe gud honeft men thus wayes maift
innocenthe and vniufthe vexed and banifled out of the realme from thair
wyffes and childring fax yeires, and at thair retourning wars handlht, as we
fall heir in the awin place. Bot as the Bifchope, withe the reft of the mifrewlars of that town war the beginnars, fa I can nocht omit vnmentioned a vennemus and malicius profecutor, whafe vnplacable hatred and infatiable greidi-
nes of thefe honeft mens gear was fic, as na kynd of dealling, credit, fawour,
or requeift of men of all fortes, rankes, and degries within the countrey, employed erneflhe for to brak and mitigat him, could purchas nor procure ony
kynd of dies at his hand.   This was Mr Jhone Arthour, ftubburnlie and dif-
pytfullie refufing all reafone, for this fpeciall caufe for that the minifters fa-
worit tham, infpyrit but queftion be the fpreit contrar to Chryft and his minifters   The pretext of his malice and auarice was, that as he wald affirme

agaınſt all the warld and treuthe ıtſelff, that James Smıthe was the ſlayer of hıs brother, agaınſt whom James haıd never anıe querrell, nor cam neir him that day ; bot was clenlie ſein and knawin to be a pair of buttes lainthe from him when he was ſlaine ; and farder, fyve hounder ſaw that onlie a poıhe of a rapper, wharof he dıed, haıffing na kynd of ſtroak or wound ma, and euerıe man ſpyed James ſword that day to be a braid ſword. Bot the treuthe was, James was rıtche, honeſt, and vpright, verteus ın hıs calling, and the vther pure, debauchit, greidie, and neidie, and therwithall a lawer, attendıng on Seſſion, and watıng to mak hıs prey of the ſoumes of contrauention, quhılk war graıt and laıge, or then thaır æquiualent be compoſition, for he kend they could nocht, nor wald nocht byde out of thaır awm countrey.

The mere pitie and ındignation of my hart (as the cerchar of harts knawes) maıd me to ındeuor what I could for the helpe and confort of that honeſt man in ſpeciall Lykas ther was na honeſt or godlie man ın the land wha ather knew him or hard of him bot meined hıs ceas and moyenned for ıt as they might, bot na grace was to be fund at a graceles manes hand.

About the middes of that yeır 1589, Françoıs, Erle of Bothewall, tuk vpe bands of men of weare, vnder the conduct of Coronell Hakerſton, vnder pretence to tak ordour wıth the Ylles, bot ıt preıved ın end a Spaniſhe papiſticall courſe, as ıs diſcoueıed ın the buik of the execution of Fentrie Hıs Capteanes leading hıs men langs the coſt ſyde, oppreſſed and troublet the Townes therof, euill fauored be going and returnıng anes. The ſecond tyme they enteıt to compas and viſit ower agaın, and cam to Kirkady, ſending thaır furrıours and commiſſars befor, to prepear for tham ſum pıces of armour and ıntertemment Bot Carell, Anſter and Pıttenweım, wıth aſſiſtance of ſum gentilmen of the countrey about, reſolued to refiſt and feght tham The quhılk when I perceaved, I maıd haſt to Court, and infoımed the King of the abbus and commotion that was lyk to be, and purchaſſed Letteıs to diſcharge the Capteanes from proceiding anıe farther, and if they wald nocht, to warrand the ſubiects to refiſt The Erle being Admiıall, diſcharges the bottes at Leithe froın giffing me paſſage ; bot taking ıorney to the Queıns ferrie, I cam wıth ſic dilıgence as I could, bot or I cam, the Coronell, wıth hıs men of wear, war feaın to tak the ſteiple of St Monians on than head, vtherwayes haid gottin ſic wages peyed tham as wald haiff interteıned tham all thaır dayes And yit ınſiſtıng, they brak the apointment quhılk the Tutor of Pıtcure (that notable Prouoſt of Dondıe,) maıd betwix tham and the Towns, and cam foıdwart to Pıttenweım ; bot at my coming wıth the Kings diſchaıge to tham, and warrand to our Townes to refift in eais of difobedience, they war fean to reteire and leaue af.   Sa it pleafed God to keipe from blod fchedding, and releiue our Townes of a grait feir and vexation.

In the beginning of wintar, the King, accompanied with the Chancellar and certean theirs of his Counfall, with twa of the Minifterie, in veric fecret maner imbarkit, few knawing till he was away, and landit at Vpflaw in Norroway, efter mikle foull wather of a ftormie wintar, and from that traucht be land to Denmark, throw maine woods and wilderies, in confermed froft and fnaw, and than maried his Quein Anna, and maid gud cheir, and drank ftouthe till the fpring tyme.   At his departing he apointed Mr Robert Bruce to be on the Counfall, and recommendit the efteat of his countrey to him. and the minifterie in fpeciall, repofing, as he profeffit, vpon him and tham aboue all his nobles.   And indeid he was nocht difapointed, for of the fawour of God than was never a mair peaceble and quyet efteat of a countrey nor during that tyme of the Kings abfence   Sa that, whar befor or fen fyne, few monethes, yea oukes, was ther without fum flauchter, ther was na fic thing during that tyme.

Boduell cam then in publict, and of his awin accord maid his repentance befor Mr Robert Bruce in the Kirk of Edinbruche, for his licentius, diffolut lyff, and all his bypaft finnes, and promifed, be Gods grace, to kythe another man in tyme coming, &c.   Bot it was a taking of Gods name in vean, and publict abufing of himfelff and the Lords peiple ; and therfor the Lord curfed him, for na thing fucceidit weill with him therefter.

1590.—In the fpring tyme of the yeir following, the Generall Affemblie conveined at Edinbruche.   At quhilk diligent tryell being taken, it was fund, that na ftenage at all was in the countrey of Papifts, of theiffes, or ame troubelfome inordinat perfones   Wharof the breithing praifit God, and apointed, efter the ordour that the Kirk of Edinbruche haid taken vpe, that thair fould be fafteing and moderat dyet vfit euerie fabathe till the Kings returning.   The quhilk cuftom being found verie meit for the exerceife of the Sabathe, was keipit in Edinbruche in the houffes of the godlie continuahe therefter.   Sa that fparing thair gros and fumptuus dinners, they vfit nocht bot a difhe of brothe or fum litle recreation till night ; and that quhilk was fpant was beftowit on the pure.   Boduell reforted to that Affemblie, and keiping hous in the Abbay in the Kings awin houffes, he haid the Quein of England be hir Ambaffator ordinar (Mr Robert Bowes wha ley at Edinbruche, a verie godlie man, and to

his vttermaiſt lowing and canfull of the peace and weill of the twa realmes
of England and Scotland,) to be his conncel, and Mr Robert Brace, my
vncle. and me, being Moderator of that Aſſemblie, invited now and then to
guid cheir, haiffing ſum grait purpofe and to luik in hand ; bot he wes neuer
lukkie nor honeſt to God nor man

At this Aſſemblie it was ordeanit, That all and euerie miniſter that haid
ma Kirks nor ane in cure ſould demit the reſt, and tak him till ane only
Alſo that the Townes of Edinbruche, Dondie, Stirling, and St Andros ſould
aggrie with ſie as they thought meit for tham. and report agame to the Aſſemblie for than tranſportation   Vpon the quhilk I wes erneſthe delt with
be all the ſaids Townes ; bot the loue of my awin flok and Preſbyterie, and
vicinitie of my vncle in St Andros, permitted me nocht to condiſcend vnto
tham   For this my parochiners aggreit amangs thamſelues to big me a hous ;
bot being vndertaken, as it comes of comoun warkes, it ſealt   Therfor my
God and heavinlie father, the giſlar and prouyder for me of all guid things,
put in my hart to tak the wark in hand myſelt : and, albeit I haid nocht fourtie pound in readie money, yit furneſit all things ſo ſtraughe to me, that
annes begoun. it ley neuer a day till it was compleit, God haiffing ſum confoit to miniſter to his awin ſervants therby from tyme to tyme thereſter
It was begun the 5 of Junij, and endit with October following 1590

In the yeir 1590. the King, accompanied with his Quein, cam hame the firſt
of May, to the grait ioy and contentment of all the countrey   Diuers prac-
teſies of witchcraft and deuilrie was againſt him, as he was certified of thereſter. bot the mercifull and mightie hand of God watched ower him, and pre-
ſerued him at the erneſt prayers of his faithfull ſervands the miniſters, whom
then he acknawlagit to be his maiſt faithfull freinds   Within a monethe or
twa efter his retourn was keipit a maiſt ſolemne action and magnifie of the
Queins Coronation, and entries in Edinbruche   At the quhilk my vncle, Mr
Andro, in tauour of the Ambaſſatours ſent from diuers Duces and Princes of
Almanie and Flanders, maid and pronuncit an Oration in vers to the grait
admiration of the hearars and than exceiding ioy and contentment, namlie of
bathe than Maieſties.   The King gaiſt him grait thankes, ſaying, he haid ſa
honored him and his countrey that day, that he could never requyt him, and
thereſter wald infiſt farder, and command him to giff the ſam to the printar,
that with diligence it might be exped, for ther was nan of the Ambaſſadours
bot haid maid him requeiſt for that eſfect.   And indeid this was the wark of
God to haiſt his awin ſervand honored, for Mr Andro haid nocht bein warnit

to this Coronation in anie convenient tyme, and haid na thing preparit bot
sic as cam in his meditation a night or twa, anent the right way of rewling
and goverment, the quhilk he vttent with a meruelus dexteritie and grace
And, at the Kings comand, the morn efter the pronuncing, gaiff it to the
prntar with an epigram of dedication to the King, and intitulat the Στεφανισκιον.
The copies of it past throw all Europe, and was mikle esteemed of be the
lernit.   Josephus Scaliger wrait to him congratulating, and said, " Nos talia
non possumus." Lipsius reiding it said " Reuera Andreas Meluinus est serio
doctus." Be the quhilk occasion, as often befor and sen syne, all the lerned
in a maner lamented that he wald nocht set himselff to wryt, quhilk was mikle memed to him be all his frinds, bot he said, that God haid callit him to
vse his toung and viue voice yit ; when he fand the calling and wariand for
the pen quhilk God wald gift it he thoucht it guid, he sould do thereftter.

The apointed ordinar Generall Assemblie was keipe at Edinbruche in August, at the quhilk it behoued me to mak the exhortation   I cam to the Kingorn the night befor, and imbarking with certean breithring, we cam within a
myle and les to Leithe, bot a contrarie wind comming iust in our teithe when
we haid vst all meanes be burding and rowing, we war compellit to go bak
agane, with a foull sdboure, and landit at Brintyland, whar na hors war to
be gottin, and being past sax hours at evin, I was to enter in iorney on my
feit to go about, when God respecting his awin wark, send the wound in the
wast with a pleasand fear night, and sa finding be the sam Prouidence a lytle
sdhollab, reposing on him whase turn was in hand, we tuk the sie, and gat
verie fear passage and cam to Edinbruche euen as nyne of the night strak, ob-
tenning of Gods mercie that nights repose, quhilk I luiked nocht for, to inable
me for the mornes action.

It sall nocht be impertinent to remember sum poincts of the doctrine vttered at that tyme vpon the 1 Thess. v ver. 12, 13.

The text being sounned and opened vpe, thir heades war insisted into :—
First, anent the weght of the charge of the ministerie , nixt, anent the honour therof ; thridlie, whow neidfull ᵒᵘδεσιx, rebuk or admonition, was in the
Kirk and amangs breithring   Vpon this last head, occasion was takin to speak
at lanthe of disciplin, quhilk also at mair lanthe I thought pertinent heir
till insert, because the course of the cheiff mater of this Storie rinnes vpon
that.

First, That discipline was maist necessar in the Kirk, seing without the saming, Chryst's Kingdome could nocht stand   For vnles the Word and Sacraments

war keipit in finceritie, and rightlie vfit and practefit be direction of the difcipline, they wald foone be corrupted And therfor certean it was, that without fum difcipline na Kirk, without trew difcipline, na rightlie reformed Kirk,
and without the right and perfyt difcipline, na right and perfyt Kirk * This
was clenlie declarit be the exemples of a Republict and Citie, and of artes of
warfear and paftorage. The Storie of the gifting, beginning, continowing,
brak and reftoring againe of the trew difcipline within the Kirk of Scotland
was recompted and callit to rememberance; and thervpon exhortation giffen
to dell with his Maieftie in maift graue and inftant maner, That his Maieftie wald fchaw that taken of trew thankfulnes to God for the grait benefit of
his faiff preferuation and retourning with his Quein from Denmark, as to re-
fchinde and abolifhe obfcure and dangerus lawes maid in preiudice of the difcipline and libertie of Chryfts Kingdome within this realme, haiffing fund in
guid experience in his abfence, as alwayes befor, the guid will, fidelitie, loue
and cear of the minifterie as of thair God, and Chryft Jefus his king, be him
anointed and fett over all, whafe caufe this was quhilk he haid put in the
hands of his pure fervants, &c

Alfo the haill breithring war erneftlie exhorted to ftudie the difcipline diligentlie, and practife it cearfullie, that they might be able at all occafiones to
ftand in defence therof, as it hes bein of Gods grait fawour with the treuthe
of the doctrine fett doun out of the Word of God , and the practife of the fam
fund maift halfome and profitable within the Kirk of Scotland. And that at
this tyme, for thrie cauffes namlie; firft, becaufe of the efteat of the godlie,
guid, and zealus breithring in England, our nibour Kirk, ftanding for the
treuthe therof, and fearlie fuffering for the fam Secondlie, becaufe thefe
Amaziafes belligod bifchopes in England, be all moyen, yea and money, war
feikand conformitie of our realme with thairs till invert and pervert our Kirk,
as did Achaz and Vrias with the King and Altar of Damafcus. Thridlie,
becaufe we haid lurking within our awin bowelles a poifonable and vennemus Pfyllus, a warlow I warrand yow, fa empoifoned be the vennome of that
auld ferpent, and fa altered in his fubftance and naturall, that the deadlie poifone of the vipere is his familiar fuid and nuriture, to wit, lies, falfhode, malice and knauerie, wha hes bein lurking a lang tyme hatching a cocatrice eagg.
and fa fynlie inftructed to handle the whiffall of that auld inchantar, that na

---

* At this the Englifhe Ambaffatour being prefent, fturred, and conferrit with me therefter at
lainthe, whom I fatisfeit.

Pſyllus, Circe, Medea, or Pharmaceutrie could euer haiff done better   This is
Patuk Adamſone, fals biſchope of St Audios, wha at this tyme was in making
of a buik againſt our diſcipline, quhilk he intytles Pſyllus, and dedicates to
the King, the epiſtle dedicatorie wharof is in my hand, wharin he ſchawes his
purpoſe to be, to ſouk out the poiſone of the diſcipline of the Kirk of Scotland, as the Pſylli a vennemus peiple in Afric ſoukes out the vennoin of the
wounds of ſic as ar ſtangit with ſerpents   But I truſt in God (ſaid I) he ſall
proue the foole als madhe as did theſe ſillie Pſylhes, of whom Heiodot in his
Melpomene wryttes, that they periſhed altogidder in this maner : When the
South wound haid dryed vpe all thair conſernars and ciſterns of water, they
tuk counſall all in a mynd to ga againſt it in armes for advengementt, but coming amang the deſerts and dry ſandes, the wound blew hichlie and owerwhelmde
thame with ſand, and deſtroyed tham euerie man.   Sa I dout nocht ſall
come of this obſtmat, malitius foolle, whilas he intends nocht onlie to ſtope
the breathe of Gods mouthe, bot alſo to be advengit vpon it, becauſe it hes
ſtrukken him ſa, that he is blaſted therwith and dryed vpe, and maid voide of
all ſape and moiſture of heavinhe lyff   But alas ! my breithring, (ſaid I,) giff
yie wald do that quhilk I think yie bathe might and ſould do at this tyme, to
wit, to ratefie and approue that ſentence of excommunication maiſt iuſtlie and
ordourlie pronuncit againſt that vennemus enemie of Chryſts Kingdome, as I
am aſſuit it is ratefeit in the heavines, as cleirlie may appeir be the effects
therof, na les then in the dayes of Ambroſe, when Sathan ſenſiblie poſſeſit ſic
as war delyveit to him be excommunication, he wald feill better his miſera-
ble tohe, and be woun againe to Chryſt if he be of the number of the elect
The quhilk, if yie do nocht, my breithring, by a ſoar experience nocht lang
fyne paſt befor, I may foretell yow a thing to come, giff God in meicie for his
Chryſts ſeak ſtey it nocht ; that yie will find and feill yit mair permtiuſhe the
refeined poiſone of that Pſyllus in branghng the diſcipline of the Kirk, and
puniſſing of our vndewtifull neghgence

An vther poinct of the doctrine then vttered I hald it nocht vnprofitable
heir to inſert, becauſe of the neceſſitie therof yit abyding vnamendit.   This
was anent the dewtie of the flockes to thair paſtors and watchmen.   The
flocks aught to loue their paſtors denhe be this text and vther of Hohe Scripture ; they aught to prouyde for tham all things neidfull and confortable for
this lyff, and to giff tham that honour quhilk apertemes to the ambaſſatours
of Chryſt.   God biddes thee honour him in the miniſterie of his worſchiping,
and thy ſaluation with the beſt of thy ſubſtance ; and giff thow do nocht this

way acknawlage the awnar of all thy fubftance and giffin therof, thow art bot an vnthankfull theiff, and nocht a lawfull profleffor therof with guid con- fcience, and at that day of Gods iuftice court, thow fall heir the dome and feill the punifment of a theift, if thow prevent nocht be repentance

But heir our flockes excufes thamfelues, faying, Our teinds ar rigurullie exacted and taken vpe from ws, therfor this burding lyes vpon tham that gettes the teinds, &c. Anfwer, If men pitie thair awin faulles, it is na ex- cufe for tham, for giff they war neuer fa fear fpulyied and oppreffed, wald they want the neceffar fuid of the body, and reyment than of, fa lang as they haid anie thing left, yea or could beg or borrow? Na: They wald vfe the reddieft for the prefent neceffitie, and picafe to remead the oppreffion and wrang, by what meanes they could And why will they nocht vfe the lyk for the fude and reyment of the faull and inwart man? Is it waife then the bodie? Is it nocht to be ceared for? Or is ther nocht a faull, a heavine, a hell, a God, a Deuill? Na, I am fure my breithring, if this doctrine foundit often in publict and privat amangs the pure famifing faulles in this land, a guid number at leaft wald be walkned and moued to feik paftors on thair awin charges.* I fpeik be guid experience, I thank God for it : Tak peanes and diftruft nocht God, he will work and bring furthe fum guid effect. I neuer faw yit a piece of fathfull peanes taken vprightlie for the honour of God, and faluation of pure faulles, bot it fand a blefling and fucces worthie of all, and it haid bein ten tymes mair Nather yit, euer knew I in Scotland a man of guid confcience, that durft in confcience come to the fchaking af of the duft of his feit againft anie town or congregation. And for my awin pairt, I fand euer the fault mair in the peanes of the paftor, nor the purs of the peiple if they haid it. Yea, can it be poffible that a man fall geau or fordar a faull to Chryft and the lyff euerlafting, and nocht receaue of his purs and things of this lyff as he may fpear, and it war to fpeare it on himfelff? Na, nocht poffible, for a thankfull hart getting mon giff againe : and if nocht thankfull, na Chriftian ; and winning the mans hairt and faull to Chryft and thie, the man himfelff, and what he hes, mon be at thy command in Chryft.

O bot they will fay, Sall the facrilegius then pas frie, and bruik the teinds? Na, nocht fa : Bot let the flocks and paftours ioyne togidder, and cry

* NOTA That nochtwithftanding of the ordinance of the laft Affemblie, men war leathe to quyt the multitud of Kirks, faying ther wald na ftipends be gottin to Kirks, and men could nocht enter to charges without ftipends.

and craue at the King, Counfall, and Efteattes, and be bot als erneſt in that mater concerning the ſervice of God, and the weill of thair awin faulles, as gentilmen and vthers ai in things twitching thair heritage, honour, and vther ciuill or criminall actiones, and J will warrand they ſall com ſpeid. For whow ather could they, or durſt they, be refuſed in ſa reaſonable a petition, &c. Bot what is the kirks dewtie in this ceas ? That we leaue na thing vndone that Chryſt hes put in our hands, and requyres of ws, according to our office in the rewling of his Kirk and Kingdome. Ar we the trew Kirk ? Ar we the lawfull Miniſterie ? Haiff we the authoritie and powar of his ſchapter ? Haiff we that fyre that deuores the aduerſar, and that hammer that braks the rokkes ? Yea, and haiff we nocht that ſcharpe twa eagit ſword ? or is it ſcharpe and drawin onlie againſt the pure and mean annes, and nocht potent in God for oweithrawing of hauldes, for doing vengeance vpon haill nationes, cheſteſing of peiples, yea binding of kings in channes, and the maiſt honoura-ble princes in fetters of yron, to execut vpon thaim the iudgment wryttin ? And finalie, is thair exception ather of perſones or ſinnes befor the iudgment ſeat of Chryſt ? or ſall his ſword or cenſour ſtrik vpon the pure adulterar or fuinicator being contumax, and ly in the ſcabart ruſting from the ſacrilegius, ſuffering thaim to go on contemptnuſlie obſtinat ? Na, na ! deir breithring, I man vtter the advys that God hes put in my hart, ſubmitting alwayes my ſpreit to the prophettes

Fuſt, I wald the Kings Maieſtie ſould be traueled withe for his fawour and concurrence, wha is neir als far hurt in this mater as the Kirk is. We haiff his will ; we haiff his promiſe ; we haiff manifold exemples and reaſones to ley befor him. We, and the graitteſt and beſt number of our flockes, haiff bein, ar, and mon be, his beſt ſubiects, his ſtrynthe, his honour A guid mi-niſter (I ſpeak it nocht arrogantlie, bot according to the treuthe,) may do him mair guid ſervice in a houre, nor manie of his ſacrilegius courteours in a yeir, &c.

Nixt, I wald wis that from this preſent Affemblie, war directed to the cheiff ſacrilegius perſones in all the ſchyres of this Realme, choſin men of godlie grauitie and authoritie, full of the Holie Ghoſt, till inſtruct, admoniſe, and charge thaim in the name of God, and of his ſone Chryſt Jeſus till amend but deley, &c

Laſt, that a frequent and honourable Affemblie war keipit, affiſted be the Kings awin preſence in perſone, ſolemnlie ſanctified with the exerceis of faſt-ing and hvmiliation, with a guid number of gentilmen and burgeſſes, directed in commiffion from euerie paroche and brouche thervnto : Befor the quhilk certean of the fpecialles of thefe facrilegius perfones might be callht and compeiring, inquyrit if they war of Chryft, and of the trew members of his Kirk or nocht   If they antwered they war, then let them teftifie it be hering of his voice and the voice of his Kirk. If nocht, let be fchaw in tham that Chryft commands to hald tham as Publicanes and Ethniks.

O then, me thinks I heir fum crying, Will ye excommunicat tham ? That will breid a giart fchifme and vproare ; they are the cheiff that faught for relligion ; yie will ryde with a thinne court if yie want tham   Soft, I pray yow, and heir reafone.   I wald afk tham wither it war the nam or the mater of excommunication that they abhorrit and fearde   Giff it be the mater, ar they ignorant of that quhilk is fa aft dung in tham heides, to wit, that ipfo facto befor God they ar excommunicat, fa lang as induidlie againft thair confcience they ly vnder the curs of that execrable facrilage ? And as for the effects and inconvenients alleadgit, I afk onlie if this be that dewtie that God bids ws do, and requyres of ws conforme to our office ? When anie abyds in finne wherby God is diſhonorit, the Kirk hurt and fklandent, and the perfones felf indangerit of condemnation, can the paftors be anfwerable for the difcharge of than dewtie, except they deall with that perfone be all the meanes that God prefcryvit to than calling, wharof the fpeciall ar the word and difciplne ? And if it be our dewtie, what haiff we mair to do bot to obey and do it, leaving to God the effects, quhilk ar in his hand alleanerlie ?

And yit to anfwer by guid appeirrance, this mater fall proceide fa fearlie and clenlie, that nan can repung therto, except they will planlie ganftand God, the Kirk, the King, and all guid reafone, and fa doing wilbe fa weak, that they may be eafilie owercom   As to thair number, it is na thing in refpect of the multitude of pure faulles that wants thair fpirituall fuid, and are oppreffed in thair teinds, and of the number of guid men that fean wald for reformation   As for thair feghting for relligion, fa did facrilegius Achan for the inheritance of Canaan, Saull for Ifraell, Joab and the fonnes of Seruia for the kingdome of Dauid ; bot they war nocht approued of God. It is nocht the feghtar that is commendit and allowit, but he that feghtes rightlie and lawfullie. The praife of planting of relligion in this land appertenies to the Lord of Hoftes alleanerlie, and when euer they boft of that, they fall in a dowble and luchar degrie of facrilage, arrogating to tham the glorie of God, and that maift falflie, nocht being fa mukle as Gods guid inftrument.

· For if they refufe that quhilk we craue, they declar euidentlie they faught

2 B

neuer for God nor relligion, bot for the kirk gear, to disturbe the posseffours therof that they might invade the fam , they taught neuer againft the Papifts. bot againft the Titulars of the Teinds and rents of the Kirk ; they fett nocht thamfelues to hauld out Jefuiftes, bot the fuddarts that clamed right to Chryfts cott . they wald nocht rut out the feminarie preifts, bot the feid of the Kirk, guid lerning, and all relligion.   Sa that if God, if Chryft, if relligion, if minif-terie, falbe reclamers of the Teinds and Kirk gear agame, they fall at an in-ftant becom to tham, Satan, Anti Chryft, Papiftrie, and Jefuittes   And now if it falbe the number of fic that fall mak out our number, war it nocht better to be few ? or fic courteours to fett out our court, war it nocht better to be courtles ?

Whairfor, deir breithring, (faid I) to be fchort, and conclud my opinion, that it may receaue ather your approbation or cenfure, my exhortation is, that we be cearfull till vnderftand our dewtie, and what command we haiff of God in this poinct. and weying it righthe, that we be about canfullie to put it in practife, leaving to God the euent and effect, repofing ourfelues, what euer fall out, vpon the warrand of his will, and the teftimonie of a found and vpright confcience   Let ws nocht fay with the flugart, " Thei is a lyon in the way ;" nor for fear of ftorme wound or wather leaue af to faw and fcheat the Lords land.   Gif Chryft and his Apoftles haid fa done, the Gofpell haid neuer bein preatched.   And if thefe noble inftruments ftenred vpe in this laft age, even in this countrey, haid been fa terrified, we haid neuer emoyed this libertie and fruict therof   Let ws be then incuragit in the fraimthe of our almightie God, and in the authoritie of his lie calling ; and the mair that facrilegius auarice carie men away from God and relligion, let ws the mair erneftlie feik efter him, and procure the weill and confort of the faulles concredit to ws.   And without queftion we falbe terrible to whatfumeuer enemie and contraire powar. and fall want na guid thing   We fall feid fweither and better on a difhe of pottage, nor they on than kinghe fear. ferving an God trewhe, and ftryving with our Chryft againft the vnthankfull waild.   It was God, euen our God, wha almoft by all meanes begoud the wark merueloufhe, and na les merueloufhe by all meannes hes continowed it in defpyt of all contraire craft and powar ; and the fam, our guid God in the fam fort will croun and end it That all praife therof haillelie may be his, to whom be it for euer.   Amen

This doctrine and advys was weill lyked and approuit of all, bot was nocht thought expedient to be practifed at that tyme be the wefdome of the politik and warldhe wyfe.   And fielyk concerning the bifchope, whom they percea-

vit to be fallin alreadie gif he war lettin alean; bot if he war put at, the King
wald tak his part, thinking it was for his caufe he war put at. Onlie this was
concludit, That euerie minifter fould haiff a copie of the Book of Difcipline
and perufe it; and euerie Prefbyterie fould caufe thair haill members fubfcryve the fam, and the refufars to be excommunicat, purpofing therby to
ather caufe the Bifchope fubfcryve the fam, or then to be of new excommunicat: Bot God wrought that mater better.

The Bifchope being a man that delt deceatfullie with all, and neuer difchargit fa mikle as a ciuill dewtie according to the lawes, repofing vpon the
Kings fawour, at laft the King was fa fafchit with complents of all fortes of
men vpon him, that he was fa often denuncit to the Horn, and fa lang lying
regiftrat therat, and vnderftanding therwith that he was infamus and euill
loued be all men, he was efchamed of him and cuft him af; and for dar difponit his lyfrent to the Duc of Lennox, with the temporalitie of the bifchoprik,
wherby the miferable bifchope fell in extream pouertie, and therwithall in a
heauie difeafe of body and mynd. Bot he haid fimulat fa often feiknes that
nan beleiued him till he was brought till fic neceffitie that he was compellit to
wrait to Mr Andro, my vncle, mak confeffion of his offences againft God and
him, and craue his helpe; wha, but for dar, vifited him, and fuppoirted him fa,
that the fpace of diuers monethes he leiued on his purfe. At laft he befought
him to get him fum collection of the breithring in the Town, and for than
fatiffaction promifed to prefent the pulpit and mak publict confeffion Bot
whither he femyit excufes, or that it was fa indeid that God wald nocht permit him, I knaw nocht, bot he haid neuer that grace to prefent the pulpit
againe. In the end of that wintar he fend to the Prefbyterie, and maid humble futt to be relaxed from excommunication, and the breithring, douting wither it was that he felt the dint therof in effect vpon his confcience, or to be
a mean to infinuat him in the breithrings pitie, to gett wharby to fuftein him,
fend Mr Andro Moncreiff, of guid memorie, and me, with fum others to try
him. We fand him in a miferable efteat, and whowfone he marked me, he
plukked af the thing on his head, and cryed, "Forgiff, forgiff, me for Gods
feak, guid Mr James, for I haiff offendit, and don wrang to yow manie wayes'
I fchawing him his fine againft Chryft and his Kirk, exhorted him to vn-
feinyit repentance, and therwith conforted him in the mercie of God, and forgaiff him with all my hart Then propoming to him anent his excommunication, giff he acknawlagit it lawfullie done, and felt the force of it in his confcience, he interrupted me, and cryed pitiouflie out in thefe words: "Loufe

me for Chryft feak,' dyvers tymes ower and ower. The quhilk when we reported to the breathing, with prayer and thankfgiffing he was relaxit

1591 —At the Prouinciall Affemblie conveined in St Andros the 6 of
Apryll 1591, Mr Jhone Caldcleuche prefented in his name, to the Affemblie,
certean Articles of Recantation, wryttin in Latine. The quhilk being red, the
Affemblie directs Mr Andro Meluill, (chofine that yeir Rector of the Vniuerfitie in the roum of Mr James Wilkie, lathe departed, a guid, godlie, honeft
man) Mr Robert Wilkie, Dauid Fergufone, and Mr Nicol Dalglaifhe, to the
faid Mr Patrik Adamfone, bifchope, to craue of him, in the name of the Affemblie, a mair clen and ample recantation, and that in vulgare langage, that
all might underftand the fam   The faid Bifchope fendes the fam fubfcryuit
with his awin hand as efter followes :

The Recantation of P. Sant Androfe, direct to the Synod convenit at St And 6 of Apr. 1591.

BRETHRINE being troublet with feiknes, that I might gift confeffion of that doctrine wherin I
hope that God fall call me, and that at his pleafoure, I aught depart in an vnitie of Chriftian fathe,
I thought gud to vtter the faming to your Worfchips, and lykwyfe to craue your godlie Worfchips affiftance, nocht for the reftitution of anie warldlie pompe or preeminnence, quhilk I lytle
refpect, as to remoue from me the fklanders quhilk ar reafit in this countrie concerning the varietie of doctrin, fpeciallie vpon my part, wherin I proteft befor God, that I haift onlie a fingle refpect
to his glorie, and be his grace I fall abyde herin vnto my lyves end
    Firft, I confes the trew doctrine and Chriftian relligion to be teatched and rightlie annunceit with-
in this realme, and deteafts all papiftrie and fuperftition, lyk as, bleffed be God, I haift detefted
the fam in my hart the fpace of threttie yeirs, fen it pleafed God to giff me the knawlage of the
treuthe, vharin I haift walkit vprightlie, alfweill hen as in vther Countries as the Lord beares me
record, vnto this laft dayes wherin, perthe for ambition and vean glore to be preferit to my breithring, and perthe for couetoufnes, I haift poffeffit grendehe the pelft of the Kirk, I did vndertak this
office of Bifchoprik, wherwith milhe the fincereft profeflioms of the Word hes fund fault, and hes
condemnit the faming as impertinent to the office of a fincere paftor of Gods Word.   And albeit
men wald cuilor the faming and imperfectiones therof be diuers clokes, yit the fam can nocht be
concilit from the fpirituell eis of the fathfull, nather yit can the men of God, when they ar put to
than confcience diffemble the fam.
    Nixt, I confes I was in an erroneus opinion, that I beleuit the government of the Kirk to be lyk
the Kingdomes of the erthe, plean contrar to the commandment of our Maifter Chryft, and the
monarche wherwith the Kirk is governit, nocht to be onlie in the perfone of our Sauiour Chryft
(as it is,) bot in the Minifters wha ar na thing but vaffalles, and vndei I im in an æquallitie amangs
thamfelues
    Thirdlie, That I maried the Erle of Huntlie contrar to the Kirks command without the confeffion
of his fathe, and profeffion of the fincere doctrine of the Word, I repent and craues God pardone.
    That I trauelit, bathe be reafoning and vther wayes, to fubiect the Kirkmen vnto the Kings or-

dinance in things that apertenes to ecclesiastik maters, and things of conscience I ask God mercie, wharvpon grait enormities hes fallen furthe in this Countrey

That I beleued and sa teachit, the Presbyteries to be a foolithe invention, and wauld haiff it sa esteemed of all men, quhilk is an ordinance of Chryst, I craue God mercie

Fordar I submit my selff to the mercie of God and the iudgment of the Assemblie, nocht misfuring my offences be my awin selff, nor infirmities of my awin ingyne, bot to the guid iudgement of the Kirk, to the quhilk alwayes I submit my selff, and besaiks vow to mak intercession to God for me, and to the Kings Maiestie, that I may haif sum moyen to liue, and consume the rest of this my wretched tyme, for whase cause and fauour I committed all thir errors, and God hes sithe recompensed me in his iudgments

And wharas I am burdenit to haiff bein the settar furthe of the buik called the Kings Declaration, wherin the haill ordour of the Kirk is condemnit and traducit, I protest befor God that I was sa commandit to writ be the Chancellar for the tyme, bot chieflie be the Secretar, wha himselff pennit the second Act of Parliament concerning the powar and authoritie of Iudicatour to be absoluthe in the Kings powar, and that it sould nocht be lesume to anie subiect to reclame from the saming vnder the penaltie of the Actes, quhilk I suppose was treasone.

Item, Whar it is alleagit that I sould haiff condemnit the doctrine announced and teatched be the Ministers of Edinburche, to haiff allowit onlie concerning obedience to the Prince my doctrine, I confes and protestes befor God, that I neuer vnderstud nor knew anie thing bot sinceritie and vprightnes in the doctrine of the ministers of Edinburche in that point nor na vther

Fordar, I confes that I was author of the Act discharging the Ministers stipends, that did nocht subserue the Actes of Parliament, wherwith God hes sithe recompenced my selff

The premisses and diuers vther poincts conteined in the Buik of the Assemblie war dyted be Mr Patrik Adamsone, and wrytten at his command be his seruant Mr Samuel Cunninghame, and subscryvit with his awin hand, befor thir witnes, directed to him from the Synodall, because of his inabilitie of body till repear to the Assemblie, James Mompennie, fear of Pitmillie, Andro Wod of Streawithie, Dauid Murray, portionar of Ardet, Mr Dauid Russall, bailyie of St Andros, Mr Wilyeam Murray, Minister at Dysart, with vthers diuers.

This man haid manie grait giftes, bot specialle excellit in the toung and pen ; and yit for abbusing of the sam aganist Chryst, all vse of bathe the ane and vther was takin from him, when he was in graittest miserie and haid maist neid of tham. In the latter end of his lyff his neirest frinds was na confort to him, and his supposed graittest enemies, to whom indeid he offerit graittest occasion of enmitie, was his onlie frinds, and ceased nocht to recompence guid for euill, namlie my vncle Mr Andro, but fand small takings of anie spiritual confort in him, quhilk specialie he wald haiff wissit to haiff sein at his end

Thus God delyverit his Kirk of a maist dangerus enemie, wha, if he haid bein endowit bot withe a comoun ciuill piece of honestie in his delling and conuerfation, he haid ma meanes to haiff wrought miſcheiff in a Kirk or Coun-trey nor ame I haiff knawin or hard of in our Yland.

Mr Dauid Blak, a man mightie in doctrine and of fingular fidelitie and dili-gence in the miniſterie, haid be the cairfull procurment of my vncle at the Generall Affemblie, bein apointed Miniſter of St Andros, Mr Robert Wilkie taking him to a part therof within the Collage of St Lenords, as maiſt aggrie-able with his naturall and giftes. He attendit maiſt charitable vpon the Bi-ſchope, furneſing him confort bathe for bodie and faull, to whom the biſchope promifit diuers dayes to com to the pulpit, and fuppleing his roum to mak publict conteffion ; bot fo often was Mr Dauid difapointed and maid to occu-pie his awin roum with the les preparation. He crauit of his Wyff, and tham that wated on him, that in ame ceas he fould be aduertifed of the tyme when they faw him weakeſt, for Mr Dauid wald haiſt fellou tean fein fum confort-able mark of Gods Spreit working with him ; bot being warmt, came and fand him as he leivit fenfles of fpirituall fanctification fa to die, therfor comend-ing him to the mercie and gud pleafour of God with a heavie hart departed.

That yeir alſo Boduell loſt the Kings fawour, the quhilk being exceffiuelie indulgent towards him diuers yeirs, turned at laſt in implacable hatred. He maid manie attempts for furpryfing of the Kings persone, quhilk was the caufe of manie pitifull executiones, wharof a number I faw with my eis, as tragicall fpectacles in the theater of this miferie of mans lyff. But things done be forme of Juſtice had with tham royned fum confortable confideration, but the murdour done of the Erle of Murray at Dinnibirfall be the Erle of Hounthe on fear day light, the King luking on it with forthought, fellon hamfukin and treafone vnder tryſt, maiſt crewalie with fyre and fworde, yit mightehe cryes and vnportunes the ear of the righteus inquyrar and revengar of bloode.

1592.—The aw of Bodualls remeaning alwayes within the Countrey, and often tymes hard about the Court, togidder with the horrour of the deid of Din-nibirfall, quhilk the vnburied corps lyand in the Kirk of Leithe, maid to be nocht onlie vnburied amangs the peiple, but be comoun rymes and fangs keipt in recent deteſtation, alfimkle as the publict threatning of Gods iudg-ments therupon from pulpites, obteined (at the Parliament hauldin at Edin-bruche in the monethe of Junie 1592, for better expeding of the forfaultrie of Boduall), by our expectation that quhilk haid coſt ws mikle pean in vean monie yeirs befor, to wit, the Ratification of the libertie of the trew Kirk,—of

Generall and Synodall Affemblies,—of Prefbyteries,—of Difciplne; the tennor wharof, becaufe it is the fpeciall euident of our difciplne amangs ciuill men, and for that it coft me a piece of peanes, I could nocht bot heir inregiftrat.

The Ratification of the Libertie of the trew Kirk , of Generall, Synodall Affemblies, Presbyteries and Difcipline ; and Lawes in the contrar abrogat Parl. June, 1592

OUR Soueraine Lord and Eftaites of this prefent Parliament, following the louable and gude exemple of thair predeceffours, hes ratified and approued, and be the tenour of this prefent Act ratifies and approues all liberties, priuileges, immunities and freidomes whatfumeuer giuen and granted be his Hienes, his Regents in his name, or anie of his predeceffours to the trew and halie Kirk, prefenthe eftablifhed within this Realme, and declared in the firft Act of his Hienes parliament the twentie day of October, in the yeir of God, a thowfand fyve houndrethe threefcore nyntein yeirs, and all and whatfumeuer Actes of Parliament and ftatutes maid of befoir be his Hienes and his Regents, anent the libertie and freidome of the faid Kirk And fpecialie the firft Act of Parliament haldin at Edinburche the twentie four day of October, the yeir of God, a thowfand fyve hounder fourfcore ane yeirs, with the haill particular Actes there mentioned, quhilk falbe als fufficient as gif the fam war heire expreffed , and all vther Acts of Parliament maid tenfme in fawour of the trew Kirk And ficlike ratifies and approues the Generall Affemblies apointed be the faid Kirk, and declares that it falbe lawfull to the Kirk and Minifters, euerie yeir at the leaft and after pro re nata, as occafion and neceffitie fall requvie, to hald and keipe Generall Affemblies, prouyding that the Kings Maieftie or his Commiffionars with them to be apointed be his Hienes be prefent at ilk Generall Affemblie, befor the diffoluing therof, nominat and apoint, tyme and place, when and whare the next Generall Affemblie falbe haldin , and in cafe nather his Maieftie nor his faid Commiffionars beis prefent for the tyme in that town whaire the faid Generall Affemblie beis haldin, then and in that cafe it falbe leifum to the faid Generall Affemblie be thamfelues to nominat and appoint tyme and place, whare the next Generall Affemblie of the Kirk falbe keipit and halden, as they haue bein in vfe to do thir tymes bypaft And als ratefies and approuues the Synodall or Prouinciall affemblies to be haldin be the faid Kirk and minifters twyfe ilk yeir as they haue bein and are prefenthe in vfe to do within euerie prouince of this Realme

And als ratefies and approuues the Prefbyteries and particular Seffions apointed be the faid Kirk, with the haill iurifdiction and difcipline of the fam Kirk aggreit vpon be his Maieftie in conference haid be his Hienes with certean of the minifters conuened to that effect Of the quhilk articles the tenor followes —Maters to be intreated in Prouinciall Affemblies : Thir affemblies are conftitut for weghtie maters, neceffar to be intreated be mutuall confent and affiftance of breithring within the prouince as neid requyres. Thir affemblies hes powar to handle, ordour, and redres all things omitted or done amifs in the particular Affemblies It hes powar to depofe the office bearers of that prouince, for gude and iuft caufe deferving depriuation And generalie thir affemblies hes the haill powar of the particular Elderfchipes wharof they ar collected —Maters to be intreated in the Prefbyteries The powar of the Prefbyteries is to giue diligent laboures in the boundes comitted to ther charge , that the kirks be keipit in gude ordour , till inquyie diligenthe of nauchtie and vngodlie perfones ; and to trauell to bring tham in the way again be admonition or threatning of Gods iudgments, or be correction. It apertenes to the Elderfchipe to tak heide that the Word of God be puilie pretched within their bounds , the facraments righlie miniftered ,

the diſciphne intertened, and ecclefiaſticall gudes vncoruptlie diſtributed. It belanges to this kynd
of aſſemblies to caufe the ordinances maid be the Aſſemblies Prouincialles, Nationalles and Gene-
ralles, to be keipit and put in execution, to mak conſtitutiones qulnlk conceines τότριπον in the
Kirk for decent ordour in the particular kirk what they govern, prouyding that they alter na rewles
maid be the Prouinciall or Generall Aſſemblies, and that they mak the Prouinciall aſſemblies forſaid prinie of the rewles that they fall mak: And to aboliſhe conſtitutiones tending to the hurt of
the fam. It hes powar till excommunicat the obſtinat, formall proces being led, and dew interuall
of tymes obferued. Anent particular kirks, gif they be lauchtulhe reuled be fufficient miniſterie
and feſſiou, they haue powar and iuriſdiction in than awin congregationes in maters ecclefiaſticall.
And decernes and declares the faids Aſſemblies, Preſbyteries and Seſſiones, Iuriſdiction and Diſciphne therof toreſaid to be in all tymes coming maiſt iuſt, gude and godlie in the felfi, nochtwithſtanding of whatfumeuer ſtatutes, actes, canon, ciuill or municipall Lawes maid in the contraie.
To the qulnlks, and euerie an of tham, this prefentes fall nocht expres derogation. And becaufe
there ar diuers Actes of Parliament maid in fauour of the Papiſticall kirk, tending to the preiudice
of the libertie of the trew Kirk of God prefenthe profeſſit within this Realme, iuriſdiction and diſciphne therof, qulnlk ſtandes yit in the burkes of the Actes of Parliament, nocht abrogated nor annulled, therfor his Hienes and Eſteates fonfaids hes abrogated, caſſed and annulled, and be the
tenor hen of abrogates, caſſes and annulles, all actes of parliament maid be his Hienes predeceſſouis
or annie of tham, for meantenance of fuperſtition and ydolatrie, with all and whatfumeuer actes,
lawes and ſtatutes maid at anie tyme befor the day and dait hen of againſt the libertie of the trew
Kirk, iuriſdiction and diſciphne therof as the fanning is vſed and exerceiſed within this realme.

And in ſpeciall that part of the Act of parliament, halden at Stirling the fourt of Nouember, the
yen 1443, commanding obedience to be giſſen to Eugenius, the Pape for the tyme, the Act maid
be King James the Thride, in his parliament, halden at Edinbruche the 21 Februar 1480, and all
vther Actes, wharby the Papes authoritie is eſtabliſhed. The Act of King James the Thrid, in his
parliament, halden at Edinbruche, 20 Nouember 1469, anent the Satterdey and vther vigilles to be
halie dayes from euen-fang to euen-fang.

Item, that part of the Act maid be the Quein Regent, in the parl. haldin at Edinbruche, 1 Februar
1551, griuing ſpeciall licence for halding of Peace and Zuill.

Item, the Kings Maieſtie and Eſteates forfaids declares, that the 129 Act of the parliament
haldin at Edinbruche the 22d day of May, the yen of God a thowfand fyve houndrethe fourfcore
foui yens fall na waves be preiudiciall, nor derogat anie thing to the priuilage that God hes giffen
to the fpirituall office beaiers concerning heads of Relligion, maters of herefie, excommunication, collation or depriuation of Miniſters, or anie fidyk eſſentiall cenfers, ſpeciahe groundit, and hafaand warrand of the Word of God. Item, oui Soveran Lord and Eſtates of Parliament forfaids abrogattes,
caſſes and annulles the Act of the fam Parliament, halden at Edinbruche the faid yen 1584, granting
Commiſſiones to Biſchopes and vthers, Judges conſtitut in ecclefiaſticall cauſſes, to receaue his
Hienes prefentationnes to benefices, to giue collation thervpon, and to put ordour in all cauſſes ecclefiaſticall, qulnlk his Maieſtie and Eſtaits forfaids declares to be expyred in the felfi, and to be
null in tyme coming, and of nan auaill, force nor effect, and therfor ordeanes all prefentationnes to
benefices to be direct to the particular preſbyteries in all tyme coming, with full powar to giue col-
latiounes thervpon, and to put ordour to all maters and cauſſes ecclefiaſticall within their bounds, according to the diſciphne of the Kirk. Prouiding the forfaid Preſbyteries be bund and afflicted to
receaue and admit whatfumeuer qualified Miniſter prefented be his Maieſtie or laik patrones.

This Act is maift remarkable, for the paffing thereof was flatlie denyed till it was extract, and being extract and fund to haift bein publifhed and giffen out with the reft, it was mikle rowed and detefted in anno 1596. And in deid the Kirk is addettit to Mr Jhone Mettellan, Chancellar for the tyme, for the fam, wha inducit the King to pas it at that tyme, for what refpect I leaue it to God, wha workes for the confort of his Kirk be all kynd of inftruments, to whom therfor be all praife and thankes for euer.

Ther was that yeir, in the monethe of Nouember, a Convention keipit at Edinbruche of a number of breithren, conveined from diuers partes of the countrey, to forefie and prevent the dangers imminent to the relligioun and profeffouns therof   The quhilk I mention and fett down of purpofe, to fchaw the cuftom of our Kirk, louablie and profitablie obferuit hentofore in tyme of neid and danger, quhilk, to the grait perrell of the Kirk, is now reftraint and difchargit

At Edinbruche, the 15, 16, 17, 18 and 20 dayes of Nouember, in the yeir 1592.

THE quhilk dayes the breithring, conveined from diuers partes of the country, to forefie and prevent the dangers imminent to the relligion and profeffouns therof, after incalling of the name of God, haifing communicated mutuallie than intelligences, hes fund the enemies of the trenthe with- in this countrey verie diligentlie laboring for fubuerfion of the relligion, and findrie crewall and dangerus plottes concludit and intendit to be execut with all poffible diligence, vnles the Lord, of his mercie, difapointed than interpryfe. For remead wharof it is concludit, that ther be a Generall Fail in all the Kirks of this countrey the 17 and 24 dayes of December nixt, that be trew humi- liation and vnfenyed repentance, the teirfull iudgments of God that hingethe ower this land may be prevented.

The Cauffes of the Generall Faft.

1 The practifes of the enemies without and within this countrey, intending till execut the blodie decrie of the Counfall of Trent againft all that trewlie profes the relligioun of Chryft, to the vtter fubuerfion therof and of the Kings efteat and perfone, whafe ftanding and decey thay acknawlage to be ioyned with the ftanding and decey of Relligion

2. A miferable defolation of the graitteft pairt of the countrey, perifhing in ignorance throw leak of paftors and fufficient moyen to interteam the Word of God amangs tham, with a cairlefnes of the Magiftrats to remead thir miferies.

3 A fearfull defection of a grait number of all efteats in this land to Papiftrie and Atheifine, fpe- ciallie of the nobilitie, throw the refoirting and trafecting of Jefuites, Semmarie Preifts and vther Pa- pifts, without execution of anie Law againft thame.

4 The generall diiordour of the haill efteat of the Comoun Wealthe, overflowing with all kynd of impietie, as contempt of the Word, blafphemie of the name of God, contempt of the Magiftrat, treffon, innocent blood fchede, adulteries, witchcrafts and fic vther abominnable crymes.

2 c

'Thir cautles to be inlargit and eiked be the diſcretion of euerie brother, according as he ſall haiff fure knawlage and ſenſe of the premiſſes.

Item, it is ordeanit that euerie preſbyterie trauell within thair awin bounds till inform the ſpecialles and beſt affected gentilmen amang tham of the practiſe of the enemies, and to moue tham to be vpon than gaird, and in readines vpon aduertiſment for defence of Relligion and profeſſouis therof, and reſiſting of the enemie; and to tak vpe and compoſe all feiddes, namlie amang tham that ar tiew profeſſours, or at the leaſt aſſurances, whar full aggriement can nocht be preſentlie procured, and to refaue thair ſubſciiptiones vnto the generall band at leſt what it ſalbe thought requiſit, at the diſcretion of euerilk Preſbyterie. And becauſe the Preſbyteries vnderwiytten, for diueis conſiderationes, cranes the aſhſtance of ſum vther breithring, the breithring heir conueined hes apointed Mr Robert Pont to concure with the Preſbyterie of Aberdein for the effect aboue wrettin, Mr Robert Rollok with the Preſbyterie of Dalkethe, and Mr Robert Bruce and Dauid Lindſay with the Preſbyteries of the Waſt for vptaking of the deadlie feiddes betwix the Maiſter of Eglintoun and the Erle of Glencairn, the Lairdes of Garlies and Blakwhean, &c   And to this effect, that they obtein his Maieſties Commiſſion, and procure his Maieſties Commiſſionais may be direct with thame, and they till attend on this as than letar will ſerue. And in the mean tyme, that his Maieſties Letters be obteined to moue the parties till aſſure, and the Preſbyteries to trauell ſa far as they may be thair awin labours.

Item, that the breither acquent thamſelues with the hiſtories of the crewaltie of the confederates of the Councell of Trent, practeiſed againſt the faithfull in vther countreyes, and inform thair congregationes thairof, as lykwayes of the lyk crewelties againſt thamſelues, gif they preueall in thair wicked attempts   And in reſpect of the ſubtiltie and ſecreit craft of the aduerſars, wha now ſa deiplie hes lerned to diſſemble than proceidings, that ſpeciall ſutt be maid to God in our publict prayers, that the plats and hid practiſes of the enemies may be diſcouered, brought to light and diſapointed.

Item, It is ordeanit that ther be an ordmarie counſeill of the breithring vnderwrytten, viz Maiſters Robert Bruce, Dauid Lindſay, Robert Pont, Jhone Dauidſone, Walter Balcanquall, James Balfour, Patrik Galloway, Jhone Dunkeſone, wha ſall conuein ordmarlie euerie ouk ans, and ofter as occaſſion ſall craue, to confult vpon ſic aduertiſment as ſalbe maid to them from diueis partes of the countrey or vtherwayes, and prouidere in omnibus ne quid eccleſia detrimenti capiat   And for the better execution of than conclutionnes, it is ordeanit that ther be ane ordinarie Agent to attend in Edinbruche vpon tham, viz. Mr James Carmichael, till the nixt Aſſemblie Generall, whaſe office ſall confiſt in the poincts following —

Imprimis, He ſall trauell diligentlie be all meanes to be informed of the practiſes of Papiſts, as be merchants and paſſingers coming from vther countreyes, and all ſic as from anie part of this countrey reſorts to Edinbruche. For the quhilk cauſe alſo, the Miniſters in euerie part ar commandit to mak ceaitull aduertiſment of all kynd of practiſes againſt the relligioun of all Papiſts, Jeſuiſtes and refeatters of tham within thair bounds, and all vther weghtie enormities that ſall fall cut and com to thair knawlage, and that in forme as efter followes :—

Mr Andro Cramby and Mr George Monro for Ros, Mr Thomas Howiſone for Inuernes, and Jhone Forſtar for Forrefe, ſall ſend than aduertiſinents to Mr Alexander Dowglas, Miniſter of Elgean

Mr Alexander Dowglas for Elgean ſall ſend to Mr Piter Blakburn, Miniſter of Aberdein. Mr George Hay for Banff, Mr James Duff and Mr Gilbert Gardin for Straithbogy, Mr Jhone Strathanthſone for Mar, Mr George Paterſone for Garioch, and Mr Douncan Dauidſone for Dear, ſall ſend

to Mr Dauid Cunningham, Minister at Aberdein. Mr Piter Blakburn and Mr Dauid Cunning-
hame fall send thair aduertisments to Montrose Mr Andro Miln for Mernes, Jhone Duiv for
Breachin, Mr Arthur Futhie for Arbrothe, Mr James Nicoltone for Meigle, fall send to Wilyeam
Chrystifone, Minister of Dondie. Wilyeam Chrystifone fall send to Mr Adam Mitchell, Minister
at Cowpar, and Mr Adam to Mr Thomas Biggar, Minister at Kuigorn, and Mr Thomas to Mr
Walter, Minister at Edinburche

Mr Wilyeam Glas for Dunkeld fall send to Mr Jhone Malcolme at Perthe, Mr Jhone Mal-
colme to Mr Walter at Edinburche Mr Wilyeam Stirling for Dumblean, Mr Patrik Simsone for
Stirling, Mr Jhone Spotswode for Linlithgow, Mr Adam Jhonstoun for Dalkethe, James Gipsone
for Hadintoun, Mr Robert Habroun for Dumbar, Mr Archbald Dowglas for Peapbles, Jhone
Clapperton for Hutton, Mr Wilyeam Meslan for Dunse, Mr Jhone Knox for Melrose, Mr Andro
Clayhill for Jedbrouche, Mr Hew Foullarton for Drumfreise, Mr Dauid Blythe for Kirkcowbrie,
Mr James Dauidtone for Wigtoun, Mr Andro Hay for Glasgw, Mr Robert Dairouche for Hamil-
ton, Mr Robert Lindsay for Lannerik, Dauid Fergusone for Dumfeimling, all thir fall send thair
aduertifments directlie to Mr Walter Balcanquall in Edinburche.

Jhone Porterfeild for Are, Mr Robert Wilkie for Irwing, Mr Jhone Rose for Dumbartan,
Mr Andro Knox for Pasley, fall send to Mr Andro Hay in Glasgw, and he to Mr Walter in
Edinburche

Mr Andro Melvill for St Andros, Mr Thomas Bowchanan for Cowpar, fall send to Mr Thomas
Biggar, Minister at Kingorn, and he to the said Mr Walter, and last, Mr Dauid Spense for Kirkady to the sam Mr Walter Prouyding that it ame of the aboue writtin breithring haist the commoditie of a truttie bearer vtherwayes, or it the mater be of sic weght that it will nocht suffer delay, in that case they fall send to Edinburche to the said Mr Walter immediatlie And to the end
that the forsaid breithring may haist the man sure intelligence, it is ordeanit that euerie brother
within the Presbyterie fall gift tham sure information at all occasionnes neidfull.

Secondlie, Efter the said agent fall receaue thir intelligences and aduertifments, he sall at the first
meitting communicat tham to the conceill of the breithring, and if the mater requyre haist, the
Agent fall convein the Counceill for that effect, and being found be tham to requyre fordar
advyse of vther breithring, the said Agent fall convocat them be his Lettres, according as he sall
receaue direction fra the Counceill.

Thirdlie, Whatsoeuer fall happin to be concludit be the Councall of the breithring to be suted at
his Maiestie, Counsall, Session, Provest and Balyies of Burrowes, Convention of Esteates, Burrowes
or Barones, or vthers whatsumeuer, the said Agent fall attend faithfullie and diligentlie for executing
thairof, and report his diligence to the Counceill.

The said Agent fall seik out and extract all Letteres, Acts, and Decreits anent the caus committed to him, and vse and direct tham as they aught to be, and to communicat tham, togidder
with the conclusiones of the Conceill, to sic Presbyteries and partes of the countrey as the Conceill fall direct, according to the forme, and be the persones aboue wryttin, ordine retrogrado.

The said Agent fall wryt the Memoirs of the Kirks proceidings and dealling with the Prince,
Councall and Lsteattes of this realme, fra tyme to tyme sen the Reformation of Relligion, to be a
mo nument to the posteritie And for that effect it is ordeanit, that from all Presbyteries, sciolles,
wryttes and ame pirces that ar in the haldin of ame breither, salbe directed to Mr Walter Balcanquall to be delyuerit to him. And lykwyse all proceidings and deallings, quhilk the Kirk fall haist
with the King, to be noted be him heirefter, &c.

Item, It is ordeanit, that thair be a comoun purs for furneising of neceflarie expences for the effaires forfaids, without the quhilk they can nocht tak effect   And that for the prefent, Mr Robert Bruce, with fic as he thinks gaid to adioyne to him, fall men the want of this comoun expences in fa dangerus a tyme to tie men of all efteates as he knawes to be weill affected, that be thair liberalitie this want may be fupplied, untill fum gaid ordinarie mean be fund out for that effect   And that the foumes collected be put in a box wharof thair falbe twa or thrie keyes in the hands of twa or thrie breithring of the Councall, wha fall deburs therof as the faid Councall fall command thame

Item, It is ordeanit, that the faid Counfall fall trauell ernestlie with his Maieftie and Countfall that the Articles following may be granted —

That his Maieftie, be publict proclamation, mak his gaid affection toward the Relligion and profeffours therof knawin to his haill fubiects, and promite to meantein and defend it againft all enemies without and within, to the uttermaift of his powar, and that he accompt all the enemies therof to be enemies of his efteat and perfone and of this Comounwealthe, charging heirfor his haill fubiects to ioyne thamefelues in a unitie and profeffioun of the trew religion profeffed within this countrey, and fubferyue the generall band for the meantenance therof againft whatfoeuer enemies, quhilk falbe prefented to tham be the Miniftrie

That a Commiffion be granted till a certean of the beft affected noble men, barrones and gentilmen and magiftrats within borrowes, that is to fay, to the Proveft and bailyies of euerie brought within thair towns and liberties therof, Robert, Lile of Orkney, James, Lord Zetland, Michall Balfour of Montwhanie, for Orkney, &c to execut all Acts of Parliament and Counfall againft whatfumeuer Jefuites, Seminarie Preifts, excommunicat and trafecting Papifts and thair refeatters and to caufe mak Wapinfchawings, and convein the countrey in armes, at all occafions neidfull for defence of the trew relligion, and refifting of the enemies therof

That a fufficient number of the wyfeft of the noble men, barrones and beft affected to relligion his Maiefties efteat and ftanding, and the weill of this Commoun welthe, be apointed upon the Secret Counfall and mak thair refidence in Edinburghe this wintar, and forder, ay whill the confpiracies plattes and attempts of the enemies of relligion within this countrey be difapointed and reprefled

That all Papifts and practefars againft the Relligion be remoued from his Maiefties companie and debarred from all publict charge, Commiffioun, Lieutenandrie or publict office

That all Skippars and Maifters of fhippes fall prefent to the Magiftrat and Counfall of the place whar they fall aryve, all paffingers, merchants and utheis that fall com with tham in thair fhippes, wha fall gift thair confcience and aithe of all perfones and packets of letters or bukis whatfumeuer, quhilks they haill recavit at anie port fen thair departour, to be deluuent to anie perfone or perfones within this countrey or without. And giff thay haill fett on land at anie part anie perfone or perfones, or deluuent packets or bukis, coffais or kifts to anie whatfoeuer, under pean of confifcation of fhippes, guds and gear

That a Commiffion be giften to the perfones underwrittin, viz   , to fett down a conftant form of prouifion of Minifters ftipends at euerie congregation within this countrey ; and that to be ratefied in Secret Counfall Seffion and Chacker to baift the ftrainthe of a Law quhill Parliament, and then to be ratefied be the haill Liteatts.

Laft, It is ordeanit that ther be a Generall Affemblie at Edinburghe the nynt of Januar mxtocom, in cais the Parliament hald and gif the Parliament be continowed, that the Prefbyterie of

Edinbruche giff adueitifment therof to the breithei of all Piefbyteiies, that they mak na wall
nauell.

And thir things deuyfit be my vncle Mr Andro with the reft of the breithring, Mr James Nicolfone and I war ordeanit to pen and fett in ordoui

Betwix this Convention and the Generall Affemblie following apointed, the
Lord euei watchfull ovei his Kiik, detected a ftiange confpiracie of ceitean
of our nobles in manei following   A ceitean young gentilman, Mr George
Car be nam, was attending on a fhipe at the Waft fie, whan his priuie con-
veifation being efpyed and his fpeitches taken heid to, it was perceavit him
to be a papift paffing to Spean, and firft graithe fufpected, and theiefter ceiteanlie knawin be fum of his familiaies that he was a tiafectar directed with
commiffion in word and wryt to the King of Spean be fum Scotes noble men
Of this Mr Andro Knox, minifter at Pafley, being ceiteanlie infoimed, accompanied with fum of his fiinds, went aboide on the fheppe, fche being readie to
mak feale, and apprehends the faid Mr George, and ceifing his coffeis, finds
diuers lettei and blankes, directed tiom George, Erle of Hountbe, Frances,
Erle of Arioll, and Wilyeam, Eile of Angus, fubfcryvit with thair hands,
wiyttin, fum in Latin and fum in Fiencbe, togidder with thair cachets, fig-
nets, &c * He being thus apprehendit is brought with diligence to the King,
and put in preffione   Vpon the quhilk alfo the faid Erle of Angus is put in
the Caftell of Edinbruche, and a moft fiequent Generall Affembhe, convent
at Edinbruche of a giait number of Baiones fiom all the paites of the
Realme, befought the King to tak oidour with thefe vnnaturall fubiects, be-
tiayers of ther couutrey to the crewall Spainyeaid   With the quhilk the
King tuk nocht weill at the fiift, quaiieling the barones for thaii conveaning
in fic number at the Minifteis waining without his calling for and licence
To the quhilk they anfwerit fieihe, that it was na tyme to attend on warn-
ings when thair rellignon prince, countiey, than lyves, lands, and all was
biought in ieopard be fic treafonable delling   Therfoi the King fattehng,
aggreagit thaii cryme veiie hihe, and faid it was of the natuie of the things
that was aboun him, and withe the quhilk he could nocht difpenfe, and therfoi
pi omiffit to tak tiyell theiin with diligence, and put ordoui theito with all
feueritie to thair contentment.   Neuertheles the Erle of Angus efchaped out
of the Caftle of Edinbruche.   The reft wer overfein, quhilk wrought a giait

* Vide, the Difcouerie, &c. and examination of Mr George Cai and Dauid Grame of Fentri,
publiit in print at the execution of the faid Dauid.

fufpition and mifcontentment in the harts of all the guid fubiects of the land towards the King.*

In that Summer the Deuill fteired vpe a maift dangerus vproar and tumult of the peiple of St Andros againft my vncle Mr Andro, to the extream perrell of his lyff, if God haid nocht bein his protection and delyverance. The wicked, malitius mifcewlars of that Town, of whom I mentioned befor in the trouble of the honeft men therof, hated Mr Andro, becaufe he could nocht bear with than vngodlie and vniuft delling, and at thair drinking, incenfit the rafcals be tals information againft Mr Andro and his Collage, making tham to think that he and his Collage fought the wrak and trouble of the Town; fa that the barme of thair drink began to rift out crewall thretnings againft the Collage and Mr Andro   They being thus prepeared, the Deuill denyfes tham an ap- peirance of iuft occafion to fall to wark.   Ther war a certean of Students in Theologie, wha weireing to go out of the Collage to thair exerceife of bodie and ghain, caufit big a pear of buttes in the Collage garding, ioyning to a wynd and paffage of the town   Wharat a certean of tham fhootting a efter noone, amangs the reft was Mr Jhone Caldclenche, then an of the Maiflers of Theologie, bot fkaife yit a fchollar in Archerie, wha miffing the butt and a number of thak houffes beyonde, fhoottes his arrow down the hie paffage of the wynd, quhilk lightes vpon a auld honeft man, a matman of the town, and hurts him in the crag   This coming to the eares of the forfaid malitius and feditius, they concitat the multitud and popular crafts and rafcall, be thair words and found of the comoun bell; wha fetting vpon the Collage, braks vpe the yet therof, and with grait violence vnbefets the principall chalmer, ding- ing at the forftaire therof with grait geftes, crying for fyre. &c. Bot the Lord affifting his fervant with wefdome and courage, maid him to keipe his chalmer ftouthe, and dell with fum of tham fearlie, whom he knew to be abbufit, and with vthers fcharplie, whom he knew to be malitius abbufars of the peiple. Be the tranelles of Mr Dauid Blak now entred to his minifterie, and Mr Ro- bert Wilkie, primarius of St Leonard with vther maifters and fchollars of the Vniuerfitie, efter lang vexation and mikle adoe, the peiples infurrection was fattelit

The King, be the Cancellars Counfall and moyen, was graitlie offendit with this, and calling the Magiftrats and certean of the ring-laders, ordeamt tham

to be tryed in particular be the barones and gentilmen of the countrey about
St Andros　Bot be that occasion getting graitter bands and mair threat abone
the heids of the town for slaying of the lyk in tyme coming.　Seing God haid
keipit bathe the honest man that was schot, and the Collage from grait hurt.
Mr Andro overpassit and forgaiff bygeanes, vpon a humble submission and band
of preventing and absteining from sic fasones in tyme to come.

1593.—This yeir 1593 in the monethe of August, the 28 day, being Tysday,
efter fyve years cessing, my wyff brought furthe a dauchtar, quhilk I named
Margret　Sche never leuche in this lyff, bot within sax or sevin moneths died,
the onlie corps that past out of my hous these diffon of yeirs.　Of the quhilk
visitation I thank God I gat a softned hait and grait confort quhilk I can
nocht omit vnremembent to his praise.　For the quhilk I wrot this Epitaphe :—

> Sen all mon enter into pression strang
> 　Of erdlie fleche, and ther remean a space,
> They ar, but dout, maist happie all amang
> 　Wha shortest tym remeanes in sic a place.
>
> I o' this hes bein my luk and happie ceafe,
> 　Abone sax moneths nocht to ly opprest
> Withe erdlie bands, when God of his gud grace
> 　Has tean me ham to his æternall rest.
>
> Sen Chryst hes then receau'd me in his glore,
> 　Deir mother, ceate, lament for me no more.

In the monethe of September 1593, the Provinciall Assemblie convenit at
St Andros, wharin the Lords watchmen of the schyr of Fyff, being informit
of the bissines and dangerus delling of the papist Erles and Lords, throw un-
punitie and oversight of the Prince, began to wey the mater grauelie and efter
gud and throuche aduysment, condiscendit all in on voice to pronunce the
sentence of excommunication vpon certean of the cheiff of tham.　The quhilk
was done be my mouthe, Moderator for the tyme, and the quhilk God sa
blessed that the haill Kirk of Scotland approuit the sam. and the quhilk the
Lord maid to be a speciall mean of preventing extreame danger ot wrak of
the Kirk and Comoun weill of Scotland, and bringing of the enemies to forfaultrie and exyll.　The names of the excommunicat was Wilyeam, Erle of
Angus, George, Erle of Hounthe, Francis, Erle of Atroll, Jhone, Lord Home,
Sr Patrik Gordoun of Achindown, and Sr James Chisholme, Knights.　This
our Synod communicat with diligence to all the provinces of the Land, and

erauit a meiting of Commiſſionars from thame to be keipit at Edinbruche in October following, for profecuting of the mater

That Convention at Edinbruche was frequenthe keipit bathe be miniſters and barones, wherin it was thought guid that Commiſſionars theirfra bathe of the miniſtrie and gentilmen and burgeſſes ſould be direct to the King, craving ordour taking with theſe excommunicat papiſt Lords; namlie it was verie greiws to the breithring to heir that the ſaids excommunicat Lords haud repearit to his Maieſtie and ſpokin him at Faley, euen immediatlie befor the meiting of the Kirk   This was geuin in Commiſſion to be regratit   The King at this tyme was in Jedbruche, and the mater ſuffered nocht delay, for theſe papiſt Lords was making grait preparation of armes, and amaſſing thair frinds to repear to the King and ceaſe about his perſone   Therfor it behoued me, (all vther refuſing except Mr Patrik Galloway, the Kings ordinar miniſter, wha was to go thither,) to tak iorney to Jedwart, accompanied with twa barrones, the Lairds of Merchiſtoun and Caderwoode, and twa burgeſſes of Edinbruche; whar finding the King, war bot bauchlie lukit vpon   Our aſſemblie of Fyff was bitterlie inveyit againſt, namlie my vncle Mr Andro and Mr Dauid Blak.   I anſwerit for all, as it pleaſit God to gift, and efter the Kings coler appeaſit, we ditchargit our Commiſſion in maiſt humble and fectfull maner   The King againe was crabit at the Convention of Edinbruche, namlie at the barrones and burgeſſes, wha ſtude honeſtlie be it, ſaying it was in trew and vpright haites, with all dewtie and reuerence to his Maieſtie for preventing of imminent euill and danger to his Stat, Religion, and Countrey   Sa that night delyuering our petitiones in wryt, betymes on the morn, we gat our anſwers in wrait feau aneuche, and returned on the thride day to the breithring   Ane of the ſpeciall anſwers was, That the King ſould hauld a Convention at Lithgow ſoone efter his retouin from the Southe, whar he ſould tak ordour with all theſe maters.

Bot the breithring, certeanlie informit that the papiſt Erls was conveining all thair frinds of purpoſe to be preſent at the ſaid Convention, and place thamſelues about the King, thought meit that all ſould with diligence retourn hain to thair countreyes, and mak warning thanof to thair barrones and brouches, ſchawing the Kings guid anſwers and the enemies purpoſe; deſyring therfor all to be in readines to keipe the ſaid Convention for diſapointing the aduerſar; and for that effect to repear till Edinbruche a few dayes befor, ther till advys anent thair proceedings. The quhilk was done be euerie Commiſſionar with exact diligence.

Ther was a Convention of the barones of Fyff keipe at the sam tyme at Cowpar, to the quhilk my vncle Mr Andro and I halting, maid tham to direct speciall barrones of than number with certean of the ministerie, to the town of Perthe to incurage tham, and to promise tham assistance for keiping of thair town against the excommunicat Erls and thair forces. The quhilk they did, till, be the Kings charge, they war constreanit to receane tham. The best and maist zealus barrones, gentilmen and burgesses, war on fut in readines to keipe the dyet at Edinbruche, namlie heiring of the Erls of Hountlie and Erriols forces come to St Jhonstoun, till the King send expres discharge of the said Erles forces, and commandit tham withe a few of thair frinds to abyde quyethe in Perthe, attending his will anent thair effeares. Quhilk being vnderstud, leaving ther armes, commissionars coming from euerie paroche and presbyterie, keipit the dyet at Edinbruche, at quhilk they resoluit to direct from that Convention a commission of barrones, burgesses, and ministers to the King and Convention of Esteattes at Linlithgow, withe petitiones as of befor. Sa the number send to Jedwart being dowblit, cam to Lithgow, amangs the quhilk (because, as they said, best acquented with the haill proccadour of the mater,) I was chosin to be speitchman and presentar of the petitions. Bot the Chancellar Mattellan haid dressit all to our coming, sa that than was nocht mikle ado at that dyet, bot all remitted to a new Convention of Esteats, to be haldin at Edinbruche the monethe following. The Erles papists turning bak, and all our folks going ham, with thankfull haits to God for disapointing of a maist dangerus interpryse as euer was of all be papists in this land.

The Convention at Edinbruche followit efter in the monethe of December, whar I, withe vthers apointed, presented of new our former petitions; the quhilk the King receaving, contentedlie promisde to satisfie at efter noone. At quhilk tyme we attending, ther was offers of satisfaction to the Kirk and the Kings Maiestie, giffin in be the Erls agents, whervpon the nixt day the King, with large discourse, schawes to the Esteattes whow dangerus the mater was, for giff the offers of these noble men war refusit, they wald desperatlie go to armes, and get forean assistance, quhilk might wrak king, countrey, and relligion. And sa be that and sic lyk arguments, induceit the Esteates, (wha seing the Kings inclination vses nocht to gainstand, for manie of tham that ar called ar prepeared befor hand for the purpose,) to condiscend to an vptaking of the mater. And sa diuers dayes was denysit that Act of Abolitioun, of the quhilk I will nocht speak, nocht being my purpose to wryt a Storie ather ciuill or ecclesiastik, but onlie to minut in Memours the things quhilk God maid me to

2 D

heir and fie ; bot trewlie quhilk my hait pitied fallen feai. The King, by
this dealling, brought himfellf in graitt fufpition and miflyking of his beft
fubiects, bathe for fauoring of Papifts, and of him wha haid fa notoriouflie
committed that filthie murdour of the Eile of Murray at Dombirfall.

My vncle Mr Andro, vfing alwayes to fpeak planlie with zeall and birning
affectiones to the honour of God and the Kings weill, gaifl him at this tyme
a maift fcharpe and frie admonition concerning his euill thinking and fpeaking
of the beft frinds of Chryft and himfelfi, the Guid Regent, Mr Knox, and Mr
George Bowchanan ; and his thinking weill and fauoring of Chryft and his
graiteft enemies the papifts, and namlie that Hous of Hounthe, defyring
confidenthe that fie as war his counfallours therin fould kythe in prefence of
the Efteatts, and giff he conuicted tham nocht of fals, treafonable and maift
pernitius doing therin againft Chryft, the Kings perfone, his efteat and realme,
he fould nocht refufe to go to the gibbet for it, prouyding they being conuict
fould ga the fam gett. Withe the quhilk the King and his Counfallors com-
ported, and paft ower the mater with finylling, faying the man was mair zealus
and coleric nor wys

On the Michelmes that yeir, the crafts and burgefles of St Andros changing
their prouest, for the Lard of Darfie, chofit Capitan Wilyeam Murray, quhilk
maid Darfies frinds to rage fa, that Burley cam vnder fylence of night and
tuk an honeft man out of his hous and caried him away ; at the quhilk braue
exployt, Burley was mutilat of a fingar to begin his warrs withall. His man
Mylles, another night, with certean companiones, his complices, cam to an
vther honeft mans hous and reft away his dauchtar And laft, the faid Laird
of Darfie maid a grait conuocation of his frinds, with the quhilk in armes he
purpofed to enter in the Town and abbufe certean citiemers therof at his pleafour, and that indeid of the beft fort The quhilk, when it was meined to my
vncle Mr Andro, being then Rector of the Vniuerfitie, and fa a ciuill Magiftrat, conuocat the haill Vniuerfitie, and fchew tham whow thair nibours of
the Town wai oppreffed, and what Gods law and manes bathe erqued in
fic a ceas And fa refoluit to tak armes for helpe and defence of the town,
and confortablie affifted with my Lord Lindfay, Sr George Dowglas, and diuers gentilmen of the countrey, maid the invadder team, for all his forces, to
byd out, and tak reafone in part of payment. He merchet mikle of that day
withe a whart fpeare in his hand, as he wear a corflet therefter at the dinging
down of Streabogy

The wintar following, God prouydit in the place of Mr Jhone Robertfone, an of the Maiſters of the New Collage, a godlie, honeſt, and lerned man, Mr Jhone Jhonſton, wha, efter diuers yers peregrinatioun for the ſtudie of gud letters in Germanie, Geneu, France, and England, cam ham and contented to tak part with my vncle, Mr Andro, in the ſaid Collage ; and wha ſen ſyne hes bein a grait helpe and confort to my ſaid vncle, and ornament to the Collage and Vniuerſitie. Mr Jhone Caldcleuche withſtud his electioun, and troublit the Collage and Vniuerſitie verie mikle, and laſt raiſit ſoummonds and callit ws befor the King and Counſall. Bot he was ſend ham the graitter fooll, whar for his violation of the actes and troubling of the Vniuerſitie, he was depoſit from all office bearing within the ſam. God warnit me of that trouble be a dream of fyre and water, quhilk moued me mikle, and wharof I fand a notable effect be an extream danger of drowning going ower the Ferne of Kingorn, at Granton Cragges, to keipe a dyet in that mater. And a wounderfull de-lyverance alas for thankfulnes ! THE XX DAY OF MERTCHIL AT GRANTON CRAGES

1594.—About the ſpring tyme in the yeir following, 1594, the outlaw Bod-nall kythe openlie with forces at Leithe and at Preiſtfeild, bot withe lyk ſuc-ces as often tymes befor. He tuk vpe men of war in ſecret vpe and down the countrey, and gaiff out that it was at the Kirks employment againſt the Pa-piſts, quhilk maid me, being then mikle occupied in publict about the Kirks effeares, to be graithe ſuſpected be the King, and bak ſpeirit be all meanes. Bot it was hard to find quhilk was neuer thought. For I neuer lyket the man, nor haid to do with him directhe or indirecthe ; yea, efter gud Archbald, Erle of Angus, whom God called to his reſt a yeir or twa befor this, I kend him nocht of the nobilitie in Scotland that I could communicat my mynd with anent publict effears, let be to haiff a delling with in action.

The Generall Aſſemblie conveined at Edinbruche in the monethe of May, my vncle Mr Andro, choſin Moderator. Than compeired the Lord Home, making humble ſupplication to be relaxed from excommunication. It was granted vpon certean conditiones verie ſtreat, the quhilk in cais he ſould ther-efter contrauein or nocht fulfill, he ſould be of new denuncit accuſit. Bot the ſaid Moderator nocht finding ſic takens of trew repentance as he wald haue cravit, and thought neidfull to be ſein be the Kirk, namlie ſic grait number and force of enemies being in the countrey, efter he haid ſchawin his reaſones to the Aſſemblie, wald nocht pronunce the ſentence of abſolution ; Bot Mr Dauid Lindſay being laſt moderator did it.

Therefter the fentence pronuncit be the Synod of Fyff againft the reft was appronen and ratefied be the haill Affemblie, acknawlaging therin the fpeciall benefit of Gods prouidence in fteirmg vpe the fpreits of his fervants to be wacryff, cearfull, and curagius in the wark of his gloire and caufe of his Kirk. And during the tyme of Affemblie was directed, with Commiffionars, certean Articles and Petitiones to the King.   Amangs the quhilk commiffionars I being named, fum faid it was nocht convenient, being fufpected and euill lyked of be the King   To the quhilk opinion the Affemblie beginning to inclyne, I ftud vpe and faid, I haid bein employed in commiffion oft tymes againft my will, and when things was man peanfull and dangerus, even when vthers refufit, bot now even for the reafone quhilk was alleagit, I wald requeaft for it as a benefit of the breithring to fend me, quhilk wald be the onlie way to clen bathe them and mie of fufpition and fklander, for even vther wayes I mened to prefent myfelff at Court befor the King, to fie gif ane man haid aught to fay to me   Of this the breithring war glaid, and refolued in a voice to fend me   Sa coming to Sterling, whar the King was, far by our expectatioun we war maift gratioufhe accepted   All our Articles war reafonit and anfwerit be his Maiefties awin hand wryt vpon the margent, and that verie fauorablie to our grait contentment; and therefter, I that was the grait tratour, with the reft callit in to the Cabinet with the King allean   His Maieftie beginnes to regrat that he could nocht find that freindlines in the Kirk quhilk he craut and wiffed.   I haiffing the fpeitche anfwered, Ther was a peccant humor in the body quhilk behoued to be purged, or it could nocht be out of danger of difeafe, yea deathe.   The King afked me what that was.   I faid it was fufpition on ather fyde; for purging wharof it war beft we fould be fire on ather fyde, and fhaw our greiffs and occafiones of fufpecting the warft, the quhilk being remouit, the body wald be curit and haill.   The King thought it maift meit and pertinent, and begins and expones what he haid: 1 Concerning the affembling of his fubiects without his licence   To the quhilk we anfweit, we did it be the warrant of his Maiefties lawes, and of Chryft, according to the Word, and cuftom of our Kirk fen the beginning, quhilk nather haid, nor be Gods grace euer fould be to his Maiefties hurt, bot honour and weill. 2. Concerning the excommunicating of his fpeciall fervant and noble man the Lord Home.   We anfwerit, That he was a profeft dangerus papift, in courfe with the reft, and whowfone he repented and reteued from them, as we war in gud hope he fould do, and approue himfelff to the prefent Affemblie, he fould be relaxed and his Maieftie fatiffeit theranent.   The

3 and laft, was concerning Mr Andro Hountar, minifter, wha haid kythed in open fields with Bodwell We anfwerit, that incontinent thereftei the Pref- byterie of St Andros haid proceidit againft him, and had depofit him of his office of minifterie. Then his Maieftie ceaffing, I afked if his Maieftie haid anie thing to fay to me. He anfwerit, Na thing mair nor to all the reft, faifi that he faw me ane in all commiffiones. I anfwerit, I thanked God therfor, for therin I was ferving God, his Kirk, and the King publictlie, and as for anie privat vnlawfull or vndewtifull practife, I wald wis traducars (if anie was of me to his Maieftie) fould be maid to fchaw thair face befor ther King, as I prefentlie haid procured of the Kirk to do of fett purpofe And thereftei exponing all our greiffs and petitiones, receavit, as faid is, verie guid anfwers, namlie a promife of a Parliament with all convenient diligence, wharin thefe excommunicat papift Erles fould be forefaultit, and thereftei proceidit againft with fyre and fword. Eftei the quhilk, the King taking me afyde, cauffit vfhe the Cabinet, and ther confeirit with me at lainthe alean of all purpofes, and gaiff me fpeciall commendationes and directiones to my vncle Mr Andro, whom with me he acknawlagit to be maift fathfull and truftie fubiects. Sa of the ftrang working of God, I, that cam to Sterling the Trator, retourned to Edinbruche a grait Courteour, yea a Cabinet Counfallour ; and fa indeid con- tinowed till thefe papift Eils war brought hame and reftored againe, as we will heir at lainthe heireftei.

The Parliament according to promife was folemnizet in the moneth of Junij, 1594, at quhilk the excommunicat Eils forfaid war, vpon the intercepted wryttings and blanks, forfaulted, ftreat actes maid againft Mes henars and papifts, and moine guid in fawoui of the Kirk, for minifteis leivings, gleibs, and manfes. And I being then in grait credit, purchaffit be the Kings awin fpeciall ceai and fawour, ane Act in fawouis of the honeft men of St Andros, James Smithe and Jhone Walwode, for retourning of tham from exyll to than awin countrey, citie, hous, wyff, and childring.

In the herveft quaiter thereftei, the Erle of Argyll, authorifed with the office of Lieutenantrie, prepeaied a giait armie, with the quhilk he cam vpon the Erle of Hounthe, and faught him at Glenninnes, aboue Muiiay land, with vncertan victorie, bot giaitteft los to Hounthe ; for excommunicat Auchin- down was ther flean, with vther diueis gentilmen of his kin, ther horfes all fpoilled, and a grait number of the beft heavilie woundit, quhilk maid tham vnable therefter to mak anie refiftance to the Kings armie.

This was in the end of September, and in the beginning of October following the King, with companies of horſmen and futtmen vnder wages. by the
comoun forces gathered be proclamation, paſt northe againſt theſe Rebelles,
whom my vncle Mr Andro and I, with vthers of the miniſterie accompanied
alſo at his Maieſties deſyre, to bear witnes of his peanes and ſeuear proceidings againſt theſe, becauſe the peiple war yit gealous ower the King for his
knawin and kythit fawour to the Erle of Hountlie   At our coming to Aberdein we fund na reſiſtance, bot the enemies fled and darn'd. Yit the King
reſoluit to go fordwart to thair cheiſt houſſes for demoliſhing therof; bot extremitie of wather ſteyed him till almaiſt the firſt monethe was conſumed,
and for the nixt ther was na pay to the wagit horſmen and futmen, wherin
ſtud the forces that war repoſit on to do the turn.   It was therfor be his Maieſtie and Counſall thought a turn wheron the haill cauſe dependit. to direct
a man of credit, fathfulnes, and dilligence to moue the brouches and weill af-
tected of all rankes to ſend with dilligence the ſecond monethes pay, for the
quhilk I was maird choiſe of be the King, Counſall and Breithring.   Wharof
I mak mention to the praiſe of my guid God, wha keipit me, and directed all
aright, the meſſage being maiſt peantull and perrillus, bathe for my perſone
and fame and eſtimation.   The iorney was lang to go to Edinbruche and retourn again with dilligence to Aberdein in extremitie of euill wather, the countrey broken and dangerus, and that quhilk eſhayed me maiſt, I was commandit to wrait to England to Mr Bowes ordinar Ambaſſatour, and to aſſure
the breithring of the miniſterie of Edinbruche and all vther, yea to preatche
it, that ſeing the Rebels war fugitiue. thair principall houſſes ſould be demoliſhed to teſtifie the Kings vtter indignation againſt thame   And yit the
treuthe was, I was nocht twa dayes on my iorney, when ſic moyen was maid
that thair ſould be na mair done bot a vewing of the places and returning
againe.   Bot the Lord my God haiſſing a cear of me ſaued all, except my
man, wha at my retourning, throw exces of trauell, tuk ſeiknes in Cowy and
died. I haid alſo a ſpeciall frind behind whom God vſit as inſtrument to work
that wark and faiff my creadit. This was my vncle Mr Andro, wha being at
Strеabogy, and preſent in Counſall daylie, when be manieſt vottes it was in-
clyning to ſpear the hous, he reaſoned and bure out the mater ſa. be the aſſiſtance of the guid Lord Lindſay and Capteans of horſmen and futmen, that
at laſt the King takes vpon him, contrar to the graiteſt part of the Counſall,
to conclud the demoliſhing of the hous, and giff command to the maiſter of
wark to that effect, quhilk was nocht lang in executing be the ſouldiours   When

all was done, lytle found meining and finall effect tordar was producit   For the King returned Southe, and left the Duc, Lieutenant behind to accomplis the mater, wha tuk vpe rigoruſlie the penalties of countrey peiple that obeyed nocht the proclamationes, and componed eaſelie with the affiſtars of the rebels, he auaritius and craftie counſallars wha war left with him, quhilk raſed a grait offence and out cry, and htle vther gud.   Alwayes in end theſe papiſt excommunicat and forfaultit Eils war compellit to pas aff the countrey. and ſa God triumphit ower tham, till in his iuſtice for our ſinnes they war retournit and ſett vpe againe.   Bot becauſe therefter my dihgence was thought ower grait, and my ſpeitches ower frie in that mater for my awin releiff and defence I haiff thought gud till inregiſter heu the wrytings quhilk I gat at that tyme from the King and Breithring

To our trafi frnds the Miniſters of the Euangill at Edinbruche.

TREST FRINDS, We greit yow hartlie weill.   At the leat Conventionn of our Eſteats aſſemblit for the preventing of the dangerus practeiſes of the Papiſts, and vthers our vnnaturall ſubiects roynit and conſpyring the ſubuerſion of Religion, the wrak of our perſone and eſtcat, and perpetuall thraldome of our countrey to maiſt mercilſs ſtrangers, it was reſoluit that we ſould with all celeritie haiſt in expedition toward the Noithe, left gift tymous remead war nocht prouydit than expected ſtrangers might arryue, and for the better effectuating therof, it was thoucht requiſit that we ſould haiff our ordinarie force of Loiſmen and futmen, (of the quhilks our burrowes verie kyndlie, and of gud will yeildit to a fowme for tuſteining of a thowſand futmen the ſpace of twa monethes, as we ourſelff prouydit be our awin priuat moyen the firſt monethe to our hois men,) the wathei being verie unſeaſonable, and ſic ſpaittes of waters, as with grait dihicultie, and nocht without perrell of a grait part of our armie could we attein to this town befor the halff of the firſt monethe was expyrit   Wherby, and be the retreat of our Rebelles conceiredlie to corners and luddilles, thinking to weirie ws, and abyding the itchew of the pay of our waigit men, as things heu ar lyk to draw to grantter lamthe then we expected, yit ſeing what our departour from this might import and whow manie dangers ar imminent, we ar fullie refolued to mak our refidence heu, and to depart na whar elles, whill we haue fullie ſetled this part of the countrey, and put it to ſic pointt as htle danger ſalbe fearit, gift we be aydit be your kyndlie helpe and promiſed releiſl.   We will, therfor, maiſt effecteouſlie defyre yow, that vie wilbe inſtant be all meanes to moue that our hrouche of Edinbruche, and the reſt of our burrowes, to haue at ws in this town befor the xxiij of this inſtant the ſecond monethes pay, with the reſt of the fiift monethes, wherof onlie that an halff yit is reſlaued   Without the quhilk we wilbe conſtreanit to leaue this guid and neceſſar wark vndone, wharby the aduerſanes wilbe ſa incouragit, as they will luk for na refiſtance, and haiff the countrey opin to ſtrangers, quhilk, befor it ſould fall out in our tyme, or anie blam might be imput to ws we haid rathei giff croun, lyff, and whatſoeuer God hes put in our hands   Be nocht therfor cauld noi ſlaw in this mater, but employ your haill means, and ſic the ſam effectuated, whilk we dout nocht bot ye will do, and interpon all your guid trauelles and dihgence to that eftect. Fordar, we commit to this bearar, Mr James Meluill, whom we hauff expreslie chosin to this meſſage, and we wis yow to credit as ourſelſt Sa we comit yow in Gods holy protectioun From Aberdein the xvj of October, 1594.

Sic ſubſcribitur.

JAMES R.

To our treſt frinds the Proueſt, Bailyies and Counſell of our brouche of Edinbruche, and the reſt of our burrowes.

TRAISI FRINDS, We greit vow bai the weill.—This bearer, Mr James Meluill, being an of the Miniſterie that hes accompanied ws in this haill iorney, and therth now beſt acquented with all our proceidings in the way, and ſince our hen coming, We hauff takin occaſion annes earand to direct him toward yow, to ſignifie to yow particularlie, whow we hauff bein occupied, and what our intention is befor our retourn. As allwa hauff inſtructed him in ſic things as he ſall ſpecialie impairt to yow in our name, anent the furtherance of the cauſe in hands, whom we will deſyre yow firmlie to credit as ourſelft And ſa remitting the mater to his ſufficiencie, and the particular Letter of the reſt of the miniſterie heir, We commit yow to God From Aberdein, the xv of October 1594

Sic ſubſcribitur.

JAMES R.

To our right worſchipfull and deir Breithring the Miniſters of Edinbruche.

Manie ar the tribulations of the righteus, but the Lord delyuereth tham out of tham all

RIGHT WORSCHIPFULI and deir breithring: Albeit the Lord in iuſtice thretned this Land with e heauie iudgments for the contempt of his fauour, yit we find that in the middes of wrathe he remembreth mercie, and ouercome the when he is iudged. For the King and his Counſall, with his haill companie dayhe growes in erneſt affection to advance the guid cauſe againſt the enemies therof, and hes reaſoluthe concludit be the grace of God, nocht to remoue out of thir partes befoi the vtter overthrow of the aduerſarie caus, wherin, as we haue iuſt occaſion to prais God, ſa we erneſthe recommend to your prayer the guid and happie ſucces of this actioun. Requyſting yow lykwayes to employ yourſelfis with our brother Mi James Meluill, the bearer, at the hands ot your awin Town, that a guid cauſe be nocht forſaken at the vtmaiſt poinct, and ſall throw leak ot ſufficient moyen to bear it furthe, as we dout nocht to find your effectuall affiſtance according to your zeall. The reſt to the bearer whom yie will creadit. The Lord preſerue yow, and direct all your proceidings to his glorie From Aberdein the xvj of October, 1594.

Your breithring and fellow laborars in the Lords herveſt,

Sic ſubſcribitur.

AN MELUILE.
Mᴿ. P. GALLOUAY
JA. NICOLSON

1595.—The yeir following* Mr Dauid Blaks ministerie in St Androis, quhilk haid wrought notable guid effects, bathe in the town for the weill of all the peiples faulles, and thair republict, and guid ordour of prouisioun for the pure, as alſo to landwart for purpoſe of bigging of kirks, and in the Preſbyterie moving non reſidents to tak tham to than kirks and charges, began now be the deuill invying it to be branght. The inſtruments war the Mantemoungaı, (ſa Mr Dauid named him,) Wilyeam Balfour and his fawouaıs, wha fearing Mr Dauid prenaling againſt him, and euicting of his hous in the Abbay to be a manſe to the minifter, cauſit, be diuers courtious and vtheıs, the Kings eares to be filled with calumnious informationes of the ſaid Mr Dauid his doctrine and minifterie. As lykwayes be his occaſioun of Mr Andro, my vncle, Rector of the Vnnerſitie, being the principall mean of the ſaid Mr Dauids bringing and placing thair, and meanteiner and affiſtar of him in his minifterie

Sa, in the monethe of Auguſt 1595, the ſaid Mr Dauid and my vncle ar chargit to comper befor the King and Counſall at Falkland to anſwer for certean ſpeitches vttered be tham in thair doctrin againſt his Maiefties progenitoуs; of the quhilk I knew na thing bot be aduertiſment fra my vncle from St Androis to keipe the dyet. Coming to Falkland, the King inquyres of me, What I thought of Mr Dauid Blak? I anſweıt, "I thought him a guid and godlie man, and a mightie preatchour, and a man whaſe minifterie had bein veıie forcible and fruitfull in St Androis."—" O," ſayes the King, · yıe aı the firſt man and onlie that euer I haid ſpeak guid of him amangs minifterie, gentilman or burgeſſes."—" Surlie, then, (ſay I), I am veıie ſorie, ſir, that your Maieftie hes nocht ſpokin with the beft ſort of tham all."—" I ken,' ſayes the King in coler, " the beft, and hes ſpoken with tham; bot all your ſedituis deallings ar cloked, and hes bein with that name of the beft men "—" Then, ſurlie, (ſay I.) ſir, your Maieftie ſall do weill to gifſ Mr Dauid a fyſe of ame in all tha thrie ranks, excepting nan bot ſic as hes knawin particulars; and gifſ they fyll him. I ſall ſpeak na maiı in this maner to your Maiefti, till

* An. 1595.—In the monethe of Meıche, 27, being Twidday about alleavin houres of the night, in place of a ſaıe las that neveı leuche, God gaue me of my wyſſ deaihe beloued, a pleaſand boy, wha during his infancie, being of a fyne ſanguine complexioun, was a paſtyme and pleaſoun, nocht onlie to my haill famihe, bot almoſt throw all the town whaı euer he was caried. Sa it is a guid thing to tak in patience whateuer God ſends. His guid thyı, Jhone Durie, being with me at that tyme, gaue him the bage of baptiſme, and called him Jhone, in remembrance of the inſpeakable grace of God beſtowit on him and his ſucceſſioun. The God of grace mak as mikle to kythe in him, coming to age, if ſa be his pleaſure as appeıes in the youthe inwaıthe and outward

your Maieſtie find what he is in effect" The King. flipping away fra me. goes to a ſpeciall courtier, and ſayes to him, " Fathe, Mr James Meiuill and I ar at our graitteſt, for I perceaue he is all for Mr Dauid Blak, and that fort" The King, leſt he fould irritat the Kirk be calling befor his Counſall anie miniſter for thair doctrin, quhilk haid nocht fucceidit weill of befor, called onlie a nomber of the breithring of the miniſterie, (namlie fic whilk war offendit with Mr Dauids ſcharpe and plean form of doctrine, ſparing nather King nor miniſter,) to try this mater and iudge thervpon

Mr Dauid compeiring, declynit the Kings iudicator in doctrine; and as for the breithring. he refuſit tham nocht, being ane fort of Aſſemblie of the Kirk. righthe callit for that effect, or vtherwayes in privat to confer with thame, and ſatiſfie tham in ane dout conceavit of his doctrine. The King ſummarhe and confuſedllie paſſit ower all, and put nan of theſe things to interloquutor, bot called for the witnes And Mr Dauid, called to fie what he haid to ſay againſt tham, anſwerit, git that was a Judicator, he fould haiff an anſwer concerning the vnlawfulnes and incompetencie allcagit; as lykwayes, but ceas it war, as it is nocht, he fould haiff an accuſar fortifeit with twa witnes according to the rewll of the Apoſtle, &c That in lyk maner is paſt and a nomber of witnes is examined: Burley the delatter and accuſar being always preſent. Whilk, when my vncle Mr Andro Meluill perceaving, chapping at the chalmer dure, whar we war, comes in, and efter humble reuerence done to the King. he braks out with grait libertie of ſpeitche, letting the King planlie to knaw, that quhilk dyvers tymes befor with fmall lyking, he haid tooned in his ear, " That than was twa Kings in Scotland, twa Kingdomes, and twa Iuriſdictiones Thir was Chryſt Jeſus, &c And gif the King of Scotland, ciuill King James the Saxt, haid ane iudicatour or cauſe thair preſenthe, it fould nocht be to iudge the fathfull meſſanger of Jeſus Chryſt, the King, &c. bot (turning him to the Laird of Burley, ſtanding there,) this trator, wha hes committed diuers poincts of hie treaſone againſt his Maieſties ciuill Lawes, to his grait diſhonour and ofience of his guid fubiects, namlie taking of his peacable fubiects on the night out thair houſſes, rauiſhing of weimen, and receattting within his hous of the Kings rebels and forfault enemies," &c

With this Burley falles down on his knies to the King, and craues Juſtice " Juſtice !" fayes Mr Andro; " wald to God yow haid it, yow wald nocht be heir to bring a iudgment from Chryſt vpon the King, and thus falſhe and vniuſthe to vex and accuſe the fathfull ſervants of God " The King began with fum countenances and ſpeitches to command ſilence and daſhe him; bot he, infurging with graiter bauldnes and force of langage, bini out the mater fa, that the King was fean to tak it vpe betwix tham with gentill termes and minne talk ; faying, " They war bathe litle men, and than hart was at than mouthe," &c. Sa that meitting was demiflit the fornoone   Nether war we affemblht again in ame forme of Judicator ; bot, when I perceauit the King to be inceufed, and verie euill myndit bathe againft Mr Andro and Mr Dauid, I fpak the Erle of Mar, being at Court, informing him of the treuthe of maters, and whow dangerus a thing it was to his Maieftie at fic a tyme to brak out with the Kirk, whill as Boduell haid confedirt with the Papift Lords, and as he knew ther was prefentlie a grait commotion in all the Bordars, befought him therfor to counfall his Maieftie aright, and mitigat thefe maters. The quhilk he did fathfullie.   And fa the King callit Mr Dauid to him felft in privat and hamlie maner, defyring to vnderftand the treuthe be way of conference : the quhilk Mr Dauid fchew him to his fatiffactioun   In lyk maner, Mr Andro, wha, efter his tafone, maift frielie reafonit with the King, and tauld him his mynd betwix tham to the Kings contentation ; and fa in end his Maieftie directed me, efter lang conference on thir maters, to go to St Andros and teatche, and declar the mater, fa as the peiple might be put out of euill opinion, bathe of his Maieftie and than minifter, and whow that all was weill aggreit   Whilk I did vpon the morn in St Andros, teatching the 127 Pfalme ; and becaufe I knew it wald be marked, I fett down the haill poincts I was to fpeak in wriat vpon that mater, as followes :

Now, I am fure, guid Chriftianes and breithring, yie wald fean haiff newes from this laft dyet, whilk we haue keipit with his Maieftie at Falkland. And, indeid, the Kings Maieftie and breithring of the minifterie thei convenit, fearing that quhilk in effect is fallen out, viz. the fafones of euill fame, quhilk euer reports of all thrngs to the warft, and oftentymes fawes abrod lies for ventie, and euill newes for guid, as we hen it hes bein reported amang yow, that the King haid begoun to put at the Kirk, and to plunge in maters with the minifterie, nanlie haid mel'de with your paftor, and ather put him to exyll, warde or fylence, whilas, indeid, thei is na thing les, therfor hes his Maieftie and the faid breithring directed me to this place to teftifie and declar the treuthe. Firft, then, it is of veritie, that a grait number of euill reports hes bein caried from this place to the King, fa biffie hes men bein, fpecialie fic as war twitched in than particulars, quhilk might haue eafelie moued and crabet the King, bot he fufpendit his opinion, and referrit all to a ruft tryell, as occafion might beft ferue for the faming.

Amangs the reft, a delatoun of leat was maid maift offenfiue and odius, That Mr Dauid, your paftor by name, fonld haue publictlie from pulpit traducit the Kings mother maift vyllie, to mak his Maieftie contemptible in the eis of his peiple, and to ften vpe the feditius to treafonable and dangerus attempts againft his Maiefties eftcat and perfone, the quhilk could nocht be fuffent vnput to tryell   Compeiring then befor his Maieftie, and a guid number of the breithring of the ministrie, bathe the accusar and acculit, the accusar affirmed that your Pastor haid spokin neuer a guid word of the Kings mother, but mikle euill, the quhilk, gif he sould nocht proue be sufficient witnes ther present, he sould be content to tyne his land, his lyff and all.

Your Pastor answered, he haid comendit his Maiesties mother for manie grait and rare gifts, and excellent verteus, and onlie vene sparinglie and soberlie haid twitched the treuthe of the iudgments of God, quhilk haid com on hir for refusing the wholsome admonitioun of the Word of God. Sa the witnes war producit and examined. It was fund clen in end, that your pastor, contrar to the accusation haid spoken mikle guid of the Kings mother, as also haid spoken concerning the iudgments of God vpon hir in hir fall.

The King could nocht think it altogidder vnlawfull to vse his mother for exemple, bot thought it na wayes expedient in his tyme, because of the peiple, that is euer readie to draw that to the contempt of his Hienes persone, and of the seditius and treasonable, whairof ther is manie in the land, wha ar euer readie to grip therat, as thought the forme of mens dealling againit hir, quhilk was extraordinar, might be drawin in exemple, and sua be tham. Therfor it was thought expedient be the haill breithring ther, that nather Mr Dauid nor na minister sould speak a word of his Maiesties mother, till that a certean Act of the Generall Assemblie, maid therament at Dondie, war sein and confiddent, and in all tymes coming the tennour therof to be keipit preceislie.

And for satiffaction of his Maiestie, the said Mr Dauid cam maist humblie in his Maiesties presence, and acknawlagit ther, that, as he sould mak answer to God, vpon the vsage of his ministerie, he thought nocht that his speitches could be offensiue to his Maiestie, nor anie wayes meant to haif offendit his Hienes, bot onlie vsit that exemple to beat down sinne in the persone quhilk he was rebuiking; nather yit wald he heirefter vse that speitche, nor anie vther wilfullie or vndewtifullie, to his Maiesties offence or displeasour, bot as his hart wes asauld, vpright and maist affectioned to his Maiestie, as anie subiects or ministers in the realme, fa wald he mak it knawin in experience, and all dewtie to his Hienes heirefter. Wharwith his Maiestie was weill pleasit, and in guid fawour dimiffit the said Mr Dauid. Conceaue therfor righthe and reuerenthe, and stand in guid opinion bathe of your Prince and Pastor, for the difcharge of all dewties addettit to tham, and pray God to keipe his Maiestie in guid concord and aggriment with his faithfull and trew seruands, deteafting from your harts the euill difpolition of fic persones, that for thair particular is sett to the contrar.

This piece of feruice was weill aneuche lyked and accepted on bathe the partes; bot my court grew les therefter, and, as we will heir, at the hamcoming of the papists Lords, clein deceyit. And to leaue the treuthe of my courting testified befor God, befor whom I walked, I sought it nocht, but it fell on me be the occasion reherfed. When it cam on, I interteaned it as I could in confcience, (quhilk, indeid, was haird to do, and coft me manie foar prik in hart,) cheiflie and firft, to mak the King to ken that we loued him deirlie, and wald do anie thing that ley in ws for his pleafuring with the warrand of God and a guid confcience, that, by his throuche lyking and coniunction with the Kirk, maters, bathe in Kirk and polecie, might go right and weill fordwart. And trewlie, I thank God, during my twa yeirs court, it was fa   Bot as I was thus about to win the King as in me lay to the Kirk. fa was he in winning of me to the Court; and when on ather syde all meanes was vsit, and bathe keipit our groundes, without grait vantage an of another we relented and fearhe reteired, as the contniowing of this Storie will in the awin place declar   The onlie particular quhilk I haid, was the pitifull esteat of the gud honest men of St Andros, whase cause and condition was ioyned fa with the esteat of the Kirk and gud breithring, that therwith it stud and fell.   Bot for myselff, as God knawes, I haid neuer a croun be my contem, bot spendit euerie yen the halff of my stipend theron ; and the treuthe was I neuer fought nane, and I gat nan vnfought.

In the monethe of September following, the Eile of Orkney, be the Laird of Burleyes moyen, cam to St Andros, as direct from the King, and reconcyled the faid Lard with Mr Andro Melvill, Rector, and Mr Dauid Blak, and Mr Robert Walace, ministers of St Andros, and that verie craftelie, vnder pretext therof to draw again the peiple to the hous of Darsy, and cause tham change thair Provest again, as they did : For Captean Murray, perceaving the changeablenes of the peiple, and the weght of the office, demitted the sam willinglie ; and fa be the vther faction of the peiple fauored be Court, the Lard of Darsy wes receavit again. That coft ws a fafchus iorney to St Jhonstoun. Returning fra the quhilk, certean newes cam of the Chancellar, Mr Jhone Metellans departour, whom Mr Andro, Mr Robert Bruce and I haid visited nocht lang befor, and left at a verie gud esteat for the lyff to come   He was a man of grait lerning, wisdome and stoutnes, and kythe in end to haue the feir of God, deing a gud christian and louar of Chryfts servants.   And, indeid, he was a grait instrument in keiping the King af the Kirk, and fra fawworing of Papists, as the yeir efter it kythed clenlie.

1596 —That Wintar the haill officiars of Esteat war alterit, and the Kings haill effeares concerning his patrimonie, propertie and casualities war put in the hands of aught, and fa almaist the haill adminiftratioun of the realme ; and therfor named OCTAUIANS ; the an halff wharof war sufpected papifts, and the reft litle better   This was mikle thought of, and portendit a grait alteration in the Kirk, whilk fell out the yeir following, 1596,* quhilk may be markett

* This yeir had twa prodigius things, quhilk I marked amang ws, on the coft syd   Ane in the feinzie ouk etter Pace, the day being tean about noon, ther tell a cloud of rean vpon Kelhe Law, and the monteanes befvd, that for a space conered them with running watei, the quhilk defending therfra, safit fa at ane instant the strypes and burnes, that they war vnpaffable to the trauellars,

for a fpeciall periodic and fatall yeir to the Kirk of Scotland, and therfor man
tak mair pean to fchaw the maters that fell out therin. It haid a ftrange varietie and mixtuie : The beginning therof with a fchaw of profit in planting
of the Kirks with perpetuall locall ftipends ; the mids of it verie confortable
for the exercerfe of Reformatioun, and renewing of the Covenant ; bot the end
of it tragicall, in wafting the Sion of our Jerufalem, the Kirk of Edinbruche,
and thretning na les to manie of the reft. The redeiming wharof, I feir be
tyme, falbe fund to haue coft ws deirar be the los of the haill libertie of
Chryfts kingdome in Scotland, nor giff all annes haid bein wafted and over-
rune. Wherin I pray God of his mercie, that my feir may be fund foolifhe.

The occupatioun and continuall laboring to efchew ruting out, maid me befor nocht to mention ame peanes takin vpon planting, whowbeit ther was mikle at diuers tymes, namlie in the yeirs fourfcore ten, twoll and threttein
veirs. Wharanent we haid diuers commiffiones from Parlament and Generall Affemblie, and quhilk indeid was bathe peanfull and expenfive to me
amangs vthers : bot becaufe I can recompt na effect of tham,* I fall fett down
this yeirs wark alleanarlie, when Commiffiones war giffen out vpon an Act of
Parliament and Letters, to dell with Taxmen and all Titulars of teinds for
effectuating of the beft conftant Plat, that etter lang aduyfment takin amangs
ws wes put in ordour and pennit be Mr Jhone Lindfay, fecretar, and the
quhilk to ferue for all thofe biotik maters, I thought meit to be hen infert,
if that firft I mark a thing that I haid Mr Alexr Hay, Clerk Regifter, a
man of ame in Scotland maift exercerfed in tha maters, and the faid Mr Jhone
Lindfay, a man of the graiteft leirning and folid naturall wit joyned with that,
I knew, controuert diuers tymes, bathe be word and wrait anent that Plat.
The an halding that it was an impoffibilitie as things ftud in Scotland to deuyfe
a conftant Plat, or giff it war deuyfit, to effectuat it, and deid in that opinion ,
the vther, to wit Mr Jhone, halding that bathe was poffible, and therfor fett
himfelff to devyfe the fam, and put it in mundo as followes ; bot concerning
the effectuating therof he died in the fam fathe with the Clark Regifter.

whowbeit weill borft   The burn of Anftruther was neuer fein fa grait in mans memorie, as it rafe
within an hour. The read fpeat of frefhe water market the fie man nor a myll and a halft. That
brought grait barrennes vpon the land the yeirs following. The vther was a monftruus grait
whaale befor the herveft cam in, vpon Kinerag Sandes.

* For the Generall, whowbeit I man remember to the grait praife of God, that our particular
trauelles war fa blifit, that wharat our coming to St Andros ther was nocht paffing four or fyve
Kirks therabout planted with minifters, ther is this day faxtein or feuintein in the Prefbyterie therof, manie of them alfweill prouydit as in anie of the Countrey, 1600.

The New and Conftant Plat of Planting the haill Kirks of Scotland, penned to be prefented to the King and Efteats in An 1596

OURE SOUERANE LORD, with confent of his thrie Eftaits in Perliament, vnderftanding that be the Law of God it is expreflie commandit, lykas alfwa for interteinment of relligioun and Gods fervice, it is man nor neceffar that the minifters of his Holie Word haift fufficient rents for than honeft fuftentatioun, Confidering alfo that the rents and patrimonie quhilk perteined of auld to the Kirk is grsatumlie damnified and exhauft be the annexatioun of the haill temporalitie therof to his Hienes Croun, and be the erectionnes of a grait part of the faid temporall lands of the Kirk with diuers Kirks and Teinds includit therwith in new temporall lordfchipes, and be the new fafoue of fetting of lang takes of the faid teinds for diuers nyntein vers, and lyff rents fucceffiue for peyment of fmall filuer dewtie nawayes equiualent to the haiff of the reafona-ble valor of the faids teinds, and be the pretendit rightes of fa monie perfones lythrents, afhig-nationnes, and vther difpofitionnes of the lands teinds and dewties of Taks, and be his Ma-iefties rights of the Thrids fuperplus, comonn Kirks, firft frnets, and tyft penme of ilk bene-fice, rights and difpofition of the fam, proceiding fiom his Hienes efter his perfyt age, and fra his Graces predeceffours, for the maift part ratefied in Parliament.—Wharby ther is na moyen left prefenthe to augment the finall ftipend of anie pure minifter, albeit he haid neuer fa grait ne-ceffitie, nor yit to plant anie new minifters at anie congregation, albeit the maift part of all the pa-roche Kirks of Scotland ar altogidder deftitut of all exerceife of Relligioun: And that ther is a grait number of minifters nocht prouydit, but avating vpon fum fpeciall charge and vocatioun, lyk-as a grait number of guid fchollars of the youthe of this Realme, for the lyk pouertie, is compellit to pas to France to the grait danger of apoftafie fra Relligioun, whar vtherwayes they might be profitable to the Kirk, and might be honefthe interteined vpon the faid Teinds. Quhilks teinds nocht onlie befor the wryttin Law of God, and therefter be expres commandment of the fam, bot alfo be the confent of all nationnes, and fpecialie of this Realme, hes euer perteined to the Kirk, wher-by of all reafone the Kirk, haueing na vther patrimonie, aught to be meanteined in the right pof-feffioun of the faids Teinds, at leift ay and whill they be fufficienthe prouydit vtherwayes Con-forme to the quhilk, diuers Actes hes bein maid in Parliament, that befor the new prouifion of anie prelat, the minifters at the Kirks and Paroches vnited to the faid prelacie fould be firft prouydit to fufficient ftipends, vtherwayes the prouifioun of the prelacie to be null And lykwayes in the tent Act of the Parliament, haukdin 1567, it is ordeanit, that the haill thrddes fould be firft employed to the vfe of the minifters ay and whill the Kirk com in poffeffioun of than awin patrimonie, quhilk is the Teinds And als in the faid Act of Annexatioun, and diuers vther louable actes, it is exprefhe prouydit, that the Minifters fould be fufficienthe prouydit of leivings furthe of the beft and readieft of the fpirituahties, and that they fould be prouydit in tytle to all finall beneficces, that they fould be prouydit to Manfes and Gleibs for thair refidence at than Kirks, and that laic Patrones fould pronyde quahfiet perfones, whilk actes hes nocht tean fulhe effect, but in the contrar the leivings of the faid minifters left incerteanhe to be fought from ver to yer at his Hienes Chec-quer, out of the thrids with infinit proces in Law, be reafone of the manifald difpofitiones of the faid thrides to vther laic perfones proceiding fra his Hienes as haueing right to the haill thrids, co-moun kirks, fuperplus, fyft penme and temporalitie of ilk benefice, and be reafone of the collation of benefices pleno iure to perfones na wayes qualefied, contrar to the guid meining and intentioun of the forfaids Actes of Parliament, to the vtter wrak and diftructioun of the Kirk be plean poner-tie as the proteft enemies of Chryft wald haue done of auld, gif fpedie remeadie be nocht fund.

Marginal notes:

Kirk rent d ow[n] ad be Annexatiouns Erectiounes

Setting of lang Taks Peyment of filuer dewtie,

Lyfrents, Affignationnes Penfionnes,

Kings fuperplus Comoun kirk.. Firft Fruits, Lyft Penme, Patronages, Difpofitions of bene-fices,

Ratificatiounes i[n] Parl.

Teinds be all Law the Kirks iuft right

Na new prouifioun to Prelatts befor the Ministers of the Kirks be prouydit.

Act of Parl. 67

Act of Annexatio n

Gleibs

All Teinds the proper patrimonie of the Kirk

Local stipends of a modifiet quantitie of victuall out of sic and sic Towns in euerie Paroche, with Gleib and Manse, nocht-withstanding anie mans right whatsumeuer.

THAIRFOR his Hienes remembering that thair is na thing mair proper to his royall office nor to be the nurtilar of the trew Kirk, and to be cairfull of the advancement of the trew religioun, and continowing thairof to the posteritie, with consent of the Estaits in Parliament, be the tennour of this Act, DECLARES, That the haill Teinds of this Realme, baith of personages and vicarages, alweill vnited to prelacies and vther dignities as nocht vnited, and vther Teinds whatsumeuer, hes perteined in all tymes bygean, and sall perteine in all tymes coming, to the Kirk as thair proper patrimonie   And of new, with consent forsaids, gifts, grants, and dispones, and perpetualie mortefies the saids Teinds of all personages and vicarages and vther benefices whatsumeuer within this realme, to the Kirk to remean thairwith as thair awin proper patrimonie conform to the tennour of this present Act in all tymes coming   And with advys forsaid, statutes and ordeanes that the Lords of Checquer with fic of the ministerie as salbe apointed heir vnto, being of æquall number with the saids Lords, sall modifie and affing out of certean townes of ilk paroche a certean quantitie of victuall of the Teind scheaues thairof, and vther dewties of the Vicarage, as the nature of the ground may pay, with the manse and haill gleib land, gift the sam remean yit vnlewed, and gif the said gleib be sewed, four-akers of the said gleib, wither the sam be of the Persones, Vicars, Bischopes, Pryors or Pryoreffes, Deans or Subdeans, Abbayes, or anie vther Kirk land for the gleib, as an locall stipend to ilk paroche Kirk of this Realm, without exception, for sustentation of the minister thairat sufficientlie and honestlie in all respects of the truncs of the paroche itfelft, nocht-withstanding the saids Kirks be annexed to prelacies or vther benefices or nocht, doted to Colleages or Vniuersities, or vther wayes perteining to auld pofleffions of whatfumeuer degrie, or to minisers newlie prouydit in tytl thairto, at the Kings presentation or laic patrones, denydit amangs manie Prebendaries, Dignities or Chaplanries, or nocht denydit, comoun Kirks, or vther whatfum-euer qualitie or conditioun the faid paroche Kirks hes bein, or be whatfumeuer maner of way the teinds thairof hes bein branked in tymes bypaft , and nochtwithftanding all and whatfumeuer right his Maieftie may haift or pretend to the thirds, fuperplus, firft truncs and fyft penme of the faids benefices , and nochtwithftanding of all penfiones, takes, affignationes, lyftrents, erectionnes, of the faid Teinds, or anie part thairof, in an temporall Lordflchipe, prouifion to prelacies, or vther bene-fices, vniones or diuifiones of the faids paroches and vther difpofitionnes of the faids Teinds, or anie part thairof whatfumeuer proceiding from his Maieftie or his predeceffours, efter his or thair perfyt age confirmed in Parliament, with whatfumeuer folemnitie or vtherwayes, to whatfumeuer cai-telles, collages or vniuerfities, particular perfone of whatfumeuer degrie   And nochtwithftanding whatfumeuer vther taks, penfionnes, lyftrents, fewing of the faids Teinds, with Landes, and fewing of the faids gleibs, and vther difpofition whatfumeuer maid be prelates or beneficed per-fones, with confent of thair Chaptours to whatfumeuer particular perfone, collage or vniuerfitie for whatfumeuer fpace of yeirs or zeirlie dewtie   And nochtwithftanding the priuilage of Lords of Seffioun, and actes of Parliaments, and vther Lawes bygean, vniones, annexationnes and incorpora-tiones of feuerall paroche Kirks to a prelacie or vther benefice, or diuifion or the fruicts of a paro-chine amang manie prebendaries, or chapleans, or vthers , and nochtwithftanding of all vther impe-diments quhilk anie way may ftay the full execution of this prefent Act

DECLARING all and whatfumeuer the forfaids prouifions of benefices, vniones, incorporationes, diuifiones, takes, penfionnes, lyftrents, erectiones, and fewing of Teinds, Manfes, Gleibs, Priuilages, Actes, Lawes, and Conftitutionnes, format and vther difpofitiones whatfumeuer of the faids Teinds, Manfes and Gleibs proceiding from his Maieftie, or his Maiefties predeceffours, or fra whatfumeuer vther beneficed perfone with whatfumeuer folemnitie, to be null in tyme coming, in fa far as they may mak anie preiudice to this prefent act, and to the particular locall affignatioun of ftipeads to

I attenco to ilk paroche kuk, conform therto, and to the full executioun therof but ame vther reaction or recmatour of law Withe powar to the faids Lords and Mmifters to tak new tryall of the valour of the faids Temds, and to apomct, ordean, and affigne the lands perpetuall locall ftipend at ilk paroche out of fic fpeciall Townes and Lands of the faid paroches, and to vnent feuerall paroches in an, or diffiuer and feparat an in ma, withe confent of the parochmars And to mak a fpeciall Buik thervpon and generalhe to do all thmgs neceffar for this effect Whilk locall affignationes of ftipends and temds whatfumeuer of the particular Townes and Lands to be fpecified therm, fall pertem als fiehe to the mmifter of the faid paroche as gift he haid bem prouidit of auld in tytle therto. Withe powar to the faid mmifter to collect, gather, and intromeat with, and to mak warnmgs and mhebitionnes agamft the poffeffours of the faids Temds, Manfes, and Globs, with als grant effect as ame Perfone or Vicar, or ame vther beneficed perfone might haue done in ame tymes bypaft nochtwithftandmg all impedmments forfands and vther whatfumeuer, but preiudice of the faids mmifters rightes to the hail remanent of the faids benefices, when the fam fall veak and fall in thair hands be deceas of the prefent poffeffours, reducing or expyring of Takes, or vtherwayes whatfumeuer, and of the true difpofitioun thervpon as accordes of the Law, and conform to this prefent Act in all pomcts And for the better executioun of the premifes, Our Soueraine Lord, with advys forfaid, diffolues expreffhe all and whatfumeuer vmones of feuerall paroche Kuks to prelacies, benefices of dignitie and vthers, and fuppreffes and abrogattes the name and ftylles of the faid prelacies and dignities, and vnites of new the Temds of ilk paroche whar the fam was denydit of auld amangs mame Prebandaries, Chapleanes, or vthers in a haill benefice, and ordeanes that mmifters be prouydit in tytle to ilk paroche kuk in particular, quhilk was befor vnited to prelacies now vacand, or quhilk hes vacked in his Graces hands fen the parhament halden at   .   An. 1584, or quhilk fall in ame wayes venk hencfter be dimiffioun, depriuatioun, or vtherwayes whatfumeuer, and to all vther feuerall paroches, vacand bathe to the parfonnges and vicarages therof, with the manfe and gleib of four aikers of land, conform to the formar actes mand anent the faids gleibs and manfes, at the quhilk kuks the faid mmifters falbe oblefit to mak thair refidence, and fall haift intromiffioun with the fruicts therof, contoim to this prefent Act and Buik of Perpetuall Modificatioun of the locall ftipends to follow henvpon And efter than diceas, demiffioun or depriuatioun, vther qualefiet perfones to be prefinted therto be his Hienes and his Grace fucceffours, and be vthers haueand the right of prefentatioun and patronage therof, and that na new Prebandenes falbe prouydit efter the deceis of the prefent poffeffours, bot the rent to accres to the leiving of the mmifter, conform to this Act, etc

And becaufe it is maift neceffar that the faids locall ftipends be of a certean quantitie according to the nature of the ground, and out of certean fpeciall landes maift eweft to the Kuk and commodius for the mmifter, that the mmifter may knaw whom of to craue his dewtie And feing it is impoffible to the Lords of Checquar to knaw what landes till apomct for peyment henof, be reafone they knaw nocht nather the names of the lands, nor the valour of the Temd ficheaves of ilk particular town and lands within this realme Thairfor his Hienes, with advys forfaid, ordeans, that ilk Prefbyterie within this Realme, with advys of thrie barrones or landit gentilmen, wha hes thair refidence within the faid prefbyterie, of guid relhgioun, and leift participant of Kuk rents, chofin be advys of the Generall Affemblie, and failyeing of the concurrence of the faids barrones, that the faids Prefbyteries be thamfelues fall haue powar till eftimat reefonabhe the valour of temds, bathe Perfonage and Vicarage, of ilk particular townes and landes lyand within ilk ane of the faids paroches of thair prefbyteries, and of the commodmfies therof to the fuftentatioun of the mmifter Whilk eftimatioun falbe publift vpon twa feuerall Sondayes in tyme of divyne fervice in

2 F

the faid paroche Kirks, with promifioun, that whatfumeuer partie entereft in anie wayes be the faid eftimatioun, and pleife to complean thervpon, fall haift mantt fummar remead, befor the faids Lords of Checquer, efter fummarie cognitioun of the caufe betwix the faid prefbyterie and particulan minifter of the paroche Kirk and generall procutour for the Kirk, or vtheis hauing enteres on the an part, and the faid partie compleaner on t' · vther part

Attour, becaufe the dilapidatioun of the rents of the Kirk hes proceidit for the maift part fra the Kirk men thamfelues, wha haid ower grait libertie to fett fie lang Takes and Fewes, and for fie dewtie as they pleafit, the folemnitie of ordinar Chaptours ferving nocht to retire a the faid dilapidatioun for the quhilk they war fuft inftitut, bot rather to authorife the fam, quhilk Chaptours for the maift part ar now worn away. THERFOR, Our Soueraine Lord, with aduys forfaid, ftatutes and ordeanes, that na minifter or beneficed perfone fall haue powar to fett in tak, or mak anie kynd of difpocitioun, alteratioun or change in anie wayes, the effeat of the locall ftipends of the paroches, with whatfumeuer confent or folemnitie, nather to fett new Taks or to renew auld Takes of whatfumeuer vther Teinds of his Paroche, or of anie part therof, or mak whatfumeuer difpofitioun of the fam in tymes coming, without the confent of the haill or maift part of the Prefbyterie, wherin the paroche lyes, affemblit at their ordinarie day of conveining, efter reafoning twa former ordinarie dayes anent the requitie of the fetting, renewing, or making of the faids Taks and difpo-

fitiounes. And declares that the converting of victuall or vther dewties in filuer, falbe expres diminutioun of the rentall, and a caufe of nullitie or reduction. And for efchewing of antedatting of Takes and rightes of Teinds whatfumeuer, and of the infinit tyme for the quhilk the fam is fett in tyme bypaft, his Hienes, with aduys forefaid, ordeanes, That all and whatfumeuer Taks of whatfumeuer Teinds fett in anie tyme preceiding the dait herof for whatfumeuer langer tyme of manie nynten yeir takes or lyftrents fuccefiue, fall induie onlie for the fpace of nyntein yeirs efter the dait of the faids Taks. Withe promifion, that whattun euer nyntein yeirs Taks or lyffrent of Teinds, quhilk hes nocht begoun in the fettars tyme, falbe null and of nan aveall, albeit an vther nyntein yeir tak or lyffrent continued in that fam Tak hes begoun or run out in the faid fettars tym. And that all former takes of Teinds preceiding the dait herof, lyffrents, affignatiounes, penfiounes, erectiounes, fewes, and vther difpofitiounes of Teinds falbe product befor the Lords of Checquaire before the   day of   nixtocome, and regiftrat in the buiks of the Collectorie. At the leift fa mikle of the faids erectiounes and fewes to be regiftrat as concernes the right of Teinds content therin. And the dait of the regiftratioun therof, and the perfone ingiffar of the faids Taks and vther rights to be regiftrat therwith in lyk maner, and market and fubfcryvit be the Collectour Clark vpon the bak of the faids Taks, and rightes for efchewing of all fraudes quhilk may be herin, withe certificatioun that the Takes and vther rightes of whatfumeuer teinds nocht regiftrat, as faid is, falbe null, and mak na faithe in iudgment nor without. And that the imprenting or publicatioun of this Act, falbe fufficient intimatioun herof, and of the certificatioun forfaid, without anie vther fpeciall Lettres, etc.

MAIROUER, becaufe the minifters and vther beneficed or laic perfones, hauing the right of Teinds of vther menes heritage, oftymes muftbe troubled bathe thamfelues and the lawfull poffefſouis of the faids Teinds, with Inhibitiones and Actiounes of Spuilyie, wherby they compell tham to height thair teinds aboue the reafonable valor, Tharfor Our Soveran Lord, with advys forfaid, declares and ordeanes, that whatfumeuer perfone is lawfulae in the naturall poffeffioun of Teinds be the leading and intromeatting therwith, the heritage or prefent right of poffeffioun of the land being his awin, and makes guid and thankfull peyment within   daves efter ilk term of the dewtie of the faid Teinds, conform to the eftimatioun aboue writtin, to be meid be the Prefbyteries forfaid to the ministers and vthers havmg right to the said Temds, in that cais, the said persone salbe frie of all actioun of Spulyie and danger quhilk may follow vpon inhibitiounes led aganist him theranent. Prouyding alwayes, that whatsumeuer persone committes anie violence in erecting of an vther faith of the naturall possessioun of leadding of Temds, salbe subiect ather to the actioun of Spulyie, or to the quadruple of the estimatioun forsaid, at the optioun of the partie erected, as said is. Lykas also it is prouydit, that whar the right, bathe of the propertie, and present right of the actuall possessioun of the Land, and als of the Teinds concurres in a mans persone, it sall be leisume to him to vse Inhibitiounes, and conform to the auld ordour, apprehend possessioun of his awin temds, payand alwayes the dewtie and valuatioun theirof to the minister, or vthers having right. In the quhilk cais, the offer of the estimatioun forsaid salbe na releuant defence to refeind the naturall possessioun of the Teinds of an vther persones heritage. And to eschew the danger of Spulyie in preiudice of him wha hes the right bathe of the Lands and Temds, as said is, and in fawour of him wha hes na present right to the actuall possessioun of an vther mannes land, nor yit of the Teinds theirof, etc. Attour, be reasone that the said patrimonie of the Kirk sould also sustein and vphauld Scholes and Pure with the comoun esleares of the Kirk and vther godlie vses, Therfor Our Soueran Lord, with advys forsaid, statutes and ordeanes that a perfyt rentall be maid of the superplus of the rents of ilk paroche kirk, by and attoure the forsaids locall stipends, conteining the rightes, be the quhilk the superplus of ilk benefice is presentlie possessit, and that the minister, albeit he be prouydit in tytle to the haill benefice, and haiff the collectione of the haill fructs theirof, and libertie to reduce takes or fewes, as anie vther beneficed persone might haue done of befor, yit the saids ministers sall nocht haue the frie dispositioun of the said superplus to thair awin vse, bot salbe comptable therfor to tham wha sall obtein the right theirof. And in ceas ot than failyie in thankfull peyment, or commit violence, they salbe subiect to the dangers of spulyies duble or quadruple of the estimatioun forsaid, sykyk as vthers that makes nocht peyment thankfullie to the said ministers thamselues, conform to the formar Article.

And as for the said superplus of the rent of ilk particular paroche Kirk, by and attour the locall and perpetuall stipend apointed for the minister, whilk superplus ather presentlie perteines to the Kirk be vacking of the benefice or vtherwayes, or sall heirefter pertein or fall in the Kirks hands, be expyring or reductioun of Taks and vther rightes, deceis of the present possessiours, or vtherwayes whatsumeuer, Our Souerain Lord, with advys foresaid, ordeanes and statutes that the said superplus salbe dispont be the advys of the Lords of Checquar, and brether of the ministerie apointed for modificatioun of ministers stipends. First to the Collages and Lords of Sessioun, and auld possessiours of the benefices induring than lyfftymes, forsamikle as salbe trein fra tham be the present ordoun. Nixt, that the comoun esleares of the Kirk be sufficientlie sustemed theirvpon. Thridlie, that reasonable consideratioun be had of the pure, of strangers, of weidowes and orphelings, reparatioun of brigges, kirks, hospitalles and vther godlie warks. And gif ther be anie rest, the sam salbe collected and keipit to the vse of the kirk, and at thair dispositioun alleanerlie. And whatsumeuer particular persone, collage, or vther sall obtein assignatioun of anie part of the superplus be the saids Lords and modifiers, thair said assignatioun and letters theirvpon salbe specialie in quantitie, and out of what townes and landes the sam is assigned, and the saids letres salbe specialie directed against the tenents and actuall possessiours of the saids particular lands, and the minister of the paroche alleanerlie, fra that na lettres in tyme coming be directed generall against all and sindrie parochiners, etc., and of the best and readiest of the fructs quher the right quhervpon the lettres passes extendes onlie to ane part of the fructs, and nocht to the haill fructs of the paroche, as wes of befor, quhilk was the occasioun of grait confusioun.

7 The l
Sep rplu

8 Distri
Superplu

The con o
of the Kir
Scholles, c
to be prou
the superp
c enil c f r

9 Commissioners from Presbyteries to vott in Parliament.

And becaufe the Prelacies in effect war befor diffolut, the haill temporalities therof being annext to the Croun, and Minifters ftipends ordeanit to be tean out of the paroche kirks vnited and incorporated therwith, lyk as be this ordour the haill fpiritualitie and teinds is of new deftinat, gevin and mortchied to the Kirk, quherby the faids prelacies is allutterlie diffolut, and fa ceiffis in tymes coming to be an of our efteattes in parliament. Therfor our Soueraine Lord, with advys forfaid, ftatutes and ordeanes that in tyme coming, ilk prefbyterie fall fend, of thair awin number, ane Commiffionar to the Parliament, out of the quhilk haill nomber of Commiffionars the reft of the Fifteattes fall chufe fa manie as, being ioyned with the auld poffeffouris of the prelacies quha falbe prefent for the tyme, may mak out the full and complent number of tham wha hes vott in Parliament for the efteat of the Kirk, quhilk number falbe æquall with the number of anie of the vther efteattes. And efter the deceis of the haill prefent poffeffouris of prelacies, the haill number of the Kirks efteat falbe elected, and tean of the faids Commiffionars of Prefbyteries, wha fall haue fic vott, priuileages and liberties in Parliament as the faids prelattes haid of befor, etc.

And to the effect that the rightes of na parties be farder preiudget, Our Soueran Lord, with advys forfaid, Ratifies all actes and ftatutes maid of befor in tawour of the Kirk, in fa far as the fam agrees, or may in anie way fortifie this prefent act. And fpecialie the Act be Secret Countall, Seffioun, and Checquaie, vpon the 14 of Februar, 1587. And in lyk maner all Actes and Statutes maid in tawour of Fewes, Takes, Patronages, Penfiounes, Erectiounes, and vther difpofitionnes of the Kirk rents, in fa far as they ar nocht contrare or anie wayes repugnant to this prefent act, and full executioun therof. Quhilk Actes, togidder with all and whatfumeuer rights perteining to priuat perfones and parties, fic as fewes, promifioun of their benefices, erectionnes, takes, lyffrents, penfiounes, patronages, affignationnes, and difpofitionnes whatfumeuer of the Teinds, fall ftand in the fam force as of befor the making of thir prefents, exceptand planlie in fa far as they ar exprefslie premdgit be the faid locall ftipend to be apointed at euerie particular paroche, conform to the tennour of this prefent Act, and Buik of particular modificatioun to follow thervpon, and vther prouifiouns and reftrictiounes exprefslie conteined herin. Lykas our Soueran Lord, with advys forfaid, abrogates all former lawes, actes, conftitutiounes, practiques, and ordinances whatfumeuer, quhilk may in anie wayes hinder, ftope, or imped this prefent act and full force and executioun therof. And declares whatfumeuer falbe done in the contrar therof, or anie part of it, the ferlyie and controuention falbe tryed, and the right, difpofitioun or vther deid whatfumeuer done contrar to the tennour herof, falbe reducit and annullit, as weill be way of exceptioun, reply, or duply, as be way of actioun. Lykas our Soueran Lord, with advys forfaid, commands that na Judges remit to an actioun, or delay the proponar of the faid nullities be way of exceptioun, reply or duply, bot proceid inftanthe to the tryell of the faid nullitie as faid is.

10 The Moderateing of the locall stipend proportionablie.

Attour, becaufe than is diuers and findrie perfones wha prefenthe brukes the rents of ilk a paroche kirk, Our Soueran Lord, with advys forfaid, ordeanes that the quantitie of the locall and perpetuall ftipends fould be æqualie tean fra ilk an of the faids perfones proportionalie, at the leaft ilk an to releiue vthers proportionalie, according to the fre profit quhilk they receaue of the faids Teinds, at the difcretioun and fummar cognitioun of the faids modifiers, wha falbe onlie iudges herin, and fall try, iudge, and cognos fummarlie vpon the æquitie of the releiff betwix the poffeffouris of the faids Teinds, fic as what ther is an Prelat or auld prouydit man, an or ma Takfmen or penfionars, new erected lordfchipe, with Teinds includit, wich the tewes of lands, tewes of fermes, and whatfumeuer vther varietie thair is of rightes, be the quhilk the poffeffioun of the Teinds of ilk paroche refpectiue brukes the fam. And what releiff the reft aught to mak to tham fra whom immediathe the rightes of the Teinds is tean, quhilk falbe affigned for the perpetuall locall ftipend of ilk paroche Kirk, quherin alfo falbe confidderit the right quhilk our Soueran Lord haid to the

The Kings right at d releiff

thriddes or anie vther partes of the beneficies, togidder with sic vther actionnes for the quhilk his Maiestie might haue chargit the poslessours of the said Teinds. Lykas also the saids Lords of the Checquar, in the making of the said releiff, sall considder immunities and priuilages and rightes quhilk parties haid of befor, and validitie therof, with all vther circumstances ex æquo et bono. And for this effect Our Soueran Lord, with advys forsaid, giffes powar to the saids Lords of Checquar, and Ministers specialie to be apointed, be his Hienes commissioun, being alwayes æquall in number with the saids Lords, to interpret all obscurities, and to decyde summarlie all controuersies, quhilk sall aryse vpon this present act, and vpon the forsaid releiff, betwix all parties subiect therto.

FINIS.

This Plat was thought the best and maist exact that euer was denysit or sett down, and wald, sum litle things amendit, haist bein gladlie receavit be the brethring of best iudgment, gif in the monethe of August 1596, ther haid nocht bein ane Act of Esteattes denysit anent the renewing of the takes of teinds to the present takismen for thair granting to the perpetuall Plat quhilk in effect maid the Teinds in all tyme comming heritable to tham; thir locall stipends and a portioun to the King sett afyde in ilk a paroche. To the quhilk, nather the Kirk, nor gentilmen whase teinds was in vther mens possessioun, could nor wald condissend to. And sa, as I mentioned befor, the cheiff of this wark gaif it ower as a thing nocht lyk to be done in his dayes.

The Generall Assemblie, convenit at Edinbruche in the monethe of Apryll that yeir 1596, be the motioun of sum godlie fathers and guid zealus brething, was almaist haillelie occupied in tryall of thair members and exerceis of repentance and reformatioun of corruptionnes in the office and lyves of the ministerie; and remembering whow the peiple of God vpon diuers occasiones, namlie a grait apprehensioun of thair sinnes and Gods iudgments iminnent therfor, did tak tham to humiliatioun and fasting, and renewing the covenant of mercie and grace with thair God for preventing of his iudgments and continuance of his gratius fauour. As in the plean of Moab, be the motioun and direction of Moses, Deut. xxix and xxx; in the field of Sichem at Silo be Iosua, Jos. xxiv; be Samuel in Mizpa, 1 Sam. vii; at Ierusalem in the hous of the Lord, be Ioiada, ii. Cornicl xxiii, sie lyk in the sam place be Iosia, ii. Kings xxiii; as also be Ezra and Nehemias; they thought it maist neidfull to giff thamselues to the saming, beginning ther presentlie amang the pastors at that Assemblie, and be that exemple to pas to the Synods in euerie prouince, and from tham to the Presbyteries, and sa to euerie Congregatioun in particular. The quhilk, of the grait mercie and blessing of God, was effectuat, the Lord preparing his servants and kirk for a tryall following, be a maist profitable and confortable exerceis going befor, yea, making that tensull invasioun

of the deuill to com on when his feruants war beft fett and maift happche occupied, quhilk giffes me yit afluiance that God will yit in mercie repear the
brakes and decayes of his Jerufalem.   Firft, certean breithing of fcharpeft
and beft infight war fett afyde to pen the enormities and corruptiones of the
miniftene, and the remead therof, the quhilk returnit to the Affemblie, was
hard, confiderit, and allowit.   The tennour in fubftance wharof followes:

THE TENNOUR OF THL ADVISL OF THE BREITHRING DEPUT FOR PENNING OF THF ENOR-
MITILS AND CORRUPTIONS OF THF MINISTRIE, AND REMEAD THEROF
ALLOWIT BE THL GENERAIL ASSLMBLIE, APR. 1596.

Corruptiones in the Office.

FORSAMIKLI as be the over fudden admifhioun and light tryall of perfones that entres in the
miniftene, it comes to pas that manie fklanders falles out in the perfones of minifters, It wald be
ordeannt for remead in tyme coming, that man diligent inquifition and tryall be vfit of all fic perfones as fall enter in the miniftne   As fpecialhe in thir poincts, That the intrant falbe pofit vpon
his confcience in the prefence of God, and that in maift grane manei, what mones him to accept
the office and charge of the miniftne vpon him   If it be a trew mynart motioun and defyre to
terue God and win faulles to Chryft, or warldlie moyen of lyff and preferment: That it be inquyrit gift anie, be fohſtation or moyen directlie or indirectlie, pres to enter in the faid office.   And
it being fund, that the fubftai be repellit, and that the Prefbyterie repell all fic of thair numbei
ira voting in the electioun or admiſhioun as falbe fund moyennars for the folicitar, pofit vpon thair
confcience to declar the treuthe for that effect

Becaufe be prefentationnes manie are intrufit forcible in the miniftne and vpon congregationnes,
that vtters thereftei that they war nocht callit be God, It wald be prouydit that nan feik prefentationnes to benefices without advys of the Prefbyterie within the bounds wharof the benefice lyes
and giff anie do in the contrare to be repelled as rei ambitus

That the tryall of perfones to be admitted to the miniftene heirefter, confift nocht onlie in thair
lerning and abilitie to preitche, bot alfo in confcience and feiling, and fpirituall wefdome, and namlie in the knawlage of the bounds of thair calling in doctrine, difcipline and wefdome, that he may
behaue himfelft accordinglie with the diuers rankes of perfones within his flock, as namlie Atheifts,
rebellius, and thofe that ar vexit with diuers tentationes, and ar weak in confcience, and fic vthei
wherin the paftorall charge is maift kythed, and that he be meit to ſtope the mouthes and convince
the aduerfars   And fic as ar nocht fund qualifeit in thir poincts, to be deleyit till fordai tryall, if
ther be appenance they may be fund qualefiet.   And becaufe men may be meit for fum places that
ar nocht for vther, it wald be confiddent that the principall places of the realme be prouydit be
men of maift worthie gifts, wefdome, and experience, and that nan tak the charge of graitter numbei of peiple nor they ai able to govern; and that this Affembhe tak ordour therwith.

That fic as falbe fund nocht gevin to thair buik and ftudie of Scriptures, nocht cairfull to haue
buikes, nocht gevin to fanctificatioun and prayer, that ftudie nocht to be powerfull and fpirituall in
doctrine, nocht applying the fam to euerie corruptioun, quhilk is the paftorall gift, obfcure and
over fcholaftic befor the peiple, cauld and wanting fpirituall zeall, neglhgent in vifiting of the feik,
and caring for the pure, indiftreit in fchofing of parts of the Word nocht meit for the flok, flatterers,

and diffembling at publict finnes, namlie of grait perfonages in their congregationes for ather flatterie or feir That all fic perfonnes be cenfured according to the degries of thair faults, and if they amend nocht, bot continow thervnto, to be deprivned

That fic as be fleuthfull in the miniftratioun of the Sacraments, and irreuerent profaners thereof, receaving clein and vnclein, ignorant and fcnlles profan, making na confcience of thair profeffioun in thair calling and families, omitting dew tryall and examinatioun or ving light or nan at all, or having in tham tryell refpect of perfones, wharin ther is manifald corruptiones, that all fic be fcharplie rebuked, and if they continow therin, depofit

Giff anie be fund fellars of the Sacraments or colludars with fklanderus perfones in difpenfing and ower feing tham for money, be depofit fimpliciter

. That euerie Minifter be chargit to haue a Seffioun eftablifhed of the mcitteft men in his congregatioun, and that difcipline, ftrik nocht onlie vpon gros finnes, as hurdome, blodfhed etc bot vpon all finnes repugnant to the Word of God, as blafphemie of Gods nam, fwearing in vean, banning, profaning of the Sabathe, difobedience to parents, idle, vmewlie annes without calling, drunkards and fic lyk deboufht men as hes na confcience in thair lyff and rewling of thair families, fpeciallie in bringing vpe of thair bernes, hars, fklanderers, bakbyters, braullars, vncharitable, merciles brakers of promife, &c and this to be an vniuerfall rewll throuchout the realme And fic as be negligent herin, and continow efter admonitioun in thair neghgence, to be depofit.

That ther be a cair in receaving of fic as fall in publict fklander, to fie tham nocht onlie gif outward obedience be confteent, quhilk is the Magiftrats office, bot to find appeirand warrand in confcience of thair trew conuerfioun, finding in tham bathe a feiling of thair fine and apprehenfioun of mercie, and that nocht onlie in that opin fine wherin they ar tean bot in far graitter couered finnes committed againft God, and knawin to him And fa to vfe this occafioun to win the faull throuhe to Chryft be all dihgence in doctrine and exhortation, and namlie of repentance, quhilk nocht being trewlie practifed then, that place is abbufit, and the perfone caften in graitter fin and God maire heilie offendit for publict profanatioun and mockage.

Dilapidatioun of benefices, demitting of tham for fawom or money, that they becom new patronages without the aduys of the Kirk to the wrak therof, fiellyk interchanging of benefices be tranfactioun, and tranfporting of thamfelues be that occafioun without the knawlage of the Kirk precedie to be punifhed Sielyk fetting of fakks, without the confent of the Affemblie, be punifhed according to the Actes, and that the demifhoun in fawours for money or vtherwayes to the effect aboue wryttin be punifhed as dilapidators.

Corruptiones in thair Perfons and Lyfs

That all fic as ar light and wanton in behauiour, as in gorgeus and light apparrell in fpeitche, corrupt communications, morologie, aifchrologie, entrapelie, vfing vean and profan companie, vnlawfull gaming as dancing, carting, diceing and fielyk, nocht befeiming the graniee of a paftor, be fcharplie and grauhe rebukit be the Prefbyterie according to the degrie therof, and continowing therin efter dew admonitioun, that fic be deprivit as fklanderus to the Gofpell

That minifters being fund fwearars or banners, profaners of the Sabbathe, drunkards feghtarguiltie of all this or anie of tham, be depofed fimpliciter and fic lyk leiars, detracters, flatterers, brekers of promife, brawlars, and quarrellars, efter admonitioun continowing therin incur the lyk punifhment.

That Minifters gevin to vnlawfull and incompetent traids and occupationnes for filthie game as haulding of hoftillaries, taking of othar befyd confcience and guid lawes, and bearing wauldlie offices in noble and gentilmens houfles merchandice, bying of victualles, and keiping of tham to the dairthe, and all fic lyk wauldlie occupatiounes as may diftract tham from thair charge, and that may be fklanderus to that paftorall calling, be admonifhed and brought to the acknawlagment of thair finnes and if they continow therin, to be depofit

That Minifters nocht refident at thair flockes be depofit according to the Actes of the Generall Affemblie and Lawes of the Realme, vtherwayes the buiding to be leyed vpon the Prefbyteries, and they to be centured therfor.

That the Affemblie command all thair members, that nan of tham await on the Court and effaires therof without the advys and allowance of thair Prefbyterie   Item that they intend na actioun ciuill without the faid advys, and for remeading of the neceffitie that fum minifters hes to enter in pley of Law, that remead be craunt for fummar and fchort procefles to be vfit in minifters actiones

That minifters tak fpeciall cair in vfing godlie exerceis in thair families, in teatching of thair wyfles, childring, and fervands, va vfing ordinar prayers and reiding of Scriptures, in removing of offenfiue pertones out of thair families, and in lyk vther poincts of godlie connerfatioun and guid exemple   And that they at the vifitatioun of thair Kirks try the minifters families in thir poincts fortud, and fic as ar fund neghgent in thir poincts efter dew admonitioun, falbe adiudgit vnmeit to govern the hous of God according to the rewll of the Apoftle.

That Minifters in all companies thryve to be fpirituall and profitable, and to talk of things pertenning to Godlines, as namlie of all fic as may threinthen in Chryft, inftruct in thair calling, and of the meanes whow to haue Chryfts Kingdome better eftablifhit in congregatiounes, and to knaw whow the Gofpell florifhethe in flockes, the hinderances and remeadies therof, etc wharin and anent than is manifauld corruptiounes bathe in our companeing with ourfelues and vthers.   That the contravemars herof be tryed and fcharplie rebukit

Finalie, If a Minifter be fund to contumance, procure, or affift a publict offendar put at be his awin minifter, and to ben with him, as tho his awin minifter war over feuere vpon him, he be rebuikit, &c.

FINIS

Thir corruptiones and remeads being read in the Affemblie was recommendit to the confideratioun of all the brcithring betwix God and thair confcience, and all war exhorted to prepar thamfelues again the day following to the exerceife of the Word, fafting and prayer, and fa to the actioun of renewing the Couenant

The day following, the haill breithring war affemblit in the Leffar Kirk of Edinbruche, tham alean without the peiple, whar a godlie zelus father, Mr Jhone Daudfone, haid the doctrin and directioun of the actioun being the mouthe of the reft in prayer   His doctrine was vpon the 41, 42, 43, 44, 45, and 46 verfes of the 12 of Luc Evangell : verie plean, particular, and powerfull, in fic fort as the grautie and motion of the man himfelff, with the mightie force of the Word. moued the haill breithring exceidinglie   Efter the quhilk all war directed to thair privat meditationes, confeffioun, and prayer a large fpace ; efter the quhilk the forfaid mouthe maid publict confeffioun and deprecatioun, during the quhilk tyme teares war fhed aboundanthe. Thereftei the Moderator declaring the purpofe and end of the actioun, as he teares and countenance of the brething vnfenyit forow and humiliatioun was teftified, fa he defyrit that be the lifting vpe of thair haudes they fould fignifie the defyre and refolution quhilk they haid of amendment of all bypaft finnes, in commiffioun or omiffioun, againft God and dewtie in thair office and perfones, promifing, be his grace, an erneft indeuour for the fam ; and fa a entring of new againe in Covenant with than God in Jefus Chryft, the grait paftor of the faulles and Mediator of the Covenant, &c. Efter the quhilk, prayer being maid be the Moderator for obteining of grace, and working of the Spreit for that effect, the bleffing was pronuncit, and the actioun endit, quhilk lafted about the fpace of thrie houres and man.

The Coufnant renewed in the Synod of Fyff, 12 May 1596

In the fourt feffioun therof, anent the making of a new Covenant betwix God and his Minifterie within this realme, ordeanit in the laft Generall Affemblie to be done in euerie Synodall throuchout the land, the prefent Affemblie of Fyff, apprehending the weghtines, tending ather to an effectuall reformatioun of all things amis, (fa far as can ly in the waiknes of man,) in the paftors firft, and fyne in thair flockes, or then to involue all in a mair feirfull giltmes and danger of horrible judgment, be fealling vpe a new and maift graue teftimonie and witneffing againft all, thought it maift neidfull that all meanes fould be vfit that might moue and fteir vpe the hartes of the breithring to an erneft confideratioun and feilling of thair vndewtifulnes and tranfgreffiones in thair offices, families, and perfones, to bring tham to a trew humiliatioun, forrow and greiff therfoi, to a plean confeffioun of the fam in the prefence of God, a cearfull feiking of mercie for Jefus Chryfts feak, an avowing and promifing of amendment in tyme to come, be the affiftance and mair effectual working of the Spreit of Grace, and a vehement folifting of God be prayer for that effect. And fa caufit firft to reid in the publict audience of the Affemblie, diftinctlie, the Articles of Reformatioun fett down in the laft General Affemblie, the quhilks war ordeanit to be infert in the Buik of the Synod, and euerie Prefbyterie commandit to haiff the copie therof in than buiks, and to caufe euerie an of thair members to extract to tham felff a copie therof for thair remembrance. Nixt, for preparatioun of the hartes, ordeanit the

Paftor of the place, Dauid Fergufone, to keipe his awin place and houie of doctrine the day following, and fludie to fram his doctrin for the purpofe; and be the vottes of the maift part, all maid chois of Mr Dauid Blak to teatche the nixt day therefter, to be keipit with preceife abftinence. Immediathe efter the quhilk doctrine, the haill breithring fould convein in the place of the Affemblie for the folem renewing of the faid Couenant; and in the mean tyme, erneft exhortatioun was maid be the Moderator to wey the mater and wark they war about maift deiphe, and ernefthe with than God in thair confidence, with meditation of the forfaid poincts of Reformatioun, and rememberance of that curs vpon fie as does the Lords wark neghgenthe and deceatfullie Alfo to call to God ernefthe for the breithring apointed to deall in doctrine.

Sa vpon the 13 day of May, being Furifday, efter the doctrin delyuerit be Mr Dauid Blak, vpon the ground, the 13 chap of Ezecq. and laft vers of the 5 Pfalme, the quhilk was copius, powerfull, percing and pertinent, the breithring of the Minifterie, and Commiffionars of euerie paroche prefent, haillelie and immediathe convening in the place of the Synodall, the Moderator, for the better difpofing of the harts, and exemple of ordourlie proceiding in the actioun, red the laft chaptour of the buik of Jofua, wherin Jofua, calling togidder the heades and rewlars of the peiple, recomptes the benefites of God beftowit vpon tham, and fettes the faid rewlars and heades of the peiple to advyfiment, Whidder they war refolut and vprighthe meined to ferue that God in vprightnes and treuthe, vtherwayes to leaue af anie profeffioun of his fervice, and tak tham to Idolatrie; and fa efter diuers demands, and anfwers gevin be the peiple, he fettes down the Contract and Couenant in forme, and regifters the fam in the buik of the Law, and fetts vpe a ftan vnder an ake trie, in a monument therof for a memorandum in all tyme to come. The quhilk exemple and form was followed poinct be poinct Firft, be commemoration of the benefites of God beftowit on the Kirk of Scotland in planting and gairding the fame from the Caftalians, Obenittes, Spaniarts, Bifchope Balaam, and lait confpiracie of the papift Erles. The quhilk being endit, and a lytle begoun to be fpokin of vnthankfulnes and vndewtifulnes in caring trewlie and ernefthe over that wark of God, and watching over the flockes of Chryft committed to the paftors charge, and over the quhilk the Lord haid fett tham fa lang with fic libertie and eafe, the Lord fteirit vpe fic a motioun of hart, that all war forcit to fall down befor the Lord, with fobbes and teares in aboundance, euerie man mightelie conmouit with the affectionnes of thair con-

fcience in the prefence of thair God, in privat meditatioun rypping out than
wayes, confefling and acknawlaging thair vnworthines and craving erneftlie
grace for amendment, and that a lang fpace

Efter the quhilk, the hartes being fattcht, the Moderator, as comoun mouthe
of all, at grait launthe maid open confefiioun of vnthankfulnes, forgettfulnes
vndewtifulnes, negligence, and caldnes, hardnes of hart. darknes, fenflefnes,
inftabilitie, vanitie of mynd, ftubburnes and rebellioun in will, foulnes and vn-
cleinnes in affectionnes, vndantoned feritie in pertubationes, vnfauonnes and
folie in fpeiche, and of converfatioun facioned efter the warld, cafehar and
man reddehe drawin efter the maners and cuftome therof from God, then
having force of holines and of the fpicit in word and actioun to draw the
peiple from thair vean converfatioun to God, and the feiking of thair lyff and
faluatioun :   And finalie, with trimbhng and maine teares for the offence of
fa guid and gratius a Lord and Father, mifufing of fa grait and honourable
a calling, and quakking for feir of fic a weght of wrethe hinging on for the
blud of fa manie faulles lying on our heids, we all bitterhe weipit and erneftlie fought for a blefling and grace to vfe the prefent occafioun of the grait
mercie and lang fuffering of God grantit to ws righthe and fathfulhe for
amendment.

Efter the quhilk confeffioun, the Moderator, entering again to deall in doc-
time vpon the dialogifme or conference of Jofua with the eldais and rewlars
of the peiple, and firft, infifting firm what vpon the reiecting of the confent
as a thing impoffible to tham to ferue God, wha was hohe, angrie, and idling,
to mak the breithring try out than awin finceritie and vpright mening of
thair hart, he refoluit the dout of impoffibilitie, and the greifl of experience
of relapfe, fchowing that the graiteft perfectioun we can attem vnto in this
lyff is to ken and feill our awin imperfectioun, and ftryve and labour againft
the faming in treuthe and vprightnes of hart ; abfteining from all things that
may quench the fpreit, and cearfull vfing of all that may ften vpe the fam.
fending all vnto Chryft Jefus, the guid and gratius paftor, and to his fulnes
and perfectioun.

Nixt, vpon the thrid confent of the peiple, and reply of Jofua, commanding
tham to caft away thair Idolles, the Moderator infifted erneftlie vpon the
cafting away of our Idolles, that is, all thefe things of this warld wharof we
tak mikle thoucht, and wharin oftentymes we tak mair pean, and delytes
mair nor in God, his fervice, or our calling ; fchawing that it was our part in
this Contract and Covenant, to giue ourfelues haillehe to ferue the Lord in

treuthe, vprightnes and fidelitie. And the part of God was to be our God, to keipe ws from all euill, and prouyde for ws all things guid for ws ; the quhilk his part he wald, but dout, fulfill aboundanthe, if we haid a cair of our part. But alas ! whill as forgetting our part, and leaving it vndone, we tak on the part of God, caring for prouifion defence and preferuatioun of ourfelffs, we fall in infidelitie and diftruft of him, yea and in proude idolatrie, placing our- felues and moyens of this warld in the roum and dignitie of God Almightie. etc

And fa, etter diuers vther poincts of doctrine, admonitiones, and exhorta- tiones, for the purpofe, be lifting vpe of the hand, euerie an teftified befor God, and mutualie an to an vther, the finceare and erneft purpofe of the hart to ftudie till amend and ferue God better in tyme to come, bathe in thair priuat perfones and in the office of that grait minnftene of Gods honour and faluation of the peiple concredit to thame, etc

And laft, the Moderator fpak vpon thefe words, " You ar witneffes this day againft yourfelffs,' etc. and anent the monument of the ftean fett vnder the ake, and the wreitting of the Couenant in the buik of the Law, preiffing to imprent and ingraue in the harts of the breithring and his awin, the remem- berance of this Covenant, that it fould nocht be forgot, and maid irrit, and of na effect (quhilk was ottymes caft vpe to the peiple of Ifraell be the prophetes thereftei), declaring whow the Lord God haid our awin confciences to bear witnes againft ws, out of the quhilk the memoriall of this actioun fould nocht be deleit : he haid his angelles and all his creatouns ; he haid that fam place, yea the verie pillars of ftean ftanding in that kirk, lykas by than awin con- fent this minut and foum of the haill actioun fould be infeit and regiftrat in the buik of the Synodall Affemblies, ther to remean for our admonitioun and rememberance during our tyme, and for example to the pofteritie.

Therefter the Moderator, remembering of the defectioun mentioned foone etter the deathe of Jofua, and the fathers and eldars that haid fem the warks of God in than dayes, for preventing of the lyk defectioun, and faftning of this new Covenant the mair firmlie in the hart, for that effect, of all the breith- ring of finaller age, requyrit certean fathers, godlie and zealus breithring thair prefent, to fpeak as thay haid fem, hard and helpit to do in the grait wark of God, in planting and preferuatioun of the Gofpell and libertie of Chryftes Kingdome, trewlie and finceihe within this land.

And fa Dauid Fergufone, paftor of Dunfermnlhng, a reuerend father, fpak verie pleafandlie and contortablie of the beginning and fucces of the minifterie ; namhe whow that a few number, viz onlie fax, wharof he was an, fa mightelie went fordwart in the wark, but feir or can of the world, and prenaht, when ther was na name of ftipend haid tell of ; when the authoritie bathe ecclefiaftik and cnull opponit themfelues, and fkarfhe a man of name and eftimatioun to tak the caufe in hand, etc   But now it was fallen to that the feir or flatterie of men, cair of getting, or lothnes of lofing, of ftipend and moyen of lyff, haid weakned the harts of a multitud of minifters, etc —ioyning thervnto exhortatioun meit for the purpofe.

Mr Jhone Daudfone, a zealus graue father, directed from the Generall Affemblie to vifit our Synodall, followit, and fpak verie mouinglie and profitabhe. faying, That as the fathers of the peiple of the Jewes, efter thair retoun from Babylon, luking vpon the building of the new repearit Temple, and comparing it with the facioun of the auld that they haid fein, weipit bitterlie ; even fa was he movit when he beheld the prefent eftat of our Knk in the perfones and converfatioun of the minifterie and profeffours, and conferrit the fam with the beginning that he haid fein, being fa vnlyk in godlines, zeall, grauitie, loue and hartlines, ftoutnes, cair and peanfulnes, mightines and powar of doctrin, etc with erneft admonitiounes and graue exhortatiounes moving the breithing to indewoui to find the fructs of that dayes wark, etc   He mennt alfo mikle the want of lerning in the minifterie, having fa guid educatioun, and fa grait tyme and occafioun of letters and knawlage, that yit he could fkarfhe meit with an, that could talk or reafone in an exact and lerned maner of hard places of Scripture or controuerfit queftionnes ; or that could fhaw takens of reidding of antient doctors of the knk, or the hiftorie therof, ioyning the precept of the Apoftle, Attendite lectiom, etc.

Mr Patrik Simfone, Minifter of Sterling, being prefent with the faid Mr Jhone, and ioynit with him in commiffioun from the Generall Affemblie, requyrit be the Moderator fpak verie halelie and weill anent a poinct of Reformatioun, viz. of the mouthes of the minifters quhilk fould be the Oracle of God, whafe lippes fould keipe knawlage, and at whafe mouthes the Law of the Lord fould be fought as the Meffingers of the Lord of hofles, as fayes the prophet.   And yit to be fa comounlie and openlie defylit and abufit with foolifhe, vean gefting and vnfauorie fpeitches and talk, evin at tables in open audience, fchowing an vnclem and vnfanctifeit hart, cearles of the honour of God, and ædificatioun of his peiple.

Vther breithring alfo being requyrit in generall as God gave it, and movit thair harts to continow that maift profitable and confortable exerceife for leaving of a deipe ftampe of the actioun in the harts of the breithring.   Mr

Dauid Blak, an of the paftors of St Andros, fpak of the dekey and falling
abak of relligioun, finceritie, zeall, and vprightnes quhilk he haid efpyit, being
yit bot a fchollar in St Andros, be the default and warldlie and vnfpirituall
behauiour of tham that fucceidit in the minifterie and rewling of the Vniuerfitie, vnto thefe godlie and vpright men that preceidit tham : That the greiff
therof haid bein giait in his hart during his abyding out of the countrey, except fa far as he haid haird of Mr Andro Meluin, and returning in the countrey he haid fund the fam falling to almaift a remediles miferie, and yit haid
bein thruft in be God and his Kirk in that roum, and fa fchawing his inde-
uous wiflit the concurrance of the breithring and helpe of thair prayers; exhorting verie powerfullie euerie an till attend vpon thair awin charge in a new
manner, according to the doctrin delyverit be the laft Moderator, repeated
againe be himfelff that day, and now promifit and adwowit folemlie to be
obfervit and preffit vnto be all and euerie an of the breithring in this prefent
actioun, etc.

Mr Andro Meluill, Rector of the Vniuerfitie of St Andros, followit furthe
the fam purpofe, and infifting on the feir of defectioun, warnit the breithring
of a lait experience of a giait waiknes and flyding away, when the holie difcipline was perfecut and fought to be overthrawin; whow maine, for feir of
the want of thair ftipend onlie, war brought to a fort of denying of Jefus
Chryft be fubfcryving to the wicket Actes of Parliament in the yeir 1584,
wharby the libertie of his throne and kingdome was intendit to be vtterlie
fubuerted   What fould be luiked for then gif the Spainyards, wha haid leat-
lie takin Calis, fra quhilk in few houres they might eafelie tranfport tham
felues to this Yland, yea in our awin Futhe, he fould effay our conftancie
with fyne and exquifit torments of than Inquifitioun, vpon the quhilk piece of
fervice our excommunicat forfaultit papift Erles war attending.   Wherby he
mightelie exhorted all the breithring to tak heid to thamfelues, and fixt the
doctrin quhilk they haid haird that day, and this prefent actioun and Covenant in thair memories, and till vfe fathfullie this guid occafioun of reft and
libertie that God fa giatiuflie geves, to be maimit and preparit againft the day
of tryall, quhilk was nocht far of

Thir fpeitches endit, efter treating and finifing of vther incident maters,
erneft prayer was powred out be the Moderator for getting of grace to remember, practife and pey the wowes ther maid, and efter hairtie thankgiffing for
that memorable benefit of God, the Affemblie was dimiffed about four etter
noone, als full of fpirituall ioy in the faull, as emptie of corporall fuid, euerie

brother with exceiding grait gladnes glorifeing God for that actioun aboue all vther that euer they haid bein partakers of : To whom onlie be all praise and honour for euer   AMEN.

THE COUENANT RENEWIT IN THE PRESBYTERIE OF ST ANDROSE.

Vpon the penult Fuirsday of the monethe of July, 1596, the Covenant was renewit in the Presbyterie of St Andros, be a verie frequent Assemblie of gentilmen and burgesses, prepared for the purpose befor be thair ministers in euerie paroche; wherin, as the Synod befor, sa the Presbyterie appointed me the comoun mouthe, keiping the form sett down before as neir as might be. The generall heides of the exhortatioun war these :

The Covenant of God is the contract, securitie, and warrand of all our weilfear, maid with Adam efter his fall, renewit with Noe efter the flud, then with Abraham, etc.

This Covenant is broucht to rememberance, and sa in a maner renewit as often as the Word is pretched, the Saciament vsit, or exerceis of fasting and publict repentance keipit

Bot in a speciall maner it hes bein vsit amangs the peiple of God, efter a grait threatning and appeirance of manie plagges, and grait danger for sinne and vnthankfulnes, sic as hes bein espyed be the Siers and Watchmen in this land, wha therfor hes begoun at thamselues in thair Generall and Synods.

The maner therof is first : To try the brakes of the Covenant of God maid with ws, in the privat persone of euerie an, in thair families, in nibourhead, and in discharge of publict offices in Kirk and Comoun weill : 2. In acknawlaging and confessing the sam with vnfenyit sorow and repentance : 3. In craving mercie for the Mediator of this Covenant his seak, with trew fathe beleiving in him : And last, in taking ernest purpose, and making promise and vowes of amendment, with a faithfull endewour of keiping and peying of the sam in all the lyff therefter.

The Covenants of Ezra and Nehemia, whilk they maid with the peiple efter thair retourn from Babylone, quhilk with fasting and prayer war maid, wryttin, sealled, and sworn, was read distinctlie, and conform to these heads, doctrin, and exhortatioun vsit; and efter meditatioun in privat and publict prayer, be haulding vpe of hands, thir promises and vowes war maid in speciall, for testefeing of a trew conuersion and change of mynd. 1. The exerceise of reiding the Word with prayer and thankfgeving, and catecheising of child-

ing and fervants to be vfit and done be the father of euerie famlie ordinarlie within the fam   2. The refifting of all enemies of relligioun, without feir
or fawour of anie perfone. 3 The planting of the miniiterie of Gods honour,
and faluatioun of the peiple within than paroches, beftowing coft theron to
thair abiltie, and feiking the Kirk dewties to be recouerit for that effect. 4 To
tak ordour with the pure that thair be nocht vagabund beggars.   5 To keipe
better publict conventiones, and difcharge offices and comoun dewties for the
weill of Kirk and Countrey : And laft, to tak cair of comoun warks, namlie of
the ftanding and repearing of brigges. Sa efter prayer to God for grace to per-
torm, left vnto all the formar tranfgreffiounes the giltines of horrible periurie
was adioyned, to haften the extremitie of iudgment, etc. the action endit

Efter the quhilk, the fpeciall barrones and gentilmen convenit with ws in
the place whar the Prefbyterie fittes, whar be confeience, vnderftanding that
thei was grait word and appenrance of invafioun of Spainyeards, and that the
excommunicat forfaulted papift Erles war com ham quietlie, the gentilmen
offerit thamfelues verie frache for refiftance, and named thair capteanes of
horfmen and futmen, and fett down in ordour anent thair armour and prouifioun ; wharof it was thought guid the King fould be aduertifed, to whom
for that effect the Laird of Renas and I war directed, bot war nocht takin
weill withe, and thei was an vther degrie of decay of my Court, for the King
haid determined to bring ham the papift Lords again, and lyked of nan that
wald nocht wag as the bus waggit.

*A Soum of the Doctrine of the Couenant renewit in the Kirk of Scotland, and namlie within
the Prouince of Fyff, and in the Congregatioun of Kilrunny, the fyft of Sept.
1596 , fet down in maner of Confeirence for the vfe of the Peiple.*

M. Thow henes that God hes movit the watchmen and fathfull paftours of the Kirk of Scotland and this Prouince of Fyff beginning at thamfelues to call and labour to moue all to a tryall
of the biak of his Couenant, and an exerceife of renewing of the faming   What does thow think
and efteim of the Couenant of God ?

P I think and efteim of the Couenant of God, as the onlie euident, right, fecuritie and warrand
of all my weilfear.

M Whartor fa ?

P. Becaufe it is the contract, band, and obligatioun wharbe God binds and oblefes himfelff to be
my louing God and Father in Chryft, fa as therby I am fure to want na guid thing, and to be
keipit from all evill.

M What war thy ceas and efteat if thow wanted this warrand ?

P Even that maift miferable efteat of Nature, without God, without Chryft, a chyld of wrathe, alian from the Comoun weill of his peiple, vnder the flauerie of the Deuill and Sinne, and, finalie, a faggot of helles fyre.

M. What is then the fubftance and tennour of this Covenant?

P God obleſes himſelff of his fie grace to be my God and father in his Sonne Jefus Chryſt and I with the reſt ar bound to be his fervants and childring.

M. Wha hes moyenned this Contract and Covenant, and knit it vpe betwix God and thie and his peiple?

P. The onlie Mediator and Reconcylar my Lord Jefus Chryſt, and that be his awin pretius blood, and bitter paſhoun and deathe.

M. And what is the conditioun on thy part, whaiby thow maybe kend his fervand and chyld in Chryſt?

P. Git I embrace this promife of Gods grace and benefeit of the bliffed Covenant (purchaſſit be Jefus Chryſt) be a new fathe, and teſtifie the fam in loue, halines, and obedience.

M. I perceaue then the Contract is mutuall, fa that God is nocht bund to thie, gif conditioun be nocht keipit on thy part. What then gif thow hes broken? Is nocht the Contract diſſolued, and maid to thie of na ſtead, force, or effect?

P. Yes in verie deid, gif God ſould enter in iudgment with ws, and deall ſtreathe and preceiſlie according to his iuſtice and right.

M And what ſould then becom of thie?

P. Even to be caſt away in the former miferie and condemnatioun with the deuilles, and that fa mikle the mair, as we ar become fathles and mean ſworn, brakers of his halie mutuall band and covenant

M Thow then, tell me, hes thow enterit in this Covenant with God? and hes thow compromitted with him according to the tennour of this Contract and mutuall band?

P. Yes indeid I haue, or then I war maiſt miferable.

M When enterit thow therin?

P Even when I was firſt baptifed, and hes profeſſit the fam ny fen I cam to anie wit or knawlage, be giffing confeſhoun of my fathe, and vſing of the Holie Supper.

M. And hes God keipit his part to thie?

P. Bleſſed be his holie nam and heavinlie Maieſtie, for he hes bein alwayes to mie a gratius God and bountifull lowing father

M But what hes bein thy part againe to him?

P. Alas! I haue broken and tranſgreſſed maiſt vnthankfulhe, finning fearlie at all tymes againſt my guid God, my nibour, and my awin faull. And fa if he fould deall with me in iudgment according to his right, I can haue na fecuritie or wairande of weilfear to produce, bot man cloſe my mouthe and contes I ly maiſt miferablie vnder danger of Gods wrathe, and all his pleagges and iudgments, temporall and eternall

M. Now, what if God might be moued to forget and remit all bygeans, and enter in a new covenant and contract with thie, wald thow nocht be glade to embras he grace?

P O! with all my hart, bot whow fall that be?

M. Gift thow erneſtlie repent thy finnes bypaſt, tak vpe a fectfull purpofe of amendment, with a faithfull promife and vow of the fam vnto the Lord by his grace for the tyme to come, and by aſſurit fathe clerue to the Lord Jefus in whom is all holines and perfectioun.

P. That is daylie crauit of ws be the Word of God, vfe of the holie facraments, and often tymes in the exerceife of faſting and publict repentance.

2 H

M. Treuthe indeid, for the Covenant and purpofe is all an and the fam Bot becaufe dayhe we break, it haird neid dayhe to be renewed to ws, and nimhe efter a lang fparing and large bountifulnes of God and manie toull finnes and grait vnthankfulnes, tending to an vtter defectioun from God, and procuring of the extremitie of his wrathe and iudgments. When God wotchaffes then, as he mait mercifullie does at this tyme, to call ws, be his fervants the watchmen, to the renewing of the Covenant, that he may vit defer his plagges, and continow his mercifull guidnes toward ws, fould we nocht be glaid therof, and indenour ourfelues with all cair and reuerence to meit the Lord offering mercie and grace ?

P Now the God of mercie grant we may fa do, and work in my hart in fpeciall be his Halie Spreit for that effect. Bot alas ' I have fett mytelfi oftentymes to repent, and promifed and advowit amendment with myfelfi, bot could never attein to the performance, and therfor, I feir I fall do na vther thing at this tyme bot involue myfelfi in a new giltines of meinfwearing and brak of promife

M. Gift thy hart be vpright and trew toward God, and if thow find anie erneft defyre of amendiment, with a laboring ftryving, and preaffing thervnto, whowbeit thow can nocht attein to that thow wald, fen nocht, for God requyres nocht perfectioun of ws in this lyfi, quhilk he knawes we can neuer attein vnto, becaufe he will nocht gift it. Wha is the God of ordour that hes apointed a tyme of feghting and a tyme of triumphing, a tyme of foiourning and wandring, and a tyme of habitatioun and dwelling, and finalie, a tyme of warfling and fuffering hein, to mak us conform to Chrift, that we may heireftei ring with him in glorie Therfor, heir we haue to ftryve againft our awin imperfectiones, and againft his enemies and ours, the deuill, the warlde, and fleche, and be trew fathe to cleue to that perfectioun of his Sone the Lord Jefus Chrift our Sauiour, in whom he is weill appleafit, and of whofe perfectioun he will accept of as ours, for Chryft is the Cautionar of the Covenant and Contract for ws, and fa principall deattei, taking the fam vpon him to fatifie in all what we ar vnable Onlie remember this, whar Chryft dwelles in the hart be fathe, then is a continuall grouthe and progres in knawlage and halines during this lyfi, quhilk hes the awin perfectioun in the lyfi to come, fulfilled euen in ws be the quickning fpreit of Chryft, working then without all contradictioun, impediment or ftay.

P O! that effhayes aie mainft of all, for alas ' I find na grouthe or going fordwart, bot rather a decay and bak turning

M Surlie, it thow be the chyld of God, thow mon grow vpe to the iuft ftature of a perfyt man in Chryft, and be lyk the pleafand plants in the Lords oitchyeard Bot tak heid I pray thie, whom God fa difpofes and moues (for ther is nocht monie of that fort,) as it is weill done to think na thing of thyfelfi, fa be war till extenuat the grace of God and working of his Spreit, quhilk fould be alwayes acknawlagit with thankfull hartes to his praife For it is in that poinct with the godlie in fpirituall giftes, as with the waildhngs in temporall, that an thinks litle or na thing of that quhilk they haue atteined to and gotten, bot ay wald be at fordar and mair, and fa does that vther Alfo ther wilbe a decey in appeirance for a fardei grouthe, and a grouthe quhilk will nocht be perceavit, vnles it be narowlie luked vnto, even as in the tries and plantes in the wintar feafone, quhilk nochtwithftanding the canld troft and fnaw, having the iutt faft in the ground, is euer growing ather within or without the eide, in hight, graitnes or fum way, yea, and that quhilk is farder in the Elect of God, comonnlie ther is graitter grouthe and going fordwart when they think and feilles leift, and leift when they feill and think mainft; for, but queftion, then ar we beft in Gods fight and eftimatioun when we ai warft in our awin and contrar. And feilling is na fure rewell of fathe, for we will feill mair a whittell in our fingar, nor the helthe of the haill body. Yet for treuthe, the man felling of the foarces of finne, the grattei mifloure of grace, for it is by grace that we can feill finne fan   Aflure thyfelff, therfor, of a guid cais it thow find that feillmg, yea, or the forow for want therof, with defyre to haue it, for that is nocht of fleche and bluid, bot of the fprett of grace, quhilk can work bathe the will and deid in that mifloin that he knawes meit for thie, with the quhilk be content

P. Weill, Sir, I thank God with all my hart, of your confortable inftruction, wherby I am brought to be weill refoluit to indeuour myfelff in this actioun, befeikand vow alfo to fchaw me whow I fall proceid therinto.

M. Fuft, be preparatioun trauehng comfulhe to try and find out thy finnes and tranfgreffiones of Gods hohe law   Nixt with an feillng difpofitioun in remorfe and forow for the finnes committed, crauing mercie and forgiftnes therof, and with a fecefull purpofe promifing be his grace till amend I hindlie, in trauehng for fruict efter the actioun, be marking thefe finnes in fpeciall quhilk maift greiues thy confcience, or thow knawes to be offenfiue to the godlie, and indeuoring but delay to amend the fam.

Anent all the quhilk thow wilbe at lynthe inftructed in the doctrine quhilk God of mercie fall witchaft to grant for that effect, and therfor pray emeftlie to God to grant giftes to his fervants of knawlage, feillng and vtterance to delyver, and to thyfelfl, and the reft of the peiple, grace to receaue the fam with light of vnderftanding, and cair to practife

Now the grauus Lord, for Jefus Chryft his Sonnes feak, be thair Holie Sprett of grace mot work it in ws all AMEN.

Thus was our peiple catechifed the haill monethe of Auguft, and vpon the firft Sabbathe of September, the Covenant with the hohe communion celebrat to thair grait confort.

And as efter all our faftes (quhilk I haiff pretermitted in this Storie, becaufe I haue wraitten a fpeciall Treatife therof,) fa efter this exercefe we wanted nocht a remarkable effect.   For if God hand nocht extraordinarlie prouydit for Scotland victualles, (coming in fic ftore and aboundance out of all vther countries, as never was fein in this land befor, fa that, be the æftimatioun of the cuftomers and men of beft iudgment, for euerie mouthe that was in Scotland ther cam in at leaft a boll of victuall), thowfandes hand died for houngar ; for nochtwithftanding of the infinit number of bolls of victuall that cam ham from vther partes, all the herveft quarter that yeir, the meall gaue aught, nyne, and ten pound the boll, and the malt alleavin and twoll, and in the fouthe and waft partes manie died

I dar nocht bot mark it, whowbeit againft my will, that the Minifters of Edinbruche and Kirk therof, neglected and omitted this actioun of the Covenant, with the effect of a feirfull defolatioun, gif we daur iudge

About the end of Auguft the King calles a Conventioun of the Efteattes to Falkland, euen of fic as be fauour and frindfehipe wai neireft ioyned with the excommunicat, forfaultit papift Erls, whar Alexander Setoun, Prefident of the

Seffioun, a papift, maid a prepared harang, wharby to perfwade the King and
Efteattes to call hame thefe Erles, left, lyk Coriolanus the Roman, or Themif-
tocles the Athenian, they fould ioyne with the enemies, and creat an vnrefift-
able danger to the efteat of the countrey Diuers of the minifterie wai wraitten for to that Conventioun, bot fic as the King knew he could mak. But
Mr Andro vnderftanding therof, and being a Commiffionar apointed be the
Generall Affemblie to fie to the dangeis of the Kirk at all occafiones, cam
thither, and prefented himfelff with the reft. Whom when the King faw, he
fend to him, afking of his earand and willing him to go hame , bot he faid
he haid a commiffioun fiift to difchaige in Gods nam and the Kirks, to the
King and Efteattes

When the King and Efteattes wai fett doun, the King cauffes the Minifteis
to be callit vpon be nam and lettin in, leaving out Mr Andro, who cam in
with the formaift The King finding fault with him that cam ther vncallit.
he anfwers, " S¹, I haue a calling to com heir be Chryft Jefus the King, and
his Kiik, wha hes fpeciall entres in this toun, and againft quhilks diiect-
lie this Conventioun is mett; charging yow and your Efteattes in his nam,
and of his Kirk, That yie fawour nocht his enemies whome he hattes, nor go
nocht about to call hame and mak citizeners. thefe that hes trateroufhe fought
to betrey thair citie and natiue countrey to the crewall Spainyard, with the
overthrow of Chryfts Kingdome, fia the quhilk they haue bein therfor maift
nufthe cutt of as rotten members, certifeing, if they fould do in the contrair,
they fould feil the dint of the wrathe of that King and his Efteattes " And
braking on in particular vpon the graittelt part of that Conventioun, with
plane fpeitche and mightie force of zeall, he challengit tham of hiche treafone
bathe againft Chryft and the King, againft the Kiik and Countrey of Scotland,
in that purpofe and counfall they war about Bot the King interrupted him,
and commandit him to go out, whafe command he obeyit, thanking God that
they haid knawin his mynd, and gottin his meffage difchargit Mr Dauid
Lindfay, Mi James Nicolfone. Mr Patrik Galloway, and I, that remeanit and
hard all, and fpak in the contrar, and adhering in effect to that quhilk Mr
Andro haid vtteied, bot in fic fort, that the King with fear promifes fatiffeit
over cafelie and removit. In end, the Efteattes concludes, that the King and
Kirk being fatiffeit, it war beft to call tham hame, and that his Maieftie fould
heir thair offeries for that effect

In the monethe of September following, the Commiffionars of the Generall
Affemblie, with diuers vther guid breithring, conveinit in Cowper, and vnder-

ſtanding certeanlie of the retourn of the papiſt Lords. and of thair plattes purpoſes, and biſſines, with thair fauorars and aſſociattes, thought guid to direct certean of the breithring thair preſent to the King being in Falkland, to mein the mater to him, and craue a diſcharge of his dewtie, namlie that ſeing without his licence and knawlage, as was certefeit to the Kirk be his Maieſties Miniſters, theſe rebelles was com ham, and war about to mak inſurrectioun in the countrey, ther dangerus indewous ſould be matu he prevented be his Maieſtic, his authoritie and powar. Alſo that ther ſould be a meitting again of the breithring in Edinbruche the monethe October following

Sa Mrs. Andro Melnill, Patrik Galloway, James Nicolſone, and I, cam to Falkland, whar we ſand the King verie quyet. The reſt leyed vpon me to be ſpeaker, alleaging I could propone the mater ſuſtantiuſlie, and in a myld and ſmothe maner, quhilk the King lyked beſt of. And entering in the Cabinet with the King alan, I ſchew his Maieſtie, That the Commiſſionars of the Generall Aſſemblie, with certean vther breithring ordeanit to watche for the weill of the Kirk in ſa dangerus a tyme, haid conveint at Cowper At the quhilk word the King interrupts me, and crabbothe quarrels our meitting. alleaging it was without warrand and ſeditius, making ourſelues and the countrey to conceaue feir what ther was na cauſe. To the quhilk, I beginning to reply in my maner, Mr Andro doucht nocht abyd it. bot brak af vpon the King in ſa zealus, powerfull, and vmeſiſtible a maner, that whowbeit the King vſed his authoritie in maiſt crabbit and colerik maner, yit Mr Andro bure him down and outtered the Commiſſioun as from the mightie God, calling the King bot " Gods ſilhe vaſſall," and taking him be the ſleiue, ſayes this in effect, throw mikle hat reaſoning and maine interruptiones : " Sr, we will humblie reuerence your Maieſtie alwayes, namlie in publict, but ſen we haue this occaſioun to be with your Maieſtie in privat. and the treuthe is, yie ar brought in extream danger bathe of you lyſſ and croun, and with yow the Countrey and Kirk of Chryſt is lyk to wrak, for nocht telling yow the treuthe. and giffen of yow a fathfull counſall, we mon diſcharge our dewtie therin. or els be trators bathe to Chryſt and yow. And therfor, Sir, as diuers tymes befor, ſo now again I mon tell yow, ther is twa Kings and twa Kingdomes in Scotland. Thair is Chryſt Jeſus the King, and his kingdome the Kirk. whaſe ſubiect King James the Saxt is, and of whaſe kingdome nocht a king. nor a lord, nor a heid, bot a member. And they whome Chryſt hes callit and commandit to watche ower his Kirk, and governe his ſpirituall kingdome. hes ſufficient powar of him, and authoritie ſa to do, bathe togidder and ſeueralie :

the quhilk na Chriftian King nor Prince fould controll and difcharge, bot fortifie and affift. vtherwayes nocht fathfull fubiects nor members of Chryft
And, Sir when yie war in your fwadling cloutes, Chryft Jefus rang fribe in
this land in fpyt of all his enemies, and his officers and minifters content and
affemblit for the rewling and weill of his Kirk, quhilk was euer for your weil-
tear, defence, and prefernatioun alfo, when thir fam enemies was feiking your
deftructioun and cutting af   And in fa doing, be than affemblies and meittings fen fyne continowalie hes bein terrible to thefe enemies, and maift ftedable for yow   And will yie now, when ther is man nor extream neceffitie of
the continowance and fathfull difcharge of that dewtie, drawin to your awin
deftructioun be a dewilhfhe and maift pernitius counfall, begin to hinder and
difhart Chryfts fervants, and your beft and maift fathfull fubiects, quarrelling
tuam for thair conveining and cair that they haiff of than dewtie to Chryft
and yow, when yie fould rather commend and countinance tham, as the godlie
kings and guid emperouris did   As to the wifdome of your counfall, quhilk I
call dewilhfhe and pernitius, it is thus, that yie mon be feruit be all fort of men
to cum to your purpofe and grandom, Jew and Gentill, Papift and Proteft-
ant, and becaufe the Minifters and Proteftants in Scotland is ower ftark, and
controlles the King, they mon be wakned and brought law be fteiring vpe a
partie to tham, and the King being æquall and indifferent. bathe falbe fean to
flie to him ; fa fall he be weill feruit. Bot, Sir, gif Gods wefdome be the onlie
trew wifdome, this will proue meire and mad folie, for his euis can bot light
vpon it, fa that in feiking of bathe. yie fall los bathe. wharas in cleuing
vprightlie to God, his trew fervants fould be your fure friends and he fould
compell the reft counterfithe and lenghe, to gift ouer thamfelues and ferve yow
as he did to Dauid " Thir things, and manie vther, was fpoken be occafioun
in conference with grait libertie and vehemance, till at laft the King fatteht
and dimitted ws pleafandlie, with manie atteftationes that he knew nocht of
the papift Lords haincoming till they war in the countrey ; and whowbeit the
Efteates haid licenced tham to mak thair ofters, they fould nocht be receaued
till they thamfelues war furthe of the countrey again, and ofter what they
wald, they fould gett na grace at his hand till they fatifhed the Kirk.

The 20 of October the Commiffionars of the Generall Affemblie. and from
diuers Synodalls, convened at Edinbruche. the haill proceidings wharof from
that day vntill the xvij day of Decem that accurfed wrakfull day to the
Kirk and Comoun weill of Scotland. becaufe they ar at lainthe. and particularlie in forme of Ephemerids fett doun be me in a buik be thamfelff, for con-

tracting of this volum, I mon remit the reidar therto Only heir I will infert
the offers quhilk the Erle of Hountlie maid to the Synod of Murray, be his
Lady the 19 day of the forfaid monethe of October, that it may be knawin
whow trew the Lord hes euer bein in his promifes to his Kirk, in making
thair and his enemies leinglie yeild, and to gift ower thamfelues vnto his
Dauid

*The Offers prefented be the Lady Henriet Stewart, Countes of Hountly, hauing commiffion from
her housband in his abfence, to the Synodall Affemblie of the Presbyteries within the
Diocefe of Murray, conuenit in Elgen the xii day of October, 1596.*

At the firft hening, and hauing intelligence that your worfchips hen conuenit, and remanent of
the Kirk of this Realm, hes bein in tyme paft, and as yit remanes euill informit be fuggeftioun of
mifreportes of my Lord and Spoufe, that he fould be a Trafeetar with ftrangers fen his departing
out of this realme, in preiudice of the relligioun prefenthe proteftnt in the fam, and of the effeat of
his natiue countrey, I, as hauing commiffioun in his nam, offers nocht onlie to mak his purgatioun
of the finifter mifreportes of him aboue wrytten, bot alfo that he fall abyd and fubmit himfelff to
all lawfull tryall theranent , and if he beis tund culpable and giltie therof to fufter and vnderly the
cenfours of your Worfchips, King, and Counfall

Secondlie, I offer that he fall mak fufficient fecuritie nather till attempt, affift, nor deuyfe anie
thing in tymes cumming, tending to the alteratioun or inuerfioun of the relligioun prefenthe pro-
teftit within this Realme

Thridlie, offers that he fall banifhe and erect from his companie and focietie all Jefuites, Seminarie Preifts, excommunicat perfones, and notoriuf knawin Papifts

Feurdlie, he is, and falbe content to intercomoun and conter with quhatfumeuer of the minifterie
your Worfchips and haill Kirk apoint , and in cais he may be mouit be guid arguments and reafones, and therby perfuadht in his confcience to leaue the relligioun prefenthe proteft be him, he
fall embrace the relligioun profeft within this Realme.

Fyfthe, offeres that he fall reffaue an ordinar minifter in his companie for his better inftructioun,
on his awin charges , and in mean tyme fall keipe guid ordour

Sexthe, for better affurance of his guid menning, he is content till affift your difcipline in punifh-
ing of vyce.

Seuinthe, in confideratioun of the premiffes I will defyre your Worfchips to giff and concead a
reafonable tyme whairin my Lord my Spoufe may be refolued in his confcience, and that it will
pleis your Worfchips to fchaw him that fauour to abfolue him fra the proces of excommunicatioun
and that he may haue, be your mediatioun and interceiding, his Maiefties fauour and ouerfight, to
remean within the countrey vntroublit during the tyme of the conterence.

And for your perfwafioun to the premiffes, I offer in his name, that he fall mak fufficient fecuritie for obferving of the Articles aboue writtin , and in teftimonie of his guid intentiounes, fall
affift the planting of minifters in the Kirks defolat within his bounds.

Thus fubfcryuit,

HENRETT COUNTESS OF HOUNLEY

Thir Articles war prefentit be the baiones vnderwryten : Sʳ Walter Ogilbie of Findlater, Knight, Robert Innes of that Ilk, Sʳ Jhone Goidown of Pitluig, Knight, Wilyeam Sutherland of Duffes, Jhone Vrquhart of Tullo, Tutoi of Crommeitie

Vpon thu offeres the papift Eiles war fuffered to bruik the countrey, yea ther awin houffes and leivings till the monethe of May therefter, when at the Geneiall Affemblie hauldin at Dondie, they war abfolued. Quhilk was eafie to effectuat, the miniftiie of St Andios and Edinbruche, and fa of the haill fouthe, being ather defated or drawin to the Kings deuotioun ; and the miniftrie of the northe haillelie be fear and flatteiie maid for the puipofe. And thus oui vndew tifulnes did lofe agaii that giait victorie quhilk God haid conqueift ower thefe enemies ; the quhilk I pray his meicie they be nocht maid iuft fcurges to the minifterie in fpeciall therfoi.

Immediathe efter that xvij day of December, the miniflers of Edinbruche Maifteis Robeit Biuce, James Balfoui, Walter Balcanquall, and Wilyeam Watfone, war nocht onlie counfallit, bot cineftlie vigit be thair flok to fle Twa of the quhilk, Mr Robert and Walter paft fouthe in England. The vther twa cam noithe ower to Fyff, whar they war attendit vpon and receavit in a hous quhilk the Lord haid prepait for the confoit of his feivants. Ther, vnder the winges of Gods prouidence, they iepofit, and thei thair hoft penned the Apologie of thair caufe, following :

A Declarationᵃ of the iuft caufes quhilk moued the Miniſters of Edinbruche to withdraw tham felues fiom thair flokes for a feafone in the moueth of December 1596, giueing place to the wiathe of the Prince, to refirue thamfelues for a better tyme.

Ther hes bein, in all ages, is, and falbe, fum profefht malitius enemies to the Lord Jefus and his fervands Sum that wald profes fundtilupe to tham, bot the loue of this waild fa oweriewles than affectionnes, that when the frindfchipe of the an and the vther comes in comparifone, fa that of neceffitie they man forfeak an of tham, lyk the ritche man in the Gofpell, with heavines of hait they depart from Chryft : Sum weak and infirm bieithing that haid neid nocht onlie of righteus infoimatioun in the treuthe, bot alfo of continuall confoit And fum wyfe and fiong fauoiais wha leakes na thing bot intelligence of the proceidings of mateis that they may meantem the caus, and ftand theivnto againft whatfoeuei calumnie or fklander.

Conceiming the firft, wharof we mein nocht to tyne tyme in waffing of fic Moores, nor contiai to the command of oui maifter, to caft oui halie things to dogges, and fitt oui peules befoi fic fwyne, feiking to find and faue fic whom the Lord will haue loft and deftroyed, and therfoi in his iighteus iudgments giffes tham ovei to thair awin tantafies to forge out ftumbling blokes, and caft tham in thair awin way to fall on, and go from cuill to warfe, deceauing and being deceauit, to tham awin iuft condemnatioun.

As for the second fort, it war bot loft labour alfo to preas to perfwad tham of the treuthe for it fearethe with tham as with an fa affectionat to his frind that he menes never to fpen his quarrell, what euer be done, what euer be faid, right or wrang, trew or fals, fafthlie or aduyfedlie fa it tend anie wayes to the hurt or hinderance of his affectionat frind, it is all an, yea, he is fa ather blindit or wilfullie addicted to his fond frindfchipe, that the leaft appenance of the hurt ther-of makes right, treuthe, wefdome, aduyfitnes in his conceat to alter bathe name and nature, and be efteemed and giffen out for contrarie vyces. Sa ar they to the frindfchipe of than gear and this waild.

Our onlie ceir is of the twa rankes that remeanes, rightlie till informe that an of the iuft and wechtie cauffes mouing ws to withdraw ourfelues from our charges, and leaue af the exerceite of our minifterie amangs our flocks of our awin accord for a feafone, (quhilk wthervayes we fould haue bein compelled to do againft our willes, to the los of our lyues and graitter difavantage of the comoun caufe, as euidenthe will appeir in our Apologie efter following) and togidder heirw.fhall to fubioyne fum comfort alfo for the confirmatioun of that wther, befeikand tham bathe to accept of the faming rightlie and lowinghe in the tender bowelles of the Lord Jefus.

Than is twa things as we vnderftand blawin abrode of ws for our difcredit and the hurt of the caufe of Jefus Chryft. An, that we haue left our flockes, and fa becom, of paftors, hyrlings. The wther, that we ar fled from the lawes, and fa of guid fubiects becom rebelles and outlawes. The quhilk crymes ar befor God and man, in all reformit kirks and comoun weilles, fa hynous and odius, that gif we haid nocht the teftimonie of a guid confcience in the contrare to vphold ws befor God, and euident reafones to clen ourfelues befor the reafonable and godlie, we wald efteim ourfelues of all men maift miferable.

For as concerning the flight from our flockes, we haue the command of our Maifter bidding ws being perfecut in a citie, to flie to an vther, and conform to the faming his awin exemple, and the exemple of his apoftles, namlie St Paull, who, being let down in a bafket by night ouer the walles of Damafcus, efchaped, and the manifold flightes of maine reuerend fathers of the antient kirk and namlie of the godlie and zealus Athanafius, weill thought of and approvin of all Chriftianitie. And wha, I pray yow, fpeaking in confcience, will or can deny our perfecutioun? Hauing fic bludie bod-waits coming to ws from court continuallie, fic fechoring to pluk ws out of our pulpites, fic bitter and malitius realling againft ws at tables, and in confcrence of counfallours, fic blafphemus traducing in publict, be proclamatiounes at mercat croffes with found of trumpet, whan befor that euer we war callit or hard, we war convict of feditioun and treafone, and proclamed to be fic perfonnes, namlie in that maift malitius and blafphemus proclamatioun, wherin was deducit the proces led againft Mr Dauid Blak, in the felft maift informall, impius, and miuft, and we inuoluit in the giltmes of the fam alleagit crymes, to be maid partakers of the fam punifment at the pleafur and will of the Prince, wha, God wattes, and man bathe, what guid will he hathe vttered towards ws and all out matters feruands, fen the receaving of our deidlie cnemies the papift Erles in his fauour: For the quhilk, we humblie pray the Lord to be mercifull to the King, and gift him repentance in tyme befor that grant iudge of the waild fett his iuftice court, enter in reductioun of that proces, and pronunce a feirfull fentence in his contrar, to be execut in wrathe without delay. And at laft a maift crattelie deuyfit tumult and infurrectioun motioned be our enemies, and moued be the fimple populace, the quhilk nochtwithftanding, be our diligence and authoritie, it was affwagit without anie violence or tort done to anie man, praifit be God. Yit, forfuthe, the fam is fa lithe aggreagit, that it is giffen out to the waild for a confpiracie of ws and our affociattes, of hie treaffone againft his Maiefties perſone and counſallours, and maid to be a ſufficient cauſe, wharfore we ſould be apprehendit as ſeditius tratois, committed to warde, and condemnit to ſchamfull execution

For what better could we haue luiked foi at the hands of our accuiſed enemies, the excommunicat papiſt Liles, whaſe ſpeciall finds ard fauouiars hes nocht onlie alienat the hart of his Maieſtie fiom ws, bot ſa incenſit the ſaming in hatied and wrathe againſt ws, ſteiied vpe be oui fiie rebuking of ſinne, and faithfull admonitiounes giffen from tyme to tyme to his Maieſtie foi eſchewing of the ſinfull iudgments of God, that his awin mouthe hes biathed out bludie ſentences and domes againſt ws   The quhilk thing, when our bietliring the Commiſſionars of the Generall Aſſemblie haird eſpyed and confiddent befoi than departing of the town, foicit to leaue ws be that ſtreat charge and proclamatioun, they gaiſt ws thair ſpeciall advys and counſall, that in cais oui Magiſtrates and flock wald nocht pieſerue ws ſaiſt fiom violent inuaſioun and craftie dint of deidlie malice, in that ceaſ we ſould withdraw oui ſelffs for a tyme, and ieſerue ourſelffs to a better occaſioun, when we might ſerue oui God and his peiple be oui miniſtrie in ſaftie and fieidome   And it is of veritie, that ſa far was oui bailyies and counſall from that abilitie oi dewtie, that they war fean for feir of thair awin eſteattes to ieceaue a commiſſioun to tak and apprehend ws, and put ws in ſtrent warde and ſure firmance, to be producit at the pleaſom of our enemies, and maid a piey to the recent anger of an incenſit King, whoſe wrathe is as the ioaring of a lyonn, or as a boare iubbit of hir whelpes, as ſpeakes the Scripture   The quhilk they haird nocht feaiit to haue effectuat indeid, gift God of his guid Proudence haird nocht caiit for oui preſeruatioun, and movit the haill bietliring of our Preſbyterie, and vthers out of diuers partes of the countrey, being thei for the tyme, togidder with oui awin Seſſioun and diuers of oui flock better affected, to counſall ws caiifullie and maiſt vigentlie to moue ws to eſchew the preſent tuiie and danger, and keipe ourſelues to the toic foi the wark of God at a better tyme   Giſt then it be lawfull, comendable, and honeſt for the ſtoutteſt to ſein whan thei is iuſt cauſe and flie to that end they may fight againe, namlie to paſtois when thei is na danger of infecting of than flockes with heieſie, and euident danger intendit againſt than lynes, and if the premiſſes and mikle man, clenlie knawin to the conſciences of all men of caii and fight in proceidings of mateis, be tiew, it is mainfeſt that ſic was the ſtat in deid of ws and oui flockes   Ther is nan of found and ſanctiſied iudgment that will blam ws as mercenarie defeitours of our charges, bot rather piaiſe God, wha hes of his gratius guidnes wotchaiſed ſa to direct and piotect ws to be reſerued in hope of faider imployment in the wark of his gloiie and giace in Jeſus Chriſt.

Now to the vthei heid of oui accuſatioun, twitching oui fleing fiom the lawes, we ſtand iuſtlie to the flat denying theiof   For we flie nocht fiom the law, bot fiom the wrathe and euill diſpoſitioun of the iudge that may eaſelie pervcit the law, oi rather from the partie wha intends, be pretence of law, to be reuengit vpon ws, as vpon than noy ſome enemies, wha, as they alleage, hes nocht ceſiit, be oui iuſt iebuking of than ſinnes, quhilk they term ſeditius ſeimontes, to diſgrace tham befoi the peiple, and theiby at laſt hes concitat the ſaming againſt iham to bereaue tham of thair lyves and honois   Giff it be nocht ſa, we appeill thair conſcience befoi God, and if it be ſa, as it is indeid, haue we nocht reaſone to declyne the iudgment of our partie, and flie from a craftie and crewall intendit reuenge of a deidlie and malitius enemie.

For to be pleain in this our neceſſar apologie, we ar foicit vnto for defence of the æſtimatioun of our office, and creadit of our calling amangis the peiple of God, nocht we onlie, bot all men of guid and æquitable iudgment, thinks it all an to be iudgit be the preſent counſall as be the Eile of Hounthe, in whafe fauour the advancment of the ſpecialles of tham, ſpeak what they will, hes bein procurit, and for whaſe effect thair credit is continowed and increaſſit at Court.   And we ar ſure nan will esteim ws foolifhe or fleyed for fleing from the iudgment of that crewall trator, as from the burning of Dumbirfall or Spanifhe Inquifitioun.

And as to the Kings Maieftie, we flie nocht from his lawtull authoritie, but from his vnlawtull wrathe, nocht from his euill naturall (quhilk of itfelff is maift clement,) but from his preiudicat difpofitioun and euill opinioun conceavit againft ws be the maift fubtill and importune fubiettioun of craftie ferpentes, from whafe pernitius poifone our continuall prayer to God is, that his Maieftie may be fauff, and nocht therby flean in body and faull. For as to his Maiefties Judicatorie, we mein nocht to declyne it in this caufe, nather, whowbeit we haue be all law maift iuft caufe of appellatioun therfra, being fa inormlie grevit and hurt be all his proceidings againft ws, yit we mein nocht fimplie till appell from his Hienes throne to anie Cæfars, kings or princes, in the eithe, but a Rege male confulto et affecto ad melius. Sa that whow foone foueuer it pleis God to delyver him from the companie and counfall of wicked Papifts and malitius Atheifts, and turn his hart and affectioun to the trew profefíours of the right Chriftian religioun and faithfull minifters therof, wha withont all queftioun is, hes bein, and will prone his onlie fure frinds and gud fubiects, we fall in all readines and humilitie prefent ourfelues befor his Maieftie, fitt dow fauld our feit, and tholl an affyfe of anie honeft men of whattfumeuer rank, for all art, part, read or counfall of that infurrectioun, or anie vther interpryfe at anie tyme attempted againft his Maieftie.

Wharfor, dear breithring, we erneftlie exhort yow in the bowelles of our comoun Sauioun to conceaue of our caufe and doings aright, and nocht onlie to fatifhe yourfelft with the æquitable reafones and motiues therof, whereby all occafioun of offence and miflyking may eafche be removed, bot alfo of Chriftian dewtie and loue to play the aduocat for ws at the hands of vthers, namlie of he as may have acces to deall with his Maieftie for the treuthe, and moue his Hienes to a better difpohtioun.

For, as concerning our dewtie to his Maieftie, the God of heavin, the cearfar of all hartes, bears ws witnes, that we inioy a gud and quiet confcience theranent, quhilk accufes ws nocht of omitting anie thing we oucht of dewtie to his Maieftie, nor committing of anie thing againft his Maiefties perfone or efteat, vnles it haue bein be the exces of affectioun or zeall, fearing for his danger, and caring for his weill and prefervatioun againft all fort of trators. That lyk as his Maieftie haid gud pruff and experience therof againft Boduall, from whafe attempts he could never be fre till we put to our hand, and efter redding of his Maieftie diuers tymes out of his claues, at laft maid him fean, being excommunicat, till abandone the countrey, fa he might haue the fam againft thefe graitter and mair dangerus trators, the faid Bodualles confederattes at Menmure, the excommunicat papift Erles, wha feikes maift fubtilhe to betrey his Maieftie in body faull, kingdom, lyf temporall and euerlafting. Gif heirin we haue offendit, let the King pardone and forgift ws.

But alas! wald to God the wrang war done to ws onlie, the pure fervants of the Lord Jefus and nocht directlie to himfelff, whafe croun and kingdome is violenthe invadit, withe whome the King enterit in actioun for redding of merches, and in the mean tym maid irruptioun violenthe within the middes of his vndoutted poffefíioun, and vnder conference of things alleagit queftionable betwix his erthlie kingdome, and the kirk, the fpirituall kingdome of Chryft Jefus, fatt down in iudgment, tuk decreit to himfelff, and therby acclamed the fpeciall priuilages of the croun of Chryft, to wit, the iudicator of the pretching of the Word, and conceaving of prayer, and annulling of the conftitutionnes and commiffionnes of his fupream affemblie within this realme. Giff anie gentillman of the countrey haid bein fa vfed with his nibour in queftioun of his mertches, wald he nocht be thought to haue iuft occafioun of compleant, yea iuft caufe and quarrell to war his greit land, himfelff and all that wald tak his part for redres therof? And yit fall nocht the Lord Jefus be hard to complean? Sall his fervants be declant trators, becaufe they mein his caufe? Sall his officers be rebelles, becaufe they warn his finds to cognos vpon the wrang and fie it repeant? And fall he oppreffioun and tyranme pas vnrepreffit? Sall he wha has receiued the haill lands and coffes of the erthe for a nift poffeffioun, vea, all powar in heavin and in eid from the grait Creator therof, fuffer himfelft to be thus handlit and vfit? Sall the Pagan Ture, the Cam of Tartarie, the Mulcout and Sophie of Pers, defend than bounds and conqueft kingdomes? Sall baftard Chriftiannes, fic as Prefter Jhone in Afric, bene impyre, and Philpe of Spean mak the warld agaft, inlarging his dominiones from the weft to eft, and in the mean tyme the han of the warld, the king of glorie, be oppreffed fpulied, and difhonored be a litle erthlie Regulus? Na, alas! wald to God the King knew what he war doing, and tuik vpe rightlie, and confiddent the fathfull, loving, and cearfull hartes of the miniftrie, wha fies the hat wrathe of Jehoua kindlit againft him, for helping the wicked and tawoning of than whom God haittes, and of the Lord Jefus, King of Kinges, for invadding of his poffeffiounes, and vfurping vpon his fpiritnall croun and kingdome. And therfor mon cry the alarme and gift the warning in tyme to leaue at and repent, befor he be confunnt therby, and maid a fearfull fpectacle to the rewlars of the erde.

Alas! his confcience, and the confcience of all, may weill ken it is nather ritches, honour, land nor rent, nor na warldlie particular that we craue, as does his comtiouns, wha goes about to cla and counfall him nocht according to his wealfeare, bot efter his affectioun and prefent dangerus difpofitioun, and fa when they haue gotten that quhilk they fought, they car na man for him, bot wald haue another in his place, of whom they might gett man, to ferue than infatiable appetett. Bot our can onlie is left he offend his God, and fa be left deftitut of his grace and protectioun, and tall in the hands of fic as feiks his wrak and diftructioun. And vit, forfuthe, they ar the finds, and we the enemies, they the wyfe and difcreit, and we the mordinat foolles, they the faueals of his honour and primileages of his croun, and we the empeaars therof, and fic as feikes to difgrace him befor the peiple. But alas! wald to God his Maieftie faw than plattes, and knew than demifies, he wald flie from than as from the fword, or confumption of raging fyre, for, as Solomon fpeakes of the harlot, "Honnie is in ther mouthe, but the fting of bitter deathe is in than end." Let the King perfew ws as he pleafes, we fall nocht ceas to requayt him with erneft prayer to our God to preferue his Grace from the miferable experience quhilk fall clor this caufe to the haill warld, gif he brak nocht at his finnes be repentance, and turn to God in tyme.

Now in end, we turn to vow our dear afflicted flok, for the faftie of whafe faulles we hope, be Gods grace, to gift our lyves gift neid beis, whowbeit we efteim the prefent los of your gear of lytle avcall, in refpect of that fervice quhilk vit in this lyft we may do to Chryft and his Kirk. What euer be the doings of men in this your vifitatioun, luik vie to the hand of God, iufthe working that quhilk fa often be our mouthes he forwarned yow of, for the contempt of his Gofpell, and trintles paffing ower the lang fimmer and feafonable heruett therof. He hes moued the tohe of a mad and contuint multitude to minifter to your troublers the occafioun of your prefent perplexitie, vea of his heanie plag vpon your hartes, bodies and genre, to the fpilling be appearance of a guid caufe, and moving of the wrathe of an erdlie prince againft yow. Bot we befeik yow therin to perceaue and tak vpe the angrie face and crabbit comntenance of the Lord of Hoftes, wha hes the coupe of his vengeance, inixit with mercie and iuftice, in his hand, to propyne to this haill land, and euerie member therof, in what rank and degrie fo euer they be. Of the quhilk the fervants of his awin hous, and yie in fpeciall, hes gottin the brend to drink. Drink it patientlie, for whowbeit it be bitter, it is a halfome potionn of repentance propynit to yow in mercie, bot be affurit for your confort, when that hathe wrought weill vpon yow and ws for our humiliatioun and amendi-

ment, the thik dreg of that read wyne of the Lords vengeance is preparit in wraithfull iustice
for the enemies to drink, the quhilk they fall drink, will they, will they, to thair horrible destruc-
tioun and confusioun euerlasting. AMEN

At the beginning of Januar, the King, with grait forces of the Homes,
Cares, and southland gentell men, cam to Edinbruche, quhilk put the town in
grait fen, and thair was keipit a frequent Conventioun of Esteates, wharin
war maid manie strange and seueir actes, the tytles wharof followes ·

Imprimus, Thrie actes of Counsall confirmed be than authoritie, an, finding the vproare at Edinbruche the xvij of December to be hicheft treasone,
and the authors and partakers, with thair fauorars, to be tratois in the hicheft
degrie. An vther, discharging the ministeis stipends that wald nocht subscryve
a band acknawlaging the King to be onlie Judge in maters of treassone or vther
ciuill and criminall cauffes, committed be preatching, prayer, or what way fo
euer   The thrid, ordeaning all prouests and bailyies, shireffes, stewarts, and
vthers of authoritie, that sould happen to be present at anie sklanderus speitches
of his Maieftie, in pulpit or vther wayes, to stay tham from anie farder proceiding, tak and apprehend, keipe and detein tham, till they sould vnderstand
his Hienes pleasure anent thair offence.

Item, Ther past an act with thir, finding his Maieftie to haue powar to charge
and difcharge a Minifter to teatche at anie tyme or place, as he sould think
conuenient.

Item, Ane Act difcharging all Generall and Synodall Affemblies and Prefbyteries to be keipit at anie tyme henefter within the brouch of Edinbruche,
and the Prefbyterie of Edinbruche to sitt in Muffelbruche or Dalkethe

Item, Ane Act ordeaning the Miniſters hous in Edinbruche to be appropriat
in tyme coming to his Hienes vfe, be reasone of the treasonable and seditius
complottes ther deuysit at sindrie tymes be the formar inhabitantes ; and therwithall the Nather Counsall hous, for that it was sum tymes imployed to be a
gaid hous, to be a Chacquer hous in all tymes coming

Item, Ther was a form of Band to be subscryvit be the prouest and bailyies
of Edinbruche, and therefter to be presented to the remanent Magistrates
within brouches, bearing a maist streat aithe of fidelitie to his Maieftie, and
oblefing tham neuer to suffei anie Minifter blafpheam his Maieftie, his Counfall and Efteattes, vnapprehendit, vnder the pean of periurie against the haill
thrie persones of the Godheid, and vnder a grait pecuniall soum in cais of
failyie

Item, The Town of Edinbruche bund neuer to admit thair former Minifters to teatche agan within the Town without his Maiefties confent, never to chufe ame vther in thair place without his Maiefties allowance , fiklyk neuer to chufe a Magiftrat without his Maiefties approbatioun , and the prefent Magiftrats to dimit and refing thair offices ower in his Hienes hands, to the intent he may with the advys of Counfall elect fic vthers as he pleafes. And fordar, was mioyned to tham, athei to find out the principall offendars, and mak thair proces clen that thei reft na thing but executioun befor the laft day of this inftant, or els the proveft, bailyies, deacones, and counfall, reprefenting the haill body of the town, till enter thair perfones in warde within the town of Perthe, vpon the firft of Februar nixt, ther till vnderly the law for the faid treafonable vproare, and for thair letting to libertie of Mr James Balfour, efter his apprehenfioun

Item, The Seffioun to be tranfported to Perthe, ther to fitt the firft day of Februar nixt, and his Maieftie and the Checquer to remean till then at Lithgow.   The Commiffars and Shiref Court to fit at Leithe.

At the fam Conventioun was read on a day bot thrie billes : An of the Erle of Hountlies, an vther of the young Lard of Bonitones, and the thrid of the Lord Sachars, thrie excommunicat Papifts In the twa firft, Aberdein was chargit to hen thair offers, and, finding tham agriable to the Law of God, confcience and quietnes of the realme, to accept tham, and to releiue the compleaners of the fentence of excommunicatioun ; vther wayes, to compeir befor the Counfall within 15 dayes therefter, and fchaw a reafonable caufe why : with certificatioun, in cais of failyie, letters fould be direct to charge tham fimpliciter thereto

And laft, Ther was apointed a number to fitt in euerie quarter of the town of Edinbruche, and examine fic as they pleafit, or fould be giflen in row to tham   Of whafe depofitionnes ther was wryttin monie quaires of paper, and yit amangs all nocht fa mikle fund as might iuftlie mak a man, to let be a minnfter, fudjutius of ame confpuracie or fordeuyfit vproar, that could publiethe be punifhable.

The King, finding this wantage and occafioun, pouffes fordwart the fam to the conquering of the libertie, bathe of the Kirk and borrowes within this land ; and pubhffes in print a nomber of queftiones, wharby he calles in dout the haill difciplne and ordour of the Kirk, ordeaning the fam to be difputed and concludit in a folem Conventioun of the Kirk and Efteattes of the Realme, to be convenit be him at St Jhonftoun about the end of Februar.

Whairfor the Synod of Fyff, cairfull of than dewtie at fa neidfull a tyme, convenit at Cowper the 8 of Februar, ordeanit euery Prefbyterie to nommat and direct twa of thair maift difcreit, wyfe, and refolut breithing to meit within the citie of St Andros vpon the Munday etter the xvj of that inftant, thei to confer, reafone, and refolue with comoun and vniform confent on maift folid and fubftantius anfwers to be fett down in wryt verie fchortlie for refolutioun of the Kings queftionnes.

Alfo, efter erneft in calling of the nam of God, and graue and weghtie confideratioun of the dangers the haill efteat of the Kirk might fall into, if the government therof, manie yeirs ago eftablifhed be the Word of God and lawes of the countrey, and peacable practife accompanied with a rare blifling of finceritie and concord, voide of all errour and fchifme even vnto this day, fould be now callit in controuerfie, and brought in doutfull and vncertain reafoning amangs men vnfkilled in the Scriptur and Kirk effeares, without the advys of a Generall Affemblie, or anie inferiour affemblie of the Kirk, namlie at fic a tyme when the notour enemies therof ar, etter fa lang preparatioun, now in full readines to accomplis thair attemptats to hir vtter overthrow,—the Synod did nommat and ordean certean of than maift graue, godlie, and difcreit breithring, to wit, Dauid Fergufone, Mr Thomas Buchanan, Mr Robert Wilkie, Mr Robert Durie, Mr Wilyeam Scot, Mr Thomas Dowglas, and Mr Jhone Fearfull, to pas from the prefent affemblie in Commiffioun to the Kings Maieftie, and in all humble reuerence and dewtifull maner, be all guid arguments and reafones to trauell with his Maieftie, that this apointed affemblie at Perthe may defeit and be left of, or at leift be prorogat and continowit vnto the tym the laft apointed Generall Affemblie be the haill Kirk, with confent of his Maiefties Commiffionars, according to the Act of his Maiefties Parliament, convein in St Andros in the monethe of Apryll nixtocome, and giff thair advys anent his Maiefties intentionnes and purpofe publifhed in print; declaring to his Maieftie in fpeciall, that na Prefbyterie hes powar to gift commiffioun to anie of thair breithring to caft in queftioun or put in dout the determinationnes and conclufionnes of a Generall Affemblie, na mair nor a particular brouche may call in controuerfie his Maiefties Actes of Parliament: Sa that whowbeit the Prefbyteries fall direct thair Commiffionars to his Maieftie at Perthe* at the day apointed, for teftifeing thair dew obedience, they

* Nota The King wrot to all prefbyteries throw the countrey to fend thrie of thair number to the Affemblie apointed at Perthe.

can on na wayes com inftructed for the purpofe mentionat therin, to put in
queftioun or alter ame conftitutioun of a Generall Affemblie

In lyk maner, that it wald pleis his Maieftie to relax the Minifters of Edinbruche from the horn, and repon tham agane in thair awin roumes ; as alfo
Mr Dauid Blak to his awin chairge in St Andros, certefeing his Maieftie, that
he can do na thing man to the contentment and winning of the hartes of all
the fathfull and godlie of this land at this prefent tyme

And fordar, to befeik his Hienes nocht to fuffer ame thing to be publifhed
in print anent the proceiding of maters betwix his Maieftie and the Kirk of
leat, having therin a fpeciall cear of his Maiefties honour and eftimatioun,
quhilk can nocht bot be impairit amang the godlie and fincere profeffours in
all realmes, if our controuerfies com in than hands.

The faid Synod alfo condifendit vpon certein inftructionnes to be giffen to
the Commiffionars, to be chofin be thair Prefbyteries, to keipe the apointed
dyet be the King at Perthe, as followes :

Inftructions geven be the Synod of the Prouince of Fyff to the Commiffionars to be chofine be
euerie Prefbyterie within the faid Synod, to go to the Conventioun, appointed be his
Maieftie at Perth , the quhilk the faid Synod ordeamt tham and euerie
an of tham preceyhe to keipe

FIRST, we fall fchaw that we ar com for obedience to his Maieftie, and nocht for that we acknawlage that to be a lawfull Generall Affemblie, be reafone it was nocht apointed be the laft generall, nor convoint be the advys of the Commiffionars of the laft Generall Affemblie, as hes bein
the practife of the Kirk at all tymes befor within this realme, warranted be the Word of God and
lawes of the countrey.

Item, we fall fchaw that we may nocht condifend in anie wayes to the reafoning or putting in
queftioun the maters of the polecie of the Kirk, becaufe the Generall Kirk of this realme, to quhilk
we ar fubiect, hes alreadie determined the faming, quhilk determinatioun we haue alfo fubfcryvit
vnto, and nan may call the fam in dout, and put thim in reafoning, but a Generall Affemblie.
Therfor, we fall defyre his Maieftie, in all humilitie, for continuation of the reafooning to the ordinar affigned Generall Affemblie, to be hauldin at St Androus the xxvj of Apryll nixtocome.

Item, gif na continuatioun can be obteined, and we ar urged to proceide, we fall proteft for the
libertyes of the Kirk, and planlie difaffenting, keipe yourfelffs free of euerie thing that falbe done
theranent

Item, becaufe the Conventioun is apointed be his Maieftie onlie for the queftionnes, we fall nocht
mell in anie maner of way withe the receaving of Hounthe or vther excommunicats, or anie vther
thing remitted from Synodall, or Prefbyteries, or properlie belanging to a Generall Affemblie.

Item, in cais the brethring amangs thamfelues, or his Maieftie, or anie of his Counfall, enter in
reafoning with yow, or anie of yow in privat, that we hauld faft be thir generall grounds .—1. That

the haill externall goveinment of the Kirk mon be tean out of the Word of God. 2. That the ordinar pastors and doctors of the Kirk mon schaw the will of God out of his Word and that onlie to be followed 3 That the pastors and doctors of the Kirk of Scotland hes with lang and graue deliberatioun sett down and constitut the haill externall disciplne and government of the Kirk, according to the quhilk it hes bein thir manie yeirs sa happilie governit and rewlit, that na heresie, schisme, or dissentioun hes haid place therin vnto this houre, and that ther is nan bearing office in the Kirk, wha calles the sam in dout It wald, therfor, pleis his Maiestie nocht to suffer the ran and maist peaceable and decent constitutioun therof to be disturbit be exagitating of fruictles questionnes, namlie at this tyme, quhen Papists preasses, be that mean of disputatioun namlie, to brangle and pervert all.

Item, yie sall trauell with the ministers, baronnes, and noblemen, that sall happin thair to be conveinit, that an vniform supplicatioun may be maid and giften in for restoring of the ministers of Edinbruche, and Mr Dauid Blak again to than flockes; and behaue yourselues heirin in the feir of God and loue of Chryst and his kingdome, faithtullie and providentlie, with all dewtifull reuerence to the Kings Maiestie.

FINIS.

In this Assemblie also was read the Band quhilk the King and Counsall deuysit to be subscryvit be all ministers, vnder pean of tinsall of than stipends, in effect to rescind the declinator subscryvit be all of befor at the calling of Mr Dauid Blak befor the King and Counsall in the monethe of December. The quhilk band the Assemblie iudged to be vnlawfull and superfluus for manie and diuers reasones, quhilks, togidder with the poincts of the forsaid supplicatioun, yie sall find in the volum mentioned befor, of the particulars that fell out in the monethes of Nouember and December.

Vpon the 21 of this monethe, Februar, the breithring apointed out of euerie presbyterie conveined at St Andros, and diuers dayes towteing the Kings Questionnes,* the schort soum wharof, togidder with the questionnes tham selues, followes:

The Questionnes proponed be the King, to be resoluit at the Conventioun of the Estaits and Generall Assemblie, appointed to be at the brouche of Perthe, the last of Feb 1596

ANSWER—1. Tim. 6.

GIF anie man teatche vthervayes, (viz. then the Apostle hes taucht concerning the government of the hous of God, quhilk is his Kirk,) and consentes nocht to the halfome words

---

* NOTA Mr Jhone Lindsay was suspected to be the author of thir Questiones. I wat he was cheiflie on the counsall of tham, bathe in deuysing and following furthe of tham

2 K

of the Lord Jefus Chryft, and to the doctrin quhilk is according to Godlines, he is putt
vp and knawes na thing, bot dotathe about queftionnes and ftryft of words, wharof
cumes invy, ftryft, realings, euill furmifings, vean difputation of men of corrupt mynds,
and deftitut of the treuthe, quhilk think that gean is godlines, from fic feparat thy felff.

Queft 1 May nocht the maters of the externall gubernation of the Kuk be difputed, falua fide
et religione ?

Ans They may nocht —1. The government of the Kuk being alreadie eftablifhed and conftitut
vpon guid groundes of the Word of God, be lawes of the countrey, and man not threttie years
poffeffioun 2. Namlie at fic a tyme when the Papifts ar readie bent to fi hak and overthrow the
Kuk and Gofpell 3 When that vnformall conformitie is fought be our inbour enemies of the
difcipline, the Bifchopes of England 4 In fa difficult eftait of a lawles and mitterles peiple. 5
When na edificatioun bot diftruction and breidding of fchifme and diffentioun within the bowelles
of the Kuk may aryfe therof 6 When nane of the paftors or doctors of the Kirk douttes ther-
ment 7 Let the King and Counfall confidder whow intolerable they wald think it to call in
dout the fundamentall lawes of the kingdome, and Actes of Parliament , or gif anie man wald put
in arbitriment or reafoning his vndoutted poffeffioun, lenning vpon a law, and decreit, and right
vinedment.

Queft 2. Is it the King feneralie, or the paftor feueralie, or bathe comunethe, that fould eftablifhe
the Actes anent the externall gouernment of the Kuk, or what is the form of thair conunction to
mak lawes ?

Ans All Actes of the Kuk fould be eftablifhed be the Word of God, conterned in Holie Scripture, the ordinar interpretars wharof ar the paftors and doctors of the Kirk The extraordinar in
tyme of corruptioun of the haill efleat of the Kuk, ar prophettes, and fic as God indowes with extraordinar giftes , and kings and princes aucht, be than ciuill authoritie, to ratifie and aproue that
be than lawes, and vindicat be than ciuill fanctioues, quhilk they declar to be Gods will out of his
Word

Queft 3 Is nocht the confent of the marft part of the flock, and alfo of the patron, neceffar in the
electioun of the paftors ?

Ans The electioun of paftors fould be maid be tham wha ar paftors and doctors lawfullie called,
and wha can try the giftes neceflathe belanging to paftors, be the Word of God ; and to fic as ar
fa chofine, the flok and patron fould gift than confent and protectioun.

Queft 4. Is it lanfull for the paftor to leaue his flok againft than willes, albeit he haue the confent of the Prefbyterie , and for what caufe fould the Prefbyterie confent therto ?

Ans When the flok will fin and obey men and nocht God, and nocht kiepe thair fathfull paftors
from wrang and dint of deadlie malice and violence, in fic ceas the paftors, be confent of than
Prefbyteries, may leaue than flockis

Queft 5 Is it lawfull for a minifter to vfe farder application nor that quhilk may edifie his awin
flock , or is the haill warld the flock of euerie particular paftor ?

Ans A minifter may declar and apply the Word of God throw out the haill Scripture, and his
warks wrought throuchout the haill warld, for the glorie of God and eydificatioun of his particular
flock

Queft. 6 Is he a lawfull paftor, wha wants impofitionem manuum ?

Ans. Impofitioun, or laying on of hands, is nocht eflentiall and neceffar, bot ceremoniall, and in-
difleient in the admiffioun of a paftor

Queft. 7 Is it lawfull to paftors to exprefs particular mens names, counfalhs, or magiftrats in pulpit, or fo vithe to deferue tham that the peiple may vnderftand whom be they mein, without notorius declurit vices and priuat admonitions preceiding ?

Ans The Canon of the Apoftle is cleir, Them that publiche fin rebuik publichtlie, that the reft may fear And fa mikle the man gift the publict fmue be in a publict perfone, bearing publict office and charge, quhilk nocht being corrected, might indanger the publict effeat Nather can anie fear be healed without the plafter be particularlie applyed to the perfone and place of his feare Vthervaves, he does na thing of the paftorall dewtie aright and fic as finds fault therwith, thinks mair ill to be called vitius nor be vitius indeid, and, lyk foolies and bernes, chufe rather to die in than difcafe nor abyde the cure

Queft 8 For quhilk vyces fould admonitiones and reprouing of magiftrats pas publichtlie from pulpits in thair abfence or prefence, refpectiue ?

Ans For all publict vyces, againft the firft and fecond Table of the Law of God, and that in all congregationes, becaufe all hes interes in thair King and fuperiour magiftrats, therfor all fould ken thair danger, and be moued to pray for tham

Queft 9 Is the application of doctrin in pulpits lauchfull quhilk is foundit vpon informatiouns, bruits, and rumors, fufpitions, conditions gif this be and that be, probabilities, liklines or vnliklines in things to come in ciuill maters, quhilk all may be fals, and confequentlie the doctrine following therypon, or fould all applicatiouns be vpon the veritie of knawin and notorius vyces ?

Ans Ther is na bruted vyce or corruptioun but may fall in the perfones and offices of men, and comounlie the fin is mikle war nor the bruit, therfor thouche this war, ther war na grait perrell of ane fpeaking treuthe therin Albeit ther nather hes bein, or is anie applicatioun vfed but againft ouer notorius veritie of vyces.

Queft 10 Is the text, quhilk is read in the pulpits, the ground wherupon all the doctrine fould be buildit, or may all things be fpokin vpon all texts fo that the reiding therof is bot a ceremonie ?

Ans. The Apoftle to Timoth Epift. ii. chap 3 anfwers cleirlie, that ther is na fcripture quhilk is nocht fa nithlie infpirit be God, that it is profitable for doctrin, refutatioun, correctioun, admonitioun, yea, even to mak the man of God perfyt for all guid wark, and to the Rom. xv. whatever is writtin is for inftructioun and confolatioun Sa this is but ane ignorant or ceremonius queftioun

Queft 11 May a fimple paftor exercefe anie iurifdictioun but confent of the maift part of his particular feffioun ?

Ans He may with confent of the beft part, quhilk comounlie is nocht the maift, for he being the meffinger of God and interpreter of his Word, hes mair authoritie with a few, nor a grait multitud in the contrare

Queft 12 Is nocht his feffiour iudge to his doctrine ?

Ans. The Word of God and exponars therof the paftors and doctors, ar onlie iudge of his doctrin. The fpirit of the prophetes ar fubiect to the prophetes. 1 Cor. xiv.

Queft 13 Sould nocht the Moderator of the Seffion be chofin veirlie of anie wha has vot therin ?

Ans. The cheiff burding of moderatioun ouer the haill flock, lyes on the paftor or paftors. And becaufe of the meffage, gift, office, and committioun by the Word quhilk he beares, the eldars and deacones mon be moderat be him alfo

Queft. 14 May the Seffioun be lawfullie elected by Minifters onlie, but the confent of the haill congregatioun ?

Ans. Nocht, for the minifters directs and moderates the electioun be the Word, and the congregatioun obeyes and gifes confent therto.

Queft. 15. Why fould nocht eldars and deacones of ilk particular feffioun be elected ad vitam ?

Ans They ar elected ad vitam except iuft canffes of depriuatioun interven   Bot becaufe the kirk leiving is faerilegiuflie fpoiled, quhilk fould fuftem thaim, they may nocht euerie yeu leaue than occupationes and attend on that office , and therfor of a number lawfullie elected fucceffiuhe fum releiues vthei, yit all abyding kirk officers , and this is of neceffitie till the Kirk get hir awin leuing.

Queff 16. How manie Prefbyteries is meit to be in the haill countrie, in what places, and whow manie paftors of kirk in ilk prefbyterie ?

Ans Plant the countrey weill with kirks out throw, and the kirks with paftors and doctors, and this queftioun wilbe foone folued , bot if this form of doing hauld on, thei wilbe fewar or they be ma

Queff. 17. Sould nocht the eldars and deacons of ilk particular feffioun haue vot in the prefbyteries, or the paftors only ?

Ans Eldars alfo hauing commiffioun from thair feffioun in maters of maners, lyk as alfo deacones in the pures effeares and patrimonie of the kirk

Queft 18 What is the maters of the iurifdiction of the prefbyterie quhilk may nocht be intreated in particular feffions ?

Ans The bulk of the polecie of the Kirk of Scotland fett down be the Generall Affemblie, and the firft Act of the Parl. haldin at Edinbruche in An. 1592, anfwers heirto fufficientlie, and to manie of all thir queftiones , and therfor wald neuei haue bein proponit gif the auld affectioun haid remeanit towards the Kirk.

Queft. 19. What form of procefs in libelling and citation, termes and dyattes, probation and pronuncing of the fentence, fonld be vfit befoi the faid particular feffiouns and prefbyteries refpectiuè ?

Ans. Echo I orm fuminar, æquitable, graue and fpirituall, as beft may ferue for the end of thair delling to win faulles from Sathan and his fnares of finne, to God be trew repentance, and purging and preferuing of the Kirk from fklander and dangei of corrupt and pernitius members refpectinè

Queff 20. What maters fould the fynod intreat vpon, quhilk may nocht be decydit in the prefbyteries ?

Ans. The anfwer to the 18 anfwers to this.

Queft 21. Sould nocht all wha hes vot in the prefbyteries, and als in the particular feffions, haue vot in the Synodall Affemblies ?

Ans. The paftors, doctors, and fic as hes commiffioun from particulai feffionnes of congregationnes hes vott, except in maters of doctrin, wherin onlie they that labors in the Word may vott and iudge.

Queft 22 Sould ilk Vniuerfitie or ilk Collage, or ilk Mafter or Regent within ilk Collage, haue vot in the prefbyteries or fynodals in the touns or countries whai they ar , and fic lyk, what form of vot fould they haue in the Geneiall Affemblies ?

Ans. Doctors and Profeffours of Theologie and ordinar inftructars of the youthe in the groundes of relligioun fould vott.   The firft, becaufe they ai ordinar office bearers within the kirk , the fecond being lawfullie calht to be Symprefbyters

Queft. 23. Is it lefum to connocat the Geneiall Affemblie by his Maiefties licence, he being pius et Chriftianus magiftiatus ?

Ans Gif he be pius et Chriftianus, he will alwayes allow and protect the affemblies of the office beareis of the Kirk for governing of the fam wha hes thair office and wariand of conveining for difcharge therof, nocht of anie eithlie or mortall king, but of Chryft Jefus, whom the Father hes anointed his king on his holie montan; and therfor may conven in his nam, and sould whenfoeuer they he the weill of the Kirk, and doing of than office to requyre the fam.

Queſt. 24 Is it neceſſar that the Generall Aſſemblie be ordinar, or onlie extraordinarlie conuened for waightie cauſſes concerning the Kirk ?

Ans. The neceſſitie hes bein, is now, and yit lyk to be, in this land ſa grait, that bathe the an and vther is neidfull. The ordinar for the ordinar cauſſes conteined in the buik of diſcipline; the extraordinar for preventing of dangers, et pro re nata

Queſt. 25 Hes nocht all men of guid lerning and relligion vot in the Generall Aſſemblie ?

Ans. Nan may vott bot he as hes lawfull calling, viz Commiſſionars from Synods and Preſbyteries: yit all the godlie and faithfull may aſſiſt, hou, or ſpeak, in a graue, ordourlie, and comlie maner, with leaue aſked and given be the moderator.

Queſt 26 Is ilk particular paſtor obleſit to repear to the Generall Aſſemblie, or is it ſufficient that onlie Commiſſionars com fra ilk particular Seſſioun, Preſbyterie, or Synodall ?

Ans. Commiſſionars ar ſufficient for votting, but the haill faithfull for aſſiſtance, giff they pleiſe and neid be

Queſt 27. Wha ſould ſchuſe the Commiſſionars to cum fra ilk ſchyre to vot in the Generall Aſſemblie ?

Ans. The provinciall Synodes.

Queſt 28 Quhat is the number of votters neceſſar to the lawfulnes of the Generall Aſſemblie, and whow manie of the haill number ſould be paſtors, and how manie vther men ?

Ans A certean of euerie prouince, and few ar or ma as the maters to be intreated of craues

Queſt 29. May anie thing be acted in the Aſſemblie to the quhilk his Maieſtie conſents nocht ?

Ans. The King ſould conſent to, and be his lawes approue, all that be the word of Gods maieſtie is concludit in his aſſemblies. Bot the actes therof hes ſufficient authoritie from Chryſt, wha hes promiſed that whatſoeuer twa or thrie conveined in his nam ſall agrie vpon in erde to ratche it in the heavins. The lyk wharof na king nor prince hes, and ſa the actes and conſtitutionnes of the Kirk is of graitter authoritie nor anie king erdlie can gift, yea even ſic as ſould command and overruell kings, whaſe graitteſt honour is to be members and nurisfathers and ſervants to the king Chryſt Jeſus, and his ſpouſe and quein the Kirk.

Queſt 30. Is it nocht expedient that the twa part of tham, wha hes his ſuffragu, ſould conſent to anie thing decernit in eccleſiaſticall iudgment, that maters pas nocht be a vot ma or les ?

Ans. We haue to thank God alwayes for that ſpreit of vnitie in iudgment quhilk hes accompanied our aſſemblies to this houre, in ſic ſort that na thing of importance euer paſſit till all war fullie reſoluit, and in an voice votted thervnto, namlie in the haill poincts of the diſcipline. God grant that thir queſtiones and Court delling breid nocht contradictioun

Queſt. 31. Hes nocht ilk iudgment inferior to the Generall Aſſemblie an territor limitat, outwith the quhilk they haue no powar of citation or iuriſdiction ?

Ans. They haiſl, Lot in ſic ſort, that if vther perſones commit ſklanderus crymes within than bounds, they may proceid againſt tham ther, vntill they ſatisfie and remoue the ſklander from the part they haue committed the crymes into. And whar citatioun is requiſit, the aſſemblie within whaſe bounds the perſone is reſident, cites him and cauſes him to compeir, etc., bot contra hoſtem communem et publicum, it is lawfull to anie member to deall.

Queſt 32 What is the ordinar eccleſiaſticall iudgment to the diſcipline of his Maieſties houſhold and counſall, remouable with his Maieſtie to anie part of the realme ?

Ans. The ſeſſioun of his Maieſties hous, and preſbyterie within the bounds whar his Maieſtie makes refidence for the tyme, or the prefbyterie within the quhilk the fklander is or was committed, pro ratione delicti

Queft. 33. Sould than be libellit precepts conteining the caufe of the citation and certificatioun of the cenfures befor all ecclefiafticall judgments or onlie till anfwer fuper inquirendis?

Ans. They that ar cited to ecclefiafticall judgments ar cited comounlie for a deleated or arrifk'n comoun fklander, athet be word or wryt, but ofteft be word, pairthe for fchortnes of proces, pairthe for want of the kirk leiving to fullom a clark, with certificationnes as eftenes, as the caufe, or falus ecclefie aut perfonæ, fall requyre

Queft. 34. Hes the inferior judgment powar to fummond to compen befor anie fuperior judgment, or fould men be fummoned onlie be the authoritie of that judgment befor quhilk they fould compen?

Ans. Grant fklanders wharwith inferiour judgments can nocht weill tak ordour, wilbe referrit to the fuperior or graitter judgments, and the perfones giltie chargit till anfwer ther, as having a warrand fa to do in fic caufes fra the fuperiour affemblie

Queft. 35. Is it nocht neceffar that priuat admonitionnes, with reafonable interualles of tym, pas befor all maner of citationnes?

Ans. Whare the fklander is becom publict, the place of priuat admonitioun is paft, and na citatioun befor a publict judgment befor the fklander brak out. Sa the queftioun is anfwerit negatiue.

Queft. 36. What interualles of tym is neceffar betwix priuat admonitioun, and betwix the laft admonitioun and the firft citation, and betwix the citation and the day of compenance befor ilk an of the faids judgments?

Ans. The officers of Chryfts kingdom ar men of weifdome and æquitable difcretion, occupeit in maters of chief importance, concerning the glorie of God and faluatioun of his peiple, and therfor fould nocht be impeft but with trifling queftiomes

Queft. 37. Whow manie citationnes fould infer contumacie?

Ans. Ane may infer contumacie, bot the Kirk, vnles ther be publict danger, vfethe pluralitie, bathe of publict and perfonall as beft may ferue for the winning of the offendar. The law fayes, Vna citatio contumaciam inducere poteft, fi fcientia citationis apprehendent citatum, atque ita compenatur, maleciofe latitare. Hoc vna pro omnibus dicitur.

Queft. 38. Is fimple contumacie, but probation of a cryme, or is anie cryme but contumacie, fufficient caufe of excommunication?

Ans. Coniunctlie and feueralie. for the cryme may be fa hainous that for purging of the Kirk, and moving of the perfone to a graitter humiliatioun, he may be excommunicat, whowbeit obedient in feliort tymes outward appearance. And being called for befor the Kirk, gif he compen nocht, nather fchaw a juft caufe why, he bewrayes a pryde and corruptioun of hairt, teftifeing him nocht to regard the Kirk or haue anie focietie therwith, and fa wordie to be declarit and publictlie fignified fic a an as he is indeid.

Queft. 39. Is ther nocht diuers kynds of cenfures, fic as prohibitio priuati conuictus, interdictio à cœnâ, nocht publifhed to the peiple, and laft of all, publica traditio Satanæ?

Ans. We haue in comoun vfe of our Kirk, as was in the antient, but twa, abftentos à cœnâ, et excommunicatos. As for the reft of the fortes, luik our Theologs comoun places, and our anfwer to the Bifchope of St Andros appellatioun

Queft. 40. Sould the prefbyteries be judges of all things that imports fklander, and gif fa be, wharof ar they nocht judges?

Ans. The prefbyteries fould pleafe to purge than bounds from all fklander, and feparat euerie

tauli from than fklandcrus knawin fine, lcft it fla h111, and his blude be craunt at than hands And
as Martyr fayes, Nihil eft ad quod Dei verbum fe non extendit, ac proinde cenfuie ecclefiaftic r
And yit in the mean tyme it nather confidders nor twitches that quhilk the cimil magiftrat does,
nor for that end Vide fupra in Mr Androes Letter, wrytten to the Kirks of Geneu and Ligium

Quefl 41 Can excommunication be vfed againft theiftis, murderars, vfurars, or nocht peyers of
thair dettes, and if fa it may be, why ar nocht all the Bordour and Hieland theifts curfed, as als
all the manfwering merchants and occuriars amangs the Borrowes?

Ans It can verie weill, bot gif the magiftrat do his dewtie, it neids nocht. And gif the Hiland
and Bordour Kirks war planted, thei wald be les thift Alfo, he merchants ar curft indeid, and
brybing Lords of Seffioun to

Quefl 42. Is thei anie appellation fra the inferiour to the fuperior iudgment, and is nocht the
fentence fufpendit during the appellation?

Ans Ther is appellationn from the inferiour iudgment to the fuperiour vpon iuft caufies, ay and
whill it com to the fupream, quhilk is the Generall Affembhe, fra the quhilk thei is nan. And as
to the fentence, gif the appellation be admitted, it is fufpendit for iuft and reafonable caufie, gif
nocht admitted, bot iniflie repellit, not.

Quefl. 43 Sould nocht all procefs and Actes be extracted to parties hauand intereft?

Ans In foro poli this may be or nocht as the Judge fies beft to be for the honour of God, weill
of the Kirk, and faithng of the perfone from the danger of his finne, and feing the ecclefiafticall
iudgments is nocht affiicted alwayes to a wryttin procefs for diuers reafones, they can nocht be
bund to gift ane extract in wyt alwayes.

Quefl 44. Is fummar excommunication lauchfull in anie cace, but admonitionnes and citationnes
preceiding?

Ans. In fum ceafes it is, fic as of Boduall, Spot, and the Papift Erles, and wantes nocht guid
warrand of reafone and Scripture, with exemples of the primiue Kirk.

Quefl 45 Hes anie vther nor the paftors of the Kirk vott in excommunication?

Ans Doctors that interp:ettes the Word, and eldars that watches over the maners, hes vott alfo.
Whowbeit chieflie that centur is deducit, directed, and execut be the paftors, the ordinar ministers
of the Word of Wefdome, λογου σοφιας.

Quefl 46. Hes ilk ecclefiafticall iudgment alik power to excommunicat?

Ans Euerie ecclefiafticall iudgment weill conftitut, hes powar to excommunicat within than
bounds; whowbeit, in refpect of the weghtines of that cenfure, it is thought guid that the Seffiones
proceid nocht without the advys of than Prefbyterie.

Quefl. 47. Is it lawfull till excommunicat fik Papifts as profeffit neuer our religion?

Ans A Papift refident within our bowelles, efteimed of communioun, and vnder fchaddow therof,
indangering the Kirk, may, by excommunicationa, be deconered and maid knawin for fic a an as
he is.

Quefl. 48 A woman being excommunicat, hauing a faithfull houfband therefter, fould he abftein
from hir compame?

Ans. Excommunicatioun cuttes nocht at the dewties of mariage nor nature, fa they be vit but
danger of the Kirk, offence of the godlie, and ftay of the medicin applyed, quhilk is to moue the
perfone to be efchamit of than deteffed eftent, and feik to be releivit therfra.

Quefl 49. Is it nocht reafonable, that befor anie letters of horning be granted be the Seffion vpon
the procefs of excommunication, that the partie fould be fummoned to hen tham granted?

Ans The ordoum preferyvit henanent in the Act of Parliament, is guid and reafonable. As to this fummonding, it can ferne for nan vther end but to mak the Seffioun iudge in the proces.

Queſt 50. Hes nocht a Chriſtian King powar to annull an notorius iniuſt fentence of excommunication?

Ans Na man nor to excommunicat; or the kuk hes till annull an notorius iniuſt fentence of horning or forfaultne

Queſt 51. May anie Counfall or Vniuerfitie be excommunicat, for what caufe, whom be, and manei therof?

Ans Sum Counfall or Vniuerfitie may be, viz Wherof euerie member or indiuiduum and perfone, is fklanderus for fic crymes, as be the Word of God deferues excommunicatioun. And this fould be done be than ordinai iudgment ecclefiaftic in manei fett down, confoim to the Word of God

Queſt 52. When the paſtors does nocht thair dewtie, or when a iurifdiction vfurpes aboue an vther, or anie vther fchifme falles out, fould nocht a Chriſtian King mend fic difordeis?

Ans. A Chriſtian King fould imploy his authoritie for mending of all difordeis, as the paſtors and doctors of the Kuk declares be Gods Word au to be amendit ordinarlie; and extraoi dinarlie be an extraordinar warrand. But na king nor prince fould tak vpon hand mending oi refoimatioun, but with the advys of the watchmen and at the fight of the Siers, wha hes the gift and calling to tak vpe the iuſt caufes, confoim to the Word of God

Queſt 53. May faſtes, for generall caufes, be proclamed be a Chriſtian prince command?

Ans. Be the advys of the Watchmen and at the fight of the Siers, wha hes the gift and calling to efpy the iuſt cauffes of humiliatioun by the Word of God, they may.

Queſt 54. May onie ecclefiaſticall iudgment compell a man to fwear in fuam turpitudinem?

Ans. A man fklanderit in caufa turpi, gif witneſſes can nocht be gottin, and weghtie prefumitiones and motiues being confirming the fufpitiones of the fklandei, that fklandei can nocht be remouit, the Kirk fatisfeit, nor the perfone pui git, but be the aithe of the Lord interpont, quhilk, be the Word of God, determines all douttes and controuerfies.

Queſt. 55. Sould ther onie thing be intreated in the ecclefiaſticall iudgment, preiudiciall to the ciuill miniſdiction oi priuat mens rights, and may nocht the ciuill magiſtrat lauchfullie ſtay all fic proceedings?

Ans Nane of tham fould preiudge another, bot bathe fonld iudge as breither for ther mutuall helpe and confort, according to the diuerfitie of the gittes and calling beſtowit vpon tham be God and fett down in his Word, wharby all mens lawfull rightes falbe helped, and nan haue occafioun to ſtay, bot bathe to fordai and advance vthei mutualie.

FINIS.

Coming to Perthe the laſt of Februar, we fand the miniſters of the Northe conveined in fic number as was nocht wount to be fein at our Aſſemblies, and euerie ane graitter courteours nor vther. Sa that my eis faw a new fight, and eares haid new voces: viz. flockes of miniſters going in and out at the kings palace, let at night and betymes in the morning. For Sᵣ Patrik Murray, the diligent apoſtle of the northe, haid maid all the northland miniſters acquentance with the King, wha began then to luik big on the mater, and find fault

with the minifters of the Southe and the Popue of Edinbruche, quhilk haid
nocht handlit maters weill, and almoft lofit the King, etc. Grevit at the hart
with this, we difchargit our commiffioun from our Synod, and vfit our inftructiones bathe privathe and publicthe in fic fort, that, do what they could,
wee delayit the haulding of ame Affemblie thrie dayes, till my fpeciall com-
lito and companioun in Chryft, wha alfo at that tyme was my bedfallow, was
caried in to the King be Sr Patrik, and keipt from his bed weill twoll houres
of the night.   At quhilk home coming in and lying down befyde me, he tuk
twa or thrie houres fleipe and thereíter finding me walking, begoud to tell
me whow he haid bein fend for to the King, and what lang confeience haid
bein betwix tham, mixed with thretning and flatterie   In end he was altent in
opinioun, " For I perceaue," faid he, " the king will nocht feall to wrak himfelff
and the Kirk bathe, vnles that our maters be better luked vnto, and he yeildit
vnto fa far as we may of confcience, yea fuppofe we lofe fum thing rather nor
all." I anfwent, " I could fie na better refolutioun then we haid bein vpon in
all ftreattes bygean, quhilk was to feik be prayer and cerfing and conference
of the Word to ken our dewtie, and be about fathfulhe to difcharge it better
and better, leaving the events and effect to God, whofe the caufe was   Bot as
for yeilding and granting ame thing againft that wherof we haid fufficient
warrand in Gods Word, and poffeffioun with fic confortable fruicts fa lang, for
nather thretning, fear of danger nor flatterie be Gods grace I fould never ; for
in my iudgment at fic a tyme the paffing from ame poinct, and it war never
fo finall wald be a fchaking ws loufe and findrie, difarming of ws of the truft
in the treuthe of our caufe and vnitie, wharby we haid ftronghe ftand to that
houre, and fa our difgrace and weakning, the aduerfars incouragment and
fardar hope, to the fchamfull wrak of the caufe of Chryft and his Kirk." Efter
lang conference anent thir maters, we reafe and paft out to our meditationes
in the Inche, and meiting agame, we that war wcount wounderfulhe to confent
and aggrie in all things, began then firft to differ in opiniones ' Weill," faid
he in end, " yie ar to be fend for to, and peraduentou, when yie haue hard
that I hard, yie will think as I think : for the King begoud with me in thir
words,—' As I faid to Mr James Melvill and yow in Edinbruche. when I tuk
yow twa by and fpak with yow laft in my chamber, that I haid a fpeciall
quarrell againft yow twa, wha bathe was difcreit and wyfe men, and fic as I
lipned in, etc ,'—therfor prepear yow for it." Yit we put af that fore noone
alfo with grait refoning and delling bathe in privat with dueirs brethring. and
with a number togidder in a Yll of the Kirk ; till at efter noone Sr Patrik

was fend with a command, that all fould meit and refolue be reafoning and
votting ather to hauld Affemblie or nocht. The queftion being proponit, Mr
Piter Blakburn tuk the affirmatiue as being indeid of that opinion, and I gat
the negatiue as being indeid of the contrar. We reafonit the mater at grait
lainthe, till the graitteft part of the breithring thoucht it aneuche and inely-
ned to my part, defyring the mater to be voted ; when my faid commilito
began a lang difcourfe, wharby he fupplied the wants of the formar reafoning,
he fpeitches in appenrance verie wyfe and perfwafiue, quhilk, with the kings
authoritie, careid a grait number from our fyde, fa that when it cam in votting, the number of the Northland minifters and Angus preuealed   Quhilk,
when I perceavit fa to ga, with grait greiff of mynd, I withdrew my felff, reiding in that entrie a dangerus courfe of defectioun that followed   And efter a
heauie regrat vnto God, and confideratioun of my awin weaknes, in refpect
fpecialie of him in whafe vertew I confydit maift amang all the breithring
prefent, (for Mr Andro was abfent, being Rector of the Vniuerfitie, the choife
wharof fell iuft at that tyme), and yit with a nghts conference of the king,
I faw him fa ftranghe alterit, what could I promife to myfelff ?

Therfor, efter the breithring of our Commiffioun haid maid honeft and
plane proteftatioun of thair difaffent from all that form of proceiding from
that pretendit Affemblie, and all that fould be done therin, to keipe thamfelues clein and trie therof, vnderftanding that diuers war direct from the
King of my frinds and weilwillars to deall with me, and bring me to his Maieftie, I quyetlie withdrew myfelff from the town   And this mikle in generall as I know concerning that Affemblie   Now for the particulars

We haid thrie or four meittings and conferences with certean Lords apointed be the King befor that Conventioun was named a Generall Affemblie,
wherin thir Articles following war towtced, and anfwers fett doun vnto, quhilk,
as I hard, haid the approbatioun of the Affemblie thereafter :—

*Certean Articles proponit be his Maiefte at Perth 2 and 3 of Merch 1596, and an-
fuerit in Conference be certean breithring conuenit there.*

Art. I. That it be nocht thought vnlawfull, nather to the Prince nor till anie of the paftors, at
anie tyme heirefter to moue douttes, reafone, or craue reformatioun in anie poinct of the externall
polecie, difciphne, and government of the Kirk, that ar nocht effentiall concerning faluatioun, or is
nocht anfwerit affirmatiue or negatiue be anie expres part of Scriptuie, prouyding it be done de-
center in the right tyme and place, and animo ædificandi non tentandi

An. The breither conuened giues thair advys in the fift Article,—that it is nocht expedient to mak a law or act twitching this, leaft a durre fould be opened to curious and turbulent fpirites Vtherwayes they think it lawfull to the King, be himfelff, or his Commiffionars, to propon in a Generall Affemblie whatfumeuer poinet he defyres to be refoluit of, or to be reformit in fpecie externi ordinis, feing fubftantia externæ adminiftratiounis ecclefiafticæ is plenifhme tradita in facris literis And as the Generall Affemblie may accept of this from the King fa may the Generall Affemblie do anent anie thing that is done be his Hienes in anie conventioun, meitting or Affemblie confent be him henefter

Ar. 2 Seing that the ciuill and politic gouernment of the countrie belangs onlie to the kings office and Counfallars, and is in na way pertinent to the fpirituall miniflerie of the Word, That na minifter heirefter fall mell with anie mater of efteat in the pulpit, or with anie of his Maiefties lawes, flatutes, and ordinances, bot gif anie of the miniflerie think tham hurtfull to relligioun or contrar to the Word, they fall priuatlie complean theron to the king and his counfall

An The aduys to the 2d article is, That lawes alreadie maid, hurtfull to relligioun or preiudiciall to the libertie of the Word, be declarit to be expyrit, as the fam falbe particularlie co ifendit vpon, and na law be henefter maid twitching relligioun, without the advys and confent of the Kirk, wha ar declarit to be the thrid efteat of the countrey ; and that na Act whatfumeuer be maid contrare to the Word, the preatching whairof the miniflers hes concredit to tham. Whilk, gif it fall fall out, as God forbid, they think that euerie paftor, be the advys of his Prefbyterie, Synodall, or Generall Affemblie, fould firft complean, and feik remeadie of the fam, quhilk remeadie nocht being gottin, they fould direct the force of the Word againit the fam with all libertie And, as concerning maters of efteat, the breithing defyres the explaning of this poinet of the article.

Ar. 3 That it fall nocht be lawfull to paftors to name anie particular menes nan es in the pulpit, or fa vmehe to deftryve them, as may be æquiualent with thair naming, except vpon the notorietie of a cryme, quhilk notorietie may onlie be detynit be the giltie being fugitiue for the cryme, or fylit be an affyfe, or excommunicat for the fam.

An Na manes name fould be expreffit to his rebuk in pulpit, bot whar the fault is notorius publiet, yit they efteim notorietie mon be defynit vtherwayes then by being fugitiue, fylit be affyes, or excommunicat. For contumacie efter citatioun, publiet commiffioun of murdour, adulterie, or ficlyk, as was Bodualls coming to the Abbay, the murder of Dumburfall, and manie vther of that fort, makes notorietie, as alfo when the fact is fa euident, that the notorietie therof may be maid out befor the Judge Ordinar As to the viue defcriptioun æquiualent to the naming, it is haird to fett a law therto, feing a giltie perfone will apply to himfelff, whowbeit the preatchour neuer thought on him

Ar. 4 That euerie minifter, in his particular applicatioun fall haue onlie refpect to the ædificatioun of his awin flock and prefent auditour, without expatiating vpon vther difcourfes na wayes pertinent to the congregationnes

An Na paftour fould vfe applicatioun wharin he hes nocht refpect to the ædificatioun of his awin flock and prefent auditor.

Ar. 5 That euerie Prefbyterie falbe comandit to tak dihgent accoumpt of euerie paftors doctrin, that he keipe himfelft within the bounds of thefe premiffes.

An. It is the dewtie of euerie Prefbyterie to tak accoumpt of euerie paftors doctrine, that he keipe himfelft within the bounds of the Word of God.

Ar. 6 That fummar excommunicatioun be vtterlie difchargit as inept, and that thrie citationnes at leaft, of aught dayes interuall betwin ilk ane of tham, preceid the fentence.

An. In the Generall Affemblie hauldin at Montros, it was ordeanit that euerie Prefbyterie fould reik out the warrands of fummar excommunicatioun pro et contra, and produce the fam, to be confiddent in the next Generall Affemblie, that decifioun might be taken therin according to the Word of God. And feing the Commiffionars from Prefbyteries at this prefent hes nocht brought with tham the faid reafones, it is beft to leaue this mater to the ordinar Generall Affemblie. In the mean tyme, the Act of Montrofe to be keipit.

Ar. 7. That na Prefbyterie or Synodall vfe than cenfures vpon nan bot tham that ar refident within the bounds committed to thair charge, vtherwayes the decreit and fentence to be null

An. The Generall Affemblie hes apointed euerie offendar to be cenfurit in the place whar he offendes, quhilk they can nocht ga by, nifi in caufa communi.

Ar 8. That all fummonds contein a fpeciall caufe and cryme, and nan to be fuper inquirendis, quod eft mere tyrannicum.

An Fiat.

Ar. 9 That na meittings and conventionnes be amang the paftors, but his Maiefties knawlage and confent, excepting alwayes thair ordinarie Seffiones, Prefbyteries, and Synodes.

An. This article is againft the meitting of paftors neceffar, as vifitatioun of Kirks, admiffioun of Minifters, concurrance of breithring in mailt lawfull earends, as in taking vpe feaddes, refoluing of queftionnes, and fic lyk. Therfor, befyde thair Seffiones, Prefbyteries, and Synods, prouinciall and generall the breithring thinks all meittings for difcharge of thair office aught to be allowit.

Ar. 10. That in all principall Townes, minifters be nocht chofin without the confent of thair awin flock and his Maieftie, and this ordour to begin prefentlie in the planting of Edinbruche.

An. This article is anfwerit be an Act of the Generall Affemblie, quhilk ftatutes that the principall Townes falbe planted with minifters be the aduys of the Generall Affemblie, at the quhilk his Hienes Commiffionars ar and fuld be prefent.

Ar. 11. That all maters concerning the haill reft of his Maiefties articles fall reft on mellit withe, ather in pulpit or anie of thair Judicatois, whill firft all his Hienes vther queftionnes be fullie decydit, and in fpeciall, that all maters importing fklander com nocht in befor tham in the mean tyme, wherin his Maiefties royall authoritie is hihe preiudgit, but onlie in caufes that ar mere ecclefiafticall.

An. This article importes a difcharge of manie poinctes of our difcipline, fa as it can nocht be prefentlie anfwerit.

FNDS THE ARTICLES.

Ane vther particular was, the morn efter it was concludit and named an extraoidinar Generall Affemblie, the King callit it in to his palice, and, in the grait hall therof ioynit it with his Conventioun of Eftates, and ther began to reafone his queftionnes; whar the Moderator and brethring, refufing to put anie of the poincts of the difcipline of the Kirk in queftioun and dout, the King wald neids haue reafoning, and maid grait prouocatioun therfor. Mr Thomas Buchannan, an of our Commiffionars, maks anfwer, faying, "S^r, it is nocht that we diftruft our caufe, or that we want reafone to refolue anie that douttes of our maters, fa that they cam in a lowing and weilwilling ma-

ner to inquyre ; but we perceaue the purpofe is bot to canves and towt our
maters heir a whyll, that theretter men of lytle fkill and les confcience may
decern into tham as they pleis." And fa, etter diuers pertinent proteftationnes,
he entent, in his maner, verie fcharphe, folidlie, and ott tymes farcaftiche, he
gaiff tham reafoning ther filles, and trewhe played a ftout, honeft, and fathfull part that day.

And laft a grait and large commiffioun was giffen for converfioun and receaving again in the bofome of the Kirk, the Eile of Hountle with his complices, the diligence therof to be reported to the nixt Generall Affemblie.
apointed to be hauldin at Dondie in the monethe of May following ; and all
vther maters remitted thervnto.

But in the meantyme this Affemblie, and confequenthe all that flowed therfra, or followed thervpon, was efteimed, of the beft and moft godlie, to be null
in the felff, and of na force or effect, for manifald reafones.

1 Firft, Becaufe it was convocat vnlawfullie, that is, againft the lawes ot
the countrey ordeaning the Generall Affemblies to be apointed be thamfelues,
with advys of the King or his Commiffionars Bot fa it is that this was convocat be the King againft the advys of the Kirk, to preiudge the ordinar
apointed Generall Affemblie in St Andros.

2 Becaufe it was nocht till edifie, bot to demolifhe the difcipline eftablifhed, as was euident be the printed queftionnes, cafting in dout the haill difcipline, therby at leaft to gean fum advantage againft the fam.

3 Becaufe it was nocht fenfit nor fanctefied be the word of God and prayer,
conceavit and done be the mouthe of the laft Moderator, Mr Robert Pont,
according to the ordour obfervit in all Generall Affemblies fen the firft beginning.

4 Becaufe ther was na Moderator chofine but an, fubornde be court, Mr
Dauid Lindfay, intrufit himfelff, wherof proceidit confufioun and vnaccuftom-
ed immoderat behauiour

5 Becaufe the ordinar fcrybe being fen the laft affemblie departed this lyff,*
ther was na fcrybe chofine, fworn, or admitted.

6 Becaufe almaift the halff of the Commiffionars from Prefbyteries according to thair commiffionnes difaffentit therfra, and protefted againft it.

7. Becaufe it was efter four dayes deley be flatterie and boft of Court, be a

---

* This was Mr James Riche, a godlie, lerned, fathfull, guid, honeft man, with whom the honeftie and vprightnes of our affemblies is lyk to end , whofe deathe that yeir, and Mr Andro Mon-
creiffs, minifter at Carell, a godlie, fathfull, and vpright brother, war ominofe to the Kirk of Scotland.

tew vottes ma, fkarfhe at laft thiawin out, and named ane extraoidinai affemblie, as it was indeid

8 Becaufe when it was fett down for ane affemblie, ther was nather halhe,
graue, noi oidourhe proceiding therin

9 Becaufe ther was na clen proponing of mateis, bot convoyit and dreffit
for the purpofe.

10. Ther was na aiticle giaulie reafonit therin, nor na wayes reafonit.

11 Ther was nan votted.

12 Ther was nan concludit Ther was indeid named a certean breithring
of eueiie province to heir his Maiefties Aiticles, and giff thair advys to the
Affemblie : the quhilk being haid in opin and full meitting, was weill lyked of
and approvin.

13. Bot the fam therefter was vpon poft haft altered, eiked and peared, and
maift confufedhe parbuilyied. And nochtwithftanding of the difaffenting and
proteffing of diueis breithing againft the faming, yit without reafoning or
votting, was be the mouthe and pen of an vnchofin moderator and clark, concludit and put out in wiyt

And fa it was of the giant mercie of God that na mair ill was done there :
and that the ill was done, was done in fic a fort as it may for thir manifald
nullities be iufthe eftimat as vndone.

1597 —The 27 of Aprill. an. 1597, Mi Robert Pont, Modeiator of the laft lawfull Generall Affemblie, cam to St Andros of purpofe to keipe the dyat apointed
for the Generall Affemblie ; bot finding nan convenit thei bot the province of
Fyff, cam to the New Collage Scholl. the place apointed for the faid affemblie,
and thei, efter incalling of the nam of God, and humble confeffioun of fine,
that haid procured that brak and defolatioun, crauit mercie, and fenfit the
affemblie ther oidourhe in the name of God, taking notes and documents of
proteftatioun for the libertie of the Kirk.

But alas ! even then that libertie began to be almoft loft. For therefter,
to vtter it in a word, whar Chryft bydit befoi, the Couit began then to govern
all : whar pretching befor preualit, then polecie tuk the place ; and finalie,
whar deuotioun and halie behauiour honor'd the minifter, then began prank-
ing at the chaie, and pratling in the ear of the Prince, to mak the minifter to
think himfelff a man of eftimatioun.

rii ce betwix the
Generall As-
fhes, and the
r

And heir annes to mark the difference betwix the Affemblies Generall following, and thefe that paft befoi. 1. Chryft, be his fpirituall office bearers con-

vocat, and apointed tymes and places befor; now the King, bearing na fpirituall chaige in the Kuk, vfurpes that allancihe. 2 Chryft piofeidit be his
Word and Spiit, diiecting the Moderator and breithring; now the King, his
lawes and polecie of efteat diiectes, I will nocht fay contiolles, Moderator and
breithring 3 Maters war propomt fimplie, and the breithring fend to feik
light therin out of the Woid of God, be reafoning, confeience, meditatioun,
piayer. Now, plattes and courfes ai wyfhe leyit befor, moyenes and meanes
ar apointed to bring tham about; all is denyfit and advyfit in the Kings Cabbinet, accoiding theito is the proceiding. Tent is weill tean in publict, in
privat, what may fordar, what may hinder the fam, thei is mater to win ciea-
dit at Court. He is the Kings man, an honeft man, a guid peaceable minifter,
that goes that way; and they aie feditius, troublefome, cappit, factius againft
the King, as meines or ieatones in the contrar. 4 In ieafoning, the Woid
was alleagit, the text fighted, the ieafone weyit at grait lamthe and lafour,
and accoiding to the waight theiof, it buie the conclufioun away be a plean
foice of cleir treuthe; the quhilk being ans fund out, he that helde the contrar, willinglie and pleafandlie yeildit, and all acquiefcit. Now, the Word is
ather as a thing knawin and comoun, paft and pofted ower; or gif it coin
directlie and cleir againft the leyed purpofe, then the Kings man, that is quic-
eft of ingyne, man denyfe a glofe oi diftingo; and giff it be infifted vpon, the
King himfelff mon fall on him, and beaie him doun, and put him to filence
with reafone, laugage, and authoritie 5 The veiitie was vpiightlie and indifferentlie foucht without ieipect of this fyde or that, this purpofe or that,
quhilk maid men fattletlie, giauhe, and quethe to bring out than ieatones,
and fpeak thair opiniones. Now, the purpofe mon be ieipected and delt for
with hat and contentioun, or they can nocht be thought frak aneuche in the
caufe. 6. The feir of God, the loue of Chiyft, the cair of the Kuk, lerning
in fcripture, the powar of pietchiing, the motioun and foice of prayei, and the
eis and prefence of thofe in whom thefe giftes fpeciallie fehyned, wrought
amangs all, æftimatioun, reueience, and guid ordoun Now, it is the perfone,
prefence, purpofe, fawour, and regard of the Piince that beares out and contiolles all. 7. Giff ame had a gift and miffour by vtheis of leining, vtterance,
vprightnes, zeall, erneftnes in prayer, force in exhortatioun, it was fpyed out
and fpeciallie employed be confent of all at thefe affemblies. Now, the plattes
ai leyed whow nan fall haue place bot fic as ferues foi the purpofe. 8 Gifi
au offenfiue woid or gefture haid fallen out in a brother, it was incontinent
cenfured, and rediefiit. Now, gif a tieuthe be vtteied frilie and in zeoll, it

is met with a fquar ly, and he that is for the Kings caufe, may vfe what countenance, gefture. and langage he pleis.   9. And votting was wount to be vfit
for na vther purpofe bot to teftefie an vnuerfall confent and aggriment in a
cleirit and found out veritie, fa that fkar fhe yie wald haue fund an non liquet,
becaufe that tyme and all meanes war granted and vfed for refolutioun. And
now, reafoning is vfed but for the fafone, and na thing is fufferit to com in
determining, bot that quhilk is fure to be born away be manieft vottes, and
therfor the catalog of Commiffionars man be pervfed, to ken wha is with ws,
and wha is againft ws   10. In end, the end of the affemblies of auld was,
whow Chryfts kingdome might ftand in halines and friedome. Now, it is whow
kirk and relligioun may be framed to the polytic eftent of a frie monarchie,
and to advance and promot the grandom of man, and fupream abfolute authoritie in all cauffes, and over all perfones, alfweill ecclefiafticall as civill

Sic an Affemblie then as this, firft cam in, and was haldin at Dondie the . .
day of May, 1597. In the quhilk the twa chieff purpofes was, ane to relax
from excommunicatioun the papift Erls, ane vther to gett the Articles, alleagit
concludit in ane Generall Affemblie at Perth, declarit and ratified at that prefent affemblie, and as far furthe further as might be atteined vnto   For preparatioun to the quhilk, the King perceaving the eftats of the minifters of
Edinbruche, and of Mr Dauid Blak to be mikle memed, for purchaffing ther
fauour and forderance to his pui poffes, he heires fic as trauelit in thair caufe,
and makes his awm men of the minifterie till obtein fa mikle at his hand as to
bring the minifters of Edinbruche to his conference; efter the quhilk, he
grantes tham to be relaxit from the horn, and libertie to do thair effeares abrod
as frie fubiects, yea to come to Dondie to the Affemblie to knaw farder of his
mynd.   In lyk maner to Mr Blak licence from his warde to com to Dondie.

Alfo ther was a grait plat leyed, and mikle ado vfit, (plewing alwayes with
our hiffers,) whow to gett a Moderator meit for the purpofe. For this effect,
Mr Thomas Buchannan was woun be the grant of a verie weill lyked futt
for the guid Lord Lindfayes relaxing and reftitutioun, wha haid at tutorie, in
a maner, Mr Robert Rolloc, Principall of the Collage of Edinbruche, a guid,
godlie, lernit man bot fellon fimple and pufillanime, and fa as he was eafelie
caried with counfall, fa efter the affemblie was lawfulhe fenfed be the doctrine
of the laft Moderatour lawfull, viz. Mr Robert Pont, and a clark chofine, viz.
Mr Thomas Nicolfone, it was drifted and wearied be the Kings command till
the coming of the faid Mr Robert Rolloc, nocht being prefent at the firft;
and then be the foreprouydit fure courfe of manieft vottes moyennit be manie

and grait perfuafiones and motiues vfit with the breithning bathe in publict and privat, the faid Mr Robert was declarit Moderator ; whom, when the King and his men hard dreffit for thair purpoffes, the Affemblie is keipit frequenthe, imperatore prefidente, with grait congratulatioun

With this all men of anie mark or valour was practifed be Sᵣ Patrik, and he as war alreadie woun, and brought to be acquented, and to confer with his Maieftie. This was the exerceife morning and euening diuerfe dayes. On a night at evin, I fitting at my fupper, Sᵣ Patrik fends for me to confer with him in the kirk yeard   I, raifing from fupper, cam to him.   The mater was anent my vncle Mr Andro, whom the King could nocht abyde.   I wald do weill to counfall him to return ham, or the King wald difchairge him.   I anfwerit it wald be bot in vean to me fa to do, for he wald nocht tak that counfall ; and gif the King wald vfe his authoritie, he wald fuffer patienthe, bot I was certean that deathe wald nocht caufe him do againft his confcience " Surlie," fayes he, " I fear he fuffer the dint of the Kings wrathe " " And trewlie," faid I, " I am nocht fearit bot he will byd all." Returning to my vncle, whar I left him at fupper, I tauld him, whale anfwer I neid nocht to wrait

Vpon the morn befor Affemblie tyme, I was commandht to com to the King, and Mr Andro withe me, wha, entering in his Cabbinet, began to dell verie fearlie with my vncle ; bot therefter entering to twitche maters, Mr Andro brak out with his wounted humor of fredome and zeall, and ther they heeled on till all the hous and clos bathe hard, mikle of a large houre.   In end the King takes vpe and dimiffes him fauourablie.

The things that war done at that Affemblie I can nocht exacthe recount Ther was, at the chofing of the Clark, an ordonance, that at the penning of euerie Act ther fould be certean brethei with the Clark, wharof I was an, and Mr James Nicolfone an vther ; bot whill as I cam till attend, they war commandit to com to the King with the Minutes, and fa I gat nocht acces againe Alfo it was ordenit that all fould be read in publict befor the diffoluing of the Affemblie, bot nocht keipit.

The Articles proponit at St Jhonftoun, and anfwerit, war hard again at this Affemblie   It was fchawin and verifiet to the Affemblie, whow they hand paft, bot litle mendit ther ; whowbeit a guid number of guid honeft breithring did honeftlie ther part as they might.

The Lords excommunicat war be a worfchipfull commiffioun ordeanit to be relaxit, and that be a few vottes ma, efter fic reafoning, as when a fpeciall frind afked me, coming out of the Affemblie the Seffioun befor, to fchaw him my iudgment in effect becaufe it dependit on his credit, wither I thought they wald be ordeanit to be abfoluit at that tyme, I tauld him, as I thought, that in my iudgment they wald gett na abfolutioun at that Affemblie nor the nixt. till they kythed better fruicts of repentance. Bot by votting and dealling the Kings will was wrought.

The minifters of Edinbruches mater and Mr Blak, I refer to thamfelff.

Mr Jhone Lindfay, Secretar, intendit an accufatioun againft Mr Robert Walace, minifter of St Andros, befor his prefbyterie, wha was ther challangit alfo, bot all thefe ar leiving, and can declar thair awin cauffes better nor I

In end was deuyfit a certean Commiffionars, to haue powar from the Affemblie to convein with the King at what tyme and place his Maieftie fould requyre, to keipe concord betwix the Kirk and King, and to intreat of all maters that might ferue or apertein to that effect. The quhilk, as experience hes provin fen fyne, hes deuoluit and tranfferit the haill powar of the Generall Affemblie in the hands of the King and his ecclefiaftic counfall thefe Commiffionars: for bathe in Generall Affemblies and without they rewill all.

In the monethe of June, immediatlie efter his retoun from the Affemblie, the King enters in practife with his Commiffionars conveuit at Falkland, and calling the prefbyterie of St Andros, reducit a fentence of depofitioun pronuncit againft Mr Jhone Rutherfurd from his miniftrie of Kinnouchar be the faid prefbyterie, and approvin be the Synod of Fyff. The quhilk, nocht-withftanding, I am certean was ratefied in the heavines, for he never did giud in the minifterie fen fyne.* The faid Mr Jhone purchaffit his court be calumnies and dilationnes of Mr Dauid Blak and his minifterie.

And within a fourtein dayes therefter the King commandit Mr Jhone Lindfay to com to St Andros, (as the faid Mr Jhone allegit,) and intend the profecutioun of his actioun againft Mr Robert Wallace befor him and his Commiffionars, takand it out of the hands of the Prefbyterie

Mr Robert was to teatche vpon the morn efter the Kings coming, according to the cours of his office in the minifterie of St Andros. The king coming to his doctrin, henes him till he cam to applicatioun, at the quhilk he interrupted him and fpak againft him publictlie. For the quhilk, all vthers being fylent, Mr Andro Meluill rebukit the King maift fcharplie, thretning him with fenfull iudgments gif he repented nocht, and thofe Commiffioners of the Kirk, and his particular minifters alfo, for nocht difcharging a fathfull and maift necef-

---

* And now hes renunced the minifterie and taken him to be a medicıner.

far dewtie to him in that refpect. Thus God afliftcd his fervant woundei fulne.
nochtwithftanding he knew that the cheifl purpofe of thair coming was againft
him. For his caufe they intendit a vifitatioun and reformatioun of the Vniuerfitie, they fought out all they could gett or find againft him :* I faw betoi the
King lying, and thereftcr haid in my hand, a quaie of peiper of calummies in
feai wrait giffen vpe to the King. They called him diuei fe tymes, they leyed
diuers things to his charge, they haid all his miflykers, euill willars, and fic
as haid anie complents againft him; bot God was fa withie him, with fic courage, vtterance and powar of his image, that they could do na thing to him
in end, but mak a new chofe of the Rector of the Vniuerfitie   At the quhilk,
according to the cuftome, he willinglie dimitted his office, wherof he wald
haue gladlie bein quyt for manie cauffes, namlie tor that it_importethe a mixture of the ciuill magiftracie with the minfterie ecclefiaftic, war nocht from
yeir to yeir the haill Vniuerfitie haid burdenit him therwithe.   And yit they
fearit fa the publict opinioun, that they gaiff him ane office als honourable and
mair fetting and aggreiable to him in all refpects, to wit, to be Dean of the
Facultie of Theologie, the quhilk indeid they could nocht giff by him to nan
vther bearing euer the fam in effect, without compear or matche for his in-
comparable leiming ; and yit of that quhilk they behoued to do of necefitie,
they wald moyen thanks bathe at his hands and the comoun æftimatioun.

As they wald haue thankes in this, fa wald they in the mater of the minifterie of Edinbruche, for whom they fuffent tham to be futed and intreated
that they fould be enterit againe euerie an in ther awin roumes, and that to
thair feuerall flocks with a new ftampe of impofitioun of hands.   Bot all this
was to the wrak of the thrid, viz. the minfterie of St Andros ; that that being
done, the reft might be the eafier prey as occafioun feined therefter.   And fa
Mr Robert Wallace was proceidit againft and remouit from St Andros be turn
form of kinghe commiffionar proceiding and proces.   Bot Mr Dauid Blak was
neuer annes called, and yit of mere kinghe powar it behouit him to be debar-
rit St Andros and tak him to an vpeland roum, or then want all roum in his
natiue countrey ; and with poft diligence fummarlie Mr George Gladfteanes
placed in his roum

To receaue Mr Robert Bruce, minifter of Edinbruche, and giff him impofi-

* Ther was a number of ftrangers, Polonians, Denees, Belgians, and Frenchmen, fchollars, wha
at the fame of Mr Andioes lerning cam to the Vniuerfitie of St Andros that yeir, and war refident
within the fam, quhilk crabit the King mikle, and reftramt his purpofe againft him. This is remarkable for Gods prouidence.

tioun of handes, war apointed be his Maieftie and Commiffionars, Mr Thomas Buchannan and Mr James Nicolfone, wha apprehendit fie a feare of leying on of the handes of the peiple vpon tham,* that it ftak to than ftomak all that yeir efter hend: and was the occafioun of a verie tafchius antipathie and contradictioun betwix the Minifters of Edinbruche and the Commiffionars, whom git the King haid nocht flouthe with might and mean affifted, the faid Commiffionars haid gottin lytle thank, and all thair awin trauell at the nixt Generall Affemblie   And as it was, they fpak na thing les thamfelues, bot that they haid gottin peyment for thair trauell of that coyne and ftreak.

About the fam verie tyme that the King interrupted Mr Robert Wallace, and vndid the miniflerie of St Andros, ther was an erthquak quhilk maid all the north parts of Scotland to trimble from St Jhonftoun throw Athall, Bredalban and all thefe hie lands to Ros, and therin and Kinteall, quhilk was fchawin me for certean be fum of our Merchantes wha war in Ros and Crommartie fiue for the tyme, and as the countrey peiple ther reported it to myfelff, being directed that fam yeir in the monethe of October be the King and Generall Affemblie, to the vifitatioun of the Northe.

This maid fie as haid red the florie of the King of Iuda, Vzzias, to remember, whow that when he at a folemne teaft vfurped the Preiftlie office, and went in to the Temple to offer incenfe on the Golden Altar, the Lord fent a mightie erthquak quhilk reafed the halff of the montean Eroge, fituat on the fouthe and weft of Jerufalem, and caried it four ftades, that is, halff a myll, toward the Eft, and lighted on the fyde of the Mont of Offence, condamnit the hie way, and fpilt all the Kings Gardings   Therwith alfo the temple reaue, and a beam of the fune coming throw ftrak the King in the face wharby he becam leproufe, and fa be the preifts was caft out of the temple, yea of his kingdome, and finalie died of melancholie and greiff, as wryttes Jofephus. lib 9. Antiq. Jud. cap 11. Wharof alfo by the florie of the kings, Amos and Zacharie the prophetes mentiounes.   Anent the quhilk this dix-huitame was maid :—

> Vziah king contented rocht to bruke
>   The cuill fword of Judas gouernment,
> Bot puftlie office proudlie vndertuke
>   Till oftei incenfe at the altai bent.

* The peiple of Edinbruche was almoft in an vproar that day, at leaft the Commiffionars war effrayit of it

God fchuk the Eid, and hohe temple rent,
  And maid a montan fkipe out of his place;
(Of fenfull wrath a' feet maift euident)
  Whilk kinghe gets and gardings did difgrace

The King him felf with Leprofie in face,
  Was ftrucken fa for fchamles facrilage,
That he was forf"t, with manie loud alace!
  To quyt his crown, and die in hermitage

King James the Saxt, this yeir thow faft afpyrs,
Ou're Chyft, his Knk, to compas thy defyr's.
  O wey this weill, and heire exemple tak,
Left Chyft, wha this yeir fchnk thy northwall parts,
And withe echpfed Snn amat'de the harts,
  For kings to com the iuft exemple mak.

A heavie fact for all the hartes of the godlie and honeft, and maift deteft-
able, traterus and crewall in refpect of the deuyfars and committars, fell furthe
vpon this alteratioun of the minifterie of St Andros.   For the forementioned
malitius, craftie miffewlars of the citie, feing now the auband of that minifterie remount, and all fic as lyked of the beft minifters to be miflyked at Court,
and that they haid gottin a minifterie that wald go throuch with thair factioun, they fteir vpe and incitats four debofhit young limmers, and wattes that
maift notable man amangs all the merchants of St Andros, and for godlines
and vertew nocht interior to manie in the land, James Smithe. as he was
coming ham at night from the coft fyde, and crewallie demeanes and murdares
him   The gud honeft man was maift innocent of anie cryme or wrang done
to anie, as we fchew befor, (whowbeit perfones led with the fpirit of that
murdarar and liar from the beginning, nocht contented to haue murderit his
body, preffes yit to murdar his gud fame, bot in vean, amangs the childring
of godlines and treuthe) and thinking it was bot gear they fought, was refoluit to haue bought pace with large foumes; and for aggrement theranent the
King himfelf haid apointed the day following to be keipit be frinds and a commiffionar directed from him expreffie for that effect. and thus vnder tryft was
cut of   Ther was never a cais that befell a man that woundit my hart fa faire.
and caft me in fa terrible a tentatioun of doutting of the prouidence of God,
feing fa gud a man left in the hands of fa vyll lowns   I knew the innocence
and gudnes of the man fa weill, the vylnes of his maift wicked enemies, and
the veritie of his caufe. I was even drounde, a certean dayes, even almaift in

a deadlie and fencles difpear, till my deir father of mercie and God of all confolatioun haid pitie on me, and brought me in the light of his fanctuarie, and
maid me better to knaw and beleiue therby, that ther was a hell prepared for
the wicked, and a heavine for the godlie hereifter; and all the reft of the
poincts of that maist deipe and confortable doctrine of his prouidence.

I haid a grait ceai of that mans efteat for the onlie reafone befor fchawin;
and feing that alteratioun coming on, I often faid to him, that he haid a thing
graithe for his confort, that the caufe of Chryft and his Kirk in Scotland was
fa royned with his, that fa lang as the an went weill, I fould warrand the
vther, bot when the an alterit I fearit the vther. And often hes he anfwerit
me, that was over grait honour for fie a vyll worme, and that maift gladlie
wald he tak his pairt in the hardeft fort as in the beft   At the tyme of that
alteratioun I was mikle and verie inftanthe vrget be the King to mak the fermont at the receaving of Mr George. Fallon leathe was I, and foar was it
againft my hairt for manie weghtie reafones, bot feing tha gmd honeft men was
at ane extream poinct of wrak, hauing ane interlocutor of the Seffioun paft
againft tham of ten thowfand mark, quhilk tendit to thair vtter hearfchipe. I
indented with the King for the ftaying of that decreit, and compofing of that
mater, (wherin I heid fa lang trauelit with his Maieftie,) I wald condifcend to
do that quhilk vther wayes my hart could nocht fufter me to do: For I thoucht
ther could be na ill don in teatching the Word trewlie; and I thank God therin I fatiffeid my confcience, bot the doing of it, at that tyme, and by fic a com-
pactioun, was a grait huuk in my hart, and wrought fear remorfe at the newes
of his deathe. Bot as the cerfar of hairts and reanes knawes the overthraw of
that minifterie of St Andros was a heanie overthraw to the joy and pleafure of
my faull, fa far was I from art, pairt, read, counfall, confenting therto, or
allowing therof. And wheras I tuk grait peanes thereifter in placeing of Mr
Blak at Mr George kuik, I did it becaufe I kend the fathfull, honeft, brothers
danger; for the King and Commiffionars bathe war cairles of him, and defyrit nocht better nor to caft him lous on his awin default (as they wald alleage),
that throw neceffitie he might be compelled till abandone the countrey

James Smithe was my deir frind whill he leivit, and from whom I parted
in my awin hous about twa houres befor his flauchter, with als grait fweitnes
and joy of hairt, arriffin of a heavinlie conference, whilk haid ftow in twa houres
from ws or we was awar, as euer I haid in this warld; during the quhilk me
thought that he and I bathe was caried from the erthe and delyting our
faulles in that lyff and glorie purchaffed be the deathe of the Mediator and

Sauiour Jefus Chryft; till Mr George Mernfe, bailyie of St Andros for the tyme, a gud fimple man, and his frind, cam and tuk him out of my maift hairthe embracing, fear againft my will, for I was determined to keipe him with me that night, and go with him to St Andros on the morn for keiping of that tryft of agriment apointed be the King.

Gif the reidar be holelie affectionat in trew and godlie frindfchipe, he will nocht lothe of the poeticall paffioun quhilk pleafit and eafit me for the tyme, and therfor for my frinds fak I can nocht fuffer to peanfhe, whowbeit bot a dwabbling countrey ryme, meittar to be fwipped away with the moufe wobbes nor byd as a picture in the palace of Apollo

A dulfull Lamentation for Sin, quhilk hes procurit the thraldome of the Kirk, and crea all murdar of James Smithe, Merchant and Citicner of Sanct Androfe.   Sept 1597

(With the toone of " Alas, I die, etc.)

Alas! the tyme, that euer I did offend
Againft thy huche and dreidfull mageftie,
Alas! the veirs and feafons I hane fpend
In erdlie tourns and waildlie vanitie;
    Alas! the mounths, alas! the wkes and dayes,
    That I contain'd in foolifhe fportis and playes
        Alas! alas! for verie greifi and peine
        Alas! for fin, alas! for fin againe

This pretius lofs, quhilk I fa feare lament
Withe murnfull mean, is of the tyme of Grace,
When God fa lang his Gofpell till ws lent,
Till ofter lyf with euerlafting peace
    For all repentand, fathfull, halie anaes
    This wounds my hart, my flaifhe my blud, and brans
        Alas! alas! etc.

I may lament with manie loud alace!
I may regrat with manie reuthfull reare,
The lichtleing of the fauour and the grace
Of thie, my God, alas! with fiches faire
    Whare grace is gean, what retts but mortall greifi
    With dulfull deathe, and wa without releifi.
        Alas! alas! etc.

And yit. the graitteft mater of my greif
Is nocht this heauie faull with pean replent,
Bot that my finnes hes wrought fa graat mifcheifl
To crabe my heavinlie father, den and fweit ,
    And moue him nocht to fpeare his erthlie glore
    His deneft Knk quhilk did this Land decore
      Alas ! alas ' etc

For whare the fcepter of thy Chryft did gyde,
And gouern be his Word and Halie Ghaite,
It is contemn'd, alas ! and fet afyde,
And fantafies of flaithe for it is plafle .
    Sa fin gets not his iuft and frie rebuik,
    The godlie grones, the wicked proudlie luik
      Alas ' alas ! etc.

The ftandart of thy treuthe is troden down,
And lies, and falfhod hes the vpperhand ,
Reftor'd again ar Trator, thiff and loun,
And honeft men ar murdrit in the Land
    Whar Chryft did gyd, now Court does gouern all.
    O wratched ceafs' O miferie and thrall '
      Alas! alas ' etc

But na thing man effrayes and terrifies,
Then the renewing of that Couenand
At grait Affemblie, Synods, Prefbyteries,
And all our Kuks, bathe vp and down this land,
    Whare mome woued, and promif'd till amend
    Bot vthers hiche in rank did vilipend
      Alas ' alas ' etc.

The purpofe therof was to purge the land
From filthie fin, that God therin might dwell
Bot Sathans fleaues wald na waves vnderftand
That guid intent, nor yit the purpofe tholl
    And fa this tow hes put vpon our rok
    And brought our fredom vnder boundage yok
      Alas ' alas ' etc.

And euer alas! for fiham and weill-awa,
Even we our felfs, wha promifʼde all the beft,
Be fen and flatterie caried clein awa,
Permits thy fpreit in ws to be repreft.
          Yea, fum in hart, are led a contrar courfe,
          Of all this wa, the fontean and the fourfe
               Alas! alas! etc.

Sa by that heape of hynous finnes before,
Whilk cry'd a vengeance to the heavinnes hie,
We haue incenfte the mightie King of glore,
Be brak of promife, and withe penurie.
          Till ather quyt his juftice and his right,
          Or then to call ws clein out of his fight.
               Alas! alas! etc.

And fen the frie rebuk of fin is gean,
And of our cenfures the feueritie
The Papifts, Atheift, mockars euerilk an,
And beaftlie flaues to fenfualtie,
          At fredome now they vant and work thair will,
          Reuyling God, his word, and feruants ftill.
               Alas! alas! etc.

FINIS.

J. S.

A crewall deid that heirvpon enfewed,
With woundit hart I wofullie record,
That all the giltie grewthie may rew'd,
Haft for to render recompence, O Lord,
          I mein the murder of that meakles man,
          Amang tham all St Andros did belang
               Alas! alas! etc

2 N

Guid James Smithe, thy fathe and feir of God,
Thyn honeflie in lyft and conuerfation,
Thy vertues rare diffeminat abiod,
And weill bekend throw manie Chrift'an nation ,
    Thy gentilnes and trew humilitie,
    Thyn vpright meining and fidelitie.
      Alas ! alas ! etc

Thy courteffie, thy fafones fear and fyne,
Thy dealling ruft and fquare can name concell,
Thy kyndnes, frindfchipe, and thy fpreit devyne,
In lyking polecie and comoun-well :
    Thy loue of right, and hatred of all wrang,
    Excelling all thy citicines amang
      Alas ! alas ! etc

Bot fpecialie, thy lyking of Gods word,
And interteining of his fervants trew,
Maid Satans flanes to tak the blodie fword,
And ftrik tha ftrakes, quhilk they fall euei rew.
    They did pretend a forgget caufe of fead,
    Bot verelie thy vertew was thy dead.
      Alas ! alas ! etc.

For certeanlie thow was an innocent ;
To God and man approued weill be tyme ,
Altho malicius greidie men war bent
On thie, maift falflie, for to lay a cryme,
    Than confciens ay the contrar did tham tell,
    As they at yit convicted be tham fell
      Alas ! alas ! etc

For why the ground of ftryft and deadlie fead ?
It is from Sathan fen that firft he fell,
Whafe fprit the wicked reprobat does lead,
And maks tham fift to hat the Lord him tell ,
    And fyn abhore fic as him loues and feirs,
    Whafe fprit and lyff is contrarie to theirs
      Alas ! alas ! etc.

Invy and malice, lang mueterat,
Did bowden in the breist of craftie men,
Withe Satans vennom haill intoxicat,
As God at laft will mak the waild to ken,
    Wha houndit furthe thefe ratches vnder night,
    On Lambe alan, haill foui to fet thair might
        Alas ' alas ' etc.

And that at vnawars behind his bak,
They interpryt'd thair himmers crewaltie,
Quhilk fouldart lyk they durft nocht vndertak,
Sic was his manhead and actiuitie
    When he was paffing lyk a feakles lam
    Thcfe crewall craftie wolfs vpon him cam.
        Alas ! alas ! etc

Wa to yow, foolifhe, filthie, feible fallows,
Yie ai mad faggets to the fyre of hell.
Lyk lowns and himmers youi carkathe for the gallows,
Your curfed faull for Beelzebub him fell
    As vagabounds, lyk Cam, to be kend,
    Till that yie mak a maift vnhappie end
        Alas ! alas ! etc.

I y ! on the himmer Lindfay, by the leaue,
Thow might haue clam'd fum kinred by thy name,
Bot making thie to flaues a filthie flaue,
Thou'it blotted out with euerlafting fcham.
    Ah ' flaue to Satan, and to flauerfhe beafts
    Ah ! flafhar tyk, whom all the land detenfts
        Alas ' alas ' etc.

Yie venturars beveall his Tragedie,
Yie kend him euei godlie, guid and wyfe
Yie mariners and tradars be the fie,
Amang voui merchants he haid eu'r the pryie,
    All honeit men, all buigcffes of towns,
    Will mein his ceats, vnles they be bot lowns.
        Alas ! alas ' etc.

But maift of all the honeft pure will mifs
His merchandife with mercie euer mixt,
He gat a thowfands bennefone and blifs,
They wanted nocht wha kep't thair tym affixt.
      Yea manie an, he quat full liberallie,
       That was by hafard put to pouertie
         Alas! alas! etc.

O Kirk and King whow grathe ar ȝie wrang'de!
Alas! for lofing of fa rare a man.
Gif hounders of fic knaues wai tean and hang de,
War in compear a wildgufs foi a wran
      A better fubiect, noi a better fone,
       Haid nocht the King nor Kirk this land within.
         Alas! alas! etc.

Then if yow will efchew the vengeance grait,
Of feakles blud that owei this land does hing,
Tak pean to purge, fet heir your haits delait,
Think this befeats a godlie kirk and king.
      For, gif that therin ȝie be negligent,
       I am fure to leat ȝie fall it feaie repent.
         Alas! alas! etc.

And thow, O Fyff! fa filthelie defyl'de
Withe fore thought fellons bludie crewaltie,
I rather be a ftranger fai exyl'de,
Noi Eile, or Lord, oi baron, into thie ·
      Vnles thow kythe thir murders to deteaft,
       That in thy Waft, this ither in thyn Eaft.
         Alas! alas! etc.

I red thie, therfor, dull for Dunmbirfall,
And for St Androfe now, to fobbe full feai,
Or thow fall feill thy iudgment, fchaipe as thirfall,
Vpon thy bak, and in thy buttoks bear:
      For why what feakles blud fa faft cryes out,
       The righteus God mon punifhe ther, but dout
         Alas! alas! etc.

Bot O St Androfe ! fearlie fall thow rew
The tym that thow brought out that wicked race ,
For thow fall drink of that quhilk thow did brew
With mikle wa, and manie loud alace !
  For fure thyn eis fall verelie behauld,
  What euer thy fathfull paftors to thê tauld.
   Alas ' alas ' etc.

And namlie yie, wha lauching in your fleine,
Now maks this mater feage vnto your drink ,
For furlie God fall then his awin releiue,
When yie your craft and malice fall forthink.
  Lauche on, and fport yow with your guid fucceſs.
  Our God is in heavin, wha fies, and will redreſs
   Alas ' alas ! etc.

Bot weil's thie weidow, fuppofed miferable,
God giue thie grace to knaw thy happines.
The deuill hes done mifcheif intolerable,
Yit God his grantai guidnes fall expreſs.
  Whilk thow fall find with wonderfull delyt,
  To thair malicius wicked harts difpyt
    O confort ! confort ! ftedfaft to remean.
    O confort ment to mitigat thy pean

God hes reten'd thy houfband to his reft,
And him inrol'd, for to mak out that number
Of righteus martyrs whom he loues ay beft,
Into this lyft perfew'd with crofs and cumber,
  Beneathe that Altar bleffed famets amang ;
  Whilk cryes, Haft Lord, reuenge our bluid and wrang
    Than cled in whait he plefand fall remean
    O confort ment to mitigat thy pean.

Bot certeanlie God fall thy houfband bie,
And father to thy childring an and all ,
He fall yow freethe from all this miferie ,
He fall yow heir, and giue yow hart to call.
  He fall yow daylie grace and blefling fend ,
  He fall yow gyd vnto that bleffed end
    O confort ! confort ! ftedfaft to remean.
    O contort ment to mitigat thy pean.

Den damſelles l leaue af your dreme mean,
And grow in godlines to womanhead,
Yie fall nocht liue lyk orphelings alean,
Altho your eithlie father now be dead,
     Your heavinlie fathers guidnes yie fall feill,
     He fall yow touchar all, and marie weill
       O confort, etc. etc.

Thow home boy, conceaued and brought vpe,
Miraculuſlie by ame expectation,
Into thy youthe, reiofe to tholl the whupe,
Thy God falbe thy ſcheild and preſeruation
     He fall thie bliſs, and mak thie fie at eaſe,
     A feirfull curſs on all thy fathers faes.
       O confort, etc etc

Sa, efter God hes maid yow meit for him,
Be all your ſuffrings and tentationnes
He's mak yow on the ledder Chryſt to clim,
And end your greifs and tribulationnes,
     Surmounting far the ſkyes and ſternes bright,
     Yie's enter in the Lords eternall light
       Ther meit with him and neuer part again.
       O confort meit to mitigat your pean '

Now Chryſt our King, triumphar ouer the deuills,
Ou'r fin, our deathe, our hell, this warld and all,
Behauld from heavin thu maiſt miſcheiws euills
And heire the plaint of fie as on thie call.
     And ather ſtanche the rage of thair impyre,
     Or come and caſt them in æternall fyre
       O com ! O com ' O com ! without delay
       O com ! and iudge, Lord Jeſus, we thie pray

     AMEN.

In the monethe of October therefter, with a heaue hart, grait pean in body
be a diſtillatioun fallin on my teithe, and with grait expences, I entered in
iorney with the reſt apointed, and viſited the provinces of Aberdein, Murray,
and Ros. At ther Synods and Preſbyteries we tryed the miniſters, particularlie in doctrine, knawlage and lyff : Sum we depoſit ; ſum we admoniſhed ;

funn we incuragit; manie we helped in ther gleibs, manſes, and leivings We delt with all the noble men and cheiff barrones for prouyding of thair Kirks. be doctrine and privat delling, and gat fubſcriptionnes to the particular prouiſionnes fett down in wrait anent euerie Kirk. Wherin the penitents recentlie receavit paſt befor be guid exemple, the Erles of Hounthe and Arroll, becaufe they war nocht yit reſtored in Parliament; but fenſyne I hen litle of the performance But therin MakinTofhie warred all the reſt, wha meitting ws at Enneines, fett down the plat of all his Kirks with fufficient prouifioun, and when he haid done, he fubſcryvit it with his hand befor ws, and faid, " Now it may be thought I am liberall," fayes he, " becaufe na miniſter will venture to com amangs ws, therfor get me men and fey me, and I will find fufficient cautioun for faifftie of ther perfones, obedience to ther doctrine and diſcipline. and guid peyment of thair ſtipend and intertemnment in St Jhonſtoun, Dondie or Aberdein." And indeid I haue euer fenſyne regrated the eſteat of our Hielands, and am fure gif Chryſt war pretched amangs tham, they wald fcham monie Lawland profeſfours, and gif peanes war taken bot als willinghe for winning of tha faulles be the prince and paſtors to plant ther Kirks. as ther is for wrakking and diſplanting of the beſt conſtitut, Chryſt might be pretched and beleiued bathe in Hielands and Bordous.

In that iorney, be occaſioun of conference be the way with Sr Patrik Murray, Mr James Nicolſone, and Mr Piter Blakburn, I fineld out the purpofe of erectioun of Biſchopes againe. The quhilk, coming to Edinbruche to the parliament in the monethe of December, I faind planlie going to wark, and therfor left my litle court commiffionarie, and all fordar dealling with tham in anie courfe or purpofe, and reteired my felfi ham to my awin calling From the quhilk, whowbeit I was often abſent of befor, occupied euer in comoun cauffes to my grait peanes and ſpending of all I haid, yit I haid confort in my confcience and ioy in ſpreit therefter, remembering fium guid done to the contentment of the godlie But when I perceavit my peanes and expences to be dowblit, and to reape na thing in end bot greiff of mynd, and euill eſtimatioun amangs guid folks, I thought it hie tyme to reteire. And yit twa turnes fell out that tyed me, as efter we will heir.

At the parliament in December, the mater was convoyed and brought in this maner The Commiffionars, in nam of the Kirk, fought be petitioun a vott in parliament, wharof they thought they haid fufficient warrand, becaufe it haid oftentymes, yea almoſt at euerie parliament, compleamt, that men ſatt and votted in parliament in nam of the Kirk, that nather brue office in the

Kirk, nor haid anie commiffioun therfra The Abbots, Priours, Lords of
Seffioun, and fic as they drew of the Nobilitie, war againft the Kirk; yit be
erneft delling of the King, wha haid promift mikle guid to be done to the
Kirk at that parliament, they condifend and aggreis, that fic of the minifterie
heirefter, as his Maieftie fould promot to the dignitie, office, place and title
of prelacie, bifchope, abbot or vther, fall haue vott in parliament, fiklyk and
als frilie as any vther ecclefiafticall prelat haid at anie tym bygean, etc.

Now this, forfuthe, was a grait benefit for the Kirk obteined at that parliament when the papift Erles war reftorit, and for the quhilk the Kirk behoued to receaue tham in fawour For the Kirk had lyen long in contempt and
povertie, quhilk the King and his commiffionars foar pitied, and this was the
way to mend that : To gett of the godheft, wyfeft and beft of the minifterie,
vpon the Counfall of the Realme, conventionnes of Eftcattes and hicheft
Court of Parliament, ther they fould reafone and vott in ther awin cauffes,
and bring hame againe the Kirk leiving, and nocht ftand at the durre geiffing
in peapers of petitiones, and fharfhe when they haid raked on manie dayes,
gott fa mikle as a fear anfwer And indeid, gif warldlie honour and ritches
haid bein to be fought for to the Kingdome of Chryft, as it was, and is of the
Antichryft, or gif ther haid bein honour and ritches to be gottin in Scotland,
euen bot fic as was wount to be to thefe tytles, dignities and offices of prelates, I wald haiff eafelie bein moued and carried away with thefe arguments,
wanting the grace and gouernment of Gods fpreit ; bot Chryft teatching ws,
and making ws to teatche his peiple the contrar, and the peiple in fic a cleir
light of the Gofpell feing and fpying the wandring away of ther gydes in the
mift of Court vanitie, and therfor the mair efteimed ther, the mair difpyfit
and contemptible befor tham, and the les able for anie guid ædificatioun to
the confcience, maid me altogidder to avoid and abhore it And heir again
my forfaid commilito and I war in contradictorie opiniones

Our Synod of Fyff convenit in St Andros in Februar following To it was
Sr Patrik direct from the King to moyen for the mater of Bifchopes. It was
far and fearlie brought about with a Letter theranent from the Kings Maieftie
to the Prefbyteries Item, an vther from the Commiffionars with a copie of
the Act of Parliament, fchawing whow hardlie it haid obteined by the Kings
grait peanes and authoritie at the hands of the Lords of Articles, and what
commoditie might therby com to the Kirk. Therefter the queftioun was proponit, Gif it war expedient and profitable for the Kirk, that the minifters
fould haue vot in parliament for and in nam of the Kirk. The quhilk feim-

ing guid be manıeſt vottes of the breithring to be anſwerit affirmatiuè, I planlıe diſcouerıt vnto thaıme the purpoſe, to the graıt offence of the Kıngs Commıſſionar, ſchawıng thaım that it being annes fund profitable and expedıent. that minıſters ſould vott ın parlament, theſe mınıſterſ behoued to be bıſchopes and prelates, or els they wald nocht be admıtted to vott, and ſa we ſould fall to waık and bıg vpe bıſchopes qulılk we haıd beın all our dayes dıngıng down. Mr Andıo Melwıll inſıſted herın ın lıs vehement maner; wha taken vpe rudlıe be Mı Thomaſ Buchanan, that he ſould nocht haue place ın the Aſſemblıe, (meming becauſe of the mıſordoiu qulılk the Kıng and Commıſſionarſ haıd maıd in the Vnıuerſıtıe, debarııng the maıſterſ therof, namlıe of Theologie, fıom the Aſſemblıes), he anſwerıt. " My profeſſioun was to reſolue queſtionnes ın the Kıık of God out of lıs Word, and to ıeaſone, vott and moderat ın Aſſemblies, when youı was to teatclıe the grammar ıewlleſ " Qulılk anſwer contented and moued the bıeıtlııng verie mıkle. Etter the qulılk Danıd Ferguſone, the auldeſt mınıſteı that tyme ın Scotland, ſpak grauhe, cleıılıe and at lamtlıe, whow the corruptıoneſ of that office of Bıſchopes haıd beın eſpyed be the Kirk of Scotland from the begınıng ; what peaın haıd beın taken bathe in doctıın trom pulpites and ın aſſemblies, ior purging and alluteılıe puttıng away therof. And now he perceavıt a purpoſe tıll eıect thaım of new, conveyed ın ſie a maner as he could compear to nathıng better nor that qulılk the Greıiauſ vſit for the oveıthraw of the antıeut cıtıe and kingdome of Tıoy, buſking vpe a bıaue hoıs, and be a craftıe Sınon peıſuading thaım to pluk down the walles wıth thaır awın hands to ıeceaue that ın for thaır honour and weılfear, qulılk ſeıuıt for thaır vtter wıak and dıſtructıoiu. Theıfor he wald, with the breıtlıiing that haıd gıffen guid waınıng, cıy, Equo ne credıte Teucıi.

Mr Jhone Dauıdſone, an of the antıent fatheıs of the Kıık, was preſent with ws at that Aſſemblıe, and mightelıe and gıauelie warmt, infoımıt and movıt the bıeıtlırıng. Amangş the ıeſt he ſaid mırrclıe, " Bıſk, buſk, buſk him as bonılıe as yie can, and tetche him in als feaılıe as yıe will, we ſie hıın weıll aneuche,—we ſie the hoınes of lıs Mytıc."

In memoııall whaıof thıs Decateſſaıad was maıd, when the mater wrought fordar on thereftcr .

By Pallaſ art the Greciauſ built an hoıſ,
Alſ hudge aſ hıll, pıeſentıng hım to Tıoy,
And cıaſtıe Sınon, taken aſ paı foıſ,
Peıſwadıt them to bıak thaıı walles wıth ıoy

Be thar awin hands, this horfs for to convoy,
And fet him vpe in than maift facrat place
Bot therout vihing capteans did diftroy
With fyre and fword thair citie foone, alace!
Tho Dardan prophets cry'd and bad tham ceafe,
Alluring tham to work thair awin releift
Yit foolifhe madnes fpuilziet tham of grace,
Sa God, for fin, brought on thair laft mifcheiff.
This horfs, this Sinon, and this Troian fak,
Methinks I fie, whill we our Bifchops mak.

In that Februar, betwix the Synods Provinciall and Generall, was that
maift confpicuus eclipfe* of the Sunne, quhilk ftrak all creatours with fic
eftonifhment and fear, as tho the day of Judgment haid bein com   I knew
befor it was to com ; I was nocht ignorant of the naturall caufe therof ; and
yit when it cam to the amazfull, vglie, alriche darknes, I waft caft on my
knies, and my hart almaift fealled   On that I gaue this warning :

In Februar, the twentie fyue exack,
   We faw the Sunne, the tent hour of the day,
   Begin to lofs his light, and turn to blak,
   Whilk piece and piece his what did weare away
The caufe is this, as lerned men do fay,
   The darkfum bodie of the changing moone
   Cam in betwix our fight and Phœbus gay,
   And hid from ws his halfome light fa foone.
Amid the meitings of our Kirk this done,
   Portends the dark and variable waild
   Sall com betwix the Kirk and Chryst aboue,
   And mak his paftors crewked, blind and thral'd.
Then ftathe ftaris flik fall and tak gud tent
The dragons taill will reng the firmament.

* Ouer notable effects of this eclipfe kythe the zeu following in the deathe of notable lights of
the Kirk of Scotland, Mr Thomas Bowchanan, Mr Robert Rollok, Dauid Fergufone, and Mr Adam
Jhonftoun, alfo of Mr Jhone Lindfay, for naturall iudgment and lerning the graitteft light of the
policie and counfall of Scotland.   In lyk maner of gud James Smithe, the fune amangs the merchants.
    A mair fenfull eclipfe was of the Sun, and fall of ftarnes from the heavin, when in the Kirk of
France the men of graiteft lerning and eftimatioun, (intyfit be the flatterie and gifts of the King for
eftablifhing of that peace quhuik he haud fantifeit in his brean betwix the papifts and proteftants for
the commoditie and fuines of his efteat,) war maid to fet and imploy than thought, pen, and trauell
to erect and fet furthe ane mid and weill mixed relligioun and new Chriftianitie, the effectuating
wharof haid nocht feallit, gif God haid nocht cutted fchort thair dayes with exemplar forts of
deathe.   The names of the chief war Vadianus, Serranus, Rotanus, Egbergius, and Martinus.

1598.—In the monethe of Merche following, 1598, the Generall Affembue held at Douche. Ther the King and Commiffionars met befor togidder, and leyed all the plattes and cou[ffes, being in grait fear that the Commiffionars fould be foarhe centiurit for than proceidings, and that ther fould be na forderance in than cheiff purpos of erecting of bifchopes. Ther was ther biffines day and night to mak and try all in euerie province. The Moderator was befor hand preparit, and all and euerie an that fould teatche and open thair mouthe in pulpit : and finalie all things framed for the purpofe, fa far as wit or diligence might mak with the prince authoritie.

The King profeffit to ftand be the Commiffionars, and they be him. The vther partie war the minifters of Edinbruche and St Andros, with all fic as ftud vprightlie for the eftablifhed difcipline and fredome of the Kirk. The Commiffionars offerit tham to giff a compt of than proceidings to the Affembhe, bot fa in effect that they war iudges thair felff, for they war fure befor hand the graitteft number fould be on thair part. Manie greiffes war giffen in be Edinbruche, St Andros, and vther prefbyteries ; grait hait and altercatioun was, fa that fic an affembhe was never fein in Scotland fen reformatioun of religioun : and that quhilk was warft, the graitteft enemies of the miniterie, the lat excommunicat forfaultit papift Lils, war brought in to tak than paftyme of the imperfectionnes of the breithring, and fkrape togidder mater of fklander and calumnie to ventilat and faw athort amangs the enemies bathe within and without the land. My vncle Mr Andro was happie in that at his firft prefenting to the affemblie, he was difchargit, nather wald the King com in nor fuffer anie thing be done till he was away, (yit he paft nocht on vttering his mynd to the breithring in his auld maner.) And nocht fatiffeit that he was out of the affembhe, he was chargeit af the town vnder all heeft peanes. And furhe, I fay, he was happie that hard nocht the things quhilk woundit our hartes throuche ; better to be buried, as they war ordeanit in end, nor euer rememberit.

Efter that a large tyme was euill tint vpon the greiffes, and they (Male Malcontent, mother of the greives*) buried, the queftioun moyennit at all the fynods befor, cam in, Whither minifters might vot in parliament ? It was reafonit at lynthe, wherin I had my large part, as they follow heirefter ; but at laft when it cam to the roll, Mr Gilbert Body led the ring, a drunken Orkney afs, and the graitteft number followit, all for the bodie, but refpect of the

---

* This nam was giffen to that dealling in derifion be the people.

ſpreit   And yit, praiſit be God, a guid number of honeſt breithring glorifiet
God, bathe in reaſoning and votting directlie againſt : Another ſort war miſ-
takine bathe in reaſoning and votting   And the number that caried the concluſioun away, war nocht ſic that laborit or haid ſkill in the word, bot lait
commiſſionars wha votted with the King and thair miniſters. Efter the quhilk
concluſioun, Mr Jhone Dauidſone, of whom I haue diuers tymes ſpoken befor,
maid publict proteſtatioun againſt it in his awin nam, and the nam of the
breithring that diſaſſented, firſt in word, and thereafter gaiff in in wryt, deſyring the clark to inſert it

Thereafter going fordwart to the reſt of the queſtionnes, befor they ſould be
reaſonit, to mak tham the mair plauſible and eaſie to be paſt, the haill deuys
and forge of the new Biſchoprik was brought furthe falon weill buſket, and
fearlie and at lynthe red befor the Aſſemblie. Then war they maid clein of all
corruptioun of Papiſtrie, Antichriſtian and Anglicall biſchopries, fyned of new
in the furnace, caſt in a new mould, and maid of a freche ſtrak : and finalie
embarrit and meloſit with ſic caueats, as range and fling thair filles tho they
war wyld, they ſould never win out. Yit when the reſt of the queſtiones war
read they perceaving that the breithrings hartes, wha haid aſſented to the
firſt, began to ſtand and ſwidder, for the beſt part thought it meitteſt to tak
tyme to mollefie and moyen maters left they ſould grow fouſome at the firſt ;
and ſa was ordeanit, that efter advyſinent in preſbyteries, the Synods of euerie
province ſould aſſemble in May, and efter reaſoning of the queſtiones ther
ſould direct thrie of thair number, quha ſould convein with the King at the
tyme and place to be apointed be his Maieſtie.

It was alſo concludit at this Aſſemblie, that this office of votting in parliament was of a mixt qualitie, and therfor the electioun therto behoued to be
mixt, partlie be the King and partlie be the Kirk ; and the nomber of vottars
to be fittie.

Our Synod of Fyff convenit in Dumfermling in the monethe of Junie. Ther
war Commiſhonars from his Maieſtie, the Lord of Towngland, and Sr Patrik
Murray. Reaſoning was, and the iudgments of all the preſbyteries and breithring, giffen in thir queſtiones . 1. Efter what maner he ſall be choſin wha ſall
vot in parliament for the Kirk : Wither the Kirk, the nominatioun, and the
King the choſe, or e contra ? Cuper Preſbyterie, quhilk Mr Thomas Buchanan
gydit, thought that the Kirk ſould nominat fyve or ſax, out of the quhilk the
King ſould chuſe an. The vther thrie Preſbyteries aggreit in an, that the Kirk
ſould mak choſe of ther awin Commiſſionars, and therwith the King ſould

content and accept the sam, as the barrones and burrowes does   2 Whow
lang fould they continow ? Cuper faid, tota vita nifi internemat culpa   The
vther thrie in an, from a Generall Affemblie to an vther   3 Whow they
fould be callit ? Cuper thought it a thing indifferent wither they war callit
Bifchopes or Commiffionars.   The vther thrie in an, thought the confequens
of the nam of graitter importance, becaufe the verie nam of bifchope now im-
portethe corruptioun and tyrannie in the Knk, therfor that they fould be called
Commiffionars of the Knk   4. Concerning the rent ? All aggreit in that it
fould be but hurt of vther kirks, and nocht hinder the diffolutioun of benefices

For my awin part I protefted I wald haue na thing ado with the forging
or blocking of it in ame fort ; for as I faw it working, the beft of it wald be
bot a corruptioun and tyrannie brought in within the Knk to the wrak
therof.

But all the cair and trauell of the Kings Commiffionars, was to gett fic thrie
men nominat as the King lyked beft of : grait deuyfes and mikle biffines was
about that.   In end they fand the way to put vpon the lyttes a gud number
of the thrie Prefbyteries that war againft tham, that they might be quyt of
than vottes ; and fa haiffing moyenned the reft behind, they gatt thair intent, viz. Mr George Gladfteanes, Mr Thomas Buchannan, and Mr Jhone Fearfull   Whilk, when the gud brethring efpyed, they wald giff tham na vther
commiffioun bot to report fathfullie thair iudgment in the queftiones, and
attending therto, to reafone, vot. and conclud, and fie ne quid ecclefia detrimenti capiat. Promitten, to approue and allow na thing bot that quhilk
they did lawfullie in that mater

That Conventioun of the Synodicall Commiffionars was keipit with the
King at Falkland in the monethe of Auguft therefter, wharin what was done
I can nocht righthe fett down, becaufe I was nocht ther. For, efter the Conventioun of Perthe, I was neuer at Affemblie nor meitting bot againft my will,
except in Prefbyterie ; and my opinioun and wis was, ther fould be na generall meittings, Rege prefidente, vnles it pleafit God to turn and fett his hart
vtherwayes, for I faw and was certean, we fould ay be farder and farder behind in the finceritie and libertie of Chryfts kindome ; and they fould euer, a
way or vther, gett thair intentes brought about.

Allwayes in generall, they fand nocht fic fordar in the purpofe as they
luiked for : and therfor the Generall Affemblie, that was apointed to be the
yeir following, was prorogat almoft a yeir, for aduyfment and better dreffing
of maters

Thus yeir I cawſt print my Catechiſme for the profit of my peiple It coſt me fyve hounder marks, quhilk God prouydit be the motion of a maiſt godlie and loving friends hart Of the quhilk ſoum I abyde addettit, bot neuer could gett a hounder mark of it again to this hour.

1599 —In the ſimmer of the 99 yeir, ther was a meitting of manie breither with the King and Commiſſionars in St Andros, for a purpoſe of aggreiment and concord ; and when all profeſſit friindſchipe and brotherlie loue ane to another, and onlie the difference was in opiniones of proceidings, and anent the concluſiomes paſt, it was thought meit to refer that to a conference, quhilk was keipit therefter in Nouember in Edinbruche I trow to mitigat my vncle and mak him amends, it was then that Montroſe was maid Chancellar of the Vniuerſitie, Mr George Gladſteanes, Vice Chancellar, and Mr Andro Meluill, Dean of the Facultie of Theologie

In the mean tyme, at our Synod in September, 1599, a weill meining brother, my colleg, gaiff in to the Aſſemblie a certean Anglopiſcopapiſticall concluſiomes, wherof he haid over guid a warrand of the Kings buik, intitulat Βασιλικα δωρον, bot becauſe it haid but of accident cum in his hand, and was nocht publiſhed, he could nocht be plane The Synod iudget tham treaſonable, ſeditius, and wicked, thinking that ſic things could nocht be, and directed tham to the King. The King, knawing the warrand durſt nocht be exhibit, gettes knawlage of the brother that gaiff tham in, and ſends to apprehend him ; bot God watched over him, and ſaued him. This maid me fean, when I haid reſolut nocht to keipe the Conventiones of the Commiſſionars, whowbeit wraitten for, to giff obedience, and tak grait peanes, faſcherie, and expences, with greiff of mynd, till attend vpon ſum guid occaſioun to gett my brother and colleag relaxit from the horn, and reponed in his awin roum againe * And this was an of the cauſſes formentioned why I conteinowed in my Commiſſionarie, leyed on me be the King and Aſſemblie. Whilk occaſioun I gat never till the fact of St Jhonſtoun fell out, and immediathe thereſter the cauſe of the miniſters of Edinbruche teathent me again, ſa that I could nocht gett frie till that was diſpairit ; and God leyed his hand vpon me be ſeiknes, wharof heirefter in the awin place

The concluſiones, wharby we gatt certean knawlage of the Kings determi-

---

* Strange and vehement war the exerceiſes of my mynd during that tyme, quhilk God, wha hes a ſecret dealling with his awin ſecret annes, knawes.

nat mynd in our maters of the Kirk, war namlie thefe fett down in that buik as in Teftament to his Sonne.

1. The office of a King is a mixed office betwix the ciuill and ecclefiatick eſteat
2. The rewling of the Kirk weill is na fmall part of the Kings office
3. The King ſould be iudge if a minifter vag from his text in pulpit
4. The minifters fould nocht mell with maters of efteat in pulpit
5. The minifter that appealles from the Kings Judicator in his doctrine from pulpit, ſould want the head
6. Na man is man to be hated of a King noi a proud Puritane.
7. Pauitie amangs the minifters can nocht agrie with a monarchie.
8. The godlie, lerned, and modeſt men of the minifterie, ſould be preferred to biſchopries and benefices
9. Without Bifchops, the thrie eſteats in Parliament can nocht be reeftabliſhed, therfoi Bifchops mon be, and partie baniſhed and put away
10. They that preatches againft bifchopps, ſould be puniſhed with the rigoui of the law.
11. Puritans ar pefts in the Comoun weill and Kirk of Scotland.
12. The principals of tham ar nocht to be ſuffered to bruik the land.
13. For a prefeiuatiue againft thei poiſone, ther mon be bifchops.
14. The minifters fought till eftabliſhe a democratie in this land, and to becom Tribuni plebis thamſelues, and lead the peiple be the nofe, to beat the ſwy of all the gouernment
15. The minifters quarrell was euer againft the King, for na vther caufe bot becaufe he was a King.
16. Partie is the mother of confufion, and enemie to vnitie, quhilk is the mother of ordour
17. The minifter thinks be tyme to diaw the policie and ciuill gouernment, be the exemple of the ecclefiafticall, to the fam partie
18. Na conventionnes or meittings of Kirkmen to be ſuffered bot be the Kings knawlage and permiſſion.

Finis.

In the monethe of Nouember therefter, the King, maid to vnderftand that a conference amangs the breithring of all fortes wald mak maters to go fordwart peacablie, and all purpofes to pas at the nixt Generall Affemblie, fend his miſſiues athort all prouinces, and convocat the ſpecialles of the minifterie from all partes to Edinbruche againft the 17 of Nouember. The foum of the quhilk conference, als fathfullie and nen as I could collect and remember it immediathe therefter, I fett down as followes:

The righteus Chryst knawes what wrang he and his sers inds gittes hur

THE SOUM OF THE CONFERENCE KEIPIT AT HALIRUDHOUSE,
THE 17 OI NOVEMBER 1599

The Preface.

BI CAUSE the meittings of the laft Generall Affemblies war factius, tumultuus, confufe, haitt and vnordour lyk, leaft the lyk fould fall out at the nixt, his Maieftie, withe advys of the Commiffionars, thought meit till apoinct this prefent Conference, and call thervnto of all fortes of the minifterie, zealus and tyrie, modeft and graue, wys and indiffeient, wherin maters might be quyetlie and grauhe reafonit, and a way prepearit to a decent and peaceable Affemblie, wherin they may be decydit and concludit.

The Propofition.

THE propofition was : That it was permitted to euerie an ther conveined, fiiely to reafone and fchaw thair mynd, bathe vpon things concludit in Affemblies and Conferences befor ; as allo on things to be concludit that war yit in deliberatioun : Piovyding alwayes, that na reafone war brought againft things concludit in Affemblies, but onlie out of Scripture, quhilk may iuftlie be brought and vfed againft the conftitutionnes of anie Affemblie.

The breithring that ftud for the eftablifhed difcipline, and difaffented from whatfoeuer conftitutiones, actes, or oidinances maid in the leat and new form of Affemblies, preiudiciall to the fam, anfwerit, they nathei could noi wald reafone in thefe maters, nocht being preparit therfor, nor meining to preiudge the Generall Affemblie following. In the quhilk, efter the inftructioun ot Gods Word, and calling for his wefdome, they purpofed, be his grace, being called therto, to fpeak thair mynd cleirlie and tullie, as God fould furnife abilitie and warrand be his Word and Spieit.

It was anfwered, that ther was na preiudice meinit to the Affemblie, bot onlie a preparatioun for it ; and in cais anie having occafioun to fpeak now, being wryttin for be the King for that effect, and keipe vpe his reafones and mynd to ftand in the head of a factioun therwith therefter in the Affemblie, he might be counted a fals knaue.

The breithring, being thus vrged, accordit to fpeak as they could remember prefenthe, protefting alwayes the faftie of the caufe from hurt, that the Affemblie war nocht preiudgit, and that it might be leifome to tham to helpe

thair prefent fpeitches and reafones, and bring out fordar as they might attein vnto, for the weill of the caufe at the nixt aſſemblie

Sa the conclufiones of the Aſſemblie of Donche was read, bearing—That it
was neidfull and expedient that miniſters fould vott in Parliament ; and that
that office was of a mixed qualitie, partlie ciuill, partlie ecclefiaſticall, &c   In
lyk maner, was read the thing done at the Conventioun of Falkland efter the
faid Aſſemblie, with the caueattes for keiping of the faids votters in Parliament from all epifcopall corruptioun, &c. And fa returning to the former conclufion, the cheiff poinct of all, it was proponit to be reafonit vpon firft, and the
faid breithring requyrit what they haid to fay againſt the faming.

The breithring anſwerit : They knew na warrant of the Word of God for
fic a conclufioun ; defyrit, therfor, they might be inftructed of the [fame] be
Scripture, quhilk, gift they could find, they wald willinglie aggrie and ſtand
content ; giff nocht, that conclufioun could nocht be maid in fathe, and therfor wrang, and to be reformed in thair judgment.

Na Scripture was producit, onlie a reafone buildet vpon this principall ·
Euangelium non deſtruit polytiam —Atqui hæc eſt pars politiæ. Ergo To
the quhilk it was anſwerit be diftinction of *polytia* in lawfull and vnlawfull ;
and the lawfulnes therof behouethe to be ſchawin be the Word of God, els
Ethnik, Turkiſhe, and Jewiſhe policie might ſtand withe the Gofpell. It was
anſwerit, It was aneuche that the policie was nocht repugnant to the Word
of God, whowbeit the warrand of euerie part of policie, and Act of Parliament, or ciuill law, war nocht producit ; therfor (faid they) ſchaw ye the affirmatiue, that it is repugnant to the Word, the probatioun wherof now comes
vpon yow.*

It was therfor provin repugnant to the Word of God, and concludit be this
fyllogifine .—

" That miniſters fould be inuoluit and intanglit with effears of this lyff,
namlie of policie, ciuill iudicators, and effeares of comoun weill, is againſt the
exprefs Word of God

---

* Ther was an vther argument rather meinit nor proponit · Miniſters war *ciues* and *libera capi-
ta* , and, therfor, according to policie, behouethe to gift thei confent to the making of lawes in
Parliament.

Anſw Gif a confent be neceſſar, it is douted. But ceas it be, they confent to the law in Parliament, athei be the Lords or barones of the ſchyre whar they war born and remeanes, or be the
Commiſſionar of the brouche wherin they war born or dwelles , for, as to his miniſterie it is na
part nor poinct of policie nor ciuill burgeſchipe , or, if the mouth of the Lord be to be confulted,
the Commiſſionar, directed from the Generall Aſſemblie, fould be heard.

" But this conclusioun and office therby imposit, will intanggle and inuolue tham. Ergo "

The propositioun is proven be the expres Word, 2 Tim. 2. μηδεὶς ϛρατευομένος ἐμπλέκιται ταις του βιου πραγμαleίαις, whau the word πραγματεια memes propelhe, effeaes of law, iurisdictioun, and rewling of the comoun weill ; as I. Cor. 6. πραγμα, for a ciuill actioun or caufe

It was anfwent, That that place tuk nocht away naturall, œconomic and polytic dewties quhilk neceffarhe this lyff requyres ; and the quhilk man be done, and may be done of euer ilk an, fa that they inuolue nocht thamfelues, and intangle therin to the hinder of thair calling.

To that it was aggreit, That ther was certean dewties and fimple actionnes to be difchaigit now and then for nature, œconomie and polecie, be euerie an, and fa be inmifters alfo. for the helpe and nocht hinder of thair cheiff and propie callings Bot ther was a giait difference betwix fic actiones and dewties, to be done at certean tymes and occafionnes of vrgent neceffities, and the difchaiging of a fett and ordinai office in a comoun weill, namhe in the twa gianttest poinets of the mageftie and princelie ftat, νομοθητικη and δικασικη, that is, the making of lawes in a comoun weill, and iudging of the fubiects accoiding to the fam in the Parhaments, Counfalls, and Conventionnes of Efteattes of the Realme, quhilk could nocht be done without intangling and inuoluing in effeaies, and fa diftractioun fia the cheiff charge ; as the place itfelff cleirlie declarit what intangling was, viz whatfoeuer might hinder the warioui from doing the dewtie of a fouldait, and pleafing his capteau.

For the quhilk purpofe alfo. the weghtines of the charge of the minifterie, and graitnes of the cure of faulles, was infifted into ; and planlie affirmed they knew neuer nor felt never the weght therof, that thought a ciuill office of gouernment in the comoun weill might be vndertakin and ioyned therwith. Whai minieche was caft in the fpeitche of the Quein of Eingland, when fche makes a Biichope :—" Alas ' for pitie, (fayes fche,) for we haue marred a guid pretchour to day."   And the King exhorted nocht to mar his pretchours fa

For corroborating and ftrynthning of the reply, this fyllogifine was fubioymit :

" That minifters fould be diftracted fiom preatching the Word, is againft the Word of God.

" But this will diftract tham.   Ergo "

The expres word, Luc 9. ver 59, 60, 61, 62, Chryft fayes to an, Follow me ; wha anfwerit, Let me fift go burie my father. Chryft anfwers, Let the dead go burie the dead, and go thow and preatche the Gofpell of the kingdome of God   Another fayes, I will follow thie, but let me firft go and tak ordour with my hous   Chryft anfwers, Na man putting hand to the pleuche, and lukes bak, is meit for the kingdome of God. Heu ar maift neidfull naturall dewties and œconomic, qultlk Chryft expreffie torbiddes for fteying of the pretching of the Gofpell, and attending vpon his minifterie. Whow mikle mair then incompetent offices, *quæ funt Cæfaris et Reipublicæ*, as we will fchaw heirefter ?

The expres word is the faxt of the Actes.—The twoll Apoftles fayes to the reft of the difciples, It is nocht æquitable, or to be approued, that we fould leaue the Word of God and ferue the Tables ; therfor, let deacones be chofine and apointed   Gift the Apoftles wald nocht leaue the preatching of the Word of God for an ecclefiaftic office, becaufe of diftractioun, mikle les wald they that minifters fould leaue thair minifterie of the Word for ciuill and impertinent

Thridlie, The Scripture calles the minifters ἀφοριζομένους, Rom 1 —feparat and fett apart : And whar fra ? Queftionles fra the occupationes of this lyff, to faue the peiple and thamfelues, and draw tham be the Gofpell to the lyff euerlafting,—to fifhe tham out of the fie of this warld to God and his kingdome of heauin   Sa the haill nature of ther calling is feparat and fett apart from the warld, to the quhilk they fould nocht be callit bak again, mikle les therin involued and drownit.

Fourthe, The Lords minifterie vnder the law is callit a warfear, Num. 4 and his minifters wariours ; and fa in the place alleagit in the New Teftament, the facrament and aithe whar of is maift ftreat, and na wayes fuffers diftractioun. For tham was allotted na inheritance, but haid the Lord for thair inheritance, Deut 18 1 ; Jofu. 13, 14. They fay to thair father, I refpect him nocht ; they ken nocht thair breithring, they acknawlage nocht thair fonnes, but keipes the Lords words, and obferues his Covenant , teatches Jacob his judgments and his law to Ifraell, fettes incenfe before his face, and brunt offerings on his altar, Deut 33. Then mikle mair the minifters of the New Teftament, becaufe of a grnatter and cleirar grace, fpirituall and frie from beggerlie cerimonies and elements of this warld.

And, laft, to conclud this poinct with that maift wechtie and graue atteftatioun of the Apoftle to Timothè, 2 4. : " I atteft thie befor God, and the Lord Jefus Chryft, wha fall iudge the quick and the dead at his appeirance and kingdome : Pretche the Word ; be inftant in tyme, and out of tyme ; convict, reproue, exhort with all lang fuffring and doctrine " And in the fourt of the firft, " Tak cear of thir things, be about thir things ' And ar thir things fpoken to Timothè onlie, and nocht to all ministers and pastors? And gif they be spoken to all, what tyme, I pray yow, is left to be imployed at Parliament, and in the effeares of the comoun weill? The deuill is a bissie bischope, and goes about lyk a roaring lyon; and wha sall gift a compt of the torn scheipe, or stollen in the pastors absence? And, finalie, that thrisfauld demand to Piter, *Amas me?* and charge, *Pasce Agnos,* &c perteines it nocht to all?

It was obiected, that we fell in the sam absurditie with the Papists, that gatherit thair Celibatum out of the words of the Apostle, I Cor. 7 *Conjugatus curat quæ sunt mundi, quomodo placeat uxori.* And gif ane with a ecclesiastic or pastorall charge may haue the charge of wyff and familie, wharfor nocht of the comoun weill? And the Apostle sayes, That he that ceares nocht for his familie, is wars nor an infidell.

It was answerit, That the Papists argument was friuolus from the abbus of mariage to the taking away of the benefit therof, being apointed be God, and rightlie seruing for the helpe of man in his calling; and na thing lyk vnto this, wherin an euident intangling and distractioun may be sein And to answer for the caring for the hous and tham that ar therin, that is memed for instructioun and rewling therof be Christian disciplne, as is euident out of the 3 Chap. ver. 4. be the word προστῆαι, he that can nocht rewall and gouern his awin hous, whow sall he haue cair επιμελϞτι of the Kirk of God? For the Apostle is cleir in that poinct, I Cor. 9. That the flocks sould prouyde for thair pastors, tham and thair famihes, the things that ar neidfull for this lyff, as the Captan or Prince for his souldarts, and they maid frie till attend on thair seruice

It was infisted, that ther was als mikle distractioun and tyme spendit in our commissions and visitationnes, in avatting on plattes and pleying of stipends, attending on parliaments and conventionnes, &c

Answerit: That thefe war the wantes, imperfectiones and corruptiones of our Kirk, as yit nocht weill constitut, wharof the fault is in the Magistrat and flockes, schawin, compleanit vpon, and rebuked at all occasionnes be the Word of God, quhilk hes na place to proue anie thing in this mater, *ubi quæritur, quid fieri debeat, non quid fiat?* And as for Commissionars for visitatioun, we ar occupied therin in our awin subiect in pretching the Word, exerceising disciplne, and vsing of censures; and that nocht ordinarlie or be sett office, bot *ex necessitate ecclesiæ et pro re nata.*

It was fordar infisted, that we grantit till obey and com to the Kings Maiestie when soeuer he called for ws, quhilk was all an with that in question.

Anſwerit · His Maieſtie now or then calling for ws, we might repear to his Hienes, and giff our advys in all things *de iure diuino*, or vtherwayes as cues, ſa that the benefit redounding to the Kirk or Comoun weill therby, preponderat and weyed down the hurt of our particular charge   Bot it was *longe aliud* to haue an ordinar office to diſcharge in the Kings Counſall and Parliament , for, as was twitched befor, ther is a grait difference betwix a certean actioun to be done now and then, as neceſſitie and occaſioun craueth, and a ſett office to be ordinarlie diſcharged

It was obiected, that the Generall Aſſemblie haid alwayes from tyme to tyme crauit this votting in Parliament, and now when the King offers it, it was euill thought of and refuſit.

Anſwerit . The Aſſemblies haid oftentymes crauit that nan ſould vott in Parliament in nam of the Kirk, bot ſie as bun office within the ſam, and haid commiſſioun therfra. Bot that anie Generall Aſſemblie, befor the laſt in Dondie, haid determined that miniſters ſould vott in parliament, it was flatlie denyed   And it was ſchawin that often tymes that queſtion haid bein agitat in Aſſemblies and amangs breithring, bot could neuer be fund whow it could ſtand with the office of a miniſter to be a Lord in Parliament, nor was able to be ſchawin be the Word of God

It was then demandit wha could vott for the Kirk, giff nocht miniſters ?

Anſwerit : It might ſtand better with the office of an Eldar and Deacon, nor of a Miniſters, they hauing commiſſioun fra the Kirk, and ſubiect to rander a compt of thair doing at the Generall Aſſemblies.   And that indeed we wald als fean haue the Kirk moeying hir awin priuilages as ame vther, and haue his Maieſtie ſatiſfeit, and the effeares of the Comoun Weill helped, bot nocht with the hinder, wrak and corruptioun of the ſpirituall miniſterie of Gods worſchiping and ſaluatioun of his perple.

It was replyit, That it war better for the miniſters to be than awin caruers, and ſie to the weill of the Kirk, bathe in the ordering and prouiſion therof thamſelues, rather nor commit it to vthers, wha wald cean bot ſklanderihe for it.

Anſwerit . That the King and his Nobles gaue the miniſterie credit and onlie place in ſpirituall maters, ſa that they wald nocht tak the ſacraments. nor vther benefites of the Kirk at ther awin hands, nor of the hands of na vther   They wald nocht think thair bernes weill bapteiſed, nor the Supper weill miniſtrat, nor thair mariages bleſſed bot be ſum miniſter   And git his Maieſtie gaue ws ſic credit, authoritie and place, in things perteining to the faull, and proper to our office, why fould we nocht giff him and his Lord the lyk in things perteining to the body, and this lyff, as proper to tham and thair office, and think it als grait abfurditie to mell therwith our felues, &c. ⁹

It was obiected, That the Kirk was in poffeffioun of voting in Parliament be bifchopes, viz. Mis Jhone Dowglas, Patrik Adamfone, Dauid Cuningham and vthers.

Anfwer : Sen the Generall Affemblie haldin at Dondie, an. 1580, whar that office of a bifchope was declarit vnlawfull be the Word of God, the Kirk cryed out contiunalie againft tham, and excepted againft all ther doings in parliament or els what, as hauing na lawfull office in the Kirk, nor na commiffioun fra the faming.

Thereftei place being given, thei was producit ane vther aigument to fchaw the conclufioun repugnant to the Word of God.

" That Minifteis fould bear fupremacie, dominioun, and be called Loids, is againft the Word of God.

" But the conclufioun imports that   Ergo "

The propofitioun is clear out of the thrie Evangelifts, Math. 20, Marc 10 Luc 22, and I. Peter, 5, 3.; and, *Nolite vocari Rabbi*, etc. This reafone was nocht infifted into, nor anfwerit for want of tyme. Lykas alfo ane vther in the fam maner :

" The confounding and mingling of Jurifdictions diftinguift in the Word of God, is repugnant thervnto

" But the conclufioun imports that. Ergo.'

The propofitioun is euident of the 2 Chron 19, and, *Quis conftituit me Judicem;* and, *Date quæ funt Cæfaris Cæfari, et quæ Dei Deo.* etc. Chryft refufed to denyd the inheritance amangs brethring, to iudge the adulteres, Jhon 8. He refufed to be maid King, and profeffed that his kingdome was nocht of this waild.

Heir was declarit lainthe and verie weghtelie be Mr Andro, be what meanes and degries the Pape was hoifed vpe into that chaire of peftilence, wherout of he tyrannifes over all Kirks and Comoun Weills, tramping Kings vnder his feit, and tranfferring thair crownes and dominiones at his pleafur; and all from this vfurping of bathe the powars and fwords, the ciuill and ecclefiaftic. In end a ficcer caveat was given to the King, to be war he fett nocht vpe fic as fould caft him or his down. And this mikle anent the conclufioun of the laft Generall Affemblie, as memorie might ferue.

Therefter was proponit the twa poincts left be the faid Affemblie to the meitting at Falkland, and ther alfo left vndecydit or determined vpon 1 Gif thefe votters in Parliament, being annes chofin be his Maieftie and the Kirk, fould bear that office ad vitam or culpam, and fa be perpetuall ; or, gif they fould be alterable fra tyme to tyme at the Affemblies pleafour. 2. Gif they fould bear the nam of Bifchopes or nocht.

Againft the perpetuitie, the diftractioun fra thair fpirituall office of the minifterie was mikle vigit againe, fchawing clenlie that fie a continuall chairge and burding lying on a few, could nocht bot debaufh and diftract tham alluterlie from the paftorall attending and teidding of thair flockes ; the quhilks they behoued to commit to fum Vicares and fum fuffraganes.

For the perpetuitie thir arguments war vfit :

Firft, that ther wald na man tak the peanes and mak the expences vpon the tytle of the benefice, to gift it over the next yeir to an vther.

It was anfweirt, That we war nocht vpon mans particular commoditie, bot feing what might be for the helpe and gud of the Kirk and Comoun weill . to the quhilk fie wald neuer do gud wha war feiking ther awin honour and welthe.

Nixt it was reafonit, That the hinder of all comoun turnes was be twa inleakes chieffie ; ane of fkill and vnderftanding of maters, and right way of proceiding therin ; ane vther of continuance and attendance conftantlie on tham being annes begoun, till they war brought to fum gud poinct and effect Bot fa it was, that gif thefe comoun men fould be changable, they could nather lern fkill, nor profecut things. Ergo.

Anfwer : They might gett mair fkill of the wit and lawes of men, and les of the wefdome and buik of God ; mak mair attendance on Court and the Warld, bot les on Chryft and his Kingdome. And it was haird to perfwad ws that a few wald fie fa mikle for the weill of the Kirk as a haill Generall Affemblie conveinit for that effect, or follow out a gud comoun caufe better and mair conftantlie, feing experience alwayes teatched, that they wha wilbe ritche and honourable, are mikle about the faming, and verie litle for Chryft

At laft thir reafones and inconvenients war brought out dilated and infifted into againft perpetuitie :

Firft : It wald brak the barres of all thair Caveattes, and, but dout. eftablifhe lordfchipe over the breithering, tyme ftrynthning opinioun, and cuftome confirming conceat. And gif the beft denyce hes be tyme turned to corruptioun, mikle mair this of the lawfulnes wharof we mifthe dout.

To this was anfwent, That paritie amangs minifters was nocht to be lyk.

and wald nocht be   And put the cais, it behoued to ftand, becaufe of ou1
conflitutiones and o1dour. They fould be *pares* and al) k as mini{te1s, whow-
be1t, in refpect of thair civill office and Lo1dfchipe, they war abon the reft.

Nixt, perpetuitie wald bereaue and defraud the Ki1k of the benefit and libertie of electioun and cho1fe of the meitteft fo1 the tu1n *pro 1e1 natæ commodo,*
tor 1t is fure that all men ar nocht meitteft for all turnes, etc   Anfwerit:
The meitteft fould be chofin at the beginning, wha wald g1ow ay meittar and
meitta1 : alfo that it was f1ie to the Ki1k till adioyne fic as they pleafit to
tham for counfall and affiftance   It was 1eplyit, That fic as wa1 adioyned
wald nocht be ha1d to reafone nor vott in Pa1hament, Conventiones and
Counfall

Thi1dlie : Mame alterationnes befalls to mortall men : They may be feik in
body, fall in offences, quhilks albe1t nocht mak tham wo1thie to be depofit,
(*nam difficilius e)icitu1 quam non admittitur ho)pes),*)1t may difg1ace them fa,
that they becom vnable and vnme1t to do ame guid in comoun turnes ; they
may tyne the gifts of mynd and vtterance, etc   In fic cea{{es this pe1petuitie
will de{raude the Ki1k of an in that roun ; for fic a man, an or ma, can nocht,
nor will nocht, be depofit, and a Commiffionar in his place will nocht be admitted

It was anfwe11t, The number of minifte1s admitted and o1deined to vott,
viz fiftie, was fa g1a1t, that whowbe1t an, twa, th1ie, four or ten or twoll, wa1
away, ther might be a new behind   Replyed : It wald be lang or fic a num-
be1 war we1ll fett down and p1onydit with guid Lo1ds le1ving in Scotland ;
and when they wa1, the1 might be a new, and ma1r nor a new, behind of the
gu1dnes they wald be of ; bot an guid man might be ma1r ftedable to the
Kirk nor an and fiftie of that fo1t.

Fou1the : Git thefe men ferue for the p1ince and fteat, whowbe1t againft
the we1ll of the Ki1k, the p1ince will meantem tham ather be his authoritie
and moyen amangs the b1e1th1ing in Affemblies, ha1ing ther lyff and gear in
his powar, fa that they will nocht fea1 depofit1oun ; or whowbe1t the Affemblie wald depofe tham of the miniftene, yit wald the King caufe him ke1pe his
Lo1dfchipe and Le1ving   And fa fould they fett thamfelues to be advengit on
the Ki1k to hi1 wrak.

Anfwerit : The1 was na thing fa guid bot might be bathe ill fufpected
and abbufit, and fa we fould content with na thing. Replyed : That we dout-
ted of the gu1dnes, and had over 1uft caufe to fufpect the euill of it.   Du-
ply1t : That the1 was na fault bot we war all trew aneuche to the craft.—Bot
God mak ws all trew aneuche to Chryft, fay we.

Fyftlie and Laft: This perpetuitie will overthraw the powar and libertie of the Affemblies of the Kirk, and altar the Chriftian government of the Kirk to Antichriftian hieraichie, placing perpetuall Commiffionars or Bifchopes aboue minifters and ther Affemblies, and fyne finn minifteriall head mon be abon tham, the lie way to Papiie. At leaft the haill powar of the Kirk and Generall Affemblie falbe in the hands of thefe twoll or threttein, wha I warrand yow, will tak na limitat Commiffioun from the Generall Kirk, bot to reafone and vott as they think beft for the weill of the Kirk forfuthe, fa this Epitome will abolifhe the grait wark, and the Generall Affemblie will becom to be bot a Chaptour of thefe Bifchopes, and fkarfhe that

Anfwer: Thefe Caveattes hes prouydit for all thefe inconvenients weill aneuche. Reply: Thefe comentares wilbe tedius to reid, and ill to remember, and the text taken to be fchoit and cleir aneuche in the felff

In end ther was alleadgit a number of inconvenients that fould fall out giff thefe vottars war nocht perpetuall ·—1. That his Maieftie and Efteattes wald nocht admit tham in parliament vtherwayes, and fa we fould lofe the grait benefit. Anfwer, *Facilis iactura*. 2. That the minifters fould ly in contempt and povertie. Anfwer: It was thair maifters cais befor tham; it may ferue tham weill aneuche to be as he was; and better povertie with finceritie, nor promotioun withe corruptioun. 3 That vtheirs wald be promout to that roum in parliament, (for his Maieftie could nocht want his thrie Efteattes,) wha wald oppres and wrak the Kirk Anfwer: Let Chryft, the King and advengar of the wraugs done to his Kirk, and tham dell togidder as he hes done befor; let fie wha gettes the warft. 4. That it could nather ftand for the weilfear of King nor Kirk, nor Comoun weill. Anfwer: It was beft that God thought beft. 5. That it wald be fafhius and confufe ilka yeir to chufe Commiffionars. Anfwer: Na profit nor pleafure without pean taken, and experience haid proven it maift eafie and ordoulie. 6. That it wald breid variance and contentioun, whill a end wald preas to haue fic, and another fic, and fa forthe. Anfwer: Tak away profit and honour, and contentioun will ceas 7. Men wald be that way difgraced, now fett vpe, and now fett by and caft down, and fa difcuragit from doing guid. Anfwer: He, that thinks it difgrace to be employed as Gods Kirk thinks guid, hes lytle grace in him, for grace is given to the lawlie.

Thus after a thrie or four houres dealling in the formar heades, it was thought infifted lang aneuche theron; and therfor the poinct remeaning conceining the nam of thcfe vottars in parliament fould bear, was proponit to be reafoned vpon.

It was reafoned for the affirmatiue: That aggreing vpon the mater and fubftance, it maid nocht what nam war giffen it   And feing the parliament laft haid granted to the mater, vnder conditioun the minifters votting in parliament fould bear the nam and office of bifchopes, quhilk was alfo a name of Scripture, we fould nocht ftand till aggrie therto, left the refufing of the name fould mak the benefit to be refufed, quhilk his Maieftie haid gottin paft in fawours of the Kirk with grait peanes and difficultie.

It was anfwerit: That the nam ἐπίσκοπος being a Scripture nam, might be giffen tham, prouyding, that becaufe ther was fum thing mair put to the mater of a bifchopes office then the Word of God could permit, it fould haue a lytle eik put to the nam quhilk the Word of God ioyned to it, and fa it war beft to baptife tham with the nam that Piter 1 Cap. 4 giffes to fic lyk officers, calling tham ἀλλότριεπίσκοπους, wai nocht they wald think fcham to be meifchallit with fic as Piter fpeakes of ther, viz. murderars, theiffs and malfactors   And verelie that goffope* at the baptifine (gif fa I dar play with that word) was na litle vokie for getting of the berns name.

But in erneft it was reafonit on the contrai, That the nam of Bifchope could nocht be giffen tham for thefe reafones, the quhilk war nocht fullie handlit, noi replyed vnto, partlie for want of tyme, and partlie for want of patience, becaufe of litle fpeid in the purpofe.

1. Gif they fould gett the nam of Bifchope, they behoued to haue it ather as it was taken properlie in the Word, or as it was comounlie conceauit be the peiple   Bot nather of the twa could thay: Nocht as in the Word, becaufe it fould be applyed to fignifie that quhilk could nocht ftand with the Word, as hes bein declarit, except it war, *Judas epifcopatus*   And nocht as it is comounlie taken, becaufe then it fould import the corruptioun of Antichriftian and Anglican bifchopes, contrar to the Caueats.

2. That quhilk offendes the Knk of God fould be efchewit, altho a thing indifferent, for fa it becomes euill.   Bot this nam of bifchope offendes the Knk of God in this land.   Ergo.

3 That quhilk iuftlie may fklander the minifters and bring tham in difgrace fould be avoidit, bot giffing to them of that name will iuftlie fklander tham ; becaufe, thefe twentie yeirs thair doctrin from the pulpit hes foundit againft bifchopes, till they war vtterlie ouerthrawin : And now fa foone to turn

---

* This was Mr Andro.

our toung for hope of ritches and promotioun, and change our not, with the clok on the vther ſchoulder, will it nocht offer iuſt occaſioun of ſklander ?

4. That quhilk may and will bring in tyranie and corruptioun in the Kirk, is nocht to be admitted within the ſam. Bot this will do it : For bearing that nam that caries with it the ſignificatioun of biſchopes corruptiones amangs the peiple, all the Caveattes will nocht keip it theirfra, namlie from inæqualitie, preeminence and lordſchipe over the breithring. For they wilbe ſa eſteimed and ſaluted amangs the reſt of the Lords in Parliament and Court, and I warrand yow thair maneis and factiones will eaſelie fram thervnto, bringing from Court to Kirk ſic behauiour as they drink in ther ; for being callit Lord at ilk a word, and bruking principall roumes in Court and Parliament, they will luik verie ſoure gif they want the ſam in Kirk and amangs the breithring and peiple ; yea and be ſiccar in ther even at plat, Court and vtherwayes, whom they think to contemne tham, and nocht giff tham thair ſtylles and honois.

And ſa for that night leat we war dimiſſit.

Vpon the xix of Nouember, the breithring wryttin for being aſſemblet again with his Maieſtie, the Moderator reported ſchortlie the things conferrit vpon the laſt day, requyring yit, that gif ther was anie man wha was nocht ſatiſfeit anent the heads conferrit vpon, that they wald yit inſiſt, and gif all war ſatiſfeit, they ſould proceid to the poinct remeaning anent the nam.

It was anſwerit planlie be the brething that ſtud againſt this new forging of biſchopries, that they haid hard to and fra reaſoning vpon the poincts propontit ; they war throuche and ſatiſfeit in their awin iudgments for the treuthe, and rather confirmed fordar therinto nor anie wayes moued to the contrar, for ought that haid bein ſpokan ; wherin they haid haid na thing out of the Word of God quhilk might warrand that concluſion of the laſt Aſſemblie to thair conſcience, or anie thing yit buildit, or to be buildet thervpon. And in ſpeciall Mr Andro appealit the Moderator, Mr Dauid Lindſay, maiſt weghtelie and vehementlie on his conſcience, That ſeing he was an of the antient fathers of the Kirk, wha was preſent at ſa manie godlie and graue aſſemblies, hauldin ſa manie yeirs anent theſe maters, and wharin they war cleirlie decydit be the Word of God, whow could he now mak ſic a propoſitioun, or think that anie ſatthit man in the treuthe, could, be a light conſcience, wherin the Word of God haid bein rather profaned then holelie, reuerenthe and grauelie vſit, be moued to alter his iudgment, and be ſatiſfeit in the contrair.

The word of the profaning of the Scripture was takin in verie euill part
be the King, and anſwerit courteouſhe with a ſ ſL ; whowbeit, the ſpeaker
condemnit himſelff for vndewtifull handling of the Word, als weill as ame
vther   Sa the King in end brak af the conference thus in effect :—That he
haid bein mount be the Commiſſionars to aponct this conference, for ſatiſfac-
tioun of ſic as war nocht reſolut. that mateis might proceid mair paceablie
and vniformahe : bot ſeing he perceavit men to be ſa full of than awin conceattes, and preoccupied in iudgment, that they plaſed thamſelues man and
man, and war rather obfirmed in thair opiniones, nor moued to giff place to
reaſone, he wald leaue the mater to the Aſſemblie   Giff the Aſſemblie wald
receaue the benefit quhilk he offered, and conclud in the mater accoidinghe,
he wald ratefie thair concluſioun with a ſanctioun ciuill of his law, that nan,
following thair particulai and privat conceatt and opinioun, ſould be permitted
to ſpeak againſt the publict oidinance of the Aſſemblie.   Gif the Aſſemblie
wald nocht embrace the benefit, let them wait themſelues giff giaittei povertie
and contempt caim vpon the Kirk   As for him, he could nocht want an of
his eſtcates : he wald put in that ioum, and theſe offices, ſic as he thought
gud. wha wald accept theroi, and do thair dewtie to him and his countrey

FINIS

1600 —The laſt night of Februar therefter, my father in law Jhone Durie
departed this lyff, wha, as he leived happehe, walking with God in prayer
day and night, ſa he died, glorifeing God with giait ioy and aſſuiance of euerlaſting lyfi and weilfear   For efter he haid called for the Magiſtiats and
Counſall of the biouche. and exhoited tham, and admoniſhed of certean things
for thair weill, bathe togidden and ſeueiahe, and ſiclyk the Eldars of his Seſſioun, and diuers of the biething of the miniſterie ; and at laſt, efter he haid
put his hous in ordour, and directed, inſtructed and confoited his wyff and
childring preſent, he takes him to privat meditatioun and piayer, and therefter inquyres what day of the monethe it was ; and being anſwerit to him,
that it was the laſt of Februar, and the morn the firſt of Meiche, " O ' then, `
ſayes he, " the laſt day of my wietched pilgiimage, and the morn the firſt of
my reſt and glorie "   Nocht lang therefter, delyvering his ſaull in the hands
of God throw Jeſus Chryſt, leaning his head to his eldeſt ſonnes breiſt, wha
held him in his armes, maiſt quyetlie and ſweithe giffes vpe the ghaſt.   He
was vpright, zealus and falon familiar with God. Sa that, gif anie thing haid
bein heauie and doutſome, he haid na reſolutioun, reſt nor releiff, till he haid

fund it in meditatioun apart with God. And furhe, bathe in his particular tuines and publict effeares, when things femed falou hard and dangerus, whowbeit of nature melancolius and feirfull, he wald gett grait affiuances, as namlie of our retoun out of England, and of our faiftie fra the Spanyars, he fchew me oft tymes that his God affured him, night and day therof. Whateuer haid com comfortable to him, incontinent apart to prayer and thankfgiffing, his haill conference and fpeaking vpon the warks of God to the glorie of his name; all vther things was (as he vfit that word oft, *tyn tyme*) bot vanitie and tinfall of tyme, to him. Sa that I may fay, the haill courfe of his lyff that I knew, was an vnweircing and conftant occupatioun in doctrine, prayer and praife. The mair I think on him, the mair I thank God that euer I knew him; praying God, that, as I haue fein the outgeat of his conuerfatioun, (as the Apoftle fayes, Heb. xiii, 7,) fa I may follow the fam in fathe. He oft regrated and inveyit vpon the warldlie fafones and biffines of the ministerie, faying, he fearit they fould becom als vyll in the peiples eis as euer the preifts war. And as concerning this mater of bifchopes, my vncle Mr Andro expreffit his mynd therin in his Epitaphes, quhilk being maift pertinent for that quhilk was euer at his deathe in hand, I haue heir infert. He defyrit, indeid, erneftlie to haue levit till the Affemblie, quhilk was haird at hand, that he might haue difchargit his mynd to the King and breithing; bot that quhilk alyve he could nocht, Mr Andro fupplied fathfullie efter his deathe.[*]

EPITAPHIUM D JOAN. DURÆI, PASTORIS INTEGERRIMI ET FIDISSIMI CELURCANI, QUI DIEM EXTREMUM CLAUSIT, CAL MART: 1600.

Durius ore tonans, Edena paftor in Vibe:
  Arcuit a ftabulis, quos dabat aula lupos.
Celurcâ in cœlum migrauit nunc, quia non quit
  Arceie a ftabulis quos dabit aula lupos.

IPSE DE SE, SIUE J. D. PASTORIS FIDELIS, TESTAMENTUM ET EXTREMA VOLUNTAS

Intonui ipfe tuba grandi, cum ius fuit et fas;
  Arceie a ftabulis quos dabat aula lupos.
Nunc cedo ftatione lubens, cum non datur vltrâ
  Arcere a ftabulis, quos dabit aula lupos.

[*] Nota.—It is guid to be honeft and vpright in a guid caufe, for the guid caufe will honour fic a perfone, bathe in lyff and deathe.

ALIUD DE SYNODIS.

Res grata ac iucunda fuit, mihi cœtibus inter-
    effe facris, quando fancta corona fuit
Nunc patribus fanctis, quia fuccreſiere profani;
    Quæ mihi cum diis ipes vlulare lupis?

ALIUD.

Cum fuit Archi vnus mihi Chriſtus epiſcopus; vni
    Vinere et in vita hac, vita, placere fuit.
Nunc poſtquam Archi-vnus non Chriſtus epiſcopus, vni
    Vt Chriſto moriar ſtat mihi vita mori

ALIUD

Cœluicæ expectabam, vltro regemque patrefque,
    Et fanctum in Lethi limine concilium
Quo multum obteſtarei ego regemque patrefque
    Tſt qui ouium cuſtos, ie fiet inde lupus.
Nunc quia me e terris fublimem ad ſydera cœli,
    Dux meus imperio de ſtatione vocat,
E cœlis obteſtor ego regemque patrefque,
    Eſt qui ovium cuſtos, ne fiet inde lupus.

AD SUMMISTAS.

Ardua res, totumque hominem, hæc res vna requirit
    Cœleſte in terris paſcere ouile Dei.
Huc vocat ille ovium Paſtor bonus, ille vocatos
    Et regni atque aliis avocat a ſtudiis,
Hanc vnam imponit cum follicitudine curam,
    Quam feret impenfam, præmia magna terens.
Cœtera de manibus veſtris non ille requiret:
    Neglecti at pœnas exiget offcii.

EXTREMA VOLUNTAS ET VERBA, AD REGEM

Compellat Regem diuino carmine vates
    Durius, in fati limine dulcis olor.
Inclyte Rex, qui tam mihi regum a rege fecundus,
    Quam fpe reque omni rege priore prior,
Pro te vitam vltro obieci vel mille periclis,
    Pro te vota Polo milha multa tuli;

Pio te quo pugnam animo, qua mente peccatus,
  Hac mente, hoc animo, hoc te precor unum abiens.
Ne regnum cœleste geras mortalibus ausis,
  Neu facei Antistes rex tua sceptra gerat.
Mystica pertractent mystæ, regalia Reges,
  Publica quæ suo, publicus ordo gerat
Da munia Deo: cape rex tua, sint sua plebi
  Distinctum imperium sub Joue Cæsar habet.

FINIS.

THE EPITAPHES OF A MAIST VPRIGHT AND FAITHFULL PASTOR, JHONE DURIE MINISTER OF MONTROSE, WHA DIED THE FIRST OF MERCHE, 1600

In Edinbrouche the thoundring of Jhone Durie weill was harde,
When courtlie wolffes from Chryftes flok he flegged and debarde.
Now in Montrose to heavin he flites, for greiff that he can nought
The courtly wolffes debar from Kirk, quhilk Chryft hes den he bought

HIS TESTAMENT OR LETTER WILL, HE VTTERING IT OF HIMSELLE.

I blew a trumpet terrible, when right and fredom feiu'd,
To mak Chryfts flock from courtlie wolffes be keiped and preferud,
Bot now I willinglie man yield, ten that we may na man
Keipe Chryft his flock from courtlie wolffes, wherof we ftand in fair

ANE VTHER OF THE ASSEMBLIE.

A gratfull and a pleafand thing to me it was to bie
Ay prefent in Affemblies, whare Gods feruands I might fie
Bot now for holie fathers, when profane fturpes the place,
To byd and yeaule with wicked wolfles, I can nocht haue a face.

ANE VTHER.

When Chryft was onhe Arche-bifchope, I pleafure haid to byde,
To him to liue, and him to pleifs, I lyked tyme and tyde
Bot now fen onhe Chryft is nocht Arche bifchope, I do chufe
To die to him, and ay to liue, and all the warld refufe.

Ane vther.

I lmked gladlie for the King and breithring at Montrofe,
And at the dur of Deathe to lie Affemblie maid of thofe ,
That I might erneftlie obteft the King and breithiing all,
That keippars of the fcheipe fould nocht to wolffiflie fafones fall.

Bot fen that now from eid till heavin, my Captan does me clam
According to his right, I do beferk tham all for fchame,
Furtlie of the heavines obtefting bathe the breithing and the King ,
That keipars of the flok of Chryft, do nocht as Wolffes owering

To his fellow Minifters.

A thing maift hard, and qululk requyres the man all haill indeid,
Is hene on erthe the heavinlie flock of Chryft to gyd and feid.
That paftor guid to this does call, the fam does feparat
The called from all wauldlie cares, as to him dedicat ,
And this as onlie cear he does withe grait follicitude
Impone, and of rewards for it does promfe multitude,
And as for vther things, he will nan of your hands requyre,
Bot fathles negligens of this, he plagges with burning fyre.

His Letter Will and Words to the King

Jhone Durie with a vers deuyne, does call vpon the King,
As fweithe finging fwan, when deathe his dayes till end did bing.
O noble King, whom I efteem to bruik the fecond place
Nixt vnder him wha is abon, and firft in euerie cace
For thie I ieopard haue my lyff in danger mame an ,
For thie my praer hes aydant bein, bathe public and allan,
And withe what mynd I praed for thie, and with what hart I taught,
Withe that fam mynd and hart at deathe, this on thing I haue faught ,
Let nocht the heavinlie Kuk of Chryft be rewlde on eithlie wayes ,
Let nocht the paftors for to twitche thy fceptter interpryfe.
Let minifters, all myftic things, and Kinglie Kings intreat,
Set counfallars for ciuill things, and Lords into thy feat.
Giff things devyne to God,—tak thyne—let peiple haue thei awin ,
For vnder Chryft, the King impyre, diftinguift hes and knawin

Finis.

The Generall Affemblie convenit at Montrofe in Merche 1600   Ther was
the King in maner wounted occupied with his Commiffionars. The Modera-

tor laſt,* delyverit verie gud doctrine befor noone, bot he was brought in effect to recant it at the efter noone befor the haill Aſſemblie, to the grait greiff of gud breithring, a grait ſtepe from a precerie honeſt miniſter to a biſchope of the new ſtrak, quhilk he becam the yeir efter

The ſam polecie was vſit to gett a Moderator for thair purpoſe, quhilk was in the Synod of Fyſf formentioned. For they put a nomber of the beſt and maiſt eſtimed breithren vpon the leittes, wharby the ring leaders in votting was removed, and the vottes of the beſt breithring diſtracted, ſum giffen till a man, an ſum to an other; and in the meantyme, ſie as the King was ſure of, ged all a gett.

Nixt it was thought beſt to put the choiſe of the haill Aſſemblie vpon the conference, and ther to reaſone all maters, wharby they might knaw what to bring in publict, and whow

In the conference firſt was intendit a treatie for vniform conſent and aggreement in opiniones, and therfor it was thought gud that four of the an opinioun, and four of the vther, ſould go aſyde to a chalmer tham alean, and confer togidder; the quhilks aggreing, wald giff guid hope of an vniverſall Thir aught ſpendit an efter noone verie fructfulle, for we war verie plean, ſquar, and compendius, efter proteſtatioun befor God to be ſecret, and indeid I luked for ſum gud effect of our trauelles But on the morn, when we on our part war readie to continow and go fordwart, the King wald haue na mair of that form, but wald haue the reaſoning in the publict conference befor him-ſelff and certean of his Counſall, with the haill number of tham that war no-minat be the Aſſemblie vpon the conference And ſa we entered in reaſon-ing as followes:

Certean Arguments vſed and propofted in the Conference at the Generall Aſſemblie hauldin at Montroſe in the moneth of Merche, 1600, with the Anſuer giffen at that tyme, ſhortlie minuted

FIRST, the Act of Parliament 1597. the title wharof is, " *That all Miniſ-ters prouydit to prelacies ſould haue vot in Parliament,*" was requyrit to be redde,—the tenor wharof followes:

Our Soueraine Lord and his Eſteattes in Parliament, haueand ſpeciall conſideratioun and regard of the grait privileges and immunities granted be his Hines predeceſſouris of maiſt worthie memorie, to the halie Kirk within this realme, and to the ſpeciall perſones exerceiſing the offices, titles and dignities of prelacies within the ſam, quhilks perſones hes euer repreſented an of the eſteattes of

* Mr Peter Blakburn, now Biſchope of Aberdein.

this realme in all conventiones of the faids efteattes. And that the faids privileges and fridomes hes bein from tyme to tyme renewed and confermed in the fam integritie and conditioun whairin they war at anie tyme of befor Sa that his Maieftie acknawlages the faming now to be fallin and becoming vnder his Maiefties mait fauorable protectioun Therfor his Maieftie, of his great zeall and fingular affectioun, quhilk he alwayes hes to the advancement of the trew relligioun prefenthe profefint within this realme, with advys and confent of his Hines efteattes, ftatutes, decernes and declares That the Kirk within this realme, wherin the fam religioun is protefled, is the trew and halie kirk, and that fic paftors and minifters within the faming, as at anie tyme his Maieftie fall pleife to prouyde to the office, place, tytle, and dignitie of a bifchope, abbot, or vther prelat, fall at all tyme henefter haue vott in pairliament, fiklyk and als frielie as anie vther ecclefiafticall prelat haid at anie tyme bygean. And als declares that all and whatfumeuer bifchopries prefenthe vacand in his Hines hands, quhilks as yit ar vndifponit to anie perfone, or quhilks fall happin at anie tyme henefter to veak, falbe onlie difponit be his Maieftie to actuall preatchars and minifters in the Kirk, or to fic vther perfones as falbe fundin apt and qualified to vfe and exerceife the office and functioun of a minifter and preatcher, and wha in thair promiffionnes to the faid bifchopries fall accept in and vpon tham, to be actuall paftors and minifters, and according therto, fall practife and exerces the faming therefter Item, as concerning the office of the faids perfones to be prouydit to the faids bifchopries, in than fpirituall poleeie and government in the Kirk, the Liteates of Parliament hes remitted, and remittes the faming to the Kings Maieftie, to be aduyfit, confulted, and agreit vpon be his Hines with the Generall Affemblie of the minifters, at fic tymes as his Maieftie fall think expedient to treat with tham thervpon but preiudice alwayes in the mean tyme, of the iurifdictioun and difcipline of the Kirk, eftablifhed be Actes of Parliament, maid in anie tyme preceiding, and permitted be the faids actes to all Generall and Prouinciall Affemblies, and vther whatfumeuer Prefbyteries and Seffionnes of the Kirk

" That the Conftitutioun of the Generall Affemblie hauldin at Dondie 1598, takin as it is meined efter the mynd of the fore fett down Actes of Parliament, is flat repugnant to the Word of God."

Argum. 1.

" Antichriftian and Anglican epifcopall digniries, offices, places, and tytles, and all ecclefiafticall prelacies, ar flat repugnant to the Word of God. Luc. 22 : 1. Tim. 3 ; Tit. 1. ; 1. Pit. 5 ; Math. 23, etc.

" Bot fic is that quhilk is fett down in the act of parliament foreplaced, and meined in effect be the conftitution of the faid Affemblie Ergo."

Anfwerit : That all corruptionnes of thefe bifchopries ar damned and reiected ; and as to the act of parliament, it was alleagit to be formed and fett down be the invyours of the Kirks weill, of purpofe that the benefit might be refufed, and the kirk to ly over in the auld miferie and contempt.

Argum 2.

" That the Minifters of God feparat from the comoun effeares of the warld, fanctefied and confecrat to the minifterie of Gods worfhipping and faluatioun of his peiple fould turn agane to the waild and bear a comoun office and charge therin and effeaies therof, is flat repugnant to the Word of God

" But fa it is that this Conftitutioun will impon that on the minifters of God. Ergo."

The piopofitioun is proven be thir places following Num 3, 11, 15. " And the Lord fpak vnto Mofes, faying, Tak the Leuites for all the firft born of the childring of Ifraell, and the Leuits falbe myn : I am the Lord" Num. 18, 6 " For lo, I haue taken the Leuites from the childring of Ifraell, quhilk as a gift ar giuen to the Lord, to do the feruice of the Tabernacle of the Congregatioun.' Deut. 10, 8 " The fam tym the Lord feparat the tryb of Leui, to bear the Aik of the Couenant of the Lord, to ftand befor the Lord to minifter vnto him, and to blefs in his nam, vnto this day" Deut 18, 9. " The priefts and the Leuites fall haue na part nor inheritance with Ifraell, for the Lord is than inheritance, as he faid vnto tham" Acts, 13, 2. " Now as they minifted vnto the Lord, and tafted, the Holie Ghoft faid, Separat me Barnabas and Saull for the waik wheruuto I haue called tham" Rom 1 1. " Paull, a feruant of Jefus Chryft, put apart to pretche the Euangell of God"

The affumptioun is proven be the Act of Parliament, whar, vnto the minifterie is adioyned an office to be giffen be the King, called the office and dignitie of a bifchope or ecclefiafticall prelat ; and in the conftitutioun of the Affemblie, it is determined to be of a mixt qualitie partlie, or halff ciuill, halff ecclefiaftic.

This argument was anfwered be denying the affumptioun, and fa the Act of Parliament and conclufioun of the Affemblie ; and planlie declarit that they fould bear na comoun office nor charge in things ciuill.

Argum. 3.

" That the Minifters of Chryft fould be diftracted from preatching of the Word and doctrin, is flat repugnant to the Word of God

" Bot this office and dignitie of a bifchope, votting in parliament, &c wilt diftract Ergo"

Luc. 9, 59 " Chryft fayes to an, Follow me ; wha anfwerit, Let me firft go bune my father. Chryft anfwerit Let the dead bune the dead ; and go thow and preatche the gofpell of the kingdom of God Another fayes, Maifter. I will follow thé, bot let me firft go and tak ordour with my houfe Chryft anfwerit, Na man putting hand to the pleuche, and luking bak, is meit for the Kingdom of God '

Deut. 33, 8. " And of Leui he faid, Let thy Thummim and thy Vrim be withe the holie on ; faying to his father, and to his mother, I have nocht fein him, nather knawes he his breithing, nor his awin childring, bot obferues thy word, and keipes thy couenant. They teache Jacob thy iudgments, and Ifraell thy law ; they put incenfe before thy face, and brunt offrings vpon thyn altar "

Act. 6, 2. " Then the twoll called the multitud of the difciples togidder, and faid, It is nocht meit that we fould leaue the Word of God to ferue the Tables "

The argument takin from thir places, concludes ftronglie.   For giff thefe maift neceffar, naturall, œconomic, yea, and ecclefiafticall offices, fould nocht diftract from the preatching of the Word, mikle les fould ciuill effeares and offices haue place to diftract.

To the quhilks it was anfwerit, that they fould nocht be diftracted, bot ne-ceffarlie imployed in pretching of the Word, and in doctrine at thefe folem and comoun tymes, for the weill of the haill Kirk and Comoun Weill.

Argum. 4.

" Whofoeuer ar in tyme and out of tyme, day and night, to be occupied in the biffines of thair calling, fould be freed and haue immunitie from all \ther tunnes   Bot fa aught and ar the Paftors of the Knk to be occupied. Ergo."

1. Chron 9, 33 " Thefe ar the cheiff fathers of the Leuites, abyding in the chalmers (of the temple) exemed (from warldlie tunnes,) becaufe day and night the wark (of the temple) lay on tham."

II. Timoth 4 " I atteft the befor God, and the Lord Jefus Chryft, wha fall nidge the quik and the dead at his appeirance and kingdome : Preatche the Word , be inftant in tyme, and out of tyme ; convict, reproue, exhort with all lang fuffring and doctrine   Watche in all, fuffer aduerfitie, fulfill thy mi-nifterie "

I. Tim. 4, 15, 16 " Tak cean of thir thungs ; be occupied in thir ; that thy forderance may be manifeft to all men. Tak heid to thy felf, and to the doc-tiin ; abyd or remean thervpon : for in doing fa, thow fall faue bathe thy felf and them that heirs the "

Johan. 21, 15, 16, 17 "So, when they had dyned, Jefus faid to Simon Pi-ter, Simon, fone of Jonas, lowes thow me mair nor thefe ? He faid vnto him, Yea, Lord ; thow knawes that I loue the. He faid vnto him, Feid my Lambes. And fo thryfe."

Act 20 20 " I pretched publiclie and throw euerie houfe ; I warned euerie an, night and day, with teares."

Anfwer to this was : They falbe occupied in na thing by ther calling.

Argum. 5.

" To mak the charge of faulles fa light, that therwithall another may be ioyned and born is direct againft the Word of God   Bot, Ergo."

Ezech. 34, 1, etc.   " And the word of the Lord cam vnto me, faying, Sone of Man, prophefie againft the Paftors of Ifraell, and fay vnto tham : Thus fayeth the Lord God. Wo be to the paftors that feid thamfelues ¹ fould nocht the fcheiphird feid the flocks ? Yie eat the fatt and cleithe yow with the woll, bot yie feid nocht the flock   The weak haue yie nocht ftramthined ; the feik haue ye nocht healed, nather haue yie bund vpe the broken, nor brought again that whilk was driuen away, nather haue yie fought that quhilk was loft, etc. They war fkattered without a fchiphird, and the fcheipe wandrit," etc

Zachar 11, 17.   " O, idoll fcheiphird that leaues the flok, the fword falbe vpon his arm, and vpon his right ei   His arme falbe clein dryed vpe, and his right ei falbe vtterlie darkned."

Act. 20, 20.   " I keip bak from yow na thing that was profitable, but haue fchawed yow, and haue taught yow opinlie, and throw euerie houfe   26. I tak yow to record this day that I am puire fra the blood of all men.   28. Tak heid vnto yourfelues, and to all the flock, whair of the Halie Ghaft hes maid yow owerfiars, to feid the Kirk of God, quhilk he hes purchaffed with his awin blod   31. Therfor watche, and remember, that be the fpace of thrie yeirs I ceafed nocht to wairn euerie an, bathe night and day withe teares."

Pit 5, 2.   " Feid the flock of God, cairing for it with a readie mynd.   8. Be fober, and watche; for your aduerfar the deuill goes about lyk a roaring lyon, feiking whom he may deuore."

II. Cor. 2, 15.   " For we ar vnto God the fweit fauour of Chryft, in tham that ar faiffed, and in tham that periffhe   16 To the an we ar the fauour of death vnto deathe, and to the vther the fauour of lyft vnto lyff : and wha is fufficient for thefe things ?   17. For we ar nocht as manie, quhilk mak merchandis of the Word of God, but as of finceritie, but as of God, in the fight of God we fpeak in Chryft."

Heb 13, 17.   " Obey your gydes, and be fubiect to tham, for they watche ouer yowr faulles, as fic as fall giff a compt for tham."

The Anfwer was be denying the affumptioun, and fa, as in all ther an-fwers, in effect denying the thing they war doing.

Argum. 6

" The rumbling and confounding of Jurisdictiones and callings, quhilk God hes diftinguifit in perfones and maner ot handling, is againft the Word : Bot fa it is that this Conftitution imports that expreffie, terming thair office to be of a mixt qualitie Ergo."

Num. 18, 4, 7 " Yie fall keip the charge of the Tabernacle of the Congregatioun, for all the feruice ot the Tabernacle, and na ftranger fall com nen to yow The ftranger that cometh neir falbe flaine "

The minifters then [ar] ot Gods feruice, and the ciuill adminiftratois ar ftrangers ane to an vther, and fould nocht be confoundit vnder pean ot deathe

II Chron 19, 11 " Behauld, Amaria the preift falbe cheif ower yow in all maters of the Lord , and Zebadia the fone of Ifmaell, a rewlar of the houfe ot Juda, falbe for all the Kings effeares. '

Math. 22, 21. " Giue vnto Cæfar that quhilk is Cæfars, and to God quhilk is Gods "

Deut. 22, 9. 10. 11. " Thow fall nocht faw thy vynyeard with diuerfe kynd of feids, leaft thow defyll the increafs of the feid quhilk thow hes fawin, and the fruict of the vynyeard Thou fall nocht plow with an ox and an afs togidder. Thow fall nocht wear a garment of diuers fortes, as ot wollen and limning togidder."

This was anfwerit be a denyall of rumling and confufioun, bot with a granting ot comoyning and connunctioun, and fa all ane, and bewraying of the purpofe quhilk they fenned befor to deny, viz. to comoyne a ciuill office with an ecclefiaftic.

Argum. 7.

" That the officiars of Chryfts Kingdome fould meddle with things nocht pertenning therto, is ἀλλοτριοεπισκοπεῖν againft the Scripture. I. Pit. 4, 15 Bot polytic and ciuill effeares ar fic. Ergo "

Johan. 6, 15. " Jefus then knew that they war to com and tak him and mak him thair king, he withdrew himfelf vnto the montan alan "

Johan. 18, 36. " Jefus anfwert and faid vnto Pilat, My kingdom is nocht of this warld."

Luc. 12, 13, 14. " An of the multitud faid vnto him, Maifter, fpeak to my breithring, that he may deuyd the heritage with mie. He faid vnto him, O man, wha maid me iudge or parter ower yow ?"

Johan. 8, 11 " Jefus faid to the adulteres, Nather do I iudge thie ; go, and fin na mair."

It was anſwerit, That the ſpirituall and ciuill functiounes differs nocht in ſubiect, bot in maner and form of handling and treatting of ane and the ſam ſubiect to diuers endes; and that Chryſts officers ſalbe vigit to handle things ciuill na vther wayes bot ſpiritualie.

Argum 8

" That Chryſts miniſters ſould bear warldlie preemmence, bruik ambitius ſtylles, and be callit εὐεργεται, gratius Lords, is againſt the Word of God But this conſtitutioun will permit, yea, and mak tham ſa to do. Ergo"

Math. 23, 6. "The Scribes and Pharifies loue προτοκλιϲιαν at ſoupers, and προτοκαθεδριαν in the Synagoge, ſalutatioun in the mercats, and to be called Rabbi. Bot be yie nocht callht Rabbi, for yie haue a Maiſter καθηγηἴης, Chryſt; and yie ar all brethring, &c. Let him that is grait amang yow be ſeruant, for whaſoeuer will lift himſelf vpe ſalbe caſt doun, and he that will demit himſelff ſalbe lift vpe."

Luc. 22, 25. "Ther enterit a contention amang them wha ſould be the maiſt or graitteſt. But he ſaid vnto tham, The Kings of the nations bears rewll ower tham, and ar called εὐεργεται, gratius Lords Bot be yie nocht ſa; bot he that is maiſt amang yow, let him be as leaſt, and he that is the gyd as the ſeruant."

Math. 20, 26. "Bot it ſall nocht be ſa amangs yow; bot whoſoeuer wilbe grait amangs yow, let him be your ſeruant"

To this was anſwerit, That this quhilk they war about to do, ſould nather permit nor mak warldlie preemmence nor ambitius ſtylles.

Argum. 9.

"That the ſouldiour of God ſould be involued in the effeares of this lyff, is flat repugnant to the Word of God: Bot this will involue him Ergo."

Num. 4, 3. "From threttie yeir auld, and aboue vnto fiftie yeir, all that is meit to tak on this warfear, to do the wark in the Tabernacle of the congregation"

II. Tim. 2, 3, 4 "Thow therfor ſuffer affliction; as a gud ſouldiour of Jeſus Chryſt. Na man that warreth, intanglit him ſelff with the effears of this lyff; that he may pleaſe him wha hes ſchoſen him to be a ſouldier," &c

Anſwerit: They ſall nocht be involuit, nor ſould nocht, be the nature of ther calling.

Argum. 10.

" The magiftrat and ciuill rewlars pretched nocht the Word, nor minifters facraments, nor exerceifes fpirituall difcipline, acknawlaging thefe things impertinent to than functioun. Ergo, Nather fould the minifters mak euull lawes, nor iudge and rewell conform thei to.'

Anfwer : It was nocht meinit be that voting in Parliament, that the minifters fould vfe indicator ciuull or criminall, or anie part of the magiftrats office. For that the King was onlie Judge in the Parliament, and the Efteattes gaue but thair aduys.

Argum. 11

" That quhilk wantes bathe precept and exemple in the Evangels, Actes and Epiftles of the Apoftles, and in the haill ftorie and wreittings of the Chriftian Kirks, till almoft aucht hounder yeirs efter Chryft, and at what tyme the Papes cam to that fchamles vfurpatioun of bathe the fwoirds, and fett himfelff in that chair of peftilence and pryde, treadding on the neks of emperours and kings, &c is na wayes to be admitted or fufferit in our reformed Kirk.

" Bot lie is this new office of a mixed qualitie. Ergo "

For anfwer to this was broucht furthe the exemples of the Auld Teftament : Melchizedek, King and Preift ; the government of the Kirk in the families of the Patriarches. Item, Mofes and the Leuittes, wha war apointed iudges and interpreters of the law athort the land

To this repl) ed : Melchizedek. Mofes, nor the Hie Preift, can nocht be exemples for the Evangelicall minifterie, being types of the heid and foveran hiche King and preift, the Lord Jefus Chryft Alfo Mofes and Aron war breithring indeid ; bot efter Arones confecratioun buir diftinct offices, fchawing ws that the ecclefiaftic and ciuull rewlars fould liue as breithring, bot euerie an to be about thair awin office and calling for vthers mutuall weilfear. As for the government of the families, ther was an vther reafone therof, then of cities and comoun weilles, in fa far as he that rewles his familie, rewles bot himfelff ; bot wha rewles a citie or comoun welthe. governs manie families ; therfor Arift. 1. Pol makes an effentiall difference betwix the adminiftrationnes of a republic and familie And finalie, as for the Leuittes, they reprefentit na ecclefiaftic euangelicall office ; and concerning thofe that war apointed שׁפרים שׁפתים שׁפרים, called in the Gofpell γράμματεις, giff they reprefented anie office vnder the Evangell, it was the office of *doctores*, fa that therby the Doctors fould be apointed votters in Parliament

Argum 12.

"The fubiect of the office of a miniſter, and of a ciuill warldlie office, ar diuers and contrai ; therfoi an can nocht be occupied in bathe."

Rom. 8, 5, 6, 7. "They that ar efter the fleſhe, fauour the things of the fleſhe ; but they that ar efter the fpicit, the things of the fpiit. The wefdome of the fleche is deathe ; but the wifdom of the fpiit is lyff and peace　The wefdome of the fleſhe is enemie againſt God : it is nocht fubiect to the Law of God, nather indeid can be"

1 Cor. 2, 12. "We haue nocht receaued the fpiit of the warld, but the fpreit quhilk is of God, that we may knaw the things that ai giffen to ws of God ; but the natuiall man perceaues nocht the things of the fpiit of God ; for they ar folifhnes to him　Nather can he knaw tham, foi they ar fpiritualie decernit."

1 Jhon 2, 15, 16. "Loue nocht the warld, nor the things that ai in the warld : Giue anie man loue the warld, the loue of the father is nocht in him , for all that is in the warld (as the luſt of the fleche, the luſt of the eis, and the pryd of lyff) is nocht of the father, but of the warld　And the warld paffethe away, and the luſt therof, but he that fulfilleth the will of God, abyds for euer.

It was anfwerit : That this aigument was againſt warldlie, vnchriſtian, and vnfanctified ciuill offices and actionnes. Replyed : That manie alleadgit Chriſtian war maii impius and innuſt, nor the Perfian, Grecian, and Roman

Argum 13.

"The maner of doing of the an is in lyk maner aduers to the vther, as is euident of the fam places, and maine vther　Eigo"

And heir was pertinenthe vfed the Apollog of Æfope anent the Colziar and the Wakar ; whaiof the Colziar defyiit to dwell befyde and with the Wakar, alleagihg manie commodities that might com to bathe. Bot the Wakar, weill advyfit, refufed altogidder ; "For it is nocht poffible, fayes he, but thy occupatioun will mar myne, for thow makes blak, and I mak whait"

Argum 14.

"Thair end ar alfo contrar : The miniſteis office being to fiſhe men out of the fie of this warld vnto God ; quhilk they can nocht do giff they ly plunging in the warld thamfelues."

Thus faid Chryſt to his difciples, Piter, Jhone, &c.—"Follow me, and I will mak yow fifchais of men."

2 s

Argum. 15.

" The experience of the Kirk in all ages fen that corruptioun enterit in, and namlie in our awin age, nocht onlie amangs the Papifts, bot in our mbour land of Eingland, and amangs ourfelues, cleirlie proues, and loudlie cryes, That it is nocht poffible that they can ftand togidder   Therfor the Quein of Einglands dictum is, when fche makes a bifchope, · Alas ¹ for pitie ¹ for we haue maried a guid preatchour to day'   And what geppes of gear our bifchopes hes bein in Scotland, and is, the haill cowntrie kennes.

" The experience alfo of the godlie paftors teatches tham this, when they haue bein bot neuer fa lytle, and of neceffitie occupied in the waild, whow hard it is to gather thamfelues again, and gett the hart fett towards God and thair fpirituall dewties and actionnes—Qui ambulat in fole, coloratur ; qui tangit picem inquinatur : qui frequentat aulam et curiam, profanatur   Forum Pontificis Petrum ad Chrifti abnegationem adegit   Quæ eft corporum conftitutio, ea eft et morum   Circumpofito aere calido calefcimus, et rurfus frigido frigefcimus.   Sic cum fanctis fanctus eris, cum peruerfis peruerteris.

" Math. 6. 24. " No man can ferue twa maifters ; ather fall he hait the an, and loue the vther, or cleiue to that an, and defpyfe the vther : Yie can nocht ferue God and Mammon "

Argum. 16.

" Nature and the fam experience hes dyted this axiom and prouerbe. A office for a man is aneuche ; and, Manie yrons in the fyre, fum will cull   Therifor, the wyfe men in nature, Plato and Ariftotle, in thair Republics, fetts down the fam εἰς προς ἓν, and baniffes therfra ὀβελισκολυχνιον and δορυδρηπανον, inftruments ferving for ma vffes at annes, as vnprofitable, and that fpilles things, &c

" Now gif in a ciuill comoun weill by the light of nature, *in fubiecto homogenio*, a turn and office is aneuche for a man, furlie it is na wayes conuenient nor poffible, that *in fubiecto heterogenio*, viz. bathe in Kirk and Comoun weill. a man can bear twa offices."

Argum. 17.

" That quhilk hes bein as a peft efchewit, ftreatlie forbiddin be Actes, and ftouthe ftand againft in publict doctrine, and at all affemblies, fen the firft planting of the finceritie of the Gofpell within this realm, fould nocht now be perfwafioun and moyen of Court, be brought in within the Kirk · But fic is this   Ergo."

The Actes of our Generall Affemblies forbids a minifter to ioyne with his miniftene the office of a notar, houfbandrie, or laboring of land, hoftelarie, &c vnder pean of depofitioun.

Theod Beza ad Knoxium, Epift 79 :—" Sed et iftud (mi Knoxe) te ceterof-que fratres velim meminiffe, quod iam oculis pene ipfis obverfatur ficut epif-copi papatum pepererunt, ita fpeudo epifcopos papatus reliquias, epicureif-mium terris invecturos. Hanc peftem caueant qui faluam ecclefiam cupiunt, et cum illam e Scotia in tempore profligaris, ne quæfo illam vnquam admittas, quantum vis vnitatis retinendæ fpecie, quæ veteres etiam optimos multos fefel-lit, blandiatur."

Argum. 18

And Laft : The iudgment of the fathers and doctors of the Kirk, antient and modern, auld and new :—Tertullian, Cyrillus, Prinafius, Ambros, etc

Tertull deIdololat. cap 18.—" Si poteftatem nullam ne in fuos quidem ex-eremit Chriftus, quibus fordido minifterio functus eft, fi regem fe fieri, confcius fui regni refugit, pleniffime dedit formam fius dirigendo omni faftigio et fug-geftu, tam dignitatis quam poteftatis. Quis enim magis his vfus fuiffet quam Dei filius? quales enim fafces producerent? quale aurum de capite radiaret nifi gloriam fæculi alienam, et fibi et fius iudicaffet?

" Ideo, quæ noluit reiecit, quæ reiecit damnauit, quæ damnauit in pompa diaboli deputauit."

Cyrillus in Joan lib. 3, cap 20 :—" Honor et gloria mundi fugienda funt iis, qui volunt gloriam Dei confequi."

Prinafius in 2 Tim 2 .—" Comparatione militum vtitur, vt oftendat multo magis, nos a negociis fecularibus liberos effe debere vt Chrifto placeamus, ti etiam feculi milites, a reliquis feculi actibus vacant, vt poffint regi fuo placere

Ambros. in Epift 2, Tim. 2 :—" Ecclefiafticus autem idcirco Deo fe probat vt hunc deuotus officium impleat quod fpopondit, in Dei rebus follicitus, a fecu-lari negocio alienus Non enim convenit vnun duplicem habere profeffionem.

Bernard. de Confider. lib. 2. cap. 4 :—" Apoftolis interdicitur dominatus, ergo tu vfurpare aude, aut dominus apoftolatum, aut Apoftolus dominatum, plane ab vtraque prohiberis; fi vtrumque fimul habere voles, perdes vtrumque "

Idem.—" Non monftrabunt vbi quifquam Apoftolorum aliquando iudex fe-derit hominum, aut diuifor terminorum, aut diftributor terrarum, ftetiffe de-nique lego apoftolos iudicandos, fediffe iudicantes non lego."

Can. Apoft. Can. 80 :—" Dicimus quod non oportet Epifcopum aut preſbyterum, publicis fe adminiftrationibus immittere fed vacare, et commodum fe exhibere vfibus ecclefiafticis. Animum igitur inducito hoc non facere aut deponitor. Nemo enim poteft duobus dominis feruire."

Vide Gregor. lib. 1. Epiftolarum. Epift. 5. ad Theotiftam, Imperatoris fororem

Synod Nicen. Can. Syla et Conftant —" Nemo clericus vel diaconus vel preflyter propter caufam fuam quamlibet intret in curiam, quoniam omnis curia a cruore dicta eft : Et fi quis clericus in curiam introeat, anathema fufcipiat, nunquam rediens ad matrem ecclefiam.'

Damafus et Conc. Neocar. et Antioch. Anno 371:—" Epifcopi qui fecularibus intenti curis greges chorepifcopis vel curis commendant, videntur mihi meretricibus fimiles, quæ ftatim vt pariunt, infantes fuos alus nutricibus tradunt educandos, quo fuam citius libidinem explere valeant. Sic et ifti infantes fuos, i. populos fibi commiffos alus educandos tradunt, vt fuas libidines expleant, i. pro fuo libitu fecularibus curis inhibent, et quod vnicuique vifum fuerit liberius agant. Pro talibus enim animæ negliguntur, oues pereunt, morbi crefcunt, hærefes et fchifmata prodeunt, deftruuntur ecclefiæ, facerdotes vitiantur, et reliqua mala proueniunt. Non taliter dominus docuit nec Apoftoli inftituerunt Sed ipfi qui curam fufcipiunt ipfi peragant, et ipfi proprios manipulos domino reprefentent. Nam ipfe ouem perditam diligenter quæfiuit, ipfe inuenit, ipfe proprius humeris reportauit, nofque id ipfum facere perdocuit Si ipfe pro ouibus tantam curam habuit, quid nos miferi dicturi fumus, qui etiam pro ouibus nobis commiffis curam impendere negligimus, et alus eas educandas tradidimus? Audiant quæfo quid beatus Jacob dixerit focero fuo :—' Viginti annos fui tecum ; oues tuæ et capre fteriles non fuerunt ; arietes gregis tui non comedi, nec captum a beftia oftendi tibi, ego dammum omne reddebam, et quidquid furto perierat a me exigebas : die noctuque æftu vrgebar et gelu ; fugiebat fomnus ab oculis meis.' Si ergo fic laborat et vigilat qui pafcit oues Laban, quanto labori, quantifque vigiliis debet intendere qui pafcit oues Dei ? Sed in his omnibus nos inftruat qui pro ouibus fuis dedit animam."

Caluinus in Epift. ad 1 Tim. 2. :—" Semper paftorem meminiffe oportet veteris proverbii, Hoc age, quod fignificat ita ferio incumbendum effe peragendis facris, vt ftudium eius et intentionem nihil aliud impediat."

P. Martyr, in loc Com Clas. 4. cap. 13.—" Diftingui oportet has functiones ciuilis et ecclefiaftica, quia vtraque earum feorfim totum hominem requirit : imo vix vllus vnquam repertus eft qui alterutram recte obire poffet, adeo eft difficilis vtraque prouincia."

Synodus 4 Carthaginenfis.—" Vt Epifcopus nullam rei familiaris curam ad fe reuocet, fed vt lectioni et orationi et verbo prædicationis tantum modo vacat."

Synod Calcedon Œcumenica. confeffu 15.—" Ne epifcopi, clerici et monachi rebus fe polyticis impliceent, aut prædia aliena conducant

Sexti Vniuers Synodus Conftantinopolita. Con. 80 —' Epifcopis non competere ecclefiafticam et politicam eminentiam Epifcopus aut prefbyter aut diaconus, militiæ vacans, et volens vtrumque, principatum romanum et facerdotalem dignitatem deponitor : Nam quæ Cæfaris funt Cæfari, et quæ Dei Deo."

Ex Epiftola Concilii Africani ad Papam Celeftinum.—" Executores etiam clericos veftros quibufque potentibus nolite mittere, nolite concedere ne fumofum typhum feculi in ecclefiam Chrifti quæ lucem fimplicitatis et humilitatis diem Deum videre cupientibus præfert videamur inducere "

Synod. Macrenfi.—" Nec Rex, pontificis dignitatem, nec pontifex regiam poteftatem fibi vfurpare præfumat. Sic actionibus proprius dignitatibufque a Deo diftinguntur ; vt et Chriftiani reges pro æterna vita pontificibus indigerent. et pontifices pro temporalium rerum curfu regum difpofitionibus vterentur. quatenus fpiritualis actio a carnalibus diftaret in curfibus, et ideo militans domino minime, fe negotiis fecularibus impliceret, ac viciffim non ille rebus diurnis prefidere videretur."

Synodus Romana, an. 1215.—" Vniuerfis clericis interdicimus, ne quis prætextu ecclefiafticæ libertatis fuam de cætero iurifdictionem extendat in præiudicium iufticiæ fecularis : vt quæ funt Cæfaris reddantur Cæfari, et quæ funt Dei, Deo."

Bohemi quatuor articulos Bafilhenfi Synodo proponunt, quorum fecundus eft :—" De ciuili dominio, quod interdictum clericis diuina lege dicebant — Gefnerus de Synodis."

Of thir and the lyk places, the Ancients and Neotoriks are full and clen when euer they treat of this mater.

Thir arguments being fa ftrang and cleir, could nocht be denyit, therfor in effect they war all granted ; and yit they fought be all the labor and meanes they could, to gett it paft in affemblie be manieft vottes, " That thefe vottars in Parliament fould ftand in the perfones chofen, ad vitam.' Bot it was be mame honeft and gud breithing mightelie withftud in open affemblie, fa that in votting it paft againft tham, and was concludit *annuatim*.

My vncle, Mr Andro, cam to that affemblie, bot the King called for him and

quarrelit him for his coming ; wha, efter the auld maner, difchargit his confcience to him with all fredome and zeall ; and going from the King in grait
teruencie, faid, putting his hand to his crag :—" S', tak yow this head, and
gar cut it af, gif yie will ; yie fall fooner get it, or I betray the caufe of
Chryft." And fa he remeanit in the town all the whyll, and furnifit arguments to the breithring, and mightelie ftrynthned and incuragit tham.

This yeir, in the monethe of Auguft, the fyft day therof, the Erle of Gowrie, and his brother Mr Alexander, war flean be the Kings folks at St Jhonftoun, for a maift hid and horroble confpiracie, intendit be tham to haue cut
of the King ;* and, in the monethe of Nouember therefter, for faultit in Parliament. &c. The King immediatlie therefter fend ower the word to the Counfall that was at Edinbruche, commanding the minifters of Edinbruche to pub-
lis the maner in pulpit, and moue the peiple to giff thankes with tham to God
for the Kings preferuatioun The minifters gladlie aggreit to thank God for
the Kings delyverance, but to declar and preache the maner in particular as
a treuthe of God out of pulpit, becaufe the informationes war diuers and vncertean, they refufit. This occafioun was gripped at till vndo that minifterie,
quhilk ofteneft and maift croſit the Court in all euill proceidings, and was the
graiteft auband and terrour to Seffioun, nobilitie, and all the land, to keipe
tham from impietie, inuftice, and all wickednes The King cam to Edinbruche, whar he was receavit with grait concourfe, and paft in perfone to the
mercat cors of Edinbruche, and thair caufit his awin minifter, Mr Patrik Galloway, mak a declaratioun of the mater to the peiple, the quhilk the King
himfelff fecoundit and confirmit, to moue the peiple to dewtie and thankfulnes Therefter fatt in counfall with his ordinarie counfallours, and gaue out
a facrilegius fentence againft the minifters of Edinbruche, vfurping Chryft
and his Kriks place and authoritie, depofit tham from pretching the Gofpell
within his countrey for euer ; quhilk was a houndreth tymes war nor if be
forme of ciuill proces he haid hangit tham ; becaufe of the vfurpatioun of

---

* A little befor, or haid about the day of this accident, the fie at an inftant, about a law water,
debordet and ran vp abon the fie mark, hier nor at anie ftream tyd, athort all the coft fyde of Lyfi,
and at an inftant reteired agan to almaift a law water, to the grait admiratioun of all, and fkaithe
don to fum
      About that fam tym, lying in Kinkell, I dreamed my wyff was dead, and wakning apprehendit
the fam, fa that with grait heavines of hairt, I murned for hir all that day, even efter I knew the
contrai And indeid therefter fche was ftrucken with fic infirmitie, that fche could nocht be a
wyff to mie.

Chryftis iurifdictioun and his Kirks, wha hes oulie powar to call and depofe his fervants

> The Dron, the Doungeoun, and the Diaught,
> Did mak then cannon of the King,
> Syn fenfullie withe ws they faught,
> And doun to dirt they did ws ding.

Thereftei the Commiffionars war wrettin for to Falkland,* whai the matei was fchawin ws at lainthe, and ordeanit that the Synodalls fould convein and aggrie anent a form of publict thankfgiffing, and apoint a certean to convein at Edinbruche in the monethe of October following, to tak ordour with the miniftene of Edinbruche

At that Synod hauldin at Dumfermling, I, being Moderator, cam from it to the King at Falkland, and fchew his Maieftie the forme of thankfgiffing concludit. And vfing that occafioun, maid humble fute for my colleg Mr Jhone Dykes; and, God moving the Kings hart, obteined libertie to him to glorifie God again, in the exerceis of his miniiterie at our awin Kirk

Bot being freed from that quhilk was na fmall exerceis to my mynd, being then refolued to haue left Commiffionarie, Court, and all that courfe, I was compelled of confcience to continow with a mair heavie and greiws tafcheiie, labour and pean, bathe of mynd and body for that miniftene of Edinbruche; for twa of the breithring being all commandit af the town, cam to my hous and vigit me to continow in my Commiffionarie foi thair caufe. The King wald haue bein at the planting of Edinbruche with vthers. I fchew him this could nocht be till the prefent minifters wai depofit be the Kirk, or be his ciuill iudicator iuftlie cut af, giff fa they haid deferuit, for na honeft man wald tak ther roumes ower thair heid: and certean I was that nan of the twa could be iuftlie done Sa that of neceffitie they behoued to be repofit in than awin roumes, or the places to veak, alfo the peiple of Edinbruche thamfelues was a grait helpe, for they ftud honeftlie affected to thair awin, and wald agrie to nan vther

The meitting of the Commiffionars from all the provinces was at Halyrudhous in October. Thei was lang reafoning and denyfing anent the miniftene of Edinbruche; bot do what the King could, they could nocht gett by that

---

* At that tyme being in Falkland, I faw a funambulus, a Frenchman, play ftrang and incredible protuiks vpon ftented takell in the palace clos befor the King, Quein, and haill Court This was poltuklie done to mitigat the Quein and peiple for Gowiies fleuchter. Even then was Henderfoun tryed befor ws, and Gowries pedagog wha haid bein buted.

quhilk I haid fpoken. Therfor the King declaring his determinatioun that they fould neuer come in Edinbruche againe, and the Kirk thinking it hard that that miniſterie fould veak, it was thought meit that the cais fould be fchawin to the miniſters of Edinbruche thamſelues, and ſie giff they wald content of than awin accord to yeild to tranſportatioun. For the quhilk purpofe, the King and breithring convenit directed Mr Wilyeam Scot, Jhone Carmichaell and me to fchaw this mater to the breithring of Edinbruche, and report thair anſwer. And when we war abfent, the King with his Commiffionars, and the breithring ther conveined, in what form I can nocht tell, nominats and chuſes thrie Biſchopes, Mr Dauid Lindſay, Biſchope of Ros ; Mr Piter Blakburn, Biſchope of Aberdein ; and Mr George Gladſteanes, Biſchope of Catnes, apointing tham to vott for the Kirk in the nixt Parliament at the forfaulterie of the Erl of Gowrey, without anie regard had to the Caveates or Concluſioun of the laſt Generall Affemblie Wharof we knew na thing till that Convention was dimiſſit.

1601 —Sa that mater of the miniſterie of Edinbruche keipit me catching heir and ther all that wintar, with grait heavineſſe of hairt for the wrak of the libertie of Chryſts Kirk, overthraw of the Sion of his Jeruſalem, the Kirk of Edinbruche, and baniſſing from his natiue countrey of that maiſt notable, vpright, and halie ſeruant of Chryſt, Mr Robert Bruce ; till in the ſpring tyme, at the begining of Apryll, it pleaſit my God, in fatherlie cear and affectioun, to delyver me from theſe publict vexationnes, be leying his hand on my awin perſone, and rifiting me with peanes and perplexties, of heavie ſeiknes of body, and grait conflictes of mynd, quhilk his Maieſties guid fprit and myne only knawes, and fall keipe in ſecret till it pleaſe him to infpyre ; fa that theſe exerceiſes of my ſpreit may be publiſhed to his glorie, and confort of fic conſciences as militattes vnder the ſtandart of Chryſt, in the feghting feilds of this erd and lyff My feiknes, with the manifald ſchowies of the vexationnes of mynd, continowed yeir and day ; bot he wha vphalds and confortes the contreit and humble, did vphald and confort me, to whom therfor be euerlaſting praiſe—Amen.*

In the tyme of my feiknes, the Generall Affemblie, apointed to be hauldin

* MEMOR.—The Conference of Brintyland in the monethe of Merche. Item, the Synod of St Andros againſt the Papiſts, whar Mr Jhone Hamilton was excommunicat, therat I taucht vpon the Teſtament of Moſes concerning Leui, and pennit Articles and petitiones, preſentit tham to the King at Halirudhous, with lytle thanks or effect.

at St Andros was, be the Kings proclamation at Mercat crosses, commandit to be keipit with him at Brunteyland in the monethe of May To the quhilk whow beit feik and vnable, it behoued me to wryt The quhilk Letter th King tuk out of the Moderatois hand and suffent it nocht to be read, but keipit it in his awin poutche, and hes it leyed vpe, as I am informed, amangs his priuie wryttes as yit, for what purpose tyme will declar. The copie wharof, word be word, I thought therfor guid to fett down here.

To the godlie Fathers and Brethring conuent in this present Generall Assemblie at Bruntsland, May 1601, J. M wisethe grace, mercie, and peace from God throw Jesus Chryst, with the spreit of freedome vprightnes and faithfulnes

HAUING manie waves a calling to be present with yow at this Assemblie, (godlie fathers and deir brethring) and flext onlie be infirmitie of bodi, efter a lang and fore seiknes, I could nocht at least but communicat my mynd with yow tchorthe in wryt And first as concerning his Matie. Sen it hes pleasit God to irdew him with fic a raie and singular grace, as to refolue to bestow him self his flat and all that God hes giffen him in possessioun, or tytle for glorefeing of Chryst, King of Kings, in the maantenance of his gospell and trew religioun, and now to put hand to iustice againit impietie, wrang and all oppressioun, to kythe in effect the trew and earnest disposiitioun of his hart I think it all our partes to praise God vncessantlie therfor, and to concur and royne with his Maiestie in our calling to our vttermaist, namlie in stirring vpe and moving the harts of his peiple to his reuerence and obedience, yea, to bestow thair liues and all that they haue with his Hines in that caufe and in all his Maiesties esteates that may ferue for the weill therof. And trewlie they ar worthie to be accmfsd, and nocht brunk the nam of Christian nor Scottes men, bot esteemed enemies to God, Rellgioun, and his Hines, that will nocht willinglie yeild hervnto, as Deborah cryes, ' Cuise Meroi, savethe the angell of the Lord, curse, becaufe they cam nocht to assist the Lord agaritt the mightie.' I wald wis therfor for this effect, as in the dayes of Asa and Joas kings of Juda, namlie according to the directioun of guid Jehoiada the preist that folemne couenants and bands, the Word of God and prayer going befoi, war maid betwix God and the King, God and the peiple, and betwix the King and the peiple, beginning in this present Assemblie and sa going to Prouincialles, Presbyteries, and throw euerie Congregatioun of this land.

Nixt, as concerning the Ministerie of Edinbruche, I hald faft that aggreement of the brethring conuenet in Bruntsland in the monethe of Merche laft, and wald befork the brethring of the Assemblie till instit with his Maieftie, with the reafonnes sett down at that conference, and fic vther as God will turnene, ioyning prayer to God wha hes the Kings hart in his hand, wherby his Hines might be brought to veild thervnto, as a speciall weill nocht onlie of the Kirk, but of his Maiesties estreat and estreares (gif God hes giffen me anie eis to fie anie thing in tham.) For by that, that the chieff blokhous of the Lords Jerusalem in this land can nocht, in my iudgment, be weill fortefied without tham In my confcience I knaw nocht brauer trompettes to incurage, moue and fett

* NOTE.—The King haid maid grait profession and promifes anent rellgioun, vnderstanding that the Jesuites in England war his concurrit enemies, and haid lathe execut iustice vpon grait perfonages for oppresfioun notablie.

toidwait the peiple to his Maiefties obedience and afliftance, when occafioun of his Maiefties weehtieft eftears may craue the fam And trewlie, when I pas throw the formes of proceidings with my felft to fpy out what may befall in end, I can nocht tie gif it be weill, bot it wilbe repofieffioun, tor proceffes wilbe fund hard, tranfpoitatioun full of faichene and inconvenients, and in end feetles wanting contentment, therfoi the beft mon be repofieffioun, whervnto I pray God his Maiefties hait may be inclyned as the haill breitheringes ar I am fure.

Bot thei is heir an incident (deir breither) of graitter importance nor all the reft, wheianent I mon nocht onlie exhort yow, bot in the nam of Chryft chaige and adiure yow, as yie will anfwer to Him vpon your fidelitie in his feruice, that yie endenour to redres it This is that intereft quhilk Chryft fuftenit be that act and decieit of Counfall, wheiby the minifteis of Edinbruche ai depofit tiom pretching in ane tyme heneftei, becaufe they refafit to pretche and gift thankes as was enioyned to tham be the faid Counfall, the graitteft intereft that euei Chryft fuftenit in this land, tor gif he hes nocht foll powai to chuft, call and depofe his awin meflingeis and ambaffadours, he hes na powar at all. His Maieftie hes fchawin him felff, in my hering diuers tymes, willing that this fould be amendit, bot I fen the decieit ftands in the buiks without ane not theirpon Forgett nocht this, bot remembei it as the graitteft poinct yie haue to do And let nocht, I humblie befeik, his Maieftie and Counfall be unfcontent with the bringing of this in heid, for the honour of Chryft, and feir of his iuft wraithe againft fic as fav, Nolumus hunc regnan e fupra nos, (Luc. 19, 14, 27) conftianes me, the quhilk I wis to be als fai fiom his Hienes and honoumable Counfall, as tiom my awin hait and fanll, bot contraiie waves that in the fawour, and be the bleffing of Chryft, his throne, as the throne of Dauid, may be eftablifhed and flourihe as the palme.

Now as to the reft, remife your Caueattes, for corruptioun creipes faft on, and is corroborat be cuftom, fight the conclufioun of your laft Affemblie, and fic gift maters hes proceidit conform thervnto or nocht, giff it may pleife his Maieftie to permit thir thinges to be done at this tyme, (quhilk indeid ar maift neceffai to be done, vtheiwayes it is nocht poffible to keipe fra corruptioun). Forda, the reftrining of the fridome of our Generall Affemblies in the ordinar conventionnes thanof, wald be leavelie compleanit vpon and regratit to his Maieftie, for feing we haue full powai and expres charge of Chryft, the onlie King of his Kirk, to meit and convem togiddei for the government theiot, and hes our ordinaiie conventiones annes in the yeir at leaft, and oftei pro re nata approven be his Maieftie in his lawes and Actes of Parliament, (Parl 1592, Act 1) Whairfoi fould our meittings depend on licences, letters and proclamationes, namlie whill vthei efteattes, as of barrones and brouches, ar permitted to vfe ther priuilage frelie ? Sall the Kirk of Jefus Chryft be les regardit, and reftranit in hir fredome and priuilage, in a fetht and conftitut efteat vndei the protectioun of a raie Chriftian magiftrat ? God foibid !

Finalie, my den breithing, chaiitie and the loue of Chryft comands me to mak yow warning be my experience, that in all your fpeitches vie refpect the trew profit of the Kirk, and of his Maiefties efteat ioynit theiwith, and nocht prefent pleafining. Now the trew profit is that quhilk hes the wariand in the law and the Prophetes, whowfoeuer the reafone of men think of it. We fould be the monthe of God to all. His law fould be in our lippes, and trew wifdome in our mouthes. Our fpeitches fould be the fpeitches and oiacles of God. And, as the laweis fayes, It is ficham to fpeak without a law, mikle man fay we, It is fcham befoi God and his angeles, and befor the Kirk of God, to the difpenfator of the heavinlie myfteries, to fpeak without Scriptoure and wairand of the Word of God Tak heed to this, wtheiwayes when God beginnes to tak vow afyde and iacken with yow, and ley on his hand, as I thank his fatherlie affectioun he hes done with me, vie will detest from your hart the factionnes of this warld, the wisdome of fleche and bluid, the exemple and maner of doing of this tyme in speciall, yea, vie will repent and rew that euer vie knew or followed tham

In conclusioun, I ley down at your feit my Commissioun, as the prinnom does his burding when he is owerleyed. It hes spendit that wharon my numerous familie could haue bein suistened, it hes greivit my mynd continuahe, and now, in end, it hes brought me in extream danger of my lyff, wharfor I beseik yow burding me na man with it, vnles yie wald haue my skine. Now the Lord Jesus, of the sam loue that moued him to gift his lyff for his Kirk, govern and keipe the sam tra the pollutionnes of this last age, and mak ws, and all the laborars within the sam euer myndfull of that grait day, when he sall com and call ws to a compt of our dispensatioun. Amen. From the bed of my Infirmitie, the 12 of May, 1601

Whow beit. the King concealht this Letter, and wald nocht suflei it to be red, vit he follow it the aduys of the first part therof, and renewit the Covenant, to the grait confort of all the Knk at that Assemblie. and ordeannt the sam to be done throwout the land. The King ther, as I haid, maid a confortable confessioun of his sinnes and his fathe; and promesit mairst weghtelie and solemnhe to abhor all papistrie, idolatrie and superstitioun, and to liue and die in the trew relligioun wherin he was brought vpe, and whilk was pretched and professit within his realme of Scotland presenthe; also to execut iustice, and do all dewties of a godhe and Christian King, better then euer befor

A MEMORIALL EUCHARISTIC AND LUCTIC EFTER MY SEIKNES IN THE YEIR 1601

AMANGS the milliones of thy mercies I ord.
Whilks thow hes heaped on me all my dayes,
This benefit of freche I mon recorde,
To steue me vp to thankfulnes alwayes.
 For euen as Nature dytts, and all men sayes,
He is a wratche vnworthe of the light,
Wha is ingrat, and namhe in thy fight.

And first tor to recompt my cairfull cafe
I was about the tivall of my lyf,
The quhilk, as I may inflhe say, alafe!
I fand of euerie sin exceiding ryf.
 I thank thy grace, with battell, greift and stryf,
But oftentyms ouer whelm'd, ouercom aad win,
Be Sathans flight, the wicked warld and sin.

For whilk I fasted, pray'd, and meditat
Vpon the Word full oft and earnestlie .
I did indure the chastisments I gat,
And sed my self in godlie companie
    For all this sa my self I could nocht flie,
But fand a woundrouse force that did withstand,
And oftest sin to haue the vpperhand.

Then said I, LORD, I sie ther's na remead
For to put end to this offending thie,
All meanes I vse in vean   Its onlie dead
That will releue me of this miserie
    Therfor, O ! LORD, git thow may pleased bie,
Cut af this sinfull dayes and tak me hame ,
Na gratter gift nor this I can acclame

Thus efter praer, I paused a whyle on deathe,
And thoucht it passing sweet to think vpone,
Till I perceaued an altering in my breathe,
With schuddring cauld and ganting , then anone
    I hasted hame becaufe I was alone,
And cal'd for chamber, tyre and bead sa hand,
And skarslie now vpon my feit might stand.

I went to bead, and on my bouk atteans,
A creuall feuer ther vpon me seas'd,
Wilk brunt vpon my flesche, my bluid and beans,
That I imposed now it hard thie pleas'd
    Of all my troubles me for till haue eas'd
Be sending deathe, the messinger of grace,
To tak me hame vnto my resting place

This message, whill I gladlie did abyde,
Concluding with my self assuredlie,
Be grait incressing fearnes in my syde,
In my conceat it was a pleurasie ,
    And sa indeid it kythe at last to bie,
And past sum critik dayes withoutin cure,
Whilk maid me think my deathe wes fellon sure.

I thank thy grace a houndreth thowsand syse,
I was resolu d and haithe weill content,
Yit, left the meanes of lyft I sould dispyse
They for the Doctor and Chirurgian sent,
   Thow lukked sa, they cam incontinent,
And cantulhe on me they did than cure,
Bot O that whyll what pean did I indure!

O pean, the ghen, the torment, and the rak,
Whow fear art thow to sillie fleche and blude,
Whow vexes thow the head, the hart and bak,
But pruff thy preats can nocht be vnderstude
   Whils in thow insiches with thy schowrs sa rude
Ther is na rest in bodie nor in mynd,
Nor nought can please the pitifullie pynd

I thought it sweit with deirest deathe to ludge,
Yit felt the passage peantull, foule and hard,
I wald haue tean bent at my last refuge,
Bot pean and seanes fluiing me debar d.
   I lyked nocht for to retene in nar'd.
Bot all mens loue to liue did me allure,
And muirning flock, wherof I had the cure

For frinds and flock for me did fast and pray
The pyn'de, the weidow, and the fatherles
Did cry on thee, and sobbing fear did tey.
" Delyuer, Lord, our helper from distres
   (Bot I, alas! my God, vnworthie was,
For I am nought, and thow art all in me,
To whom pertenes all praise æternalie.)

Thus thow did moue than hart, and hard than prayer,
And blest the meanes was sused to mak me heall
My seiknes ceased dayhe mair and mair,
Till now all force of fiver clein did teall.
   Bot efter in my hand begau to beall
A crewall Catarh, working mikle wa,
Bathe mynd and bodie was tormentit sa.

My mynd was vex't with ftrange imaginations,
My bodie haill tormented was with pean,
Whilk did airyle of tympathetic pafnons,
And na remead in man did now remean.
    Then I on thie, my God, to call was fean,
And maid my prayer in fa ern'ſt a ways
As I hope to remember all my days.

To memorie I cal'd quhilk I had taught,
And meditat into my mynd full oft,
' (Gods Word beleiue, when euer it's teatch'd we aught
Bot then its beft, when it is deneft coft.
    We all in eafe ar lothfome, weak and foft;
Bot when the crofs maks fleche to feill the neid,
Then is the Word right ſtedable indeid)'

The fpeciall poinct was whow the Lord fuſteins
His awin in tym of thair maift ſharpe tentations,
Withe pitie graut, and mercie he tham meins
Induring than extreuitie and paffions.
    Syn, efter pruft and tryall of vexations,
He tham releiues, and giues tham reft in end,
With graitter pleafure nor euer they war pen'd

The praer was ithe, the practife very hard
For to beleiue and weat withe patience,
Sic grieuous pean tormented me, and mard
That I could ſkarſhe keip me but offence,
    Till nen difpearing void of confidence,
Thow turn'd thy face, and gaue a pleafand blink,
Quhilk perf't my hart, and deiphe ther did link

Me thoucht I faw thyn ers with mortall fight,
But weill I wat I felt th' effect indeid,
For wha had faid to pafs an vther night
Thow fall haue ſtraithe, I wald haue thought they leid
    And yit that link began atteans to breid
Sic courage, confort, ſtrynthe and patience,
As I haue euer to praife thyne excellence.

As Sydrak, Mifak and Abednego
Ley in the flaming turnace fire of harme
Sa fullie was I fenc d againft my fo,
That thouche as tyre, fa burning was myn arme,
　I but it ly, as it had bein hot warme ,
And full fax dayes indurit patienthe,
Till thow at laft with ioy releiued mie.

Let anie iudge whow grait my pean could bie
When fourtie dayes at fullie paft and fpent,
And yit the matter runnes abonndanthe
Out of my hand, and litle does relent ,
　All praile to God wha mad me patient,
Wha weill will cure this, and all vther woundc,
That I for euer his benefits may founde

And to confes the treuthe vnto his glore
I find ten fauld of ioy and pleafure fweit ,
Mair than my feiknes and my pean before
Bathe in my bodie, and in to my fpreit.
　Lord, put in mie thouchts, words and warks that's meit
To be a lafting facrifice to thie,
Of thankfulnes euen to the day I die

LORD, mak this lyft be feiknes fa perfen'd,
And keep by thie, ftill ferue vnto thy glore
LORD, mak this lyff, that s fa be thie renev d
A new lyft, for to praife thie more and more ,
　LORD, let the ritches of thy mercies ftore,
Thus in he plentie powred vpon mie,
Be to thy praife and glore æternalie.

And fen from hopped herbrie I mon now
I amche furthe again into the ftormie fies ,
I humblie prav thie, LORD, thyne care to bow,
And grant to me as thow kens beft agries,
　Me to preferue in all difficulties
And caufe me fyne aryue into that port,
Where thy redeimed maks than beft refort

Thy fyne and conſtant ſpreit, O LORD, therefore
For Jeſus feak in whom thou at weill content
Set in my faull that dewlie till adore
Thie God in Chryſt, by him I may be bent,
    To fuilie truſt and rightlie to repent
In rin my courſe, and ply my voyage out,
Till I be faued and paſt all kynd of dout.

And namlie fen the quarrell of thy CHRYSr
Within this Land, requyrs a dewetie
Of doing, fuffring, mame turn and tryſt
Myn initant tauli befaks ſucceſſantlie,
    Tuit, what thow will, that I may planlie fie
Syn to be ſtout withe reache vpright hart,
Amangs the reſt to play an honeſt part

1 INIS

Merch 1602.

QUATORZA M

SE VRSL fin my right fyd paſt the pituis peau
    Of pungent pleurefie, when Catarha
Maiſt curtlhe kyth hir force to haue me fleau,
    Syn ſoone cam on this crewall Colica
In this reſpect amangs tham waiſt of a
    Becauſe the ſetles fa in my left fyd,
That moneths ten can nocht hir weare awa,
Bot ſukand ſtill ſhe ſlubburnlie dois byd
And namlie when I think I may confyd
    Sa in my helthe, that I may do my turns,
Sic grenuus gripps she maks me till abyd,
    Of feiknes feare, that all wha fies me murns
      But, LORD, fen they ar pledges of thy Loue,
      Draw me be tham to CHRYST in heaven aboue

Dreame

Lyke as the raging tempests in the sie
Does crosse the courfe of merchants in the tort,
That they ar tean to yeild, and let it bie,
And caft about, and feik the nerreft port
So when I'm fet my peiple to comfort
And for my faulles cate to ferue my God,
This crewall Cofte giues me battell mort,
And dings me dead when I wald be abrod
        But fen fic ftormes ar fend from God alone,
        Lord, grant contentment, Let thy will be done

Amen

THE END

ALTERATIONS AND CORRECTIONS

Pro *cluking*, p 102, l 38 lege *clunking*, p 101
Pro *skaffat*. p 103, l 25, lege *skaffald*, p. 102.
Pro *bamsses*, p. 114, l 31, lege *banssed*, p. 111.
That is p 116, del p 116
Pro *for abbat*, p 121, l 27, lege *sie abbat*, p 117
Pro *is* p. 119. l. 9 from foot, lege *as*, p 116
Pro *stark*, p. 122, l 1, lege *starts*, p. 118
Pro *assembluet*, p 136, l 26, lege *assemble*, p. 129
Pro *Cambuskinnoll*, p. 142, lege *Cambuskinnott*, p 134
     Note. The Editor has, however, been informed, that *Cambuskinnoll* is some-
     times used by old writers.
Pro *Asaes* p. 146, l. 19, lege *Ahaz*, p 137.
We thus, p, 150, l. 29, deleted.
Pro *5 psalme*, p 151, l 30, lege *50 psalme*, p. 140
Pro *nocht*, p. 158, l 9, lege *not*, p. 145.
Pro *Linthgow*, p 165, l. 7 lege *Linlithgou*, p. 151.
Pro *ludwg*, p 186, l 19, lege *ludging*, p. 168
Pro *had ridden*, p 190, Note, l 2, lege *hat ridden* p. 173.
Pro *a Calles*, p 194, l 16, lege *at Calles*, p. 176
Is, p 208, l 1, deleted
Pro *bebins*, p. 223, l 29, lege *debirs*, p 204,
Pro *Linland*, p 233, l. 13, lege *England*, p. 211.
Pro *put* p. 238, l. 17, lege *but*, p 218
Pro *bein gladlie haiff receauit*, p 255, l 22, lege *haiff bein gladlie receauit* p 229.
And, p 268, l 11 from foot, delete
Lord Sachars, p. 289, should be *Lord Sanchar* [Sanquhar], p. 251.
Pro *of*, p. 298, l 21, lege *to*, p 261
Pro *ratified*, p. 298, l. 28, lege *ratifie it*, p 261.
Pro *indiffentlie*, p 310, l 16, lege *indifferentlie*, p. 271
Ye, p 329, Note, l 2, deleted
Pro *They quhilks*, p 339, last line, lege *The quhilks*, p. 303
Pro *Deut.* 18. 12., p 352 l 16, lege *Deut* 18 9, p. 315.
Qlk p 354, l 10, delete.
Pro *the*, p. 357. l 25, lege *they*, p 320

INDEX.

INDEX.

Lightning Source UK Ltd.
Milton Keynes UK
UKOW05n1555221216
290672UK00001B/118/P

9 781356 199976